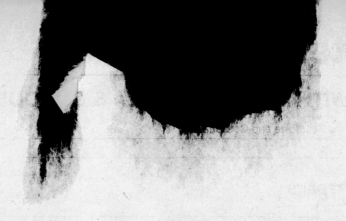

THE BOOK ®

Seat Ibiza & Cordoba
Service and Repair Manual

A K Legg LAE MIMI and Steve Rendle

Models covered

(3571 - 336 - 6AD1)

Seat Ibiza Hatchback and Cordoba Saloon, Estate (Vario) & Coupe

Petrol engines: 1.0 litre (999 & 1043cc), 1.3 litre (1272cc), 1.4 litre (1390cc SOHC & 1391cc),
1.6 litre (1595cc & 1598cc) & 2.0 litre (1984cc)
Diesel engines: 1.9 litre (1896cc), including turbo-diesel

Does not cover 1390cc DOHC or 1781cc petrol engines, or revised ranges introduced October 1999

© Haynes Publishing 2002

A book in the **Haynes Service and Repair Manual Series**

ISBN 1 85960 571 0

British Library Cataloguing in Publication Data
A catalogue record for this book is available from ~

ABCDE
FGHIJ
KLMNO
PQ

Printed in the USA

Haynes Publishing
Sparkford, Nr Yeovil, Somerset BA22 7JJ, England

Haynes North America, Inc
861 Lawrence Drive, Newbury Park, California 91320, USA

Editions Haynes
4, Rue de l'Abreuvoir
92415 COURBEVOIE CEDEX, France

~ublishing Nordiska AB
~751 45 UPPSALA, Sverige

Conte

LIVING WITH ▓▓▓▓▓▓ ▓A & ▓▓▓DOBA

Contents

REPAIRS AND OVERHAUL

Engine and associated systems

Transmission

Brakes and Suspension

Body Equipment

Wiring Diagrams

REFERENCE

Index

The Ibiza and Cordoba models covered by this manual were first introduced to the European market in the Autumn of 1993. Mechanically there is a fundamental similarity to the Golf and Vento models produced by Seat's parent company, VW, although there are a number detailed differences, especially in areas of styling and equipment.

Models have been produced with a wide range of engines, from the economical 999 cc petrol engine, to the performance-orientated 1984 cc 16-valve petrol engine, as well as normally-aspirated and turbocharged diesel engines. All petrol engines use fuel injection, and are fitted with a wide range of emission control systems. All the engines are of a well-proven design and, provided regular maintenance is carried out, are unlikely to give trouble.

Ibiza models are available in 3- and 5-door Hatchback bodystyles, whilst Cordoba models are available in 4-door Saloon, 2-door Coupe, and 5-door Estate (Vario) form.

Fully-independent front suspension is fitted, with the components attached to a subframe assembly; the rear suspension is semi-independent, with a torsion beam and trailing arms.

A five-speed manual gearbox is fitted as standard to all models.

A wide range of standard and optional equipment is available within the model range to suit most tastes, including an anti-lock braking system and air conditioning.

For the home mechanic, Ibiza and Cordoba models are straight-forward vehicles to maintain, and most of the items requiring frequent attention are easily accessible.

Seat Ibiza 1.8 GLXi

Seat Cordoba 2.0 GTi

The Seat Ibiza and Cordoba Team

Haynes manuals are produced by dedicated and enthusiastic people working in close co-operation. The team responsible for the creation of this book included:

Authors	**A.K. Legg** LAE MIMI **Steve Rendle**
Sub-editor	**Louise Brown**
Page Make-up	**Steve Churchill**
Workshop manager	**Paul Buckland**
Photo Scans	**John Martin**
Cover illustration & Line Art	**Roger Healing**
Wiring diagrams	**Steve Tanswell**

We hope the book will help you to get the maximum enjoyment from your car. By carrying out routine maintenance as described you will ensure your car's reliability and preserve its resale value.

Your Seat Ibiza and Cordoba Manual

The aim of this manual is to help you get the best value from your vehicle. It can do so in several ways. It can help you decide what work must be done (even should you choose to get it done by a garage). It will also provide information on routine maintenance and servicing, and give a logical course of action and diagnosis when random faults occur. However, it is hoped that you will use the manual by tackling the work yourself. On simpler jobs it may even be quicker than booking the car into a garage and going there twice, to leave and collect it. Perhaps most important, a lot of money can be saved by avoiding the costs a garage must charge to cover its labour and overheads.

The manual has drawings and descriptions to show the function of the various components so that their layout can be understood. Tasks are described and photographed in a clear step-by-step sequence. The illustrations are numbered by the Section number and paragraph number to which they relate - if there is more than one illustration per paragraph, the sequence is denoted alphabetically.

References to the 'left' or 'right' of the vehicle are in the sense of a person in the driver's seat, facing forwards.

Acknowledgements

Thanks are due to Champion Spark Plug who supplied spark plug information. Thanks are also due to Draper Tools Limited, who provided some of the workshop tools, and to all those people at Sparkford who helped in the production of this manual.

We take great pride in the accuracy of information given in this manual, but vehicle manufacturers make alterations and design changes during the production run of a particular vehicle of which they do not inform us. No liability can be accepted by the authors or publishers for loss, damage or injury caused by any errors in, or omissions from, the information given.

Working on your car can be dangerous. This page shows just some of the potential risks and hazards, with the aim of creating a safety-conscious attitude.

General hazards

Scalding

• Don't remove the radiator or expansion tank cap while the engine is hot.
• Engine oil, automatic transmission fluid or power steering fluid may also be dangerously hot if the engine has recently been running.

Burning

• Beware of burns from the exhaust system and from any part of the engine. Brake discs and drums can also be extremely hot immediately after use.

Crushing

• When working under or near a raised vehicle, always supplement the jack with axle stands, or use drive-on ramps. *Never venture under a car which is only supported by a jack.*
• Take care if loosening or tightening high-torque nuts when the vehicle is on stands. Initial loosening and final tightening should be done with the wheels on the ground.

Fire

• Fuel is highly flammable; fuel vapour is explosive.
• Don't let fuel spill onto a hot engine.
• Do not smoke or allow naked lights (including pilot lights) anywhere near a vehicle being worked on. Also beware of creating sparks (electrically or by use of tools).
• Fuel vapour is heavier than air, so don't work on the fuel system with the vehicle over an inspection pit.
• Another cause of fire is an electrical overload or short-circuit. Take care when repairing or modifying the vehicle wiring.
• Keep a fire extinguisher handy, of a type suitable for use on fuel and electrical fires.

Electric shock

• Ignition HT voltage can be dangerous, especially to people with heart problems or a pacemaker. Don't work on or near the ignition system with the engine running or the ignition switched on.

• Mains voltage is also dangerous. Make sure that any mains-operated equipment is correctly earthed. Mains power points should be protected by a residual current device (RCD) circuit breaker.

Fume or gas intoxication

• Exhaust fumes are poisonous; they often contain carbon monoxide, which is rapidly fatal if inhaled. Never run the engine in a confined space such as a garage with the doors shut.

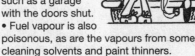

• Fuel vapour is also poisonous, as are the vapours from some cleaning solvents and paint thinners.

Poisonous or irritant substances

• Avoid skin contact with battery acid and with any fuel, fluid or lubricant, especially antifreeze, brake hydraulic fluid and Diesel fuel. Don't syphon them by mouth. If such a substance is swallowed or gets into the eyes, seek medical advice.
• Prolonged contact with used engine oil can cause skin cancer. Wear gloves or use a barrier cream if necessary. Change out of oil-soaked clothes and do not keep oily rags in your pocket.
• Air conditioning refrigerant forms a poisonous gas if exposed to a naked flame (including a cigarette). It can also cause skin burns on contact.

Asbestos

• Asbestos dust can cause cancer if inhaled or swallowed. Asbestos may be found in gaskets and in brake and clutch linings. When dealing with such components it is safest to assume that they contain asbestos.

Special hazards

Hydrofluoric acid

• This extremely corrosive acid is formed when certain types of synthetic rubber, found in some O-rings, oil seals, fuel hoses etc, are exposed to temperatures above 400°C. The rubber changes into a charred or sticky substance containing the acid. *Once formed, the acid remains dangerous for years. If it gets onto the skin, it may be necessary to amputate the limb concerned.*
• When dealing with a vehicle which has suffered a fire, or with components salvaged from such a vehicle, wear protective gloves and discard them after use.

The battery

• Batteries contain sulphuric acid, which attacks clothing, eyes and skin. Take care when topping-up or carrying the battery.
• The hydrogen gas given off by the battery is highly explosive. Never cause a spark or allow a naked light nearby. Be careful when connecting and disconnecting battery chargers or jump leads.

Air bags

• Air bags can cause injury if they go off accidentally. Take care when removing the steering wheel and/or facia. Special storage instructions may apply.

Diesel injection equipment

• Diesel injection pumps supply fuel at very high pressure. Take care when working on the fuel injectors and fuel pipes.

⚠ *Warning: Never expose the hands, face or any other part of the body to injector spray; the fuel can penetrate the skin with potentially fatal results.*

Remember...

DO

• Do use eye protection when using power tools, and when working under the vehicle.

• Do wear gloves or use barrier cream to protect your hands when necessary.

• Do get someone to check periodically that all is well when working alone on the vehicle.

• Do keep loose clothing and long hair well out of the way of moving mechanical parts.

• Do remove rings, wristwatch etc, before working on the vehicle – especially the electrical system.

• Do ensure that any lifting or jacking equipment has a safe working load rating adequate for the job.

DON'T

• Don't attempt to lift a heavy component which may be beyond your capability – get assistance.

• Don't rush to finish a job, or take unverified short cuts.

• Don't use ill-fitting tools which may slip and cause injury.

• Don't leave tools or parts lying around where someone can trip over them. Mop up oil and fuel spills at once.

• Don't allow children or pets to play in or near a vehicle being worked on.

The following pages are intended to help in dealing with common roadside emergencies and breakdowns. You will find more detailed fault finding information at the back of the manual, and repair information in the main chapters.

If your car won't start and the starter motor doesn't turn

☐ Open the bonnet and make sure that the battery terminals are clean and tight.
☐ Switch on the headlights and try to start the engine. If the headlights go very dim when you're trying to start, the battery is probably flat. Get out of trouble by jump starting (see next page) using a friend's car.

If your car won't start even though the starter motor turns as normal

☐ Is there fuel in the tank?
☐ Is there moisture on electrical components under the bonnet? Switch off the ignition, then wipe off any obvious dampness with a dry cloth. Spray a water-repellent aerosol product (WD-40 or equivalent) on ignition and fuel system electrical connectors like those shown in the photos. Pay special attention to the ignition coil wiring connector and HT leads.

A Check the condition and security of the battery connections.

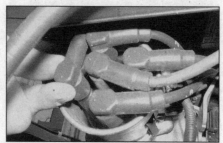

B Check that the spark plug HT leads are securely connected on the distributor cap.

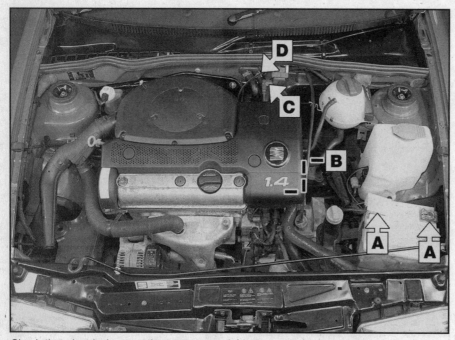

Check that electrical connections are secure (with the ignition switched off) and spray them with a water dispersant spray like WD-40 if you suspect a problem due to damp

C Check that the main HT lead is securely connected on the ignition coil.

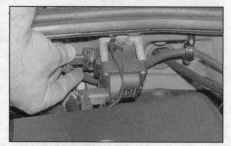

D Check that the LT wiring plug at the ignition coil is securely connected (petrol engine models).

Jump starting

HAYNES HiNT

Jump starting will get you out of trouble, but you must correct whatever made the battery go flat in the first place. There are three possibilities:

1 *The battery has been drained by repeated attempts to start, or by leaving the lights on.*

2 *The charging system is not working properly (alternator drivebelt slack or broken, alternator wiring fault or alternator itself faulty).*

3 *The battery itself is at fault (electrolyte low, or battery worn out).*

When jump-starting a car using a booster battery, observe the following precautions:

✔ Before connecting the booster battery, make sure that the ignition is switched off.

✔ Ensure that all electrical equipment (lights, heater, wipers, etc) is switched off.

✔ Take note of any special precautions printed on the battery case.

✔ Make sure that the booster battery is the same voltage as the discharged one in the vehicle.

✔ If the battery is being jump-started from the battery in another vehicle, the two vehicles MUST NOT TOUCH each other.

✔ Make sure that the transmission is in neutral (or PARK, in the case of automatic transmission).

1 Connect one end of the red jump lead to the positive (+) terminal of the flat battery

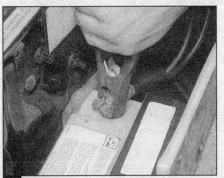

2 Connect the other end of the red lead to the positive (+) terminal of the booster battery.

3 Connect one end of the black jump lead to the negative (-) terminal of the booster battery

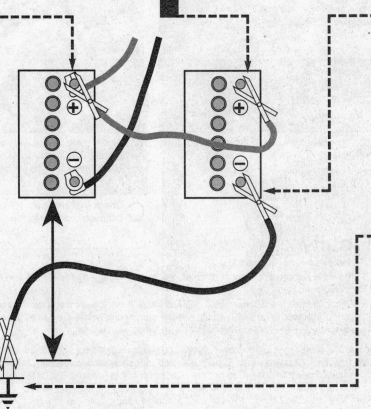

4 Connect the other end of the black jump lead to a bolt or bracket on the engine block, well away from the battery, on the vehicle to be started.

5 Make sure that the jump leads will not come into contact with the fan, drive-belts or other moving parts of the engine.

6 Start the engine using the booster battery and run it at idle speed. Switch on the lights, rear window demister and heater blower motor, then disconnect the jump leads in the reverse order of connection. Turn off the lights etc.

Wheel changing

 Warning: Do not change a wheel in a situation where you risk being hit by another vehicle. On busy roads, try to stop in a lay-by or a gateway. Be wary of passing traffic while changing the wheel - it is easy to become distracted by the job in hand.

Preparation

- ☐ When a puncture occurs, stop as soon as it is safe to do so.
- ☐ Park on firm level ground, if possible, and well out of the way of other traffic.
- ☐ Use hazard warning lights if necessary.

- ☐ If you have one, use a warning triangle to alert other drivers of your presence. One may be provided in the rear luggage compartment.
- ☐ Apply the handbrake and engage first or reverse gear.

- ☐ Chock the wheel diagonally opposite the one being removed – a couple of large stones will do for this.
- ☐ If the ground is soft, use a flat piece of wood to spread the load under the jack.

Changing the wheel

1 The spare wheel and tools are stored in the luggage compartment, under the floor covering. Release the retaining strap, and lift out the jack and wheel changing tools out from the centre of the wheel. Unscrew the retaining nut and lift the wheel out of the vehicle.

2 Remove the wheel trim/hub cap. The full-size wheel trim is removed by gripping it and pulling it from the wheel. The hub cap is removed by inserting the screwdriver from the tool kit and levering it off; some models are fitted with both wheel trims and hub caps.

3 Loosen each wheel bolt by a half turn, using the wheelbrace.

4 Locate the jack below the reinforced point on the sill, indicated by the triangular indentations (not at *any* other point on the sill). On models with a sill skirt, a plastic cover must be removed before locating the jack. Turn the jack handle clockwise until the wheel is raised clear of the ground.

5 Unscrew the wheel bolts and remove the wheel.

6 Fit the spare wheel, and screw in the bolts. Lightly tighten the bolts with the wheelbrace then lower the vehicle to the ground.

7 Securely tighten the wheel bolts, then refit the wheel trim/hub cap. Note that the wheel bolts should be tightened to the specified torque at the earliest opportunity.

Finally...

- ☐ Remove the wheel chocks.
- ☐ Stow the punctured wheel and tools back in the luggage compartment and secure them in position.
- ☐ Check the tyre pressure on the wheel just fitted. If it is low, or if you don't have a pressure gauge with you, drive slowly to the nearest garage and inflate the tyre to the right pressure.
- ☐ Have the damaged tyre or wheel repaired as soon as possible.

Note: *If a temporary space-saver spare wheel has been fitted, special conditions apply to its use. This type of spare wheel is only intended for use in an emergency, and should not remain fitted any longer than it takes to get the punctured wheel repaired. While the temporary wheel is in use, do not exceed 50 mph (80 km/h), and avoid harsh acceleration, braking or cornering. Note that, besides being narrower than a normal roadwheel, the temporary spare wheel is of smaller diameter; therefore, since ground clearance will be slightly reduced with the temporary spare in use, take care when travelling over rough ground.*

Identifying leaks

Puddles on the garage floor or drive, or obvious wetness under the bonnet or underneath the car, suggest a leak that needs investigating. It can sometimes be difficult to decide where the leak is coming from, especially if the engine bay is very dirty already. Leaking oil or fluid can also be blown rearwards by the passage of air under the car, giving a false impression of where the problem lies.

 Warning: Most automotive oils and fluids are poisonous. Wash them off skin, and change out of contaminated clothing, without delay.

> **HAYNES HiNT** *The smell of a fluid leaking from the car may provide a clue to what's leaking. Some fluids are distinctively coloured. It may help to clean the car carefully and to park it over some clean paper overnight as an aid to locating the source of the leak.*
> *Remember that some leaks may only occur while the engine is running.*

Sump oil

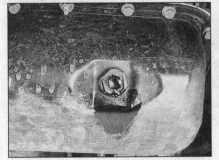

Engine oil may leak from the drain plug...

Oil from filter

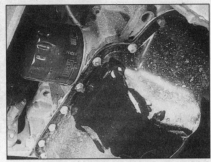

...or from the base of the oil filter.

Gearbox oil

Gearbox oil can leak from the seals at the inboard ends of the driveshafts.

Antifreeze

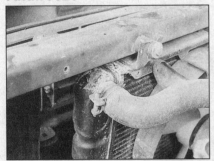

Leaking antifreeze often leaves a crystalline deposit like this.

Brake fluid

A leak occurring at a wheel is almost certainly brake fluid.

Power steering fluid

Power steering fluid may leak from the pipe connectors on the steering rack.

Towing

 Warning: To prevent damage to the catalytic converter on petrol models, do not tow or push-start a vehicle more than 50 metres. Where possible, use jump leads (see Jump starting).

When all else fails, you may find yourself having to get a tow home – or of course you may be helping somebody else. Long-distance recovery should only be done by a garage or breakdown service. For shorter distances, DIY towing using another car is easy enough, but observe the following points:

□ Use a proper tow-rope – they are not expensive. The vehicle being towed must display an ON TOW sign in its rear window.

□ Always turn the ignition key to the 'on' position when the vehicle is being towed, so that the steering lock is released, and that the direction indicator and brake lights will work.

□ A rear towing eye is provided behind a cover on the right-hand side of the rear bumper (see illustration). The front towing eye is provided behind the cover/foglight on the right-hand side of the front bumper. Use a screwdriver to prise out the appropriate cover.

□ Before being towed, release the handbrake and select neutral on the transmission.

□ Note that greater-than-usual pedal pressure will be required to operate the brakes, since the vacuum servo unit is only operational with the engine running.

□ On models with power steering, greater-than-usual steering effort will also be required.

□ The driver of the car being towed must keep the tow-rope taut at all times to avoid snatching.

□ Make sure that both drivers know the route before setting off.

□ Only drive at moderate speeds and keep the distance towed to a minimum. Drive smoothly and allow plenty of time for slowing down at junctions.

Rear towing eye

Introduction

There are some very simple checks which need only take a few minutes to carry out, but which could save you a lot of inconvenience and expense.

These *Weekly Checks* require no great skill or special tools, and the small amount of time they take to perform could prove to be very well spent, for example;

☐ Keeping an eye on tyre condition and pressures, will not only help to stop them wearing out prematurely, but could also save your life.

☐ Many breakdowns are caused by electrical problems. Battery-related faults are particularly common, and a quick check on a regular basis will often prevent the majority of these.

☐ If your car develops a brake fluid leak, the first time you might know about it is when your brakes don't work properly. Checking the level regularly will give advance warning of this kind of problem.

☐ If the oil or coolant levels run low, the cost of repairing any engine damage will be far greater than fixing the leak, for example.

Underbonnet check points

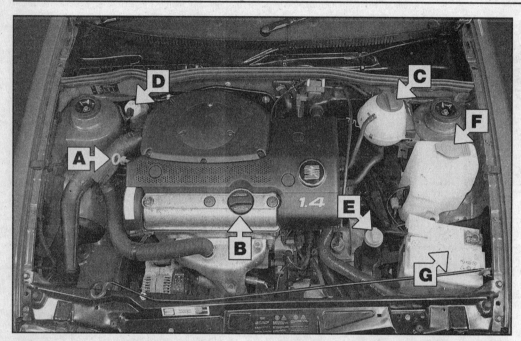

◀ 1.4 litre petrol

A Engine oil level dipstick
B Engine oil filler cap
C Coolant expansion tank
D Brake fluid reservoir
E Power steering fluid reservoir
F Screen washer fluid reservoir
G Battery

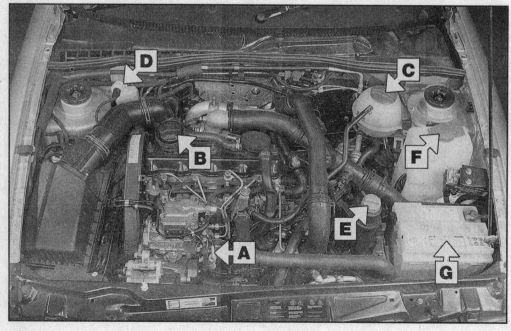

◀ 1.9 litre diesel

A Engine oil level dipstick
B Engine oil filler cap
C Coolant expansion tank
D Brake fluid reservoir
E Power steering fluid reservoir
F Screen washer fluid reservoir
G Battery

Engine oil level

Before you start
✔ Make sure that your car is on level ground.
✔ Check the oil level before the car is driven, or at least 5 minutes after the engine has been switched off.

The correct oil
Modern engines place great demands on their oil. It is very important that the correct oil for your car is used (See Lubricants and fluids).

Car Care
● If you have to add oil frequently, you should check whether you have any oil leaks. Place some clean paper under the car overnight, and check for stains in the morning. If there are no leaks, then the engine may be burning oil.

● Always maintain the level between the upper and lower dipstick marks (see photo 3). If the level is too low severe engine damage may occur. Oil seal failure may result if the engine is overfilled by adding too much oil.

1 The dipstick is brightly coloured for easy identification (see *Underbonnet check points* for exact location). Withdraw the dipstick.

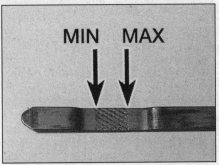

3 Note the level on the end of the dipstick, which should be between the upper (MAX) and lower (MIN) mark.

2 Using a clean rag or paper towel, wipe all oil from the dipstick. Insert the clean dipstick into the tube as far as it will go, then withdraw it again.

4 Oil is added through the filler cap. Unscrew the cap and top-up the level. A funnel may help to reduce spillage. Add the oil slowly, checking the level on the dipstick frequently. Avoid overfilling (see *Car care*).

Coolant level

⚠ **Warning: DO NOT attempt to remove the expansion tank pressure cap when the engine is hot, as there is a very great risk of scalding. Do not leave open containers of coolant about, as it is poisonous.**

Car Care
● With a sealed-type cooling system, adding coolant should not be necessary on a regular basis. If frequent topping-up is required, it is likely there is a leak. Check the radiator, all hoses and joint faces for signs of staining or wetness, and rectify as necessary.
● It is important that antifreeze is used in the cooling system all year round, not just during

the winter months. Don't top-up with water alone, as the antifreeze will become too diluted.

● Seat state that if the coolant in the expansion tank is red in colour (G12 coolant) or blue in colour (G11 coolant), on no account should this be mixed with any other type of coolant, even the small amounts likely to be required for topping-up.

1 The coolant level varies with the temperature of the engine. When the engine is cold, the coolant level should be between the MIN and MAX marks.

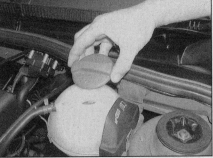

2 If topping-up is necessary, wait until the engine is cold. Slowly unscrew the cap to release any pressure present in the cooling system, and remove the cap.

3 Add a mixture of water and antifreeze to the expansion tank until the coolant level is on the MAX mark.

Brake (and clutch) fluid level

Note: Some models are fitted with a hydraulic clutch which shares the brake fluid reservoir.

Before you start:
✔ Make sure that the car is on level ground.
✔ Cleanliness is of great importance when dealing with the braking system, so take care to clean around the reservoir cap before topping-up. Use only clean brake fluid.

Safety First!
● If the reservoir requires repeated topping-up this is an indication of a fluid leak somewhere in the system, which should be investigated immediately.

● If a leak is suspected, the car should not be driven until the braking system has been checked. Never take any risks where brakes are concerned.

Warning:
● **Brake fluid can harm your eyes and damage painted surfaces, so use extreme caution when handling and pouring it.**
● **Do not use fluid that has been standing open for some time, as it absorbs moisture from the air, which can cause a dangerous loss of braking effectiveness.**

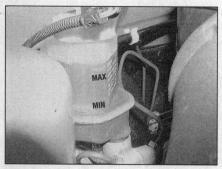

1 The MIN and MAX marks are indicated on the reservoir. The fluid level must be kept between the marks at all times.

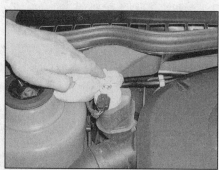

2 If topping-up is necessary, first wipe clean the area around the filler cap to prevent dirt entering the hydraulic system. Unscrew the reservoir cap.

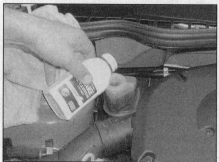

3 Carefully add fluid, taking care not to spill it onto the surrounding components. Use only the specified fluid; mixing different types can cause damage to the system. On completion, securely refit the cap and wipe away any spilt fluid. With the ignition switched on, check the operation of the brake fluid low level warning lamp by having an assistant depress the button on the top of the reservoir cap.

Power steering fluid level

Before you start:
✔ Make sure that the car is parked on level ground.
✔ Set the steering in the straight-ahead position.

✔ The engine should be stopped.
✔ For the check to be accurate, the engine should be at operating temperature, and the steering must not be turned once the engine has been stopped.

Safety First!
● The need for frequent topping-up indicates a leak, which should be investigated immediately.

1 The reservoir is located next to the battery. The power steering fluid level is checked with a dipstick attached to the reservoir filler cap. Unscrew the filler cap from the top of the reservoir.

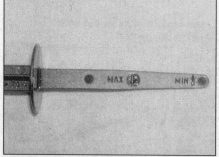

2 Wipe all the fluid from the dipstick with a clean rag or paper towel. Refit the reservoir cap, then remove it once more. Note the fluid level on the dipstick. The fluid level should be between the MIN and MAX marks on the dipstick.

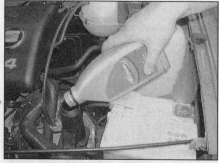

3 Top-up with the specified type of fluid if necessary, and securely refit the reservoir cap on completion.

Tyre condition and pressure

It is very important that tyres are in good condition, and at the correct pressure - having a tyre failure at any speed is highly dangerous. Tyre wear is influenced by driving style - harsh braking and acceleration, or fast cornering, will all produce more rapid tyre wear. As a general rule, the front tyres wear out faster than the rears. Interchanging the tyres from front to rear ("rotating" the tyres) may result in more even wear. However, if this is completely effective, you may have the expense of replacing all four tyres at once! Remove any nails or stones embedded in the tread before they penetrate the tyre to cause deflation. If removal of a nail does reveal that the tyre has been punctured, refit the nail so that its point of penetration is marked. Then immediately change the wheel, and have the tyre repaired by a tyre dealer.

Regularly check the tyres for damage in the form of cuts or bulges, especially in the sidewalls. Periodically remove the wheels, and clean any dirt or mud from the inside and outside surfaces. Examine the wheel rims for signs of rusting, corrosion or other damage. Light alloy wheels are easily damaged by "kerbing" whilst parking; steel wheels may also become dented or buckled. A new wheel is very often the only way to overcome severe damage.

New tyres should be balanced when they are fitted, but it may become necessary to re-balance them as they wear, or if the balance weights fitted to the wheel rim should fall off. Unbalanced tyres will wear more quickly, as will the steering and suspension components. Wheel imbalance is normally signified by vibration, particularly at a certain speed (typically around 50 mph). If this vibration is felt only through the steering, then it is likely that just the front wheels need balancing. If, however, the vibration is felt through the whole car, the rear wheels could be out of balance. Wheel balancing should be carried out by a tyre dealer or garage.

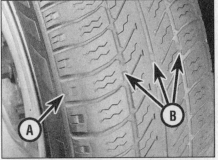

1 Tread Depth - visual check
The original tyres have tread wear safety bands (B), which will appear when the tread depth reaches approximately 1.6 mm. The band positions are indicated by a triangular mark on the tyre sidewall (A).

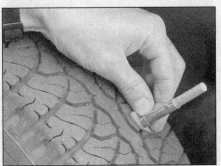

2 Tread Depth - manual check
Alternatively, tread wear can be monitored with a simple, inexpensive device known as a tread depth indicator gauge.

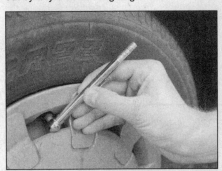

3 Tyre Pressure Check
Check the tyre pressures regularly with the tyres cold. Do not adjust the tyre pressures immediately after the vehicle has been used, or an inaccurate setting will result.

Tyre tread wear patterns

Shoulder Wear

Underinflation (wear on both sides)
Under-inflation will cause overheating of the tyre, because the tyre will flex too much, and the tread will not sit correctly on the road surface. This will cause a loss of grip and excessive wear, not to mention the danger of sudden tyre failure due to heat build-up.
Check and adjust pressures
Incorrect wheel camber (wear on one side)
Repair or renew suspension parts
Hard cornering
Reduce speed!

Centre Wear

Overinflation
Over-inflation will cause rapid wear of the centre part of the tyre tread, coupled with reduced grip, harsher ride, and the danger of shock damage occurring in the tyre casing.
Check and adjust pressures

If you sometimes have to inflate your car's tyres to the higher pressures specified for maximum load or sustained high speed, don't forget to reduce the pressures to normal afterwards.

Uneven Wear

Front tyres may wear unevenly as a result of wheel misalignment. Most tyre dealers and garages can check and adjust the wheel alignment (or "tracking") for a modest charge.
Incorrect camber or castor
Repair or renew suspension parts
Malfunctioning suspension
Repair or renew suspension parts
Unbalanced wheel
Balance tyres
Incorrect toe setting
Adjust front wheel alignment
Note: *The feathered edge of the tread which typifies toe wear is best checked by feel.*

Battery

Caution: Before carrying out any work on the vehicle battery, read the precautions given in Safety first at the start of this manual.

✔ Make sure that the battery tray is in good condition, and that the clamp is tight. Corrosion on the tray, retaining clamp and the battery itself can be removed with a solution of water and baking soda. Thoroughly rinse all cleaned areas with water. Any metal parts damaged by corrosion should be covered with a zinc-based primer, then painted.

✔ Periodically (approximately every three months), check the charge condition of the battery as described in Chapter 5A.

✔ On batteries which are not of the maintenance-free type, periodically check the electrolyte level in the battery - see Chapter 1.

✔ If the battery is flat, and you need to jump start your vehicle, see **Roadside Repairs**.

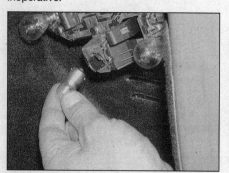

Battery corrosion can be kept to a minimum by applying a layer of petroleum jelly to the clamps and terminals after they are reconnected.

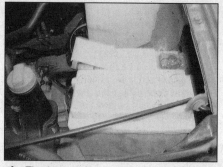

1 The battery is located on the left-hand side of the engine compartment. The exterior of the battery should be inspected periodically for damage such as a cracked case or cover.

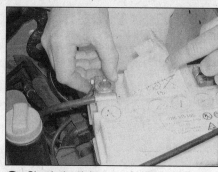

2 Check the tightness of battery clamps to ensure good electrical connections. You should not be able to move them. Also check each cable for cracks and frayed conductors.

3 If corrosion (white, fluffy deposits) is evident, remove the cables from the battery terminals, clean them with a small wire brush, then refit them. Automotive stores sell a useful tool for cleaning the battery post . . .

4 . . . as well as the battery cable clamps

Electrical systems

✔ Check all external lights and the horn. Refer to the appropriate Sections of Chapter 12 for details if any of the circuits are found to be inoperative.

✔ Visually check all accessible wiring connectors, harnesses and retaining clips for security, and for signs of chafing or damage.

HAYNES HiNT

If you need to check your brake lights and indicators unaided, back up to a wall or garage door and operate the lights. The reflected light should show if they are working properly.

1 If a single indicator light, brake light or headlight has failed, it is likely that a bulb has blown and will need to be replaced. Refer to Chapter 12 for details. If both brake lights have failed, it is possible that the brake light switch operated by the brake pedal has failed. Refer to Chapter 9 for details.

2 If more than one indicator light or headlight has failed, it is likely that either a fuse has blown or that there is a fault in the circuit (see *Electrical fault finding* in Chapter 12). The main fuses are in the fusebox under the lower driver's side of the facia. For access to the fuses, remove the driver's side glovebox (see Chapters 11 and 12).

3 To replace a blown fuse, pull it from its location in the fusebox. Fit a new fuse of the same rating, available from car accessory shops. It is important that you find the reason that the fuse blew (see *Electrical fault finding* in Chapter 12).

Washer fluid level*

On models with a headlight washer system, the screen washer fluid is also used to clean the headlights. The underbonnet reservoir also serves the tailgate washer.

Car Care

● Screenwash additives not only keep the winscreen clean during foul weather, they also prevent the washer system freezing in cold weather - which is when you are likely to need it most. Don't top up using plain water as the screenwash will become too diluted, and will freeze during cold weather.

 Warning: On no account use engine coolant antifreeze in the screen washer system - this may damage the paintwork.

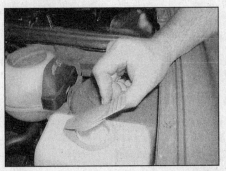

1 The screenwash fluid reservoir is located on the left-hand side of the engine compartment, in front of the suspension turret. The screen washer fluid level can be seen through the reservoir body. If more fluid is required, first open the cap.

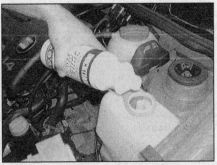

2 When topping-up the reservoir, a screen-wash additive should be added in the quantities recommended on the bottle.

Wiper blades

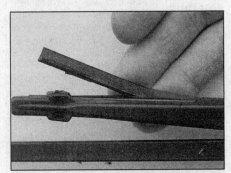

1 Check the condition of the wiper blades; if they are cracked or show any signs of deterioration, or if the glass swept area is smeared, renew them. For maximum clarity of vision, wiper blades should be renewed annually, as a matter of course.

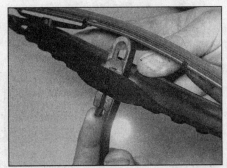

2 To remove a windscreen wiper blade, pull the arm fully away from the screen until it locks. Swivel the blade through 90°, press the locking tab with your fingers, and slide the blade out of the hooked end of the arm.

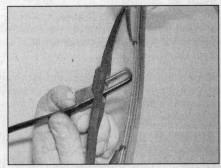

3 Where applicable, don't forget to check the tailgate wiper blade as well. To remove the blade, depress the retaining tab and slide the blade out of the hooked end of the arm.

Lubricants and fluids

Engine

Petrol . . . . Multigrade engine oil, viscosity SAE 5W/40 to 20W/50, to API SG/CD
(Duckhams QXR Premium Petrol Engine Oil, or Duckhams Hypergrade Petrol Engine Oil)

Diesel . . . . Multigrade engine oil, viscosity SAE 5W/40 to 20W/50, to API SG/CD
(Duckhams QXR Premium Diesel Engine Oil, or Duckhams Hypergrade Diesel Engine Oil)

Cooling system* . . . . Ethylene glycol based antifreeze
(Duckhams Antifreeze and Summer Coolant)

Manual transmission . . . . Gear oil, viscosity SAE 75W to API GL5
(Duckhams Hypoid Gear Oil 80W GL-4)

Braking system** . . . . Hydraulic fluid to SAE J1703F or DOT 4
(Duckhams Universal Brake and Clutch Fluid)

Power steering reservoir . . . . Seat/VW hydraulic oil G 002 000

*Note: *Refer to coolant renewal in Chapter 1A or 1B for details of Seat/VW G11 and G12 coolant.*
**Note: *And clutch hydraulic system where applicable*

Choosing your engine oil

Engines need oil, not only to lubricate moving parts and minimise wear, but also to maximise power output and to improve fuel economy. By introducing a simplified and improved range of engine oils, Duckhams has taken away the confusion and made it easier for you to choose the right oil for your engine.

HOW ENGINE OIL WORKS

• Beating friction

Without oil, the moving surfaces inside your engine will rub together, heat up and melt, quickly causing the engine to seize. Engine oil creates a film which separates these moving parts, preventing wear and heat build-up.

• Cooling hot-spots

Temperatures inside the engine can exceed 1000° C. The engine oil circulates and acts as a coolant, transferring heat from the hot-spots to the sump.

• Cleaning the engine internally

Good quality engine oils clean the inside of your engine, collecting and dispersing combustion deposits and controlling them until they are trapped by the oil filter or flushed out at oil change.

OIL CARE - FOLLOW THE CODE

To handle and dispose of used engine oil safely, always:

• **Avoid skin contact with used engine oil.** Repeated or prolonged contact can be harmful.
• **Dispose of used oil and empty packs in a responsible manner in an authorised disposal site.** Call 0800 663366 to find the one nearest to you. Never tip oil down drains or onto the ground.

Tyre pressures (cold)

	Ibiza - bar (psi)		Cordoba - bar (psi)	
	Front	Rear	Front	Rear
155/80 tyres:				
Half load	2.1 (30)	1.9 (28)	-	-
Full load	2.2 (32)	2.5 (36)	-	-
175/70 tyres:				
33, 37 and 44 kW petrol engines:				
Half load	2.1 (30)	1.9 (28)	2.1 (30)	2.2 (32)
Full load	2.2 (32)	2.5 (36)	1.9 (28)	2.4 (35)
47 kW diesel engines:				
Half load	2.2 (32)	1.9 (28)	2.1 (30)	2.2 (32)
Full load	2.3 (33)	2.5 (36)	1.9 (28)	2.4 (35)
55 kW petrol engines:				
Half load	2.1 (30)	1.8 (26)	2.1 (30)	2.2 (32)
Full load	2.2 (32)	2.4 (35)	1.9 (28)	2.4 (35)
55 kW diesel engines:				
Half load	2.2 (32)	1.9 (28)	2.2 (32)	2.3 (33)
Full load	2.3 (33)	2.5 (36)	1.9 (28)	2.4 (35)
66 kW petrol engines:				
Half load	2.1 (30)	1.8 (26)	2.2 (32)	2.3 (33)
Full load	2.2 (32)	2.4 (35)	1.9 (28)	2.4 (35)
185/60 tyres:				
44 kW petrol engines:				
Half load	2.1 (30)	1.9 (28)	2.1 (30)	2.2 (32)
Full load	2.2 (32)	2.5 (36)	1.9 (28)	2.4 (35)
47 and 66 kW diesel engines:				
Half load	2.2 (32)	1.9 (28)	-	-
Full load	2.3 (33)	2.5 (36)	-	-
55 kW petrol engines:				
Half load	2.1 (30)	1.8 (26)	2.1 (30)	2.2 (32)
Full load	2.2 (32)	2.4 (35)	1.9 (28)	2.4 (35)
55 kW diesel engines:				
Half load	2.3 (33)	2.1 (30)	-	-
Full load	2.4 (35)	2.5 (36)	-	-
66 petrol engines:				
Half load	2.1 (30)	1.8 (26)	2.2 (32)	2.3 (33)
Full load	2.2 (32)	2.4 (35)	1.9 (28)	2.4 (35)
74 kW 8V petrol engines:				
Half load	2.1 (30)	1.8 (26)	2.2 (32)	2.3 (33)
Full load	2.2 (32)	2.4 (35)	2.1 (30)	2.6 (38)
74 kW 16V petrol engines:				
Half load	2.2 (32)	2.1 (30)	-	-
Full load	2.3 (33)	2.5 (36)	-	-
85 and 95 kW petrol engines:				
Half load	2.4 (35)	2.0 (29)	2.4 (35)	2.5 (36)
Full load	2.5 (36)	2.6 (38)	2.2 (32)	2.7 (39)
185/55 tyres:				
66 and 74 kW petrol engines:				
Half load	2.3 (33)	2.4 (35)	2.2 (32)	2.4 (35)
Full load	2.2 (32)	2.6 (38)	2.1 (30)	2.6 (38)
85 kW petrol engines:				
Half load	2.4 (35)	2.2 (32)	2.5 (36)	2.5 (36)
Full load	2.5 (36)	2.6 (38)	2.2 (32)	2.7 (39)
95 kW petrol engines:				
Half load	2.4 (35)	2.2 (32)	2.3 (33)	2.5 (36)
Full load	2.5 (36)	2.6 (38)	2.2 (32)	2.6 (38)
195/45 tyres:				
Half load	2.6 (38)	2.3 (33)	-	-
Full load	2.7 (39)	2.7 (39)	-	-
Emergency spare wheel	4.2 (61)	4.2 (61)	4.2 (61)	4.2 (61)

Advanced driving

Many people see the words 'advanced driving' and believe that it won't interest them or that it is a style of driving beyond their own abilities. Nothing could be further from the truth. Advanced driving is straightforward safe, sensible driving - the sort of driving we should all do every time we get behind the wheel.

An average of 10 people are killed every day on UK roads and 870 more are injured, some seriously. Lives are ruined daily, usually because somebody did something stupid. Something like 95% of all accidents are due to human error, mostly driver failure. Sometimes we make genuine mistakes - everyone does. Sometimes we have lapses of concentration. Sometimes we deliberately take risks.

For many people, the process of 'learning to drive' doesn't go much further than learning how to pass the driving test because of a common belief that good drivers are made by 'experience'.

Learning to drive by 'experience' teaches three driving skills:

☐ Quick reactions. (Whoops, that was close!)
☐ Good handling skills. (Horn, swerve, brake, horn).
☐ Reliance on vehicle technology. (Great stuff this ABS, stop in no distance even in the wet...)

Drivers whose skills are 'experience based' generally have a lot of near misses and the odd accident. The results can be seen every day in our courts and our hospital casualty departments.

Advanced drivers have learnt to control the risks by controlling the position and speed of their vehicle. They avoid accidents and near misses, even if the drivers around them make mistakes.

The key skills of advanced driving are **concentration,** effective all-round **observation, anticipation** and **planning.** When **good vehicle handling** is added to

these skills, all driving situations can be approached and negotiated in a safe, methodical way, leaving nothing to chance.

Concentration means applying your mind to safe driving, completely excluding anything that's not relevant. Driving is usually the most dangerous activity that most of us undertake in our daily routines. It deserves our full attention.

Observation means not just looking, but seeing and seeking out the information found in the driving environment.

Anticipation means asking yourself what is happening, what you can reasonably expect to happen and what could happen unexpectedly. (One of the commonest words used in compiling accident reports is 'suddenly'.)

Planning is the link between seeing something and taking the appropriate action. For many drivers, planning is the missing link.

If you want to become a safer and more skilful driver and you want to enjoy your driving more, contact the Institute of Advanced Motorists on 0208 994 4403 or write to IAM House, Chiswick High Road, London W4 4HS for an information pack.

Chapter 1 Part A:
Routine maintenance & servicing - petrol models

Contents

Degrees of difficulty

| Easy, suitable for novice with little experience | | Fairly easy, suitable for beginner with some experience | | Fairly difficult, suitable for competent DIY mechanic | | Difficult, suitable for experienced DIY mechanic | | Very difficult, suitable for expert DIY or professional | |

Lubricants and fluids

Refer to end of *Weekly checks* on page 0•16

Capacities

Engine oil (including 0.5 litres for filter)

Engine codes AER, AAU, AAV, AEX, APQ, ABD, ABU, AEE, ALM	3.5 litres
Engine codes 2E, AGG, 1F, ABF, AFT	4.0 litres

Cooling system (approximate)

Engine codes AAU, AAV, ABD	4.2 litres
Engine codes AER, AEX, APQ, ABU, AEE, ALM, 2E, AGG, 1F, ABF, AFT .	5.5 litres

Transmission*

085 gearbox:	
Up to 26/2/96	3.1 litres
From 27/2/96	2.7 litres
020 gearbox	2 litres
02A gearbox	2.1 litres

* Refer to Chapter 7, Section 1, for identification details

Braking system

All models	2.0 litres

Power steering

All models	0.7 to 0.9 litres

Fuel tank

All models (approximate)	45 litres

Washer reservoir

Models with headlight washers	7.0 litres
Models without headlight washers	3.0 litres

Engine

Oil filter:

Engine codes AAU, AAV, ABD, AEX, ABU	Champion C161
Engine codes AFT, 2E, AGG, ABF, 1F	Champion C160

Cooling system

Antifreeze mixture:

40% antifreeze	Protection down to -25°C
50% antifreeze	Protection down to -35°C

Note: *Refer to Section 31 and antifreeze manufacturer for latest recommendations.*

Fuel system

Air filter element:

Engine codes AAU, AAV, ABD, AEX, ABU, AFT	Champion W102
Engine code AER	Champion type not available
Engine codes ABF, 2E, AGG, 1F	Champion U586
Fuel filter	Champion L201

Ignition system

Ignition timing	Controlled by engine management system

Spark plugs:

	Type	**Electrode gap***
Engine codes AAU, 2E, AGG, AEE	Champion RN8VTYC4	Not adjustable
Engine code AAV	Champion N7BYC	0.7 mm
Engine codes ABD, AEX, ABU, 1F, AER, APQ	Champion RN10VTYC4	Not adjustable
Engine code AFT	Champion RC8VTYC4	Not adjustable
Engine code ABF	Champion C6VPYC	0.8 mm
Engine code ALM	Champion type not available	

*Gap setting as recommended by Champion for use with their specified plugs. If non-Champion plugs are to be used, the Seat recommendations for electrode gap are given below

Electrode gap (Seat recommendation):

All engine codes except ABF	0.7 to 0.9 mm
Engine code ABF	0.6 mm

Brakes

Brake pad minimum thickness (including backing plate)	7.0 mm
Brake shoe friction material minimum thickness	2.5 mm

Torque wrench settings

	Nm	lbf ft
Roadwheel bolts	110	81

Torque wrench settings (continued)	Nm	lbf ft
Spark plugs:		
Engine codes AAU, AAV	20	15
Engine codes AER, AEX, APQ, ABU, ABD, 1F, 2E	25	18
Engine code AEE, ALM, AFT, AGG, ABF	30	22
Sump drain plug	30	22
Transmission filler/level plug	25	18

Maintenance schedule - petrol models

The maintenance intervals in this manual are provided with the assumption that you, not the dealer, will be carrying out the work. These are the minimum intervals recommended for vehicles driven daily. If you wish to keep your vehicle in peak condition at all times, you may wish to perform some of these procedures more often. We encourage frequent maintenance, since it enhances the efficiency, performance and resale value of your vehicle.

When the vehicle is new, it should be serviced by a dealer service department, in order to preserve the factory warranty.

Every 250 miles (400 km) or weekly

☐ Refer to *Weekly checks*

Every 10 000 miles (15 000 km) - OEL on interval display

In addition to the items listed in the previous services, carry out the following:

☐ Renew the engine oil and filter (Section 3)
☐ Check the front (and rear where applicable) brake pad thickness (Section 4)
☐ Reset the service interval display (Section 5)

Every 12 months - IN 01 on interval display

Note: *If the vehicle is covering less than 10 000 miles (15 000 km) a year, also carry out the tasks listed above.*

☐ Check operation of all lights and horn (Section 6)
☐ Check the condition of the airbag unit(s) (Section 7)
☐ Check the operation of the washer system(s) (Section 8)
☐ Lubricate all hinges, locks and door check straps (Section 9)
☐ Check engine management and other systems for fault codes (Section 10)
☐ Check battery electrolyte level - where applicable (Section 11)
☐ Check all underbonnet components and hoses for fluid leaks (Section 12)
☐ Check the transmission and driveshaft gaiters for leaks and damage (Section 13)
☐ Check the braking system for leaks and damage (Section 14)
☐ Check the rear brake shoe lining thickness (Section 15)
☐ Check the condition of the exhaust system and its mountings (Section 16)
☐ Check the steering and suspension components for condition and security (Section 17)
☐ Check the headlight beam adjustment (Section 18)
☐ Carry out a road test (Section 19)
☐ Reset the service interval display (Section 5)

Every 20 000 miles (30 000 km) - IN 02 on interval display

Note: *If the vehicle is covering more than 20 000 miles (30 000 km) a year, also carry out all the operations described above*

☐ Renew the spark plugs on pre-1996 models only (Section 20)
☐ Renew the pollen filter element (Section 21)
☐ Check the condition of the auxiliary drivebelt(s), and renew if necessary (Section 22)
☐ Check the manual transmission oil level (Section 23)
☐ Check underbody protection for damage (Section 24)
☐ Check the timing belt for condition and wear (Section 25)
☐ Check exhaust emissions (Section 26)
☐ Reset the service interval display (Section 5)

Every 40 000 miles (60 000 km) or 2 years

In addition to the items listed in the previous services, carry out the following:

☐ Renew the air filter element (Section 27)
☐ Renew the fuel filter (Section 28)
☐ Renew the timing belt (Section 29)

Note: *Seat specify a timing belt renewal interval of 60 000 miles (90 000 km) however, if the vehicle is used mainly for short journeys, we recommend that this shorter interval is adhered to. The belt renewal interval is very much up to the individual owner but, bearing in mind that severe engine damage will result if the belt breaks in use, we recommend the shorter interval.*

Every 60 000 miles (90 000 km)

In addition to the items listed in the previous services, carry out the following:

☐ Renew the spark plugs on 1996-on models only (Section 20)
☐ Check and adjust the clutch pedal freeplay where applicable (Section 30)

Every 2 years (regardless of mileage)

In addition to the items listed in the previous services, carry out the following:

☐ Renew the coolant (Section 31)
☐ Renew the brake fluid (Section 32)

1A

Underbonnet view of a 1.4 litre petrol engine model (engine code APQ)

1 Engine oil dipstick
2 Engine oil filler cap
3 Coolant expansion tank
4 Washer fluid reservoir
5 Power steering fluid reservoir
6 Brake (and clutch) fluid reservoir
7 Front suspension strut upper mountings
8 Ignition coil
9 Battery
10 Air cleaner housing
11 Clutch cable
12 Exhaust manifold hot air shroud
13 Alternator
14 Fuel evaporative system charcoal canister
15 Oil filter

Front underbody view (1.4 litre petrol engine model shown - other models similar)

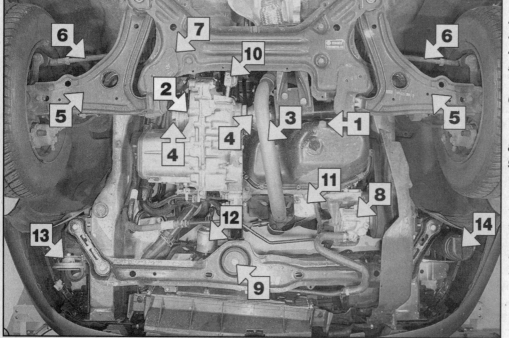

1 Engine oil drain plug
2 Transmission oil drain plug
3 Exhaust front pipe
4 Driveshafts
5 Front suspension lower arms
6 Steering track rods
7 Front suspension subframe (crossmember)
8 Power steering pump
9 Engine front mounting
10 Transmission gearchange linkage
11 Oil filter
12 Radiator electric cooling fan
13 Horn
14 Fuel evaporative system charcoal canister

Rear underbody view

1 Exhaust silencer and tailpipe
2 Fuel tank
3 Rear towing eye
4 Rear axle
5 Rear suspension strut lower mounting bolts
6 Handbrake cables

Underbonnet view of a 2.0 litre petrol engine model (engine code AGG)

1 Engine oil dipstick
2 Engine oil filler cap
3 Coolant expansion tank
4 Washer fluid reservoir
5 Power steering fluid reservoir
6 Brake (and clutch) fluid reservoir
7 Front suspension strut upper mountings
8 Ignition coil
9 Battery
10 Air cleaner housing
11 Clutch cable
12 Distributor
13 Alternator
14 Oil filter

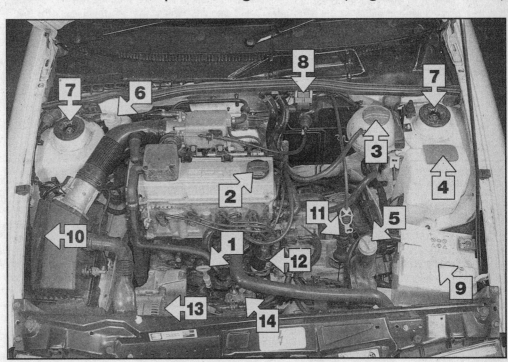

1 Introduction

General information

This Chapter is designed to help the home mechanic maintain his/her vehicle for safety, economy, long life and peak performance.

The Chapter contains a master mainten-ance schedule, followed by Sections dealing specifically with each task in the schedule. Visual checks, adjustments, component renewal and other helpful items are included. Refer to the accompanying illustrations of the engine compartment and the underside of the vehicle for the locations of the various components.

Servicing your vehicle in accordance with the mileage/time maintenance schedule and the following Sections will provide a planned maintenance programme, which should result in a long and reliable service life. This is a comprehensive plan, so maintaining some items but not others at the specified service intervals, will not produce the same results.

As you service your vehicle, you will discover that many of the procedures can - and should - be grouped together, because of the particular procedure being performed, or because of the proximity of two otherwise unrelated components to one another. For example, if the vehicle is raised for any reason, the exhaust can be inspected at the same time as the suspension and steering components.

The first step in this maintenance programme is to prepare yourself before the actual work begins. Read through all the Sections relevant to the work to be carried out, then make a list and gather all the parts and tools required. If a problem is encountered, seek advice from a parts specialist, or a dealer service department.

Service interval display

All models are equipped with a service interval display indicator in the instrument panel. Every time the engine is started, the panel will illuminate for a few seconds, providing a handy reminder of when the next service is required:

Display shows IN 00 - no service required.
Display shows OEL - 10 000 mile (15 000 km) service required.
Display shows IN 01 - 12 monthly service required.
Display shows IN 02 - 20 000 mile (30 000 km) service required.

The display should not necessarily be used as a definitive guide to the servicing needs of your car, but it is useful as a reminder, to ensure that servicing is not accidentally overlooked. Owners of older cars, or those covering a small annual mileage, may feel inclined to service their car more often, in which case the service interval display is perhaps less relevant.

The display should be reset whenever a service is carried out, and the procedure for this is described in Section 5.

2 Regular maintenance

1 If, from the time the vehicle is new, the routine maintenance schedule is followed closely, and frequent checks are made of fluid levels and high-wear items, as suggested throughout this manual, the engine will be kept in relatively good running condition, and the need for additional work will be minimised.
2 It is possible that there will be times when the engine is running poorly due to the lack of regular maintenance. This is even more likely if a used vehicle, which has not received regular and frequent maintenance checks, is purchased. In such cases, additional work may need to be carried out, outside of the regular maintenance intervals.
3 If engine wear is suspected, a compression test (refer to the relevant Part of Chapter 2)

will provide valuable information regarding the overall performance of the main internal components. Such a test can be used as a basis to decide on the extent of the work to be carried out. If, for example, a compression test indicates serious internal engine wear, conventional maintenance as described in this Chapter will not greatly improve the performance of the engine, and may prove a waste of time and money, unless extensive overhaul work is carried out first.
4 The following series of operations are those most often required to improve the performance of a generally poor-running engine:

Primary operations

a) *Clean, inspect and test the battery (Weekly checks and Section 11, where applicable).*
b) *Check all the engine-related fluids (Weekly checks).*
c) *Check the condition and tension of the auxiliary drivebelt (Section 22).*
d) *Renew the spark plugs (Section 20).*
e) *Inspect the distributor cap and rotor arm (Chapter 5B).*
f) *Check the condition of the air filter, and renew if necessary (Section 27).*
g) *Check the fuel filter (Section 28).*
h) *Check the condition of all hoses, and check for fluid leaks (Section 12).*
i) *Check the exhaust gas emissions (Section 26).*

5 If the above operations do not prove fully effective, carry out the following secondary operations:

Secondary operations

All items listed under Primary operations, plus the following:
a) *Check the charging system (Chapter 5A).*
b) *Check the ignition system (Chapter 5B).*
c) *Check the fuel system (Chapter 4A or 4B).*
d) *Renew the distributor cap and rotor arm (Chapter 5B).*
e) *Renew the ignition HT leads (Chapter 5B).*

Every 10 000 miles (15 000 km)

3 Engine oil and filter renewal

1 Frequent oil and filter changes are the most important maintenance procedures which can be undertaken by the DIY owner. As engine oil ages, it becomes diluted and contaminated, which leads to premature engine wear.

The oil change interval given in this Manual is the same as quoted by the manufacturer,

but owners of older vehicles (or those covering a small annual mileage) may feel justified in changing the oil and filter more frequently, perhaps every 5000 miles.

2 Before starting this procedure, gather all the necessary tools and materials. Also make sure that you have plenty of clean rags and newspapers handy, to mop up any spills. Ideally, the engine oil should be warm, as it will drain better, and more built-up sludge will be removed with it. Take care, however, not to touch the exhaust or any other hot parts of the

engine when working under the vehicle. To avoid any possibility of scalding, and to protect yourself from possible skin irritants and other harmful contaminants in used engine oils, it is advisable to wear gloves when carrying out this work.
3 Access to the underside of the vehicle will be greatly improved if it can be raised on a lift, driven onto ramps, or jacked up and supported on axle stands (see *Jacking and vehicle support*). Whichever method is chosen, make sure that the vehicle remains level, or if it is at an angle, that the drain plug is at the lowest point. Where applicable, remove the engine compartment undertray.

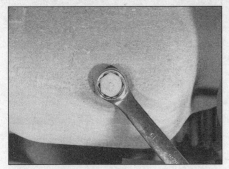

3.4 Unscrewing the sump drain plug

4 Using a socket and wrench or a ring spanner, unscrew the drain plug about half a turn **(see illustration)**. Position the draining container under the drain plug, then remove the plug completely **(see Haynes Hint)**. Recover the sealing ring from the drain plug.

5 Allow some time for the old oil to drain, noting that it may be necessary to reposition the container as the oil flow slows to a trickle.

6 After all the oil has drained, wipe off the drain plug with a clean rag, and fit a new sealing washer. Clean the area around the drain plug opening, and refit the plug. Tighten the plug to the specified torque.

7 Move the container into position under the oil filter, which is located on the front of the cylinder block. On engine codes AER, AAU, AAV, ABD, ABU, AEX, APQ, AEE, ALM, it is screwed directly into the cylinder block **(see illustration)**, however on engine codes AFT, 1F, 2E, AGG, ABF, it is screwed into a housing on the front of the cylinder block.

8 Using an oil filter removal tool, loosen the filter initially, then unscrew it by hand the rest of the way **(see illustration)**. Empty the oil in the filter into the container.

9 Use a clean rag to remove all oil, dirt and sludge from the filter sealing area. Check the old filter to make sure that the rubber sealing ring has not stuck to the engine. If it has, carefully remove it.

10 Apply a light coating of clean engine oil to the sealing ring on the new filter, then screw it into position on the engine. Tighten the filter firmly by hand only - **do not** use any tools.

11 Remove the old oil and all tools from under the car, then lower the car to the ground (if applicable).

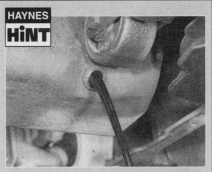

Keep the drain plug pressed into the sump while unscrewing it by hand the last couple of turns. As the plug releases, move it away sharply so the stream of oil issuing from the sump runs into the container, not up your sleeve!

12 Remove the dipstick, then unscrew the oil filler cap from the cylinder head cover. Fill the engine, using the correct grade and type of oil (see *Lubricants and fluids*). An oil can spout or funnel may help to reduce spillage. Pour in half the specified quantity of oil first, then wait a few minutes for the oil to drain into the sump **(see illustrations)**. Continue adding oil a small quantity at a time until the level is up to the bottom of the hatched area on the dipstick. Add more oil until the level is up to the top of the hatched area on the dipstick, then refit the dipstick and the filler cap.

13 Start the engine and run it for a few minutes, checking for leaks around the oil filter seal and the sump drain plug. Note that there may be a few seconds delay before the oil pressure warning light goes out when the engine is started, as the oil circulates through the engine oil galleries and the new oil filter before the pressure builds up.

14 Switch off the engine, and wait a few minutes for the oil to settle in the sump once more. With the new oil circulated and the filter completely full, recheck the level on the dipstick, and add more oil as necessary. Refit the tray to the underside of the engine, where applicable.

15 Dispose of the used engine oil safely, with reference to *General repair procedures* in the *Reference* section of this manual.

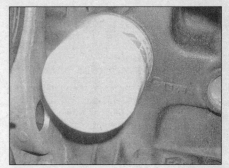

3.7 Oil filter location (engine code APQ)

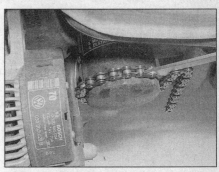

3.8 Loosening the oil filter using a chain-type removal tool

4 Front and rear brake pad check

1A

Front brake pads

1 Firmly apply the handbrake, then jack up the front of the car and support it securely on axle stands. Remove the front roadwheels.

2 For a comprehensive check, the brake pads should be removed and cleaned. The operation of the caliper can then also be checked, and the condition of the brake disc itself can be fully examined on both sides. Refer to Chapter 9 **(see Haynes Hint)**.

3.12a Remove the oil filler cap . . .

3.12b . . . then fill the engine using the correct grade and quantity of oil

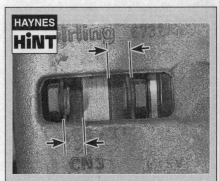

For a quick check, the thickness of the friction material on each brake pad can be measured through the aperture in the caliper body

3 If any pad's friction material is worn to the specified thickness or less, *all four pads must be renewed as a set.*

Rear brake pads (models with rear disc brakes)

4 Chock the front wheels, then jack up the rear of the vehicle and support it on axle stands. Remove the rear roadwheels.
5 For a quick check, the thickness of friction material remaining on each brake pad can be measured through the top of the caliper body. If any pad's friction material is worn to the specified thickness or less, all four pads must be renewed as a set.
6 For a comprehensive check, the brake pads should be removed and cleaned. This will permit the operation of the caliper to be checked, and the condition of the brake disc itself to be fully examined on both sides. Refer to Chapter 9 for further information.

7 If any pad's friction material is worn to the specified thickness or less, *all four pads must be renewed as a set.*

5 Resetting the service interval display

Refer to Chapter 12, Section 14.

Every 12 months

6 Lights and horn operation check
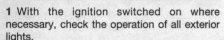

1 With the ignition switched on where necessary, check the operation of all exterior lights.
2 Check the brake lights with the help of an assistant, or by reversing up close to a reflective door or window. Make sure that all the rear lights are capable of operating independently, without affecting any of the other lights - for example, switch on as many rear lights as possible, then try the brake lights. If any unusual results are found, this is usually due to an earth fault or other poor connection at that rear light unit.
3 Again with the help of an assistant or using a reflective surface, check as far as possible that the headlights work on both main and dipped beam.
4 Replace any defective bulbs with reference to Chapter 12.

 Particularly on older vehicles, bulbs can stop working as a result of corrosion build-up on the bulb or its holder - fitting a new bulb will not cure the problem in this instance. When replacing any bulb, if you find any green or white-coloured powdery deposits, these should be cleaned off using emery cloth.

5 Check the operation of all interior lights, including the glovebox and luggage area illumination lights. Switch on the ignition, and check that all relevant warning lights come on as expected - the vehicle handbook should give details of these. Now start the engine, and check that the appropriate warning lights go out. When you are next driving at night, check that all the instrument panel and facia lighting works correctly. If any problems are found, refer to Chapter 12.
6 Finally, choose an appropriate time of day to test the operation of the horn.

7 Airbag unit check

On models fitted with an airbag, inspect the airbag(s) exterior condition checking for signs of damage or deterioration. If an airbag shows signs of damage, it must be renewed (see Chapter 12).

8 Washer system(s) check

1 Check that each of the washer jet nozzles is clear and that each nozzle provides a strong jet of washer fluid. The tailgate and headlight jets (where applicable) should be aimed to spray at a point slightly above the centre of the screen/headlight. On the windscreen washer nozzles where there are two jets, aim one of the jets slightly above the centre of the screen and aim the other just below to ensure complete coverage of the screen. If necessary, adjust the jets using a pin.
2 Check that the wiper system(s) operate correctly.

9 Hinge and lock lubrication

1 Lubricate the hinges of the bonnet, doors and tailgate with light general-purpose oil. Similarly, lubricate all latches, locks and lock strikers. At the same time, check the security and operation of all the locks, adjusting them if necessary (see Chapter 11).

2 Lightly lubricate the bonnet release mechanism and cable with a suitable grease.

10 Engine management system fault code check

1 This check is part of the manufacturer's maintenance schedule, and involves interrogating the engine management control unit (and the brake ABS module, if applicable) using special dedicated test equipment. Such testing will allow the test equipment to read any fault codes stored in the electronic control unit memory.
2 Unless a fault is suspected, this test is not essential, although it should be noted that it is recommended by the manufacturers.
3 It is possible for quite serious faults to occur in the engine management system without the owner being aware of it. Certain engine management system faults will cause the system to enter an emergency back-up mode, which is often so sophisticated that engine performance is not apparently much affected. If a problem has caused the system to enter its back-up mode, this will usually be most apparent when starting and running from cold.

11 Battery electrolyte level check

⚠️ *Warning: The electrolyte inside a battery is diluted acid, therefore it is a good idea to wear suitable rubber gloves when handling the battery. When topping-up, don't overfill the cells so that the electrolyte overflows. In the event of any spillage, rinse the electrolyte off without delay. Refit the cell covers and rinse the battery with copious quantities of clean water. Don't attempt to siphon out any excess electrolyte.*

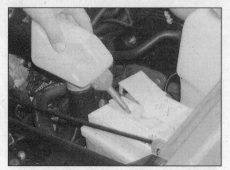

11.3 Topping up the battery electrolyte level using a battery top-up bottle with automatic level spout

1 Some models covered by this Manual may be fitted with a maintenance-free battery as standard equipment, or may have had one fitted as a replacement. If the battery in your vehicle is marked Freedom, Maintenance-Free or similar, no electrolyte level checking is required (the battery is often completely sealed, preventing any topping-up).

2 Batteries which do require their electrolyte level to be checked can be recognised by the presence of removable covers over the six battery cells - the battery casing is also sometimes translucent, so that the electrolyte level can be more easily checked.

3 Remove the cell covers and either look down inside the battery to see the level indicator, or check the level using any markings provided on the battery casing. The electrolyte should cover the battery plates by 2.0 or 3.0 mm. If necessary, top up a little at a time with distilled (de-ionised) water until the level in all six cells is correct - don't fill the cells up to the brim. Wipe up any spillage, then refit the cell covers **(see illustration)**.

12 Hose and fluid leak check

1 Visually inspect the engine joint faces, gaskets and seals for any signs of water or oil leaks. Pay particular attention to the areas around the camshaft cover, cylinder head, oil filter and sump joint faces. Bear in mind that, over a period of time, some very slight seepage from these areas is to be expected - what you are really looking for is any indication of a serious leak **(see Haynes Hint)**. Should a leak be found, renew the offending gasket or oil seal by referring to the appropriate Chapters in this manual.

2 Also check the security and condition of all the engine-related pipes and hoses. Ensure that all cable-ties or securing clips are in place and in good condition. Clips that are broken or missing can lead to chafing of the hoses, pipes or wiring, which could cause more serious problems in the future.

3 Carefully check the radiator hoses and heater hoses along their entire length. Renew

any hose that is cracked, swollen or deteriorated. Cracks will show up better if the hose is squeezed. Pay close attention to the hose clips that secure the hoses to the cooling system components. Hose clips can pinch and puncture hoses, resulting in cooling system leaks.

4 Inspect all the cooling system components (hoses, joint faces etc.) for leaks. A leak in the cooling system will usually show up as white- or rust-coloured deposits on the area adjoining the leak. Where any problems of this nature are found on system components, renew the component or gasket with reference to Chapter 3.

5 With the vehicle raised, inspect the fuel tank and filler neck for punctures, cracks and other damage. The connection between the filler neck and tank is especially critical. Sometimes a rubber filler neck or connecting hose will leak due to loose retaining clamps or deteriorated rubber.

6 Carefully check all rubber hoses and metal fuel lines leading away from the fuel tank. Check for loose connections, deteriorated hoses, crimped lines, and other damage. Pay particular attention to the vent pipes and hoses, which often loop up around the filler neck and can become blocked or crimped. Follow the lines to the front of the vehicle, carefully inspecting them all the way. Renew damaged sections as necessary.

7 From within the engine compartment, check the security of all fuel hose attachments and pipe unions, and inspect the fuel hoses and vacuum hoses for kinks, chafing and deterioration.

8 Where applicable, check the condition of the power steering fluid hoses and pipes.

13 Transmission and driveshaft gaiter check

1 Raise the front of the vehicle and support on axle stands. Alternatively, drive the car onto ramps.

2 Inspect around the transmission for any sign of leaks or damage. In particular, check the area around the driveshaft oil seals for

A leak in the cooling system will usually show up as white- or rust-coloured deposits on the area adjoining the leak

leakage **(see illustration)**. Slight seepage should not be of great concern, but a serious leak should be investigated further, with reference to Chapter 7.

3 Check the security and condition of the wiring and wiring plugs on the transmission housing.

4 With the vehicle raised and securely supported on stands, turn the steering onto full lock, then slowly rotate the roadwheels. Inspect the condition of the outer constant velocity (CV) joint rubber gaiters, squeezing the gaiters to open out the folds. Check for signs of cracking, splits or deterioration of the rubber, which may allow the grease to escape, and lead to water and grit entry into the joint **(see illustration)**. Also check the security and condition of the retaining clips. Repeat these checks on the inner CV joints. If any damage or deterioration is found, the gaiters should be renewed (see Chapter 8).

5 At the same time, check the general condition of the CV joints themselves by first holding the driveshaft and attempting to rotate the wheel. Repeat this check by holding the inner joint and attempting to rotate the driveshaft. Any appreciable movement indicates wear in the joints, wear in the driveshaft splines, or a loose driveshaft retaining nut.

1A

13.2 Driveshaft inner CV joint, showing driveshaft seal (arrowed)

13.4 Check the condition of the driveshaft gaiters (arrowed)

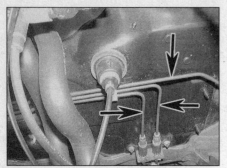

14.1 Hydraulic brake pipes located on the left-hand side of the bulkhead

15.2 Rear brake backplate inspection hole (arrowed) for assessing brake lining wear

14 Braking system check

1 Starting under the bonnet, examine the brake fluid reservoir and master cylinder for leaks. When a brake fluid leak occurs, it is normal to find blistered or wrinkled paint in the area of the leak. Check the metal pipes from the master cylinder for damage, and check the brake pressure regulator, servo/ABS unit and fluid unions for leaks **(see illustration)**.
2 With the vehicle raised and securely supported on stands, first inspect each front brake caliper. In particular, check the flexible hose leading to the caliper for signs of damage or leaks, especially where the hose enters the metal end fitting. Make sure that the hose is not twisted or kinked, and that it cannot come into contact with any other components when the steering is on full lock.
3 From the caliper, trace the brake pipes back along the car. Again, look for leaks from the fluid unions or signs of damage, but additionally check the pipes for signs of corrosion. Make sure the pipes are securely located by the clips provided on the vehicle underside.
4 At the rear of the vehicle, inspect each rear brake and its flexible hose. Examine the handbrake cables, tracing them back from each rear brake and checking for frayed cables or other damage. Lubricate the handbrake cable pivots and other moving parts with general-purpose grease. Also check that the rear wheels are locked when the handbrake lever is fully applied.
5 If any damage is found, refer to Chapter 9 for further information.

15 Rear brake shoe check

1 Chock the front wheels, then jack up the rear of the vehicle, and support it securely on axle stands.
2 For a quick check, the thickness of friction material remaining on one of the brake shoes can be observed through the hole in the brake backplate which is exposed by prising out the sealing grommet **(see illustration)**. If a rod of the same diameter as the specified minimum friction material thickness is placed against the shoe friction material, the amount of wear can be assessed. A torch or inspection light will probably be required. If the friction material on any shoe is worn down to the specified minimum thickness or less, all four shoes must be renewed as a set.
3 For a comprehensive check, the brake drum should be removed and cleaned. This will allow the wheel cylinders to be checked, and the condition of the brake drum itself to be fully examined (see Chapter 9).

16 Exhaust system check

1 With the engine cold (at least an hour after the vehicle has been driven), check the complete exhaust system from the engine to the end of the tailpipe. The exhaust system is most easily checked with the vehicle raised on a hoist, or suitably supported on axle stands, so that the exhaust components are readily visible and accessible.
2 Check the exhaust pipes and joints for evidence of leaks, severe corrosion and damage. Make sure that all brackets and mountings are in good condition, and that all relevant nuts and bolts are tight **(see illustration)**. Leakage at any of the joints or in other parts of the system will usually show up as a black sooty stain in the vicinity of the leak.
3 Rattles and other noises can often be traced to the exhaust system, especially the brackets and mountings. Try to move the pipes and silencers from side to side. If the components are able to come into contact with the body or suspension parts, secure the system with new mountings. If necessary, separate the joints (if possible) and twist the pipes as necessary to provide additional clearance.

17 Steering and suspension check

Front suspension and steering check

1 Raise the front of the vehicle, and securely support it on axle stands.
2 Visually inspect the balljoint dust covers and the steering rack-and-pinion gaiters for splits, chafing or deterioration. Any wear of these components will cause loss of lubricant, together with dirt and water entry, resulting in rapid deterioration of the balljoints or steering gear.
3 On vehicles with power steering, check the fluid hoses for chafing or deterioration, and the pipe and hose unions for fluid leaks. Also check for signs of fluid leakage under pressure from the steering gear rubber gaiters, which would indicate failed fluid seals within the steering gear.
4 Grasp the roadwheel at the 12 o'clock and 6 o'clock positions, and try to rock it **(see illustration)**. Very slight free play may be felt, but if the movement is appreciable, further investigation is necessary to determine the source. Continue rocking the wheel while an assistant depresses the footbrake. If the movement is now eliminated or significantly reduced, it is likely that the hub bearings are at fault. If the free play is still evident with the footbrake depressed, then there is wear in the suspension joints or mountings.

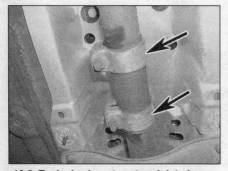

16.2 Typical exhaust system joint clamps (arrowed) - check that the nuts and bolts are tight, with no sign of leaks

17.4 Check for wear in the hub bearings by grasping the wheel and trying to rock it

5 Now grasp the wheel at the 9 o'clock and 3 o'clock positions, and try to rock it as before. Any movement felt now may again be caused by wear in the hub bearings or the steering tie-rod balljoints. If the inner or outer balljoint is worn, the visual movement will be obvious.

6 Using a large screwdriver or flat bar, check for wear in the suspension mounting bushes by levering between the relevant suspension component and its attachment point. Some movement is to be expected as the mountings are made of rubber, but excessive wear should be obvious. Also check the condition of any visible rubber bushes, looking for splits, cracks or contamination of the rubber.

7 With the car standing on its wheels, have an assistant turn the steering wheel back and forth about an eighth of a turn each way. There should be very little, if any, lost movement between the steering wheel and roadwheels. If this is not the case, closely observe the joints and mountings previously described, but in addition, check the steering column universal joints for wear, and the rack-and-pinion steering gear itself.

Rear suspension check

8 Chock the front wheels, then jack up the rear of the vehicle and support securely on axle stands.

9 Working as described previously for the front suspension, check the rear hub bearings, the suspension bushes and the strut mountings for wear.

Suspension strut/ shock absorber check

10 Check for any signs of fluid leakage around the suspension strut/shock absorber body, or from the rubber gaiter around the piston rod. Should any fluid be noticed, the suspension strut/shock absorber is defective internally, and should be renewed. **Note:** *Suspension struts/shock absorbers should always be renewed in pairs on the same axle.*

11 The efficiency of the suspension strut/shock absorber may be checked by bouncing the vehicle at each corner. The body

will return to its normal position and stop after being depressed. If it rises and returns on a rebound, the suspension strut/shock absorber is probably suspect. Also examine the suspension strut/shock absorber upper and lower mountings for any signs of wear.

18 Headlight beam alignment check

Accurate adjustment of the headlight beam is only possible using optical beam-setting equipment, and this work should therefore be carried out by a Seat dealer or service station with the necessary facilities.

Basic adjustments can be carried out in an emergency, and further details are given in Chapter 12.

19 Road test

Instruments and electrical equipment

1 Check the operation of all instruments and electrical equipment.

2 Make sure that all instruments read correctly, and switch on all electrical equipment in turn, to check that it functions properly.

Steering and suspension

3 Check for any abnormalities in the steering, suspension, handling or road feel.

4 Drive the vehicle, and check that there are no unusual vibrations or noises.

5 Check that the steering feels positive, with no excessive sloppiness, or roughness, and check for any suspension noises when cornering and driving over bumps.

Drivetrain

6 Check the performance of the engine, clutch (where applicable), gearbox/ transmission and driveshafts.

7 Listen for any unusual noises from the engine, clutch and gearbox/transmission.

8 Make sure the engine runs smoothly at idle, and there is no hesitation on accelerating.

9 Check that, where applicable, the clutch action is smooth and progressive, that the drive is taken up smoothly, and that the pedal travel is not excessive. Also listen for any noises when the clutch pedal is depressed.

10 Check that all gears can be engaged smoothly without noise, and that the gear lever action is not abnormally vague or notchy.

11 Listen for a metallic clicking sound from the front of the vehicle, as the vehicle is driven slowly in a circle with the steering on full-lock. Carry out this check in both directions. If a clicking noise is heard, this indicates wear in a driveshaft joint, in which case renew the joint if necessary.

Check the operation and performance of the braking system

12 Make sure that the vehicle does not pull to one side when braking, and that the wheels do not lock prematurely when braking hard.

13 Check that there is no vibration through the steering when braking.

14 Check that the handbrake operates correctly without excessive movement of the lever, and that it holds the vehicle stationary on a slope.

15 Test the operation of the brake servo unit as follows. With the engine off, depress the footbrake four or five times to exhaust the vacuum. Hold the brake pedal depressed, then start the engine. As the engine starts, there should be a noticeable give in the brake pedal as vacuum builds up. Allow the engine to run for at least two minutes, and then switch it off. If the brake pedal is depressed now, it should be possible to detect a hiss from the servo as the pedal is depressed. After about four or five applications, no further hissing should be heard, and the pedal should feel considerably harder.

1A

Every 20 000 miles (30 000 km)

20 Spark plug renewal

1 The correct functioning of the spark plugs is vital for the correct running and efficiency of the engine. It is essential that the plugs fitted are appropriate for the engine (a suitable type is specified at the beginning of this Chapter). If

this type is used and the engine is in good condition, the spark plugs should not need attention between scheduled replacement intervals. Spark plug cleaning is rarely necessary, and should not be attempted unless specialised equipment is available, as damage can easily be caused to the electrodes.

2 Before removing the spark plugs, allow the engine time to cool.

3 To gain access to the spark plugs on engine codes AER, AAU, AAV, ABD, ABU, AEX, APQ,

AEE, ALM, refer to Chapter 4A or 4B as applicable, and remove the air filter housing complete or alternatively leave the hoses connected and move the housing to the rear of the engine compartment. On some models, it may also be necessary to unclip the accelerator cable. On engine code AFT remove the upper section of the inlet manifold with reference to Chapter 4B. On engine codes 1F, 2E, AGG, ABF, the spark plugs are accessible without removing any other components.

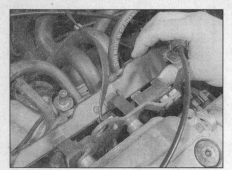

20.4 Where applicable, pull the HT lead clip out of the retaining brackets on the rear of the cylinder head

20.5 Pull the HT lead end fittings off the plugs

20.7a Use a spark plug spanner to unscrew the plugs

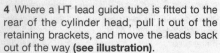

4 Where a HT lead guide tube is fitted to the rear of the cylinder head, pull it out of the retaining brackets, and move the leads back out of the way (see illustration).

5 If the marks on the original-equipment spark plug (HT) leads cannot be seen, mark the leads 1 to 4, to correspond to the relevant cylinder (No 1 cylinder is at the timing belt end of the engine). Where metal heat shields are fitted to the lead end fittings, take care not to burn your hands if the engine is still warm. Pull the leads from the plugs by gripping the end fitting, not the lead, otherwise the lead connection may be fractured (see illustration).

6 It is advisable to remove the dirt from the spark plug recesses using a clean brush, vacuum cleaner or compressed air before removing the plugs, to prevent dirt dropping into the cylinders.

7 Unscrew the plugs using a spark plug spanner, suitable box spanner or a deep socket and extension bar (see illustrations). Keep the socket aligned with the spark plug - if it is forcibly moved to one side, the ceramic insulator may be broken off. As each plug is removed, examine it as follows.

8 Examination of the spark plugs will give a good indication of the condition of the engine. If the insulator nose of the spark plug is clean and white, with no deposits, this is indicative of a weak mixture or too hot a plug (a hot plug transfers heat away from the electrode slowly, a cold plug transfers heat away quickly).

9 If the tip and insulator nose are covered with hard black-looking deposits, then this is indicative that the mixture is too rich. Should the

plug be black and oily, then it is likely that the engine is fairly worn, as well as the mixture being too rich.

10 If the insulator nose is covered with light tan to greyish-brown deposits, then the mixture is correct and it is likely that the engine is in good condition.

11 The spark plug electrode gap is of considerable importance as, if it is too large or too small, the size of the spark and its efficiency will be seriously impaired. Where the gap can be adjusted, it should be set to the value specified at the start of this Chapter. **Note:** *Spark plugs with multiple earth electrodes are becoming an increasingly common fitment, especially to vehicles equipped with catalytic converters. Unless there is clear information to the contrary, no attempt should be made to adjust the plug gap on a spark plug with more than one earth electrode.*

12 To set the gap, measure it with a feeler blade and then bend open or close the outer plug electrode until the correct gap is achieved. The centre electrode should never be bent, as this will crack the insulator and cause plug failure, if nothing worse. If using feeler blades, the gap is correct when the appropriate-size blade is a firm sliding fit.

13 Special spark plug electrode gap adjusting tools are available from most motor accessory shops, or from some spark plug manufacturers (see illustration).

14 Before fitting the spark plugs, check that the threaded connector sleeves are tight, and that the plug exterior surfaces and threads are

clean. It's often difficult to screw in new spark plugs without cross-threading them - this can be avoided using a piece of rubber hose (see Haynes Hint).

15 Remove the rubber hose (if used), and tighten the plug to the specified torque using the spark plug socket and a torque wrench. Refit the remaining spark plugs in the same manner.

16 Reconnect the HT leads securely in their correct order, and where applicable refit the guide tube.

17 Refit the items removed in paragraph 3 according to engine code.

21 Pollen filter renewal

1 The pollen filter (where fitted) is located beneath the windscreen cowl panels; it is located on the right-hand side on left-hand drive models, and the left-hand side on right-hand drive models.

HAYNES HiNT

It is very often difficult to insert spark plugs into their holes without cross-threading them. To avoid this possibility, fit a short length of 5/16 inch internal diameter rubber hose over the end of the spark plug. The flexible hose acts as a universal joint to help align the plug with the plug hole. Should the plug begin to cross-thread, the hose will slip on the spark plug, preventing thread damage to the aluminium cylinder head

20.7b Removing a spark plug from the cylinder head

20.13 Adjusting a spark plug electrode gap with the special tool

2 Remove the windscreen cowl panel as described in Chapter 11.

3 Unscrew the two plastic nuts and remove the plastic grille panel from the pollen filter.

4 Depress the two retaining tabs at the front of the pollen filter, and lift the filter from its housing.

5 Fit the new filter using a reversal of the removal procedure.

22 Auxiliary drivebelt check and renewal

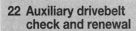

Checking

1 Apply the handbrake, then jack up the front of the vehicle and support it on axle stands (see *Jacking and vehicle support*). Loosen the right-hand front wheel bolts.

2 Remove the right-hand front roadwheel.

3 Turn the steering to full right-hand lock. Where applicable, remove the fasteners, and lower the wheel arch liner and/or engine undertray for access to the drivebelt. Models with power steering may have a cover fitted over the drivebelt - if so, release the fasteners and remove it.

4 Using a socket and wrench on the crankshaft sprocket bolt, rotate the crankshaft so that the full length of the auxiliary drivebelt(s) can be examined. Look for cracks, splitting and fraying on the surface of the belt; check also for signs of glazing (shiny patches) and separation of the belt plies. If damage or wear is visible, the belt should be renewed. If there is any evidence of contamination by oil, grease or coolant, the reason should be investigated without delay.

5 Where the drivebelt tension is adjustable, check and if necessary adjust its tension with reference to Chapter 2A.

6 On completion, refit the wheel arch liner and engine undertray (as applicable), then refit the roadwheel and lower the car to the ground. Tighten the roadwheel bolts to the specified torque.

Renewal

7 For details of auxiliary drivebelt renewal, refer to Chapter 2A.

23.2a 085 transmission oil filler/level plug (arrowed) - models up to October 1995

23 Manual transmission oil level check

1 Park the car on a level surface. The oil level must be checked before the car is driven, or at least 5 minutes after the engine has been switched off. If the oil is checked immediately after driving the car, some of the oil will remain distributed around the transmission components, resulting in an inaccurate level reading.

2 On pre October 1995 models equipped with the 085 transmission, the filler/level plug is located above the left-hand driveshaft, and the drain plug is located below the driveshaft. For easier access, turn the steering onto full left lock. Do not raise the car, because the level must be checked with the car resting on its wheels, on a level surface. On October 1995-on models equipped with the 085 transmission, the filler/level plug is located on the front of the transmission housing, and can be accessed from above **(see illustrations)**. If preferred, however, the plug can be reached from below.

3 On models equipped with the 020 transmission, the filler/level plug is located on the left-hand end of the transmission, and the drain plug is located below the final drive and driveshaft position. On the 02A transmission the filler/level plug is located on the front of the transmission **(see illustrations)**.

4 Wipe clean the area around the filler/level

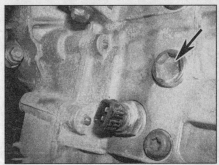

23.2b 085 transmission oil filler/level plug (arrowed) - models from October 1995

plug. A 17 mm hexagonal socket (or a large Allen key) will be required to remove the plug **(see illustration)**.

5 The oil level should reach the lower edge of the filler/level hole. A certain amount of oil will have gathered behind the filler/level plug, and will trickle out when it is removed; this does **not** necessarily indicate that the level is correct. To ensure that a true level is established, wait until the initial trickle has stopped, then add oil through the hole as necessary until a trickle of new oil can be seen emerging. The level will be correct when the flow ceases; use only oil of the specified type.

6 Filling the transmission with oil is an extremely awkward operation; above all, allow plenty of time for the oil to settle properly before checking it. If a large amount is added to the transmission, and a large amount flows out on checking the level, refit the filler/level plug; take the vehicle on a short journey so that the new oil is distributed fully around the transmission components, then recheck the level when it has settled again.

7 If the transmission has been overfilled so that oil flows out when the filler/level plug is removed, check that the car is completely level (front-to-rear and side-to-side), and allow the surplus to drain off into a suitable container.

8 When the level is correct, refit the plug, tightening it to the specified torque, and wipe off any spilt oil.

1A

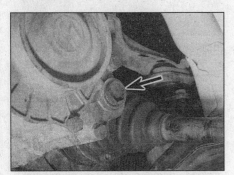

23.3a Manual transmission oil filler/level plug location (Type 020 transmission)

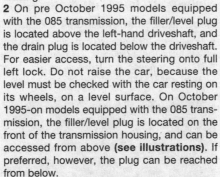
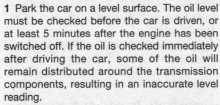

23.3b Manual transmission oil filler/level plug location (Type 02A transmission)

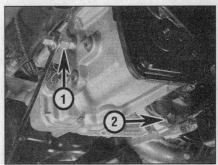

23.4 Loosening the filler/level plug (1) on the later 085 transmission using a hex adapter - also shown is the transmission oil drain plug (2)

24 Underbody protection check

Raise and support the vehicle on axle stands. Using an electric torch or lead light, inspect the entire underside of the vehicle, paying particular attention to the wheel arches. Look for any damage to the flexible underbody coating, which may crack or flake off with age, leading to corrosion. Also check that the wheel arch liners are securely attached with any clips provided - if they come loose, dirt may get in behind the liners and defeat their purpose. If there is any damage to the underseal, or any corrosion, it should be repaired before the damage gets too serious.

25 Timing belt check

1 Refer to Chapter 2A and remove the upper timing belt covers for access to the timing belt.
2 Using a socket on the crankshaft pulley bolt, turn the engine slowly while thoroughly checking the timing belt for signs of damage and wear, especially at the roots of the belt teeth. Also check for oil contamination which may have come from the crankshaft oil seal.
3 Fit a new oil seal where necessary, and a new timing belt if required with reference to Chapter 2A.
4 Check and where necessary adjust the tension of the timing belt with reference to Chapter 2A.

5 Refit the upper timing belt covers.

26 Exhaust emissions check

This check is part of the manufacturer's maintenance schedule, and involves testing the exhaust emissions using an exhaust gas analyser. Unless a fault is suspected, this test is not essential, although it should be noted that it is recommended by the manufacturers. In the majority of cases, adjusting the idle speed and mixture is either not possible, or requires access to dedicated test equipment. Exhaust emissions testing is included as part of the MOT test.

Every 40 000 miles (60 000 km) or 2 years

27 Air filter renewal

Single-point injection models

Rectangular side-mounted air cleaner

1 Prise open the retaining clips and lift the top cover from the air cleaner. Unclip the vacuum hose where applicable **(see illustrations)**.
2 Remove the air cleaner filter element, noting which way up it is fitted.

Inlet manifold/throttle body mounted air cleaner

3 On models with a round-type air cleaner, prise open the retaining clips and lift the cover from the top of the air cleaner.
4 Remove the filter element.

Multi-point injection models

Rectangular side-mounted air cleaner

5 Prise open the retaining clips and lift the top cover from the air cleaner. On engine code AGG, disconnect the hose from the inlet resonator first **(see illustrations)**.

6 Remove the air cleaner filter element, noting which way up it is fitted **(see illustration)**.

Inlet manifold/throttle body mounted air cleaner

7 There are eight screws visible on the air cleaner top cover, and four of them are marked 1 to 4 on the top cover - these four screws secure the housing to the inlet manifold. The remaining four screws secure the air cleaner top cover to the air cleaner housing, and must also be removed to renew

27.1a Release the air filter cover clips . . .

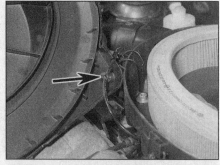
27.1b . . . then lift off the cover and unclip the vacuum hose (arrowed)

27.5a Prise open the retaining clips . . .

27.5b . . . disconnect the inlet resonator hose . . .

27.6 . . . and remove the air filter element (engine code AGG)

27.7a Unscrew the cover retaining screws . . .

the filter element **(see illustrations)**. Remove all eight screws, noting that they are of different lengths.

8 Lift off the air cleaner top cover, and take out the filter element **(see illustration)**.

All models

9 Remove any debris that may have collected inside the air cleaner and wipe it clean.

10 Fit a new air filter element in position, making sure it is correctly seated.

11 Refit the air cleaner top cover and secure with the screws or clips, as applicable.

28 Fuel filter renewal

Refer to Chapter 4A, Section 6

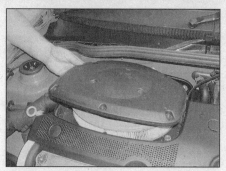

27.7b . . . pull the housing forwards and lift off the cover . . .

27.8 . . . then remove the air filter element

29 Timing belt renewal

Note: *Seat specify a timing belt renewal interval of 60 000 miles (90 000 km) however, if the vehicle is used mainly for short journeys,* we recommend that this shorter interval is adhered to. The belt renewal interval is very much up to the individual owner but, bearing in mind that severe engine damage will result if the belt breaks in use, we recommend the shorter interval.

Refer to Chapter 2A for the renewal procedure.

Every 60 000 miles (90 000 km)

30 Clutch pedal freeplay check

Note: *This Section only applies to models with a 085 or 02A transmission fitted with manually-adjusted clutch cable. All other models are fitted with either a self-adjusting cable or hydraulically-operated clutch which* automatically compensates for wear of the clutch friction plate linings.

Refer to Chapter 6 for details of adjusting the pedal/cable freeplay.

Every 2 years (regardless of mileage)

31 Coolant renewal

1 Two types of coolant are specified by the manufacturers for use in the coolant system, and it is important not to mix them as they have different characteristics. The G11 coolant is for use in cast iron engines, and the G12 coolant is for use in both cast iron and aluminium engines. G11 coolant is a dark blue-greenish colour, and G12 coolant is a reddish colour. If G12 coolant appears brown, this indicates that it has been mixed with another antifreeze additive, in which case the cooling system must be flushed out then filled with a fresh solution.

2 The expansion tank should have a mark or label on it indicating which type of coolant to use, however as from August 1996, all engines are filled with G12 solution. Earlier engines may have G11 solution and may continue to have this type, however, if preferred it may be replaced by G12 solution. Change the marking or label if the solution is changed.

Cooling system draining

⚠️ *Warning: Wait until the engine is cold before starting this procedure. Do not allow antifreeze to come in contact with your skin, or with the painted surfaces of the vehicle. Rinse off spills immediately with plenty of water. Never leave antifreeze lying around in an open container, or in a puddle in the driveway or on the garage floor. Children and pets are attracted by its sweet smell, but antifreeze can be fatal if ingested.*

3 With the engine completely cold, cover the expansion tank cap with a wad of rag, and slowly turn the cap anti-clockwise to relieve the pressure in the cooling system (a hissing sound will normally be heard). Wait until any pressure remaining in the system is released, then continue to turn the cap until it can be removed.

4 Where necessary, remove the engine compartment undertray. Position a suitable container beneath the radiator bottom hose connection, then release the retaining clip and ease the hose from the radiator stub. Alternatively, disconnect the hose from the thermostat housing and bend the hose down into the container. If the hose joint has not been disturbed for some time, it will be necessary to gently manipulate the hose to break the joint. Do not use excessive force, or the radiator stub could be damaged. Allow the coolant to drain into the container.

5 If the coolant has been drained for a reason other than renewal, then provided it is clean and less than two years old, it can be re-used.

6 Once all the coolant has drained, reconnect the hose to the radiator (or thermostat housing) and secure it in position with the retaining clip.

Cooling system flushing

7 If coolant renewal has been neglected, or if the antifreeze mixture has become diluted, then in time, the cooling system may gradually lose efficiency, as the coolant passages become restricted due to rust, scale deposits, and other sediment. Flushing the system clean can restore the cooling system efficiency.

8 The radiator should be flushed independently of the engine, to avoid unnecessary contamination.

Radiator flushing

9 To flush the radiator, disconnect the top and bottom hoses and any other relevant hoses from the radiator, with reference to Chapter 3.

10 Insert a garden hose into the radiator top inlet. Direct a flow of clean water through the radiator, and continue flushing until clean water emerges from the radiator bottom outlet.

11 If after a reasonable period, the water still does not run clear, the radiator can be flushed with a good proprietary cooling system cleaning agent. It is important that the manufacturer's instructions are followed carefully. If the contamination is particularly bad, insert the hose in the radiator bottom outlet, and reverse-flush the radiator. This is best carried out with the radiator removed from the vehicle.

Engine flushing

12 To flush the engine, remove the thermostat as described in Chapter 3, then temporarily refit the thermostat cover.

13 With the top and bottom hoses disconnected from the radiator, insert a garden hose into the radiator top hose. Direct a clean flow of water through the engine, and continue flushing until clean water emerges from the radiator bottom hose.

14 On completion of flushing, refit the thermostat and reconnect the hoses with reference to Chapter 3.

Cooling system filling

15 Before attempting to fill the cooling system, make sure that all hoses and clips are in good condition, and that the clips are tight. Note that an antifreeze mixture must be used all year round, to prevent corrosion of the engine components.

16 Remove the expansion tank filler cap, and fill the system by slowly pouring the coolant into the expansion tank. If the coolant is being renewed, begin by pouring in a couple of litres of water, followed by the correct quantity of antifreeze, then top-up with more water. Once the level in the expansion tank starts to rise, squeeze the radiator top and bottom hoses to help expel any trapped air in the system. With all the air expelled, top-up the coolant level to

the MAX mark and refit the expansion tank cap.

17 Start the engine and run it until it reaches normal operating temperature and the electric cooling fan operates, then stop the engine and allow it to cool.

18 Check for leaks, particularly around disturbed components. Check the coolant level in the expansion tank, and top-up if necessary. Note that the system must be cold before an accurate level is indicated in the expansion tank. If the expansion tank cap is removed while the engine is still warm, cover the cap with a thick cloth, and unscrew the cap slowly to gradually relieve the system pressure. Wait until any pressure remaining in the system is released, then continue to turn the cap until it can be removed.

Antifreeze type and mixture

19 The antifreeze should always be renewed at the specified intervals. This is necessary not only to maintain the antifreeze properties, but also to prevent corrosion which would otherwise occur as the corrosion inhibitors become progressively less effective.

20 Always use the correct antifreeze (refer to paragraphs 1 and 2). The quantity of antifreeze and levels of protection are indicated in the Specifications.

21 Before adding antifreeze, the cooling system should be completely drained, preferably flushed, and all hoses checked for condition and security.

22 After filling with antifreeze, a label should be attached to the expansion tank, stating the type and concentration of antifreeze used, and the date installed. Any subsequent topping-up should be made with the same type and concentration of antifreeze.

23 Do not use engine antifreeze in the washer system, as it will cause damage to the vehicle paintwork.

---

32 Brake fluid renewal

 Warning: Brake hydraulic fluid can harm your eyes and damage painted surfaces, so use extreme caution when handling and pouring it. Do not use fluid that has been standing open for some time, as it absorbs moisture from the air. Excess moisture can cause a dangerous loss of braking effectiveness.

1 The procedure is similar to that for the bleeding of the hydraulic system as described in Chapter 9, except that the brake fluid reservoir should be emptied by siphoning, using a clean poultry baster or similar before starting, and allowance should be made for the old fluid to be expelled when bleeding a section of the circuit.

2 Working as described in Chapter 9, open the first bleed screw in the sequence, and pump the brake pedal gently until nearly all the old fluid has been emptied from the master cylinder reservoir.

 Warning: On models with ABS, under no circumstances should the hydraulic unit bleed screws be opened.

 Old hydraulic fluid is often much darker in colour than the new, making it easy to distinguish the two.

3 Top-up to the MAX level with new fluid, and continue pumping until only the new fluid remains in the reservoir, and new fluid can be seen emerging from the bleed screw. Tighten the screw, and top the reservoir level up to the MAX level line.

4 Work through all the remaining bleed screws in the sequence until new fluid can be seen at all of them. Be careful to keep the master cylinder reservoir topped-up to above the MIN level at all times, or air may enter the system and greatly increase the length of the task.

5 On models fitted with a hydraulic clutch, bleed the system as described in Chapter 6.

6 When the operation is complete, check that all bleed screws are securely tightened, and that their dust caps are refitted. Wash off all traces of spilt fluid, and recheck the master cylinder reservoir fluid level.

7 Check the operation of the brakes before taking the car on the road.

Chapter 1 Part B:
Routine maintenance & servicing - diesel models

Contents

1B

Degrees of difficulty

Easy, suitable for novice with little experience	**Fairly easy,** suitable for beginner with some experience	**Fairly difficult,** suitable for competent DIY mechanic	**Difficult,** suitable for experienced DIY mechanic	**Very difficult,** suitable for expert DIY or professional

Lubricants and fluids

Refer to end of *Weekly checks*

Capacities

Engine oil (including 0.5 litres for filter)
All engines .... 4.5 litres

Cooling system (approximate)
Engine codes 1Y, AAZ .... 6.5 litres
Engine codes 1Z, AHU, AEY, AFN .... 5.5 litres

Transmission*
020 gearbox .... 2 litres
02A gearbox .... 2.1 litres
* Refer to Chapter 7, Section 1, for identification details

Braking system
All models .... 2.0 litres

Power steering
All models .... 0.7 to 0.9 litres

Fuel tank
All models (approximate) .... 45 litres

Washer reservoir
Models with headlight washers .... 7.0 litres
Models without headlight washers .... 3.0 litres

Engine

Oil filter:
    Engine codes 1Y, 1Z, AAZ .... Champion C150
    Engine codes AEY, AHU, AFN .... Champion type not available

Cooling system

Antifreeze mixture:
    40% antifreeze .... Protection down to -25°C
    50% antifreeze .... Protection down to -35°C
Note: *Refer to Section 32 and antifreeze manufacturer for latest recommendations.*

Fuel system

Air filter element:
    Engine codes 1Y, 1Z, AAZ .... Champion U582
    Engine codes AEY, AHU, AFN .... Champion type not available
Fuel filter:
    Engine codes 1Y, 1Z, AAZ .... Champion L114
    Engine codes AEY, AHU, AFN .... Champion type not available
Idle speed:
    Engine code 1Y .... 900 ± 30 rpm
    Engine code AAZ .... 920 ± 30 rpm

Brakes

Brake pad minimum thickness (including backing plate) .... 7.0 mm
Brake shoe friction material minimum thickness .... 2.5 mm

Torque wrench settings	Nm	lbf ft
Roadwheel bolts	110	81
Sump drain plug	30	22
Transmission filler/level plug	25	18

The maintenance intervals in this manual are provided with the assumption that you, not the dealer, will be carrying out the work. These are the minimum intervals recommended for vehicles driven daily. If you wish to keep your vehicle in peak condition at all times, you may wish to perform some of these procedures more often. We encourage frequent maintenance, since it enhances the efficiency, performance and resale value of your vehicle.

When the vehicle is new, it should be serviced by a dealer service department, in order to preserve the factory warranty.

Every 250 miles (400 km) or weekly

☐ Refer to *Weekly checks*

Every 10 000 miles (15 000 km) - OEL on interval display

Note: *Every 5000 miles (7500 km) on models with engine codes 1Y and AEY.*
In addition to the items listed in the previous services, carry out the following:

☐ Renew the engine oil and filter (Section 3)
☐ Check the front (and rear where applicable) brake pad lining thickness (Section 4)
☐ Drain water from the fuel filter (Section 5)
☐ Reset the service interval display (Section 6)

Every 12 months - IN 01 on interval display

Note: *If the vehicle is covering less than 10 000 miles (15 000 km) a year, also carry out the tasks listed above.*

☐ Check operation of all lights and horn (Section 7)
☐ Check the condition of the airbag unit(s) (Section 8)
☐ Check the operation of the washer system(s) (Section 9)
☐ Lubricate all hinges, locks and door check straps (Section 10)
☐ Check diesel engine management and other systems for fault codes, where applicable (Section 11)
☐ Check battery electrolyte level - where applicable (Section 12)
☐ Check all underbonnet components and hoses for fluid leaks (Section 13)
☐ Check the transmission and driveshaft gaiters for leaks and damage (Section 14)
☐ Check the braking system for leaks and damage (Section 15)
☐ Check the rear brake shoe lining thickness (Section 16)
☐ Check the condition of the exhaust system and its mountings (Section 17)
☐ Check the steering and suspension components for condition and security (Section 18)
☐ Check the headlight beam adjustment (Section 19)
☐ Carry out a road test (Section 20)
☐ Check the idle speed and adjust if necessary - engine codes 1Y and AAZ only (Section 21)
☐ Reset the service interval display (Section 6)

Every 20 000 miles (30 000 km) - IN 02 on interval display

Note: *If the vehicle is covering more than 20 000 miles (30 000 km) a year, also carry out all the operations described above*

☐ Renew the fuel filter (Section 22)
☐ Renew the pollen filter element (Section 23)
☐ Check the condition of the auxiliary drivebelt(s), and renew if necessary (Section 24)
☐ Check the timing belt for condition and wear (Section 25)
☐ Check the manual transmission oil level (Section 26)
☐ Check underbody protection for damage (Section 27)
☐ Renew the air filter element (Section 28)
☐ Check exhaust emissions (Section 29)
☐ Reset the service interval display (Section 6)

Every 60 000 miles (90 000 km)

In addition to the items listed in the previous services, carry out the following:

☐ Renew the timing belt, and the tensioner roller (Section 30)
☐ Check and adjust the clutch pedal freeplay where applicable (Section 31)

Every 2 years (regardless of mileage)

In addition to the items listed in the previous services, carry out the following:

☐ Renew the coolant (Section 32)
☐ Renew the brake fluid (Section 33)

1B

Underbonnet view of a 1.9 litre diesel engine model

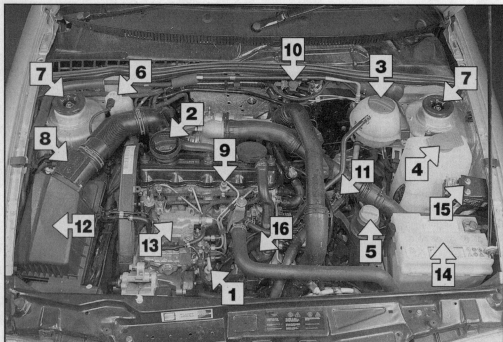

1 Engine oil dipstick
2 Engine oil filler cap
3 Coolant expansion tank
4 Washer fluid reservoir
5 Power steering fluid reservoir
6 Brake (and clutch) fluid reservoir
7 Front suspension strut upper mountings
8 Airflow sensor
9 Injector with needle stroke transmitter
10 Turbocharger boost pressure valve
11 Inlet air temperature sender
12 Air cleaner assembly
13 Fuel injection pump
14 Battery
15 Air conditioning system fusebox
16 Brake servo vacuum pump

Front underbody view of a 1.9 litre diesel engine model

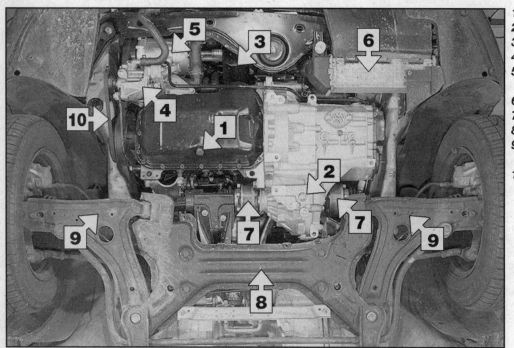

1 Engine oil drain plug
2 Transmission oil drain plug
3 Oil filter
4 Power steering pump
5 Air conditioning compressor
6 Intercooler
7 Driveshafts
8 Front subframe
9 Front suspension lower arms
10 Power steering pump drivebelt

Rear underbody view of a 1.9 litre diesel engine model

1 Exhaust silencer and tailpipe
2 Fuel tank
3 Rear axle
4 Rear suspension strut lower mounting bolts
5 Handbrake cables

1B

Maintenance procedures

1 Introduction

General information

This Chapter is designed to help the home mechanic maintain his/her vehicle for safety, economy, long life and peak performance.

The Chapter contains a master maintenance schedule, followed by Sections dealing specifically with each task in the schedule. Visual checks, adjustments, component renewal and other helpful items are included. Refer to the accompanying illustrations of the engine compartment and the underside of the vehicle for the locations of the various components.

Servicing your vehicle in accordance with the mileage/time maintenance schedule and the following Sections will provide a planned maintenance programme, which should result in a long and reliable service life. This is a comprehensive plan, so maintaining some items but not others at the specified service intervals, will not produce the same results.

As you service your vehicle, you will discover that many of the procedures can - and should - be grouped together, because of the particular procedure being performed, or because of the proximity of two otherwise unrelated components to one another. For example, if the vehicle is raised for any reason, the exhaust can be inspected at the same time as the suspension and steering components.

The first step in this maintenance programme is to prepare yourself before the actual work begins. Read through all the Sections relevant to the work to be carried out, then make a list and gather all the parts and tools required. If a problem is encountered, seek advice from a parts specialist, or a dealer service department.

Service interval display

All models are equipped with a service interval display indicator in the instrument panel. Every time the engine is started, the panel will illuminate for a few seconds, providing a handy reminder of when the next service is required:

Display shows IN 00 - no service required.
Display shows OEL - 10 000 mile (15 000 km) service required.
Display shows IN 01 - 12 monthly service required.

Display shows IN 02 - 20 000 mile (30 000 km) service required.

The display should not necessarily be used as a definitive guide to the servicing needs of your car, but it is useful as a reminder, to ensure that servicing is not accidentally overlooked. Owners of older cars, or those covering a small annual mileage, may feel inclined to service their car more often, in which case the service interval display is perhaps less relevant.

The display should be reset whenever a service is carried out, and the procedure for this is described in Section 6.

2 Regular maintenance

1 If, from the time the vehicle is new, the routine maintenance schedule is followed closely, and frequent checks are made of fluid levels and high-wear items, as suggested throughout this manual, the engine will be kept in relatively good running condition, and the need for additional work will be minimised.
2 It is possible that there will be times when the engine is running poorly due to the lack of

regular maintenance. This is even more likely if a used vehicle, which has not received regular and frequent maintenance checks, is purchased. In such cases, additional work may need to be carried out, outside of the regular maintenance intervals.

3 If engine wear is suspected, a compression test (refer to the relevant Part of Chapter 2) will provide valuable information regarding the overall performance of the main internal components. Such a test can be used as a basis to decide on the extent of the work to be carried out. If, for example, a compression test indicates serious internal engine wear, conventional maintenance as described in this Chapter will not greatly improve the performance of the engine, and may prove a waste of time and money, unless extensive overhaul work is carried out first.

4 The following series of operations are those most often required to improve the performance of a generally poor-running engine:

Primary operations

a) Clean, inspect and test the battery (Weekly checks and Section 12, where applicable).
b) Check all the engine-related fluids (Weekly checks).
c) Drain the water from the fuel filter (Section 5).
d) Check the condition and tension of the auxiliary drivebelt(s) (Section 24).
e) Check the condition of the air filter, and renew if necessary (Section 28).
f) Check the condition of all hoses, and check for fluid leaks (Section 13).
g) Check the exhaust gas emissions (Section 29).

5 If the above operations do not prove fully effective, carry out the following secondary operations:

Secondary operations

All items listed under Primary operations, plus the following:

a) Check the charging system (Chapter 5A).
b) Check the preheating system (Chapter 5C).
c) Renew the fuel filter (Section 22) and check the fuel system (Chapter 4C).

Every 10 000 miles (15 000 km)

3 Engine oil and filter renewal

1 Frequent oil and filter changes are the most important maintenance procedures which can be undertaken by the DIY owner. As engine oil ages, it becomes diluted and contaminated, which leads to premature engine wear. The oil

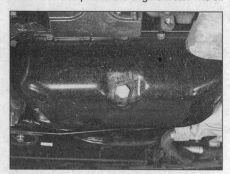

3.4 The drain plug is situated at the rear of the sump

HAYNES HiNT

Keep the drain plug pressed into the sump while unscrewing it by hand the last couple of turns. As the plug releases, move it away sharply so the stream of oil issuing from the sump runs into the container, not up your sleeve!

change interval given in this Manual is the same as quoted by the manufacturer, but owners of older vehicles (or those covering a small annual mileage) may feel justified in changing the oil and filter more frequently, perhaps every 5000 miles.

2 Before starting this procedure, gather all the necessary tools and materials. Also make sure that you have plenty of clean rags and newspapers handy, to mop up any spills. Ideally, the engine oil should be warm, as it will drain better, and more built-up sludge will be removed with it. Take care, however, not to touch the exhaust or any other hot parts of the engine when working under the vehicle. To avoid any possibility of scalding, and to protect yourself from possible skin irritants and other harmful contaminants in used engine oils, it is advisable to wear gloves when carrying out this work.

3 Access to the underside of the vehicle will be greatly improved if it can be raised on a lift, driven onto ramps, or jacked up and supported on axle stands (see Jacking and vehicle support). Whichever method is chosen, make sure that the vehicle remains level, or if it is at an angle, that the drain plug is at the lowest point. Where applicable, remove the engine compartment undertray.

4 Using a socket and wrench or a ring spanner, unscrew the drain plug about half a turn (see illustration). Position the draining container under the drain plug, then remove the plug completely (see Haynes Hint). Recover the sealing ring from the drain plug.

5 Allow some time for the old oil to drain, noting that it may be necessary to reposition the container as the oil flow slows to a trickle.

6 After all the oil has drained, wipe off the drain plug with a clean rag, and fit a new sealing washer. Clean the area around the drain plug opening, and refit the plug. Tighten the plug to the specified torque.

7 Move the container into position under the oil filter, which is located on the front of the cylinder block, at the flywheel end. Note that the filter is mounted on the bottom of the oil cooler which is attached to the oil filter bracket.

8 Using an oil filter removal tool if necessary, slacken the filter initially, then unscrew it by hand the rest of the way. Empty the oil in the filter into the container. Genuine Seat filters have a bracket on the base of the filter, for engaging a claw-type removal tool. In the absence of the proper tool, a useful substitute can be made from a strip of thick metal, gripped with a pair of pliers (see illustrations).

9 Use a clean rag to remove all oil and sludge from the filter sealing area on the oil cooler. Check the old filter to make sure that the rubber sealing ring has not stuck to the oil cooler. If it has, carefully remove it.

3.8a Loosen the oil filter using the special removal tool . . .

3.8b . . . or home-made alternative

3.10 Fitting a new oil filter

3.12a Unscrew the oil filler cap ...

3.12b ... and fill the engine with the recommended type and quantity of oil

10 Apply a light coating of clean engine oil to the sealing ring on the new filter, then screw it into position on the oil cooler. Tighten the filter firmly by hand only - **do not** use any tools **(see illustration)**.

11 Remove the old oil and all tools from under the car, then lower the car to the ground (if applicable).

12 Remove the dipstick, then unscrew the oil filler cap from the cylinder head cover. Fill the engine, using the correct grade and type of oil (see *Lubricants and fluids*). An oil can spout or funnel may help to reduce spillage. Pour in half the specified quantity of oil first, then wait a few minutes for the oil to drain into the sump **(see illustrations)**. Continue adding oil a small quantity at a time until the level is up to the bottom of the hatched area on the dipstick. Add more oil until the level is up to the top of the hatched area on the dipstick, then refit the dipstick and the filler cap.

13 Start the engine and run it for a few minutes, checking for leaks around the oil filter seal and the sump drain plug. Note that there may be a few seconds delay before the oil pressure warning light goes out when the engine is started, as the oil circulates through the engine oil galleries and the new oil filter before the pressure builds up.

14 Switch off the engine, and wait a few minutes for the oil to settle in the sump once more. With the new oil circulated and the filter completely full, recheck the level on the dipstick,

and add more oil as necessary. Refit the tray to the underside of the engine, where applicable.

15 Dispose of the used engine oil safely, with reference to *General repair procedures* in the *Reference* section of this manual.

4 Front and rear brake pad check

Front brake pads

1 Firmly apply the handbrake, then jack up the front of the car and support it securely on axle stands. Remove the front roadwheels.

2 For a comprehensive check, the brake pads should be removed and cleaned. The operation of the caliper can then also be checked, and the condition of the brake disc itself can be fully examined on both sides. Refer to Chapter 9 **(see Haynes Hint)**.

3 If any pad's friction material is worn to the specified thickness or less, *all four pads must be renewed as a set.*

Rear brake pads (models with rear disc brakes)

4 Chock the front wheels, then jack up the rear of the vehicle and support it on axle stands. Remove the rear roadwheels.

5 For a quick check, the thickness of friction material remaining on each brake pad can be measured through the top of the caliper body. If any pad's friction material is worn to the specified thickness or less, all four pads must be renewed as a set.

6 For a comprehensive check, the brake pads should be removed and cleaned. This will permit the operation of the caliper to be checked, and the condition of the brake disc itself to be fully examined on both sides. Refer to Chapter 9 for further information.

7 If any pad's friction material is worn to the specified thickness or less, *all four pads must be renewed as a set.*

5 Fuel filter water draining

1 From time to time, the water collected from the fuel by the filter unit must be drained out.

2 The fuel filter is mounted on the right-hand inner wing. First, remove the air filter assembly as described in Chapter 4C.

3 At the top of the filter unit, pull out the R-clip and lift out the control valve, leaving the fuel hoses attached **(see illustration)**.

4 Loosen the retaining bracket screw and lift the filter up slightly.

5 Position a container below the filter unit, and pad the surrounding area with rags to absorb any fuel that may be spilt.

6 Unscrew the drain plug at the base of the filter unit, until fuel starts to run out into the container **(see illustration)**. Drain about 100 cc of water/fuel from the filter.

7 Refit the control valve to the top of the filter and insert the retaining clip. Close the drain plug and wipe off any surplus fuel from the nozzle.

1B

HAYNES HINT

For a quick check, the thickness of the friction material on each brake pad can be measured through the aperture in the caliper body

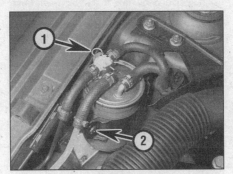

5.3 Fuel filter R-clip (1) and retaining bracket screw (2)

5.6 Unscrew the drain plug (arrowed) at the base of the filter unit

8 Remove the collecting container and rags, then push the filter unit back into the retaining bracket and tighten the bracket screw. Refit the air filter assembly.
9 Run the engine at idle, and check around the fuel filter for fuel leaks.

10 Raise the engine speed to about 2000 rpm several times, then allow the engine to idle again. Observe the fuel flow through the transparent hose leading to the fuel injection pump, and check that it is free of air bubbles.

6 Resetting service interval display

Refer to Chapter 12, Section 14.

Every 12 months

7 Lights and horn operation check

1 With the ignition switched on where necessary, check the operation of all exterior lights.
2 Check the brake lights with the help of an assistant, or by reversing up close to a reflective door or window. Make sure that all the rear lights are capable of operating independently, without affecting any of the other lights - for example, switch on as many rear lights as possible, then try the brake lights. If any unusual results are found, this is usually due to an earth fault or other poor connection at that rear light unit.
3 Again with the help of an assistant or using a reflective surface, check as far as possible that the headlights work on both main and dipped beam.
4 Replace any defective bulbs with reference to Chapter 12.

 HAYNES HINT *Particularly on older vehicles, bulbs can stop working as a result of corrosion build-up on the bulb or its holder - fitting a new bulb will not cure the problem in this instance. When replacing any bulb, if you find any green or white-coloured powdery deposits, these should be cleaned off using emery cloth.*

5 Check the operation of all interior lights, including the glovebox and luggage area illumination lights. Switch on the ignition, and check that all relevant warning lights come on as expected - the vehicle handbook should give details of these. Now start the engine, and check that the appropriate warning lights go out. When you are next driving at night, check that all the instrument panel and facia lighting works correctly. If any problems are found, refer to Chapter 12.
6 Finally, choose an appropriate time of day to test the operation of the horn.

8 Airbag unit check

On models fitted with an airbag, inspect the airbag(s) exterior condition checking for signs of damage or deterioration. If an airbag shows signs of damage, it must be renewed (see Chapter 12).

9 Washer system(s) check

1 Check that each of the washer jet nozzles is clear and that each nozzle provides a strong jet of washer fluid. The tailgate and headlight jets (where applicable) should be aimed to spray at a point slightly above the centre of the screen/headlight. On the windscreen washer nozzles where there are two jets, aim one of the jets slightly above the centre of the screen and aim the other just below to ensure complete coverage of the screen. If necessary, adjust the jets using a pin.
2 Check that the wiper system(s) operate correctly.

10 Hinge and lock lubrication

1 Lubricate the hinges of the bonnet, doors and tailgate with light general-purpose oil. Similarly, lubricate all latches, locks and lock strikers. At the same time, check the security and operation of all the locks, adjusting them if necessary (see Chapter 11).
2 Lightly lubricate the bonnet release mechanism and cable with a suitable grease.

11 Engine management system fault code check

1 This check is part of the manufacturer's maintenance schedule, and involves interrogating the engine management control unit (and the brake ABS module, if applicable) using special dedicated test equipment. Such testing will allow the test equipment to read any fault codes stored in the electronic control unit memory. **Note:** *Note that early models with engine codes 1Y and AAZ are not fitted with an electronic control unit.*
2 Unless a fault is suspected, this test is not essential, although it should be noted that it is recommended by the manufacturers.
3 It is possible for quite serious faults to occur in the engine management system without the owner being aware of it. Certain engine management system faults will cause the system to enter an emergency back-up mode, which is often so sophisticated that engine performance is not apparently much affected.

If a problem has caused the system to enter its back-up mode, this will usually be most apparent when starting and running from cold.

12 Battery electrolyte level check

⚠️ *Warning: The electrolyte inside a battery is diluted acid, therefore it is a good idea to wear suitable rubber gloves when handling the battery. When topping-up, don't overfill the cells so that the electrolyte overflows. In the event of any spillage, rinse the electrolyte off without delay. Refit the cell covers and rinse the battery with copious quantities of clean water. Don't attempt to siphon out any excess electrolyte.*

1 Some models covered by this Manual may be fitted with a maintenance-free battery as standard equipment, or may have had one fitted as a replacement. If the battery in your vehicle is marked Freedom, Maintenance-Free or similar, no electrolyte level checking is required (the battery is often completely sealed, preventing any topping-up).
2 Batteries which do require their electrolyte level to be checked can be recognised by the presence of removable covers over the six battery cells - the battery casing is also sometimes translucent, so that the electrolyte level can be more easily checked.
3 Remove the cell covers and either look down inside the battery to see the level indicator, or check the level using any markings provided on the battery casing. The electrolyte should cover the battery plates by 2.0 or 3.0 mm. If necessary, top up a little at a time with distilled (de-ionised) water until the level in all six cells is correct - don't fill the cells up to the brim. Wipe up any spillage, then refit the cell covers **(see illustration).**

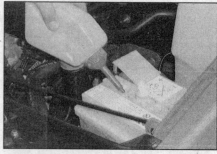

12.3 Topping up the battery electrolyte level using a battery top-up bottle with automatic level spout

A leak in the cooling system will usually show up as white - or rust-coloured deposits on the area adjoining the leak

14.2 Driveshaft inner CV joint, showing driveshaft seal (arrowed)

14.4 Check the condition of the driveshaft gaiters (arrowed)

13 Hose and fluid leak check

1 Remove the engine top cover as described in Chapter 2B, Section 17, then visually inspect the engine joint faces, gaskets and seals for any signs of water or oil leaks. Pay particular attention to the areas around the camshaft cover, cylinder head, oil filter and sump joint faces. Bear in mind that, over a period of time, some very slight seepage from these areas is to be expected - what you are really looking for is any indication of a serious leak **(see Haynes Hint)**. Should a leak be found, renew the offending gasket or oil seal by referring to the appropriate Chapters in this manual.

2 Also check the security and condition of all the engine-related pipes and hoses. Ensure that all cable-ties or securing clips are in place and in good condition. Clips that are broken or missing can lead to chafing of the hoses, pipes or wiring, which could cause more serious problems in the future.

3 Carefully check the radiator hoses and heater hoses along their entire length. Renew any hose that is cracked, swollen or deteriorated. Cracks will show up better if the hose is squeezed. Pay close attention to the hose clips that secure the hoses to the cooling system components. Hose clips can pinch and puncture hoses, resulting in cooling system leaks.

4 Inspect all the cooling system components (hoses, joint faces etc.) for leaks. A leak in the cooling system will usually show up as white- or rust-coloured deposits on the area adjoining the leak. Where any problems of this nature are found on system components, renew the component or gasket with reference to Chapter 3.

5 With the vehicle raised, inspect the fuel tank and filler neck for punctures, cracks and other damage. The connection between the filler neck and tank is especially critical. Sometimes a rubber filler neck or connecting hose will leak due to loose retaining clamps or deteriorated rubber.

6 Carefully check all rubber hoses and metal fuel lines leading away from the fuel tank.

Check for loose connections, deteriorated hoses, crimped lines, and other damage. Pay particular attention to the vent pipes and hoses, which often loop up around the filler neck and can become blocked or crimped. Follow the lines to the front of the vehicle, carefully inspecting them all the way. Renew damaged sections as necessary.

7 From within the engine compartment, check the security of all fuel hose attachments and pipe unions, and inspect the fuel hoses and vacuum hoses for kinks, chafing and deterioration.

8 Where applicable, check the condition of the power steering fluid hoses and pipes.

9 Refit the engine top cover as described in Chapter 2B, Section 17.

14 Transmission and driveshaft gaiter check

1 Raise the front of the vehicle and support on axle stands. Alternatively, drive the car onto ramps.

2 Inspect around the transmission for any sign of leaks or damage. In particular, check the area around the driveshaft oil seals for leakage **(see illustration)**. Slight seepage should not be of great concern, but a serious leak should be investigated further, with reference to Chapter 7.

3 Check the security and condition of the wiring and wiring plugs on the transmission housing.

4 With the vehicle raised and securely supported on stands, turn the steering onto full lock, then slowly rotate the roadwheels. Inspect the condition of the outer constant velocity (CV) joint rubber gaiters, squeezing the gaiters to open out the folds. Check for signs of cracking, splits or deterioration of the rubber, which may allow the grease to escape, and lead to water and grit entry into the joint **(see illustration)**. Also check the security and condition of the retaining clips. Repeat these checks on the inner CV joints. If any damage or deterioration is found, the gaiters should be renewed (see Chapter 8).

5 At the same time, check the general condition of the CV joints themselves by first holding the driveshaft and attempting to rotate the wheel. Repeat this check by holding the

inner joint and attempting to rotate the driveshaft. Any appreciable movement indicates wear in the joints, wear in the drive-shaft splines, or a loose driveshaft retaining nut.

15 Braking system check

1 Starting under the bonnet, examine the brake fluid reservoir and master cylinder for leaks. When a brake fluid leak occurs, it is normal to find blistered or wrinkled paint in the area of the leak. Check the metal pipes from the master cylinder for damage, and check the brake pressure regulator, servo/ABS unit and fluid unions for leaks **(see illustration)**.

2 With the vehicle raised and securely supported on stands, first inspect each front brake caliper. In particular, check the flexible hose leading to the caliper for signs of damage or leaks, especially where the hose enters the metal end fitting. Make sure that the hose is not twisted or kinked, and that it cannot come into contact with any other components when the steering is on full lock.

3 From the caliper, trace the brake pipes back along the car. Again, look for leaks from the fluid unions or signs of damage, but additionally check the pipes for signs of corrosion. Make sure the pipes are securely located by the clips provided on the vehicle underside.

4 At the rear of the vehicle, inspect each rear brake and its flexible hose. Examine the handbrake cables, tracing them back from each rear brake and checking for frayed

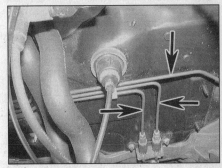

15.1 Hydraulic brake pipes located on the left-hand side of the bulkhead

1B

16.2 Rear brake backplate inspection hole (arrowed) for assessing brake lining wear

cables or other damage. Lubricate the handbrake cable pivots and other moving parts with general-purpose grease. Also check that the rear wheels are locked when the handbrake lever is fully applied.

5 If any damage is found, refer to Chapter 9 for further information.

16 Rear brake shoe check

1 Chock the front wheels, then jack up the rear of the vehicle, and support it securely on axle stands.

2 For a quick check, the thickness of friction material remaining on one of the brake shoes can be observed through the hole in the brake backplate which is exposed by prising out the sealing grommet **(see illustration)**. If a rod of the same diameter as the specified minimum friction material thickness is placed against the shoe friction material, the amount of wear can be assessed. A torch or inspection light will probably be required. If the friction material on any shoe is worn down to the specified minimum thickness or less, all four shoes must be renewed as a set.

3 For a comprehensive check, the brake drum should be removed and cleaned. This will allow the wheel cylinders to be checked, and the condition of the brake drum itself to be fully examined (see Chapter 9).

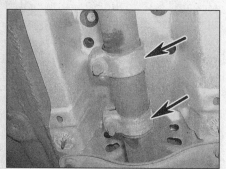

17.2 Typical exhaust system joint clamps (arrowed) - check that the nuts and bolts are tight, with no sign of leaks

17 Exhaust system check

1 With the engine cold (at least an hour after the vehicle has been driven), check the complete exhaust system from the engine to the end of the tailpipe. The exhaust system is most easily checked with the vehicle raised on a hoist, or suitably supported on axle stands, so that the exhaust components are readily visible and accessible.

2 Check the exhaust pipes and joints for evidence of leaks, severe corrosion and damage. Make sure that all brackets and mountings are in good condition, and that all relevant nuts and bolts are tight **(see illustration)**. Leakage at any of the joints or in other parts of the system will usually show up as a black sooty stain in the vicinity of the leak.

3 Rattles and other noises can often be traced to the exhaust system, especially the brackets and mountings. Try to move the pipes and silencers from side to side. If the components are able to come into contact with the body or suspension parts, secure the system with new mountings. If necessary, separate the joints (if possible) and twist the pipes as necessary to provide additional clearance.

18 Steering and suspension check

Front suspension and steering check

1 Raise the front of the vehicle, and securely support it on axle stands.

2 Visually inspect the balljoint dust covers and the steering rack-and-pinion gaiters for splits, chafing or deterioration. Any wear of these components will cause loss of lubricant, together with dirt and water entry, resulting in rapid deterioration of the balljoints or steering gear.

3 On vehicles with power steering, check the fluid hoses for chafing or deterioration, and the pipe and hose unions for fluid leaks. Also check for signs of fluid leakage under pressure from the steering gear rubber gaiters, which would indicate failed fluid seals within the steering gear.

4 Grasp the roadwheel at the 12 o'clock and 6 o'clock positions, and try to rock it **(see illustration)**. Very slight free play may be felt, but if the movement is appreciable, further investigation is necessary to determine the source. Continue rocking the wheel while an assistant depresses the footbrake. If the movement is now eliminated or significantly reduced, it is likely that the hub bearings are at fault. If the free play is still evident with the footbrake depressed, then there is wear in the suspension joints or mountings.

5 Now grasp the wheel at the 9 o'clock and 3 o'clock positions, and try to rock it as before.

Any movement felt now may again be caused by wear in the hub bearings or the steering tie-rod balljoints. If the inner or outer balljoint is worn, the visual movement will be obvious.

6 Using a large screwdriver or flat bar, check for wear in the suspension mounting bushes by levering between the relevant suspension component and its attachment point. Some movement is to be expected as the mountings are made of rubber, but excessive wear should be obvious. Also check the condition of any visible rubber bushes, looking for splits, cracks or contamination of the rubber.

7 With the car standing on its wheels, have an assistant turn the steering wheel back and forth about an eighth of a turn each way. There should be very little, if any, lost movement between the steering wheel and roadwheels. If this is not the case, closely observe the joints and mountings previously described, but in addition, check the steering column universal joints for wear, and the rack-and-pinion steering gear itself.

Rear suspension check

8 Chock the front wheels, then jack up the rear of the vehicle and support securely on axle stands.

9 Working as described previously for the front suspension, check the rear hub bearings, the suspension bushes and the strut mountings for wear.

Suspension strut/ shock absorber check

10 Check for any signs of fluid leakage around the suspension strut/shock absorber body, or from the rubber gaiter around the piston rod. Should any fluid be noticed, the suspension strut/shock absorber is defective internally, and should be renewed. **Note:** *Suspension struts/shock absorbers should always be renewed in pairs on the same axle.*

11 The efficiency of the suspension strut/shock absorber may be checked by bouncing the vehicle at each corner. The body will return to its normal position and stop after being depressed. If it rises and returns on a rebound, the suspension strut/shock absorber is probably suspect. Also examine the suspension strut/shock absorber upper and lower mountings for any signs of wear.

18.4 Check for wear in the hub bearings by grasping the wheel and trying to rock it

19 Headlight beam alignment check

Accurate adjustment of the headlight beam is only possible using optical beam-setting equipment, and this work should therefore be carried out by a Seat dealer or service station with the necessary facilities.

Basic adjustments can be carried out in an emergency, and further details are given in Chapter 12.

20 Road test

Instruments and electrical equipment

1 Check the operation of all instruments and electrical equipment.
2 Make sure that all instruments read correctly, and switch on all electrical equipment in turn, to check that it functions properly.

Steering and suspension

3 Check for any abnormalities in the steering, suspension, handling or road feel.
4 Drive the vehicle, and check that there are no unusual vibrations or noises.
5 Check that the steering feels positive, with no excessive sloppiness, or roughness, and check for any suspension noises when cornering and driving over bumps.

Drivetrain

6 Check the performance of the engine, clutch (where applicable), gearbox/ transmission and driveshafts.

7 Listen for any unusual noises from the engine, clutch and gearbox/transmission.
8 Make sure the engine runs smoothly at idle, and there is no hesitation on accelerating.
9 Check that, where applicable, the clutch action is smooth and progressive, that the drive is taken up smoothly, and that the pedal travel is not excessive. Also listen for any noises when the clutch pedal is depressed.
10 Check that all gears can be engaged smoothly without noise, and that the gear lever action is not abnormally vague or notchy.
11 Listen for a metallic clicking sound from the front of the vehicle, as the vehicle is driven slowly in a circle with the steering on full-lock. Carry out this check in both directions. If a clicking noise is heard, this indicates wear in a driveshaft joint, in which case renew the joint if necessary.

Check the operation and performance of the braking system

12 Make sure that the vehicle does not pull to one side when braking, and that the wheels do not lock prematurely when braking hard.
13 Check that there is no vibration through the steering when braking.
14 Check that the handbrake operates correctly without excessive movement of the lever, and that it holds the vehicle stationary on a slope.
15 Test the operation of the brake servo unit as follows. With the engine off, depress the footbrake four or five times to exhaust the vacuum. Hold the brake pedal depressed, then start the engine. As the engine starts, there should be a noticeable give in the brake pedal as vacuum builds up. Allow the engine to run for at least two minutes, and then switch it off. If the brake pedal is depressed

21.3 Idle speed adjustment screw location on engine code AAZ. Engine code 1Y similar

now, it should be possible to detect a hiss from the servo as the pedal is depressed. After about four or five applications, no further hissing should be heard, and the pedal should feel considerably harder.

21 Idle speed check and adjustment

Note: *This Section only applies to engine codes 1Y and AAZ.*
1 Start the engine and run it until it reaches its normal operating temperature. With the handbrake applied and the transmission in neutral, allow the engine to idle. Check that the cold start knob is pushed in to the fully off position.
2 Using a diesel tachometer, check the idle speed against the information given in the Specifications.
3 If necessary, adjust the engine idle speed by rotating the adjustment screw at the fuel injection pump **(see illustration)**.

Every 20 000 miles (30 000 km)

22 Fuel filter renewal

1 The fuel filter is mounted on the right-hand inner wing. First remove the air filter assembly as described in Chapter 4C. If wished, for improved access, detach the inlet air hose from the inlet manifold and the air cleaner, and move it out of the way.
2 Place a container below the filter, and pad the surrounding area with rags to absorb any fuel that may be spilt.
3 At the top of the filter unit, pull out the R-clip and lift out the control valve, leaving the fuel hoses attached **(see illustrations)**.
4 Slacken the hose clips, and pull the fuel supply and delivery hoses from the ports on

the of the filter unit. If crimp-type clips are fitted, cut them off using snips, and use proper fuel hose clips on refitting. Note the fitted position of each hose, in relation to the

direction-of-flow arrows on top of the filter, to aid correct refitting.
Caution: Be prepared for an amount of fuel loss.

22.3a Release the clip . . .

22.3b . . . and lift out the control valve, leaving the fuel hoses attached

22.5a Loosen the securing screw . . .

22.5b . . . and lift the filter out its retaining bracket

5 Loosen the retaining bracket screw and lift the filter out **(see illustrations)**.
6 Fill the new fuel filter with clean diesel fuel before fitting - this will make the engine easier to start. Fit the new fuel filter into the retaining bracket, and tighten the screw.
7 Fit a new O-ring seal to the control valve, then refit the control valve to the top of the filter, and insert the retaining clip.
8 Reconnect the fuel supply and delivery hoses **(see illustration)**, using the notes made during removal - note the fuel flow arrow markings next to each port. Where crimp-type hoses were originally fitted, use screw-type clips on refitting. Remove the collecting container and rags, and refit the air filter assembly.
9 Start and run the engine at idle, then check around the fuel filter for fuel leaks. **Note:** *It may take a few seconds of cranking before the engine starts, especially if the new filter was not primed with fuel before fitting.*
10 Raise the engine speed to about 2000 rpm several times, then allow the engine to idle again. Observe the fuel flow through the transparent hose leading to the fuel injection pump, and check that it is free of air bubbles.

23 Pollen filter renewal

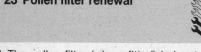

1 The pollen filter (where fitted) is located beneath the windscreen cowl panels; it is located on the right-hand side on left-hand drive models, and the left-hand side on right-hand drive models.

22.8 Reconnect the fuel supply and delivery hoses

2 Remove the windscreen cowl panel as described in Chapter 11.
3 Unscrew the two plastic nuts and remove the plastic grille panel from the pollen filter.
4 Depress the two retaining tabs at the front of the pollen filter, and lift the filter from its housing.
5 Fit the new filter using a reversal of the removal procedure.

24 Auxiliary drivebelt check and renewal

Checking

1 Apply the handbrake, then jack up the front of the vehicle and support it on axle stands (see *Jacking and vehicle support*). Loosen the right-hand front wheel bolts.
2 Remove the right-hand front roadwheel.
3 Turn the steering to full right-hand lock. Where applicable, remove the fasteners, and lower the wheel arch liner and/or engine undertray for access to the drivebelt. Models with power steering may have a cover fitted over the drivebelt - if so, release the fasteners and remove it.
4 Using a socket and wrench on the crankshaft sprocket bolt, rotate the crankshaft so that the full length of the auxiliary drivebelt(s) can be examined. Look for cracks, splitting and fraying on the surface of the belt; check also for signs of glazing (shiny patches) and separation of the belt plies. If damage or wear is visible, the belt should be renewed. If there is any evidence of contamination by oil, grease or coolant, the reason should be investigated without delay.
5 Where the drivebelt tension is adjustable, check and if necessary adjust its tension with reference to Chapter 2B.
6 On completion, refit the wheel arch liner and engine undertray (as applicable), then refit the roadwheel and lower the car to the ground. Tighten the roadwheel bolts to the specified torque.

Renewal

7 For details of auxiliary drivebelt renewal, refer to Chapter 2B.

25 Timing belt check

1 Refer to Chapter 2B and remove the upper timing belt covers for access to the timing belt.
2 Using a socket on the crankshaft pulley bolt, turn the engine slowly while thoroughly checking the timing belt for signs of damage and wear, especially at the roots of the belt teeth. Also check for oil contamination which may have come from the crankshaft oil seal.
3 Fit a new oil seal where necessary, and a new timing belt if required with reference to Chapter 2B.
4 Check and where necessary adjust the tension of the timing belt with reference to Chapter 2B.
5 Refit the upper timing belt covers.

26 Manual transmission oil level check

1 Park the car on a level surface. The oil level must be checked before the car is driven, or at least 5 minutes after the engine has been switched off. If the oil is checked immediately after driving the car, some of the oil will remain distributed around the transmission components, resulting in an inaccurate level reading.
2 On pre October 1995 models equipped with the 085 transmission, the filler/level plug is located above the left-hand driveshaft, and the drain plug is located below the driveshaft. For easier access, turn the steering onto full left lock. Do not raise the car, because the level must be checked with the car resting on its wheels, on a level surface. On October 1995-on models equipped with the 085 transmission, the filler/level plug is located on the front of the transmission housing, and can be accessed from above **(see illustrations)**. If preferred, however, the plug can be reached from below.
3 On models equipped with the 020 transmission, the filler/level plug is located on the left-hand end of the transmission, and the drain plug is located below the final drive and

26.2a 085 transmission oil filler/level plug (arrowed) - models up to October 1995

26.2b 085 transmission oil filler/level plug (arrowed) - models from October 1995

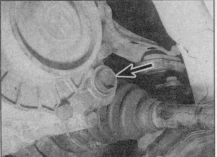

26.3a 020 transmission oil filler/level plug location

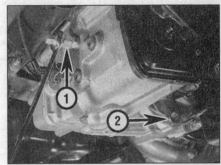

26.3b 02A transmission oil filler/level plug location

driveshaft position. On the 02A transmission the filler/level plug is located on the front of the transmission **(see illustrations)**.

4 Wipe clean the area around the filler/level plug. A 17 mm hexagonal socket (or a large Allen key) will be required to remove the plug **(see illustration)**.

5 The oil level should reach the lower edge of the filler/level hole. A certain amount of oil will have gathered behind the filler/level plug, and will trickle out when it is removed; this does **not** necessarily indicate that the level is correct. To ensure that a true level is established, wait until the initial trickle has stopped, then add oil through the hole as necessary until a trickle of new oil can be seen emerging. The level will be correct when the flow ceases; use only oil of the specified type.

6 Filling the transmission with oil is an extremely awkward operation; above all, allow plenty of time for the oil level to settle properly before checking it. If a large amount is added to the transmission, and a large amount flows out on checking the level, refit the filler/level plug; take the vehicle on a short journey so that the new oil is distributed fully around the transmission components, then recheck the level when it has settled again.

7 If the transmission has been overfilled so that oil flows out when the filler/level plug is removed, check that the car is completely level (front-to-rear and side-to-side), and allow the surplus to drain off into a suitable container.

8 When the level is correct, refit the plug, tightening it to the specified torque, and wipe off any spilt oil.

27 Underbody protection check

Raise and support the vehicle on axle stands. Using an electric torch or lead light, inspect the entire underside of the vehicle, paying particular attention to the wheel arches. Look for any damage to the flexible underbody coating, which may crack or flake off with age, leading to corrosion. Also check that the wheel arch liners are securely attached with any clips provided - if they come loose, dirt may get in behind the liners and defeat their purpose. If there is any damage to the underseal, or any corrosion, it should be repaired before the damage gets too serious.

28 Air filter renewal

1 The air filter is housed in the air cleaner located on the right-hand side of the engine compartment.

2 Prise open the spring clips and lift off the air cleaner top cover **(see illustration)**. Note: *On engine codes 1Z, AHU, and AFN, the airflow meter is integral with the top cover. Take care not to damage the wiring.*

3 Lift out the air filter element.

4 Remove any debris that may have collected inside the air cleaner.

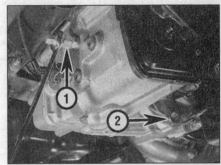

26.4 Loosening the oil filler/level plug (1) on the later 085 transmission using a hex adapter - also shown is the transmission oil drain plug (2)

5 Fit a new air filter element in position, ensuring that the edges are securely seated **(see illustration)**.

6 Refit the air cleaner top cover and snap the retaining clips into position.

29 Exhaust emissions check

This check is part of the manufacturer's maintenance schedule, and involves checking the exhaust emissions using smoke testing equipment. Unless a fault is suspected, this test is not essential, although it should be noted that it is recommended by the manufacturers. Smoke testing is included as part of the MOT test.

1B

28.2 Prise open the spring clips, and lift off the air cleaner top cover

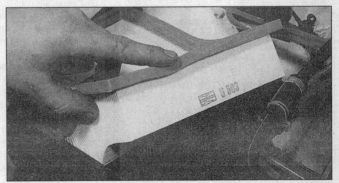

28.5 Fit a new air filter element in position, ensuring the edges are securely seated

Every 60 000 miles (90 000 km)

30 Timing belt and belt tensioner roller renewal

Note: *Seat specify a timing belt renewal interval of 60 000 miles (90 000 km) however, if the vehicle is used mainly for short journeys, we recommend that a shorter interval is adhered to. The belt renewal interval is very much up to the individual owner but, bear in mind that severe engine damage will result if the belt breaks in use.*

1 Refer to Chapter 2B for the renewal procedure for the timing belt and the tensioner roller.

31 Clutch pedal freeplay check

Note: *This Section only applies to models with a 085 or 02A transmission fitted with manually-adjusted clutch cable. All other models are fitted with either a self-adjusting cable or hydraulically-operated clutch which automatically compensates for wear of the clutch friction plate linings.*
1 Refer to Chapter 6 for details of adjusting the pedal/cable freeplay.

Every 2 years (regardless of mileage)

32 Coolant renewal

1 Two types of coolant are specified by the manufacturers for use in the coolant system, and it is important not to mix them as they have different characteristics. The G11 coolant is for use in cast iron engines, and the G12 coolant is for use in both cast iron and aluminium engines. G11 coolant is a dark blue-greenish colour, and G12 coolant is a reddish colour. If G12 coolant appears brown, this indicates that it has been mixed with another antifreeze additive, in which case the cooling system must be flushed out then filled with a fresh solution.
2 The expansion tank should have a mark or label on it indicating which type of coolant to use, however as from August 1996, all engines are filled with G12 solution. Earlier engines may have G11 solution and may continue to have this type, however, if preferred it may be replaced by G12 solution. Change the marking or label if the solution is changed.

Cooling system draining

⚠️ **Warning: Wait until the engine is cold before starting this procedure. Do not allow antifreeze to come in contact with your skin, or with the painted surfaces of the vehicle. Rinse off spills immediately with plenty of water. Never leave antifreeze lying around in an open container, or in a puddle in the driveway or on the garage floor. Children and pets are attracted by its sweet smell, but antifreeze can be fatal if ingested.**

3 With the engine completely cold, cover the expansion tank cap with a wad of rag, and slowly turn the cap anti-clockwise to relieve the pressure in the cooling system (a hissing sound will normally be heard). Wait until any pressure remaining in the system is released,

then continue to turn the cap until it can be removed.
4 Where necessary, remove the engine compartment undertray. Position a suitable container beneath the radiator bottom hose, then release the retaining clip and ease the hose from the radiator stub. Also disconnect the heater return hose from the water pump. If necessary, apply the handbrake, then jack up the front of the vehicle and support it on axle stands (see *Jacking and vehicle support*) for access to the bottom of the pump. Allow the coolant to drain into the container.
5 If the coolant has been drained for a reason other than renewal, then provided it is clean and less than two years old, it can be re-used.
6 Once all the coolant has drained, reconnect the hoses to the radiator and water pump and secure with the retaining clips.

Cooling system flushing

7 If coolant renewal has been neglected, or if the antifreeze mixture has become diluted, then in time, the cooling system may gradually lose efficiency, as the coolant passages become restricted due to rust, scale deposits, and other sediment. Flushing the system clean can restore the cooling system efficiency.
8 The radiator should be flushed independently of the engine, to avoid unnecessary contamination.

Radiator flushing

9 To flush the radiator, disconnect the top and bottom hoses and any other relevant hoses from the radiator, with reference to Chapter 3.
10 Insert a garden hose into the radiator top inlet. Direct a flow of clean water through the radiator, and continue flushing until clean water emerges from the radiator bottom outlet.
11 If after a reasonable period, the water still does not run clear, the radiator can be flushed with a good proprietary cooling system cleaning agent. It is important that the manufacturer's instructions are followed

carefully. If the contamination is particularly bad, insert the hose in the radiator bottom outlet, and reverse-flush the radiator. This is best carried out with the radiator removed from the vehicle.

Engine flushing

12 To flush the engine, remove the thermostat as described in Chapter 3, then temporarily refit the thermostat cover.
13 With the top and bottom hoses disconnected from the radiator, insert a garden hose into the radiator top hose. Direct a clean flow of water through the engine, and continue flushing until clean water emerges from the radiator bottom hose.
14 On completion of flushing, refit the thermostat and reconnect the hoses with reference to Chapter 3.

Cooling system filling

15 Before attempting to fill the cooling system, make sure that all hoses and clips are in good condition, and that the clips are tight. Note that an antifreeze mixture must be used all year round, to prevent corrosion of the engine components.
16 Remove the expansion tank filler cap, and fill the system by slowly pouring the coolant into the expansion tank. If the coolant is being renewed, begin by pouring in a couple of litres of water, followed by the correct quantity of antifreeze, then top-up with more water. Once the level in the expansion tank starts to rise, squeeze the radiator top and bottom hoses to help expel any trapped air in the system. With all the air expelled, top-up the coolant level to the MAX mark and refit the expansion tank cap.
17 Start the engine and run it until it reaches normal operating temperature and the electric cooling fan operates, then stop the engine and allow it to cool.
18 Check for leaks, particularly around disturbed components. Check the coolant level in the expansion tank, and top-up if necessary. Note that the system must be cold before an accurate level is indicated in the expansion tank. If the expansion tank cap is

removed while the engine is still warm, cover the cap with a thick cloth, and unscrew the cap slowly to gradually relieve the system pressure. Wait until any pressure remaining in the system is released, then continue to turn the cap until it can be removed.

Antifreeze type and mixture

19 The antifreeze should always be renewed at the specified intervals. This is necessary not only to maintain the antifreeze properties, but also to prevent corrosion which would otherwise occur as the corrosion inhibitors become progressively less effective.

20 Always use the correct antifreeze (refer also to paragraphs 1 and 2). The quantity of antifreeze and levels of protection are indicated in the Specifications.

21 Before adding antifreeze, the cooling system should be completely drained, preferably flushed, and all hoses checked for condition and security.

22 After filling with antifreeze, a label should be attached to the expansion tank, stating the type and concentration of antifreeze used, and the date installed. Any subsequent topping-up should be made with the same type and concentration of antifreeze.

23 Do not use engine antifreeze in the washer system, as it will cause damage to the vehicle paintwork.

33 Brake fluid renewal

⚠️ *Warning: Brake hydraulic fluid can harm your eyes and damage painted surfaces, so use extreme caution when handling and pouring it. Do not use fluid that has been standing open for some time, as it absorbs moisture from the air. Excess moisture can cause a dangerous loss of braking effectiveness.*

1 The procedure is similar to that for the bleeding of the hydraulic system as described in Chapter 9, except that the brake fluid reservoir should be emptied by siphoning, using a clean poultry baster or similar before starting, and allowance should be made for the old fluid to be expelled when bleeding a section of the circuit.

2 Working as described in Chapter 9, open the first bleed screw in the sequence, and pump the brake pedal gently until nearly all the old fluid has been emptied from the master cylinder reservoir.

⚠️ *Warning: On models with ABS, under no circumstances should the hydraulic unit bleed screws be opened.*

  HAYNES HiNT *Old hydraulic fluid is often much darker in colour than the new, making it easy to distinguish the two.*

3 Top-up to the MAX level with new fluid, and continue pumping until only the new fluid remains in the reservoir, and new fluid can be seen emerging from the bleed screw. Tighten the screw, and top the reservoir level up to the MAX level line.

4 Work through all the remaining bleed screws in the sequence until new fluid can be seen at all of them. Be careful to keep the master cylinder reservoir topped-up to above the MIN level at all times, or air may enter the system and greatly increase the length of the task.

5 On models fitted with a hydraulic clutch, bleed the system as described in Chapter 6.

6 When the operation is complete, check that all bleed screws are securely tightened, and that their dust caps are refitted. Wash off all traces of spilt fluid, and recheck the master cylinder reservoir fluid level.

7 Check the operation of the brakes before taking the car on the road.

1B

Chapter 2 Part A:
Petrol engine in-car repair procedures

Contents

Degrees of difficulty

| **Easy,** suitable for novice with little experience | | **Fairly easy,** suitable for beginner with some experience | | **Fairly difficult,** suitable for competent DIY mechanic | ✓✓ | **Difficult,** suitable for experienced DIY mechanic | ✓✓ | **Very difficult,** suitable for expert DIY or professional | ✓✓ |

Specifications

General

Engine data:

	Engine code*	Bore	Stroke	Compression ratio
999 cc, Bosch Motronic injection, 37 kW	AER	67.1 mm	70.6 mm	10.5:1
1043 cc, Bosch Mono-Motronic injection, 33 kW	AAU	75.0 mm	59.0 mm	9.8:1
1272 cc, Bosch Mono-Motronic injection, 40 kW	AAV	75.0 mm	72.0 mm	9.5:1
1390 cc				
Bosch Motronic injection, 44 kW	AEX	76.5 mm	75.6 mm	10.2:1
Bosch Motronic injection, 44 kW	APQ	76.5 mm	75.6 mm	10.2:1
1391 cc, Bosch Mono-Motronic injection, 44 kW	ABD	75.0 mm	79.14 mm	9.5:1
1595 cc				
Bosch Mono-Motronic injection, 55 kW, 10/94-on	1F	81.0 mm	77.4 mm	9.0:1
Simos multi-point injection, 74 kW	AFT	81.0 mm	77.4 mm	10.3:1
1598 cc:				
Bosch Mono-Motronic injection, 55 kW, 08/92 to 09/94	ABU	76.5 mm	86.9 mm	9.3:1
1AV multi-point injection, 55 kW	AEE	76.5 mm	86.9 mm	10.0:1
1AV multi-point injection, 55 kW	ALM	76.5 mm	86.9 mm	10.0:1
1984 cc:				
Digifant multi-point injection, 85 kW, to 10/94	2E	82.5 mm	92.8 mm	10.4:1
Simos multi-point injection, 85 kW	AGG	82.5 mm	92.8 mm	10.1:1
Digifant multi-point injection, DOHC, 110 kW	ABF	82.5 mm	92.8 mm	10.5:1

Compression pressures (wear limit) . . . . 7.0 bar to 7.5 bar (102 to 109 psi)
Firing order . . . . 1 - 3 - 4 - 2
No 1 cylinder location . . . . Timing belt end

Auxiliary V-belt tension:	**New belt**	**Used belt**
Deflection	2.0 mm	5.0 mm
Torque:		
Alternator	8.0 Nm	4.0 Nm
Power steering pump	7.0 Nm	4.0 Nm

* Note: *See* Vehicle identification *in* Reference *for the location of code marking on the engine.*

Lubrication system

Oil pump type:
  AER, AAU, AAV, AEX, APQ, ABD, ABU, 1F, AEE, ALM . . . . Sump-mounted, chain-driven from crankshaft
  AFT, 2E, AGG, ABF . . . . Sump-mounted, driven indirectly from intermediate shaft
Normal operating oil pressure . . . . 2.0 bar minimum (at 2000 rpm, oil temperature 80°C)
Oil pump backlash . . . . 0.2 mm (wear limit)
Oil pump axial clearance . . . . 0.15 mm (wear limit)
Oil pump drive chain tension (where applicable) . . . . 3.5 to 4.5 mm (approx) deflection at mid-point between sprockets

Torque wrench settings

	Nm	lbf ft
Big-end cap:		
Engine code AER:		
Stage 1	20	15
Stage 2	Angle-tighten 90°	
Engine code AAU, AAV, ABD, ABU, AFT, 1F, 2E, AGG, ABF:		
Stage 1	30	22
Stage 2	Angle-tighten 90°	
Engine code AEX, APQ, AEE, ALM:		
M8 bolt:		
Stage 1	30	22
Stage 2	Angle-tighten 90°	
M7 bolt:		
Stage 1	20	15
Stage 2	Angle-tighten 90°	
Camshaft bearing cap nuts:		
Engine codes AER, AAU, AAV, ABD, ABU, AEX, APQ, AEE, ALM:		
Stage 1	6	4
Stage 2	Angle-tighten 90°	
Engine codes AFT, 1F, 2E, AGG, ABF	20	15
Camshaft cover:		
Engine code AER:		
Stage 1	5	4
Stage 2	Angle-tighten 90°	
Engine codes AAU, AAV, ABD, ABU, 1F, 2E, AGG, AFT, ABF	10	7
Camshaft sprocket bolt:		
Engine code AER:		
Stage 1	20	15
Stage 2	Angle-tighten 90°	
Engine codes except AER	80	59
Crankshaft front oil seal housing:		
M6	10	7
M8	25	19
Crankshaft main bearing cap:		
Engine codes AAU, AAV, ABD, ABU, AEX, APQ, AEE, ALM:		
Bolts with full length thread:		
Stage 1	65	48
Stage 2	Angle-tighten 90°	
Bolts with partial length thread	65	48
Engine code AER	65	48
Engine codes AFT:		
Stage 1	65	48
Stage 2	Angle-tighten 90°	
Engine codes 1F, 2E, AGG, ABF	65	48
Crankshaft rear oil seal housing	10	7
Crankshaft pulley for the auxiliary drivebelt:		
Engine codes AER, 1F, 2E, AGG, ABF	20	15
Engine codes AAU, AAV, ABD, ABU:		
M6	10	7
M8	20	15
Engine code AFT	25	19
Crankshaft sprocket bolt:		
Engine code AER:		
Hexagonal:		
Stage 1	90	66
Stage 2	Angle-tighten 120°	
Dodecagonal (bi-hex):		
Stage 1	90	66
Stage 2	Angle-tighten 90°	
Engine codes AAU, AAV, ABD, ABU, AEX, APQ, AEE, ALM:		
Stage 1	90	66
Stage 2	Angle-tighten 120°	
Engine codes AFT, 1F, 2E, AGG, ABF:		
Stage 1	90	66
Stage 2	Angle-tighten 90°	

Torque wrench settings (continued)

	Nm	lbf ft
Cylinder head cover:		
Engine code AER:		
Stage 1	5	4
Stage 2	Angle-tighten 90º	
Engine codes except AER	10	7
Cylinder head bolts:		
Engine code AER:		
Stage 1	30	22
Stage 2	Angle-tighten a further 90º	
Stage 3	Angle-tighten a further 90º	
Engine codes AAU, AAV, ABD, ABU, AEX, APQ, AEE, ALM, AFT, 1F, 2E, AGG, ABF:		
Stage 1	40	30
Stage 2	60	44
Stage 3	Angle-tighten a further 90º	
Stage 4	Angle-tighten a further 90º	
Engine mountings:		
Engine codes 1F, 2E, AGG, AFT, ABF:		
Engine mounting to bracket	60	44
Engine mounting to crossmember/subframe	30	22
Front engine mounting bracket to cylinder block	25	19
Left-hand rear engine mounting bracket to manual transmission	35	26
Engine codes AER, AAU, AAV, ABD, ABU, AEX, APQ, AEE, ALM:		
Right-hand rear engine mounting bracket to cylinder block:		
Stage 1	40	30
Stage 2	Angle-tighten 90º	
Right-hand rear engine mounting to bracket	60	44
Right-hand rear engine mounting to subframe	30	22
Left-hand rear engine mounting top bolt	50	37
Left-hand rear engine mounting bracket to transmission	60	44
Left-hand rear engine mounting to subframe	25	19
Front engine mounting top and bottom bolt	50	37
Front engine mounting bracket to engine/transmission	45	33
Flywheel bolt:		
Stage 1	60	44
Stage 2	Angle-tighten 90º	
Intermediate shaft sprocket (engine codes AFT, 1F, 2E, AGG, ABF) ...	80	59
Intermediate shaft oil seal housing (engine codes AFT, 1F, 2E, AGG, ABF)	25	19
Oil cooler nut	25	19
Oil level dipstick tube	10	7
Oil pressure switch	25	19
Oil pump (AER, AAU, AAV, ABD, ABU, AEX, APQ, AEE, ALM)	20	15
Oil pump drive chain guide rail-to-crankcase bolt	10	7
Sump drain plug	30	22
Sump retaining bolts:		
Engines with solid gasket (AER, AAU, AAV, ABD, ABU, AEX, APQ, AEE, ALM)	15	11
Engines with liquid gasket (AFT, 1F, 2E, AGG, ABF)	20	15
Timing belt inner cover:		
M6	10	7
M8	20	15
Timing belt outer cover	10	7
Timing belt tensioner	20	15
Timing belt tensioner locknut:		
Engine codes ABF, AFT, 1F, 2E, AGG	45	33
Engine code AER	20	15
Transmission-to-engine bolts:		
Engine codes AER, AAU, AAV, ABD, ABU, AEX, APQ, AEE, ALM:		
M10	45	33
M12	80	59
Engine codes AFT, 1F, 2E, AGG, ABF:		
M10	60	44
M12	80	59

2A

1 General information

Using this Chapter

Chapter 2 is divided into three Parts; A, B and C. Repair operations that can be carried out with the engine in the vehicle are described in Parts A (petrol engines) and B (diesel engines). Part C covers the removal of the engine/transmission as a unit, and describes the engine dismantling and overhaul procedures.

In Parts A and B, the assumption is made that the engine is installed in the vehicle, with all ancillaries connected. If the engine has been removed for overhaul, the preliminary dismantling information which precedes each operation may be ignored.

Access to the engine bay can be improved by removing the bonnet and the body front panel assembly; for details, see Chapter 11.

Engine description

Throughout this Chapter, engines are identified and referred to by the manufacturer's code letters, rather than capacity. A listing of all engines covered, together with their code letters, is given in the Specifications.

The engines are water-cooled, single or double overhead camshaft, in-line four-cylinder units, with aluminium-alloy (engine code AER) or cast-iron (all other engine codes) cylinder blocks and aluminium-alloy cylinder heads. All are mounted transversely at the front of the vehicle, with the transmission bolted to the left-hand side of the engine.

The cylinder head carries the camshaft(s), driven by a toothed timing belt. It also houses the inlet and exhaust valves, which are closed by single or double coil springs, and which run in guides pressed into the cylinder head. The camshaft actuates the valves directly via hydraulic tappets, mounted in the cylinder head. The cylinder head contains integral oilways which supply and lubricate the tappets.

The crankshaft is supported by five main bearings, and endfloat is controlled by a thrust bearing fitted between cylinder Nos 2 and 3. On models with an aluminium cylinder block, the crankshaft must not be removed, otherwise the block will distort; the crankshaft and block must therefore be renewed as an assembly.

Engine coolant is circulated by a pump, driven either by the camshaft timing belt or the auxiliary drivebelt. For details of the cooling system, refer to Chapter 3.

AFT (1595 cc), 2E, AGG and ABF (1984 cc) engines are fitted with a timing belt-driven intermediate shaft, which provides drive for the distributor and the oil pump.

Lubricant is circulated under pressure by a pump, driven either by the crankshaft or by the intermediate shaft, depending on engine type. Oil is drawn from the sump through a strainer, and then forced through an externally-mounted, replaceable screw-on filter. From there, it is distributed to the cylinder head, where it lubricates the camshaft journals and hydraulic tappets, and also to the crankcase, where it lubricates the main bearings, connecting rod big- and small-ends, gudgeon pins and cylinder bores. Certain larger engines are fitted with oil jets, mounted at the base of each cylinder - these spray oil onto the underside of the pistons, to improve cooling. An oil cooler, supplied with engine coolant, reduces the temperature of the oil before it re-enters the engine.

Repairs possible with the engine installed in the vehicle:

The following operations can be performed without removing the engine:

a) Auxiliary drivebelts - removal and refitting.
b) Camshaft(s) - removal and refitting. *
c) Camshaft oil seal - renewal.
d) Camshaft sprocket - removal and refitting.
e) Coolant pump - removal and refitting (refer to Chapter 3)
f) Crankshaft oil seals - renewal.
g) Crankshaft sprocket - removal and refitting.
h) Cylinder head - removal and refitting. *
i) Engine mountings - inspection and renewal.
j) Intermediate shaft oil seal - renewal.
k) Oil pump and pickup assembly - removal and refitting.
l) Sump - removal and refitting.
m) Timing belt, sprockets and cover - removal, inspection and refitting.

*Cylinder head dismantling procedures are detailed in Chapter 2C, with details of camshaft and hydraulic tappet removal.
Note: It is possible to remove the pistons and connecting rods (after removing the cylinder head and sump) without removing the engine. However, this is not recommended. Work of this nature is more easily and thoroughly completed with the engine on the bench, as described in Chapter 2C.

2.5a Crankshaft/intermediate shaft sprocket timing marks: engine codes 1F, 2E, AGG

2 Locating TDC on No 1 cylinder

General information

Note: This sub-section has been written with the assumption that the distributor (where fitted), HT leads and timing belt are correctly fitted.

1 The crankshaft, the camshaft, and on certain engines the intermediate shaft, sprockets are driven by the timing belt, and rotate in phase with each other. When the timing belt is removed during servicing or repair, it is possible for the shafts to rotate independently of each other, and the correct phasing is then lost.

2 The design of the engines covered in this Chapter is such that potentially damaging piston-to-valve contact may occur if the camshaft is rotated when any of the pistons are stationary at, or near, the top of its stroke.

3 For this reason, it is important that the correct phasing between the camshaft, crankshaft and intermediate shaft is preserved whilst the timing belt is off the engine. This is achieved by setting the engine in a reference condition (known as Top Dead Centre or TDC) before the timing belt is removed, and then preventing the shafts from rotating until the belt is refitted. Similarly, if the engine has been dismantled for overhaul, the engine can be set to TDC during reassembly to ensure that the correct shaft phasing is restored. **Note:** On engine code ABF the intermediate shaft drives only the oil pump (ie not the distributor as well), so its alignment with the crankshaft and camshaft is not critical. On engine codes AAU, AAV, ABD, ABU, AER, AEX, APQ, AEE and ALM, the coolant pump is driven by the timing belt, but the pump alignment with respect to the crankshaft and camshaft is not critical.

4 TDC is the highest position a piston reaches within its respective cylinder - in a four-stroke engine, each piston reaches TDC twice per cycle, once on the compression stroke and once on the exhaust stroke. In general, TDC normally refers to No 1 cylinder on the compression stroke. (Note that the cylinders are numbered one to four, starting from the timing belt end of the engine).

5 The crankshaft sprocket has a marking which, when aligned with a reference marking on the timing belt cover or intermediate shaft sprocket (depending on engine type), indicates that No 1 cylinder (and hence also No 4 cylinder) is at TDC **(see illustrations)**.

6 The camshaft sprocket is also equipped with a timing mark - when this is similarly aligned, the engine is correctly synchronised, and the timing belt can then be refitted and tensioned **(see illustrations)**. Note on the ABF engine, there is also a mark on the back of the camshaft sprocket which aligns with the front, upper face of the cylinder head.

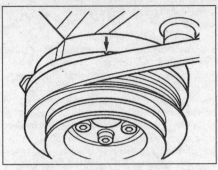

2.5b Crankshaft pulley timing marks:
engine codes ABF, AFT

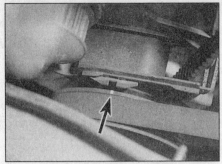

2.5c Crankshaft sprocket timing marks:
engine codes AAU, AAV, ABD, ABU

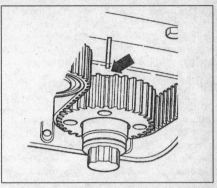

2.5d Crankshaft sprocket timing marks -
bevelled tooth (arrowed): engine codes
AER, AEX, APQ, AEE, ALM

7 In addition, on certain engines the flywheel has markings which can be observed by removing a protective cap from the transmission bellhousing. When this mark is aligned with a corresponding reference mark on the bellhousing casting, it indicates that No 1 cylinder is at TDC **(see illustration)**. Note, however, that these markings cannot be used if the transmission has been removed from the engine for repair or overhaul.

8 The following sub-Sections describe setting the engine to TDC on No 1 cylinder.

Setting TDC on No 1 cylinder - timing belt fitted

All engines

9 Before starting work, disconnect the battery negative (earth) lead (see Chapter 5A). Disable the ignition system by removing the distributor centre HT lead and grounding it on

the cylinder block, using a jumper wire. Prevent any vehicle movement by putting the transmission in neutral, applying the handbrake and chocking the rear wheels. Also remove the engine top cover where necessary.

10 On the distributor cap, note the position of the No 1 cylinder HT terminal with respect to the distributor body. On some models, the manufacturer provides a marking in the form of a small cut-out. If the terminal is not marked, follow the HT lead from the No 1 cylinder spark plug back to the distributor cap - No 1 cylinder is at the timing end of the engine - and using chalk or a pen (*not* a pencil), place a mark on the distributor body directly under the terminal.

11 Remove the distributor cap, as described in Chapter 5B.

12 Disconnect the HT leads from the spark plugs, noting their order of connection.

13 To bring any piston up to TDC, it will be necessary to rotate the crankshaft manually. This can be done by using a wrench and socket on the bolt that retains the crankshaft pulley (refer to Section 5 for more detail).

14 Rotate the crankshaft in its normal direction of rotation until the distributor rotor arm electrode begins to approach the mark that was made on the distributor body.

> **HAYNES HINT** *Remove all four spark plugs; this will make the engine easier to turn; refer to Chapter 1A for details.*

15 With reference to Section 4, remove the upper timing belt outer cover to expose the camshaft timing belt sprocket beneath.

16 Identify the timing marks on both the camshaft sprocket and the inner section of the timing belt cover (or cylinder head cover, as applicable) - refer to the accompanying illustrations. Continue turning the crankshaft clockwise until these marks are exactly aligned with each other.

17 At this point, identify the timing marks on the crankshaft sprocket (or pulley, as applicable) and the timing belt cover (or intermediate shaft, as applicable) and check that they are correctly aligned. **Note**: *On some engines, the outer part of the lower timing belt cover must be removed to expose the crankshaft sprocket timing marks.*

Engine codes 1F, 2E, AGG, ABF, AFT only

18 Locate the timing inspection hole on the transmission bellhousing, and remove the protective cap. This exposes the edge of the flywheel, on which there is a set of timing marks.

19 With the camshaft timing marks aligned, the timing mark on the flywheel should be aligned exactly with the pointer marked on the bellhousing. **Note**: *Observe from directly above the inspection hole to ensure correct alignment.*

2A

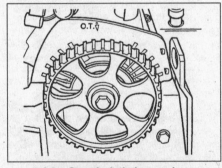

2.6a Camshaft timing marks:
engine codes 1F, 2E, AGG, ABF, AFT

2.6b Camshaft timing marks:
engine codes AAU, AAV, ABD, ABU

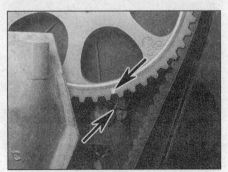

2.6c Camshaft timing marks:
engine codes AER, AEX, APQ, AEE, ALM

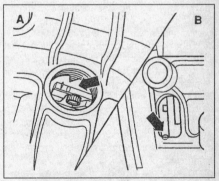

2.7 Flywheel/driveplate timing marks:
engine codes 1F, 2E, AGG, ABF, AFT

A *Flywheel*   B *Driveplate*

20 On engine code AFT, note that the intermediate shaft sprocket has no timing markings - alignment is achieved by checking that the centre of the rotor arm electrode is lined up with the No 1 terminal marking on the distributor body.

All engines

21 Check that the centre of the distributor rotor arm electrode is now aligned with the No 1 terminal mark on the distributor body. If it proves impossible to align the rotor arm with the No 1 terminal whilst maintaining the alignment of the camshaft timing marks, refer to Chapter 5B and check that the distributor has been fitted correctly.

22 When all the above steps have been completed successfully, the engine will be set to TDC on No 1 cylinder.

Caution: If the timing belt is to be removed, ensure that the crankshaft, camshaft and intermediate shaft alignment is preserved by preventing the sprockets from rotating with respect to each other.

Setting TDC on No 1 cylinder - timing belt removed

23 This procedure has been written with the assumption that the timing belt has been removed and that the alignment between the camshaft, crankshaft and where applicable, intermediate shaft has been lost, for example following engine removal and overhaul.

24 On all the engines covered in this manual, it is possible for damage to be caused by the piston crowns striking the valve heads, if the camshaft is rotated with the timing belt removed and the crankshaft set to TDC. For this reason, the TDC setting procedure must be carried out in a particular order, as described in the following paragraphs.

25 Before the cylinder head is refitted, use a wrench and socket on the crankshaft pulley centre bolt to turn the crankshaft in its normal direction of rotation, until all four pistons are positioned **halfway down** their bores, with No 1 piston on its upstroke - i.e. around 90° before TDC.

26 With the cylinder head and camshaft sprocket fitted, identify the timing marks on both the camshaft sprocket and the inner section of the timing belt cover or cylinder head cover, as applicable referring to the illustrations shown earlier in this Section.

27 Turn the camshaft sprocket in its normal direction of rotation until the timing marks on the sprocket and timing belt inner cover (or cylinder head cover) are exactly aligned.

28 On engine code AFT *only*, check that the centre of the rotor arm electrode is lined up with the No 1 terminal marking on the distributor. If this is not the case, rotate the intermediate shaft sprocket to bring them into alignment.

29 Identify the timing marks on the crankshaft sprocket (or pulley, as applicable) and the timing belt cover (or intermediate shaft, as applicable). Refer to the illustrations given earlier. Using a socket and wrench on the

crankshaft sprocket retaining bolt, turn the crankshaft through 90° (quarter of a turn) in its normal direction of rotation, to bring the timing marks into alignment.

30 On engine codes 1F, 2E, AGG, ABF, AFT, if the transmission is fitted to the engine, the crankshaft alignment can be verified by observing the timing marks on the flywheel and transmission bellhousing. Remove the protective cap from the timing inspection hole on the bellhousing, and check that the marks are aligned as described in paragraph 7. **Note:** *Observe from directly above the inspection hole, to ensure correct alignment.*

31 Check that the centre of the distributor rotor arm electrode is now aligned with No 1 cylinder terminal marking on the distributor body. If it proves impossible to align the rotor arm with the No 1 terminal whilst maintaining the alignment of the camshaft timing marks, refer to Chapter 5B and check that the distributor has been fitted correctly.

32 When all the above steps have been completed successfully, the engine will be set at TDC on No 1 cylinder. The timing belt can now be fitted as described in Section 4.

Caution: Until the timing belt is fitted, ensure that the crankshaft, camshaft and intermediate shaft alignment is preserved by preventing the sprockets from rotating with respect to each other.

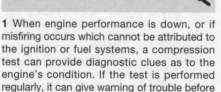

3 Cylinder compression test

1 When engine performance is down, or if misfiring occurs which cannot be attributed to the ignition or fuel systems, a compression test can provide diagnostic clues as to the engine's condition. If the test is performed regularly, it can give warning of trouble before any other symptoms become apparent.

2 The engine must be fully warmed-up to normal operating temperature, the battery must be fully charged, and all the spark plugs must be removed (refer to Chapter 1). Also remove the engine top cover where necessary. The aid of an assistant will also be required.

3 Disable the ignition system by disconnecting the ignition HT coil lead from the distributor cap and earthing it on the cylinder block. Use a jumper lead or similar wire to make a good connection.

4 To prevent possible damage to the catalytic converter, depressurise and disable the fuel injection system by removing the fuel pump fuse or relay (see Chapter 4).

5 Fit a compression tester to the No 1 cylinder spark plug hole - the type of tester which screws into the plug thread is preferable.

6 Have an assistant fully depress the accelerator, then crank the engine on the starter motor. After one or two revolutions, the compression pressure should build up to a maximum figure, and then stabilise. Record the highest reading obtained.

7 Repeat the test on the remaining cylinders, recording the pressure in each. Keep the accelerator pedal fully depressed.

8 All cylinders should produce very similar pressures; a difference of more than 2 bars between any two cylinders indicates a fault. Note that the compression should build up quickly in a healthy engine; low compression on the first stroke, followed by gradually-increasing pressure on successive strokes, indicates worn piston rings. A low compression reading on the first stroke, which does not build up during successive strokes, indicates leaking valves or a blown head gasket (a cracked head could also be the cause). Deposits on the undersides of the valve heads can also cause low compression.

9 Refer to the Specifications section of this Chapter, and compare the recorded compression figures with those stated by the manufacturer.

10 If the pressure in any cylinder is low, carry out the following test to isolate the cause. Introduce a teaspoonful of clean oil into that cylinder through its spark plug hole, and repeat the test.

11 If the addition of oil temporarily improves the compression pressure, this indicates that bore or piston wear is responsible for the pressure loss. No improvement suggests that leaking or burnt valves, or a blown head gasket, may be to blame.

12 A low reading from two adjacent cylinders is almost certainly due to the head gasket having blown between them; the presence of coolant in the engine oil will confirm this.

13 If one cylinder is about 20 percent lower than the others and the engine has a slightly rough idle, a worn camshaft lobe could be the cause.

14 On completion of the test, refit the spark plugs and restore the ignition and fuel systems.

4 Timing belt and outer covers - removal and refitting

General information

1 The primary function of the toothed timing belt is to drive the camshaft(s), but it is also used to drive the coolant pump or intermediate shaft, depending on the engine specification. Should the belt slip or break in service, the valve timing will be disturbed and piston-to-valve contact may occur, resulting in serious engine damage.

2 For this reason, it is important that the timing belt is tensioned correctly, and inspected regularly for signs of wear or deterioration.

3 Note that the removal of the *inner* section of the timing belt cover is described as part of the cylinder head removal procedure, as described in Section 11 later in this Chapter.

Removal

4 Disconnect the battery negative (earth) lead (see Chapter 5A). Apply the handbrake, then jack up the front of the vehicle and support it on axle stands (see *Jacking and vehicle support*). Also remove the engine top cover where necessary.

5 Except on engine code ABF, remove the air cleaner inlet duct and exhaust manifold hot air tube with reference to Chapter 4A. On engine code ABF, remove the air cleaner complete with reference to Chapter 4B.

6 Release the uppermost part of the timing belt cover by prising open the metal spring clips and where applicable, removing the retaining screws. Lift the cover away from the engine **(see illustration).**

7 With reference to Section 6, remove the auxiliary drive V-belt (where fitted), then remove the ribbed auxiliary drivebelt. On engine codes AFT, 1F, 2E, AGG, ABF the power steering pump tensioning and pivot bolts must be loosened first. On some engines access can be improved by removing the wheel arch liner.

8 Refer to Section 2 and using the engine alignment markings, set the engine to TDC on No 1 cylinder. Note that on some engines, it will be necessary to remove the crankshaft pulley for the ribbed auxiliary drivebelt (together with the V-belt pulley, where fitted) and timing belt lower cover first, to gain access to the engine alignment markings on the crankshaft sprocket - this operation is described in the next paragraph.

9 Undo the retaining screws, and remove the crankshaft pulley (together with the V-belt pulley, where fitted) from the crankshaft sprocket. On completion, check that the engine is still set to TDC.

 HAYNES HINT *To prevent the crankshaft pulley from rotating whilst the mounting bolts are being slackened, select 4th gear and get an assistant to apply the footbrake firmly. Failing this, grip the pulley by wrapping a length of old rubber hose or old V-belt around it.*

4.12 Relieve the tension on the timing belt by slackening the tensioner mounting nut (arrowed): engine code 2E shown

4.6 Removing the timing belt outer cover (engine code ABD shown)

10 On engine codes AFT, 1F, 2E, AGG, ABF refer to Chapter 3 and remove the coolant pump pulley to allow removal of the timing belt lower cover.

11 Remove the retaining screws and clips, and lift off the timing belt lower cover.

12 All engines *except* AAU, AAV, ABD, ABU, refer to Section 5 and relieve the tension on the timing belt by slackening the tensioner mounting nut slightly, allowing it to pivot away from the belt **(see illustration).**

13 On engine codes AAU, AAV, ABD, ABU only, slacken the coolant pump mounting bolts, then release the tension on the timing belt by rotating the pump anticlockwise - use a screwdriver inserted between the lugs on the pump casting, as a lever **(see illustration)**.

14 Examine the timing belt for manufacturer's markings that indicate the direction of rotation. If none are present, make your own using typist's correction fluid.

Caution: If the belt appears to be in good condition and can be re-used, it is essential that it is refitted the same way around, otherwise accelerated wear will result, leading to premature failure.

15 Slide the belt off the sprockets, taking care to avoid twisting or kinking it excessively. Ensure that the sprockets remain aligned with their respective timing markings once the timing belt has been removed.

Caution: It is potentially damaging to allow the camshaft to turn with the timing belt removed and the engine set at TDC, as piston-to-valve contact may occur.

16 Examine the belt for evidence of contamination by coolant or lubricant. If this is the case, identify the source of the contamination before progressing any further. Check the belt for signs of wear or damage, particularly around the leading edges of the belt teeth. Renew the belt if its condition is in doubt; the cost of belt renewal is negligible compared with potential cost of the engine repairs, should the belt fail in service. Similarly, if the belt is known to have covered more than 36 000 miles, it is prudent to renew it regardless of condition, as a precautionary measure.

17 If the timing belt is not going to be refitted for some time, it is a wise precaution to hang a warning label on the steering wheel, to remind yourself (and others) not to attempt starting the engine.

Refitting

18 Ensure that the crankshaft, camshaft and where applicable, intermediate shaft timing marks, are still correctly aligned in the TDC on No 1 cylinder position, as described in Section 2.

Engine codes AAU, AAV, ABD and ABU

19 Loop the timing belt under the crankshaft sprocket loosely, observing the direction of rotation markings.

20 Refit the lower section of the timing belt cover.

21 Fit the crankshaft pulley to the crankshaft sprocket, noting that the offset of the mounting holes allows only one fitting position, then insert and tighten the bolts to the specified torque.

22 Ensure that the timing marks on the crankshaft pulley and camshaft sprocket are correctly aligned with their corresponding reference marks on the timing belt inner cover; refer to Section 2 for details.

23 Engage the timing belt teeth with the crankshaft sprocket, then manoeuvre it into position over the coolant pump and camshaft sprockets - avoid bending the belt back on itself or twisting it excessively as you do this. Ensure that the front run of the belt is taut - ie all the slack should be in the section of the belt that passes over the coolant pump pulley.

24 Insert a stout screwdriver between the lugs on the coolant pump casting, then using the screwdriver as a lever, turn the coolant pump clockwise so that the slack in the belt is taken up (refer to illustration 4.13).

25 Test the belt tension by grasping it between the fingers at a point mid-way between the coolant pump and camshaft sprockets and twisting it; the belt tension is correct when it can just be twisted through 90° (quarter of a turn) and no further.

26 When the correct belt tension has been achieved, tighten the coolant pump mounting bolts to the specified torque (see Chapter 3).

27 Using a spanner or wrench and socket on the crankshaft pulley centre bolt, rotate the crankshaft through two complete revolutions, and reset the engine to TDC on No 1 cylinder, with reference to Section 2. Re-check the belt tension, and adjust it if necessary.

2A

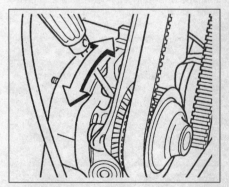

4.13 Release the tension on the timing belt by rotating the pump towards the engine - use a screwdriver as a lever

4.31a Turn the tensioner with an Allen key until the slack in the belt is taken up

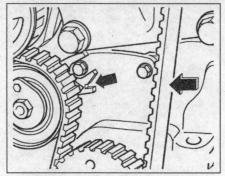

4.31b Sliding pointer should line up with the groove in the tensioner baseplate

Engine codes AER, AEX, APQ, AEE, and ALM

28 Ensure that the timing marks on the crankshaft and camshaft sprockets are correctly aligned with their corresponding TDC reference marks on the timing belt inner cover; refer to Section 2 for details.

29 Engage the timing belt teeth with the crankshaft sprocket, then manoeuvre it into position over the coolant pump and camshaft sprockets. Observe the direction of rotation markings on the belt.

30 Pass the flat side of the belt over the tensioner roller - avoid bending the belt back on itself or twisting it excessively as you do this. Ensure the front run of the belt is taut - ie all the slack should be in the section of the belt that passes over the tensioner roller.

31 Tension the belt as follows: tighten the tensioner securing bolt lightly, then insert an Allen key into the adjustment hole, and turn the eccentrically-mounted tensioner clockwise until the slack in the belt is taken up. Continue turning the tensioner until the sliding pointer lines up with the groove in the tensioner baseplate (see illustrations). On completion, tighten the tensioner securing bolt to the specified torque.

32 Using a spanner or wrench and socket on the crankshaft pulley centre bolt, rotate the crankshaft through two complete revolutions, and reset the engine to TDC on No 1 cylinder, with reference to Section 2. Re-check the alignment of the tensioner, and adjust it if necessary.

4.43 Tension the belt by turning the tensioner clockwise using circlip pliers

33 Refer to Section 5 and test the operation of the tensioner.

34 Refit the lower and upper sections of the timing belt outer cover, tightening the retaining screws securely.

35 Refit the crankshaft pulley to the crankshaft sprocket, noting that the offset of the mounting holes allows only one fitting position, then insert and tighten the retaining bolts to the specified torque.

Engine codes AFT and ABF

36 Ensure that the timing marks on the flywheel and camshaft sprocket are correctly aligned with their corresponding TDC reference marks on the transmission bellhousing and timing belt inner cover/cylinder head cover respectively; refer to Section 2 for details.

37 Loop the timing belt under the crankshaft sprocket loosely, observing the direction of rotation markings.

38 Refit the lower section of the timing belt cover.

39 Fit the crankshaft pulley to the crankshaft sprocket, noting that the offset of the mounting holes allows only one fitting position, then insert and tighten the retaining bolts to the specified torque.

40 Ensure that the intermediate shaft has not moved since the removal of the timing belt. Check that the marking for the No 1 cylinder terminal on the distributor body is still aligned with the centre of the rotor arm electrode (see Section 2).

41 Fully engage the timing belt teeth with the crankshaft sprocket, then manoeuvre the belt into position over the intermediate shaft and camshaft sprocket(s). Observe the direction of rotation markings on the belt.

42 Pass the flat side of the belt over the tensioner roller - avoid bending the belt back on itself or twisting it excessively as you do this. Ensure that the front run of the belt is taut - i.e. all the slack should be in the section of the belt that passes over the tensioner roller.

43 Tension the belt by turning the eccentrically-mounted tensioner clockwise; two holes are provided in the side of the tensioner hub for this purpose - a pair of right-angled circlip pliers is an ideal substitute for the correct manufacturer's tool (see illustration).

44 On engine code ABF, turn the tensioner hub

clockwise until the hub pointers are aligned with each other (see illustration), then tighten the central nut to the specified torque. Do not turn the hub beyond the point where the pointers align, otherwise the tension will be incorrect. In this case, loosen the nut and turn the tensioner fully anti-clockwise, then turn it clockwise slowly until the pointers are correctly aligned. Tighten the central nut to the specified torque. Depress the timing belt between the camshaft and intermediate shaft sprockets with a finger, and check that the pointers move apart, then release the belt and check that the pointers realign again.

45 On engine code AFT, turn the tensioner hub clockwise until the timing belt tension is correct. Test the timing belt tension by grasping it between the fingers at a point midway between the intermediate shaft and camshaft sprockets and twisting it; the belt tension is correct when it can just be twisted through 90° (quarter of a turn) and no further.

46 When the correct belt tension has been achieved, tighten the tensioner locknut to the specified torque.

47 Using a spanner or wrench and socket on the crankshaft pulley centre bolt, rotate the crankshaft through two complete revolutions and reset the engine to TDC on No 1 cylinder, with reference to Section 2. Re-check the timing belt tension and adjust it, if necessary.

48 Refit the upper section of the timing belt outer cover, and tighten the retaining screws securely.

Engine codes 1F, 2E and AGG

49 Ensure that the timing mark on the camshaft sprocket is correctly aligned with the corresponding TDC reference mark on the timing belt inner cover; refer to Section 2 for details.

50 Loop the timing belt under the crankshaft sprocket loosely, observing the direction of rotation markings.

51 Temporarily refit the pulley for the ribbed auxiliary drivebelt to the crankshaft sprocket, using two of the retaining screws - note that the offset mounting holes allow only one fitting position.

52 Verify that the timing marks on the

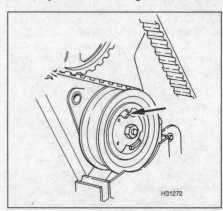

4.44 On engine code ABF, the timing belt is correctly tensioned when the pointers are aligned with each other

5.2 Slide the tensioner off its mounting stud

crankshaft pulley and the intermediate shaft sprocket are still correctly aligned; refer to Section 2 for details.

53 Engage the timing belt teeth with the crankshaft sprocket, then manoeuvre it into position over the intermediate shaft and camshaft sprockets. Observe the direction of rotation markings on the belt.

54 Pass the flat side of the belt over the tensioner roller - avoid bending the belt back on itself or twisting it excessively as you do this. Ensure that the front run of the belt is taut - ie all the slack should be in the section of the belt that passes over the tensioner roller.

55 Tension the belt by turning the eccentrically-mounted tensioner clockwise; two holes are provided in the side of the tensioner hub for this purpose - a pair of sturdy right-angled circlip pliers is a suitable substitute for the correct VAG tool (refer to illustration 4.43).

56 Test the timing belt tension by grasping it between the fingers at a point mid-way between the intermediate shaft and camshaft sprockets and twisting it; the belt tension is correct when it can just be twisted through 90° (quarter of a turn) and no further.

57 When the correct belt tension has been achieved, tighten the tensioner locknut to the specified torque.

58 Using a spanner or wrench and socket on the crankshaft pulley centre bolt, rotate the crankshaft through two complete revolutions. Reset the engine to TDC on No 1 cylinder with reference to Section 2, and check that the crankshaft pulley and intermediate shaft and camshaft sprocket timing marks are re-aligned. Re-check the timing belt tension and adjust it, if necessary.

59 Remove the pulley for the ribbed auxiliary drivebelt from the crankshaft sprocket, to allow the lower section of the outer timing belt cover to be refitted, then refit the pulley, noting that the offset of the mounting holes allows only one fitting position. Finally, insert and tighten the retaining bolts to the specified torque.

All engine codes

60 Refer to Chapter 3 and refit the coolant pump pulley, where applicable.

61 Working from Section 6, refit and tension the auxiliary drivebelt(s).

62 Restore ignition system by reconnecting the HT lead to the distributor cap, then restore the fuelling system by refitting the fuel pump relay. Also refit the engine top cover where necessary.

63 On completion, refer to Chapter 5B and check the ignition timing; adjust it if necessary.

---

5 Timing belt sprockets and tensioner - removal, inspection and refitting

Timing belt tensioner

Removal

Note: *On engine codes AAU, AAV, ABD, ABU the coolant pump is used to tension the timing belt. The following paragraphs describe removal of the timing belt tensioner on all other engines.*

1 Remove the timing belt as described in Section 4.

2 Unscrew the hub nut and withdraw the tensioner off of its mounting stud **(see illustration)**.

Inspection

3 Wipe the tensioner clean, but do not use solvents that may contaminate the bearings. Spin the tensioner pulley on its hub by hand. Stiff movement or excessive freeplay is an indication of severe wear, in which case the tensioner should be renewed.

Refitting

4 Slide the tensioner onto the mounting stud, then refit the washer and retaining nut - do not fully tighten the nut at this stage. On engine codes AER, AEX, APQ, AEE, ALM make sure that the cut-out in the tensioner plate is located over the timing cover bolt.

To make a camshaft sprocket holding tool, obtain two lengths of steel strip about 6 mm thick by 30 mm wide or similar, one 600 mm long, the other 200 mm long (all dimensions approximate). Bolt the two strips together to form a forked end, leaving the bolt slack so that the shorter strip can pivot freely. At the end of each 'prong' of the fork, secure a bolt with a nut and a locknut, to act as the fulcrums; these will engage with the cut-outs in the sprocket, and should protrude by about 30 mm

5 Refit the timing belt as described in Section 4.

Camshaft timing belt sprocket

Removal

6 Remove the timing belt as described in Section 4.

7 The camshaft sprocket must be held stationary whilst its retaining bolt is slackened. A simple home-made tool using basic materials may be fabricated as shown in the accompanying illustration **(see Tool Tip)**.

8 Using the home-made tool, brace the camshaft sprocket. Slacken and remove the retaining bolt; recover the washer (if fitted).

9 Slide the camshaft sprocket from the end of the camshaft. Where applicable, recover the Woodruff key from the keyway.

Inspection

10 With the sprocket removed, examine it for signs of damage and wear. Examine the camshaft oil seal for signs of leaking. If necessary, refer to Section 8 and renew it.

11 Wipe the sprocket and camshaft mating surfaces clean.

Refitting

12 Where applicable, fit the Woodruff key into the keyway, with the plain surface facing upwards. Offer up the sprocket to the camshaft, engaging the slot in the sprocket with the Woodruff key. On engines where a key is not used, ensure that the lug in the sprocket hub engages with recess in the end of the camshaft.

13 Hold the sprocket stationary using the home-made tool, then refit the retaining bolt and washer and tighten the bolt to the specified torque.

14 With reference to Section 4, check that the engine is still set to TDC on No 1 cylinder, then refit and tension the timing belt.

Crankshaft timing belt sprocket

Removal

15 Remove the timing belt as described in Section 4.

16 The crankshaft sprocket must be held stationary whilst its retaining bolt is slackened. If access to the correct VAG flywheel locking tool is not available, lock the crankshaft in position by removing the starter motor, as described in Chapter 5A, to expose the flywheel ring gear. Have an assistant insert a stout lever between the gear teeth and the transmission bellhousing whilst the sprocket retaining bolt is slackened.

17 Withdraw the bolt, recover the washer and lift off the sprocket **(see illustration)**.

Inspection

18 With the sprocket removed, examine it for signs of damage and wear. Examine the crankshaft oil seal for signs of leaking. If necessary, refer to Section 10 and renew it.

19 Wipe the sprocket and crankshaft mating surfaces clean.

2A

5.17 Removing the crankshaft sprocket

5.20 Crankshaft sprocket alignment tooth and keyway (arrowed)

Refitting

20 Offer up the sprocket, engaging the lug on the inside of the sprocket with the recess in the end of the crankshaft **(see illustration)**. Insert the bolt (and washer where applicable) and tighten it to the specified torque.

21 With reference to Section 4, check that the engine is still set to TDC on No 1 cylinder, then refit and tension the timing belt.

Intermediate shaft sprocket

Removal

22 Remove the timing belt as described in Section 4.

23 The intermediate shaft sprocket must be held stationary whilst its retaining bolt is slackened. A simple home-made tool using basic materials may be fabricated as described earlier in the camshaft sprocket removal sub-Section.

24 Using the home-made tool, brace the intermediate shaft sprocket and slacken and remove the retaining bolt. Recover the washer where fitted.

25 Slide the sprocket from the end of the intermediate shaft. Where applicable, recover the Woodruff key from the keyway.

Inspection

26 With the sprocket removed, examine it for signs of damage and wear. Examine the intermediate shaft oil seal for signs of leaking. If necessary, refer to Section 9 and renew it.

27 Wipe the sprocket and shaft mating surfaces clean.

6.18 Turn the rotary tensioner clockwise to release the tension

Refitting

28 Where applicable, fit the Woodruff key into the keyway, with the plain surface facing upwards. Offer up the sprocket to the intermediate shaft, engaging the slot in the sprocket with the Woodruff key.

29 With reference to Section 4, check that the engine is still set to TDC on No 1 cylinder, then refit and tension the timing belt.

---

6 Auxiliary drivebelts - removal and refitting

General information

1 Depending on the vehicle specification and engine type, one or two auxiliary drivebelts may be fitted. Both are driven from pulleys mounted on the crankshaft, and provide drive for the alternator, coolant pump, power steering pump and on vehicles with air conditioning, the refrigerant compressor.

2 The run of the belts and the components they drive are also dependent on vehicle specification and engine type, and because of this, the coolant pump and power steering pump may be fitted with pulleys to suit either a ribbed belt or a V-belt.

3 The ribbed auxiliary belt may be fitted with an automatic tensioning device, depending on its run (and hence the number of components it is driving), otherwise, the belt is tensioned by the alternator mountings, which have an in-built tensioning spring. The V-belt is tensioned by pivoting the alternator or power steering pump on its mounting.

4 On refitting, the auxiliary belt must be tensioned correctly, to ensure correct operation under all conditions and prolonged service life.

Auxiliary V-belt

Removal

5 Apply the handbrake, then jack up the front of the vehicle and support it on axle stands (see *Jacking and vehicle support*).

6 Where necessary, remove the right-hand front roadwheel then remove the wheel arch liner for access to the right-hand end of the engine.

7 With reference to Chapter 5A, loosen the alternator tension and pivot bolts then turn the adjustment rack nut to swivel the alternator towards the engine.

8 Slip the V-belt off of the pulleys.

9 Examine the belt for signs or wear or damage, and renew it if necessary.

Refitting and tensioning

10 Refit the belt by reversing the removal procedure, ensuring that it seats evenly in the pulleys.

11 Set the belt tension by turning the adjustment rack nut until the belt can be deflected under firm thumb pressure by the amount given in the Specifications. Alternatively, the rack nut can be turned to a torque of 8 Nm for a new belt or 4 Nm for a used belt to apply the correct tension. Tighten the lock bolt and pivot bolt to their specified torques on completion (see Chapter 5A).

12 Rotate the crankshaft in its normal direction of rotation through two turns, then re-check and if necessary adjust the tension.

Auxiliary ribbed belt

Removal

13 Apply the handbrake, then jack up the front of the vehicle and support it on axle stands (see *Jacking and vehicle support*).

14 Where necessary, remove the right-hand front roadwheel then remove the wheel arch liner for access to the right-hand end of the engine. Where applicable, remove the air inlet tube and hot air tube for access to the ribbed belt.

15 Where applicable, remove the auxiliary V-belt as described in the previous sub-Section.

16 Examine the ribbed belt for manufacturer's markings, indicating the direction of rotation. If none are present, make some using typist's correction fluid or a dab of paint - do not cut or score the belt in any way.

Vehicles with a roller-arm automatic tensioning device

17 Rotate the tensioner roller arm clockwise against its spring tension, so that the roller is forced away from the belt - use an adjustable spanner as a lever.

Vehicles with rotary automatic tensioning device

18 Fit a ring spanner to the tensioner centre nut, and rotate the assembly anti-clockwise, against its spring tension **(see illustration)**.

Vehicles without an automatic tensioning device

19 Slacken the alternator upper and lower mounting bolts by between one and two turns.

20 Push the alternator down to its stop against the spring tension, so that it rotates around its uppermost mounting.

All vehicles

21 Pull the belt off the alternator pulley, then release it from the remaining pulleys **(see illustration)**.

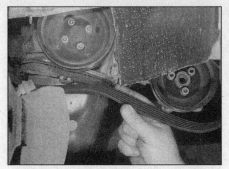

6.21 Removing the auxiliary drivebelt

6.23 Rotate the tensioner roller arm clockwise using an adjustable spanner

Refitting and tensioning

Caution: Observe the manufacturer's direction of rotation markings on the belt, when refitting.

22 Pass the ribbed belt underneath the crankshaft pulley, ensuring that the ribs seat in the channels on the surface of the pulley.

Vehicles with roller-arm automatic tensioning device

23 Rotate the tensioner roller arm clockwise against its spring tension - use an adjustable spanner as a lever **(see illustration)**.

24 Pass the belt around the coolant pump pulley or air conditioning refrigerant pump pulley (as applicable), then fit it over the alternator pulley.

25 Release the tensioner pulley arm, and allow the roller to bear against the flat surface of the belt.

Vehicles with rotary automatic tensioning device

26 Fit a ring spanner to the tensioner centre nut, and rotate the assembly anti-clockwise, against its spring tension.

27 Pass the flat side of the belt underneath the tensioner roller, then fit it over the power steering pump and alternator pulleys.

28 Release the spanner and allow the tensioner roller to bear against the flat side of the belt.

Vehicles without an automatic tensioning device

29 Repeatedly push the alternator down to its stop against the spring tension, so that it rotates around its uppermost mounting, and check that it moves back freely when released. If necessary, slacken the alternator mounting bolts by a further half a turn.

30 Keep the alternator pushed down against its stop, pass the belt over the alternator pulley, then release the alternator and allow it to tension the belt.

31 On models with power steering, tighten the alternator mounting bolts to the specified torque (see Chapter 5A).

32 On models without power steering, disable the ignition system by removing the distributor centre HT lead and grounding it on the cylinder block, using a jumper wire. Spin the engine approximately 10 turns on the starter motor, then tighten the alternator mounting bolts to the specified torque. Reconnect the HT lead.

All vehicles

33 Where applicable, refer to the previous sub-Section and refit the auxiliary V-belt.

34 Where applicable, refit the wheel arch liner and roadwheel.

35 Lower the vehicle to the ground.

---

7 Camshaft cover - removal and refitting

Removal

Engine codes AER, AAU, AAV, ABD, ABU, AEX, APQ, AEE, ALM

1 Remove the engine top cover where necessary. Disconnect the crankcase breather hose from the cover; cut off retaining clip, if it is of the crimp type - fit a worm-drive clip in its place on refitting.

2 Slacken and withdraw the three camshaft cover retaining bolts - recover the washers and seals.

Engine code AFT

3 With reference to Chapter 4B, remove the upper section of the inlet manifold and throttle body from the engine.

4 Prise the crankcase breather pressure-regulating valve from the port on the cylinder head cover.

5 Working around the edge of the camshaft cover, progressively slacken and remove the retaining nuts.

Engine codes 1F, 2E, AGG

6 Remove the engine top cover where necessary. Disconnect the crankcase breather hoses from the pressure regulator valve, mounted on top of the camshaft cover. If crimp-type hose clips are used, cut them off and replace them with standard worm-drive clips on refitting. Slacken and withdraw the retaining screws and remove the regulator valve.

7 On engine code 2E, access may be improved by removing the idling stabilisation valve; refer to Chapter 4B.

8 Working around the edge of the camshaft cover, progressively slacken and remove the retaining nuts. Where necessary, also unscrew the bolts securing the brackets to the inlet manifold.

Engine code ABF

9 Remove the engine top cover where necessary. Refer to Chapter 5B and disconnect the HT leads from the spark plugs.

10 Refer to Chapter 4B and remove the upper section of the inlet manifold and throttle body.

11 With reference to Chapter 1A, remove the spark plugs from the cylinder head.

12 Working around the edge of the camshaft cover, progressively slacken and remove the outer retaining screws. Where applicable, remove the reinforcement plates from the edge of the cover. Slacken and withdraw the two inner retaining screws from between the spark plug apertures - recover the washers.

All engine codes

13 Lift the cover away from the cylinder head; if it sticks, do not attempt to lever it off with an implement - instead free it by working around the cover and tapping it lightly with a soft-faced mallet.

14 Where applicable, lift the oil baffle plate off the camshaft bearing cap studs, noting its orientation.

15 Recover the camshaft cover gasket; note that the gasket may be made up of several pieces, depending on engine specification. Inspect each piece carefully - renew the entire gasket if damage or deterioration is evident.

16 Clean the mating surfaces of the cylinder head and camshaft cover thoroughly, removing all traces of oil and old gasket - take care to avoid damaging the surfaces as you do this.

Refitting

17 Refitting is a reversal of removal. Ensure that the gasket is not displaced as the camshaft cover is lowered into position. Tighten the retaining screws/nuts to the specified torque.

---

8 Camshaft oil seal - renewal

2A

1 Refer to Section 6 and remove the auxiliary drivebelt(s).

2 With reference to Sections 2, 4 and 5 of this Chapter, remove the auxiliary belt pulleys and timing belt cover, then set the engine to TDC on No 1 cylinder and remove the timing belt, timing belt tensioner (where applicable) and camshaft sprocket.

3 After removing the retaining bolts, lift the inner timing belt cover away from the engine block - this will expose the oil seal. *Note: On engine codes AER, AAU, AAV, ABD, ABU, AEX, APQ, AEE, ALM, the coolant pump retaining bolts pass through the timing belt inner cover; with reference to Chapter 3, drain the coolant from the engine and remove the coolant pump.*

4 Drill two small holes into the existing oil seal, diagonally opposite each other. Thread two self-tapping screws into the holes, and using two pairs of pliers, pull on the heads of the screws to extract the oil seal. Take great care to avoid drilling through into the seal housing or camshaft sealing surface.

8.7 Drive the camshaft oil seal squarely into its housing

5 Clean out the seal housing and sealing surface of the camshaft by wiping it with a lint-free cloth - avoid using solvents that may enter the cylinder head and affect component lubrication. Remove any swarf or burrs that may cause the seal to leak.

6 Lubricate the lip of the new oil seal with clean engine oil, and push it over the camshaft until it is positioned above its housing.

7 Using a hammer and a socket of suitable diameter, drive the seal squarely into its housing **(see illustration)**. **Note:** *Select a socket that bears only on the hard outer surface of the seal, not the inner lip which can easily be damaged.*

8 Refit the inner timing belt cover (and coolant pump where applicable) and tighten the retaining bolts to the specified torque.

9 With reference to Sections 2, 4 and 5 of this Chapter, refit the timing sprockets, then refit and tension the timing belt.

10 With reference to Section 6, refit and tension the auxiliary drivebelt(s).

9 Intermediate shaft oil seal - renewal

Note: *This section is not applicable to engine codes AER, AAU, AAV, ABD, ABU, AEX, APQ, AEE, ALM, which do not have an intermediate shaft.*

1 Refer to Section 6 and remove the auxiliary drivebelt(s).

2 With reference to Sections 4 and 5 of this Chapter, remove the auxiliary belt pulleys, timing belt outer cover, timing belt, tensioner (where applicable) and intermediate shaft sprocket.

3 With reference to Section 7 of Chapter 2C, remove the intermediate shaft flange, and renew the oil seal and O-ring.

4 Refer to Sections 4 and 5 of this Chapter and refit the intermediate shaft sprocket, tensioner, timing belt, outer cover and auxiliary belt pulleys.

5 Refer to Section 6 of this Chapter, and refit the auxiliary drivebelt(s).

10 Crankshaft oil seals - renewal

Crankshaft front (timing end) oil seal

1 Apply the handbrake, then jack up the front of the vehicle and support it on axle stands (see *Jacking and vehicle support*).

2 Remove the auxiliary drivebelt(s) as described in Section 6.

3 With reference to Sections 4 and 5 of this Chapter, remove the auxiliary drivebelt(s), timing belt outer covers, timing belt and crankshaft sprocket.

4 Remove the oil seal, using the same method as that described for the camshaft oil seal removal, in Section 8.

5 Clean out the seal housing and sealing surface of the crankshaft by wiping it with a lint-free cloth - avoid using solvents that may enter the crankcase and affect component lubrication. Remove any swarf or burrs that could cause the seal to leak.

6 Lubricate the lip of the new oil seal with clean engine oil, and position it over the housing **(see illustration)**.

7 Using a hammer and a socket of suitable diameter, drive the seal squarely into its housing **(see illustration)**. **Note:** *Select a socket that bears only on the hard outer surface of the seal, not the inner lip which can easily be damaged.*

8 With reference to Sections 4 and 5 of this Chapter, refit the crankshaft sprocket, timing belt, covers, and auxiliary drivebelt(s).

9 Lower the vehicle to the ground.

Crankshaft front (timing end) oil seal housing - gasket renewal

10 Apply the handbrake, then jack up the front of the vehicle and support it on axle stands (see *Jacking and vehicle support*).

11 Remove the auxiliary drivebelt(s) as described in Section 6.

12 With reference to Sections 4 and 5 of this Chapter, remove the timing belt outer covers, timing belt and crankshaft sprocket.

13 Refer to Section 15 and remove the sump. Alternatively, it may be possible to remove the oil seal housing without removing the sump, however, if the sump gasket is damaged it must be renewed.

14 Progressively slacken and then remove the oil seal housing retaining bolts.

15 Lift the housing away from the cylinder block, together with the crankshaft oil seal.

16 Recover the old gasket from the seal housing on the cylinder block. If it has disintegrated, scrape the remains off with a trimming knife blade. Take care to avoid damaging the mating surfaces.

17 Prise the old oil seal from the housing using a screwdriver.

18 Wipe the oil seal housing clean, and check it visually for signs of distortion or cracking. Lay the housing on a work surface, with the mating surface face down. Press in a new oil seal, using a block of wood as a press to ensure that the seal enters the housing squarely.

19 Smear the crankcase mating surface with multi-purpose grease, and lay the new gasket in position.

20 Pad the end of the crankshaft with a layer of PVC tape, to protect the oil seal as it is being fitted.

21 Lubricate the inner lip of the crankshaft oil seal with clean engine oil, then offer up the seal and its housing to the end of the crankshaft. Ease the seal over the shaft using a twisting motion, until the housing is flush with the crankcase.

22 Insert the retaining bolts and tighten them progressively to the specified torque **(see illustration)**.

23 Refer to Section 15 and refit the sump.

24 With reference to Sections 4 and 5 of this Chapter, refit the crankshaft sprocket, then refit and tension the timing belt. On completion, refit

10.6 Lubricate the new crankshaft oil seal, and position it over the housing

10.7 Using a hammer and a socket, drive the seal squarely into its housing

10.22 Tighten the front oil seal housing bolts to the specified torque

the timing belt outer cover, and auxiliary drivebelt(s).

25 Lower the vehicle to the ground.

Crankshaft rear oil seal (flywheel end)

26 Apply the handbrake, then jack up the front of the vehicle and support it on axle stands (see *Jacking and vehicle support*).

27 Remove the transmission (Chapter 7), and flywheel (Section 13 of this Chapter).

28 Where applicable, remove the retaining bolts and lift the engine rear plate from the cylinder block.

29 The oil seal may be removed using the same method as that described for the camshaft oil seal removal in Section 8. The alternative method is to unbolt the oil seal housing from the cylinder block then drive the oil seal from the housing (see following paragraphs), however if this method is used care must be taken not to damage the sump gasket. If the gasket is damaged, it will be necessary to drain the engine oil (Chapter 1A) and remove the sump as described in Section 15, then fit the sump with a new gasket after fitting the oil seal housing.

30 Progressively slacken and then remove the oil seal housing retaining bolts.

31 Lift the housing away from the cylinder block, together with the crankshaft oil seal.

32 Recover the old gasket and clean the mating surfaces on the seal housing and cylinder block.

33 Prise the old oil seal from the housing using a screwdriver.

34 Wipe the oil seal housing clean, and check it visually for signs of distortion or cracking.

35 Lay the housing on a work surface, with the mating surface face down. Press in a new oil seal, using a block of wood as a press to ensure that the seal enters the housing squarely.

36 Smear the cylinder block surface with multi-purpose grease, and lay the new gasket in position.

37 A protective plastic cap is supplied with genuine crankshaft oil seals. When fitted over the end of the crankshaft, the cap prevents damage to the inner lip of the oil seal as it is being fitted. Use PVC tape to pad the end of the crankshaft if a cap is not available.

38 Lubricate the inner lip of the crankshaft oil seal with clean engine oil, then offer up the seal and its housing to the end of the crankshaft. Ease the seal along the shaft using a twisting motion, until the housing is flush with the crankcase.

39 Insert the retaining bolts and tighten them progressively to the specified torque **(see illustration)**.

40 Where applicable, refer to Section 15 and refit the sump.

41 Where applicable, refit the engine rear plate and tighten the bolts.

42 Refit the flywheel (Section 13 of this Chapter), then refit the transmission (Chapter 7).

10.39 Tighten the rear oil seal housing bolts to the specified torque

43 Lower the vehicle to the ground.

44 Where applicable, fill the engine with fresh oil with reference to Chapter 1A.

11 Cylinder head and manifolds - removal, separation and refitting

Removal

1 Select a solid, level surface to park the vehicle upon. Give yourself enough space to move around it easily.

2 Refer to Chapter 11 and remove the bonnet.

3 Disconnect the battery negative (earth) lead (see Chapter 5A).

4 Referring to Chapter 1A, carry out the following :

a) Drain the engine oil.

b) Drain the cooling system.

5 Refer to Section 6 and remove the auxiliary drivebelt(s). Remove the engine top cover where necessary.

6 With reference to Section 2, set the engine to TDC on No 1 cylinder.

7 Refer to Chapter 3 and perform the following:

a) Slacken the clips and disconnect the radiator top and bottom hoses from the ports on the cylinder head and coolant pump/thermostat housing (as applicable).

b) Slacken the clips and disconnect the expansion tank and cabin heater inlet and outlet coolant hoses from the ports on the cylinder head.

8 The body front panel comprises the front bumper moulding, radiator and grille, cooling fan(s) headlight units, front valence and bonnet lock mechanism. Although its removal is not essential, its does give greatly-improved access to the engine. Its removal is described at the beginning of the engine removal procedure - refer to Chapter 2C for details.

9 With reference to Chapter 4D, unplug the lambda sensor cabling from the main harness at the multiway connector (where applicable).

10 With reference to Chapter 5B and Chapter 1A, carry out the following:

a) Remove the HT leads from the spark plugs and the distributor.

b) On engine codes AER, AAU, AAV, ABD, ABU, AEX, APQ, AEE, ALM, remove the distributor.

11 On multi-point fuel-injected models, refer to Chapter 4B and remove the throttle body, the upper section of the inlet manifold (engine codes AFT and ABF only), the fuel rail and the fuel injectors. On engine code AGG, disconnect the wiring from the oil pressure switch on the left-hand end of the cylinder head **(see illustration)**.

12 On single-point fuel-injected models, refer to Chapter 4A, remove the throttle body air box, and then remove the throttle body.

13 With reference to Sections 2, 4 and 7, carry out the following:

a) Remove the timing belt outer covers, and disengage the timing belt from the camshaft sprocket.

b) Remove the camshaft cover.

14 On engine codes AER, AAU, AAV, ABD, ABU, AEX, APQ, AEE, ALM, refer to Section 5 and remove the camshaft sprocket.

15 Slacken and withdraw the retaining screws, and lift off the inner timing belt cover(s). Note that on engine codes AER, AAU, AAV, ABD, ABU, AEX, APQ, AEE and ALM, the coolant pump securing bolts double up as fixings for the inner timing belt cover - refer to Chapter 3 and remove the coolant pump from the engine block.

16 With reference to Chapter 4A or 4B as applicable, unplug wiring harness from the coolant temperature sensor at the connector.

17 Refer to Chapter 4D and separate the exhaust downpipe from the exhaust manifold flange.

18 Where applicable, detach the warm-air inlet hose from the exhaust manifold heat shield.

19 Slacken and remove the bolt securing the engine oil dipstick tube to the cylinder head.

20 Remove the retaining screw and detach the engine harness connector bracket from the cylinder head.

21 Following the reverse of the tightening sequence shown in illustration 11.37, progressively slacken the cylinder head bolts, by half a turn at a time, until all bolts can be unscrewed by hand.

22 Check that nothing remains connected to the cylinder head, then lift the head away from

2A

11.11 Oil pressure switch (engine code AGG)

the cylinder block; seek assistance if possible, as it is a heavy assembly, especially if it is being removed complete with the manifolds.

23 Remove the gasket from the top of the block, noting the locating dowels. If the dowels are a loose fit, remove them and store them with the head for safe-keeping. Do not discard the gasket - on some models it will be needed for identification purposes.

24 If the cylinder head is to be dismantled for overhaul refer to Chapter 2C.

Manifold separation

25 Inlet manifold removal and refitting is described in Chapter 4A or 4B as applicable.
26 Progressively slacken and remove the exhaust manifold retaining nuts. Lift the manifold away from the cylinder head and recover the gaskets. Where applicable, slacken the union and detach the CO sampling pipe from the manifold.
27 Ensure that the mating surfaces are completely clean, then refit the exhaust manifold, using new gaskets. Tighten the retaining nuts to the specified torque given in Chapter 4D.

Preparation for refitting

28 The mating faces of the cylinder head and cylinder block must be perfectly clean before refitting the head. Use a hard plastic or wood scraper to remove all traces of gasket and carbon, and also clean the piston crowns. Take particular care during the cleaning operations, as aluminium alloy is easily damaged. Also, make sure that the carbon is not allowed to enter the oil and water passages - this is particularly important for the lubrication system, as carbon could block the oil supply to the engine's components. Using adhesive tape and paper, seal the water, oil and bolt holes in the cylinder block/crankcase.
29 Check the mating surfaces of the cylinder block and the cylinder head for nicks, deep scratches and other damage. If slight, they may be removed carefully with a file, but if excessive, machining may be the only alternative to renewal.
30 If warpage of the cylinder head gasket surface is suspected, use a straight-edge to check it for distortion. Refer to Part C of this Chapter if necessary.

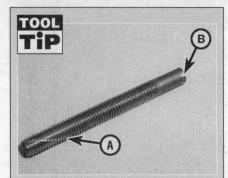

If a tap is unavailable, make a home-made substitute by cutting a slot (A) down the threads of one of the old cylinder head bolts. After use, the bolt head can be cut off, and the shank can then be used as an alignment dowel to assist cylinder head refitting. Cut a screwdriver slot (B) in the top of the bolt, to allow it to be unscrewed

31 Thoroughly clean out the cylinder head bolt holes in the cylinder block, making sure that all oil and water is removed - this is important to prevent hydraulic lock damage and inaccurate torques. Check the threads in the block for damage and if necessary use a tap of the correct size to clean them out. If a tap is unavailable, make a home-made substitute **(see Tool Tip)**.
32 The cylinder head bolts must be renewed whenever they are removed. Note that on engine codes AFT, 1F, 2E, AGG, the original cylinder head gasket is manufactured of either soft material or metal, and the cylinder head bolts are different for each type of gasket. The conventional (soft material) gasket must be fitted with the standard bolts, but the metal gasket must be fitted with bolts having three raised pips on top of their heads **(see illustration)**.
33 On all the engines covered in this Chapter, it is possible for the piston crowns to strike and damage the valve heads, if the camshaft is rotated with the timing belt removed and the crankshaft set to TDC. For this reason, the crankshaft must be set to a position other than TDC on No 1 cylinder, before the cylinder head is refitted. Set the crankshaft to TDC on No 1

cylinder, using the information in Section 2, then turn the crankshaft back by a few degrees, away from the TDC position. If preferred, for maximum safety, the pistons can be positioned halfway down their bores, with No 1 piston on its upstroke - ie 90° before TDC.

Refitting

34 Check that the new gasket is the same type as the old one removed. On engine codes AFT, 1F, 2E, AGG, the soft material gasket may be replaced by a metal one but the corresponding head bolts must be used. Lay the new head gasket on the cylinder block, ensuring that the manufacturer's TOP/OBEN mark or part number is facing upwards **(see illustrations)**. Align the holes in the gasket with the corresponding holes in the block. Note that some engines are fitted with two location dowels in the block to ensure correct location of the gasket and cylinder head. On engines without these dowels, make up two guide rods **(see Haynes Hint)**.

> **HAYNES HINT** *Where no locating dowels are fitted, it may prove difficult to accurately align the head on the block when refitting. To overcome this, two of the old cylinder head bolts can be modified to act as locating dowels. Cut the heads off two of the bolts, and then cut a slot in the top of the bolts, so that a flat-bladed screwdriver may be used to unscrew them from the block once the head is placed over them. Screw the two dowels into place either end of the head.*

35 With the help of an assistant, place the cylinder head and manifolds centrally on the cylinder block, ensuring that the locating dowels/rods engage with the recesses in the cylinder head. Check that the head gasket is correctly seated before allowing the full weight of the cylinder head to rest upon it.
36 Apply a smear of grease to the threads, and to the underside of the heads, of the cylinder head bolts; use a good-quality high-melting point grease. Carefully enter each bolt together with its washer (where applicable) into its relevant hole (*do not drop them in*) and

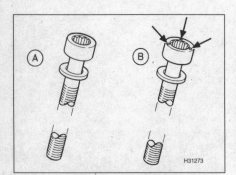

11.32 The standard head bolt (A) is for the conventional gasket, and the raised pip bolt (B) is for the metal gasket

11.34a Lay a new head gasket on the block, engaging it with the locating dowels

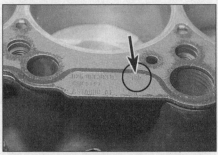

11.34b Ensure that the manufacturer's TOP mark and part number are facing upwards

screw in, by hand only, until finger-tight. With two bolts entered, the home-made locating rods can be removed.

37 Working progressively and in the sequence shown, tighten the cylinder head bolts to their Stage 1 torque setting, using a torque wrench and suitable socket **(see illustration)**.

38 Following the same sequence, tighten the bolts to the remaining stages as given in the Specifications. For the angle-tightening, it is recommended that an angle-measuring gauge is used to ensure accuracy. If a gauge is not available, use white paint to make alignment marks between the bolt head and cylinder head prior to tightening; the marks can then be used to check that the bolt has been rotated through the correct angle during tightening.

39 Refit the engine harness connector bracket to the cylinder head and tighten the retaining screw.

40 Refit the engine oil dipstick tube to the cylinder head and tighten the bolt.

41 Where applicable, refit the warm-air inlet hose to the exhaust manifold heat shield.

42 Refer to Chapter 4D and reconnect the exhaust downpipe to the exhaust manifold flange.

43 Refit the inner timing belt cover(s) and tighten the retaining screws. Note that on engine codes AER, AAU, AAV, ABD, ABU, AEX, APQ, AEE and ALM, the coolant pump securing bolts double up as fixings for the inner timing belt cover - refer to Chapter 3 and refit the coolant pump.

44 On engine codes AER, AAU, AAV, ABD, ABU, AEX, APQ, AEE, ALM, refer to Section 5 and refit the camshaft sprocket.

45 With reference to Sections 2, 4 and 7, carry out the following:
  a) Refit the camshaft cover.
  b) Engage the timing belt with the camshaft sprocket and refit the timing belt outer covers.

46 On multi-point fuel-injected models, refer to Chapter 4B and refit the throttle body, the upper section of the inlet manifold (engine codes AFT and ABF only), the fuel rail and the fuel injectors.

47 With reference to Chapter 5B and Chapter 1A, carry out the following:
  a) Reconnect the HT leads to the spark plugs and the distributor.
  b) On engine codes AER, AAU, AAV, ABD, ABU, AEX, APQ, AEE, ALM, refit the distributor.

48 With reference to Chapter 4D, reconnect the lambda sensor cabling from the main harness at the multiway connector (where applicable).

49 Refit the body front panel assembly where removed, with reference to Chapter 2C.

50 Reconnect the radiator top and bottom hoses and tighten the clips.

51 Reconnect the expansion tank and heater inlet and outlet hoses to the cylinder head.

52 Refer to Section 6 and refit the auxiliary drivebelt(s). Refit the engine top cover where necessary.

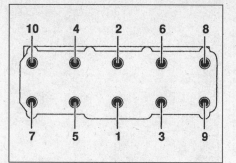

11.37 Cylinder head bolt tightening sequence

53 Referring to Chapter 1A, carry out the following :
  a) Fill the engine with oil.
  b) Refill the cooling system.

54 Reconnect the battery negative (earth) lead (see Chapter 5A).

55 Refer to Chapter 11 and refit the bonnet.

12 Hydraulic tappets - operation check

> ⚠ **Warning: After fitting hydraulic tappets, wait a minimum of 30 minutes (or preferably, leave overnight) before starting the engine, to allow the tappets time to settle, otherwise the pistons may strike the valve heads.**

1 The hydraulic tappets are self-adjusting, and require no attention whilst in service.

2 If the hydraulic tappets become excessively noisy, their operation can be checked as described below.

3 Run the engine until it reaches its normal operating temperature. Switch off the engine, then refer to Section 7 and remove the camshaft cover.

4 Rotate the camshaft by turning the crankshaft with a socket and wrench, until the first cam lobe over No 1 cylinder is pointing upwards.

5 Using a feeler blade, measure the clearance between the base of the cam lobe and the top of the tappet. If the clearance is greater than 0.1 mm (engine codes AAU, AAV, ABD, ABU, 1F, 2E, AGG, AFT, ABF) or 0.2 mm (engine codes AER, AEX, APQ, AEE, ALM), then the tappet is defective and must be renewed.

6 If the clearance is less than the specified amount, press down on the top of the tappet until it is felt to contact the top of the valve stem **(see illustration)**. Use a wooden or plastic implement that will not damage the surface of the tappet.

7 If the tappet travels more than 0.1 mm before making contact, then it is defective and must be renewed.

8 Hydraulic tappet removal and refitting is described as part of the cylinder head overhaul sequence - see Chapter 2C for details.

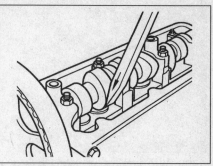

12.6 Press down on the tappet, until it contacts the top of the valve stem

13 Flywheel - removal, inspection and refitting

General information

1 The mounting arrangement of the flywheel and clutch components depends on the type of transmission fitted.

2 On vehicles fitted with the 5-speed 020 transmission (see Chapters 6 and 7), the clutch pressure plate is bolted directly to the end of the crankshaft. The flywheel is then bolted to the pressure plate. Removal of these components is therefore described in Chapter 6.

3 On vehicles fitted with the 5-speed 085 transmission (see Chapters 6 and 7), the layout is conventional. The flywheel is mounted on the crankshaft, with the pressure plate bolted to it. Removal of the flywheel is described in this Section. Removal of the manual trans-mission is described in Chapter 7, and removal of the clutch in Chapter 6.

Removal

4 Remove the transmission and clutch as described in Chapter 7 and Chapter 6.

5 Lock the flywheel in position using a home-made locking tool, fabricated from a piece of scrap metal. Bolt it to one of the transmission bellhousing mounting holes **(see illustration)**. Mark the position of the flywheel with respect to the crankshaft using a dab of paint.

6 Unscrew and remove the flywheel mounting bolts, then lift the flywheel from the end of the crankshaft. If necessary remove the rear engine plate.

13.5 Flywheel locked in position with a home-made tool

2A

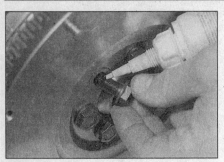

13.10 Apply locking compound to the new flywheel bolts if they are not already pre-coated

Inspection

7 If the flywheel's clutch mating surface is deeply scored, cracked or otherwise damaged, the flywheel must be renewed. However, it may be possible to have it surface-ground. Seek the advice of an engine reconditioning specialist.

8 If the ring gear is badly worn or has missing teeth, a new gear can be fitted to the flywheel by a Seat dealer or engine reconditioning specialist.

Refitting

9 Clean the mating surfaces of the flywheel and crankshaft. Remove any remaining locking compound from the threads of the crankshaft holes, using the correct-size tap, if available.

HAYNES HiNT *If a suitable tap is not available, cut two slots down the threads of one of the old flywheel bolts with a hacksaw, and use the bolt to remove the locking compound from the threads.*

10 If the new flywheel retaining bolts are not supplied with their threads already pre-coated, apply a suitable thread-locking compound to the threads of each bolt **(see illustration)**.

11 Refit the engine rear plate if removed. Offer up the flywheel to the crankshaft, using the alignment marks made during removal, and fit the new retaining bolts.

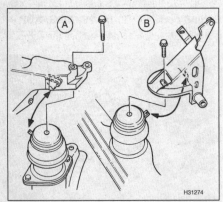

14.13 Location lugs and recesses on the right-hand rear (A) and front (B) engine mountings

13.12 Tighten the flywheel bolts to the specified torque

12 Lock the flywheel using the method employed on dismantling, and tighten the retaining bolts to the specified torque **(see illustration)**.

13 Refit the clutch as described in Chapter 6. Remove the locking tool, and refit the transmission as described in Chapter 7.

---

14 Engine mountings - inspection and renewal

Inspection

1 If improved access is required, apply the handbrake then jack up the front of the vehicle and support it on axle stands (see *Jacking and vehicle support*).

2 Check the mounting rubbers to see if they are cracked, hardened or separated from the metal at any point; renew the mounting if any such damage or deterioration is evident.

3 Check that the mounting bolts are tightened to their specified torques.

4 Using a large screwdriver or a crowbar, check for wear in the mounting by carefully levering against it to check for free play. Alternatively, enlist the aid of an assistant to move the engine/transmission back and forth, or from side to side, while you watch the mounting. While some free play is to be expected even from new components, excessive wear should be obvious. If excessive free play is found, check that the mounting

14.19 Right-hand engine mounting (viewed with the engine/transmission removed)

bolts are correctly tightened, then renew any worn components as described in the following paragraphs.

Renewal

Front engine mounting

5 Disconnect the battery negative (earth) lead (see Chapter 5A), and position it away from the terminal.

6 With the front of the vehicle supported on axle stands, position a trolley jack and wooden block underneath the engine and position it such that the jack head is directly underneath the engine/bellhousing mating surface. Raise the jack until it just takes the weight of the engine off the front engine mounting.

7 Unscrew the mounting top bolt.

8 Loosen the rear left- and right-hand engine mounting bolts several turns to prevent excessive tension in the mountings.

9 Where applicable, unscrew the bolt securing the coolant hose support to the mounting bracket.

10 Unscrew the mounting lower bolt from the crossmember.

11 Unscrew and remove the starter motor mounting bolts. If necessary, support the starter motor.

12 Raise the engine/transmission assembly slightly, then remove the mounting and bracket.

13 Refitting is a reversal of removal, noting the following points:

  a) *Ensure that the orientation lug that protrudes from the top surface of the engine mounting block engages with the recess in the mounting bracket* **(see illustration)**. *Also check that the lug on the right-hand rear mounting block engages with its recess before tightening the mounting bolts.*

  b) *Tighten all bolts to the specified torque.*

Right-hand engine mounting

14 Disconnect the battery negative (earth) lead (see Chapter 5A), and position it away from the terminal.

15 With the front of the vehicle supported on axle stands, mount an engine lifting beam across the engine bay, and attach the jib to the engine lifting eyes on the cylinder head. Alternatively, an engine hoist can be used. Raise the hoist/lifting beam jib to take the weight of the engine off the engine mounting.

16 Where necessary, move the air intake pipe to one side (refer to Chapter 4A).

17 Where necessary, remove the Lambda sensor connector support bracket from the mounting.

18 Loosen the front and left-hand rear engine mounting bolts several turns to prevent excessive tension in the mountings.

19 Unscrew the two bolts securing the mounting to the subframe **(see illustration)**.

20 Raise the engine/transmission assembly slightly, then remove the mounting from under the vehicle. If required, unbolt the bracket from the rear of the engine.

21 Refitting is a reversal of removal, noting the following points:

a) *Ensure that the orientation lug that protrudes from the top surface of the engine mounting block engages with the recess in the mounting bracket (see illustration 14.13).*

b) *Tighten all bolts to the specified torque.*

Left-hand mounting

22 Disconnect the battery negative (earth) lead (see Chapter 5A), and position it away from the terminal.

23 With the front of the vehicle supported on axle stands, mount an engine lifting beam across the engine bay, and attach the jib to the engine lifting eyes on the cylinder head. Alternatively, an engine hoist can be used. Raise the hoist/lifting beam jib to take the weight of the engine off the engine mounting.

24 Detach the gearchange control rods from the mounting bracket.

25 Unscrew the mounting top bolt.

26 Loosen the front and right-hand rear mounting bolts several turns to prevent excessive tension in the mountings.

27 Raise the engine/transmission assembly slightly, then unbolt the mounting bracket from the transmission.

28 Unscrew the two bolts securing the mounting to the subframe and withdraw the mounting from under the vehicle **(see illustration)**.

29 Refitting is a reversal of removal but tighten the bolts to the specified torque.

15 Sump -
removal and refitting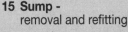

Removal

1 Disconnect the battery negative (earth) lead (see Chapter 5A), and position it away from the terminal.

2 Apply the handbrake, then jack up the front of the vehicle and support it on axle stands (see *Jacking and vehicle support*). Refer to Chapter 1A and drain the engine oil.

3 On engine codes AER, AAU, AAV, ABD, ABU, AEX, APQ, AEE, ALM, remove the exhaust system downpipe, as described in Chapter 4D, and on models with power steering remove the power steering pump pulley then unbolt the pump and tie it to one side without disconnecting the hydraulic fluid lines.

4 If necessary, to improve access to the sump, refer to Chapter 8 and disconnect the right-hand driveshaft from the transmission output flange, however this is not essential.

5 Working around the outside of the sump, progressively unscrew the sump retaining bolts. Where applicable, unbolt and remove the flywheel cover plate from the transmission to gain access to the left-hand sump fixings. On engine codes AER, AAU, AAV, ABD, ABU,

14.28 Left-hand engine mounting (viewed with the engine/transmission removed)

AEX, APQ, AEE, ALM, cut-outs are provided in the flywheel for access to the sump retaining bolts nearest the transmission - turn the flywheel as necessary to align the cut-outs. Also on these engine codes note the location of the wiring harness clips on the right-hand end of the sump **(see illustrations)**.

6 Break the joint by striking the sump with the palm of your hand, then lower the sump and withdraw it from underneath the vehicle. Recover and discard the sump gasket on engine codes AFT, 1F, 2E, AGG, ABF. Where a baffle plate is fitted, note that it can only be removed once the oil pump has been unbolted (see Section 16).

7 While the sump is removed, take the opportunity to check the oil pump pick-up/strainer for signs of clogging or disintegration. If necessary, remove the pump as described in Section 16, and clean or renew the strainer.

Refitting

8 Clean the mating surfaces of the cylinder block/crankcase and sump, then use a clean rag to wipe out the sump. Ensure that the sump and cylinder block/crankcase mating surfaces are clean and dry.

9 On engine codes AER, AAU, AAV, ABD, ABU, AEX, APQ, AEE, ALM, apply a 2 to 3 mm thick bead of suitable sealant to the sump mating surface.

10 On engine codes AFT, 1F, 2E, AGG, ABF lay a new sump gasket in position on the sump mating surface.

15.5a Removing the sump bolts (engine removed and inverted for clarity)

11 Offer up the sump and refit the retaining bolts. Tighten the bolts evenly and progressively to the specified torque.

12 As applicable, refit the driveshaft, exhaust downpipe, flywheel cover plate and power steering pump.

13 Refer to Chapter 1A and refill the engine with the specified grade and quantity of oil.

14 Reconnect the battery negative (earth) lead (see Chapter 5A).

16 Oil pump and pickup -
removal, inspection and refitting

General information

Engine codes AER, AAU, AAV, ABD, ABU, AEX, APQ, AEE, ALM

1 The oil pump and pickup are both mounted at the timing belt end of the crankcase. Drive is taken from the crankshaft via a chain and sprocket.

Engine codes AFT, 1F, 2E, AGG, ABF

2 The oil pump and pickup are both mounted in the sump. Drive is taken from the inter-mediate shaft, which rotates at half crankshaft speed.

Removal

Engine codes AER, AAU, AAV, ABD, ABU, AEX, APQ, AEE, ALM

3 Refer to Section 15 and remove the sump.

4 With reference to Section 10, remove the front (timing belt end) crankshaft oil seal and housing.

5 Unscrew and remove the bolts securing the oil pump to the end of the crankcase. Where applicable, remove the bolts and lift off the guide rail **(see illustration overleaf)**.

6 Remove the screws securing the oil pump pickup to the crankcase bracket.

7 Disengage the pump sprocket from the drive chain, and remove the oil pump and pickup from the engine.

Engine codes AFT, 1F, 2E, AGG, ABF

8 Refer to Section 15 and remove the sump.

2A

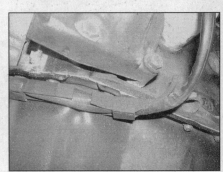

15.5b Wiring harness clips on the sump mounting bolts

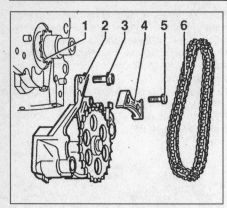

**16.5 Oil pump components -
engine codes AER, AAU, AAV, ABD, ABU,
AEX, APQ, AEE, ALM**

1	Crankshaft sprocket	4	Guide rail
2	Pump body	5	Guide rail bolts
3	Mounting bolts	6	Drive chain

9 Unscrew and remove the bolts securing the oil pump to the base of the crankcase (see illustration).
10 Lower the oil pump and pickup away from the crankcase. Where applicable, recover the baffle plate.

Inspection

11 Remove the screws from the mating flange, and lift off the pickup tube. Recover the O-ring seal. Slacken and withdraw the screws, then remove the oil pump cover.
12 Clean the pump thoroughly, and inspect the gear teeth for signs of damage or wear.
13 Where applicable, check the condition of the oil pump drive chain; if the links appear excessively worn or are particularly loose, renew the chain.
14 Check the pump backlash by inserting a feeler blade between the meshed gear teeth; rotate the gears against each other slightly, to give the maximum clearance (see illustration).

Compare the measurement with the limit quoted in Specifications.
15 Check the pump axial clearance as follows. Lay an engineer's straight edge across the oil pump casing, then using a feeler blade, measure the clearance between the straight edge and the pump gears (see illustration). Compare the measurement with the limit quoted in Specifications.
16 If either measurement is outside of the specified limit, this indicates that the pump is worn and must be renewed.

Refitting

Engine codes AER, AAU, AAV, ABD, ABU, AEX, APQ, AEE, ALM

17 Refit the oil pump cover, then fit the screws and tighten them securely.
18 Reassemble the oil pickup to the oil pump, using a new O-ring seal. Tighten the retaining screws securely.
19 Offer up the oil pump to the end of the crankcase. Fit the drive chain over the oil pump sprocket, then engage it with the crankshaft sprocket.
20 Fit the pump mounting bolts and hand-tighten them. Where applicable, fit the chain guide rail and tighten the retaining bolts to the specified torque.
21 Check the tension of the drive chain by applying finger pressure to it at a point midway between the two sprockets. Adjust the position of the pump on its mountings until the tension is within the range given in the Specifications. On completion, tighten the mounting bolts to the specified torque.
22 Fit and tighten the fixings for the pickup tube to crankcase bracket.
23 With reference to Section 10, refit the crankshaft oil seal housing, using a new gasket and oil seal.
24 Refer to Section 15 and refit the sump.

Engine codes AFT, 1F, 2E, AGG, ABF

25 Refit the oil pump cover, then fit and tighten the screws to the specified torque.

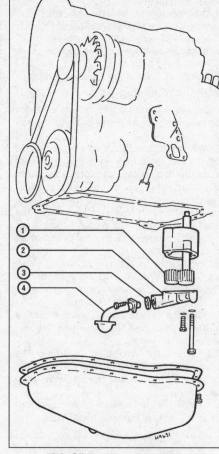

**16.9 Oil pump components -
engine codes AFT, 1F, 2E, AGG, ABF**

| 1 | Oil pump gears | 3 | O-ring seal |
| 2 | Oil pump cover | 4 | Pickup tube |

26 Reassemble the oil pickup to the oil pump, using a new O-ring seal. Tighten the retaining screws to the specified torque.

**16.14 Checking the oil pump backlash
(engine code 2E shown)**

**16.15 Checking the oil pump axial clearance
(engine code 2E shown)**

27 Where applicable, fit the crankcase baffle plate in place.

28 Offer up the oil pump to the crankcase, then fit the mounting bolts and tighten them to the specified torque.

29 Refer to Section 15 and refit the sump.

17 Oil cooler - removal and refitting

Removal

1 An oil cooler is fitted to 1.8 and 2.0 litre engines. First apply the handbrake, then jack up the front of the vehicle and support it on axle stands (see "*Jacking and Vehicle Support*"). Remove the engine compartment undertray.

2 Position a container beneath the front of the engine, then unscrew and remove the oil filter (refer to Chapter 1A if necessary). Empty the oil into the container.

3 Fit hose clamps to the two coolant hoses on the oil cooler. Alternatively, drain the cooling system with reference to Chapter 1A. Loosen the clips and disconnect the hoses.

4 Unscrew the nut from the centre tube, then lower the oil cooler from the oil filter housing, noting the fitted location of the coolant stubs. If fitted, remove the gasket, or clean the sealant from the mating faces.

Refitting

5 Clean the mating surfaces of the oil cooler and the oil filter housing. Apply sealant or fit a new gasket (as applicable) to the upper surface, the locate the cooler on the centre tube and screw on the nut. Tighten the nut to the specified torque.

6 Refit the hoses and tighten the clips. Remove the hose clamps where fitted.

7 Smear a little clean engine oil on the oil filter sealing ring, then screw on the filter and tighten by hand only.

8 Refill or top-up the cooling system with reference to Chapter 1A.

9 Start the engine and allow it to idle for several minutes. Check for oil or coolant leaks around the oil cooler, then switch off the engine.

10 Refit the engine compartment undertray, and lower the vehicle to the ground.

2A

Notes

Chapter 2 Part B:
Diesel engine in-car repair procedures

Contents

Degrees of difficulty

Easy, suitable for novice with little experience	**Fairly easy,** suitable for beginner with some experience	**Fairly difficult,** suitable for competent DIY mechanic 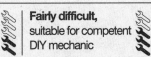

Difficult, suitable for experienced DIY mechanic	**Very difficult,** suitable for expert DIY or professional

Specifications

General

Engine code: *

1896 cc, mechanical indirect fuel injection, normally-aspirated, 47 kW .	1Y
1896 cc, mechanical indirect fuel injection, turbocharged, 55 kW	AAZ
1896 cc, electronic direct fuel injection, normally-aspirated, 47 kW ...	AEY
1896 cc, electronic direct fuel injection, turbocharged, 66 kW	1Z, AHU, AFN

Bore .... 79.5 mm
Stroke .... 95.5 mm

Compression ratio:

1Y	22.5:1
AAZ	22.5:1
AEY	19.5:1
1Z, AHU, AFN	19.5:1

Compression pressures (wear limit):

1Y, AAZ	26 bar
AEY, 1Z, AHU, AFN	19 bar

Firing order .... 1 - 3 - 4 - 2
Cylinder No 1 location .... Timing belt end

Timing belt tension:
   Engine code 1Y, AAZ (measured using Seat tool U-40021) .... Scale reading of 12 - 13 units

* Note: *See* Vehicle identification *in* Reference *for the location of the code marking on the engine.*

Lubrication system

Oil pump type .... Sump-mounted, driven indirectly from intermediate shaft
Normal operating oil pressure .... 2.0 bar minimum (at 2000 rpm, oil temperature 80°C)
Oil pump backlash .... 0.2 mm (wear limit)
Oil pump axial clearance .... 0.15 mm (wear limit)

Torque wrench settings

	Nm	lbf ft
Alternator mounting bolts	20	15
Big-end cap:		
Stage 1	30	22
Stage 2	Angle-tighten 90°	
Camshaft bearing cap nuts	20	15
Camshaft cover screws/nuts	10	7
Camshaft sprocket bolt	45	33
Coolant pump pulley	25	18
Crankshaft front oil seal housing bolts:		
M6	25	18
M8	25	18
Crankshaft main bearing cap:		
Stage 1	65	48
Stage 2	Angle-tighten 90°	
Crankshaft pulley for the auxiliary drivebelt	25	18
Crankshaft rear oil seal housing bolts	10	7
Crankshaft sprocket bolt:		
Stage 1	90	66
Stage 2	Angle-tighten a further 90°	
Cylinder head bolts:		
Stage 1	40	30
Stage 2	60	44
Stage 3	Angle-tighten a further 90°	
Stage 4	Angle-tighten a further 90°	
Engine mountings:		
Through-bolts	50	37
Front mounting block bolt	50	37
Mounting to engine	25	18
Flywheel	20	15
Injection pipes	25	18
Inlet manifold	25	18
Intermediate shaft oil seal housing	25	18
Intermediate shaft sprocket bolt	45	33
Oil cooler	25	18
Oil pressure switch	25	18
Oil pump cover screws	10	7
Oil pump mounting bolts	25	18
Oil pump pickup tube screws	10	7
Sump drain plug	30	22
Sump retaining bolts	25	18
Timing belt idler nut/locknut:		
Non semi-automatic	45	33
Semi-automatic	20	15
Timing belt inner cover	10	7
Timing belt tensioner roller bolt (1Y, AAZ, AEY)	20	15
Transmission-to-engine bolts:		
M10	60	44
M12	80	59
Vibration damper	25	18

1 General information

Using this Chapter

Chapter 2 is divided into three parts; A, B and C. Repair operations that can be carried out with the engine in the vehicle are described in Parts A (petrol engines) and B (diesel engines). Part C covers the removal of the engine/ transmission as a unit and describes the engine dismantling and overhaul procedures.

In Parts A and B, the assumption is made that the engine is installed in the vehicle, with all ancillaries connected. If the engine has been removed for overhaul, the preliminary dismantling information which precedes each operation may be ignored.

Access to the engine bay can be improved by removing the bonnet and the body front panel assembly; these procedures are described in Chapter 11.

Engine description

Throughout this Chapter, engines are identified and referred to by manufacturer's code letters, rather than capacity. A listing of all engines covered, together with their code letters, is given in the Specifications at the start of this Chapter.

The engines are water-cooled, single overhead camshaft, in-line four cylinder units with cast-iron cylinder blocks and aluminium-alloy cylinder heads. All are mounted transversely at the front of the vehicle, with the transmission bolted to the left-hand side of the engine.

The cylinder head carries the camshaft, which is driven by a toothed timing belt. It also houses the inlet and exhaust valves, which are closed by single or double coil springs, and which run in guides pressed into the cylinder head. The camshaft actuates the valves directly via hydraulic tappets, mounted in the cylinder head. The cylinder head contains integral oilways which supply and lubricate the tappets.

2.2a Remove the rubber bung from the transmission bellhousing (arrowed) . . .

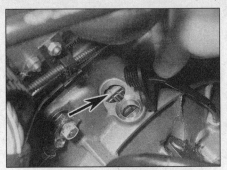

2.2b . . . to see the TDC 0 marking (arrowed) on the flywheel

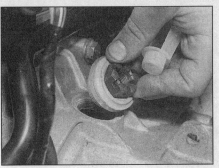

2.2c Where necessary, use a large nut to unscrew the bung from the transmission

On engine codes 1Y, AAZ (indirect injection engines), the cylinder head incorporates renewable swirl chambers. On engine codes AFN, AEY, 1Z, AHU (direct injection engines), the piston crowns are shaped to form combustion chambers.

The crankshaft is supported by five main bearings, and endfloat is controlled by a thrust bearing fitted between cylinders No 2 and 3.

All diesel engines are fitted with a timing belt-driven intermediate shaft, which provides drive for the brake servo vacuum pump and the oil pump.

Engine coolant is circulated by a pump, driven by the auxiliary drivebelt. For details of the cooling system, refer to Chapter 3.

Lubricant is circulated under pressure by a pump, driven by the intermediate shaft. Oil is drawn from the sump through a strainer, and then forced through an externally-mounted, replaceable screw-on filter. From there, it is distributed to the cylinder head, where it lubricates the camshaft journals and hydraulic tappets, and also to the crankcase, where it

lubricates the main bearings, connecting rod big- and small-ends, gudgeon pins and cylinder bores. Oil jets are fitted to the base of each cylinder - these spray oil onto the underside of the pistons, to improve cooling. An oil cooler, supplied with engine coolant, reduces the temperature of the oil before it re-enters the engine.

Repairs possible with the engine installed in the vehicle

The following operations can be performed without removing the engine:

a) *Auxiliary drivebelts - removal and refitting.*
b) *Camshaft - removal and refitting. **
c) *Camshaft oil seal - renewal.*
d) *Camshaft sprocket - removal and refitting.*
e) *Coolant pump - removal and refitting (refer to Chapter 3)*
f) *Crankshaft oil seals - renewal.*
g) *Crankshaft sprocket - removal and refitting.*
h) *Cylinder head - removal and refitting. **
i) *Engine mountings - inspection and renewal.*
j) *Intermediate shaft oil seal - renewal.*
k) *Oil pump and pickup assembly - removal and refitting.*
l) *Sump - removal and refitting.*
m) *Timing belt, sprockets and cover - removal, inspection and refitting.*

*Cylinder head dismantling procedures are in Chapter 2C, and also contain details of camshaft and hydraulic tappet removal.

Note: *It is possible to remove the pistons and connecting rods (after removing the cylinder head and sump) without removing the engine from the vehicle. However, this procedure is not recommended. Work of this nature is more*

easily and thoroughly completed with the engine on the bench - refer to Chapter 2C.

2 Location of TDC on No 1 cylinder

1 Remove the engine top cover, camshaft cover, auxiliary drivebelts and timing belt outer covers as described in Sections 17, 7, 6 and 4 respectively.

2 Remove the inspection bung from the transmission bellhousing - where a hexagon bung is fitted, use a large nut to remove it. Rotate the crankshaft clockwise with a wrench and socket, or a spanner, until the 0 mark machined onto the edge of the flywheel lines up with pointer on the bellhousing casting **(see illustrations)**.

3 To lock the engine in the TDC position, the camshaft (not the sprocket) and fuel injection pump sprocket must be secured in a reference position, using special locking tools. Improvised tools may be fabricated, but due to the exact measurements and machining involved, it is strongly recommended that a kit of locking tools is either borrowed or hired from a Seat dealer, or purchased from a reputable tool manufacturer - for example, Draper produce a kit of camshaft and fuel injection pump sprocket locking tools specifically for the range of engines covered in this Chapter **(see illustration)**.

4 Engage the edge of the locking bar with the slot in the end of the camshaft **(see illustration)**.

5 With the locking bar still inserted, turn the camshaft slightly (by turning the crankshaft clockwise, as before), so that the locking bar rocks to one side, allowing one end of the bar to contact the cylinder head surface. At the other side of the locking bar, measure the gap between the end of the bar and the cylinder head using a feeler blade.

6 Turn the camshaft back slightly, then pull out the feeler blade. The idea now is to level the locking bar by inserting two feeler blades, each with a thickness equal to *half* the originally measured gap, on either side of the camshaft between each end of the locking bar and the cylinder head **(see illustration)**. This centres the camshaft, and sets the valve timing in the reference condition.

2B

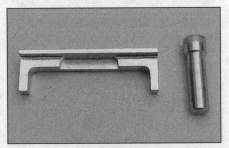

2.3 Engine locking tools

2.4 Engage the locking bar with the slot in the camshaft

2.6 Camshaft centred and locked using locking bar and feeler gauges

2.7 Injection pump sprocket locked using locking pin (arrowed) - engine code AAZ

7 Insert the locking pin through the fuel injection pump sprocket alignment hole, and thread it into the support bracket behind the sprocket. This locks the fuel injection pump in a reference condition **(see illustration)**.
8 The engine is now set to TDC on No 1 cylinder.

3 Cylinder compression test

Compression test

Note: *A compression tester specifically designed for diesel engines must be used for this test.*

1 When engine performance is down, or if misfiring occurs, a compression test can provide diagnostic clues as to the engine's condition. If the test is performed regularly, it can give warning of trouble before any other symptoms become apparent.
2 A compression tester specifically intended for diesel engines must be used, because of the high pressures involved. The tester is connected to an adapter which screws into the glow plug or injector hole. It is unlikely to be worthwhile buying such a tester for occasional use, but it may be possible to borrow or hire one - if not, have the test performed by a garage.
3 Unless specific instructions to the contrary are supplied with the tester, observe the following points:

4.8a Prise open the spring clips . . .

a) *The battery must be in a good state of charge, the air filter must be clean, and the engine should be at normal operating temperature.*
b) *All the injectors or glow plugs should be removed before starting the test. If removing the injectors, also remove the flame shield washers, otherwise they may be blown out.*
c) *The stop solenoid must be disconnected, to prevent the engine from running or fuel from being discharged.*

4 There is no need to hold the accelerator pedal down during the test, because the diesel engine air inlet is not throttled.
5 Seat specify wear limits for compression pressures - refer to the Specifications. Seek the advice of a Seat dealer or other diesel specialist if in doubt as to whether a particular pressure reading is acceptable.
6 The cause of poor compression is less easy to establish on a diesel engine than on a petrol engine. The effect of introducing oil into the cylinders (wet testing) is not conclusive, because there is a risk that the oil will sit in the swirl chamber or in the recess on the piston crown, instead of passing to the rings. However, the following can be used as a rough guide to diagnosis.
7 All cylinders should produce very similar pressures; a difference of more than 5 bars between any two cylinders indicates the existence of a fault. Note that the compression should build up quickly in a healthy engine; low compression on the first stroke, followed by gradually-increasing pressure on successive strokes, indicates worn piston rings. A low compression reading on the first stroke, which does not build up during successive strokes, indicates leaking valves or a blown head gasket (a cracked head could also be the cause).
8 A low reading from two adjacent cylinders is almost certainly due to the head gasket having blown between them; the presence of coolant in the engine oil will confirm this.

Leakdown test

9 A leakdown test measures the rate at which compressed air fed into the cylinder is lost. It is an alternative to a compression test, and in many ways it is better, since the escaping air

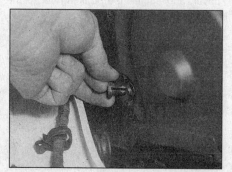

4.8b . . . and remove the press-stud fixings to remove the timing belt upper cover

provides easy identification of where pressure loss is occurring (piston rings, valves or head gasket).
10 The equipment needed for leakdown testing is unlikely to be available to the home mechanic. If poor compression is suspected, have the test performed by a suitably-equipped garage.

4 Timing belt and outer covers
- removal and refitting

General information

1 The primary function of the toothed timing belt is to drive the camshaft, but it is also used to drive the fuel injection pump and intermediate shaft. Should the belt slip or break in service, the valve timing will be disturbed and piston-to-valve contact may occur, resulting in serious engine damage.
2 For this reason, it is important that the timing belt is tensioned correctly, and inspected regularly for signs of wear or deterioration.
3 Note that the removal of the *inner* section of the timing belt cover is described as part of the camshaft oil seal renewal procedure; see Section 8 of this Chapter.

Removal

4 Disconnect the battery negative (earth) lead (see Chapter 5A).
5 Apply the handbrake, then jack up the front of the vehicle and support it on axle stands (see *Jacking and vehicle support*). Remove the right-hand front roadwheel, and where necessary remove the engine compartment undershield.
6 Remove the air cleaner housing as described in Chapter 4C and the engine top cover as described in Section 17.
7 With reference to Section 6, remove the auxiliary drivebelt(s). Where applicable, remove the tensioner roller by unscrewing the central bolt, noting that it has a **left-hand thread**.
8 Release the uppermost part of the timing belt outer cover by prising open the metal spring clips and removing the press-stud fixings **(see illustration)**. Lift the cover away from the engine
9 Refer to Section 2, and using the engine alignment markings, set the engine to TDC on No 1 cylinder.
10 Slacken and withdraw the screws, and lift off the coolant pump pulley. Slacken and withdraw the retaining screws, then remove the pulley for the ribbed auxiliary belt (together with the V-belt pulley, where fitted) from the crankshaft sprocket **(see illustration)**. On completion, check that the engine is still set to TDC.

 HAYNES HINT *To prevent the auxiliary belt pulley from rotating whilst the mounting bolts are being*

4.10 Removing the crankshaft auxiliary belt pulleys

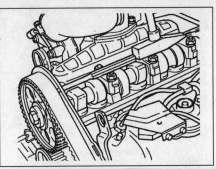

4.20 Releasing the camshaft sprocket from the taper using a thin metal drift

4.27a Tensioning the timing belt using a pair of circlip pliers in the belt tensioner

4.27b Timing belt correctly fitted

slackened, select 4th gear (manual transmission) or PARK (automatic transmission) and get an assistant to apply the footbrake firmly. Failing this, grip the sprocket by wrapping a length of old rubber hose around it.

11 Unscrew the bolts and nut, and lift off the timing belt lower cover.

12 On engines with a two-part fuel injection pump sprocket, ensure that the sprocket locking pin is firmly in position (see Section 2), then loosen the outer sprocket securing bolts by half a turn. *Caution: Do not loosen the sprocket centre nut, as this will alter the fuel injection pump's basic timing setting.*

13 With reference to Section 5, relieve the tension on the timing belt by slackening the tensioner mounting nut slightly, allowing it to pivot away from the belt.

14 On engine codes 1Z, AHU, AEY, AFN, slacken and withdraw the bolt and remove the idler roller from the top of the timing belt inner cover.

15 Examine the timing belt for manufacturer's markings that indicate the direction of rotation. If none are present, make your own using typist's correction fluid or a dab of paint - do not cut or score the belt in any way. *Caution: If the belt appears to be in good condition and can be re-used, it is essential that it is refitted the same way around, otherwise accelerated wear will result, leading to premature failure.*

16 Slide the belt off the sprockets, taking care to avoid twisting or kinking it excessively.

17 Examine the belt for evidence of contamination by coolant or lubricant. If this is the case, find the source of the contamination before progressing any further. Check the belt for signs of wear or damage, particularly around the leading edges of the belt teeth. Renew the belt if its condition is in doubt; the cost of belt renewal is negligible compared with potential cost of the engine repairs, should the belt fail in service. Similarly, if the belt is known to have covered more than 36 000 miles, it is prudent to renew it regardless of condition, as a precautionary measure.

18 If the timing belt is not going to be refitted for some time, it is a wise precaution to hang a warning label on the steering wheel, to remind yourself (and others) not to attempt to start the engine.

Refitting

19 Ensure that the crankshaft is still set to TDC on No 1 cylinder, as described in Section 2.

20 Refer to Section 5 and slacken the camshaft sprocket bolt by half a turn. Release the sprocket from the camshaft taper mounting by carefully tapping it with a thin metal drift, inserted through the hole provided in the timing belt inner cover **(see illustration)**.

21 Loop the timing belt loosely under the crankshaft sprocket. *Caution: Observe the direction of rotation markings on the belt.*

22 Engage the timing belt teeth with the crankshaft sprocket, then manoeuvre it into position over the camshaft and injection pump sprockets. Ensure the belt teeth seat correctly on the sprockets. **Note:** *Slight adjustments to the position of the camshaft sprocket (and where applicable, injection pump sprocket) may be necessary to achieve this.*

23 Pass the flat side of the belt over the intermediate shaft pulley and tensioner roller - avoid bending the belt back on itself or twisting it excessively as you do this.

24 On engine codes 1Z, AHU, AEY, AFN only, refit the idler roller to the timing belt inner cover, and tighten the retaining nut to the specified torque.

25 On engines with a single-part fuel injection pump sprocket, remove the locking pin from the fuel injection pump sprocket (see Section 2).

26 Ensure that the front run of the belt is taut - ie all the slack should be in the section of the belt that passes over the tensioner roller.

27 Tension the belt by turning the eccentrically-mounted tensioner clockwise; two holes are provided in the side of the tensioner hub for this purpose - a pair of sturdy right-angled circlip pliers is a suitable substitute for the correct Seat tool **(see illustrations)**.

28 On engines **without** a semi-automatic tensioner, test the timing belt tension by grasping it between the fingers at a point midway between the intermediate shaft and camshaft sprockets, and twisting it. The belt tension is approximately correct when the belt can just be twisted through 90° (quarter of a turn) and no further. Seat technicians use a special tool to check the tension, and it is recommended that this tool is obtained or a Seat dealer asked to check the tension on completion. If using the Seat tool, refer to the Specifications at the beginning of this Chapter for the correct setting.

29 On engines **with** a semi-automatic belt tensioner, turn the tensioner clockwise until the alignment markings on the pulley and hub are lined up **(see illustration)**.

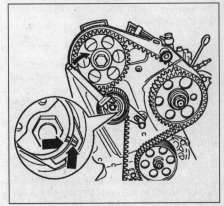

4.29 Alignment marks on pulley and hub - engines with semi-automatic tensioner

2B

5.2a Remove the tensioner nut and recover the washer

5.2b Slide the tensioner off its mounting stud

30 When the correct belt tension has been achieved, tighten the tensioner locknut to the specified torque.

31 At this point, check that the crankshaft is still set to TDC on No 1 cylinder (see Section 2).

32 Refer to Section 5 and tighten the camshaft sprocket bolt to the specified torque while holding it stationary with the home-made tool.

33 On engines with a two-part fuel injection pump sprocket, tighten the outer sprocket bolts.

34 With reference to Section 2, remove the camshaft locking bar and sprocket locking pin.

35 Using a spanner or wrench and socket on the crankshaft pulley centre bolt, rotate the crankshaft through two complete revolutions. Reset the engine to TDC on No 1 cylinder, with reference to Section 2 and check that the fuel injection pump sprocket locking pin can be inserted. Re-check the timing belt tension and adjust it, if necessary.

36 Refit the upper and lower sections of the timing belt outer cover, tightening the retaining screws securely.

37 Refit the coolant pump pulley and tighten the retaining screws to the specified torque.

38 Refit the crankshaft auxiliary belt pulley and tighten the retaining screws to the specified torque, using the method employed during removal. Note that the offset of the pulley mounting holes allows only one fitting position.

39 Where necessary, refit the tensioner roller and tighten the bolt to the specified torque.

40 Working from Section 6, refit and tension the auxiliary drivebelt(s).

41 Refit the air cleaner housing as described in Chapter 4C and the engine top cover as described in Section 17.

42 Refit the roadwheel and engine compartment undershield, then lower the vehicle to the ground.

43 Reconnect the battery negative (earth) lead (see Chapter 5A).

44 On completion, refer to Chapter 4C and check the fuel injection pump timing.

To make a camshaft sprocket holding tool, obtain two lengths of steel strip about 6 mm thick by 30 mm wide or similar, one 600 mm long, the other 200 mm long (all dimensions approximate). Bolt the two strips together to form a forked end, leaving the bolt slack so that the shorter strip can pivot freely. At the end of each prong of the fork, secure a bolt with a nut and a locknut, to act as the fulcrums; these will engage with the cut-outs in the sprocket, and should protrude by about 30 mm

---

5 Timing belt tensioner and sprockets - removal, inspection and refitting

Timing belt tensioner

Removal

1 Remove the timing belt as described in Section 4.

2 Unscrew the hub nut and withdraw the tensioner off of its mounting stud (see illustrations).

5.10 Removing the camshaft sprocket

Inspection

3 Wipe the tensioner clean, but do not use solvents that may contaminate the bearings. Spin the tensioner pulley on its hub by hand. Stiff movement or excessive freeplay is an indication of severe wear, in which case the tensioner should be renewed.

Refitting

4 Slide the tensioner pulley over the mounting stud. On engines with a semi-automatic tensioner, engage the forked end of the backplate with the timing belt pillar.

5 Refit the tensioner washer and retaining nut - do not fully tighten the nut at this stage.

6 With reference to Section 4, refit and tension the timing belt. On engines with a semi-automatic tensioner, the operation of the tensioner can be tested as follows: apply finger pressure to the timing belt at a point mid-way between the camshaft and injection pump sprockets. The tensioner pulley alignment marks should move apart as pressure is applied, and then move back and line up again as the pressure is removed.

Camshaft sprocket

Removal

7 Remove the timing belt (see Section 4).

8 The camshaft sprocket must be held stationary whilst its retaining bolt is slackened; if access to the correct Seat special tool is not possible, a simple home-made tool using basic materials may be fabricated (see Tool Tip).

9 Using the home-made tool, brace the camshaft sprocket and slacken and remove the retaining bolt; recover the washer where fitted.

10 Slide the camshaft sprocket from the end of the camshaft (see illustration). Where applicable, recover the Woodruff key from the keyway.

Inspection

11 With the sprocket removed, examine the camshaft oil seal for signs of leaking. If necessary, refer to Section 8 and renew it.

12 Wipe the sprocket and camshaft mating surfaces clean.

Refitting

13 Where applicable, fit the Woodruff key into the keyway with the plain surface facing upwards. Fit the sprocket to the camshaft, engaging the slot in the sprocket with the Woodruff key. Where a key is not used, ensure the lug in the sprocket hub engages with recess in the end of the camshaft.

14 Working from Sections 2 and 4, check that the engine is still set to TDC on No 1 cylinder, then refit and tension the timing belt with reference to Section 4.

Crankshaft sprocket

Removal

15 Remove the timing belt as described in Section 4.

5.20a Insert the crankshaft sprocket bolt . . .

5.20b . . . tighten it to the Stage 1 torque . . .

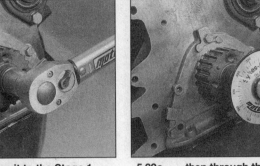

5.20c . . . then through the Stage 2 angle

16 The crankshaft sprocket must be held stationary whilst its retaining bolt is slackened. If access to the correct Seat flywheel locking tool is not available, lock the crankshaft in position by removing the starter motor, as described in Chapter 5A, to expose the flywheel ring gear. Get an assistant insert a stout lever between the ring gear teeth and the transmission bellhousing whilst the sprocket retaining bolt is slackened.

17 Withdraw the bolt, recover the washer and lift off the sprocket.

Inspection

18 With the sprocket removed, examine the crankshaft oil seal for signs of leaking. If necessary, refer to Section 10 and renew it.

19 Wipe the sprocket and crankshaft mating surfaces clean.

Refitting

20 Offer up the sprocket to the crankshaft, engaging the lug on the inside of the sprocket with the recess in the end of the crankshaft. Insert the retaining bolt and tighten it to the specified torque **(see illustrations)**.

21 Working from Sections 2 and 4, check that the engine is still set to TDC on No 1 cylinder, then refit and tension the timing belt with reference to Section 4.

Intermediate shaft sprocket

Removal

22 Remove the timing belt as described in Section 4.

23 The intermediate shaft sprocket must be held stationary whilst its retaining bolt is slackened; if access to the correct Seat special tool is not possible, a simple home-made tool using basic materials may be fabricated as described in the camshaft sprocket removal sub-Section.

24 Using a socket and extension bar, brace the intermediate shaft sprocket. Slacken and remove the retaining bolt; recover the washer, where fitted **(see illustration)**.

25 Slide the sprocket from the end of the intermediate shaft. Where applicable, recover the Woodruff key from the keyway.

Inspection

26 With the sprocket removed, examine the intermediate shaft oil seal for signs of leaking. If necessary, refer to Section 9 and renew it.

27 Wipe the sprocket and shaft mating surfaces clean.

Refitting

28 Where applicable, fit the Woodruff key into the keyway with the plain surface facing upwards. Offer up the sprocket to the intermediate shaft, engaging the slot in the sprocket with the Woodruff key.

29 Tighten the sprocket retaining bolt to the specified torque while holding the sprocket using the method employed during removal.

30 Refit the timing belt with reference to Section 4.

Fuel injection pump sprocket

31 Refer to Chapter 4C.

---

6 Auxiliary drivebelts -
removal and refitting

General information

1 Depending on the vehicle specification and engine type, one or two auxiliary drivebelts may be fitted. Both are driven from pulleys mounted on the crankshaft, and provide drive for the alternator, coolant pump, power steering pump and on vehicles with air conditioning, the refrigerant compressor.

2 The run of the belts and the components they drive are also dependent on vehicle specification and engine type. Because of this, the coolant pump and power steering pump may be fitted with pulleys to suit either a ribbed belt or a V-belt.

3 The ribbed auxiliary belt may be fitted with an automatic tensioning device, depending on its run (and hence the number of components it is driving), otherwise, the belt is tensioned by the alternator mountings, which have an in-built tensioning spring. The V-belt is tensioned by pivoting the power steering pump on its mounting.

4 On refitting, the auxiliary belt must be tensioned correctly to ensure correct operation under all conditions and prolonged service life.

Auxiliary V-belt

Removal

5 Apply the handbrake, then jack up the front of the vehicle and support it on axle stands (see *Jacking and vehicle support*).

6 Where necessary, remove the right-hand front roadwheel then remove the lower engine cover for access to the right-hand end of the engine.

7 With reference to Chapter 10, slacken the power steering pump mounting bolts and allow the pump body to pivot around its uppermost mounting towards the engine.

8 Slip the V-belt off the power steering pump pulley and where applicable, the coolant pump pulley **(see illustration)**.

9 Examine the belt for signs or wear or damage, and renew it if necessary.

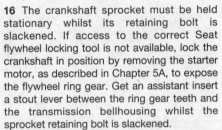

5.24 Brace the intermediate shaft sprocket, then remove the retaining bolt

6.8 Removing the auxiliary V-belt from the power steering pump pulley

2B

6.10 Tightening the power steering pump mounting bolts

Refitting and tensioning

10 Refitting is a reversal of removal, but adjust the tension as follows. Grasp the underside of the power steering pump and draw it towards the front of the vehicle. The tension is correct when the midpoint of the belt's longest run can be deflected by no more than 5 mm. Tighten the power steering pump bolts to the correct torque **(see illustration)**.

Auxiliary ribbed belt

Removal

11 Apply the handbrake, then jack up the front of the vehicle and support it on axle stands (see *Jacking and vehicle support*).
12 Where necessary, remove the right-hand front roadwheel then remove the lower engine cover for access to the right-hand end of the engine.
13 Where applicable, remove the auxiliary V-belt as described in the previous sub-Section.
14 Examine the ribbed belt for manufacturer's markings, indicating the direction of rotation. If none are present, make some using typist's correction fluid or a dab of paint - do not cut or score the belt in any way.

Vehicles with a roller-arm automatic tensioning device
15 Rotate the tensioner roller arm clockwise against its spring tension so that the roller is forced away from the belt - use an adjustable spanner as a lever **(see illustration)**.

Vehicles without an automatic tensioning device
16 Slacken the alternator upper and lower mounting bolts by between one and two turns.
17 Push the alternator down to its stop against the spring tension, so that it rotates around its uppermost mounting.
All vehicles
18 Slip the belt off the alternator pulley, then release it from the remaining pulleys.

Refitting and tensioning

Caution: Observe the direction of rotation markings on the belt, when refitting.
19 Pass the ribbed belt underneath the crankshaft pulley, ensuring that the ribs seat securely in the channels on the surface of the pulley.

Vehicles with roller-arm automatic tensioning device
20 Rotate the tensioner roller arm clockwise against its spring tension, then pass the belt around the air conditioning refrigerant pump pulley and over the alternator pulley.
21 Release the tensioner pulley arm and allow the roller to bear against the flat surface of the belt.

Vehicles without an automatic tensioning device
22 Repeatedly push the alternator down to its stop against the spring tension, so that it rotates around its uppermost mounting and check that it moves back freely when released. If necessary, slacken the alternator mounting bolts by a further half a turn.
23 Keep the alternator pushed down against its stop, pass the belt over the alternator and air conditioning compressor pulleys, then release the alternator and allow it to tension the belt.
24 Disable the ignition system by removing the distributor centre HT lead and grounding it on the cylinder block, using a jumper wire. Spin the engine approximately 10 turns on the starter motor, then tighten the alternator mounting bolts to the specified torque. Reconnect the HT lead.
25 Where applicable, refit the auxiliary V-belt as described in the previous sub-Section.
26 Refit the lower cover and roadwheel, then lower the vehicle to the ground.

6.15 Rotate the tensioner roller arm clockwise - use an adjustable spanner - and remove the belt

7 Camshaft cover - removal and refitting

Removal

1 Remove the engine top cover (see Section 17), then disconnect the crankcase breather hose and regulator valve from the camshaft cover **(see illustration)**.
2 Slacken and withdraw the three camshaft cover retaining nuts - recover the washers and seals **(see illustration)**.
3 Lift the cover away from the cylinder head **(see illustration)**. If it sticks, do not attempt to lever it off - instead free it by working around the cover and tapping it lightly with a soft-faced mallet.
4 Recover the camshaft cover gasket. Inspect the gasket carefully, and renew it if damage or deterioration is evident.
5 Clean the mating surfaces of the cylinder head and camshaft cover thoroughly, removing all traces of oil and old gasket - take care to avoid damaging the surfaces as you do this.

Refitting

6 Refit the camshaft cover by following the removal procedure in reverse, noting the following points:
   a) *Ensure that the gasket is correctly seated on the cylinder head, and take care to avoid displacing it as the camshaft cover is lowered into position (see illustration).*

7.1 Crankcase breather regulator valve

7.2 Camshaft cover retaining nut

7.3 Lift the camshaft cover away from the cylinder head

b) *Tighten the camshaft cover retaining screws/nuts to the specified torque.*
c) *When refitting hoses that were originally secured with crimp-type clips, use standard worm-drive clips in their place on refitting.*

8 Camshaft oil seal - renewal

1 Refer to Section 5 and remove the camshaft sprocket.
2 Where necessary, unbolt and remove the timing belt inner cover. Note that it may be possible to remove the old and fit the new oil seal through the hole in the inner cover.
3 Working from the relevant Section of Chapter 2C, carry out the following:
a) *Unbolt the camshaft No 1 bearing cap, and slide off the camshaft oil seal (see illustration).*
b) *Lubricate the surface of a new camshaft oil seal with clean engine oil, and fit it over the end of the camshaft.*
c) *Apply a suitable sealant to the mating surface of the bearing cap, then refit it and tighten its mounting nuts progressively to the specified torque.*
4 Where removed, refit the timing belt inner cover and tighten the bolts.
5 Refer to Section 5 and refit the camshaft sprocket.

9 Intermediate shaft oil seal - renewal

1 Refer to Section 5 and remove the intermediate shaft sprocket.
2 If necessary, unbolt and remove the inner timing belt cover.
3 Unscrew the bolts and remove the intermediate shaft flange. Remove the O-ring seal from the flange and discard it.
4 Support the flange then lever or press out the oil seal.
5 Clean the flange and cylinder block recess.
6 Press a new shaft oil seal into the housing in the intermediate shaft flange and fit a new

7.6 Ensure that the camshaft cover gasket is correctly seated on the cylinder head

O-ring seal to the inner sealing surface of the flange. Make sure the sealing lip of the oil seal faces inwards.
7 Lubricate the inner lip of the oil seal and the O-ring seal with clean engine oil, and slide the flange and seal over the end of the intermediate shaft.
8 Insert the bolts and tighten them to the specified torque.
9 Where necessary, refit the inner timing belt cover and tighten the bolts.
10 Refer to Section 5 and refit the intermediate shaft sprocket.

10 Crankshaft oil seals - renewal

Crankshaft front oil seal (leaving housing in situ)

1 Refer to Section 5 and remove the crankshaft sprocket.
2 Drill two small holes into the existing oil seal, diagonally opposite each other. Thread two self-tapping screws into the holes and using two pairs of pliers, pull on the heads of the screws to extract the oil seal **(see illustration)**. Take great care to avoid drilling through into the seal housing or crankshaft sealing surface.
3 Clean out the seal housing and sealing surface of the crankshaft by wiping it with a lint-free cloth - avoid using solvents that may enter the crankcase and affect component

8.3 Remove the camshaft bearing cap and slide off the oil seal

lubrication. Remove any swarf or burrs that could cause the seal to leak.
4 Smear the lip of the new oil seal with clean engine oil, and position it over the housing.
5 Using a hammer and a socket of suitable diameter, drive the seal squarely into its housing. **Note:** *Select a socket that bears only on the hard outer surface of the seal, not the inner lip, which can easily be damaged.*
6 Refer to Section 5 and refit the crankshaft sprocket.

Crankshaft front oil seal (incl. removal of the housing)

7 Refer to Section 5 and remove the crankshaft sprocket.
8 Refer to Section 15 and remove the sump.
9 Unscrew and remove the oil seal housing retaining bolts, then lift the housing away from the cylinder block, together with the crankshaft oil seal.
10 Recover the old gasket from the seal housing on the cylinder block. If it has disintegrated, scrape the remains off with a trimming knife blade. Take care to avoid damaging the mating surfaces.
11 Prise the old oil seal from the housing using a screwdriver **(see illustration)**.
12 Wipe the oil seal housing clean, and check it visually for damage. Lay the housing on a work surface, with the mating surface face down. Press in a new oil seal, using a block of wood as a press to ensure that the seal enters the housing squarely.
13 Smear the crankcase mating surface with multi-purpose grease, and lay the new gasket in position **(see illustration)**.

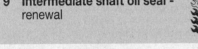

10.2 Removing the crankshaft front oil seal using self-tapping screws

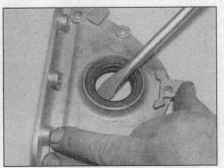

10.11 Prise the old oil seal from the housing

10.13 Locate the new crankshaft front oil seal housing gasket in position

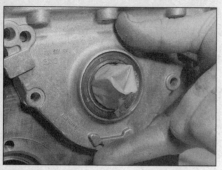

10.15 Offer up the seal and its housing to the end of the crankshaft

10.29 Locate the new crankshaft rear oil seal housing gasket in position

10.30 A protective plastic cap is supplied with genuine manufacturer's crankshaft oil seal housings

14 Wrap some adhesive tape around the end of the crankshaft; this will protect the oil seal as it is being fitted.

15 Lubricate the inner lip of the crankshaft oil seal with clean engine oil, then offer up the seal and its housing to the end of the crankshaft. Ease the seal along the shaft until the housing is flush with the crankcase **(see illustration)**.

16 Insert the bolts and tighten them to the specified torque.

17 Refer to Section 15 and refit the sump.

18 Refer to Section 5 and refit the crankshaft sprocket.

Crankshaft rear oil seal (flywheel end)

19 Apply the handbrake, then jack up the front of the vehicle and support it on axle stands (see *Jacking and vehicle support*).

20 Remove the transmission (Chapter 7), and flywheel (Section 13 of this Chapter).

21 Remove the retaining bolts and lift the engine rear plate from the cylinder block.

22 The oil seal may be removed using the same method as that described for the camshaft oil seal removal in Section 8. The alternative method is to unbolt the oil seal housing from the cylinder block then drive the oil seal from the housing (see following paragraphs), however if this method is used care must be taken not to damage the sump gasket. If the gasket is damaged, it will be necessary to drain the engine oil (Chapter 1B) and remove the sump as described in Section 15, then fit the sump with a new gasket after fitting the oil seal housing.

23 Progressively slacken and then remove the oil seal housing retaining bolts.

24 Lift the housing away from the cylinder block, together with the crankshaft oil seal.

25 Recover the old gasket and clean the mating surfaces on the seal housing and cylinder block.

26 Prise the old oil seal from the housing using a screwdriver.

27 Wipe the oil seal housing clean, and check it visually for signs of distortion or cracking.

28 Lay the housing on a work surface, with the mating surface face down. Press in a new oil seal, using a block of wood as a press to ensure that the seal enters the housing squarely.

29 Smear the cylinder block surface with multi-purpose grease, and lay the new gasket in position **(see illustration)**.

30 A protective plastic cap is supplied with genuine crankshaft oil seals. When fitted over the end of the crankshaft, the cap prevents damage to the inner lip of the oil seal as it is being fitted **(see illustration)**. Use PVC tape to pad the end of the crankshaft if a cap is not available.

31 Lubricate the inner lip of the crankshaft oil seal with clean engine oil, then offer up the seal and its housing to the end of the crankshaft **(see illustration)**. Ease the seal along the shaft using a twisting motion, until the housing is flush with the crankcase.

32 Insert the retaining bolts and tighten them progressively to the specified torque **(see illustration)**.

33 Where applicable, refer to Section 15 and refit the sump.

34 Refit the engine rear plate and tighten the bolts.

35 Refit the flywheel (Section 13 of this Chapter), then refit the transmission (Chapter 7).

36 Lower the vehicle to the ground.

37 Where applicable, fill the engine with fresh oil with reference to Chapter 1B.

11 Cylinder head, inlet and exhaust manifolds - removal, separation and refitting

Removal

1 For improved access, refer to Chapter 11 and remove the bonnet from its hinges, and if necessary raise the front of the vehicle and support on axle stands (see *Jacking and vehicle support*).

2 Disconnect the battery negative (earth) lead (see Chapter 5A), and remove the engine top cover (Section 17).

3 With reference to Chapter 1B, carry out the following:
 a) Drain the engine oil.
 b) Drain the cooling system.

4 Refer to Section 6 and remove the auxiliary drivebelt(s).

5 With reference to Section 2, set the engine to TDC on No 1 cylinder.

6 Refer to Chapter 3 and perform the following:
 a) Slacken the clips and disconnect the radiator hoses from the ports on the cylinder head.
 b) Slacken the clips and disconnect the expansion tank hose, and the heater inlet and outlet coolant hoses, from the ports on the cylinder head **(see illustration)**.

10.31 Fitting the crankshaft rear oil seal housing

10.32 Tightening the crankshaft rear oil seal housing retaining bolts

11.6 Disconnect the heater coolant hoses from the ports on the cylinder head

7 The body front panel assembly comprises the front bumper moulding, radiator and grille, cooling fan(s) headlight units, front valence and bonnet lock mechanism. Although its removal is not essential, its does give greatly-improved access to the engine; refer to the beginning of the engine removal procedure, in Chapter 2C.

8 Refer to Chapter 4C and carry out the following:

a) *Remove the air cleaner assembly and air inlet duct.*

b) *Unscrew the unions and remove the injector fuel supply pipes from the injectors and the injection pump head.*

c) *Disconnect the injector bleed hose from the injection pump fuel return port.*

d) *Unplug all fuel system electrical cabling at the relevant connectors, labelling each cable to aid refitting later.*

9 With reference to Sections 2, 4 and 7, carry out the following:

a) *Remove the camshaft cover. Also disconnect the crankcase ventilation hose from the outlet on the front of the cylinder block.*

b) *Remove the timing belt outer covers, and disengage the timing belt from the camshaft sprocket.*

c) *Remove the timing belt tensioner, camshaft sprocket and fuel injection pump sprocket.*

10 Slacken and withdraw the retaining screws and lift off the timing belt inner covers **(see illustrations)**.

11 Disconnect the wiring plug from the coolant temperature sensor and oil pressure switch **(see illustrations)**.

12 Refer to Chapter 4D and carry out the following:

a) *Remove the bolts and separate the exhaust downpipe from the exhaust manifold flange.*

b) *Where applicable, remove the turbocharger from the exhaust manifold.*

c) *Where applicable, remove the EGR valve and its connecting pipework from the inlet and exhaust manifolds.*

d) *Disconnect the supply cable from the glow plug in cylinder No 4 **(see illustration)**.*

13 Remove the retaining screw and detach

11.10a Slacken and withdraw the retaining screws . . .

11.10b . . . and lift off the timing belt inner covers

11.11a Disconnect the wiring plug from the coolant temperature sensor . . .

11.11b . . . and oil pressure switch

the engine harness connector bracket from the cylinder head **(see illustration)**.

14 Working in the reverse of the sequence shown in illustration 11.37a, progressively slacken the cylinder head bolts, by half a turn at a time, until all bolts can be unscrewed by hand. Discard the bolts - new ones must be fitted on reassembly.

15 Check that nothing remains connected to the cylinder head, then lift the head away from the cylinder block; seek assistance if possible, as it is a heavy assembly, especially if it is being removed complete with the manifolds **(see illustration)**.

16 Remove the gasket from the top of the block, noting the locating dowels. If the dowels are a loose fit, remove them and store them with the head for safe-keeping. Do not discard the gasket - it will be needed for identification purposes.

17 If the cylinder head is to be dismantled for overhaul refer to Chapter 2C.

Manifold separation and reassembly

18 With the cylinder head on a work surface, slacken and withdraw the inlet manifold securing bolts. Lift the manifold away, and recover the gasket.

19 Unbolt the heat shield **(see illustration overleaf)**, then progressively slacken and remove the exhaust manifold retaining nuts. Lift the manifold away from the cylinder head, and recover the gaskets.

20 Ensure that the inlet and exhaust manifold mating surfaces are completely clean. Refit the exhaust manifold, using new gaskets. Ensure that the gaskets are fitted the correct way around, otherwise they will obstruct the

2B

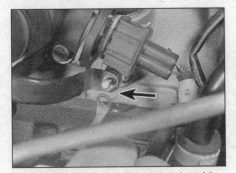

11.12 Unbolt the electrical supply cable from No 4 cylinder glow plug

11.13 Removing the engine harness connector bracket from the cylinder head

11.15 Lifting the cylinder head away from the engine

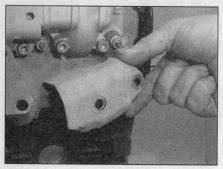

11.19 Unbolt and remove the exhaust manifold heat shield

11.20a Fit the exhaust manifold gaskets . . .

11.20b . . . then refit the exhaust manifold. Tighten the nuts to the specified torque

11.22a Fit a new inlet manifold gasket to the cylinder head . . .

11.22b . . . then lift the inlet manifold into position

11.22c Insert the retaining bolts and tighten them to the specified torque

inlet manifold gasket. Tighten the exhaust manifold retaining nuts to the specified torque given in Chapter 4D **(see illustrations)**.

21 Refit the heat shield to the studs on the exhaust manifold, then fit and tighten the retaining nuts.

22 Fit a new inlet manifold gasket to the cylinder head, then lift the inlet manifold into position. Insert the retaining bolts and tighten them to the specified toque **(see illustrations)**.

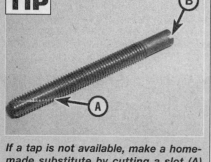

TOOL TiP

If a tap is not available, make a home-made substitute by cutting a slot (A) down the threads of one of the old cylinder head bolts. After use, the bolt head can be cut off, and the shank can then be used as an alignment dowel to assist cylinder head refitting. Cut a screwdriver slot (B) in the top of the bolt, to allow it to be unscrewed

Preparation for refitting

23 The mating faces of the cylinder head and cylinder block/crankcase must be perfectly clean before refitting the head. Use a hard plastic or wood scraper to remove all traces of gasket and carbon; also clean the piston crowns. Take particular care during the cleaning operations, as aluminium alloy is easily damaged. Also, make sure that the carbon is not allowed to enter the oil and water passages - this is particularly important for the lubrication system, as carbon could block the oil supply to the engine's components. Using adhesive tape and paper, seal the water, oil and bolt holes in the cylinder block/crankcase.

24 Check the mating surfaces of the cylinder block/crankcase and the cylinder head for nicks, deep scratches and other damage. If slight, they may be removed carefully with abrasive paper, but note that head machining will not be possible - refer to Chapter 2C.

25 If warpage of the cylinder head gasket surface is suspected, use a straight-edge to check it for distortion. Refer to Part C of this Chapter if necessary.

26 Clean out the cylinder head bolt drillings using a suitable tap. If a tap is not available, make a home-made substitute **(see Tool Tip)**.

27 On all the engines covered in this Chapter, it is possible for the piston crowns to strike and damage the valve heads, if the camshaft is rotated with the timing belt removed and the crankshaft set to TDC. For this reason, the crankshaft must be set to a position other than

TDC on No 1 cylinder, before the cylinder head is refitted. Use a wrench and socket on the crankshaft pulley centre bolt to turn the crankshaft in its normal direction of rotation, until all four pistons are positioned halfway down their bores, with No 1 piston on its upstroke - approximately 90° before TDC.

Refitting

28 Examine the old cylinder head gasket for manufacturer's identification markings. These will either be in the form of punched holes or a part number, on the edge of the gasket **(see illustration)**. Unless new pistons have been fitted, the new cylinder head gasket must be the same type as the old one.

29 If new piston assemblies have been fitted as part of an engine overhaul, before purchasing the new cylinder head gasket, refer to Section 13 of Chapter 2C and measure the

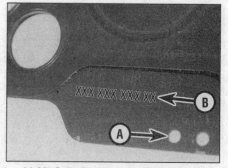

11.28 Cylinder head gasket punched holes (A) and part number (B)

piston projection. Purchase a new gasket according to the results of the measurement (see Chapter 2C Specifications).

30 Lay the new head gasket on the cylinder block, engaging it with the locating dowels. Ensure that the manufacturer's TOP and part number markings are face up.

31 Cut the heads from two of the old cylinder head bolts. Cut a slot, big enough for a screw-driver blade, in the end of each bolt. These can be used as alignment dowels to assist in cylinder head refitting **(see illustration)**.

32 With the help of an assistant, place the cylinder head and manifolds centrally on the cylinder block, ensuring that the locating dowels engage with the recesses in the cylinder head. Check that the head gasket is correctly seated before allowing the full weight of the cylinder head to rest upon it.

33 Unscrew the home-made alignment dowels, using a screwdriver.

34 Apply a smear of grease to the threads, and to the underside of the heads, of the new cylinder head bolts.

35 Oil the bolt threads, then carefully enter each bolt into its hole (*do not drop them in*) and screw in, by hand only, until finger-tight **(see illustration)**.

36 Working progressively and in the sequence shown, tighten the cylinder head bolts to their Stage 1 torque setting, using a torque wrench and suitable socket **(see illustrations)**. Repeat the exercise in the same sequence for the Stage 2 torque setting.

37 Once all the bolts have been tightened to their Stage 2 settings, working again in the given sequence, angle-tighten the bolts through the specified Stage 3 angle, using a socket and extension bar. It is recommended that an angle-measuring gauge is used during this stage of the tightening, to ensure accuracy. If a gauge is not available, use white paint to make alignment marks between the bolt head and cylinder head prior to tightening; the marks can then be used to check the bolt has been rotated through the correct angle during tightening. Repeat for the Stage 4 setting **(see illustration)**.

38 Refit the timing belt inner cover, tightening the retaining screws securely.

39 With reference to Sections 2 and 5, refit the timing belt tensioner and sprockets.

11.31 Two of the old head bolts (arrowed) used as cylinder head alignment dowels

40 Refer to Section 2 and set the engine to TDC on No 1 cylinder. On completion, refer to Section 4 and refit the camshaft timing belt and outer covers.

41 The remainder of refitting is a reversal of the removal procedure, as follows:

a) *Refer to Chapter 4D and refit the turbocharger (where applicable), the exhaust downpipe, the EGR valve (where applicable) and the glow plug cabling.*

b) *Refer to Chapter 4C and refit the injector fuel supply hoses to the injectors and the injection pump head. Reconnect all fuel system electrical cabling. Refit the injector bleed hose to the injection pump fuel return port. Refit the air cleaner assembly and air inlet duct.*

c) *Refit the engine harness connector bracket to the cylinder head.*

d) *Refit the camshaft cover (see Section 7) and crankcase ventilation hose.*

e) *With reference to the information in Chapter 2C, refit the body front panel assembly, if it was removed for greater access.*

f) *Reconnect the radiator, expansion tank and heater coolant hoses, referring to Chapter 3 for guidance. Reconnect the coolant temperature sensor wiring.*

g) *Refer to Section 6 and refit the auxiliary drivebelt(s).*

h) *Restore the battery connection.*

i) *Refer to Chapter 11 and refit the bonnet.*

42 On completion, lower the vehicle to the ground then refer to Chapter 1B and carry out the following:

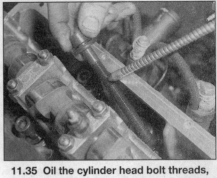

11.35 Oil the cylinder head bolt threads, then place each bolt into its hole

a) *Refill the engine cooling system with the correct quantity of new coolant.*

b) *Refill the engine lubrication system with the correct grade and quantity of oil.*

Note: *No further tightening of the cylinder head bolts is required.*

12 Hydraulic tappets - operation check

⚠️ **Warning: After fitting hydraulic tappets, wait a minimum of 30 minutes (or preferably, leave overnight) before starting the engine, to allow the tappets time to settle, otherwise the pistons may strike the valve heads.**

1 The hydraulic tappets are self-adjusting, and require no attention whilst in service.

2 If the hydraulic tappets become excessively noisy, their operation can be checked as described below.

3 Run the engine until it reaches its normal operating temperature. Switch off the engine, then refer to Section 7 and remove the camshaft cover.

4 Rotate the camshaft by turning the crankshaft with a socket and wrench, until the first cam lobe over No 1 cylinder is pointing upwards.

5 Using a feeler blade, measure the clearance between the base of the cam lobe and the top of the tappet. If the clearance is greater than 0.1 mm, then the tappet is defective and must be renewed.

2B

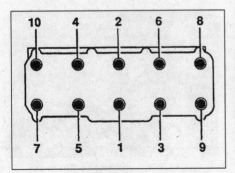

11.36a Cylinder head bolt tightening sequence

11.36b Tightening the cylinder head bolts using a torque wrench and socket

11.37 Angle-tightening a cylinder head bolt

14.10 Remove the engine mounting lower bolt

6 If the clearance is less than 0.1 mm, press down on the top of the tappet until it is felt to contact the top of the valve stem. Use a wooden or plastic implement that will not damage the surface of the tappet.

7 If the tappet travels more than 0.1 mm before making contact, then it is defective and must be renewed.

8 Hydraulic tappet removal and refitting is described as part of the cylinder head overhaul sequence - see Chapter 2C for details.

13 Flywheel - removal, inspection and refitting

Removal

1 On all diesel models, the clutch pressure plate is bolted directly to the end of the crankshaft, and the flywheel is then bolted to the pressure plate. Remove these components, therefore, as described in Chapter 6.

Inspection

2 If the flywheel's clutch mating surface is deeply scored, cracked or otherwise damaged, the flywheel must be renewed. However, it may be possible to have it surface-ground. Seek the advice of an engine reconditioning specialist.

3 If the ring gear is badly worn or has missing teeth, a new gear can be fitted to the flywheel by a Seat dealer or engine reconditioning specialist.

14.12 Removing the mounting bracket

Refitting

4 Refer to Chapter 6 for the refitting procedure.

14 Engine mountings - inspection and renewal

Inspection

1 If improved access is required, raise the front of the car and support it securely on axle stands.

2 Check the mounting rubbers to see if they are cracked, hardened or separated from the metal at any point, and renew the mounting if any such damage or deterioration is evident.

3 Check that all the mounting's fasteners are securely tightened, using a torque wrench to check if possible.

4 Using a large screwdriver or a crowbar, check for wear in the mounting by carefully levering against it to check for free play. Where this is not possible, enlist the aid of an assistant to move the engine/transmission back and forth, or from side to side, while you watch the mounting. While some free play is to be expected even from new components, excessive wear should be obvious. If excessive free play is found, check first that the fasteners are correctly secured, then renew any worn components as described below.

Renewal

Front engine mounting

5 Disconnect the battery negative (earth) lead (see Chapter 5A), and position it away from the terminal.

6 With the front of the vehicle supported on axle stands, position a trolley jack and wooden block underneath the engine and position it such that the jack head is directly underneath the engine/bellhousing mating surface. Raise the jack until it just takes the weight of the engine off the front engine mounting.

7 Unscrew the mounting top bolt.

8 Loosen the rear left- and right-hand engine mounting bolts several turns to prevent excessive tension in the mountings.

9 Unscrew the bolt securing the coolant hose support to the mounting bracket.

10 Unscrew the mounting lower bolt from the crossmember **(see illustration)**.

11 Unscrew and remove the starter motor mounting bolts **(see illustration)**. If necessary, support the starter motor.

12 Raise the engine/transmission assembly slightly, then remove the mounting bracket **(see illustration)**.

13 Refitting is a reversal of removal, noting the following points:

a) Ensure that the orientation lug that protrudes from the top surface of the engine mounting block engages with the recess in the mounting bracket **(see illustration)**. Also check that the lug on

14.11 Removing the starter mounting/transmission bellhousing bolts

the right-hand rear mounting block engages with its recess before tightening the mounting bolts.

b) Tighten all bolts to the specified torque.

Right-hand engine mounting

14 Disconnect the battery negative (earth) lead (see Chapter 5A), and position it away from the terminal.

15 With the front of the vehicle supported on axle stands, mount an engine lifting beam across the engine bay, and attach the jib to the engine lifting eyes on the cylinder head. Alternatively, an engine hoist can be used. Raise the hoist/lifting beam jib to take the weight of the engine off the engine mounting.

16 Remove the air cleaner assembly (refer to Chapter 4B).

17 Loosen the front and left-hand engine mounting bolts several turns to prevent excessive tension in the mountings.

18 Unscrew the two bolts securing the mounting to the bodywork.

19 Raise the engine/transmission assembly slightly, then remove the mounting from under the vehicle. If required, unbolt the bracket from the engine.

20 Refitting is a reversal of removal, noting the following points:

a) Ensure that the orientation lug that protrudes from the top surface of the engine mounting block engages with the recess in the mounting bracket.

b) Tighten all bolts to the specified torque.

Left-hand mounting

21 Disconnect the battery negative (earth)

14.13 Lug (arrowed) on top of the mounting engages with the recess in the bracket

lead (see Chapter 5A), and position it away from the terminal.

22 With the front of the vehicle supported on axle stands, mount an engine lifting beam across the engine bay, and attach the jib to the engine lifting eyes on the cylinder head. Alternatively, an engine hoist can be used. Raise the hoist/lifting beam jib to take the weight of the engine off the engine mounting.

23 Detach the gearchange control rods from the mounting bracket.

24 Unscrew the mounting top bolt.

25 Loosen the front and right-hand mounting bolts several turns to prevent excessive tension in the mountings.

26 Raise the engine/transmission assembly slightly, then unbolt the mounting bracket from the transmission.

27 Unscrew the two bolts securing the mounting to the subframe and withdraw the mounting from under the vehicle.

28 Refitting is a reversal of removal but tighten the bolts to the specified torque.

15 Sump -
removal, inspection and refitting

Removal

1 Disconnect the battery negative (earth) lead (see Chapter 5A) and position it away from the terminal.

2 Apply the handbrake, then jack up the front of the vehicle and support it on axle stands (see *Jacking and vehicle support*). Where applicable, remove the screws and lower the engine undertray from the vehicle. Refer to Chapter 1B and drain the engine oil.

3 If necessary, to improve access to the sump, refer to Chapter 8 and disconnect the right-hand driveshaft from the transmission output flange, however this is not essential.

4 Unscrew the bolts and remove the clutch housing cover. This is necessary for access to the sump end bolts.

5 Working around the outside of the sump, progressively slacken and withdraw the sump retaining bolts.

6 Break the joint by striking the sump with the palm of your hand, then lower the sump and withdraw it from underneath the vehicle. Recover and discard the sump gasket. Where a baffle plate is fitted, note that it can only be removed once the oil pump has been unbolted (see Section 16).

7 While the sump is removed, take the opportunity to check the oil pump pick-up/strainer for signs of clogging or disintegration. If necessary, remove the pump as described in Section 16, and clean or renew the strainer.

Refitting

8 Clean the mating surfaces of the cylinder block/crankcase and sump, then use a piece of clean rag to wipe out the sump.

9 Note that where a baffle plate is fitted, the gasket may be incorporated in the plate and it may not be possible to renew it separately. On engines without a baffle plate, ensure that the sump and cylinder block/crankcase mating surfaces are clean and dry, then apply a coating of suitable sealant to the sump and crankcase mating surfaces.

10 Offer up the sump to the engine and insert the retaining bolts. Tighten the bolts evenly and progressively to the specified torque.

11 Refit the clutch housing cover and tighten the bolts.

12 Where applicable, refit the driveshaft and engine undertray.

13 Refer to Chapter 1B and refill the engine with the specified grade and quantity of oil.

14 Reconnect the battery negative (earth) lead (see Chapter 5A).

16 Oil pump and pickup -
removal and refitting

General information

1 The oil pump and pickup are both mounted in the sump. Drive is taken from the inter-mediate shaft, which rotates at half crankshaft speed.

2 Refer to Section 15 and remove the sump.

3 Unscrew and remove the bolts securing the oil pump to the base of the crankcase.

4 Lower the oil pump and pickup away from the crankcase. Where applicable, recover the baffle plate.

Inspection

5 Remove the screws from the flange, and lift off the pickup tube. Recover the O-ring seal. Slacken and withdraw the screws, then remove the oil pump cover.

6 Clean the pump thoroughly, and inspect the gear teeth for signs of damage or wear.

7 Check the pump backlash by inserting a feeler blade between the meshed gear teeth; rotate the gears against each other slightly, to give the maximum clearance. Compare the measurement with the limit quoted in Specifications.

8 Check the pump axial clearance as follows. Lay an engineer's straight edge across the oil pump casing, then using a feeler blade, measure the clearance between the straight edge and the pump gears. Compare the measurement with the limit quoted in Specifications.

9 If either measurement is outside of the specified limit, this indicates that the pump is worn and must be renewed.

Refitting

10 Refit the oil pump cover, then fit and tighten the screws to the specified torque.

11 Reassemble the oil pickup to the oil

pump, using a new O-ring seal. Tighten the retaining screws to the specified torque.

12 Where applicable, fit the crankcase baffle plate in place.

13 Offer up the oil pump to the crankcase, then fit the mounting bolts and tighten them to the specified torque.

14 Refer to Section 15 and refit the sump.

17 Engine top cover -
removal and refitting

Removal

1 Most engines have a large plastic cover fitted over the top of the engine which acts as an acoustic shroud. Removing this cover gives access to many of the engine components.

2 Using a suitable screwdriver or similar tool, prise out the plastic covers fitted over the retaining nuts (see illustration).

3 Unscrew the retaining nuts and lift off the cover. Take care not to lose any of the rubber spacers fitted to the locating studs as the cover is removed.

Refitting

4 Refitting is a reversal of removal. Make sure that no hoses become trapped or pinched under the cover. Tighten the retaining nuts securely.

18 Oil cooler -
removal and refitting

Removal

1 Apply the handbrake, then jack up the front of the vehicle and support it on axle stands (see *"Jacking and Vehicle Support"*). Remove the engine compartment undertray.

2 Position a container beneath the front of the engine, then unscrew and remove the oil filter (refer to Chapter 1B if necessary). Empty the oil into the container.

3 Fit hose clamps to the two coolant hoses on the oil cooler. Alternatively, drain the cooling system with reference to Chapter 1B. Loosen the clips and disconnect the hoses.

17.2 Removing the plastic covers for access to the retaining nuts

2B

4 Unscrew the nut from the centre tube, then lower the oil cooler from the oil filter housing, noting the fitted location of the coolant stubs. If fitted, remove the gasket, or clean the sealant from the mating faces.

Refitting

5 Clean the mating surfaces of the oil cooler and the oil filter housing. Apply sealant or fit a new gasket (as applicable) to the upper surface, the locate the cooler on the centre tube and screw on the nut. Tighten the nut to the specified torque.

6 Refit the hoses and tighten the clips. Remove the hose clamps where fitted.

7 Smear a little clean engine oil on the oil filter sealing ring, then screw on the filter and tighten by hand only.

8 Refill or top-up the cooling system with reference to Chapter 1B.

9 Start the engine and allow it to idle for several minutes. Check for oil or coolant leaks around the oil cooler, then switch off the engine.

10 Refit the engine compartment undertray, and lower the vehicle to the ground.

Chapter 2 Part C:
Engine removal and overhaul procedures

Contents

Degrees of difficulty

Easy, suitable for novice with little experience	Fairly easy, suitable for beginner with some experience 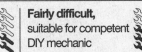	Fairly difficult, suitable for competent DIY mechanic	Difficult, suitable for experienced DIY mechanic 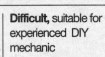	Very difficult, suitable for expert DIY or professional

Specifications

Engine codes
See Chapter 2A or 2B.

Cylinder head
Cylinder head gasket surface, maximum distortion:
  Engine codes AER, AAU, AAV, ABD, ABU, AEX,APQ, AEE, ALM, ABF . 0.05 mm
  Engine codes AFT, 1F, 2E, AGG, 1Y, AAZ, AEY, 1Z, AHU, AFN . . . . . . 0.1 mm
Minimum cylinder head height:
  Engine codes AER, AAU, AAV, ABD, ABU, AEX, APQ, AEE, ALM . . . . 135.6 mm
  Engine codes AFT, 2E, AGG . . . . 132.6 mm
  Engine code ABF . . . . 118.1 mm
  Engine codes 1Y, AAZ, AEY, 1Z, AHU, AFN . . . . Head reworking not possible
Maximum swirl chamber projection (engine codes 1Y, AAZ) . . . . 0.07 mm

Cylinder head gasket
Identification markings (punched holes), engine codes 1Z, AHU, 1Y and AAZ only*:
  Engine code 1Z, AHU:
    Piston projection:
      0.91 to 1.00 mm . . . . 1 hole
      1.01 to 1.10 mm . . . . 2 holes
      1.11 to 1.20 mm . . . . 3 holes
  Engine codes 1Y, AAZ:
    Piston projection:
      0.66 to 0.86 mm . . . . 1 hole
      0.87 to 0.90 mm . . . . 2 holes
      0.91 to 1.02 mm . . . . 3 holes
*Note: See text in Chapter 2B and in Sections 4 and 13 of this Chapter for details.

Camshaft
Endfloat, all engine codes . . . . 0.15 mm
Maximum runout, all engine codes . . . . 0.01 mm
Maximum running clearance:
  Engine codes AEY, 1Y, AAZ, 1Z, AHU, AFN . . . . 0.11 mm
  All other engine codes . . . . 0.10 mm

2C

Valves

	Inlet	Exhaust
Valve stem diameter:		
Engine code AER	6.967 mm	6.950 mm
Engine codes AAU, AAV, ABD, ABU	7.965 or 6.970 mm	7.945 or 6.950 mm
Engine codes AEX, APQ, AEE, ALM	6.963 mm	6.943 mm
Engine code AFT	6.92 ± 0.02 mm	6.92 ± 0.02 mm
Engine code 1F	7.97 or 6.92 mm	7.95 or 6.92 mm
Engine code 2E	7.97 mm	7.95 mm
Engine code AGG	6.92 mm	6.92 mm
Engine code ABF	6.97 mm	6.94 mm
Engine codes AEY (to 6/95), 1Y, AAZ	7.97 mm	7.95 mm
Engine code AEY (from 7/95)	7.95 mm	6.95 mm
Engine codes 1Z (to 6/95), AHU (to 6/95)	7.97 mm	7.95 mm
Engine codes 1Z (from 7/95), AHU (from 7/95), AFN	6.97 mm	6.95 mm

Maximum valve head deflection (end of valve stem flush with top of guide):
Inlet:
Engine codes AEY, 1Y, AAZ, 1Z, AHU, AFN . . . . 1.3 mm
All other engine codes . . . . 1.0 mm
Exhaust (all engine codes) . . . . 1.3 mm

Intermediate shaft

Maximum endfloat:
Engine codes AFT, 1F, 2E, AGG, ABF, AEY, 1Y, AAZ, 1Z, AHU, AFN . . 0.25 mm

Cylinder block

Bore diameter:	Standard	1st oversize	2nd oversize	3rd oversize
Engine code AER	67.11 mm	67.36 mm	67.61 mm	67.86 mm
Engine codes AAU, AAV, ABD	75.01 mm	75.26 mm	75.51 mm	75.76 mm
Engine codes ABU, AEX, APQ, AEE, ALM	76.51 mm	76.76 mm	77.01 mm	77.26 mm
Engine code AFT	81.01 mm	81.51 mm	N/A	N/A
Engine code 1F	81.01 mm	81.26 mm	81.51 mm	N/A
Engine codes 2E, ABF	82.51 mm	82.76 mm	83.01 mm	N/A
Engine code AGG	82.51 mm	N/A	N/A	N/A
Engine codes AEY, 1Y, AAZ, 1Z, AHU, AFN	79.51 mm	79.76 mm	80.01 mm	N/A

Connecting rods

Big-end bearing running clearance (maximum):
Engine codes AER, ABU, AEX, APQ, AEE, ALM . . . . 0.091 mm
Engine codes AAU, AAV, ABD . . . . 0.095 mm
Engine codes AFT, 1F, 2E, AGG, ABF . . . . 0.12 mm
Engine codes AEY, 1Y, AAZ, 1Z, AHU, AFN . . . . 0.08 mm

Minimum big-end bearing shell pre-tension:
Engine code AER, AEX, APQ, AEE, ALM . . . . 1.5 mm

Pistons and piston rings

Piston diameter:	Standard	1st oversize	2nd oversize	3rd oversize
Engine code AER	67.085 mm	67.335 mm	67.585 mm	67.835 mm
Engine codes AAU, AAV, ABD	74.985 mm	75.235 mm	75.485 mm	75.735 mm
Engine codes ABU, AEX, APQ, AEE, ALM	76.470 mm	76.720 mm	76.970 mm	77.220 mm
Engine code AFT	80.965 mm	81.485 mm	N/A	N/A
Engine code 1F	80.985 mm	81.235 mm	81.485 mm	N/A
Engine codes 2E, ABF	82.485 mm	82.735 mm	82.985 mm	N/A
Engine code AGG	82.475 mm	N/A	N/A	N/A
Engine codes AEY, 1Z, AHU, AFN	79.47 mm	79.72 mm	79.97 mm	N/A
Engine codes 1Y, AAZ	79.48 mm	79.78 mm	79.98 mm	N/A

Piston ring-to-groove clearance:	Standard	Service limit
Engine codes AER (all rings)	0.02 to 0.05 mm*	0.15 mm*
Engine codes AAU, AAV, AFT, 1F, 2E, AGG (all rings)	0.02 to 0.05 mm	0.15 mm
Engine codes ABD, ABU, AEX, APQ, AEE, ALM (all rings)	0.04 to 0.08 mm	0.15 mm
Engine code ABF (all rings)	0.02 to 0.06 mm	0.15 mm
Engine code AEY, 1Z, AHU, AFN:		
Top compression ring	0.06 to 0.09 mm	0.25 mm
2nd compression ring	0.05 to 0.08 mm	0.25 mm
Oil scraper ring	0.03 to 0.06 mm	0.15 mm
Engine code 1Y, AAZ:		
Top compression ring	0.09 to 0.12 mm	0.25 mm
2nd compression ring	0.05 to 0.08 mm	0.25 mm
Oil scraper ring	0.03 to 0.06 mm	0.15 mm

Pistons and piston rings (continued)

Piston ring end gap:	Standard	Service limit
Engine codes AER:		
Top compression ring	0.02 to 0.05 mm	0.15 mm
2nd compression ring	0.02 to 0.05 mm	0.15 mm
Oil scraper ring	0.02 to 0.05 mm*	0.15 mm*
Engine codes AAU, AAV, AFT, 1F, 2E, AGG:		
Top compression ring	0.02 to 0.05 mm	0.15 mm
2nd compression ring	0.02 to 0.05 mm	0.15 mm
Oil scraper ring	0.02 to 0.05 mm	0.15 mm
Engine codes ABD, ABU, AEX, APQ, AEE, ALM:		
Top compression ring	0.04 to 0.08 mm	0.15 mm
2nd compression ring	0.04 to 0.08 mm	0.15 mm
Oil scraper ring	0.04 to 0.08 mm	0.15 mm
Engine code ABF:		
Top compression ring	0.02 to 0.07 mm	0.15 mm
2nd compression ring	0.02 to 0.07 mm	0.15 mm
Oil scraper ring	0.02 to 0.06 mm	0.15 mm
Engine code AEY, 1Z, AHU, AFN:		
Top compression ring	0.06 to 0.09 mm	0.25 mm
2nd compression ring	0.05 to 0.08 mm	0.25 mm
Oil scraper ring	0.03 to 0.06 mm	0.15 mm
Engine code 1Y, AAZ:		
Top compression ring	0.09 to 0.12 mm	0.25 mm
2nd compression ring	0.05 to 0.08 mm	0.25 mm
Oil scraper ring	0.03 to 0.06 mm	0.15 mm

*Note: 3-part oil scraper ring: clearances not measurable.

Crankshaft

Maximum endfloat:
- Engine codes AER, , ABU, AEX, APQ, AEE, ALM .... 0.40 mm
- Engine codes AAU, AAV, ABD .... 0.20 mm
- Engine codes AFT, 1F, 2E, AGG, ABF, AEY, 1Y, AAZ, 1Z, AHU, AFN . 0.37 mm

Main bearing journal diameters:
- All engine codes:
  - Standard .... 54.00 mm
  - 1st undersize .... 53.75 mm
  - 2nd undersize .... 53.50 mm
  - 3rd undersize .... 53.25 mm
  - Tolerance:
    - Engine codes AER, AAU, AAV, ABU .... -0.022 to -0.037 mm
    - Engine codes AEX, APQ, AEE, ALM .... -0.017 to -0.037 mm
    - Engine codes AFT, 1F, 2E, AGG, ABF, AEY, 1Y, AAZ, 1Z, AHU, AFN .... -0.022 to -0.042 mm

Main bearing running clearances:
- Engine codes AER, AEX, APQ, AEE, ALM .... 0.13 mm
- Engine codes AAU, AAV, ABD, ABU, AFT, 1F, 2E, AGG, ABF, AEY, 1Y, AAZ, 1Z, AHU, AFN .... 0.17 mm

Crankpin journal diameters:
- Engine code AER, AAU, AAV, ABD:
  - Standard .... 42.00 mm
  - 1st undersize .... 41.75 mm
  - 2nd undersize .... 41.50 mm
  - 3rd undersize .... 41.25 mm
- Engine codes ABU, AEX, APQ, AEE, ALM, AFT, 1F, 2E, AGG, ABF, AEY, 1Y, AAZ, 1Z, AHU, AFN:
  - Standard .... 47.80 mm
  - 1st undersize .... 47.55 mm
  - 2nd undersize .... 47.30 mm
  - 3rd undersize .... 47.05 mm
- Tolerance:
  - Engine codes AER, ABU, AEX, APQ, AEE, ALM .... -0.022 to -0.037 mm
  - Engine codes AAU, AAV .... -0.030 to -0.045 mm
  - Engine codes ABD .... -0.020 to -0.035 mm
  - Engine codes AFT, 1F, 2E, AGG, ABF, AEY, 1Y, AAZ, 1Z, AHU, AFN .... -0.022 to -0.042 mm

Torque wrench settings

Refer to Specifications in Chapters 2A (petrol engines) or 2B (diesel engines).

2C

2.2a Prise out the plastic caps ...

2.2b ... undo the screws ...

When removing the engine from the vehicle, be methodical about the disconnection of external components. Labelling cables and hoses as they are removed will greatly assist the refitting process.

Always be extremely careful when lifting the engine/transmission assembly from the engine compartment. Serious injury can result from careless actions. If help is required, it is better to wait until it is available rather than risk personal injury and/or damage to components by continuing alone. By planning ahead and taking your time, a job of this nature, although major, can be accomplished successfully and without incident.

On all models described in this manual, the engine and transmission are removed as a complete assembly upwards, through the front of the vehicle. This involves the removal of the body front panel assembly, which is the assembly that forms the front of the engine compartment. Note that the engine and transmission should ideally be removed with the vehicle standing on all four roadwheels, but access to the driveshafts and exhaust system downpipe will be improved if the vehicle can be temporarily raised onto axle stands.

1 Engine and transmission removal - preparation and precautions

If you have decided that the engine must be removed for overhaul or major repair work, several preliminary steps should be taken.

Locating a suitable place to work is extremely important. Adequate work space, along with storage space for the vehicle, will be needed. If a workshop or garage is not available, at the very least a solid, level, clean work surface is required.

If possible, clear some shelving close to the work area and use it to store the engine components and ancillaries as they are removed and dismantled. In this manner, the components stand a better chance of staying clean and undamaged during the overhaul. Laying out components in groups together with their fixings bolts and screws will save time and avoid confusion when the engine is refitted.

Clean the engine compartment and engine/transmission before beginning the removal procedure; this will help visibility and help to keep tools clean.

The help of an assistant will be required since there are certain instances when one person cannot safely perform all of the operations required to remove the engine from the vehicle. Safety is of primary importance, considering the potential hazards involved in this kind of operation. A second person should always be in attendance to offer help in an emergency. If this is the first

time you have removed an engine, advice and aid from someone more experienced would also be beneficial.

Plan the operation ahead of time. Before starting work, obtain (or arrange for the hire of) all of the tools and equipment you will need. Access to the following items will allow the task of removing and refitting the engine/transmission to be completed safely and with relative ease: a heavy-duty trolley jack - rated in excess of the combined weight of the engine and transmission, complete sets of spanners and sockets as described in the front of this manual, wooden blocks, and plenty of rags and cleaning solvent for mopping up spilled oil, coolant and fuel. A selection of different sized plastic storage bins will also prove useful for keeping dismantled components grouped together. If any of the equipment must be hired, make sure that you arrange for it in advance, and perform all of the operations possible without it beforehand; this may save you time and money.

Plan on the vehicle being out of use for quite a while, especially if you intend to carry out an engine overhaul. Read through the whole of this Section and work out a strategy based on your own experience and the tools, time and workspace available to you. Some of the overhaul processes may have to be carried out by a Seat dealer or an engineering works - these establishments often have busy schedules, so it would be prudent to consult them before removing or dismantling the engine, to get an idea of the amount of time required to carry out the work.

2 Engine and transmission - removal, separation and refitting

Removal

All models

1 Select a solid, level surface to park the vehicle upon. Give yourself enough space to move around it easily.

2 Refer to Chapter 11 and remove the bonnet from its hinges. Also remove the engine top cover where necessary **(see illustrations)**.

3 Disconnect the battery negative (earth) lead, then remove the battery with reference to Chapter 5A **(see illustration)**.

4 Refer to Chapter 4A, 4B or 4C and remove the air cleaner assembly.

5 With reference to Chapter 1A or 1B as applicable, carry out the following:

a) If the engine is to be dismantled, drain the engine oil (see illustration).

b) Drain the cooling system.

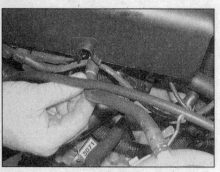

2.2c ... release the hoses from the clips ...

2.2d ... and remove the engine top cover (1390 cc engine code APQ)

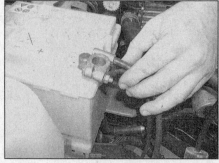

2.3 Disconnecting the battery leads

**2.5 Engine oil drain plug
(engine code APQ)**

2.6 Heater hoses on the bulkhead

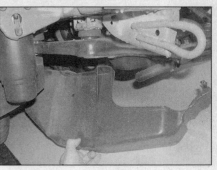

**2.9 Removing the engine compartment
undertray**

6 Refer to Chapter 3 and perform the following:
a) *Slacken the clips and disconnect the radiator top and bottom hoses from the cylinder head, and from the thermostat housing/coolant pump (as applicable).*
b) *Disconnect the coolant hoses from the expansion tank and heater inlet and outlet ports at the bulkhead* **(see illustration)**.

7 On vehicles with air conditioning, refer to Chapter 3 and carry out the following additional operations:
a) *Unbolt the air conditioning receiver/dryer from its mountings, and allow it to rest on the engine front crossmember.*
b) *Remove the retaining bolts from the clips that secure the condenser supply and return pipes to the engine crossmember.*
c) *Refer to Chapter 3 and remove the air conditioning compressor from the engine leaving the refrigerant lines connected. Support the compressor on an axle stand.*

8 Apply the handbrake, then jack up the front of the vehicle and support it on axle stands (see *Jacking and vehicle support*). Remove both front roadwheels.
9 Refer to Chapter 11 and carry out the following:

a) *Remove the undertray from the underside of the engine compartment* **(see illustration)**.
b) *Remove the screws and clips that secure the plastic inner wheel arch liners to the front valance.*

10 The body front panel comprises the front bumper, radiator, cooling fan(s), headlight units, front valance and bonnet lock mechanism. Its removal gives greatly-improved access to the engine and transmission, and is essential on models fitted with air conditioning. On some models it is sufficient to only remove the radiator. Refer to

Chapter 11 for the removal procedure of the body front panel **(see illustration)**.

Petrol models

11 Unplug the Lambda sensor wiring from the main harness at the multiplug connector (refer to Chapter 4D) **(see illustration)**.
12 Disconnect the ignition HT king lead from the centre terminal of the distributor cap, and tie it back away from the engine **(see illustration)**.
13 Disconnect the accelerator cable from with reference to Chapter 4A or 4B **(see illustration)**.
14 On vehicles with an activated charcoal canister emission control system, refer to Chapter 4D and disconnect the vacuum hose from the connection near the front suspension turret **(see illustration)**.
15 Refer to Chapter 9 and disconnect the brake servo vacuum hose from the inlet manifold **(see illustration)**.

2C

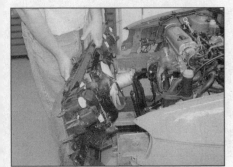

**2.10 Removing the body front panel from
the front of the car**

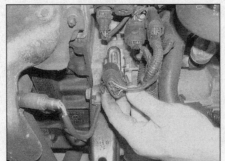

**2.11 Disconnecting the Lambda sensor
wiring (engine code APQ)**

**2.12 Disconnecting the HT king lead from
the distributor cap (engine code APQ)**

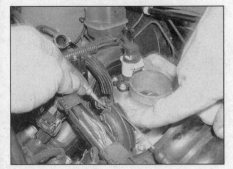

**2.13 Disconnecting the accelerator cable
(engine code APQ)**

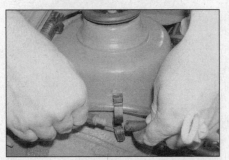

**2.14 Disconnecting the charcoal canister
emission control system vacuum hose
(engine code APQ)**

**2.15 Disconnecting the brake vacuum
servo hose from the inlet manifold
(engine code APQ)**

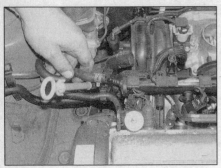

2.16a Disconnect the fuel supply hose . . .

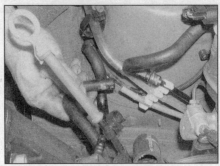

2.16b . . . and return hose (engine code APQ)

2.17 Detaching the ignition coil ground cable from the engine top cover bracket (engine code APQ)

16 With reference to Chapter 4A or 4B, depressurise the fuel system then disconnect the fuel supply and return hoses **(see illustrations)**.

17 Unscrew the nut and disconnect the ignition coil ground cable from the bracket on the cylinder head **(see illustration)**.

18 Refer to Chapter 6 and disconnect the clutch control cable from the lever on the transmission **(see illustration)**.

19 Refer to Chapter 4D, and remove the hot air shroud then detach the exhaust downpipe from the exhaust manifold. Unbolt the exhaust downpipe from the transmission bracket and move it to one side **(see illustrations)**.

Diesel models

 Warning: When dismantling any part of the air inlet system on a turbocharged vehicle, ensure that no foreign material gets into the

turbo air inlet port; cover the opening with a sheet of plastic, secured with an elastic band. The turbocharger compressor blades could be severely damaged if debris is allowed to enter.

20 Disconnect the brake servo vacuum hose from the vacuum pump (see Chapter 9).

21 On vehicles with an Exhaust Gas Recirculation (EGR) system, refer to Chapter 4D and disconnect the vacuum hoses from the EGR valve and throttle valve sensor.

22 With reference to Chapter 4C, unscrew the banjo bolts and disconnect the fuel supply and return hoses from the fuel injection pump. Also disconnect the injector bleed hose from the port on the fuel return union.

23 With reference to Chapter 4C, disconnect the accelerator cable from the injection pump.

24 On vehicles with a turbocharger, disconnect the hoses from the air mass meter and turbocharger, and also disconnect the

crankcase ventilation hose. Where necessary, disconnect the cold start cable.

25 Refer to Chapter 6 and disconnect the clutch control cable from the lever on the transmission.

26 Refer to Chapter 4D, and detach the exhaust downpipe from the exhaust manifold (or turbocharger).

27 Disconnect the brake vacuum hose from the vacuum pump.

All models

28 Disconnect the main engine wiring harness from the engine and transmission, making a note of its routing to ensure correct refitting. Disconnect the earth cables and release the wiring from the supports on the transmission. Where applicable, disconnect the engine wiring from the battery negative terminal. Disconnect the wiring from the reversing light switch **(see illustrations)**.

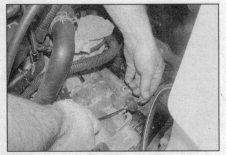

2.18 Disconnecting the clutch control cable from the lever and transmission (engine code APQ)

2.19a Removing the hot air shroud and stub from the exhaust manifold (engine code APQ)

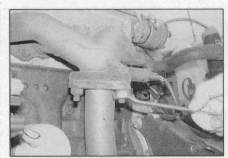

2.19b Unscrewing the exhaust downpipe to manifold retaining nuts (engine code APQ)

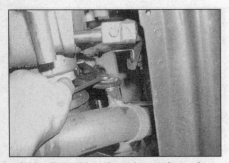

2.19c Detaching the exhaust downpipe from the transmission bracket (engine code APQ)

2.28a Disconnecting the main engine wiring harness (engine code APQ)

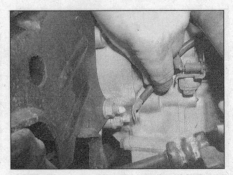

2.28b Disconnecting the earth cable from the transmission bolt (engine code APQ)

2.28c Disconnecting the engine wiring from the battery negative terminal

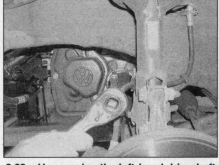

2.29a Unscrewing the left-hand driveshaft bolts

2.29b Removing the gasket from the left-hand driveshaft

29 Refer to Chapter 8 and remove the right-hand driveshaft complete. The left-hand driveshaft must be unbolted from the transmission drive flange, then tied to one side on the underbody. Note that the driveshaft inner joints are assembled to the transmission drive flanges with rubber gaskets which tend to swell up making refitting difficult. To ensure correct refitting of the gaskets, both driveshafts may be removed complete at this stage, then refitted after the engine/transmission has been installed in the engine compartment. Renew the gaskets if they are unserviceable **(see illustrations)**.
30 On vehicles with power steering, refer to Chapter 10 and remove the power steering pump from the engine without disconnecting the hydraulic lines **(see illustrations)**. Tie the pump to one side. Note that on some models,

the power steering fluid reservoir must be removed and positioned to one side. Also on some models, it will be necessary to remove the crankshaft pulley plastic cover first, for access to the power steering pump and drivebelt.
31 Disconnect the gearchange linkage from the transmission with reference to Chapter 7. Mark the linkage and shaft for position before disconnecting, to ensure correct refitting **(see illustration)**.
32 If necessary, lower the vehicle to the ground, then attach an engine lifting beam or hoist to the engine lifting eyes. Take the weight of the engine and transmission, then unscrew the three engine mounting bolts. If necessary, unscrew the nut and bolts and remove the left-hand engine mounting bracket from the transmission **(see illustrations)**.

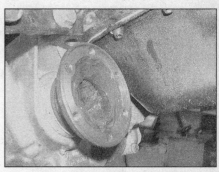

2.29c Transmission drive flange

33 Carry out a final check to ensure that nothing else remains connected to the engine, then raise the engine/transmission

2.30a Unscrew the mounting bolts . . .

2.30b . . . and remove the power steering pump (engine code APQ)

2.31 Disconnecting the gearchange linkage from the transmission (engine code APQ)

2.32a Engine lifting eye (engine code APQ)

2.32b Removing the right-hand engine mounting bolt (engine code APQ)

2.32c Removing the left-hand engine mounting bolt (engine code APQ)

2C

assembly a little, and if necessary unbolt and remove the front mounting bracket from the engine. With the help of an assistant, lift the assembly from the engine compartment being careful not to damage the surrounding components. Move the hoist away from the vehicle and lower the assembly to the ground **(see illustration)**.

Separation and reassembly

34 Refer to Chapter 5A and remove the starter motor.

35 Unbolt the flywheel cover plate from the transmission bellhousing.

36 Disconnect the wiring from the reverse switch on the transmission.

37 Unscrew the transmission flange bolts, then, with the help of an assistant, withdraw the transmission directly from the rear of the engine. Take care not to allow the weight of the transmission to bear on the clutch components.

38 Commence reassembly by smearing a little high-melting-point grease on the splines of the transmission input shaft. Do not use an excessive amount as there is the risk of contaminating the clutch friction plate. Carefully offer up the transmission to the cylinder block, guiding the dowels into the mounting holes in cylinder block.

39 Refit the bellhousing bolts and nuts, hand tightening them to secure the transmission in position. **Note:** *Do not tighten them to force the engine and transmission together.* Ensure that the bellhousing and cylinder block mating faces will butt together evenly without obstruction, before tightening the bolts and nuts to their specified torque.

40 With reference to Chapter 5A, refit the starter motor and tighten the retaining bolts to the specified torque.

Refitting

41 Attach an engine hoist to the lifting eye on the cylinder head, and raise the engine and transmission from the ground.

42 Wheel the hoist up to the front of the vehicle and with the help of an assistant, guide the engine and transmission in through the front of the engine compartment. Rotate the assembly slightly so that the transmission casing enters first, then guide the auxiliary belt pulleys past the bodywork.

43 Align the rear engine mounting brackets with the mounting points on the body. Note that alignment lugs protrude from the metal discs that are bonded to the top of each of each engine mounting; these must engage with the recesses on the underside of the engine mounting brackets.

44 Lift the front engine mounting bracket into position, then insert the bolts and tighten them to the correct torque.

45 Fit the front engine mounting rubber block into the cup in the crossmember, then insert the retaining bolt through the underside of the crossmember and tighten it to the specified torque.

2.32d Unscrewing the bolt from the front engine mounting (engine code APQ)

46 Lower the engine and transmission into position, ensuring that the locating lugs on the front engine mounting engage with the recess in the mounting bracket. Insert the front and rear engine mounting through-bolts, tightening them by hand initially.

47 Detach the engine hoist and wheel it away from the vehicle.

48 Settle the engine and transmission assembly on its mountings by rocking it backwards and forwards, then tighten the mounting through-bolts to the specified torque.

49 The remainder of the refitting sequence is the direct reverse of the removal procedure. Finally, refill the cooling system with reference to Chapter 1A or 1B. If the engine oil was drained, refer to Chapter 1A or 1B and refill the engine with fresh oil.

50 When the engine is started for the first time, check for coolant, oil and fuel leaks. If the engine has been overhauled, read the notes in Section 14 before attempting to start it.

3 Engine overhaul - preliminary information

It is much easier to dismantle and work on the engine if it is mounted on a portable engine stand. These stands can often be hired from a tool hire shop. Before the engine is mounted on a stand, the flywheel should be removed, so that the stand bolts can be tightened into the end of the cylinder block/crankcase.

2.33 Lifting the engine/transmission assembly from the engine compartment (engine code APQ)

If a stand is not available, it is possible to dismantle the engine with it blocked up on a workbench, or on the floor. Be very careful not to tip or drop the engine when working without a stand.

If you intend to obtain a reconditioned engine, all ancillaries must be removed first, to be transferred to the replacement engine (just as they will if you are doing a complete engine overhaul yourself). These components include the following:

Petrol engines

a) *Power steering pump (Chapter 10) - where applicable.*

b) *Air conditioning compressor (Chapter 3) - where applicable.*

c) *Alternator (including mounting brackets) and starter motor (Chapter 5A).*

d) *The ignition system and HT components including all sensors, distributor, HT leads and spark plugs (Chapters 1A and 5B).*

e) *The fuel injection system components (Chapter 4A and 4B).*

f) *All electrical switches, actuators and sensors, and the engine wiring harness (Chapter 4A, 4B and 5B).*

g) *Inlet and exhaust manifolds (Chapter 4A, 4B and 4D).*

h) *Engine oil dipstick and tube (Chapter 2A).*

i) *Engine mountings (Chapter 2A).*

j) *Flywheel (Chapter 2A).*

k) *Clutch components (Chapter 6).*

Diesel engines

a) *Power steering pump (Chapter 10) - where applicable.*

b) *Air conditioning compressor (Chapter 3) - where applicable.*

c) *Alternator (including mounting brackets) and starter motor (Chapter 5A).*

d) *The glow plug/pre-heating system components (Chapter 4D)*

e) *The fuel injection system components, including the fuel injection pump, all sensors and actuators (Chapter 4C)*

f) *The vacuum pump (Chapter 2B)*

g) *All electrical switches, actuators and sensors, and the engine wiring harness (Chapter 4C and 5B).*

h) *Inlet and exhaust manifolds and where applicable, the turbocharger (Chapter 4C and 4D).*

i) *The engine oil level dipstick and its tube (Chapter 2B)*

j) *Engine mountings (Chapter 2 B).*

k) *Flywheel/driveplate (Chapter 2B).*

l) *Clutch components (Chapter 6)*

Note: *When removing the external components from the engine, pay close attention to details that may be helpful or important during refitting. Note the fitted position of gaskets, seals, spacers, pins, washers, bolts, and other small components.*

If you are obtaining a short engine (the engine cylinder block/ crankcase, crankshaft, pistons and connecting rods, all fully assembled), then the cylinder head, sump and

4.6 Keep groups of components together in labelled bags or boxes

baffle plate, oil pump, timing belt (together with its tensioner and covers), auxiliary belt (together with its tensioner), coolant pump, thermostat housing, coolant outlet elbows, oil filter housing and where applicable oil cooler will also have to be removed.

If you are planning a full overhaul, the engine can be dismantled in the order given below:

a) Inlet and exhaust manifolds.
b) Timing belt, sprockets and tensioner.
c) Cylinder head.
d) Flywheel.
e) Sump.
f) Oil pump.
g) Piston/connecting rod assemblies.
h) Crankshaft.

4 Cylinder head -
dismantling, cleaning, inspection and reassembly

Note: *Reconditioned cylinder heads can be obtained from engine overhaul specialists, and it may therefore be more practical for the home mechanic to buy a reconditioned head, rather than to dismantle, inspect and recondition the original head. Note that when dealing with DOHC engines, the operations described in this Section are equally applicable to both the inlet and exhaust camshafts.*

Dismantling

1 Remove the cylinder head, and separate the inlet and exhaust manifolds from it (Chapter 2A or 2B).
2 On diesel models, remove the injectors and glow plugs (see Chapter 4C and Chapter 5C).
3 Refer to Chapter 3 and remove the coolant outlet elbow together with its gasket/O-ring.
4 Where applicable, unscrew the coolant sensor and oil pressure switch from the cylinder head.
5 Remove the timing belt sprocket from the camshaft (Part A or B of this Chapter).
6 It is important that groups of components are kept together when they are removed and, if still serviceable, refitted in the same groups. If they are refitted randomly, accelerated wear leading to early failure will occur. Stowing

groups of components in plastic bags or storage bins will help to keep everything in the right order - label them according to their fitted location, eg No 1 exhaust, No 2 inlet, etc **(see illustration).** (Note that No 1 cylinder is nearest the timing belt end of the engine.)
7 Check that the manufacturer's identification markings are visible on camshaft bearing caps; if none can be found, make your own using a scriber or centre-punch.
8 The camshaft bearing cap nuts must be removed progressively and in sequence to avoid stressing the camshaft, as follows.

Engine codes AER, AAU, AAV, ABD, ABU, AEX, APQ, AEE, ALM, AFT, AEY, 1Y, AAZ, 1Z, AHU, AFN

9 Slacken the nuts from bearing caps Nos 5, 1 and 3 first, then at bearing caps 2 and 4. Slacken the nuts alternately and diagonally half a turn at a time until they can be removed by hand. **Note:** *Camshaft bearing caps are numbered 1 to 5 from the timing belt end.*

Engine codes 1F, 2E, AGG

10 On engines with 4 caps, slacken and remove the retaining nuts from bearing caps Nos 1 and 3 first, then at bearing caps 2 and 5. On engines with 5 caps, slacken and remove the retaining nuts from bearing caps Nos 1, 3 and 5 first, then at bearing caps Nos 2 and 4. Slacken the nuts alternately and diagonally half a turn at a time until they can be removed by hand. **Note:** *Camshaft bearing caps are numbered 1 to 5 from the timing belt end* **(see illustration).**

2C

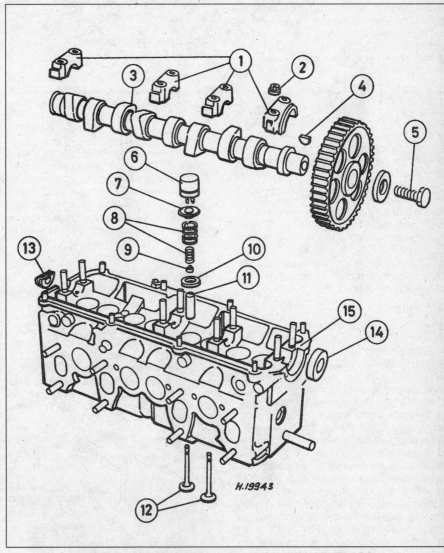

H.19943

4.10 Cylinder head components - engine codes 1F, 2E, AGG

1 Camshaft bearing cap	6 Hydraulic tappet	11 Valve guides
2 Nut	7 Valve spring upper seat	12 Valves
3 Camshaft	8 Valve springs	13 Plug
4 Woodruff key	9 Valve stem seals	14 Camshaft oil seal
5 Camshaft sprocket bolt	10 Valve spring lower seat	15 Cylinder head casting

Engine code ABF

11 At the inlet camshaft, slacken and remove the retaining nuts from bearing caps 5 and 7 plus the additional cap adjacent to the drive chain sprocket, then at bearing caps 6 and 8. Slacken the nuts alternately and diagonally half a turn at a time until they can be removed by hand. At the exhaust camshaft, slacken and remove the retaining nuts from bearing caps 1 and 3 plus the additional caps adjacent to the drive chain and timing belt sprockets, then at bearing caps 2 and 4. Slacken the nuts alternately and diagonally half a turn at a time until they can be removed by hand **(see illustration)**. **Note:** *The exhaust camshaft bearing caps are numbered 1 to 4 from timing belt end - inlet camshaft bearing caps are numbered 5 to 8 from the same end.*

All engine codes

12 Slide the oil seal from the timing sprocket end of the camshaft (exhaust camshaft on engine code ABF) and discard it; a new one must be used on reassembly.

13 Carefully lift the camshaft from the cylinder head; do not tilt it and support both ends as it is removed so that the journals and lobes are not damaged. On engine code ABF, lift out both camshafts at the same time, together with the drive chain. Mark the chain's direction of rotation, to ensure that it is refitted the same way around, when the head is rebuilt later - use a dab of paint for this purpose, do not mark the chain with a scriber or centre-punch as this will risk damaging it.

14 Lift the hydraulic tappets from their bores and store them with the valve contact surface facing downwards, to prevent the oil from draining out. Make a note of the position of each tappet, as they must be fitted to the same valves on reassembly - accelerated wear leading to early failure will result if they are interchanged.

15 Turn the cylinder head over, and rest it on one side. Using a valve spring compressor, compress each valve spring in turn, extracting the split collets when the upper valve spring seat has been pushed far enough down the valve stem to free them. If the spring seat sticks, tap the upper jaw of the compressor with a hammer to free it **(see illustrations)**.

16 Release the valve spring compressor and remove the upper spring seat, valve spring(s) and lower spring seat. **Note:** *Depending on age and specification, engines may have*

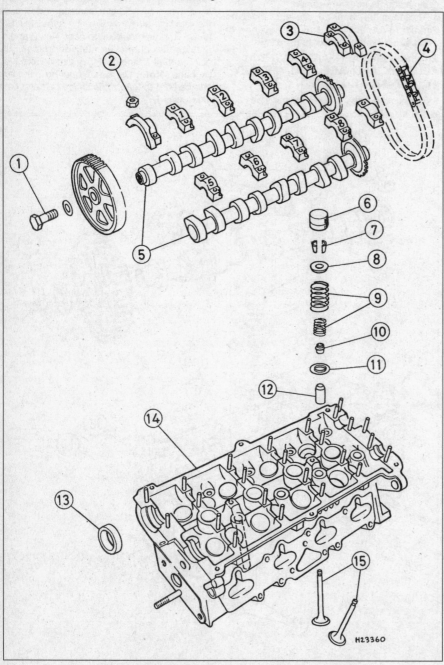

4.15a Valve spring compressor jaws located on the upper spring seat . . .

4.15b . . . and on the valve head

4.11 Cylinder head components - engine code ABF

1 Camshaft sprocket bolt	6 Hydraulic tappet	11 Valve spring lower seat
2 Camshaft bearing cap nut	7 Split collets	12 Valve guide
3 Bearing cap	8 Valve spring upper seat	13 Camshaft oil seal
4 Drive chain	9 Valve spring(s)	14 Cylinder head casting
5 Camshaft	10 Valve stem seal	15 Valves

H23360

concentric double valve springs, or single valve springs with no lower spring seat.

17 Use a pair of pliers to extract the valve stem oil seal. Withdraw the valve itself from the head gasket side of the cylinder head. If the valve sticks in the guide, carefully deburr the end face with fine abrasive paper. Repeat this process for the remaining valves.

18 On engine codes 1Y and AAZ, if the swirl chambers are badly coked or burned and are in need of renewal, insert a pin punch through each injector hole, and carefully drive out the swirl chambers using a mallet **(see illustration)**.

Cleaning

19 Using a suitable degreasing agent, remove all traces of oil deposits from the cylinder head, paying particular attention to the journal bearings, hydraulic tappet bores, valve guides and oilways. Scrape off any traces of old gasket from the mating surfaces, taking care not to score or gouge them. If using emery paper, do not use a grade of less than 100. Turn the head over and using a blunt blade, scrape any carbon deposits from the combustion chambers and ports.
Caution: Do not erode the sealing surface of the valve seat. Finally, wash the entire head casting with a suitable solvent to remove the remaining debris.

20 Clean the valve heads and stems using a fine wire brush. If the valve is heavily coked, scrape off the majority of the deposits with a blunt blade first, then use the wire brush.
Caution: Do not erode the sealing surface of the valve face.

21 Thoroughly clean the remainder of the components using solvent and allow them to dry completely. Discard the oil seals, as new items must be fitted when the cylinder head is reassembled.

Inspection

Cylinder head casting

Note: *On diesel engines the cylinder heads and valves cannot be reworked (although valves may be lapped in), therefore new or exchange units must be obtained.*

22 Examine the head casting closely to identify any damage sustained or cracks that may have developed **(see illustration)**. Pay particular attention to the areas around the mounting holes, valve seats and spark plug holes. If cracking is discovered between the valve seats, the manufacturers state that the cylinder head may be re-used, provided the cracks are no larger than 0.5 mm wide. More serious damage will mean the renewal of the cylinder head casting.

23 Moderately pitted and scorched valve seats can be repaired by lapping the valves in during reassembly, as described later in this Chapter. Badly worn or damaged valve seats may be restored by recutting; this is a highly specialised operation involving precision machining and accurate angle measurement

4.18 Swirl chamber removal (diesel engines 1Y and AAZ)

and as such should be entrusted to a professional cylinder head re-builder.

24 Measure any distortion of the gasket surfaces using a straight edge and a set of feeler blades. Take one measurement longitudinally on both the inlet and exhaust manifold mating surfaces. Take several measurements across the head gasket surface, to assess the level of distortion in all planes **(see illustration)**. Compare the measurements with the figures in the Specifications. On petrol engines, if the head is distorted out of specification, it may be possible to repair it by smoothing down any high-spots on the surface with fine abrasive paper.

25 Minimum cylinder head heights (measured between the cylinder head gasket surface and the cylinder head cover gasket surface), where quoted by the manufacturer, are listed in Specifications. If the cylinder head is to be professionally machined, bear in mind the following:

a) *The minimum cylinder head height dimension (where specified) must be adhered to.*

b) *The valve seats will need to be recut to suit the new height of the cylinder head, otherwise valve to piston crown contact may occur.*

c) *Before the valve seats can be recut, check that there is enough material left on the cylinder head to allow repair; if too much material is removed, the valve stem may protrude too far above the top of the valve guide and this would prevent the hydraulic tappets from operating correctly. Refer to a professional head rebuilder or machine*

4.24 Measuring the distortion of the cylinder head gasket surface

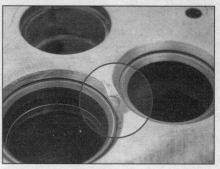

4.22 Look for cracking between the valve seats

shop for advice. **Note:** *Depending on engine type, it may be possible to obtain new valves with shorter valve stems - refer to your Seat dealer for advice.*

Camshaft

26 The camshaft is identified by means of markings stamped onto the side of the shaft, between the inlet and exhaust lobes **(see illustration)**.

27 Visually inspect the camshaft for evidence of wear on the surfaces of the lobes and journals. Normally their surfaces should be smooth and have a dull shine. Look for scoring, erosion or pitting and areas that appear highly polished - these are signs that wear has begun to occur. Accelerated wear will occur once the hardened exterior of the camshaft has been damaged, so always renew worn items. **Note:** *If these symptoms are visible on the tips of the camshaft lobes, check the corresponding tappet, as it will probably be worn as well.*

28 Where applicable, examine the distributor drive gear for signs of wear or damage. Slack in the drive caused by worn gear teeth will affect ignition timing.

29 If the machined surfaces of the camshaft appear discoloured or blued, it is likely that it has been overheated at some point, probably due to inadequate lubrication. This may have distorted the shaft, so check the runout as follows: place the camshaft between two V-blocks and using a DTI gauge, measure the runout at the centre journal. If it exceeds the figure quoted in the Specifications at the start of this Chapter, camshaft renewal should be considered.

2C

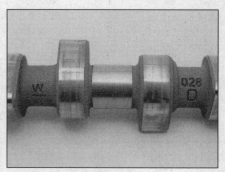

4.26 Camshaft identification markings

4.30 Checking camshaft endfloat using a DTI gauge

30 To measure the camshaft endfloat, temporarily refit the camshaft to the cylinder head, then fit the first and last bearing caps and tighten the retaining nuts to the specified first stage torque setting (on engine codes AER, AAU, AAV, ABD, ABU, AEX, APQ, AEE, ALM, only fit the third bearing cap) - refer to *Reassembly* for details. Anchor a DTI gauge to the timing pulley end of the cylinder head and align the gauge probe with the camshaft axis. Push the camshaft to one end of the cylinder head as far as it will travel, then rest the DTI gauge probe on the end of the camshaft, and zero the gauge display. Push the camshaft as far as it will go to the other end of the cylinder head, and record the gauge reading. Verify the reading by pushing the camshaft back to its original position and checking that the gauge indicates zero again **(see illustration)**. **Note:** *The hydraulic tappets must not be fitted to the cylinder whilst this measurement is being taken.*

31 Check that the camshaft endfloat measurement is within the limit listed in the Specifications. Wear outside of this limit is unlikely to be confined to any one component, so renewal of the camshaft, cylinder head and bearing caps must be considered; seek the advice of a cylinder head rebuilding specialist.

32 The difference between the outside diameters of the camshaft bearing surfaces and the internal diameters formed by the bearing caps and the cylinder head must now be measured, this dimension is known as the camshaft running clearance.

33 The dimensions of the camshaft bearing journals are not quoted by the manufacturer, so running clearance measurement by means of a

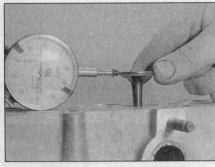

4.48 Measure the maximum deflection of the valve in its guide, using a DTI gauge

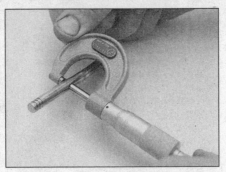

4.44 Measure the diameter of a valve stem with a micrometer

micrometer and a bore gauge or internal vernier calipers cannot be recommended in this case.

34 Another (more accurate) method of measuring the running clearance involves the use of Plastigauge. This is a soft, plastic material supplied in thin 'sticks' of about the same diameter as a sewing needle. Lengths of Plastigauge are cut to length as required, laid on the camshaft bearing journals and crushed as the bearing caps are temporarily fitted and tightened. The Plastigauge spreads widthways as it is crushed; the running clearance can then be determined by measuring the increase in width using the card gauge supplied with the Plastigauge kit.

35 The following paragraphs describe this measurement procedure step by step, but note that a similar method is used to measure the crankshaft running clearances; refer to the illustrations in Section 11 for further guidance.

36 Ensure that the cylinder head, bearing cap and camshaft bearing surfaces are completely clean and dry. Lay the camshaft in position in the cylinder head.

37 Lay a length of Plastigauge on top of each of the camshaft bearing journals.

38 Lubricate each bearing cap with a little silicone release agent, then place them in position over the camshaft and tighten the retaining nuts down to the specified torque - refer to *Reassembly* later in this Section for guidance. **Note:** *Where the torque setting is expressed in several stages, tighten the cap fixings to the first stage only. Do not rotate the camshaft whilst the bearing caps are in place, as the measurements will be affected.*

39 Carefully remove the bearing caps again,

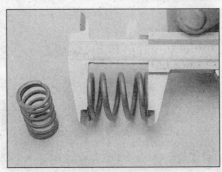

4.50 Measure the free length of each of the valve springs

lifting them vertically away from the camshaft to avoid disturbing the Plastigauge. The Plastigauge should remain on the camshaft bearing surface, squashed into a uniform sausage shape. If it disintegrates as the bearing caps are removed, re-clean the components and repeat the exercise, using a little more release agent on the bearing cap.

40 Hold the scale card supplied with the kit against each bearing journal, and match the width of the crushed Plastigauge with the graduated markings on the card, use this to determine the running clearances.

41 Compare the camshaft running clearance measurements with those listed in the Specifications; if any are outside the specified tolerance, the camshaft and cylinder head should be renewed. Note that undersize camshafts with bearing shells may be obtained from Seat dealers, but only as part of an exchange cylinder head package.

42 On engine code ABF, running clearance measurements must be carried out on both camshafts.

43 On completion, remove the bearing caps and camshaft, and clean away all remaining traces of Plastigauge and silicone release agent.

Valves and associated components

Note: *On all engines, the valve heads cannot be re-cut (although they may be lapped in).*

44 Examine each valve closely for signs of wear. Inspect the valve stems for wear ridges, scoring or variations in diameter; measure their diameters at several points along their lengths with a micrometer **(see illustration)**.

45 The valve heads should not be cracked, badly pitted or charred. Note that light pitting of the valve head can be rectified by grinding-in the valves during reassembly, as described later in this Section.

46 Check that the valve stem end face is free from excessive pitting or indentation; this would be caused by defective hydraulic tappets.

47 Place the valves in a V-block and using a DTI gauge, measure the runout at the valve head. A maximum figure is not quoted by the manufacturer, but the valve should be renewed if the runout appears excessive.

48 Insert each valve into its respective guide in the cylinder head and set up a DTI gauge against the edge of the valve head. With the valve end face flush with the top of the valve guide, measure the maximum side to side deflection of the valve in its guide **(see illustration)**.

49 If the measurement is out of tolerance, the valve and valve guide should be renewed as a pair. **Note:** *Valve guides are an interference fit in the cylinder head and their removal requires access to a hydraulic press. For this reason, it would be wise to entrust the job to an engineering workshop or head rebuilding specialist.*

50 Using vernier calipers, measure the free length of each of the valve springs. As a manufacturer's figure is not quoted, the only way to check the length of the springs is by comparison with a new component. Note that valve springs are usually renewed during a major engine overhaul **(see illustration)**.

4.51 Checking the squareness of a valve spring

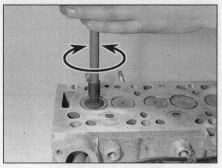

4.54 Grinding-in a valve

4.59a Fitting a swirl chamber (diesel engines 1Y and AAZ)

4.59b Swirl chamber locating recess

51 Stand each spring on its end on a flat surface, against an engineers square **(see illustration)**. Check the squareness of the spring visually; if it appears distorted, renew the spring.

52 Measuring valve spring pre-load involves compressing the valve by applying a specified weight and measuring the reduction in length. This may be a difficult operation to conduct in the home workshop, so it would be wise to approach your local garage or engineering workshop for assistance. Weakened valve springs will at best, increase engine running noise and at worst, cause poor compression, so defective items should be renewed.

Reassembly

Caution: Unless all new components are to be used, maintain groups when refitting valve train components - do not mix components between cylinders and ensure that components are refitted in their original positions.

53 To achieve a gas-tight seal between the valves and their seats, it will be necessary to grind, or lap, the valves in. To complete this process you will need a quantity of fine/coarse grinding paste and a grinding tool - this can either be of the dowel and rubber sucker type, or the automatic type which are driven by a rotary power tool.

54 Smear a small quantity of *fine* grinding paste on the sealing face of the valve head. Turn the cylinder head over so that the combustion chambers are facing upwards and insert the valve into the correct guide. Attach the grinding tool to the valve head and

using a backward/forward rotary action, grind the valve head into its seat. Periodically lift the valve and rotate it to redistribute the grinding paste **(see illustration)**.

55 Continue this process until the contact between valve and seat produces an unbroken, matt grey ring of uniform width, on both faces. Repeat the operation for the remaining valves.

56 If the valves and seats are so badly pitted that coarse grinding paste must be used, check first that there is enough material left on both components to make this operation worthwhile - if too little material is left remaining, the valve stems may protrude too far above their guides, impeding the correct operation of the hydraulic tappets. Refer to a machine shop or cylinder head rebuilding specialist for advice.

57 Assuming the repair is feasible, work as described in the previous paragraph but use the coarse grinding paste initially, to achieve a dull finish on the valve face and seat. Then, wash off coarse paste with solvent and repeat the process using fine grinding paste to obtain the correct finish.

58 When all the valves have been ground in, remove all traces of grinding paste from the cylinder head and valves with solvent, and allow them to dry completely.

59 Where necessary on diesel engines (engine code 1Y and AAZ only), fit new swirl chambers by driving them squarely into their housings with a mallet - use a block of wood to protect the face of the swirl chamber. Note the locating recess on the side of the chamber and the corresponding groove in the housing **(see illustrations)**.

60 On completion, the projection of the swirl chamber from the face of the cylinder head must be measured using a DTI gauge and compared with the limit quoted in the Specifications **(see illustration)**. If this limit is exceeded, there is a risk that the chamber may be struck by the piston, and in this case the advice of a professional cylinder head rebuilder or machine shop should be sought.

61 Turn the head over and place it on a stand, or wooden blocks. Where applicable, fit the first lower spring seat into place, with the convex side facing the cylinder head **(see illustration)**.

62 Working on one valve at a time, lubricate the valve stem with clean engine oil, and insert it into the guide. Fit one of the protective plastic sleeves supplied with the new valve stem oil seals over the valve end face - this will protect the oil seal whilst it is being fitted **(see illustrations)**.

2C

4.60 Measuring swirl chamber projection using a DTI gauge

4.61 Fit the lower spring set in place, with the convex face facing the cylinder head

4.62a Lubricate the valve stem with clean engine oil and insert it into the guide

4.62b Fit one of the protective plastic sleeves over the valve end face

4.63a Fit a new valve stem seal over the valve

4.63b Use a long-reach socket to press on the oil seal

63 Dip a new valve stem seal in clean engine oil, and carefully push it over the valve and onto the top of the valve guide - take care not to damage the stem seal as it passes over the valve end face. Use a suitable long reach socket to press it firmly into position (see illustrations).

64 Locate the valve spring(s) over the valve stem (see illustration). Where a lower spring seat is fitted, ensure that the springs locate squarely on the stepped surface of the seat. Note: Depending on age and specification, engines may have either concentric double valve springs, or single valve springs with no lower spring seat.

65 Fit the upper seat over the top of the springs, then using a valve spring compressor, compress the springs until the upper seat is pushed beyond the collet grooves in the valve stem. Refit the split

collet, using a dab of grease to hold the two halves in the grooves (see illustrations). Gradually release the spring compressor, checking that the collet remains correctly seated as the spring extends. When correctly seated, the upper seat should force the two halves of the collet together, and hold them securely in the grooves in the end of the valve.

66 Repeat this process for the remaining sets of valve components. To settle the components after installation, strike the end of each valve stem with a mallet, using a block of wood to protect the stem from damage. Check before progressing any further that the spilt collets remain firmly held in the end of the valve stem by the upper spring seat.

67 Smear some clean engine oil onto the sides of the hydraulic tappets, and fit them into position in their bores in the cylinder head. Push them down until they contact the

valves, then lubricate the camshaft lobe contact surfaces (see illustration).

68 Lubricate the camshaft and cylinder head bearing journals with clean engine oil, then carefully lower the camshaft into position on the cylinder head. Support the ends of the shaft as it is inserted, to avoid damaging the lobes and journals (see illustrations).

69 On engine ABF, locate the drive chain on the inlet and exhaust camshafts (observing the direction of rotation markings made earlier) such that the timing marks line up as shown. Lower the camshafts and chain onto the cylinder head, ensuring that the marks remain aligned (see illustration).

70 On all engine codes except ABF, turn the camshaft so that the lobes for No 1 cylinder are pointing upwards.

71 On diesel engines, with reference to Chapter 2B, lubricate the lip of a new

4.64 Fitting a valve spring

4.65a Fit the upper seat over the top of the valve spring

4.65b Use grease to hold the two halves of the split collet in the groove

4.67 Fit the tappets into their bores in the cylinder head

4.68a Lubricate the camshaft bearings with clean engine oil . . .

4.68b . . . then lower the camshaft into position on the cylinder head

4.69 On engine code ABF, ensure that the timing marks remain aligned

4.71 Fitting the camshaft oil seal (diesel engines)

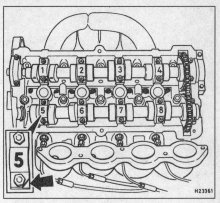

4.73 On engine code ABF, the bearing caps have recesses (arrowed)

camshaft oil seal with clean engine oil and locate it over the end of the camshaft. Slide the seal along the camshaft until it locates in the lower half of its housing in the cylinder head **(see illustration)**.

72 Oil the upper surfaces of the camshaft bearing journals, then fit the bearing caps in place. Ensure that they are fitted the right way around and in the correct locations, then fit and tighten the retaining nuts, as follows. **Note:** *New bearing cap retaining nuts must be used on reassembly for all engine codes.*

Engine code ABF

73 The bearing caps have recesses machined into one corner; these recesses must face the inlet side of the cylinder head **(see illustration)**.

74 Fit caps Nos 6 and 8 over the inlet camshaft, and tighten the retaining nuts alternately and diagonally to the specified torque.

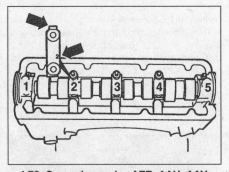

4.78 On engine codes AER, AAU, AAV, ABD, ABU, AEX, APQ, AEE, ALM, the bearing caps are fitted as shown

75 Fit the remaining inlet camshaft caps and tighten the nuts to the specified torque.

76 Fit caps Nos 2 and 4 to the exhaust camshaft and tighten the retaining nuts to the specified torque.

77 Locate the remaining caps over the exhaust camshaft, then fit and tighten the nuts to the specified torque.

Engine codes AER, AAU, AAV, ABD, ABU, AEX, APQ, AEE, ALM

78 The bearing caps have their respective cylinder numbers stamped onto them, and have an elongated lug on one side. When correctly fitted, the numbers should be readable from the exhaust side of the cylinder head, and the lugs should face the inlet side of the cylinder head **(see illustration)**.

79 Fit caps Nos 2 and 4 over the camshaft and tighten the retaining nuts alternately and diagonally to the specified Stage 1 torque.

80 Smear the mating surfaces of caps Nos 1 and 5 with sealant then fit them, together with cap No 3, over the camshaft and tighten the nuts to the specified first stage torque.

81 Tighten all bearing caps to the Stage 2 torque, then fit the bolts to bearing cap No 5 and tighten them to the specified torque.

Engine codes 1F, 2E, AGG, AFT

82 The bearing cap mounting holes are drilled off-centre; ensure they are fitted the correct way round (refer to illustration 4.85).

83 On engines with 4 caps, fit caps Nos 2 and 5 over the camshaft and tighten the retaining nuts alternately and diagonally to the specified torque. Now smear the mating

surfaces of cap No 1 with sealant and refit caps Nos 1 and 3, tightening the nuts progressively to the specified torque.

84 On engines with 5 caps, fit caps Nos 2 and 4 over the camshaft and tighten the retaining nuts alternately and diagonally to the specified torque. Now smear the mating surfaces of cap No 1 with sealant and refit caps Nos 1, 3 and 5, tightening the nuts progressively to the specified torque.

Engine codes AEY, 1Y, AAZ, 1Z, AHU, AFN

85 The bearing cap mounting holes are drilled off-centre; ensure that they are fitted the correct way around **(see illustration)**.

86 Fit caps Nos 2 and 4 over the camshaft, and tighten the retaining nuts alternately and diagonally to the specified torque.

87 Smear the mating surfaces of cap No 1 with sealant then fit it, together with cap Nos 3 and 5, over the camshaft and tighten the nuts to the specified torque **(see illustration)**.

All engine codes

88 With reference to Chapter 2A or 2B as applicable, lubricate the lip of a new camshaft oil seal with clean engine oil, and locate it over the end of the camshaft. Using a mallet and a long-reach socket of an appropriate diameter, drive the seal squarely into its housing until it bears against the inner stop - do not attempt to force it in any further **(see illustration)**.

2C

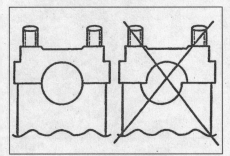

4.85 On engine codes 1F, 2E, AGG, AFT, AEY, 1Y, AAZ, 1Z, AHU, AFN, the camshaft bearing cap holes are drilled off-centre

4.87 Smear the mating surfaces of cap No 1 with sealant

4.88 Fitting a new camshaft oil seal

4.91 Fit the coolant elbow, using a new O-ring or gasket

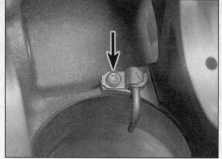

5.5a Remove the piston cooling jet retaining screw (arrowed) . . .

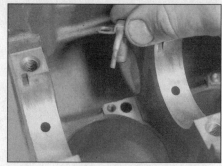

5.5b . . . and withdraw the jet from its mounting hole

89 With reference to Chapter 2A or 2B as applicable, carry out the following:
 a) *Refit the timing belt sprocket to the camshaft.*
 b) *Refit the inlet and exhaust manifolds, complete with new gaskets.*
90 Refit the coolant sensor and oil pressure switch.
91 Refit the coolant outlet elbow, using a new gasket/O-ring as necessary **(see illustration)**.
92 On diesel engines, refit the fuel injectors and glow plugs, with reference to Chapter 4C and 5C.
93 Refer to Chapter 2A or 2B as applicable, and refit the cylinder head to the cylinder block.

5 Pistons and connecting rods - removal and inspection

Removal

1 Refer to Part A or B of this Chapter (as applicable) and remove the cylinder head, flywheel, sump and baffle plate, oil pump and pickup.
2 Inspect the tops of the cylinder bores. Any

wear ridges found at the point where the pistons reach top dead centre must be removed, otherwise the pistons may be damaged when they are pushed out of their bores. This can be accomplished with a scraper or ridge reamer.
3 Scribe the number of each piston on its crown, noting that No 1 is at the timing belt end of the engine.
4 Using a set of feeler blades, measure the big-end to crankpin web thrust clearance at each connecting rod, and record the measurements.
5 Where applicable, remove the retaining screw and withdraw the piston cooling jets from their mounting holes. On engine codes 2E and ABF, the jet mounting incorporates a pressure relief valve, take care to avoid damaging it during removal **(see illustrations)**.
6 Rotate the crankshaft until pistons No 1 and 4 are at bottom dead centre. Unless they are already identified, mark the big-end bearing caps and connecting rods with their respective piston numbers, using a centre-punch or a scribe **(see illustration)**. Note the orientation of the bearing caps in relation to the connecting rod. It may be difficult to see

the manufacturer's markings at this stage, so scribe alignment arrows on them both to ensure correct reassembly. Unbolt the bearing cap bolts/nuts, half a turn at a time, until they can be removed by hand. Recover the bottom shell bearing, and tape it to the cap for safe keeping. Note that if the shell bearings are to be re-used, they must be refitted to the same connecting rod.
7 On certain engines, the bearing cap bolts remain in the connecting rod and the caps are secured with nuts. In this case the threads of the bolts should be covered with insulating tape, to prevent them from scratching the crankpins and cylinder bores when the pistons are removed **(see illustration)**.
8 Drive the pistons out of the top of their bores by pushing on the connecting rods with a piece of dowel or a hammer handle. As the piston and connecting rod emerge, recover the top shell bearing and tape it to the connecting rod for safekeeping.
9 Turn the crankshaft through half a turn and working as described above, remove No 2 and 3 pistons and connecting rods. Remember to maintain the components in their cylinder groups, whilst they are in a dismantled state.

5.6 Mark the big-end caps and connecting rods with their piston numbers (arrowed)

5.7 Cover the bolt threads with tape

10 Insert a small flat-bladed screwdriver into the removal slot and prise the gudgeon pin circlips from each piston. Push out the gudgeon pin, and separate the piston and connecting rod **(see illustrations)**. Discard the circlips as new items must be fitted on reassembly. If the pin proves difficult to remove, heat the piston to 60°C with hot water - the resulting expansion will then allow the two components to be separated.

Inspection

11 Before an inspection of the pistons can be carried out, the existing piston rings must be removed, using a removal/installation tool, or an old feeler blade if such a tool is not available. Always remove the upper piston rings first, expanding them to clear the piston crown. The rings are very brittle and will snap if they are stretched too much - sharp edges are produced when this happens, so protect your eyes and hands. Discard the rings on removal, as new items must be fitted when the engine is reassembled **(see illustration)**.

12 Use a section of old piston ring to scrape the carbon deposits out of the ring grooves, taking care not to score or gouge the edges of the groove.

13 Carefully scrape away all traces of carbon from the top of the piston. A hand-held wire brush (or a piece of fine emery cloth) can be used, once the majority of the deposits have been scraped away. Be careful not to remove any metal from the piston, as it is relatively soft. **Note:** *Take care to preserve the piston number markings that were made during removal.*

14 Once the deposits have been removed, clean the pistons and connecting rods with paraffin or a suitable solvent, and dry thoroughly. Make sure that the oil return holes in the ring grooves are clear.

15 Examine the piston for signs of excessive wear or damage. Some normal wear will be apparent, in the form of a vertical grain on the piston thrust surfaces and a slight looseness of the top compression ring in its groove. Abnormal wear should be carefully examined, to assess whether the component is still serviceable and what the cause of the wear might be.

16 Scuffing or scoring of the piston skirt may

5.10a Insert a small screwdriver into the slot and prise off the gudgeon pin circlips

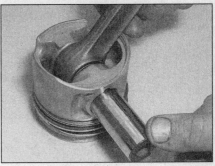

5.10b Push out the gudgeon pin and separate the piston and connecting rod

indicate that the engine has been overheating, through inadequate cooling, lubrication or abnormal combustion temperatures. Scorch marks on the skirt indicate that blow - by has occurred, perhaps caused by worn bores or piston rings. Burnt areas on the piston crown are usually an indication of pre-ignition, pinking or detonation. In extreme cases, the piston crown may be melted by operating under these conditions. Corrosion pit marks in the piston crown indicate that coolant has seeped into the combustion chamber and/or the crankcase. The faults causing these symptoms must be corrected before the engine is brought back into service, or the same damage will recur.

17 Check the pistons, connecting rods, gudgeon pins and bearing caps for cracks. Lay the connecting rods on a flat surface, and look along the length to see if it appears bent or twisted. If you have doubts about their condition, get them measured at an engineering workshop. Inspect the small-end bush bearing for signs of wear or cracking.

18 Using a micrometer, measure the diameter of all four pistons at a point 10 mm from the bottom of the skirt, at right angles to the gudgeon pin axis **(see illustration)**. Compare the measurements with those listed in the Specifications. If the piston diameter is out of the tolerance band listed for its particular size, then it must be renewed. **Note:** *If the cylinder block was re-bored during a previous overhaul, oversize pistons may have been fitted.* Record the measurements and use them to check the piston clearances

when the cylinder bores are measured, later in this Chapter.

19 Hold a new piston ring in the appropriate groove and measure the ring-to-groove clearance using a feeler blade **(see illustration)**. Note that the rings are of different widths, so use the correct ring for the groove. Compare the measurements with those listed. If the clearances are outside of the tolerance band, then the piston must be renewed. Confirm this by checking the width of the piston ring with a micrometer.

20 The gudgeon pin must be a firm sliding fit in the piston. If there is excessive play, the piston and connecting rod bush will have to be resized and a new gudgeon pin installed. An engineering workshop will have the equipment needed to undertake a job of this nature.

21 The orientation of the piston with respect to the connecting rod must be correct when the two are reassembled. The piston crown is marked with an arrow (which may be obscured by carbon deposits); this must point towards the timing belt end of the engine when the piston is installed. The connecting rod and its bearing cap both have recesses machined into them, close to their mating surfaces - these recesses must both face the same way as the arrow on the piston crown (ie towards the timing belt end of the engine) when correctly installed **(see illustration overleaf)**. Reassemble the two components to satisfy this requirement. **Note:** *On certain engines, the connecting rod big-ends are provided with offset dowels which locate in holes in the bearing caps.*

2C

5.11 Piston rings can be removed using an old feeler blade

5.18 Using a micrometer, measure the diameter of all four pistons

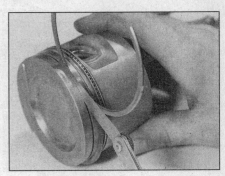

5.19 Measuring the piston ring-to-groove clearance using a feeler blade

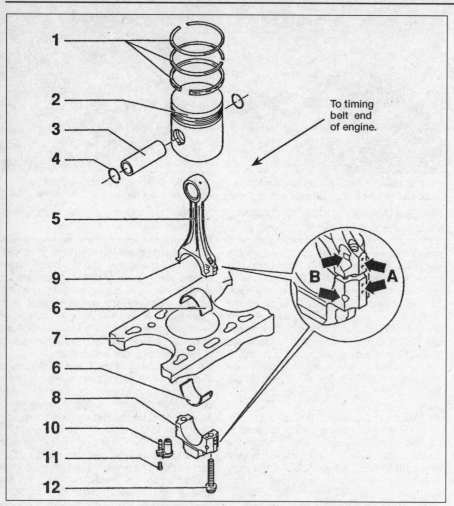

5.21 Piston assembly (engine code AAZ shown - other engines similar)

1	Piston rings	6	Big-end bearing shell
2	Piston	7	Top of cylinder block
3	Gudgeon pin	8	Big-end bearing cap
4	Circlip	9	Locating dowel (where applicable)
5	Connecting rod		

10 Oil jet for piston cooling (where applicable)
11 Oil jet retaining screw
12 Big-end bearing cap bolts

A Connecting rod/bearing cap identification marks

B Connecting rod/bearing cap orientation marks

22 Lubricate the gudgeon pin and small-end bush with clean engine oil. Slide the pin into the piston, engaging the connecting rod small-end. Fit two new circlips to the piston at either end of the gudgeon pin, such that their open ends are facing 180° away from the removal slot in the piston. Repeat this operation for the remaining pistons.

6 Crankshaft - removal and inspection

Removal

1 Note: *If no work is to be done on the pistons and connecting rods, then removal of the cylinder head and pistons will not be necessary. Instead, the pistons need only be pushed far enough up the bores so that they are positioned clear of the crankpins. The use of an engine stand is strongly recommended.*

2 With reference to Chapter 2A or 2B as applicable, carry out the following:
  a) *Remove the crankshaft timing belt sprocket.*
  b) *Remove the clutch components and flywheel.*
  c) *Remove the sump, baffle plate, oil pump and pickup.*
  d) *Remove the front and rear crankshaft oil seals and their housings.*

3 Remove the pistons and connecting rods, as described in Section 5 (refer to the Note above).

4 Carry out a check of the crankshaft endfloat, as follows. **Note:** *This can only be accomplished when the crankshaft is still installed in the cylinder block/crankcase, but is free to move.* Set up a DTI gauge so that the probe is in line with the crankshaft axis and is in contact with a fixed point on the end of the crankshaft. Push the crankshaft along its axis to the end of its travel, and then zero the gauge. Push the crankshaft fully the other way, and record the endfloat indicated on the dial **(see illustration)**. Compare the result with the figure given in the Specifications and establish whether new thrustwashers are required.

5 If a dial gauge is not available, feeler blades can be used. First push the crankshaft fully towards the flywheel end of the engine, then use a feeler blade to measure the gap between cylinder No 3 crankpin web and the main bearing thrustwasher **(see illustration)**. Compare the results with the Specifications.

6 Observe the manufacturer's identification marks on the main bearing caps. The number relates to the position in the crankcase, as counted from the timing belt end of the engine **(see illustration)**.

6.4 Measuring crankshaft endfloat using a DTI gauge

6.5 Measuring crankshaft endfloat using feeler blades

6.6 Manufacturer's identification markings on the main bearing caps (arrowed)

7 Loosen the main bearing cap bolts one quarter of a turn at a time, until they can be removed by hand. Using a soft-faced mallet, strike the caps lightly to free them from the crankcase. Recover the lower main bearing shells, taping them to the cap for safekeeping. Mark them with indelible ink to aid identification, but do not score or scratch them in any way.

8 Carefully lift the crankshaft out, taking care not to dislodge the upper main bearing shells **(see illustration)**. It would be wise to get an assistant's help, as the crankshaft is heavy. Set it down on a clean, level surface and chock it with blocks to prevent it from rolling.

9 Extract the upper main bearing shells from the crankcase, and tape them to their respective bearing caps. Remove the two thrustwasher bearings from either side of No 3 crank web.

10 With the shell bearings removed, observe the recesses machined into the bearing caps and crankcase - these provide location for the lugs which protrude from the shell bearings and so prevent them from being fitted incorrectly.

Inspection

11 Wash the crankshaft in a suitable solvent and allow it to dry. Flush the oil holes thoroughly, to ensure they are not blocked - use a pipe cleaner or a needle brush if necessary. Remove any sharp edges from the edge of the hole which may damage the new bearings when they are installed.

12 Inspect the main bearing and crankpin journals carefully; if uneven wear, cracking,

7.2 Check the intermediate shaft endfloat using a DTI gauge

6.8 Lifting the crankshaft from the crankcase

scoring or pitting are evident then the crankshaft should be reground by an engineering workshop, and refitted to the engine with undersize bearings.

13 Use a micrometer to measure the diameter of each main bearing journal **(see illustration)**. Taking a number of measurements on the surface of each journal will reveal if it is worn unevenly. Differences in diameter measured at 90° intervals indicate that the journal is out of round. Differences in diameter measured along the length of the journal, indicate that the journal is tapered. Again, if wear is detected, the crankshaft must be reground by an engineering workshop, and undersize bearings will be needed (refer to *Reassembly*)

14 Check the oil seal journals at either end of the crankshaft. If they appear excessively scored or damaged, they may cause the new seals to leak when the engine is reassembled. It may be possible to repair the journal; seek the advice of an engineering workshop or your Seat dealer.

15 Measure the crankshaft runout by setting up a DTI gauge on the centre main bearing and rotating the shaft in V-blocks. The maximum deflection of the gauge will indicate the runout. Take precautions to protect the bearing journals and oil seal mating surfaces from damage during this procedure. A maximum runout figure is not quoted by the manufacturer, but use the figure of 0.05 mm as a rough guide. If the runout exceeds this figure, crankshaft renewal should be considered - consult your Seat dealer or an engine rebuilding specialist for advice.

6.13 Use a micrometer to measure the diameter of each main bearing journal

16 Refer to Section 9 for details of main and big-end bearing inspection.

7 Intermediate shaft - removal and refitting

Note: *This Section does not apply to engine codes AER, AAU, AAV, ABD, ABU, AEX, APQ, AEE, ALM.*

Removal

1 Refer to Chapter 2A or 2B and carry out the following:

a) *Remove the timing belt.*

b) *Remove the intermediate shaft sprocket.*

2 Before the shaft is removed, the endfloat must be checked. Anchor a DTI gauge to the cylinder block with its probe in line with the intermediate shaft centre axis. Push the shaft into the cylinder block to the end of its travel, zero the DTI gauge and then draw the shaft out to the opposite end of its travel. Record the maximum deflection and compare the figure with that listed in Specifications - renew the shaft if the endfloat exceeds this limit **(see illustration)**.

3 Slacken the retaining bolts and withdraw the intermediate shaft flange. Recover the O-ring seal, then press out the oil seal **(see illustrations)**.

4 Withdraw the intermediate shaft from the cylinder block and inspect the drive gear at the end of the shaft; if the teeth show signs of excessive wear, or are damaged in any way, the shaft should be renewed.

2C

7.3a Slacken the retaining bolts (arrowed) . . .

7.3b . . . and withdraw the intermediate shaft flange

7.3c Press out the oil seal . . .

5 If the oil seal has been leaking, check the shaft mating surface for signs of scoring or damage.

Refitting

6 Liberally oil the intermediate shaft bearing surfaces and drive gear, then carefully guide the shaft into the cylinder block and engage the journal at the leading end with its support bearing.

7 Press a new shaft oil seal into its housing in the intermediate shaft flange and fit a new O-ring seal to the inner sealing surface of the flange.

8 Lubricate the inner lip of the seal with clean engine oil, and slide the flange and seal over the end of the intermediate shaft. Ensure that the O-ring is correctly seated, then fit the flange retaining bolts and tighten them to the specified torque. Check that the intermediate shaft can rotate freely.

9 With reference to Chapter 2A or 2B, carry out the following:

a) *Refit the timing belt sprocket to the intermediate shaft and tighten the centre bolt to the specified torque.*

b) *Refit the timing belt. Where applicable on petrol models, follow the intermediate sprocket alignment instructions carefully to ensure that the distributor drive gear alignment is preserved.*

8 Cylinder block/ crankcase casting - cleaning and inspection

Cleaning

1 Remove all external components and electrical switches/sensors from the block. For complete cleaning, the core plugs should ideally be removed. Drill a small hole in the plugs, then insert a self-tapping screw into the hole. Extract the plugs by pulling on the screw with a pair of grips, or by using a slide hammer.

2 Scrape all traces of gasket and sealant from the cylinder block/crankcase, taking care not to damage the sealing surfaces.

3 Remove all oil gallery plugs (where fitted). The plugs are usually very tight - they may

8.6 To clean the cylinder block threads, run a correct-size tap into the holes

7.3d . . . then recover the O-ring seal

have to be drilled out, and the holes re-tapped. Use new plugs when the engine is reassembled.

4 If the casting is extremely dirty, it should be steam-cleaned. After this, clean all oil holes and galleries one more time. Flush all internal passages with warm water until the water runs clear. Dry thoroughly, and apply a light film of oil to all mating surfaces and cylinder bores, to prevent rusting. If you have access to compressed air, use it to speed up the drying process, and to blow out all the oil holes and galleries.

 Warning: Wear eye protection when using compressed air!

5 If the castings are not very dirty, you can do an adequate cleaning job with hot, soapy water and a stiff brush. Take plenty of time, and do a thorough job. Regardless of the cleaning method used, be sure to clean all oil holes and galleries very thoroughly, and to dry all components well. Protect the cylinder bores as described above, to prevent rusting.

6 All threaded holes must be clean, to ensure accurate torque readings during reassembly. To clean the threads, run the correct-size tap into each of the holes to remove rust, corrosion, thread sealant or sludge, and to restore damaged threads **(see illustration)**. If possible, use compressed air to clear the holes of debris produced by this operation. **Note:** *Take extra care to exclude all cleaning liquid from blind tapped holes, as the casting may be cracked by hydraulic action if a bolt is threaded into a hole containing liquid.*

7 Apply suitable sealant to the new oil gallery plugs, and insert them into the holes in the block. Tighten them securely.

8 If the engine is not going to be reassembled immediately, cover it with a large plastic bag to keep it clean; protect all mating surfaces and the cylinder bores as described above, to prevent rusting.

Inspection

9 Visually check the casting for cracks and corrosion. Look for stripped threads in the threaded holes. If there has been any history of internal water leakage, it may be worthwhile having an engine overhaul specialist check the cylinder block/crankcase with professional

equipment. If defects are found, have them renewed or if possible, repaired.

10 Check the cylinder bores for scuffing or scoring. Any evidence of this kind of damage should be cross-checked with an inspection of the pistons (see Section 5 of this Chapter). If the damage is in its early stages, it may be possible to repair the block by reboring it. Seek the advice of an engineering workshop before you progress.

11 To allow an accurate assessment of the wear in the cylinder bores to be made, their diameter must be measured at a number of points, as follows. Insert a bore gauge into bore No 1 and take three measurements in line with the crankshaft axis; one at the top of the bore, roughly 10 mm below the bottom of the wear ridge, one halfway down the bore and one at a point roughly 10 mm from the bottom of the bore. **Note:** *Stand the cylinder block squarely on a workbench during this procedure, inaccurate results may be obtained if the measurements are taken when the engine mounted on a stand.*

12 Rotate the bore gauge through 90°, so that it is at right angles to the crankshaft axis and repeat the measurements detailed in paragraph 11 **(see illustration)**. Record all six measurements, and compare them with the data listed in the Specifications. If the difference in diameter between any two cylinders exceeds the wear limit, or if any one cylinder exceeds its maximum bore diameter, then *all four* cylinders will have to be rebored and oversize pistons will have to be fitted. Note that the imbalances produced by not reboring all the cylinders together would render the engine unusable.

13 Use the piston diameter measurements recorded earlier (see Section 5) to calculate the piston-to-bore clearances. Figures are not available from the manufacturer, so seek the advice of your engine reconditioning specialist.

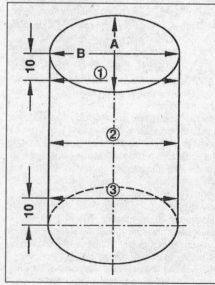

8.12 Bore measurement points

14 Place the cylinder block on a level work surface, crankcase downwards. Use a straight edge and a set of feeler blades to measure the distortion of the cylinder head mating surface in both planes. A maximum figure is not quoted by the manufacturer, but use the figure of 0.05 mm as a rough guide. If the measurement exceeds this figure, repair may be possible by machining - consult your dealer for advice.

15 Before the engine can be reassembled, the cylinder bores must be honed. This process involves using an abrasive tool to produce a fine, cross-hatch pattern on the inner surface of the bore. This has the effect of seating the piston rings, resulting in a good seal between the piston and cylinder. There are two types of honing tool available to the home mechanic, both are driven by a rotary power tool, such as a drill. The bottle brush hone is a stiff, cylindrical brush with abrasive stones bonded to its bristles. The more conventional surfacing hone has abrasive stones mounted on spring-loaded legs. For the inexperienced home mechanic, satisfactory results will be achieved more easily using the Bottle Brush hone. **Note:** *If you are unwilling to tackle cylinder bore honing, an engineering workshop will be able to carry out the job for you at a reasonable cost.*

16 Carry out the honing as follows; you will need one of the honing tools described above, a power drill/air wrench, a supply of clean rags, some honing oil and a pair of safety glasses.

17 Fit the honing tool in the drill chuck. Lubricate the cylinder bores with honing oil and insert the honing tool into the first bore, compressing the stones to allow it to fit. Turn on the drill and as the tool rotates, move it up and down in the bore at a rate that produces a fine cross-hatch pattern on the surface. The lines of the pattern should ideally cross at about 50 to 60° **(see illustration)**, although some piston ring manufacturer's may quote a different angle; check the literature supplied with the new rings.

⚠️ *Warning: Wear safety glasses to protect your eyes from debris flying off the honing tool.*

18 Use plenty of oil during the honing process. Do not remove any more material than is necessary to produce the required finish. When removing the hone tool from the bore, do not pull it out whilst it is still rotating; maintain the up/down movement until the chuck has stopped, then withdraw the tool whilst rotating the chuck by hand, in the normal direction of rotation.

19 Wipe out the oil and swarf with a rag and proceed to the next bore. When all four bores have been honed, thoroughly clean the whole cylinder block in hot soapy water to remove all traces of honing oil and debris. The block is clean when a clean rag, moistened with new engine oil does not pick up any grey residue when wiped along the bore.

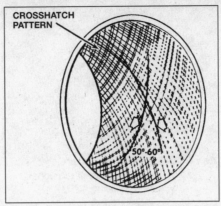

8.17 Cylinder bore honing pattern

20 Apply a light coating of engine oil to the mating surfaces and cylinder bores to prevent rust forming. Store the block in a plastic bag until reassembly.

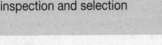

9 Main and big-end bearings - inspection and selection

Inspection

1 Even though the main and big-end bearings should be renewed during the engine overhaul, the old bearings should be retained for close examination, as they may reveal valuable information about the condition of the engine **(see illustration)**.

2 Bearing failure can occur due to lack of lubrication, the presence of dirt or other foreign particles, overloading the engine, or corrosion. Regardless of the cause of bearing failure, the cause must be corrected before

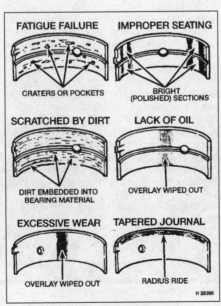

9.1 Typical bearing failures

the engine is reassembled, to prevent it from happening again.

3 When examining the bearing shells, remove them from the cylinder block/crankcase, the main bearing caps, the connecting rods and the connecting rod big-end bearing caps. Lay them out on a clean surface in the same general position as their location in the engine. This will enable you to match any bearing problems with the corresponding crankshaft journal. *Do not* touch any shell's internal bearing surface with your fingers while checking it, or the delicate surface may be scratched.

4 Dirt and other foreign matter gets into the engine in a variety of ways. It may be left in the engine during assembly, or it may pass through filters or the crankcase ventilation system. It may get into the oil, and from there into the bearings. Metal chips from machining operations and normal engine wear are often present. Abrasives are sometimes left in engine components after reconditioning, especially when parts are not thoroughly cleaned using the proper cleaning methods. Whatever the source, these foreign objects often end up embedded in the soft bearing material, and are easily recognised. Large particles will not embed in the bearing, but will score or gouge the bearing and journal. The best prevention for this cause of bearing failure is to clean all parts thoroughly, and keep everything spotlessly-clean during engine assembly. Frequent and regular engine oil and filter changes are also recommended.

5 Lack of lubrication (or lubrication breakdown) has a number of interrelated causes. Excessive heat (which thins the oil), overloading (which squeezes the oil from the bearing face) and oil leakage (from excessive bearing clearances, worn oil pump or high engine speeds) all contribute to lubrication breakdown. Blocked oil passages, which usually are the result of misaligned oil holes in a bearing shell, will also oil-starve a bearing, and destroy it. When lack of lubrication is the cause of bearing failure, the bearing material is wiped or extruded from the steel backing of the bearing. Temperatures may increase to the point where the steel backing turns blue from overheating.

6 Driving habits can have a definite effect on bearing life. Full-throttle, low-speed operation (labouring the engine) puts very high loads on bearings, tending to squeeze out the oil film. These loads cause the bearings to flex, which produces fine cracks in the bearing face (fatigue failure). Eventually, the bearing material will loosen in pieces, and tear away from the steel backing.

7 Short-distance driving leads to corrosion of bearings, because insufficient engine heat is produced to drive off the condensed water and corrosive gases. These products collect in the engine oil, forming acid and sludge. As the oil is carried to the engine bearings, the acid attacks and corrodes the bearing material.

2C

8 Incorrect bearing installation during engine assembly will lead to bearing failure as well. Tight-fitting bearings leave insufficient bearing running clearance, and will result in oil starvation. Dirt or foreign particles trapped behind a bearing shell result in high spots on the bearing, which lead to failure.

9 *Do not* touch any shell's internal bearing surface with your fingers during reassembly; there is a risk of scratching the delicate surface, or of depositing particles of dirt on it.

10 As mentioned at the beginning of this Section, the bearing shells should be renewed as a matter of course during engine overhaul; to do otherwise is false economy.

Selection - main and big-end bearings

11 Main and big-end bearings for the engines described in this Chapter are available in standard sizes and a range of undersizes to suit reground crankshafts - refer to Specifications for details.

12 The running clearances will need to be checked when the crankshaft is refitted with its new bearings (see Section 11).

10 Engine overhaul - reassembly sequence

1 Before reassembly begins, ensure that all new parts have been obtained, and that all necessary tools are available. Read through the entire procedure to familiarise yourself with the work involved, and to ensure that all items necessary for reassembly of the engine are at hand. In addition to all normal tools and materials, thread-locking compound will be needed. A suitable tube of liquid sealant will also be required for the joint faces that are without gaskets. It is recommended that the manufacturer's own products are used, which are specially formulated for this purpose.

2 In order to save time and avoid problems,

10.2 Auxiliary drivebelt tensioner (engine code APQ)

engine reassembly should ideally be carried out in the following order:

a) *Crankshaft.*
b) *Piston/connecting rod assemblies.*
c) *Oil pump (see Chapter 2A or 2B).*
d) *Sump (see Chapter 2A or 2B).*
e) *Flywheel (see Chapter 2A or 2B).*
f) *Cylinder head and gasket (Chapter 2A or 2B).*
g) *Timing belt tensioner, sprockets and timing belt (see Chapter 2A or 2B).*
h) *Engine external components and ancillaries.*
i) *Auxiliary drivebelts, pulleys and tensioners (see illustration).*

3 At this stage, all engine components should be absolutely clean and dry, with all faults repaired. The components should be laid out (or in individual containers) on a completely clean work surface.

11 Crankshaft - refitting and running clearance check

1 Crankshaft refitting is the first stage of engine reassembly following overhaul. At this point, it is assumed that the crankshaft, cylinder block/crankcase and bearings have

been cleaned, inspected and reconditioned or renewed.

2 Place the cylinder block on a clean, level worksurface, with the crankcase facing upwards. Unbolt the bearing caps and carefully release them from the crankcase; lay them out in order to ensure correct reassembly. If they are still in place, remove the bearing shells from the caps and the crankcase and wipe out the inner surfaces with a clean rag - they must be kept spotlessly clean.

3 Clean the rear surface of the new bearing shells with a rag and lay them on the bearing saddles. Ensure that the orientation lugs on the shells engage with the recesses in the saddles, and that the oil holes are correctly aligned (see illustration). Do not hammer or otherwise force the bearing shells into place. It is critically important that the surfaces of the bearings are kept free from damage and contamination.

4 Give the newly-fitted bearing shells and the crankshaft journals a final clean with a rag. Check that the oil holes in the crankshaft are free from dirt, as any left here will become embedded in the new bearings when the engine is first started.

5 Carefully lay the crankshaft in the crankcase, taking care not to dislodge the bearing shells.

Running clearance check

6 When the crankshaft and bearings are refitted, a clearance must exist between them to allow lubricant to circulate. This clearance is impossible to check using feeler blades, so Plastigauge is used. This is a thin strip of soft plastic that is crushed between the bearing shells and journals when the bearing caps are tightened up. The change in its width then indicates the size of the clearance gap.

7 Cut off five pieces of Plastigauge, just shorter than the length of the crankshaft journal. Lay a piece on each journal, in line with its axis (see illustration).

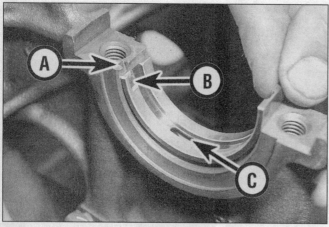

11.3 Bearing shells correctly refitted

| A | *Recess in bearing saddle* | B | *Lug on bearing shell* | C | *Oil hole* |

11.7 Lay a piece of Plastigauge on each journal, in line with the crankshaft axis

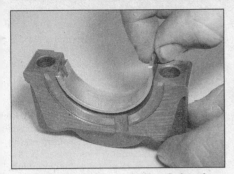

11.8 Fit the new lower half main bearing shells to the main bearing caps

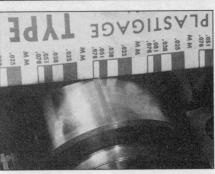

11.11 Measure the width of the crushed Plastigauge using the scale provided

11.16 Fitting the thrustwashers to No 3 bearing cap

8 Wipe off the rear surfaces of the new lower half main bearing shells and fit them to the main bearing caps, ensuring the locating lugs engage correctly **(see illustration)**.

9 Wipe the surfaces of the bearing shells and give them a light coating of silicone release agent - this will prevent the Plastigauge from sticking to the shell. Fit the caps in their correct locations on the bearing saddles, using the manufacturer's markings as a guide. Ensure that they are correctly orientated - the caps should be fitted such that the recesses for the bearing shell locating lugs are on the same side as those in the bearing saddle.

10 Working from the centre bearing cap, tighten the bolts one half turn at a time until they are all correctly torqued *to their first stage only*. Do not let the crankshaft turn at all whilst the Plastigauge is in place. Progressively unbolt the bearing caps and remove them, taking care not to dislodge the Plastigauge.

11 The width of the crushed Plastigauge can now be measured, using the scale provided **(see illustration)**. This measurement indicates the running clearance - compare it with that listed in Specifications. If the clearance is outside the tolerance, it may be due to dirt or debris trapped under the bearing surface; try cleaning them again and repeat the clearance check. If the results are still unacceptable, re-check the journal diameters and the bearing sizes. If the Plastigauge is thicker at one end, the journals may be tapered, and will require regrinding.

12 When you are satisfied that the clearances are correct, carefully remove the remains of the Plastigauge from the journals and bearings faces. Use a soft, plastic or wooden scraper as anything metallic is likely to damage the surfaces.

Crankshaft - final refitting

13 Lift the crankshaft out of the crankcase. Wipe off the surfaces of the bearings in the crankcase and the bearing caps. Fit the thrust bearings either side of the No 3 bearing saddle, between cylinders No 2 and 3. Use a small quantity of grease to hold them in place and ensure that they are seated correctly in the machined recesses, with the oil grooves facing outwards

14 Liberally coat the bearing shells in the crankcase with clean engine oil of the appropriate grade.

15 Lower the crankshaft into position so that No 2 and 3 cylinder crankpins are at TDC. No 1 and 4 cylinder crankpins will then be at BDC, ready for fitting No 1 piston.

16 Lubricate the lower bearing shells in the main bearing caps with clean engine oil, then fit the thrustwashers to either side of bearing cap No 3, noting that the lugs protruding from the washers engage the recesses in the side of the bearing cap **(see illustration)**. Make sure that the locating lugs on the shells are still engaged with the corresponding recesses in the caps.

17 Fit the main bearing caps in the correct order and orientation - No 1 bearing cap must be at the timing belt end of the engine and the bearing shell locating recesses in the bearing saddles and caps must be adjacent to each other **(see illustration)**. Insert the bearing cap bolts and hand tighten them only.

18 Working from the centre bearing cap outwards, tighten the retaining bolts to their specified torques. Where the torque is expressed in several stages, tighten all the bolts to the first stage, then repeat the exercise in the same sequence for the subsequent stage(s) **(see illustration)**.

19 Refit the crankshaft rear oil seal housing, together with a new oil seal, referring to Part A or B (as applicable) of this Chapter for details.

20 Check that the crankshaft rotates freely by turning it manually. If resistance is felt, re-check the running clearances, as described above.

21 Carry out a check of the crankshaft endfloat as described at the beginning of Section 6. If the thrust surfaces of the crankshaft have been checked and new thrust bearings have been fitted, then the endfloat should be within specification.

12 Pistons and piston rings - assembly

1 At this point it is assumed that the pistons have been correctly assembled to their respective connecting rods and that the piston ring-to-groove clearances have been checked. If not, refer to the end of Section 5.

2 Before the rings can be fitted to the pistons, the end gaps must be checked with the rings fitted into the cylinder bores.

3 Lay out the piston assemblies and the new ring sets on a clean work surface so that the components are kept together in their groups during and after end gap checking. Place the crankcase on the work surface on its side, allowing access to the top and bottom of the bores.

4 Take the No 1 piston top ring and insert it into the top of the bore. Using the No 1 piston as a ram, push the ring close to the bottom of the bore, at the lowest point of the piston travel. Ensure that it is perfectly square in the bore by pushing firmly against the piston crown.

5 Use a set of feeler blades to measure the gap between the ends of the piston ring; the correct blade will just pass through the gap

2C

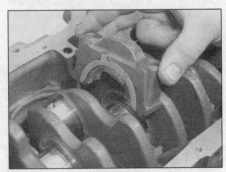

11.17 Fitting a main bearing cap in place

11.18 Tighten the bearing cap bolts to the specified torque

12.5 Checking a piston ring end gap using a feeler blade

with a minimal amount of resistance **(see illustration)**. Compare this measurement with that listed in Specifications. Check that you have the correct ring before deciding that a gap is incorrect. Repeat the operation for the remaining rings.

6 If new rings are being fitted, it is unlikely that the end gaps will be too small. If a measurement is found to be undersize, it must be corrected or there is the risk that the ends of the ring may contact each other during operation, possibly resulting in engine damage. This is achieved by gradually filing down the ends of the ring, using a file clamped in a vice. Take great care as the rings are brittle and form sharp edges if they fracture. Remember to keep the rings and piston assemblies in the correct order.

7 When all the piston ring end gaps have been verified, they can be fitted to the pistons. Work from the lowest ring groove (oil control ring) upwards. Note that the oil control ring comprises two side rails separated by an expander ring. Note also that the two compression rings are different in cross-section, and so must be fitted in the correct groove and the right way up, using a piston ring fitting tool. Both of the compression rings have marks stamped on one side to indicate the top facing surface. Ensure that these marks face up when the rings are fitted **(see illustration)**.

8 Distribute the end gaps around the piston, spaced at 120° intervals to the each other. **Note:** *If the piston ring manufacturer supplies specific fitting instructions with the rings, follow these exclusively.*

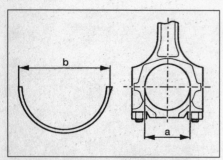

13.11 Dimensions for calculation of big-end bearing shell pre-tension (engine codes AER, AEX, APQ, AEE, ALM)

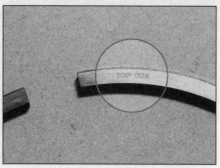

12.7 Piston ring TOP marking

13 Piston and connecting rod assemblies - refitting and big-end bearing clearance check

Big-end running clearance check

Note: *At this point, it is assumed that the crankshaft has been fitted to the engine, as described in Section 11.*

1 As with the main bearings (Section 11), a running clearance must exist between the big-end crankpin and its bearing shells to allow oil to circulate. There are two methods of checking the size of the running clearance, as described in the following paragraphs.

2 Place the cylinder block on a clean, level worksurface, with the crankcase facing upwards. Position the crankshaft such that crankpins No 1 and 4 are at BDC.

3 The first method is the least accurate and involves bolting bearing caps to the big-ends, away from the crankshaft, with the bearing shells in place. **Note:** *Correct orientation of the bearing caps is critical; refer to the notes in Section 5. The internal diameter formed by the assembled big-end is then measured using internal vernier calipers. The diameter of the respective crankpin is then subtracted from this measurement and the result is the running clearance.*

4 The second method of carrying out this check involves the use of Plastigauge, in the same manner as the main bearing running clearance check (see Section 11) and is much more accurate than the previous method. Clean all four crankpins with a clean rag. With crankpins No 1 and 4 at BDC initially, place a strand of Plastigauge on each crankpin journal.

5 Fit the upper big-end bearing shells to the connecting rods, ensuring that the locating lugs and recesses engage correctly. Temporarily refit the piston/connecting rod assemblies to the crankshaft; refit the big-end bearing caps, using the manufacturer's markings to ensure that they are fitted the correct way around - refer to *Final refitting* for details.

6 Tighten the bearing cap nuts/bolts as described below. Take care not to disturb the Plastigauge or rotate the connecting rod during the tightening process.

7 Dismantle the assemblies without rotating the connecting rods. Use the scale printed on the Plastigauge envelope to determine the big-end bearing running clearance and compare it with the figures listed in Specifications.

8 If the clearance is significantly different from that expected, the bearing shells may be the wrong size (or excessively worn, if the original shells are being re-used). Make sure that no dirt or oil was trapped between the bearing shells and the caps or connecting rods when the clearance was measured. Re-check the diameters of the crankpins. Note that if the Plastigauge was wider at one end than at the other, the crankpins may be tapered. When the problem is identified, fit new bearing shells or have the crankpins reground to a listed undersize, as appropriate.

9 Upon completion, carefully scrape away all traces of the Plastigauge material from the crankshaft and bearing shells. Use a plastic or wooden scraper, which will be soft enough to prevent scoring of the bearing surfaces.

Engine codes AER, AEX, APQ, AEE, ALM only

10 Determine the pre-tension of the big-end shell bearings, as follows. Temporarily fit the big-end bearing caps to the connecting rods (without the bearing shells), then using internal vernier calipers or a bore gauge, measure the big-end internal diameter (dimension a).

11 Now measure the *external* diameter of the bearing shell (removed) using a micrometer or vernier calipers (dimension b). The pre-tension is given by dimension a subtracted from dimension b **(see illustration)**. Compare the figure with that listed in the Specifications - if it is less than the minimum limit, then the bearing shell must be renewed.

Piston and connecting rod assemblies - final refitting

12 Note that the following procedure assumes that the crankshaft main bearing caps are in place (see Section 11).

13 Ensure that the bearing shells are correctly fitted, as described at the beginning of this Section. If new shells are being fitted, ensure that all traces of the protective grease are cleaned off using paraffin. Wipe dry the shells and connecting rods with a lint-free cloth.

14 Lubricate the cylinder bores, the pistons, and piston rings with clean engine oil. Lay out each piston/connecting rod assembly in order on a worksurface. On engines where the big-end bolts are captive in the connecting rods, fit short sections of rubber hose or tape over the bolt threads, to protect the cylinder bores during reassembly.

15 Start with piston/connecting rod assembly No 1. Make sure that the piston rings are still spaced as described in Section 12, then clamp them in position with a piston ring compressor.

16 Insert the piston/connecting rod assembly into the top of cylinder No 1. Lower the big-end in first, guiding it to protect the big-end bolts and the cylinder bores.

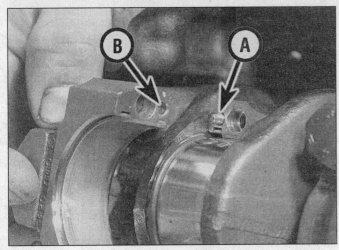

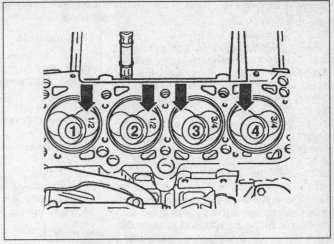

13.19 Fitting a big-end bearing cap

A Dowel   B Locating hole

13.20 Piston orientation and fitting order (engine code AFN, 1Z, AHU, and AEY)

17 Ensure that the orientation of the piston in its cylinder is correct - the piston crown, connecting rods and big-end bearing caps have markings, which must point towards the timing belt end of the engine when the piston is installed in the bore - refer to Section 5 for details.

18 Using a block of wood or hammer handle against the piston crown, tap the assembly into the cylinder until the piston crown is flush with the top of the cylinder.

19 Ensure that the bearing shell is still correctly installed. Liberally lubricate the crankpin and both bearing shells with clean engine oil. Taking care not to mark the cylinder bores, tap the piston/connecting rod assembly down the bore and onto the crankpin. Refit the big-end bearing cap, tightening its retaining nuts/bolts finger-tight at first **(see illustration)**. Note that the orientation of the bearing cap with respect to the connecting rod must be correct when the two components are reassembled. The connecting rod and its corresponding bearing cap both have recesses machined into them, close to their mating surfaces - these recesses must both face in the same direction as the arrow on the piston crown (ie towards the timing belt end of the engine) when correctly installed - refer to the illustrations in Section 5 for details. **Note:** *On certain engines, the connecting rod big-ends are provided with offset dowels which locate in holes in the bearing caps.*

20 On engine codes AFN, 1Z, AHU, and AEY, the piston crowns are specially shaped to improve the engine's combustion charac-teristics. Because of this, pistons 1 and 2 are different to pistons 3 and 4. When correctly fitted, the larger inlet valve chambers on pistons 1 and 2 must face the flywheel end of the engine, and the larger inlet valve chambers on pistons 3 and 4 must face the timing belt end of the engine. New pistons have number markings on their crowns to

indicate their type - 1/2 denotes piston 1 or 2, 3/4 indicates piston 3 or 4 **(see illustration)**.

21 Working progressively around each bearing cap, tighten the retaining nuts half a turn at a time to the specified torque **(see illustrations)**.

22 Refit the remaining three piston/ connecting rod assemblies in the same way.

23 Rotate the crankshaft by hand and check that it turns freely. Some stiffness is to be expected if new parts have been fitted, but there should be no binding or tight spots.

Engine codes AFN, 1Z, AHU, AEY, 1Y, AAZ only

24 If new pistons are to be fitted, or if a new short engine is to be installed, the projection of the piston crowns above the cylinder head at TDC must be measured, to determine the type of head gasket that should be fitted.

25 Turn the cylinder block over (so that the crankcase is facing downwards) and rest it on a stand or wooden blocks. Anchor DTI gauge to the cylinder block, and zero it on the head gasket mating surface. Rest the gauge probe on No 1 piston crown and turn the crankshaft slowly by hand so that the piston reaches and then passes through TDC. Measure and record the maximum deflection at TDC.

26 Repeat the measurement at piston No 4, then turn the crankshaft through 180° and take measurements at pistons Nos 2 and 3.

27 If the measurements differ from piston to piston, take the highest figure and use this to determine the head gasket type that must be used - refer to the Specifications for details.

28 Note that if the original pistons have been refitted, then a new head gasket of the same type as the original item must be fitted; refer to Chapter 2B for details of how to identify different head gasket types.

14 Engine - initial start-up after overhaul

2C

1 After overhauling the engine, refit the remainder of the engine components in the order listed in Section 10 of this Chapter, referring to Part A or B where necessary. Refit the engine (and transmission) to the vehicle as described in Section 2 of this Chapter. Double-check the engine oil and coolant levels and make a final check that everything has been reconnected. Make sure that there are no tools or rags left in the engine compartment.

13.21a Tightening the big-end bearing cap bolts to the Stage 1 torque . . .

13.21b . . . and Stage 2 angle setting

Petrol models

2 Remove the spark plugs, referring to Chapter 1A for details.

3 The engine must be immobilised such that it can be turned over using the starter motor, without starting - disable the fuel pump by unplugging the fuel pump power relay from the relay board; refer to the relevant Part of Chapter 4 for details.

Caution: If the vehicle has a catalytic converter, it is potentially damaging to immobilise the engine by disabling the ignition system without first disabling the fuel system, as unburnt fuel could be supplied to the catalyst.

4 Turn the engine using the starter motor until the oil pressure warning lamp goes out. If the lamp fails to extinguish after several seconds of cranking, check the engine oil level and oil filter security. Assuming these are correct, check the security of the oil pressure switch cabling - do not progress any further until you are satisfied that oil is being pumped around the engine at sufficient pressure.

5 Refit the spark plugs, and reconnect the fuel pump relay.

Diesel models

6 Disconnect the electrical cable from the fuel cut-off valve at the fuel injection pump - refer to Chapter 4C for details.

7 Turn the engine using the starter motor until the oil pressure warning lamp goes out.

8 If the lamp fails to extinguish after several seconds of cranking, check the engine oil level and oil filter security. Assuming these are correct, check the security of the oil pressure switch cabling - do not progress any further until you are satisfied that oil is being pumped around the engine at sufficient pressure.

9 Reconnect the fuel cut-off valve cable.

All models

10 Start the engine, but be aware that as fuel system components have been disturbed, the cranking time may be a little longer than usual.

11 While the engine is idling, check for fuel, water and oil leaks. Don't be alarmed if there are some odd smells and the occasional plume of smoke as components heat up and burn off oil deposits.

12 Assuming all is well, keep the engine idling until hot water is felt circulating through the top hose.

13 On diesel models, check the fuel injection pump timing and engine idle speed, as described in Chapter 4C and Chapter 1B.

14 After a few minutes, recheck the oil and coolant levels, and top-up as necessary.

15 On all the engines described in this Chapter, there is no need to re-tighten the cylinder head bolts once the engine has been run following reassembly.

16 If new pistons, rings or crankshaft bearings have been fitted, the engine must be treated as new, and run-in for the first 600 miles (1000 km). *Do not* operate the engine at full-throttle, or allow it to labour at low engine speeds in any gear. It is recommended that the engine oil and filter are changed at the end of this period.

Chapter 3
Cooling, heating and air conditioning systems

Contents

Degrees of difficulty

Easy, suitable for novice with little experience 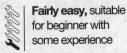	Fairly easy, suitable for beginner with some experience 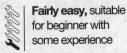	Fairly difficult, suitable for competent DIY mechanic 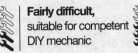	Difficult, suitable for experienced DIY mechanic 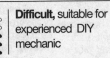	Very difficult, suitable for expert DIY or professional

Specifications

Cooling system pressure cap

Opening pressure:
Petrol engines:
    All except 1.05, 1.3 and 1.6 litre (AAU, AAV, ABD, ABU) . . . . 1.4 to 1.6 bar
    1.05, 1.3 and 1.6 (AAU, AAV, ABD, ABU) engines . . . . 1.3 to 1.5 bar
Diesel engines:
    All except engine codes 1Y and AAZ . . . . 1.4 to 1.6 bar
    Engine codes 1Y and AAZ . . . . 1.2 to 1.5 bar

Thermostat

All except 1.4 and 1.6 litre (AEX, APQ, AEE, AER and ALM) and 2.0 litre 16-valve engines:
Begins to open . . . . 87°C
Fully open . . . . 102°C
1.4 and 1.6 litre (AEX, APQ, AEE, AER and ALM) engines:
Begins to open . . . . 84°C
Fully open . . . . 98°C
2.0 litre 16-valve engines:
Begins to open . . . . 85°C
Fully open . . . . 105°C

Cooling fan

Fan speeds:
1st speed cut-in . . . . 92 to 97°C
1st speed cut-out . . . . 91 to 84°C
2nd speed cut-in . . . . 99 to 105°C
2nd speed cut-out . . . . 98 to 91°C
3rd speed cut-in (where applicable) . . . . 110 to 115°C
3rd speed cut-out (where applicable) . . . . 105 to 110°C

Torque wrench settings

	Nm	lbf ft
Coolant pump housing/coolant pump-to-engine bolts:		
Diesel engines:		
Stage 1	20	15
Stage 2	Angle-tighten through a further 90°	
1.6 litre (code AER) engine	20	15
1.05, 1.3 and 1.6 (AAU, AAV, ABD, ABU) engines	10	7
1.4 and 1.6 (AEX, APQ, AEE and ALM) engines	20	15
1.6 (AFT) engine	25	18
1.6 and 2.0 (1F, 2E and AGG) engines:		
Stage 1	20	15
Stage 2	Angle-tighten through a further 90°	
2.0 16V (ABF) engine:		
Stage 1	20	15
Stage 2	Angle-tighten through a further 90°	
Coolant pump pulley bolts:		
All except 1.6 and 2.0 (1F, 2E and AGG) engines and 2.0 16V (ABF) engine	25	18
1.6 and 2.0 (1F, 2E and AGG) engines and 2.0 16V (ABF) engine	20	15
Coolant pump-to-coolant pump housing bolts (diesel engines, 1.6 litre (codes AFT and 1F), and 2.0 litre petrol engines)	10	7
Thermostat cover bolts	10	7

1 General information and precautions

A pressurised cooling system is used, comprising a pump, an aluminium crossflow radiator, an electric cooling fan, a thermostat and a heater matrix, aswell as the interconnecting hoses. The system functions as follows. Cold coolant from the radiator passes through the hose to the coolant pump where it is pumped around the cylinder block and head passages. After cooling the cylinder bores, combustion surfaces and valve seats, the coolant reaches the underside of the thermostat, which is initially closed. The coolant passes through the heater and is returned through the cylinder block to the coolant pump.

When the engine is cold the coolant circulates only through the cylinder block, cylinder head, expansion tank and heater. When the coolant reaches a predetermined temperature, the thermostat opens and the coolant passes through to the radiator. As the coolant circulates through the radiator it is cooled by the inrush of air when the car is in forward motion. Airflow is supplemented by the action of the electric cooling fan(s) when necessary. Upon leaving the radiator, the coolant is has cooled and the cycle is repeated.

The electric cooling fan(s) mounted on the rear of the radiator are controlled by a thermostatic switch. At a pre-set coolant temperature, the switch actuates the fan(s).

Refer to Section 11 for information on the air conditioning system fitted to certain models.

Precautions

 Warning: Do not attempt to remove the expansion tank filler cap or disturb any part of the cooling system while the engine is hot, as there is a high risk of scalding. If the expansion tank filler cap must be removed before the engine and radiator have fully cooled (even though this is not recommended) the pressure in the cooling system must first be relieved. Cover the cap with a thick layer of cloth, to avoid scalding, and slowly unscrew the filler cap until a hissing sound can be heard. When the hissing has stopped, indicating that the pressure has reduced, slowly unscrew the filler cap until it can be removed; if more hissing sounds are heard, wait until they have stopped before unscrewing the cap completely. At all times keep well away from the filler cap opening.

Do not allow antifreeze to come into contact with skin or painted surfaces of the vehicle. Rinse off spills immediately with plenty of water. Never leave antifreeze lying around in an open container or in a puddle in the driveway or on the garage floor. Children and pets are attracted by its sweet smell. Antifreeze can be fatal if ingested.

If the engine is hot, the electric cooling fan may start rotating even if the engine is not running, so be careful to keep hands, hair and loose clothing well clear when working in the engine compartment.

2.3 Disconnecting a radiator top hose

Refer to Section 11 for additional precautions to be observed when working on models with air conditioning.

2 Cooling system hoses – disconnection and renewal

Note: *Refer to the warnings given in Section 1 of this Chapter before proceeding.*

1 If the checks described in Chapter 1 reveal a faulty hose, it must be renewed as follows.

2 First drain the cooling system as described in Chapter 1. If the coolant is not due for renewal, it may be re-used if it is collected in a clean container.

3 To disconnect a hose, release its retaining clips, then move them along the hose, clear of the relevant inlet/outlet union. Carefully work the hose free **(see illustration)**. While the hoses can be removed with relative ease when new or hot, **do not** attempt to disconnect any part of the system while it is still hot.

4 Note that the radiator inlet and outlet unions are fragile; do not use excessive force when attempting to remove the hoses. If a hose proves to be difficult to remove, try to release it by rotating the hose ends before attempting to free it.

> **HAYNES HINT** *If all else fails, cut the hose with a sharp knife, then slit it so that it can be peeled off in two pieces. Although this may prove expensive if the hose is otherwise undamaged, it is preferable to buying a new radiator.*

5 When fitting a hose, first slide the clips onto the hose, then work the hose into position. If clamp type clips were originally fitted, it is a good idea to replace them with screw type clips when refitting the hose. If the hose is

stiff, use a little soapy water as a lubricant, or soften the hose by soaking it in hot water.

6 Work the hose into position, checking that it is correctly routed, then slide each clip along the hose until it passes over the flared end of the relevant inlet/outlet union, before securing it in position with the retaining clip.

7 Refill the cooling system (see Chapter 1).

8 Check thoroughly for leaks as soon as possible after disturbing any part of the cooling system.

3 Radiator – removal, inspection and refitting

 If leakage is the reason for wanting to remove the radiator, bear in mind that minor leaks can often be cured using a radiator sealant with the radiator in situ.

Models without air conditioning

Removal

1 Disconnect the battery negative lead.

2 Drain the cooling system as described in Chapter 1.

3 Remove the front grille panel as described in Chapter 11.

4 Disconnect the upper and lower hoses from the radiator, with reference to Section 2 if necessary. On 2.0 litre 16-valve models, it may be necessary to remove the HT lead housing from the inlet manifold to improve access.

5 Disconnect the electric cooling fan wiring connector, and release the wiring from the cooling fan shroud, then unscrew the bolts securing the cooling fan shroud to the radiator, and carefully manipulate the cooling fan/shroud assembly out from the top of the engine compartment **(see illustrations)**.

6 Disconnect the wiring plug from the cooling fan switch mounted in the radiator.

7 Unclip the upper part of the cooling fan air deflector from the front of the radiator, and withdraw it (this is necessary because the bonnet release cable passes through the shroud).

8 Unscrew the two bolts securing the radiator to the bonnet lock crossmember, then carefully lift the radiator out from the engine compartment, complete with the side sections of the cooling can air deflector, taking care not to damage the radiator on surrounding components **(see illustrations)**.

Inspection

9 If the radiator has been removed due to suspected blockage, reverse flush it as described in Chapter 1. Clean dirt and debris from the radiator fins, using an air line (in which case, wear eye protection) or a soft brush. Be careful, as the fins are sharp and easily damaged.

3.5a Disconnecting the cooling fan wiring connector

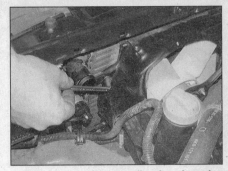

3.5b Unscrewing a cooling fan shroud securing bolt

10 If necessary, a radiator specialist can perform a flow test on the radiator, to establish whether an internal blockage exists.

11 A leaking radiator must be referred to a specialist for permanent repair. Do not attempt to weld or solder a leaking radiator, as damage may result.

12 In an emergency, minor leaks from the radiator can be cured using a suitable radiator sealant in accordance with the manufacturers instructions with the radiator in situ.

13 If the radiator is to be sent for repair or renewed, remove the cooling fan switch.

Refitting

14 Refitting is a reversal of removal, bearing in mind the following points.

a) Before refitting, ensure that the lower radiator mounting rubbers are in place on the body panel.

b) Make sure that the lugs on the top of the cooling fan air deflector engage correctly with the top of the cooling fan shroud.

c) On completion, refill the cooling system using the correct type of antifreeze as described in Chapter 1.

Models with air conditioning

Note: *Two alternative radiator/cooling fan assemblies may be fitted to models with air conditioning. For some models the procedure is as described previously for models without air conditioning. For models with the alternative assembly, proceed as follows.*

Removal

15 Proceed as described in paragraphs 1 to 3.

16 Where applicable, unscrew the bolt

3.8a Unscrew the bolts securing the radiator to the crossmember . . .

securing the air conditioning refrigerant pipe bracket to the front body panel, and move the pipe(s) clear of the working area, taking care not to strain them.

17 Remove the body front panel, as described in Chapter 11.

18 Disconnect the wiring plug from the cooling fan switch mounted in the radiator.

19 In order to gain sufficient clearance to remove the radiator, it may be necessary to carry out the following:

 Warning: Do not attempt to disconnect the refrigerant lines – refer to the warnings given in Section 11.

a) Unscrew the retaining nuts and release the air conditioning system filter/drier assembly from its mounting bracket.

b) Release the refrigerant lines from all relevant retaining clips.

c) Unscrew the retaining bolts and move the condenser as far forward as possible, taking great care not to place any excess strain on the refrigerant lines.

20 Slacken and remove the four radiator retaining bolts, then carefully manipulate the radiator out from the front of the vehicle.

Inspection

21 Proceed as described in paragraphs 9 to 13.

Refitting

22 Refitting is a reversal of removal, bearing in mind the following points.

a) Refit the body front panel as described in Chapter 11.

b) Refill the cooling system using the correct type of antifreeze as described in Chapter 1.

3

3.8b . . . then lift the radiator from the engine compartment

4.4 Withdrawing the thermostat from its housing – 2.0 litre petrol engine

4 Thermostat –
removal, testing and refitting

Diesel engines, 1.6 (AFT and 1F), and 2.0 litre petrol engines

Removal

1 The thermostat is located in an elbow beneath the coolant pump at the front timing belt end of the engine.

2 Drain the cooling system as described in Chapter 1.

3 Remove the retaining clip, and pull the plastic connecting pipe from the thermostat housing.

4 Unscrew the two securing bolts, and remove the thermostat cover, then lift out the thermostat **(see illustration)**. Recover the O-ring if it is loose.

Testing

5 A rough test of the thermostat may be made by suspending it with a piece of string in a container full of water. Heat the water to bring it to the boil - the thermostat must open by the time the water boils. If not, renew it.

6 If a thermometer is available, the precise opening temperature of the thermostat may be determined, and compared with the figures given in the Specifications. The opening temperature is also marked on the thermostat.

7 A thermostat which fails to close as the water cools must also be renewed.

Refitting

8 Refitting is a reversal of removal, bearing in mind the following points.
a) Refit the thermostat using a new O-ring.
b) Check the condition of the O-ring between the plastic connecting pipe and the thermostat elbow, and renew if necessary.
c) Refill the cooling system with the correct type and quantity of coolant as described in Chapter 1.

1.05, 1.3, 1.4 and 1.6 (code ABU, AEE, AER and ALM) litre engines

Removal

9 The thermostat is located in a housing at the left-hand end of the cylinder head.

10 Drain the cooling system as described in Chapter 1.

11 Release the securing clip and disconnect the coolant hose from the thermostat cover **(see illustration)**.

12 Unscrew the two securing bolts, and remove the thermostat cover, noting the locations of any brackets secured by the bolts, then lift out the thermostat. Recover the O-ring if it is loose.

Testing

13 Proceed as described in paragraphs 5 to 7.

Refitting

14 Refitting is a reversal of removal, bearing in mind the following points.
a) Refit the thermostat using a new O-ring.
b) Ensure that any brackets are in place on the thermostat cover bolts as noted before removal.
c) Refill the cooling system with the correct type and quantity of coolant as described in Chapter 1.

5 Electric cooling fan –
testing, removal and refitting

Models without air conditioning

Testing

1 Vehicles may be fitted with one or two cooling fans, depending on model. On most models with two cooling fans, both fans are electric, but on some early models, the second fan is belt driven from the main electric fan. The cooling fan is supplied with current through the ignition switch, cooling fan control unit (where applicable), the relay(s) and fuses/fusible link (see Chapter 12). The circuit is completed by the cooling fan thermostatic switch, which is mounted in the left-hand end of the radiator. The cooling fan has two speed settings; the thermostatic switch actually contains two switches, one for the stage 1 fan speed setting and another for the stage 2 fan speed setting. **Note:** On some models equipped with air conditioning, there is also a second switch (fitted into one of the

5.7a Two of the cooling fan shroud securing bolts (arrowed)

4.11 Disconnecting the coolant hose from the thermostat cover – 1.6 litre engine

coolant outlet housings/hoses on the cylinder head). This switch controls the cooling fan stage 3 speed setting. Testing of the cooling fan circuit is as follows noting that the following check should be carried out on both the stage 1 speed circuit and speed 2 circuit (see the wiring diagrams at the end of Chapter 12). **Note:** On models with a twin mechanical cooling fan arrangement, if only one fan is working, the drivebelt linking the fans may have broken.

2 If a fan does not appear to work, first check the fuses/fusible links. If they are good, run the engine until normal operating temperature is reached, then allow it to idle. If the fan does not cut in within a few minutes, switch off the ignition and disconnect the wiring plug from the cooling fan switch. Bridge the relevant two contacts in the wiring plug using a length of spare wire, and switch on the ignition. If the fan now operates, the switch is probably faulty and should be renewed.

3 If the switch appears to work, the motor can be checked by disconnecting the motor wiring connector and connecting a 12 volt supply directly to the motor terminals. If the motor is faulty, it must be renewed, as no spares are available.

4 If the fan still fails to operate, check the cooling fan circuit wiring (Chapter 12). Check each wire for continuity and ensure that all connections are clean and free of corrosion.

5 On models with a cooling fan control unit, if no fault can be found with the fuses/fusible links, wiring, fan switch, or fan motor, then it is likely that the cooling fan control unit is faulty. Testing of the unit should be entrusted to a Seat dealer; if the unit is faulty it must be renewed.

Removal

6 Disconnect the battery negative lead.

7 Disconnect the electric cooling fan wiring connector, then unscrew the bolts securing the cooling fan shroud to the radiator, and carefully manipulate the cooling fan/shroud assembly out from the top of the engine compartment **(see illustrations)**. On 2.0 litre 16-valve models, it may be necessary to remove the HT lead housing from the inlet manifold to improve access.

8 If desired, the cooling fan motor(s) can be removed from the shroud after unscrewing the three securing nuts and bolts **(see illustration)**. The fan blades are secured to the motor spindle with a circlip.

Refitting

9 Refitting is a reversal of removal.

Models with air conditioning

Testing

10 Proceed as described in paragraphs 1 to 5.

Removal

Note: *Two alternative radiator/cooling fan assemblies may be fitted to models with air conditioning. For some models the procedure is as described previously for models without air conditioning. For models with the alternative assembly, proceed as follows.*

11 Remove the radiator as described in Section 3.

12 Disconnect the wiring connector from the rear of the cooling fan motor.

13 Press out the pins from the centre of the fan retaining ring fasteners, and unclip the retaining ring from the cooling fan shroud.

14 Slacken and remove the motor retaining nuts, and remove the cooling fan assembly from the front of the vehicle.

15 On models with twin cooling fans, as the motor is removed, where applicable, free it from the drivebelt linking the fans, and remove the belt. If necessary, unscrew the retaining nuts and remove the second fan. No spare parts are available for the motor, and if the unit is faulty, it must be renewed.

Refitting

16 Refitting is a reversal of removal, but refit the radiator as described in Section 3, and refill the cooling system with the correct type of coolant as described in Chapter 1. On completion, check the operation of the cooling fan(s).

6 Cooling system electrical switches – testing, removal and refitting

Electric cooling fan thermostatic switch

Testing

1 Testing of the switch is described in Section 5, as part of the electric cooling fan test procedure.

Radiator-mounted switch – removal and refitting

2 The switch is located in the left-hand side of the radiator. The engine and radiator should be cold before removing the switch.

3 Disconnect the battery negative lead.

4 Either drain the radiator to below the level of the switch (as described in Chapter 1), or have ready a suitable plug which can be used to plug the switch aperture in the radiator whilst the switch is removed. If a plug is used,

5.7b Removing the cooling fan assembly

take great care not to damage the radiator, and do not use anything which will allow foreign matter to enter the radiator.

5 Disconnect the wiring plug from the switch **(see illustration).**

6 Carefully unscrew the switch from the radiator.

7 Refitting is a reversal of removal, applying a smear of suitable grease to the threads of the switch and tightening it securely. On completion, refill the cooling system with the correct type and quantity of coolant as described in Chapter 1, or top up as described in *Weekly checks*.

8 Start the engine and run it until it reaches normal operating temperature, then continue to run the engine and check that the cooling fan cuts in and functions correctly.

Thermostat housing-mounted switch – removal and refitting

9 The switch is located in the cylinder head coolant elbow.

10 Disconnect the battery negative lead.

11 Either drain the cooling system to below the level of the switch (as described in Chapter 1), or have ready a suitable plug which can be used to plug the switch aperture in the housing whilst the switch is removed. If a plug is used, to not use anything which will allow foreign matter to enter the cooling system.

12 Disconnect the wiring plug from the switch.

13 Pull out the switch retaining clip, then withdraw the switch from its housing. Recover the sealing ring if it is loose.

14 Refitting is a reversal of removal, but check the condition of the switch sealing ring and renew if necessary. On completion, refill the cooling system with the correct type and quantity of coolant as described in Chapter 1, or top up as described in *Weekly checks*.

Coolant temperature gauge sender/coolant temperature sensor – all except 2.0 litre 16-valve models

Note: *On all models except the 2.0 litre 16-valve, the sender unit is an integral part of the fuel injection/preheating system (as applicable) coolant temperature sensor.*

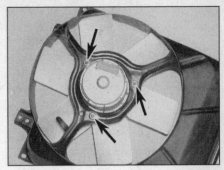

5.8 Cooling fan motor-to-shroud securing nuts (arrowed)

Testing

15 The coolant temperature gauge, mounted in the instrument panel, is fed with a stabilised voltage supply from the instrument panel feed (through the ignition switch and a fuse), and its earth is controlled by the sensor.

16 The sensor unit is clipped into the coolant outlet elbow at the left-hand end or centre of the cylinder head (depending on model). The sensor contains a thermistor, which consists of an electronic component whose electrical resistance decreases at a predetermined rate as its temperature rises. When the coolant is cold, the sensor resistance is high, current flow through the gauge is reduced, and the gauge needle points towards the cold end of the scale. If the sensor is faulty, it must be renewed.

17 If the gauge develops a fault, first check the other instruments; if they do not work at all, check the instrument panel electrical feed. If the readings are erratic, there may be a fault in the instrument panel assembly. If the fault lies in the temperature gauge alone, check it as follows.

18 If the gauge needle remains at the cold end of the scale, disconnect the wiring connector from the sensor unit, and earth the temperature gauge wire (see *Wiring diagrams* for details) to the cylinder head. If the needle then deflects when the ignition is switched on, the sensor unit is proved faulty, and should be renewed. If the needle still does not move, remove the instrument panel (Chapter 12) and check the continuity of the wiring between the sensor unit and the gauge, and the feed to the

6.5 Disconnecting the wiring plug from the cooling fan switch

3

6.20a Disconnect the wiring plug . . .

6.20b . . . then pull out the retaining clip and withdraw the coolant temperature gauge sender/coolant temperature sensor from its housing – 1.4 litre engine

6.20c Coolant temperature gauge sender/coolant temperature location (arrowed) – 2.0 litre 8-valve engine

gauge unit. If continuity is shown, and the fault still exists, then the gauge is faulty and should be renewed.

19 If the gauge needle remains at the hot end of the scale, disconnect the sensor wire. If the needle then returns to the cold end of the scale when the ignition is switched on, the sensor unit is proved faulty and should be renewed. If the needle still does not move, check the remainder of the circuit as described previously.

Removal and refitting

20 Proceed as described in paragraphs 9 to 14 for the thermostat housing-mounted cooling fan thermostatic switch, noting that the sender/sensor is located in the coolant outlet elbow at the left-hand end or centre of the cylinder head (depending on model) **(see illustrations)**.

Coolant temperature gauge sender – 2.0 litre 16-valve models

Testing

21 Proceed as described in paragraphs 15 to 19, noting that the sender is screwed into the left-hand end of the cylinder head. The coolant temperature gauge sender is the rearmost of the two senders.

Removal and refitting

22 The sender is screwed into the left-hand end of the cylinder head. The coolant temperature gauge sender is the rearmost of the two senders.

23 Proceed as described in paragraphs 10 to 12.
24 Unscrew the sender from the cylinder head.
25 Refitting is a reversal of removal. On completion, refill the cooling system with the correct type and quantity of coolant as described in Chapter 1, or top up as described in *Weekly checks*.

Coolant temperature sensor – 2.0 litre 16-valve models

Testing

26 No information on testing was available at the time of writing. It is recommended that testing of the sensor is entrusted to a Seat dealer.

Removal and refitting

27 Proceed as described in paragraphs 22 to 25, but note that the coolant temperature sensor is the one nearest the front of the engine.

---

7 Coolant pump –
removal and refitting

Diesel engines, 1.6 litre petrol engines (codes AFT and 1F), and 2.0 litre petrol engines

Removal

1 Disconnect the battery negative lead.

2 Drain the cooling system as described in Chapter 1.
3 Apply the handbrake, then jack up the front of the vehicle and support securely on axle stands.
4 Using a suitable Allen key or hexagon bit, slacken the three coolant pump pulley securing bolts **(see illustration)**.
5 Where applicable, remove the engine cover
6 Remove the air cleaner assembly, complete with the air trunking, as described in Chapter 4C.
7 On 2.0 litre 16-valve models, unscrew the two bolts securing the HT lead housing to the inlet manifold, and lift the housing until the oil separator/crankcase ventilation valve securing bolts can be unscrewed. Move the valve to one side, without disconnecting the breather tube.
8 Remove the auxiliary drivebelt(s) as described in Chapter 1.
9 Remove the alternator as described in Chapter 5A.
10 On models with power steering, remove the power steering pump as described in Chapter 10.
11 Remove the securing bolts, and lift off the coolant pump pulley **(see illustration)**.
12 On models fitted with air conditioning, unscrew the bolts securing the compressor to the mounting bracket, and carefully move the compressor to one side, taking care not to strain the refrigerant pipes. If necessary, release the refrigerant pipes from the clips on the condenser/radiator assembly to allow the compressor to be moved.
13 Remove the retaining clip, and pull the plastic connecting pipe from the thermostat housing elbow underneath the coolant pump.
14 Release the hose clips and disconnect the coolant hoses from the coolant pump.
15 Unscrew the four nuts and single bolt securing the alternator/air conditioning compressor mounting bracket to the engine, and remove the bracket.
16 Unscrew the bolt securing the timing belt cover to the coolant pump.
17 Unscrew the four bolts securing the coolant pump housing assembly to the cylinder block, then lift the housing/pump

7.4 Slacken the coolant pump securing bolts

7.11 Remove the coolant pump pulley

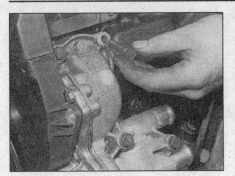

7.17a Unscrew the securing bolts . . .

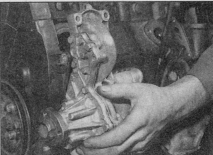

7.17b . . . then lift the housing/pump from the engine compartment . . .

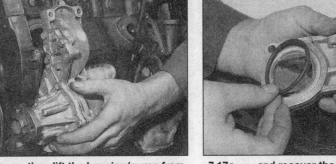

7.17c . . . and recover the gasket/sealing ring

from the engine compartment. Recover the gasket/sealing ring **(see illustrations).**
18 To separate the pump from the housing, unscrew the securing bolts. Recover the gasket(s) and, where applicable, the O-ring(s) **(see illustration).**

Refitting

19 Refitting is a reversal of removal, bearing in mind the following points.
a) *Renew the pump gasket(s) and O-ring(s), as applicable.*
b) *Use a new gasket between the pump housing and the cylinder block.*
c) *Tighten all fixings to the specified torque, where applicable.*
d) *Check the condition of the O-ring between the plastic connecting pipe and the thermostat elbow, and renew if necessary.*
e) *Refill the cooling system as described in Chapter 1.*
f) *Refit and tension the auxiliary drivebelt(s) as described in Chapter 1.*

1.05 litre, 1.3 litre, 1.4 litre and 1.6 litre (codes AER, ABU, AEE and ALM) petrol engines

Removal

20 Disconnect the battery negative lead.
21 Drain the cooling system as described in Chapter 1.
22 Remove the timing belt as described in Chapter 2A.
23 Remove the camshaft sprocket and the rear timing belt cover as described in Chapter 2A, noting that two of the rear timing belt cover securing bolts also secure the coolant pump.
24 Withdraw the coolant pump from the cylinder block, and recover the O-ring if it is loose **(see illustration).**

Refitting

25 Refitting is a reversal of removal, bearing in mind the following points.
a) *Refit the coolant pump using a new O-ring.*
b) *Refit the camshaft sprocket and the timing belt as described in Chapter 2A.*
c) *On completion, refill the cooling system with the correct type of coolant, as described in Chapter 1.*

8 Heating and ventilation system – general information

1 The heating/ventilation system consists of a four-speed blower motor (housed in the passenger compartment), face-level vents in the centre and at each end of the facia, and air ducts to the front and rear footwells.
2 The control unit is located in the facia, and the controls operate flap valves to deflect and mix the air flowing through the various parts of the heating/ventilation system. The flap valves are contained in the air distribution housing, which acts as a central distribution unit, passing air to the various ducts and vents.

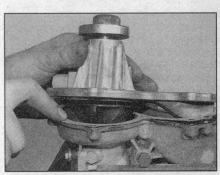

7.18 Unscrew the securing bolts to separate the pump from the housing

3

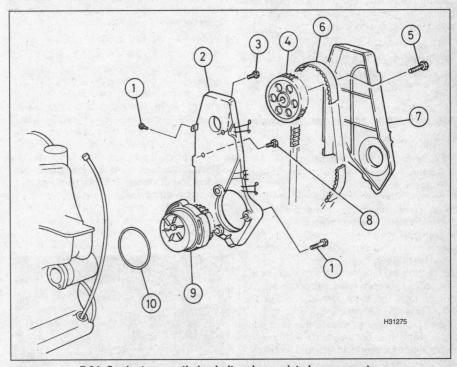

H31275

**7.24 Coolant pump, timing belt and associated components -
1.05 litre, 1.3 litre, 1.4 litre and 1.6 litre (codes AER, ABU, AEE and ALM) petrol engines**

1 *Bolt*	4 *Camshaft sprocket*	8 *Bolt*
2 *Timing belt rear cover*	5 *Bolt*	9 *Coolant pump*
3 *Bolt*	6 *Timing belt*	10 *O-ring*
	7 *Timing belt outer cover*	

9.2 Carefully prise off the heater control panel trim plate

9.3 Remove the switch mounting plate securing screws . . .

9.4 . . . and withdraw the switch mounting plate

3 Cold air enters the system through the grille at the rear of the engine compartment. On some models (depending on specification) a pollen filter is fitted to the ventilation inlet to filter out dust, soot, pollen and spores from the air entering the vehicle.

4 The airflow, which can be boosted by the blower, then flows through the various ducts, according to the settings of the controls. Stale air is expelled through ducts behind the rear bumper. If warm air is required, the cold air is passed through the heater matrix, which is heated by the engine coolant.

5 If necessary, the outside air supply can be closed off, allowing the air inside the vehicle to be recirculated. This can be useful to prevent unpleasant odours entering from outside the vehicle, but should only be used briefly, as the recirculated air inside the vehicle will soon deteriorate.

9 Heating/ventilation system components - removal and refitting

Models without air conditioning

Heater/ventilation control unit

1 Disconnect the battery negative lead.

2 Carefully prise off the heater control panel trim plate **(see illustration)**.

3 Remove the two screws securing the switch mounting plate in position below the heater controls **(see illustration)**.

4 Withdraw the switch mounting plate, and disconnect the wiring plugs from the switches **(see illustration)**.

5 Unscrew the four heater/ventilation control unit securing screws, then manipulate the unit out through the facia and disconnect the wiring plugs **(see illustrations)**.

6 Unclip the control cables and release each cable from the control unit, noting each cable's correct fitted location and routing; to avoid confusion on refitting, label each cable as it is disconnected. The outer cables are released by simply lifting the retaining clips **(see illustration)**.

7 Refitting is reversal of removal. Ensure that the control cables are correctly routed and reconnected to the control panel, as noted

9.5a Unscrew the securing screws . . .

9.5b . . . then withdraw the heater control panel

before removal. Clip the outer cables in position and check the operation of each knob/lever before refitting the switch mounting plate and the trim plate.

Heater/ventilation control cables

8 Remove the heater/ventilation control unit from the facia as described previously, detaching the relevant cable from the control unit.

9 Remove the left-hand lower facia trim panel for access to the heater control cable connections on the heater/ventilation distribution unit.

10 Follow the run of the cable behind the facia, taking note of its routing, and disconnect the cable from the lever on the air distribution/blower motor housing. Note that the method of fastening is the same as that used at the control unit.

11 Fit the new cable, ensuring that it is correctly routed and free from kinks and obstructions.

12 Connect the cable to the control unit and air distribution/blower motor housing making sure the outer cable is clipped securely in position.

13 Check the operation of the control knob then refit the control unit as described previously in this Section. Finally refit the facia trim panel.

Heater matrix

14 Unscrew the expansion tank cap (referring to the Warning note in Section 1) to release any pressure present in the cooling system, then securely refit the cap.

15 Clamp both heater hoses as close to the bulkhead as possible to minimise coolant loss. Alternatively, drain the cooling system as described in Chapter 1.

16 Release the retaining clips and disconnect both hoses from the heater matrix unions which are located in the centre of the engine compartment bulkhead **(see illustration)**.

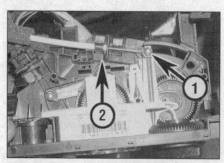

9.6 Unclip the control cable inners from the levers (1) and release the cable outers from the retaining clips (2)

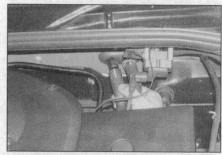

9.16 Disconnect the hoses from the heater matrix unions on the engine compartment bulkhead

9.19a Remove the front . . .

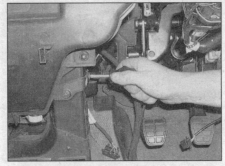

9.19b . . . and side securing screws . . .

9.19c . . . and withdraw the footwell air duct assembly

17 Remove the facia assembly as described in Chapter 12.
18 If not already done, unclip the right- and left-hand upper air ducts and remove them from the heater/ventilation unit.
19 Unscrew the two securing screws, and withdraw the centre footwell air duct assembly **(see illustrations)**.
20 Unscrew the two securing screws, and remove the driver's foot rest **(see illustration)**.
21 Working in the engine compartment, unscrew the three nuts securing the heater assembly to the bulkhead **(see illustrations)**.
22 Working inside the vehicle, unscrew the bolt securing the passenger's side of the heater assembly to the mounting bracket **(see illustration)**.
23 Disconnect the wiring plugs from the heater assembly and the blower motor unit, and unbolt the earth lead from the passenger's side footwell **(see illustration)**. Carefully

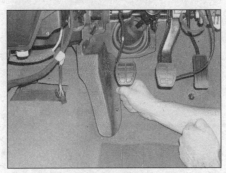

9.20 Remove the driver's foot rest

release all relevant wiring from the clips on the heater casing, noting its routing.
24 Lift out the heater assembly, complete with the heater control panel **(see illustration)**.
25 With the heater/ventilation unit removed, proceed as follows.

9.21a Unscrew the two right-hand . . .

26 Where applicable, unscrew the two screws securing the matrix to the heater/ventilation unit, then release the two securing clips, and carefully withdraw the matrix from its housing, taking care not to damage the matrix fins **(see illustrations)**.

9.21b . . . and single left-hand nuts (arrowed) securing the heater assembly to the bulkhead

9.22 Unscrew the bolt securing the heater assembly to the mounting bracket

9.23 Unbolt the earth lead from the passenger's side footwell

9.24 Lifting out the heater assembly

9.26a Release the securing clips . . .

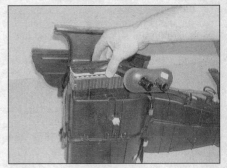

9.26b . . . and withdraw the matrix from its housing

3

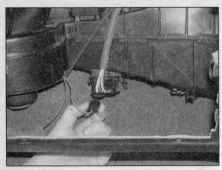

9.30a Disconnect the blower motor wiring plug . . .

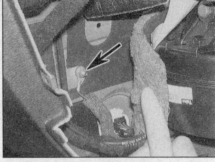

9.30b . . . and unbolt the earth wire (arrowed) from the door pillar

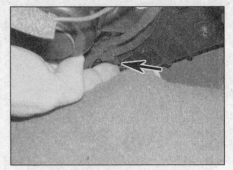

9.31a Release the retaining clip (arrowed) . . .

9.31b . . . then withdraw the motor

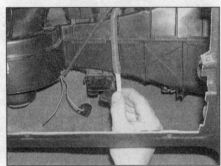

9.35 Disconnect the wiring connectors from the resistor . . .

9.36 . . . then depress the retaining tabs and withdraw the resistor

27 Refitting is a reversal of removal, bearing in mind the following points.
   a) Check the condition of the gasket which fits between the matrix pipes and the bulkhead, and renew if necessary.
   b) Take care to avoid damage to the matrix fins when sliding the matrix into its housing.
   c) Make sure that all wiring is correctly reconnected and routed.
   d) Make sure that the air ducts are securely clipped into position.
   e) Refit the facia assembly as described in Chapter 12.
   f) On completion, check the coolant level and top up if necessary as described in Weekly checks.

Heater blower motor

28 Disconnect the battery negative lead.
29 Where applicable, remove the passenger's side lower facia panel.
30 Reach under the facia and disconnect the blower motor wiring plug. Trace back the earth wire from the blower motor, and unbolt the end of the earth wire from the door pillar – Note that improved access to the earth wire can be obtained by removing the glovebox (see Chapter 11, Section 31) (see illustrations).
31 Release the retaining clip, then rotate the motor assembly clockwise and lower it out from the base of the housing (see illustrations).
32 Refitting is a reversal of the removal procedure making sure the motor is correctly clipped into the housing.

Heater blower motor resistor

33 Disconnect the battery negative lead.
34 Where applicable, remove the passenger's side lower facia panel.
35 Reach up under the facia and disconnect the wiring connectors from the resistor (see illustration).
36 Depress the resistor retaining tabs, and withdraw the resistor from its housing (see illustration).
37 Refitting is the reverse of removal.

Models with air conditioning

Heater control unit

38 The procedure is as described previously in this Section for models without air conditioning.

Heater matrix

39 On models equipped with air conditioning

10.1 Removing a passenger's side facia vent

it is not possible to remove the heater matrix without opening the refrigerant circuit (see Section 11). Therefore this task must be entrusted to a Seat dealer or an air conditioning specialist.

Heater blower motor

40 Remove the facia assembly as described in Chapter 11.
41 Disconnect the motor wiring connector.
42 Disconnect the wiring connector from the motor then remove the retaining screws and lower the motor assembly out of position.
43 Refitting is the reverse of removal.

Heater blower motor resistor

44 The procedure is as described previously in this Section for models without air conditioning, but note that the resistor is secured to the housing by a screw.

10 Heating/ventilation system vents – removal and refitting

Driver's and passenger's side vents

1 To remove a vent, carefully prise it from the housing using a small flat-bladed screwdriver (see illustration). Take care not to damage the surrounding trim.
2 To refit, carefully push the vent into position until the locating clips engage.

Central facia vents

3 Proceed as described previously for the driver's and passenger's side vents, but note that each vent must be prised progressively from both sides to release it from the housing **(see illustration)**.

11 Air conditioning system – general information and precautions

General information

An air conditioning system is available on certain models. It enables the temperature of incoming air to be lowered, and dehumidifies the air, which makes for rapid demisting and increased comfort.

The cooling side of the system works in the same way as a domestic refrigerator. Refrigerant gas is drawn into a belt-driven compressor and passes into a condenser mounted in front of the radiator, where it loses heat and becomes liquid. The liquid passes through an expansion valve to an evaporator, where it changes from liquid under high pressure to gas under low pressure. This change is accompanied by a drop in temperature, which cools the evaporator. The refrigerant returns to the compressor and the cycle begins again.

Air blown through the evaporator passes to the air distribution unit, where it is mixed with hot air blown through the heater matrix to achieve the desired temperature in the passenger compartment.

10.3 Prising out a central facia vent

The heating side of the system works in the same way as on models without air conditioning (see Section 8).

The operation of the system is controlled electronically by coolant temperature switches (see Section 6), and pressure switches which are screwed into the compressor high-pressure line. Any problems with the system should be referred to a Seat dealer or an air conditioning specialist.

Precautions

⚠ **Warning: The refrigeration circuit contains a refrigerant and it is therefore dangerous to disconnect any part of the system without specialised knowledge and equipment. The refrigerant is potentially dangerous and should only be handled by qualified persons. If it is splashed onto the skin it can cause frostbite. It is not itself poisonous, but in the presence of a naked flame (including a cigarette) it forms a poisonous gas. Uncontrolled discharging of the refrigerant is dangerous and potentially damaging to the environment. Do not operate the air conditioning system if it is known to be short of refrigerant, as this may damage the compressor.**

When an air conditioning system is fitted, it is necessary to observe special precautions whenever dealing with any part of the system, its associated components and any items which require disconnection of the system. If for any reason the system must be disconnected, entrust this task to your Seat dealer or an air conditioning specialist.

12 Air conditioning system components – removal and refitting

⚠ **Warning: Do not attempt to open the refrigerant circuit. Refer to the precautions given in Section 11.**

1 The only operation which can be carried out easily without discharging the refrigerant is the renewal of the compressor drivebelt, which is covered in Chapter 1. All other operations must be referred to a Seat dealer or an air conditioning specialist.

2 If necessary the compressor can be unbolted and moved aside, without disconnecting its flexible hoses, after removing the drivebelt.

3

Chapter 4 Part A:
Fuel system - single-point petrol injection

Contents

Degrees of difficulty

Easy, suitable for novice with little experience	**Fairly easy,** suitable for beginner with some experience	**Fairly difficult,** suitable for competent DIY mechanic	**Difficult,** suitable for experienced DIY mechanic	**Very difficult,** suitable for expert DIY or professional

Specifications

System type
Engine codes AAU, AAV, ABD, ABU, 1F .... Bosch Mono-Motronic

Fuel system data
Fuel pump type .... Electric, immersed in fuel tank
Fuel pump delivery rate .... 625 cm^3/30 secs (battery voltage of 12.0V)
Regulated fuel pressure .... 0.8 to 1.2 bar
Engine idle speed:
  Engine codes AAU, AAV, ABD*, ABU .... 750 to 850 rpm (non-adjustable, electronically controlled)
  *Engine code ABD with chassis nos 150797 to 499999 and
  700918 to 999999 .... 850 to 950 rpm (non-adjustable, electronically controlled)
  Engine code 1F .... 825 to 1025 rpm (non-adjustable, electronically controlled)
Exhaust gas CO content .... 1.0 ± 0.5%
Injector electrical resistance .... 1.2 to 1.6 ohms at 15°C

Recommended fuel
Minimum octane rating .... 91 RON unleaded

Torque wrench settings
	Nm	lbf ft
CO sampling pipe bracket to inlet manifold	13	10
Fuel connection union to throttle body	25	18
Fuel tank strap bolts	25	18
Injector retaining screw	5	4
Inlet manifold	25	18
Throttle body retaining screws	15	11

1 General information and precautions

General information

The Bosch Mono-Motronic system is a self-contained engine management system, which controls both the fuel injection and ignition. This Chapter deals with the fuel injection system components only - refer to Chapter 5B for details of the ignition system components.

The fuel injection system comprises a fuel tank, an electric fuel pump, a fuel filter, fuel supply and return lines, a throttle body with an integral electronic fuel injector, and an Electronic Control Unit (ECU) together with its associated sensors, actuators and wiring.

The fuel pump delivers a constant supply of fuel through a cartridge filter to the throttle body, at a slightly higher pressure than required - the fuel pressure regulator (integral with the throttle body) maintains a constant fuel pressure at the fuel injector and returns excess fuel to the tank via the return line. This constant flow system also helps to reduce fuel temperature and prevents vaporisation.

The fuel injector is opened and closed by an Electronic Control Unit (ECU), which calculates the injection timing and duration according to engine speed, throttle position and rate of opening, inlet air temperature, coolant temperature, road speed and exhaust gas oxygen content information, received from sensors mounted on the engine.

Inlet air is drawn into the engine through the air cleaner, which contains a renewable paper filter element. The inlet air temperature is regulated by a vacuum operated valve mounted in the air cleaner, which blends air at ambient temperature with hot air, drawn from over the exhaust manifold.

Idle speed control is achieved partly by an electronic throttle positioning module, mounted on the side of the throttle body and partly by the ignition system, which gives fine control of the idle speed by altering the ignition timing. As a result, manual adjustment of the engine idle speed is not necessary.

To improve cold starting and idling (and fuel economy), an electric heating element is mounted on the underside of the inlet manifold; this prevents fuel vapour condensation when the engine is cold. Power is supplied to the heater by a relay, which is in turn controlled by the ECU.

The exhaust gas oxygen content is constantly monitored by the ECU via the Lambda sensor, which is mounted in the exhaust pipe. The ECU then uses this information to modify the injection timing and duration to maintain the optimum air/fuel ratio - a result of this is that manual adjustment of the idle exhaust CO content is not necessary. In addition, all models are fitted with an exhaust catalyst - see Chapter 4D for details.

In addition, the ECU controls the operation of the activated charcoal filter evaporative loss system - refer to Chapter 4D for further details.

It should be noted that fault diagnosis of the Bosch Mono-Motronic system is only possible with dedicated electronic test equipment. Problems with the systems operation should therefore be referred to a Seat dealer for assessment. Once the fault has been identified, the removal/refitting sequences detailed in the following Sections will then allow the appropriate component(s) to be renewed as required. **Note:** *Throughout this Chapter, vehicles are frequently referred to by their engine code, rather than by engine capacity - refer to Chapter 2A for engine code listings.*

Precautions

⚠️ *Warning: Petrol is extremely flammable - great care must be taken when working on any part of the fuel system.*

Do not smoke, or allow any naked flames or uncovered light bulbs near the work area. Note that gas powered domestic appliances with pilot flames, such as heaters boilers and tumble-dryers, also present a fire hazard - bear this in mind if you are working in an area where such appliances are present. Always keep a suitable fire extinguisher close to the work area and familiarise yourself with its operation before starting work. Wear eye protection when working on fuel systems and wash off any fuel spilt on bare skin immediately with soap and water. Note that fuel vapour is just as dangerous as liquid fuel; a vessel that has been emptied of liquid fuel will still contain vapour and can be potentially explosive.

Many of the operations described in this Chapter involve the disconnection of fuel

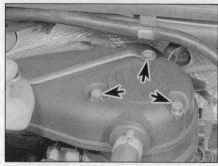

2.2 Remove the throttle body air box retaining screws (arrowed)

lines, which may cause an amount of fuel spillage. Before commencing work, refer to the above Warning and the information in Safety first! at the beginning of this manual.

Residual fuel pressure remains in the fuel system long after the engine has been switched off. This pressure must be relieved in a controlled manner before work can commence on any component in the fuel system - refer to Section 9 for details.

When working with fuel system components, pay particular attention to cleanliness - dirt entering the fuel system may cause blockages which will lead to poor running.

In the interests of personal safety and equipment protection, many of the procedures in this Chapter state that the negative cable be removed from the battery terminal. This firstly eliminates the possibility of accidental short circuits being caused as the vehicle is being worked upon, and secondly prevents damage to electronic components (eg sensors, actuators, ECUs) which are particularly sensitive to the power surges caused by disconnection or reconnection of the wiring harness whilst they are still live.

It should be noted, however, that many of the engine management systems described in this Chapter (and Chapter 5B) have a learning capability, that allows the system to adapt to the engine's running characteristics as it wears with use. This

2.8 On the round-type air cleaner, prise open the air cleaner cover retaining clips

learnt information is lost when the battery is disconnected and the system will then take a short period of time to re-learn the engine's characteristics - this may be manifested (temporarily) as rough idling, reduced throttle response and possibly a slight increase in fuel consumption, until the system re-adapts. The re-adaptation time will depend on how often the vehicle is used and the driving conditions encountered.

2 Air cleaner and inlet system - removal and refitting

Removal

Rectangular air cleaner

1 Slacken the worm drive clips and disconnect the air ducting from the air cleaner and air box.
2 Lift off the plastic cap, remove the retaining screw **(see illustration)** and lift off the throttle body air box, recovering the seal.
3 Disconnect the vacuum hoses from the inlet air temperature regulator vacuum switch, noting their order of fitment.
4 Unhook the rubber loops from the lugs on the chassis member.
5 Pull the air cleaner towards the engine and withdraw the air inlet hose from the port on the inner wing.
6 Lift the air cleaner out of the engine bay.
7 Prise open the retaining clips and lift the top cover from the air cleaner. Remove the air cleaner filter element (see Chapter 1A for more details).

Round air cleaner

8 On models with a round-type air cleaner, prise open the retaining clips and lift the cover from the top of the air cleaner **(see illustration)**. Recover the filter element, then remove the retaining nuts and lift the air cleaner from the top of the throttle body.

Refitting

9 Refit the air cleaner by following the removal procedure in reverse.

3 Inlet air temperature regulator - removal and refitting

Removal

1 Disconnect the vacuum hoses from the temperature regulator, noting their locations.
2 Remove the throttle body air box/air cleaner, as described in Section 2.
3 Prise off the metal retaining plate **(see illustration)** and remove the temperature regulator from the throttle body air box/air cleaner. Recover the gasket.

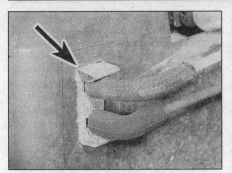

3.3 Temperature regulator metal plate (arrowed) - wing-mounted air cleaner

Refitting

4 Refit the regulator by following the removal procedure in reverse.

4 Accelerator cable - removal, refitting and adjustment

Removal

Note: *On RHD models the accelerator pedal pivot shaft extends into the left-hand passenger compartment, behind the heater assembly.*

1 Remove the throttle body air box/air cleaner as described in Section 2.

2 At the throttle body, disconnect the accelerator inner cable from the throttle valve spindle plate **(see illustration)**.

3 Extract the outer cable from the mounting bracket - it is not necessary to remove the adjustment clip from the cable ferrule.

4 Using a screwdriver, carefully prise the cap/grommet from the bulkhead. The cap is retained by three tags, and if necessary have an assistant insert a screwdriver from inside the car to help release the tags. On RHD models, the pedal lever extension is located behind the heater assembly.

5 Have the assistant lift the accelerator pedal so that the top of the extension is visible through the hole in the bulkhead on the engine compartment side. Unclip the accelerator cable end from the pedal extension lever.

6 Withdraw the accelerator cable from inside the engine compartment.

Refitting

7 Refitting is a reversal of removal, but if necessary adjust the cable as follows.

Adjustment

8 At the throttle body, fix the position of the outer cable in its mounting bracket by inserting the metal clip in one of the locating slots, such that when the accelerator pedal is depressed fully, the throttle valve is held wide open to its end stop.

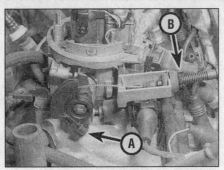

4.2 Throttle body accelerator cable mounting arrangement

A Throttle valve spindle plate
B Adjustment clip

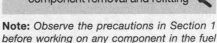

5 Bosch Mono Motronic engine management system - component removal and refitting

Note: *Observe the precautions in Section 1 before working on any component in the fuel system.*

Throttle body

Removal

1 Refer to Section 2 and remove the air cleaner/throttle body air box.

2 Refer to Section 9 and depressurise the fuel system, then disconnect the battery negative cable and position it away from the terminal.

3 Disconnect the fuel supply and return hoses from the ports on the side of the throttle body. Note the arrows that denote the direction of fuel flow, and mark the hoses accordingly **(see illustration)**.

4 Unplug the wiring harness from the throttle body at the connectors, labelling them to aid correct refitting later.

5 Refer to Section 4 and disconnect the accelerator cable from the throttle body.

6 Remove the through-bolts and lift the throttle body away from the inlet manifold, recovering the gasket.

Refitting

7 Refitting is a reversal of removal; renew all gaskets where appropriate. On completion, check and if necessary adjust the accelerator cable.

Fuel injector

Removal

8 Refer to Section 2 and remove the air cleaner/throttle body air box.

9 Refer to Section 9 and depressurise the fuel system, then disconnect the battery negative cable and position it away from the terminal.

10 Unplug the wiring harness from the injector at the connector(s), labelling them to aid correct refitting later.

11 Remove the screw and lift off the injector retaining cap/inlet air temperature sensor housing **(see illustration)**.

5.3 Throttle body fuel supply and return ports (engine code ABD shown)

12 Lift the injector out of the throttle body, recovering the O-ring seals.

13 Check the injector electrical resistance using a multimeter and compare the result with the Specifications.

Refitting

14 Refit the injector by following the removal procedure in reverse, renewing all O-ring seals. Tighten the retaining screw to the specified torque.

Inlet air temperature sensor

15 The inlet air temperature sensor is an integral part of the injector retaining cap. Removal is as described in the previous sub-Section. Check its electrical resistance using a multimeter with a resistance measurement function (refer to illustration 5.11).

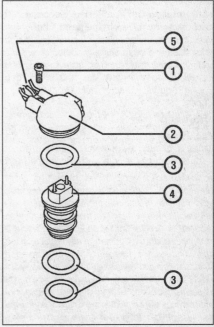

5.11 Injector components (engine code ABD shown)

1 Screw
2 Injector cap/inlet air temperature sensor housing
3 O-ring seals
4 Injector
5 Wiring harness connection

Fuel pressure regulator

Removal

16 If the operation of the fuel pressure regulator is in question, dismantle the unit as described below, then check the cleanliness and integrity of the internal components.

17 Remove the air cleaner/throttle body air box, with reference to Section 2.

18 Refer to Section 9 and depressurise the fuel system, then disconnect the battery negative cable and position it away from the terminal.

19 With reference to the relevant sub-Section, remove the screw and lift off the inlet air temperature/injector cap.

20 Slacken and withdraw the retaining screws and lift off the fuel pressure regulator retaining frame **(see illustration)**.

21 Lift out the upper cover, spring and membrane.

22 Clean all the components thoroughly, then inspect the membrane for cracks or splits - renew it if necessary.

Refitting

23 Reassemble the pressure regulator by following the removal procedure in reverse.

Throttle valve positioning module

Removal

24 Disconnect the battery negative cable and position it away from the terminal. Remove the air cleaner/throttle body air box, with reference to Section 2.

25 Refer to Section 4 and disconnect the accelerator cable from the throttle body.

26 Unplug the connector from the side of the throttle valve positioning module.

27 Remove the retaining screws and lift the module together with the accelerator cable outer mounting bracket away from the throttle body.

Refitting

28 Refitting is a reversal of removal. Note that if a new module has been fitted, the adjustment of the idle switch will need to be checked - refer to a Seat dealer for advice as this operation requires access to dedicated test equipment.

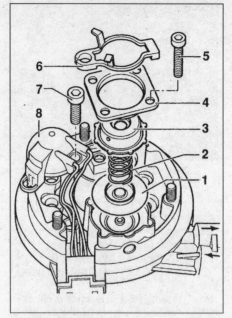

5.20 Fuel pressure regulator components

1	Membrane	6	Cable guide
2	Spring	7	Injector retaining
3	Upper cover		screw
4	Retaining frame	8	Injector cap
5	Screws		

Throttle valve potentiometer

29 Refer to the relevant sub-Section and remove the throttle body.

30 The throttle valve potentiometer is an integral part of the lower section of the throttle body and cannot be renewed separately.

Idle switch

31 Refer to the relevant sub-Section and remove the throttle valve positioning module. The idle switch is an integral part of the module and cannot be renewed separately.

32 Where a new throttle valve positioning module has been fitted, the adjustment of the idle switch will need to be checked - refer to a Seat dealer for advice as this operation requires access to dedicated test equipment.

Lambda sensor

Removal

33 The lambda sensor is either threaded into the exhaust pipe, at the front of the first silencer/catalyst, or threaded into the exhaust manifold **(see illustration)**. Refer to Chapter 4D for details.

34 Disconnect the battery negative cable and position it away from the terminal, then unplug the wiring harness from the lambda sensor at the connector, located adjacent to the right hand rear engine mounting.

35 Working under the vehicle, slacken and withdraw the sensor, taking care to avoid damaging the sensor probe as it is removed.

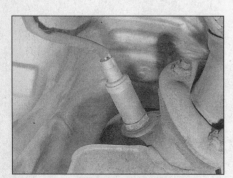

5.33 Lambda sensor (engine code ABD shown)

Note: *As a flying lead remains connected to the sensor after it has been disconnected, if the correct size spanner is not available, a slotted socket will be required to remove the sensor.*

Refitting

36 Apply a little anti-seize grease to the sensor threads only - keep the probe tip clean.

37 Refit the sensor to its housing, tightening it to the correct torque. Restore the harness connection.

Coolant temperature sensor

Removal

38 Disconnect the battery negative cable and position it away from the terminal, then refer to Chapter 3 and drain approximately one quarter of the coolant from the engine.

39 On engine codes AAU, AAV, ABD, and ABU the temperature sensor is located on the left hand side of the cylinder head, under the heater coolant outlet elbow **(see illustration)**. On engine code 1F, the sensor is mounted on top of the coolant outlet elbow, at the front of the cylinder head.

40 Unscrew/unclip the sensor from its housing and recover the sealing washer(s) and O-ring - be prepared for an amount of coolant loss.

Refitting

41 Refit the sensor by reversing the removal procedure, using new sealing washers and rings where appropriate. Refer to Chapter 1A and top-up the cooling system.

Electronic control unit (ECU)

42 The ECU is located behind the engine compartment bulkhead, under one of the windscreen cowl panels. On right-hand drive models it on the right-hand side and on left-hand drive models it is on the left-hand side. The unit is coded, and should not be removed without consulting a Seat dealer, otherwise it may not function correctly when the multi-plug is reconnected. If a new ECU is fitted, it must be adapted to the immobiliser by a Seat dealer using special equipment.

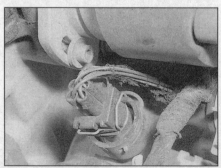

5.39 Coolant temperature sensor (engine code ABD shown)

6 Fuel filter -
removal and refitting

Note: *Observe the precautions in Section 1 before working on any component in the fuel system.*

Removal

1 The fuel filter is mounted in the fuel supply line, on the rear of the fuel tank. Access is from the underside of the vehicle.

2 Refer to Section 9 and depressurise the fuel system.

3 Park the car on a level surface, then apply the handbrake and select 1st gear and chock the front roadwheels. Raise the rear of the vehicle, support it securely on axle stands and remove the roadwheels; refer to *Jacking and vehicle support* for guidance.

4 Slacken the hose clips and disconnect the fuel lines from either side of the filter unit **(see illustration)**. If the clips are of the crimp type, snip them off with cutters and replace them with equivalent size worm drive clips upon reconnection.

5 Release the filter retaining clip/remove the cover bracket (where applicable) and lower the filter unit away from its mounting bracket.

Refitting

6 Refitting is a reversal of removal. Note the direction of flow arrow marked on the side of the filter unit casing - this must point towards the engine when fitted **(see illustration)**.

6.4 Fuel filter hose clips (arrowed)

7 Fuel pump and
gauge sender unit -
removal and refitting

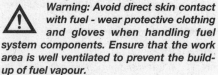

Note: *Observe the precautions in Section 1 before working on the fuel system.*

⚠ **Warning:** *Avoid direct skin contact with fuel - wear protective clothing and gloves when handling fuel system components. Ensure that the work area is well ventilated to prevent the build-up of fuel vapour.*

1 The fuel pump and gauge sender unit are combined in one assembly, which is mounted on the top of the fuel tank. Access is via a hatch provided in the load space floor. The unit protrudes into the fuel tank and its removal involves exposing the contents of the tank to the atmosphere.

6.6 Note the direction of flow arrow marked on the side of the filter unit

Removal

2 Depressurise the fuel system (Section 9).

3 Ensure that the vehicle is parked on a level surface, then disconnect the battery negative cable and position it away from the terminal.

4 Tilt the rear seat backrest forwards.

5 Unscrew the access hatch screws and lift the hatch away from the floorpan **(see illustrations)**.

6 Unplug the wiring harness connector from the pump/sender unit. The use of screwdriver may be necessary to prise the connector tab to one side **(see illustration)**.

7 Pad the area around the fuel pump with rags to absorb any spilt fuel. Where applicable, disconnect the charcoal canister pipes located over the fuel pump and position the pipe ends to one side **(see illustration)**. Disconnect the fuel supply and return lines and remove them from the ports at the sender unit **(see illustrations)**. Observe the supply

7.5a Unscrew the screws . . .

7.5b . . . and lift the access hatch from the floorpan

7.6 Using a screwdriver to release the wiring harness connector from the pump/sender unit

7.7a Disconnecting the charcoal canister pipes located over the fuel pump

7.7b Depress the buttons . . .

7.7c . . . and disconnect the fuel supply and return lines from the fuel pump/sender unit

4A

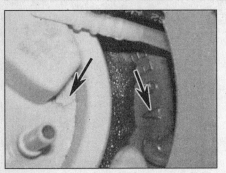

7.8a Alignment marks on the pump body and fuel tank

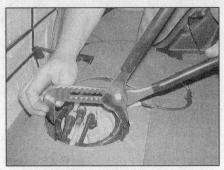

7.8b Using a pair of water pump pliers, unscrew the securing ring . . . .

7.8c . . . and remove it from the fuel pump

and return arrows markings on the ports - label the fuel hoses accordingly to ensure correct refitting later.

8 Note the pump alignment marks on the pump body and fuel tank. Unscrew the plastic securing ring and lift it out. Use a pair of water pump pliers to grip and rotate the plastic securing ring **(see illustrations)**.

9 Lift out the pump/sender unit, holding it above the level of the fuel in the tank until the excess fuel has drained out. Recover the rubber seal **(see illustration)**.

10 Remove the pump/sender unit from the vehicle and lay it on an absorbent card or rag. Inspect the float at the end of the sender unit swinging arm for punctures and fuel ingress - renew the unit if it appears damaged.

11 The fuel pick-up may be removed by releasing the plastic clip with a small screwdriver **(see illustrations)**.

12 Inspect the fuel level sender unit wiper

and track; clean off any dirt and debris that may have accumulated and look for breaks in the track. The sender may be renewed separate from the fuel pump by first releasing the upper retainer with a small screwdriver, then sliding the unit from the pump body and disconnecting the wiring **(see illustrations)**.

13 Inspect the rubber seal from the fuel tank aperture for signs of fatigue and renew it if necessary.

Refitting

14 Refit the sender unit by following the removal procedure in reverse, noting the following points:

a) *The arrow markings on the sender unit body and the fuel tank must be aligned.*

b) *Smear the tank aperture rubber seal with clean fuel before fitting it in position.*

c) *Reconnect the fuel hoses to the correct ports.*

8 Fuel tank - removal and refitting

Note: Observe the precautions in Section 1 before working on the fuel system.

Removal

1 Before the tank can be removed, it must be drained of as much fuel as possible. As no drain plug is provided, it is preferable to carry out this operation with the tank almost empty.

2 Disconnect the battery negative cable and position it away from the terminal. Using a hand pump or syphon, remove any remaining fuel from the bottom of the tank.

3 Chock the front wheels, then jack up the rear of the vehicle and support it on axle stands (see *Jacking and vehicle support*). Remove the rear roadwheels.

7.9 Lifting the fuel pump/sender unit from the fuel tank

7.11a Release the clip with a small screwdriver . . .

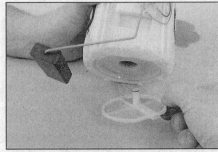

7.11b . . . and carefully remove the fuel pick-up from the bottom of the fuel pump/sender assembly

7.12a Release the upper retainer . . .

7.12b . . . then slide the fuel level sender down from the pump body . . .

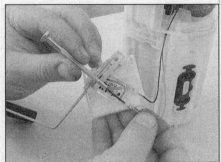

7.12c . . . and disconnect the wiring

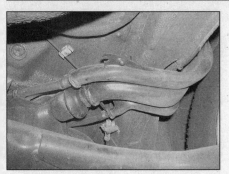

8.9 Fuel tank filler and vent pipes

4 Refer to Section 7 and carry out the following:

a) *Disconnect the wiring harness from the top of the pump sender unit at the connector.*

b) *Disconnect the fuel supply and return hoses from the pump/sender unit.*

c) *Where applicable, disconnect the hoses from the fuel evaporative emission system carbon filter.*

5 Position a trolley jack under the centre of the tank. Insert a block of wood between the jack head and the tank to prevent damage to the tank surface. Raise the jack until it just takes the weight of the tank.

6 Working inside the rear right hand wheel arch, slacken and withdraw the screws that secure the tank filler neck inside of the wheel arch. Open the fuel filler flap and remove the retaining circlip.

7 Release the mounting rubbers from the rear of the exhaust system and lower the system onto the rear axle.

8 Where necessary, unbolt the exhaust heatshield from the side of the fuel tank. Unscrew and remove the fuel tank retaining bolts, keeping one hand on the tank to steady it.

9 Lower the tank away from the underside of the vehicle and disconnect the filler and vent pipes, taking care not to damage the retainers within the fuel tank **(see illustration)**.

10 If the tank is contaminated with sediment or water, remove the fuel pump/sender unit (see Section 7) and swill the tank out with clean fuel. The tank is injection moulded from a synthetic material and if damaged, it should be renewed. However, in certain cases it may be possible to have small leaks or minor damage repaired. Seek the advice of a specialist before attempting to repair the fuel tank.

Refitting

11 Refitting is the reverse of the removal procedure noting the following points:

a) *When lifting the tank back into position ensure the hoses are not trapped between the tank and vehicle body.*

b) *When reconnecting the filler pipe, apply a little petroleum jelly (Vaseline) to the end of the pipe and to the retainers within the fuel tank.*

c) *Ensure that all pipes and hoses are correctly routed and securely held in position with their retaining clips.*

d) *Tighten the tank retaining bolts to the specified torque.*

e) *On completion, refill the tank with fuel and thoroughly check for signs of leakage prior to taking the vehicle out on the road.*

9 Fuel injection system - depressurisation

Note: *Observe the precautions in Section 1 before working on any component in the fuel system.*

⚠ *Warning: The following procedure will merely relieve the pressure in the fuel system - remember that fuel will still be present in the system components and take precautions accordingly before disconnecting any of them.*

1 The fuel system referred to in this Section is defined as the tank-mounted fuel pump, the fuel filter, the fuel injector, the throttle body-mounted fuel pressure regulator and the metal pipes and flexible hoses of the fuel lines between these components. All these contain fuel which will be under pressure while the engine is running and/or while the ignition is switched on. The pressure will remain for some time after the ignition has been switched off and must be relieved before any of these components are disturbed for servicing work. Ideally, the engine should be allowed to cool completely before work commences.

2 Refer to Chapter 12 and locate the fuel pump relay. Remove the relay from its housing, then crank the engine for a few seconds. The engine may fire and run for a while, but continue cranking until it stops. The fuel injector should have opened enough times during cranking to considerably reduce the line fuel pressure.

3 Disconnect the battery negative terminal.

4 Place a suitable container beneath the relevant connection/union to be disconnected, and have a large rag ready to soak up

10.8 Remove the retaining screws and lift out the manifold heater unit

any escaping fuel not being caught by the container.

5 Slowly loosen the connection or union nut (as applicable) to avoid a sudden release of pressure and position the rag around the connection to catch any fuel spray which may be expelled. Once the pressure has been released, disconnect the fuel line and insert plugs to minimise fuel loss and prevent the entry of dirt into the fuel system.

10 Inlet manifold - removal and refitting

Note: *Observe the precautions in Section 1 before working on any component in the fuel system.*

Removal

1 Disconnect the battery negative cable and position it away from the terminal, then refer to Chapter 1 and drain the coolant from the engine.

2 With reference to Section 5, remove the throttle body from the inlet manifold. Recover and discard the gasket and where applicable, remove the intermediate flange.

3 Slacken the clips and remove the coolant hoses from the inlet manifold.

4 Refer to Chapter 9 and disconnect the brake servo vacuum hose from the port on the inlet manifold.

5 On engine codes AAU, AAV, ABD and ABU, remove the screws and lift off the warm air collection plate. Also unbolt the CO sampling pipe bracket from the inlet manifold.

6 Disconnect the harness wiring from the inlet manifold heater at the connector.

7 Progressively slacken and remove the inlet manifold nuts and screws, then loosen the manifold from the cylinder head.

8 Make a final check to ensure that nothing remains connected to the manifold, then manoeuvre it out of the engine bay and recover the gasket. If required, remove the retaining screws and lift out the manifold heater unit **(see illustration)**.

Refitting

9 Refitting is the reverse of the removal procedure, noting the following points:

a) *Ensure that the manifold and cylinder head mating surfaces are clean and dry. Install the manifold with a new gasket and tighten its retaining nuts to the specified torque setting.*

b) *Ensure that all relevant hoses are reconnected to their original positions and are securely held (where necessary) by their retaining clips.*

c) *Refit the throttle body as described in Section 5.*

d) *On completion, refill the cooling system as described in Chapter 1.*

4A

11 Fuel injection system - testing and adjustment

1 If a fault appears in the fuel injection system first ensure that all the system wiring connectors are securely connected and free of corrosion. Then ensure that the fault is not due to poor maintenance; ie, check that the air cleaner filter element is clean, the spark plugs are in good condition and correctly gapped, the cylinder compression pressures are correct, the ignition timing is correct and the engine breather hoses are clear and undamaged, referring to Chapter 1A, Chapter 2A and Chapter 5B for further information.

2 If these checks fail to reveal the cause of the problem the vehicle should be taken to a suitably equipped Seat dealer for testing. A diagnostic connector is incorporated in the engine management system wiring harness, into which a dedicated electronic test equipment can be plugged. The test equipment is capable of interrogating the engine management system ECU electronically and accessing its internal fault log. In this manner, faults can be pinpointed quickly and simply, even if their occurrence is intermittent. Testing all the system components individually in an attempt to locate the fault by elimination is a time consuming operation that is unlikely to be fruitful (particularly if the fault occurs dynamically) and carries high risk of damage to the ECU's internal components.

3 Experienced home mechanics equipped with an accurate tachometer and a carefully-calibrated exhaust gas analyser may be able to check the exhaust gas CO content and the engine idle speed; if these are found to be out of specification, then the vehicle must be taken to a Seat dealer for assessment. Neither the air/fuel mixture (exhaust gas CO content) nor the engine idle speed are manually adjustable; incorrect test results indicate a fault within the fuel injection system.

Chapter 4 Part B:
Fuel system - multipoint petrol injection

Contents

Degrees of difficulty

Easy, suitable for novice with little experience		Fairly easy, suitable for beginner with some experience		Fairly difficult, suitable for competent DIY mechanic	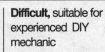	Difficult, suitable for experienced DIY mechanic		Very difficult, suitable for expert DIY or professional	

Specifications

System type
Engine code AER, AEX, APQ	Bosch Motronic 9.0
Engine code AEE, ALM	Magneti-Marelli 1AV
Engine code AFT, AGG	Simos
Engine code 2E, ABF	Digifant

Fuel system data
Fuel pump type	Electric, immersed in fuel tank
Fuel pump delivery rate	1100 cm^3 / min (battery voltage of 12.6V)
Regulated fuel pressure	Approximately 2.5 bar

Engine idle speed (non-adjustable, electronically controlled):
Engine code AER	860 to 940 rpm
Engine codes AEX, APQ, AEE, ALM	840 ± 50 rpm
Engine code AFT	790 to 890 rpm
Engine code AGG	880 ± 50 rpm
Engine code 2E	825 ± 25 rpm
Engine code ABF	820 ± 50 rpm

Idle CO content (non-adjustable, electronically controlled):
All engine codes	0.5%

Injector electrical resistance:
Engine code AER, AEX, APQ, AEE, ALM	14 to 17 ohms
Engine codes AFT, AGG, 2E, ABF	15 to 20 ohms

Recommended fuel
Minimum octane rating (all models)	95 RON

4B

Torque wrench settings

	Nm	lbf ft
Airflow meter	10	7
Earth lead to throttle body	10	7
ECU	10	7
Evaporative carbon canister	20	15
Filler neck	4	3
Fuel rail:		
Except engine code AGG	10	7
Engine code AGG:		
M6	10	7
M8	20	15
Fuel level sender/pump	75	55
Fuel tank	25	18
Hot air baffle plate (engine code 2E):		
Bolt	25	18
Nut	20	15
Idle speed control valve (engine code 2E)	20	15
Inlet manifold:		
Except engine codes 2E, AGG, AFT	20	15
Engine codes 2E, AGG, AFT	25	18
Lambda sensor:		
Except engine codes 2E, AGG, ABF	55	41
Engine code 2E, AGG, ABF	50	37
Throttle body (engine codes 2E, AGG)	10	7
Throttle valve potentiometer	10	7

1 General information and precautions

General information

The Bosch Motronic and Magneti-Marelli 1AV systems are self-contained engine management systems, which control both the fuel injection and ignition. This Chapter deals with the fuel system components only - see Chapter 5B for details of the ignition system.

The fuel injection system comprises a fuel tank, an electric fuel pump, a fuel filter, fuel supply and return lines, a throttle body, a fuel rail, a fuel pressure regulator, four electronic fuel injectors, and an Electronic Control Unit (ECU) together with its associated sensors, actuators and wiring. The two systems used are essentially very similar - the only significant differences lie within the ECUs.

The fuel pump delivers a constant supply of fuel through a cartridge filter to the fuel rail, at a slightly higher pressure than required - the fuel pressure regulator maintains a constant fuel pressure to the fuel injectors, and returns excess fuel to the tank via the return line. This constant flow system also helps to reduce fuel temperature, and prevents vaporisation.

The fuel injectors are opened and closed by an Electronic Control Unit (ECU), which calculates the injection timing and duration according to engine speed, crankshaft position, throttle position and rate of opening, inlet manifold depression, inlet air temperature, coolant temperature, road speed and exhaust gas oxygen content information, received from sensors mounted on and around the engine.

Inlet air is drawn into the engine through the air cleaner, which contains a renewable paper filter element. The inlet air temperature is regulated by a valve mounted in the air cleaner inlet trunking, which blends air at ambient temperature with hot air, drawn from over the exhaust manifold.

The temperature of the air entering the throttle body is measured by a sensor mounted on the right-hand side of the inlet manifold. This sensor also monitors the pressure in the inlet manifold. This information is used by the ECU to fine-tune the fuelling requirements for different operating conditions.

Idle speed control is achieved partly by an electronic throttle valve positioning module, on the rear of the throttle body and partly by the ignition system, which gives fine control of the idle speed by altering the ignition timing. As a result, manual adjustment of the engine idle speed is not necessary or possible.

The exhaust gas oxygen content is constantly monitored by the ECU via the Lambda sensor, which is mounted in the exhaust pipe. The ECU then uses this information to modify the injection timing and duration to maintain the optimum air/fuel ratio - a result of this is that manual adjustment of the idle exhaust CO content is not necessary or possible. All models are fitted with a catalytic converter - see Chapter 4D.

Where fitted, the ECU controls the operation of the activated charcoal filter evaporative loss system - refer to Chapter 4D for further details.

It should be noted that fault diagnosis of all the engine management systems described in this Chapter is only possible with dedicated electronic test equipment. Problems with the systems operation should therefore be referred to a VW dealer for assessment. Once the fault has been identified, the removal/refitting sequences detailed in the following Sections will then allow the appropriate component(s) to be renewed as required.

Precautions

 Warning: Petrol is extremely flammable - great care must be taken when working on any part of the fuel system.

Do not smoke, or allow any naked flames or uncovered light bulbs near the work area. Note that gas powered domestic appliances with pilot flames, such as heaters boilers and tumble-dryers, also present a fire hazard - bear this in mind if you are working in an area where such appliances are present. Always keep a suitable fire extinguisher close to the work area, and familiarise yourself with its operation before starting work. Wear eye protection when working on fuel systems, and wash off any fuel spilt on bare skin immediately with soap and water. Note that fuel vapour is just as dangerous as liquid fuel - possibly more so; a vessel that has been emptied of liquid fuel will still contain vapour, and can be potentially explosive.

Many of the operations described in this Chapter involve the disconnection of fuel lines, which may cause an amount of fuel

2.7a Undo the screws securing the air cleaner to the throttle body

2.7b The screws which secure the element cover are numbered 1 to 4

2.8 Removing the air filter element

spillage. Before commencing work, refer to the above Warning and the information in Safety first! at the beginning of this manual.

Residual fuel pressure always remain in the fuel system, long after the engine has been switched off. This pressure must be relieved in a controlled manner before work can commence on any component in the fuel system - refer to Section 11 for details.

When working with fuel system components, pay particular attention to cleanliness - dirt entering the fuel system may cause blockages, which will lead to poor running.

In the interests of personal safety and equipment protection, many of the procedures in this Chapter suggest that the negative lead be removed from the battery terminal. This firstly eliminates the possibility of accidental short-circuits being caused as the vehicle is being worked upon, and secondly prevents damage to electronic components (eg sensors, actuators, ECUs) which are particularly sensitive to the power surges caused by disconnection or reconnection of the wiring harness whilst they are still live.

It should be noted, however, that the engine management systems described in this Chapter (and Chapter 5B) have a learning capability, that allows the system to adapt to the engine's running characteristics as it wears with use. This

learnt information is lost when the battery is disconnected, and the system will then take a short period of time to re-learn the engine's characteristics - this may be manifested (temporarily) as rough idling, reduced throttle response and possibly a slight increase in fuel consumption, until the system re-adapts. The re-adaptation time will depend on how often the vehicle is used and the driving conditions encountered.

2 Air cleaner and inlet system - removal and refitting

Removal

Rectangular side-mounted air cleaner

1 Loosen the clips and disconnect the air ducting from the air cleaner/airflow meter and inlet manifold.

2 Disconnect the wiring from the airflow meter or air temperature sensor as applicable.

3 Disconnect the vacuum hoses from the inlet air temperature regulator vacuum switch, noting their order of fitment.

4 Unhook the rubber loops from the lugs on the chassis member, and withdraw the air cleaner body to the rear.

5 Prise open the retaining clips and lift the top cover from the air cleaner. Remove the air cleaner filter element (see Chapter 1A for more details).

6 On all engine codes except ABF, refer to Section 5, 6 or 7 and remove the airflow meter from the air cleaner.
Caution: The airflow meter is a delicate component - handle it carefully.

Inlet manifold/throttle body mounted air cleaner

7 There are eight screws visible on the air cleaner top cover, and four of them are marked 1 to 4 on the top cover - these four screws secure the housing to the inlet manifold. The remaining four screws secure the air cleaner top cover to the air cleaner housing, and need only be removed if the filter element is to be renewed **(see illustrations)**. If all eight screws are removed, note that they are of different lengths, so note their locations as they are removed.

8 If all eight screws have been removed, lift off the air cleaner top cover, and take out the filter element **(see illustration)**.

9 Unhook the insulated earth strap leading to the ignition coil, which is hooked into a clip on the left-hand side of the housing **(see illustration)**.

10 Disconnect the hot air hose from the shroud on the exhaust manifold, and release it from the clip on the front of the cylinder head **(see illustration)**.

11 Lift up the air cleaner housing and disconnect the crankcase breather pipe from the stub; also disconnect the vacuum hoses where applicable. Check the pipe for signs of hardening or splitting, and fit a new pipe if necessary **(see illustration)**.

4B

2.9 Unhooking the earth strap from the air cleaner

2.10 Disconnecting the hot air hose from the exhaust manifold shroud

2.11 Disconnect the crankcase breather pipe from the stub . . .

2.12 ... then remove the air cleaner housing from the engine

12 The air cleaner housing can now be removed from the engine compartment **(see illustration)**. Recover the sealing washer from the base of the housing - it may still be on the throttle body. Examine the seal condition, and renew if it provides a less-than-airtight fit.

Refitting

13 Refitting is a reversal of removal.

---

3 Inlet air temperature regulation system - general information and component renewal

General information

1 An inlet air temperature regulation system is fitted to all engines except engine codes AGG and AFT. On engine codes AER, AEX, APQ, AEE and ALM, the system consists of a wax-filled capsule mounted in the air ducting. The capsule operates an internal flap to direct hot air into the air cleaner. On engine codes 2E and ABF, the system consists of a temperature controlled vacuum switch, mounted in the air cleaner housing, a vacuum operated flap valve and several lengths of interconnecting vacuum hose. The switch senses the temperature of the inlet air and opens when a preset lower limit is reached. It then directs the manifold vacuum to the flap valve which opens, allowing warm air drawn from around the exhaust manifold to blend with the inlet air. On engine codes AGG and AFT, the inlet air temperature sensor monitors the air temperature and constantly informs the ECU.

Component renewal

Capsule system

Regulating flap unit

2 Loosen the clip and disconnect the hot air hose from the flap unit, then undo the screw and disconnect the air inlet duct.
3 Undo the screw and remove the regulating flap unit from the air cleaner **(see illustration)**.
4 Refitting is a reversal of removal.

Vacuum operated system

Temperature switch

5 With reference to Section 2, release the clips and remove the top cover from the air cleaner.
6 Disconnect the vacuum hoses from the temperature switch, noting their order of connection to ensure correct refitting.
7 Prise the metal retaining clip off the

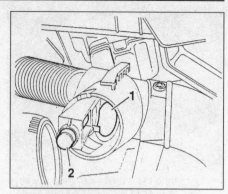

3.3 Air inlet temperature control flap valve (1) and temperature sensor (2)

temperature switch ports, then press the switch body through into the top of the air cleaner. Recover the gasket.
8 Refitting is a reversal of removal.

Flap valve

9 The flap valve is integrated with the lower section of the air cleaner and cannot be renewed separately.

---

4 Accelerator cable - removal, refitting and adjustment

Removal

Note: *On RHD models the accelerator pedal pivot shaft extends into the left-hand passenger compartment, behind the heater assembly.*

1 On engine codes AER, AEX, APQ, AEE and ALM, remove the air cleaner assembly complete as described in Section 2. Also remove the engine top cover where necessary.
2 At the throttle body, prise off the clip (if fitted) and disconnect the accelerator inner cable from the throttle valve spindle segment **(see illustrations)**.
3 Extract the outer cable from the mounting bracket - it is not necessary to remove the adjustment clip from the cable ferrule **(see illustrations)**.
4 Using a screwdriver, carefully prise the cap/grommet from the bulkhead **(see illustrations)**.

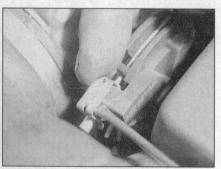

4.2a At the throttle body, prise off the clip ...

4.2b ... and disconnect the accelerator inner cable from the throttle valve

4.3a Remove the metal clip ...

4.3b ... and extract the outer cable from the bracket (engine code 2E shown)

4.4a Accelerator cable cap/grommet on the bulkhead

4.4b Removing the accelerator cable cap/grommet from the bulkhead

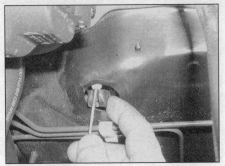

4.5 Unclipping the accelerator cable end from the pedal extension lever

4.8 Adjust the accelerator cable, then fix the cable using the metal clip in one of the slots

The cap is retained by three tags, and if necessary have an assistant insert a screwdriver from inside the car to help release the tags. On RHD models, the pedal lever extension is located behind the heater assembly.

5 Have the assistant lift the accelerator pedal so that the top of the extension is visible through the hole in the bulkhead on the engine compartment side. Unclip the accelerator cable end from the pedal extension lever (see illustration).

6 Withdraw the accelerator cable from inside the engine compartment.

Refitting

7 Refitting is a reversal of removal, but if necessary adjust the cable as follows.

Adjustment

8 At the throttle body, fix the position of the

outer cable in its mounting bracket by inserting the metal clip in one of the locating slots (see illustration), such that when the accelerator pedal is depressed fully, the throttle valve is held wide open to its end stop.

5 Bosch Motronic/ Magneti-Marelli system - component removal and refitting

Note: *Observe the precautions in Section 1 before working on any component in the fuel system.*

Throttle body

Removal

1 Remove the air cleaner housing as described in Section 2.

2 Refer to Section 4 and detach the accelerator cable from the throttle valve lever.

3 Disconnect the battery negative (earth) lead (see Chapter 5A), and position it away from the terminal.

4 Unplug the wiring connectors from the throttle body and from the inlet manifold pressure/air temperature sensor (see illustrations).

5 Disconnect the hose for the charcoal canister from the port on the throttle body (see illustration).

6 Slacken and withdraw the through-bolts, then lift the throttle body away from the inlet manifold. Recover and discard the gasket. Note that one of the bolts secures the throttle body earth strap (see illustrations).

7 If required, refer to the relevant sub-Section and remove the throttle potentiometer.

4B

5.4a Disconnect the throttle potentiometer wiring plug . . .

5.4b . . . and the inlet air pressure/temperature sensor plug

5.5 Disconnect the charcoal canister hose from the stub on the throttle body

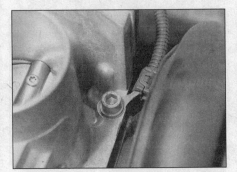

5.6a One of the throttle body through-bolts also secures the earth strap . . .

5.6b . . . remove the bolt, and move the strap to one side

5.6c Remove the remaining through-bolts . . .

5.6d ... lift away the throttle body ...

5.6e ... and recover the base gasket

5.10a Disconnect the injector wiring plugs ...

5.10b ... then unclip the harness retaining clips, and move the wiring harness to one side

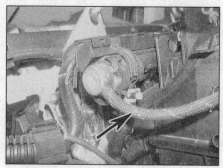

5.12 Fuel pressure regulator vacuum hose

5.13 Fuel supply and return connections at the fuel rail - note direction-of-flow arrows and colour-coding

Refitting

8 Refitting is a reversal of removal, noting the following:

a) *Use a new throttle body-to-inlet manifold gasket.*

b) *Tighten the throttle body through-bolts securely, to prevent air leaks. A tightening torque for these bolts is not specified by the manufacturers.*

c) *Ensure that all hoses and electrical connectors are refitted securely.*

d) *With reference to Section 4, check and if necessary adjust the accelerator cable.*

Fuel injectors and fuel rail

Note: *If a faulty injector is suspected, before removing the injectors, it is worth trying the effect of one of the proprietary injector-*

cleaning treatments. These can be added to the petrol in the tank, and are intended to clean the injectors as you drive.

Removal

9 Disconnect the battery negative (earth) lead (see Chapter 5A), and position it away from the terminal. Also remove the engine top cover where necessary.

10 Unplug the injector harness connectors, labelling them to aid correct refitting later. Unclip the wiring harness clips from the top of the fuel rail, and lay the harness to one side **(see illustrations)**.

11 Refer to Section 11 and depressurise the fuel system.

12 Disconnect the vacuum hose from the port on the bottom of the fuel pressure regulator **(see illustration)**.

13 Slacken the clips and disconnect the fuel supply and return hoses from the end of the fuel rail. *Carefully* note the fitted positions of the hoses - the supply hose is marked with a black or white arrow, and the return hose is marked with a blue arrow **(see illustration)**.

14 Slacken and withdraw the fuel rail mounting bolts, then carefully lift the rail away from the inlet manifold, together with the injectors. Recover the injector lower O-ring seals as they emerge from the manifold **(see illustrations)**.

15 The injectors can be removed individually from the fuel rail by extracting the relevant metal clip and easing the injector out of the rail. Recover the injector upper O-ring seals **(see illustrations)**.

16 If required, remove the fuel pressure regulator, referring to the relevant sub-Section for guidance.

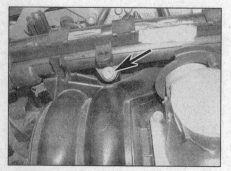

5.14a Unscrew the mounting bolts ...

5.14b ... then lift out the fuel rail ...

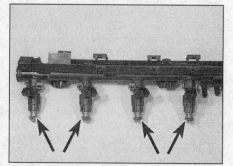

5.14c ... and recover the injector lower O-ring seals (arrowed)

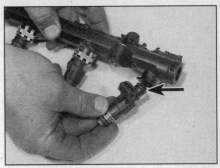

5.15a Using a suitable screwdriver, prise out the injector securing clip . . .

5.15b . . . and remove it from the fuel rail

5.15c Ease out the injector, and recover the upper O-ring seal (arrowed)

17 Check the electrical resistance of the injector using a multimeter and compare it with the Specifications.

Refitting

18 Refit the injectors and fuel rail by following the removal procedure in reverse, noting the following points:
a) *Renew the injector O-ring seals if they appear worn or damaged.*
b) *Ensure that the injector retaining clips are securely seated.*
c) *Check that the fuel supply and return hoses are reconnected correctly - refer to the colour coding described in Removal.*
d) *Check that all vacuum and electrical connections are remade correctly and securely.*
e) *On completion, start the engine and check for fuel leaks.*

Fuel pressure regulator

Removal

19 Disconnect the battery negative (earth) lead (see Chapter 5A), and position it away from the terminal. Also remove the engine top cover where necessary.
20 Refer to Section 11 and depressurise the fuel system.
21 Disconnect the vacuum hose from the port on the bottom of the fuel pressure regulator.
22 Slacken the clip and disconnect the fuel supply hose from the end of the fuel rail. This will allow the majority of fuel in the regulator to drain out. Be prepared for an amount of fuel loss - position a small container and some old rags underneath the fuel regulator housing.
Note: *The supply hose is marked with a black or white arrow.*
23 Extract the retaining clip from the top of the regulator housing and lift out the regulator body, recovering the O-ring seals **(see illustrations)**.

Refitting

24 Refit the fuel pressure regulator by following the removal procedure in reverse, noting the following points:
a) *Renew the O-ring seals if they appear worn or damaged.*
b) *Ensure that the regulator retaining clip is securely seated.*
c) *Refit the regulator vacuum hose securely.*

5.23a The fuel pressure regulator is mounted in the end of the fuel rail (arrowed)

Throttle valve potentiometer

Note: *The potentiometer is matched to the throttle body during manufacture, and is not available separately - if defective, a complete throttle body assembly will be required.*

Removal

25 Disconnect the battery negative (earth) lead (see Chapter 5A), and position it away from the terminal. Also remove the engine top cover where necessary.
26 Unplug the harness connector from the potentiometer.
27 Remove the retaining screws and lift the potentiometer away from the throttle body **(see illustration)**. Recover the gasket.

Refitting

28 Refitting is a reversal of removal, noting the following:

5.27 Throttle valve potentiometer

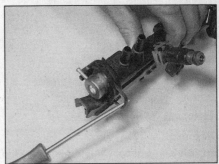

5.23b To remove the pressure regulator, prise out the retaining clip and withdraw it from the fuel rail

a) *Renew the gasket if it is damaged.*
b) *Ensure that the potentiometer drive engages correctly with the throttle spindle extension.*

Inlet manifold air temperature/pressure sensor

Removal

29 The sensor is attached to the right-hand side of the inlet manifold **(see illustration)**.
30 Disconnect the battery negative (earth) lead (see Chapter 5A), and position it away from the terminal.
31 Remove the two securing screws, and pull the sensor from the manifold. Recover the O-ring seal.

Refitting

32 Refitting is a reversal of removal, renewing the O-ring seal if necessary, and tightening the securing screws securely.

5.29 Inlet manifold air temperature/pressure sensor

4B

5.35 On engine code APQ, the Lambda sensor is located in the exhaust manifold - on some models, the sensor is in the downpipe, ahead of the catalytic converter

Road speed sensor

33 The road speed sensor is mounted on the transmission - refer to Chapter 7.

Coolant temperature sensor

34 Refer to Chapter 3, Section 6.

Lambda sensor

Removal

35 The Lambda sensor is either located in the exhaust downpipe ahead of the catalytic converter, or located in the exhaust manifold **(see illustration)**. Refer to Chapter 4D for details.

36 Disconnect the battery negative lead and position it away from the terminal - refer to the note in paragraph 3. Unplug the wiring harness from the lambda sensor at the connector, located on the right-hand side of the engine rear mounting.

37 On some models, the sensor is located accessible from below - later models have the sensor situated higher up the downpipe, and it can be accessed from above. Slacken and withdraw the sensor, taking care to avoid damaging the sensor probe as it is removed. **Note:** *As a flying lead remains connected to the sensor after is has been disconnected, if the correct-size spanner is not available, a slotted socket will be required to remove the sensor.*

Refitting

38 Apply a little anti-seize grease to the

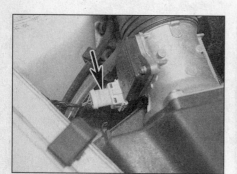

6.3 Airflow meter wiring connector (engine code AGG)

5.40 The fuel injection ECU is situated under the right-hand windscreen cowl panel on right-hand drive models

sensor threads - avoid contaminating the probe tip.

39 Refit the sensor to its housing, tightening it to the correct torque. Restore the harness connection.

Electronic control unit (ECU)

40 The ECU is located behind the engine compartment bulkhead, under one of the windscreen cowl panels. On left-hand drive models it is located on the left-hand side of the bulkhead, and on right-hand drive models it is located on the right-hand side **(see illustration)**. The unit is coded, and should not be removed without consulting a Seat dealer, otherwise it may not function correctly when the multi-plug is reconnected. If a new ECU is fitted, it must be adapted to the immobiliser by a Seat dealer using special equipment.

---

6 Simos engine management system components - removal and refitting

Note: *Observe the precautions in Section 1 before working on any component in the fuel system.*

Airflow meter

Removal

1 Disconnect the battery negative (earth) lead (see Chapter 5A). Also remove the engine top cover where necessary.

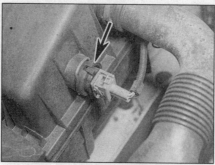

6.7 Inlet air temperature sensor (engine code AGG)

2 With reference to Section 2 , slacken the clips and disconnect the air ducting from the airflow meter, at the rear of the air cleaner housing.
3 Unplug the harness connector from the airflow meter **(see illustration)**.
4 Remove the retaining screws and extract the meter from the air cleaner housing. Recover the O-ring seal.
Caution: Handle the airflow meter carefully - its internal components are easily damaged.

Refitting

5 Refitting is a reversal of removal. Renew the O-ring seal if it appears damaged.

Throttle valve potentiometer

6 The throttle valve potentiometer is an integral part of the throttle body - refer to the information in the relevant sub-Section.

Inlet air temperature sensor

Removal

7 The sensor is mounted on the left-hand front of the inlet manifold (engine code AFT) or on the side of the air cleaner (engine code AGG) **(see illustration)**.
8 Unplug the harness connector from the sensor.
9 Unscrew the sensor from the inlet manifold or extract the clip and withdraw the sensor from the side of the air cleaner. Recover the O-ring seal.

Refitting

10 Refitting is a reversal of removal but, as applicable, fit a new O-ring seal and tighten the sensor securely.

Road speed sensor

11 The road speed sensor is mounted on the transmission - refer to Chapter 7.

Coolant temperature sensor

Removal

12 The coolant temperature sensor is mounted in the coolant outlet elbow on the front of the cylinder head (see Chapter 3). Remove the engine top cover where necessary.
13 Unplug the harness connector from the sensor.
14 Refer to Chapter 3, and drain approximately one quarter of the coolant from the engine.
15 Extract the retaining clip and lift the sensor from the coolant elbow - be prepared for an amount of coolant loss. Recover the O-ring.

Refitting

16 Refit the sensor by reversing the removal procedure, using a new O-ring. Refer to Chapter 1A and top-up the cooling system.

Engine speed sensor

Removal

17 The engine speed sensor is mounted on the front of the cylinder block, adjacent to the mating surface of the block and transmission bellhousing. If necessary, drain the engine oil and remove the oil filter (and where applicable oil cooler) to improve access - see Chapter 2A for details.

18 Unplug the harness connector from the sensor.

19 Remove the retaining screw and withdraw the sensor from the cylinder block.

Refitting

20 Refit the sensor by reversing the removal procedure.

Throttle body

Removal

21 Refer to Section 4 and detach the accelerator cable from the throttle valve lever.

22 Slacken the clips and detach the inlet air ducting from the throttle body.

23 Unplug the harness connector from the throttle positioning valve module, mounted at the rear of the throttle body.

24 Disconnect the vacuum hose from the port on the throttle body, then release the wiring harness from the guide clip.

25 Refer to Chapter 3, and drain approximately one quarter of the coolant from the engine. Slacken the clips and disconnect the coolant hoses from the ports on the throttle body, making a careful note of their fitted positions.

26 Disconnect the charcoal filter emission control system vacuum hose from the port on the throttle body.

27 Slacken and withdraw the through-bolts, then lift the throttle body away from the inlet manifold. Recover and discard the gasket.

Refitting

28 Refitting is a reversal of removal, noting the following:

a) *Use a new throttle body-to-inlet manifold gasket.*

b) *Observe the correct tightening torque when refitting the throttle body through-bolts.*

c) *Ensure that the coolant hoses are correctly refitted - the hose from the cylinder head connects to the port furthest from the inlet manifold.*

d) *Ensure that all the vacuum hoses and electrical connectors are refitted securely.*

e) *Refer to Chapter 1A and top-up the cooling system.*

f) *Check and if necessary adjust the accelerator cable.*

Fuel injectors and fuel rail

Removal

29 Disconnect the battery negative (earth) lead (see Chapter 5A). Also remove the engine top cover where necessary.

30 Unplug the injector harness connectors, labelling them to aid correct refitting later.

31 Depressurise the fuel system and described in Section 11.

32 Disconnect the vacuum hose from the port on the top of the fuel pressure regulator.

33 Slacken the clips and disconnect the fuel supply and return hoses from the end of the fuel rail. *Carefully note the fitted positions of the hoses and label them to aid refitting later.*

34 Slacken and withdraw the fuel rail screws, then carefully lift the rail away from the inlet manifold, together with the injectors. Recover the injector inserts and lower O-ring seals as they emerge from the manifold.

35 The injectors can be removed individually from the fuel rail by extracting the relevant metal clip and easing the injector out of the rail. Recover the injector upper O-ring seals.

36 If required, remove the fuel pressure regulator, referring to the relevant sub-Section for guidance.

37 Check the electrical resistance of the injector using a multimeter and compare it with the Specifications. **Note:** *If a faulty injector is suspected, before condemning the injector, it is worth trying the effect of one of the proprietary injector-cleaning treatments.*

Refitting

38 Refit the injectors and fuel rail by following the removal procedure in reverse, noting the following points:

a) *Renew the injector O-ring seals if they appear worn or damaged.*

b) *Ensure that the injector retaining clips are securely seated.*

c) *Check that the fuel supply and return hoses are reconnected correctly.*

d) *Check that all vacuum and electrical connections are remade correctly and securely.*

e) *On completion, start the engine and check for fuel leaks.*

Fuel pressure regulator

Removal

39 Disconnect the battery negative (earth) lead (see Chapter 5A). Also remove the engine top cover where necessary.

40 Refer to Section 11 and depressurise the fuel system.

41 Disconnect the vacuum hose from the port on the top of the fuel pressure regulator.

42 Slacken the clip and disconnect the fuel return hose from the end of the fuel rail. This will allow the majority of fuel in the fuel rail to drain out. Be prepared for an amount of fuel loss - position a small container and some old rags underneath the port. **Note:** *The return port faces downwards.*

43 Extract the retaining clip from the side of the regulator housing and lift out the regulator body, recovering the O-ring seals and the strainer plate.

44 Examine the strainer plate for contamination and clean it if necessary, using neat fuel.

Refitting

45 Refit the fuel pressure regulator by following the removal procedure in reverse, noting the following points:

a) *Renew the O-ring seals if they appear worn or damaged.*

b) *Ensure that the regulator retaining clip is securely seated.*

c) *Refit the regulator vacuum hose securely.*

Lambda sensor

Removal

46 The Lambda sensor is threaded into the exhaust pipe, at the front of the catalytic converter. Refer to Chapter 4D for details.

47 Unplug the wiring harness from the lambda sensor at the connector.

48 Working under the car, slacken and withdraw the sensor, taking care to avoid damaging the sensor probe as it is removed. **Note:** *As a flying lead remains connected to the sensor after is has been disconnected, if the correct spanner is not available, a slotted socket will be required to remove the sensor.*

Refitting

49 Apply a little anti-seize grease to the sensor threads - avoid contaminating the probe tip.

50 Refit the sensor to its housing, tightening it to the correct torque. Restore the harness connection.

Electronic control unit (ECU)

40 The ECU is located behind the engine compartment bulkhead, under one of the windscreen cowl panels. On left-hand drive models it is located on the left-hand side of the bulkhead, and on right-hand drive models it is located on the right-hand side. The unit is coded, and should not be removed without consulting a Seat dealer, otherwise it may not function correctly when the multi-plug is reconnected. If a new ECU is fitted, it must be adapted to the immobiliser by a Seat dealer using special equipment.

4B

7 Digifant engine management system components - removal and refitting

Note: *Observe the precautions in Section 1 before working on any component in the fuel system.*

Airflow meter (engine code 2E only)

Note: *An airflow meter is not used on engine code ABF. Engine load is sensed using a manifold pressure sensor, which is an integral part of the Electronic Control Unit and hence cannot be renewed separately.*

Removal

1 Disconnect the battery negative (earth) lead (see Chapter 5A). Also remove the engine top cover where necessary.

2 With reference to Section 2, slacken the clips and disconnect the air ducting from the airflow meter, at the rear of the air cleaner housing.

7.3 Unplug the harness connector from the airflow meter (engine code 2E only)

3 Unplug the harness connector from the airflow meter **(see illustration).**
4 Remove the retaining screws and extract the meter from the air cleaner housing. Recover the seal.
Caution: Handle the airflow meter carefully - its internal components are easily damaged.

Refitting

5 Refitting is a reversal of removal. Renew the O-ring seal if it appears damaged. **Note:** *On completion, the airflow meter must be matched electronically to the Digifant Electronic Control Unit (ECU) - this operation requires access to dedicated electronic test equipment, refer to a Seat dealer for advice.*

Throttle valve potentiometer

Removal

6 Disconnect the battery negative (earth) lead (see Chapter 5A). Also remove the engine top cover where necessary.
7 Unplug the harness connector from the potentiometer **(see illustration).**
8 Remove the retaining screws and lift the potentiometer away from the throttle body. Where applicable, recover the O-ring seal.

Refitting

9 Refitting is a reversal of removal, noting the following:
 a) *Where applicable, renew the O-ring seal if it appears damaged.*
 b) *Ensure that the potentiometer drive*

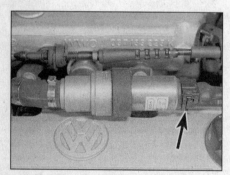

7.16 Idling stabilisation valve harness connector (arrowed)

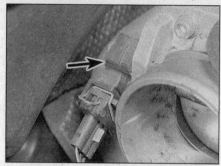

7.7 Unplug the harness connector (arrowed) from the throttle potentiometer - inlet air duct removed for clarity

 engages correctly with the throttle spindle extension.
 c) *On completion, the potentiometer must be matched electronically to the Digifant Electronic Control Unit (ECU) - this operation requires access to dedicated electronic test equipment, refer to a Seat dealer for advice.*

Inlet air temperature sensor

Removal

10 On engine code 2E, the sensor is an integral part of the airflow meter and cannot be renewed separately.
11 On engine code ABF, the sensor is located in the right-hand side of the inlet manifold.
12 Unplug the harness connector from the sensor.
13 Pull out the retaining clip and carefully extract the sensor from the inlet manifold. Recover the O-ring.

Refitting

14 Refitting is a reversal of removal. Renew the O-ring if it is damaged.

Idling stabilisation valve

Removal

15 The valve is mounted on a bracket on the inlet manifold, above the camshaft cover. On engine code ABF, remove the retaining screws and lift off the protective cover plate.
16 Unplug the harness connector from the valve **(see illustration).**

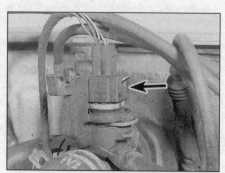

7.22 Unplug the harness connector (arrowed) from the coolant temperature sensor (engine code 2E shown)

17 Slacken the clip and disconnect the inlet air duct hose from the port on the idle stabilisation valve.
18 Slacken the mounting bracket retaining clip and carefully extract the valve from the inlet manifold.

Refitting

19 Refitting is a reversal of removal.

Road speed sensor

20 The road speed sensor is mounted on the transmission - refer to Chapter 7.

Coolant temperature sensor

Removal - engine code 2E

21 The coolant temperature sensor is mounted in the coolant outlet elbow on the front of the cylinder head (see Chapter 3).
22 Unplug the harness connector from the sensor **(see illustration).**
23 Refer to Chapter 3 and drain approximately one quarter of the coolant from the engine.
24 Extract the retaining clip and lift the sensor from the coolant elbow - be prepared for an amount of coolant loss. Recover the O-ring.

Removal - engine code ABF

25 The coolant temperature sensor is mounted on the side of the cylinder head, below and to the left of the ignition distributor.
26 Unplug the harness connector from the sensor.
27 Refer to Chapter 3 and drain approximately one quarter of the coolant from the engine.
28 Unscrew the sensor and recover the sealing washer.

Refitting

29 Refit the sensor by reversing the removal procedure, using a new O-ring/sealing washer as applicable. Refer to Chapter 1A and top-up the cooling system.

Engine speed sensor

Removal

30 The engine speed sensor is mounted on the front cylinder block, adjacent to the mating surface of the block and transmission bellhousing.
31 Unplug the harness connector from the sensor.
32 Remove the sensor retaining screw, and carefully withdraw the sensor from the cylinder block.

Refitting

33 Refit the sensor by reversing the removal procedure.

Cold start valve (engine code 2E up to 1994)

Removal

34 Refer to Section 11 and depressurise the fuel system.

35 Disconnect the battery negative (earth) lead (see Chapter 5A).

36 Unplug the harness connection from the cold start valve.

37 Slacken the clip and pull the fuel hose off the port at the rear of the cold start valve.

38 Remove the retaining screw and withdraw the cold start valve from the inlet manifold. Recover and discard the gasket.

Refitting

39 Refit the cold start valve by reversing the removal procedure, using a new gasket.

Throttle body

40 Refer to Section 4 and detach the accelerator cable from the throttle valve lever.

41 Slacken the clips and detach the inlet air ducting from the throttle body.

42 Unplug the harness connector from the throttle potentiometer. On the ABF engine, also disconnect the wiring from the idle speed switch.

43 Disconnect the vacuum hoses from the ports on the throttle body, noting their order of fitment. Release the wiring harness from the guide clip.

44 Slacken and withdraw the upper and lower through-bolts **(see illustration)**, then lift the throttle body away from the inlet manifold. Recover and discard the gasket.

45 If required, refer to the relevant sub-Section and remove the throttle potentiometer. Where fitted, the idle speed switch may be removed after undoing the retaining screw.

Refitting

46 Refitting is a reversal of removal, noting the following:

a) *Use a new throttle body-to-inlet manifold gasket.*

b) *Observe the correct tightening torque when refitting the throttle body through-bolts.*

c) *Ensure that all vacuum hoses and electrical connectors are refitted securely.*

d) *With reference to Section 4, check and if necessary adjust the accelerator cable.*

Fuel injectors and fuel rail

Removal

47 Disconnect the battery negative (earth) lead (see Chapter 5A). Also remove the engine top cover where necessary.

48 Refer to the relevant sub-Section in this Chapter and remove the throttle body.

49 On engine code ABF, refer to Section 12 and remove the upper section of the inlet manifold.

50 Unplug the injector harness at the multiway connector.

51 Refer to Section 11 and depressurise the fuel system.

52 Disconnect the vacuum hose from the port on the top of the fuel pressure regulator.

53 Slacken the clips and disconnect the fuel supply and return hoses from the end of the fuel rail. *Carefully* note the fitted positions of

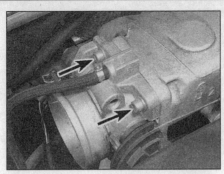

7.44 Throttle body upper through-bolts (arrowed)

the hoses - the supply hose is colour-coded black/white and the return hose is colour-coded blue.

54 Slacken and withdraw the fuel rail retaining screws, then carefully lift the fuel rail away from the inlet manifold, together with the injectors. Recover the injector lower O-ring seals as they emerge from the manifold.

55 Remove the retaining screws and lift the upper section of the fuel rail away from the lower section; recover and discard the gasket.

56 The injectors can now be carefully pressed from the fuel rail individually. Recover the injector upper O-ring seals.

57 If required, remove the fuel pressure regulator, referring to the relevant sub-Section for guidance.

58 Check the electrical resistance of the injector using a multimeter set to the resistance measurement function connected across the injector terminals and compare it with the Specifications. **Note:** *If a faulty injector is suspected, before condemning the injector, it is worth trying the effect of one of the proprietary injector-cleaning treatments.*

59 Refit the injectors to the fuel rail, noting that the recesses in the side of each injector body must align with the lugs in the lower section of the fuel rail. Moisten the lower O-ring seals with clean engine oil before refitting.

60 Refit the upper section of the fuel rail, together with a new gasket and tighten the retaining screws to the specified torque.

Refitting

61 Refit the injectors and fuel rail by following the removal procedure in reverse, noting the following points:

a) *Renew the injector O-ring seals if they appear worn or damaged.*

b) *Ensure that the injector retaining clips are securely seated.*

c) *Check that the fuel supply and return hoses are reconnected correctly - refer to the colour coding described in Removal.*

d) *Use a new gasket when refitting the upper section of the inlet manifold to the lower section.*

e) *Check that all vacuum and electrical connections are remade correctly and securely.*

f) *On completion, start the engine and check for fuel leaks.*

Fuel pressure regulator

Removal

62 Disconnect the battery negative (earth) lead (see Chapter 5A). Also remove the engine top cover where necessary.

63 Refer to Section 11 and depressurise the fuel system.

64 Disconnect the vacuum hose from the port on the top of the fuel pressure regulator.

65 Slacken the clip and disconnect the fuel supply hose from the end of the fuel rail. This will allow the majority of fuel in the regulator to drain out. Be prepared for an amount of fuel loss - position a small container and some old rags underneath the fuel regulator housing.

66 Extract the retaining clip from the side of the regulator housing and lift out the regulator body. Recover the O-ring seal.

Refitting

67 Refit the fuel pressure regulator by following the removal procedure in reverse, noting the following points:

a) *Renew the O-ring seals if they appear worn or damaged.*

b) *Ensure that the regulator retaining clip is securely seated.*

c) *Refit the regulator vacuum hose securely.*

Lambda sensor

Removal

68 The lambda sensor is threaded into the exhaust pipe, at the front of the catalytic converter. Refer to Chapter 4D for details.

69 Unplug the wiring harness from the Lambda sensor at the connector, located adjacent to the right-hand rear engine mounting.

70 Working under the vehicle, slacken and withdraw the sensor, taking care to avoid damaging the sensor probe as it is removed. **Note:** *As a flying lead remains connected to the sensor after is has been disconnected, if the correct size spanner is not available, a slotted socket will be required to remove the sensor.*

Refitting

71 Apply a little anti-seize grease to the sensor threads - avoid contaminating the probe tip.

72 Refit the sensor to its housing, tightening it to the correct torque. Restore the harness connection.

Electronic control unit (ECU)

73 The ECU is located behind the engine compartment bulkhead, under one of the windscreen cowl panels. On left-hand drive models it is located on the left-hand side of the bulkhead, and on right-hand drive models it is located on the right-hand side. The unit is coded, and should not be removed without consulting a Seat dealer, otherwise it may not function correctly when the multi-plug is reconnected. If a new ECU is fitted, it must be adapted to the immobiliser by a Seat dealer using special equipment.

4B

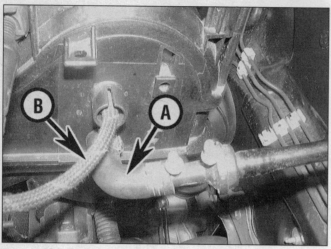

12.5 Brake servo vacuum hose (A) and distributor vacuum hose (B)

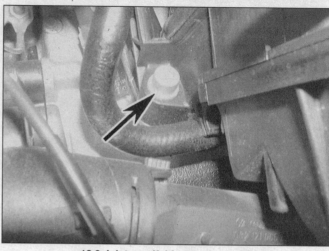

12.9 Inlet manifold mounting bolts

8 Fuel filter - renewal

Refer to Chapter 4A, Section 6.

9 Fuel pump and gauge sender unit - removal and refitting

Refer to Chapter 4A, Section 7.

10 Fuel tank - removal and refitting

Refer to Chapter 4A, Section 8.

11 Fuel injection system - depressurisation

Refer to Chapter 4A, Section 9.

12 Inlet manifold - removal and refitting

Note: *Observe the precautions in Section 1 before working on the fuel system.*

Removal

1 Refer to Section 11 and depressurise the fuel system, then disconnect the battery negative (earth) lead (see Chapter 5A). Also remove the engine top cover where necessary.
2 Refer to Section 2 and remove the air cleaner housing. Although this is not essential on models where the air cleaner is located on the right-hand side of the engine compart-

ment, it will provide additional working room.
3 Refer to Section 5, 6 or 7 as applicable and remove the throttle body from the inlet manifold.
4 Where applicable, unplug the wiring harness from the inlet manifold air temperature/pressure sensor.
5 Disconnect the brake servo vacuum hose from the port on the left-hand side of the inlet manifold. Also, where applicable, disconnect the distributor vacuum supply hose **(see illustration)**.
6 Refer to Section 5, 6 or 7 as applicable and remove the fuel rail and fuel injectors.
7 On engine codes 2E and ABF, remove the idling stabilisation valve as described in Section 7.
8 On engine code AFT, disconnect the hose from the variable intake vacuum capsule, then unbolt the upper section of the inlet manifold from the lower section and withdraw from the engine compartment. If necessary, the variable intake components and cover plate may be unbolted from the upper inlet manifold at this stage.
9 Progressively slacken and remove the inlet manifold-to-cylinder head bolts. Move the manifold away from the head, and recover the O-ring seals or gasket as applicable **(see illustration)**.

10 Where necessary, unclip the fuel supply and return hoses from underneath the manifold **(see illustration)**. Note their locations and colour-coding identification for refitting. The manifold can now be removed from the engine compartment.

Refitting

11 Refit the inlet manifold by following the removal procedure in reverse, noting the following points:
 a) Use new manifold O-ring seals or gaskets *(see illustration)*.
 b) Tighten the manifold-to-cylinder head bolts to the specified torque.
 c) Check that all vacuum, electrical and fuel system connections are remade correctly and securely.
 d) On completion, start the engine and check for fuel leaks.

13 Fuel injection system - testing and adjustment

1 If a fault appears in the fuel injection system first ensure that all the system wiring connectors are securely connected and free of corrosion. Then ensure that the fault is not

12.10 Unclip the fuel hoses from the base of the manifold, and remove the manifold from the engine compartment

12.11 When refitting the inlet manifold, use new O-ring seals due to poor maintenance; ie, check that the air cleaner filter element is clean, the spark plugs are in good condition and correctly gapped, the cylinder compression pressures are correct, the ignition timing is correct and the engine breather hoses are clear and undamaged, referring to Chapter 1A, Chapter 2A and Chapter 5B.

2 If these checks fail to reveal the cause of the problem the vehicle should be taken to a suitably equipped Seat dealer for testing. A diagnostic connector is incorporated in the engine management system wiring harness, into which a dedicated electronic test equipment can be plugged. The test equipment is capable of interrogating the engine management system ECU electronically and accessing its internal fault log. In this manner, faults can be pinpointed quickly and simply, even if their occurrence is intermittent. Testing all the system components individually in an attempt to locate the fault by elimination is a time consuming operation that is unlikely to be fruitful (particularly if the fault occurs dynamically) and carries high risk of damage to the ECU's internal components.

3 Experienced home mechanics equipped with an accurate tachometer and a carefully-calibrated exhaust gas analyser may be able to check the exhaust gas CO content and the engine idle speed; if these are found to be out of specification, then the vehicle must be taken to a Seat dealer for assessment. Neither the air/fuel mixture (exhaust gas CO content) nor the engine idle speed are manually adjustable; incorrect test results indicate a fault within the fuel injection system.

4B

Chapter 4 Part C:
Fuel system - diesel

Contents

Degrees of difficulty

Easy, suitable for novice with little experience	Fairly easy, suitable for beginner with some experience	Fairly difficult, suitable for competent DIY mechanic	Difficult, suitable for experienced DIY mechanic	Very difficult, suitable for expert DIY or professional 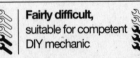

Specifications

General

Firing order	1-3-4-2
Maximum engine speed:	
Engine codes 1Y, AAZ	5200 ± 100 rpm
Engine code AEY	N/A (ECU controlled)
Engine codes 1Z, AHU, AFN	5050 ± 100 rpm (ECU controlled)
Engine idle speed:	
Engine code 1Y	900 ± 30 rpm
Engine code AAZ	920 ± 30 rpm
Engine code AEY	900 ± 40 rpm (ECU controlled)
Engine codes 1Z, AHU, AFN	900 ± 30 rpm (ECU controlled)
Engine fast idle speed:	
Engine codes 1Y, AAZ	1050 ± 50 rpm
Engine code AEY	N/A (ECU controlled)
Engine codes 1Z, AHU, AFN	N/A (ECU controlled)

Fuel injection pump

Injection pump timing, DTI reading (engine codes AAZ and 1Y):	
Test:	
Engine code 1Y	0.83 to 0.97 mm
Engine code AAZ	0.73 to 0.87 mm
Setting:	
Engine code 1Y	0.90 ± 0.02 mm
Engine code AAZ	0.80 ± 0.02 mm

Turbocharger

Type	Garrett or KKK
Maximum boost pressure:	
Engine code AAZ	0.60 to 0.83 bar at 4000 rpm
Engine code 1Z, AHU	0.50 to 0.65 bar at 3500 to 4000 rpm
Engine code AFN	1.65 to 2.20 bar at 3000 rpm

4C

Torque wrench settings

	Nm	lbf ft
Accelerator position sensor cable unit	10	7
Cold start valve (engine code AEY)	10	7
Fuel cut-off solenoid	40	30
Fuel filler neck	10	7
Fuel tank retaining strap bolts	25	18
Idle increase valve (engine code 1Y, AAZ)	20	15
Injection pump fuel supply and return banjo bolts	25	18
Injection pump head fuel unions	25	18
Injection pump sprocket:		
Engine codes 1Y and AAZ up to October 1994 - single nut	45	33
Engine codes 1Y and AAZ from October 1994-on - three bolts	25	18
Engine codes AEY, 1Z/AHU and AFN - single nut	55	41
Injection pump timing plug	25	18
Injection pump to front support bracket bolts	25	18
Injection pump to rear support bracket bolts	25	18
Injection pump top cover	10	7
Injector	70	52
Injector clamp retaining nut (engine code AEY)	20	15
Injector pipe union nut	25	18
Inlet manifold	25	18
Oil feed pipe	25	18
Oil return pipe to turbocharger	40	30
Turbocharger (engine code AAZ):		
Bolt	45	33
Nut	25	18
Turbocharger (engine code 1Z, AHU):		
Lower nut	25	18
Upper bolts	35	26
Turbocharger (engine code AFN):		
Nut	25	18
Bolt	30	22
Turbocharger oil feed union	50	37

1 General information and precautions

General information

The fuel system comprises a fuel tank, a fuel injection pump, an engine-bay mounted fuel filter with an integral water separator, fuel supply and return lines and four fuel injectors. Certain engines are fitted with a turbocharger.

The injection pump is driven at half crankshaft speed by the camshaft timing belt. Fuel is drawn from the fuel tank, through the filter by the injection pump, which then distributes the fuel under very high pressure to the injectors via separate delivery pipes.

Engine codes 1Y and AAZ

The injectors are spring loaded mechanical valves, which open when the pressure of the fuel supplied to them exceeds a specific limit. Fuel is then sprayed from the injector nozzle into the cylinder via a swirl chamber (indirect injection). Engine code AAZ is fitted with two-stage injectors which open in steps as the supplied fuel pressure rises; this improves the engines combustion characteristics.

The basic injection timing is set by the position of the injection pump on its mounting bracket. When the engine is running, the injection timing is advanced and retarded mechanically by the injection pump itself and is influenced primarily by the accelerator position and engine speed.

The engine is stopped by means of a solenoid operated fuel cut-off valve which interrupts the flow of fuel to the injection pump when de-activated.

On certain early models, when starting from cold, the engine idle speed could be raised manually by means of a cold start accelerator cable, controlled via a knob on the facia. On later models, an automatic idle boost actuator, mounted on the side of the injection pump replaced the cold start accelerator cable.

It should be noted that on later models, the fuel injection pump is equipped with an electronic self-diagnosis and fault logging system. Servicing of this system is only possible with dedicated electronic test equipment. Problems with the systems operation should therefore be referred to a Seat dealer for assessment. Once the fault has been identified, the removal/refitting sequences detailed in the following Sections will then allow the appropriate component(s) to be renewed as required.

Engine codes AEY, 1Z, AHU, AFN

The direct-injection fuelling system is controlled electronically by a diesel engine management system, comprising an Electronic Control Unit (ECU) and its associated sensors, actuators and wiring.

Basic injection timing is set mechanically by the position of the pump on its mounting bracket. Dynamic timing and injection duration are controlled by the ECU and are dependant on engine speed, throttle position and rate of opening, inlet air flow , inlet air temperature, coolant temperature, fuel temperature, ambient pressure (altitude) and manifold depression information, received from sensors mounted on and around the engine. Closed loop control of the injection timing is achieved by means of an injector needle lift sensor. Note that injector No 3 is fitted with the needle lift sensor.

Two-stage injectors are used, which improve the engine's combustion characteristics, leading to quieter running and better exhaust emissions.

In addition, the ECU manages the operation of the Exhaust Gas Recirculation (EGR) emission control system (Chapter 4D), the turbocharger boost pressure control system (except engine code AEY) and the glow plug control system (Chapter 4D). On engine code AEY, a vacuum operated throttle valve is fitted to the inlet manifold to increase the vacuum when the engine speed is less than 2200 rpm. This is necessary to operate the EGR system efficiently.

It should be noted that fault diagnosis of the diesel engine management system is only possible with dedicated electronic test equipment. Problems with the system's operation should therefore be referred to a Seat dealer for assessment. Once the fault

2.1 Disconnect the air ducting from the air cleaner assembly

2.2 Unhook the rubber loops from the lugs on the chassis member

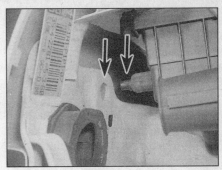

2.6 Engage the mounting lug with the recess (arrowed) in the inner wing

has been identified, the removal/refitting sequences detailed in the following Sections will then allow the appropriate component(s) to be renewed as required. **Note:** *Throughout this Chapter, vehicles are frequently referred to by their engine code, rather than by engine capacity - refer to Chapter 2B for engine code listings.*

Precautions

Many of the operations described in this Chapter involve the disconnection of fuel lines, which may cause an amount of fuel spillage. Before commencing work, refer to the warnings below and the information in Safety first! at the beginning of this manual.

⚠️ *Warning: When working on any part of the fuel system, avoid direct contact skin contact with diesel fuel - wear protective clothing and gloves when handling fuel system components. Ensure that the work area is well ventilated to prevent the build up of diesel fuel vapour.*

Fuel injectors operate at extremely high pressures and the jet of fuel produced at the nozzle is capable of piercing skin, with potentially fatal results. When working with pressurised injectors, take care to avoid exposing any part of the body to the fuel spray. It is recommended that a diesel fuel systems specialist should carry out any pressure testing of the fuel system components.

Under no circumstances should diesel fuel be allowed to come into contact with coolant hoses - wipe off accidental spillage immediately. Hoses that have been contaminated with fuel for an extended period should be renewed. Diesel fuel systems are particularly sensitive to contamination from dirt, air and water. Pay particular attention to cleanliness when working on any part of the fuel system, to prevent the ingress of dirt. Thoroughly clean the area around fuel unions before disconnecting them. Store dismantled components in sealed containers to prevent contamination and the formation of condensation. Only use lint-free cloths and clean fuel for component cleansing.

| 2 | Air cleaner assembly - removal and refitting |

Removal

1 Loosen the clips and disconnect the air ducting from the air cleaner assembly or airflow meter (as applicable) **(see illustration)**.
2 Unhook the rubber loops from the lugs on the chassis member **(see illustration)**.
3 Pull the air cleaner towards the engine and withdraw the air inlet hose from the port on the inner wing.
4 Lift the air cleaner out of the engine bay. On engine codes 1Z, AHU, and AFN, disconnect the wiring from the airflow meter, and if necessary separate the airflow meter from the air cleaner by removing the retaining screws. Handle the airflow meter carefully, as it is a delicate component.
5 Prise open the retaining clips and lift the top cover from the air cleaner. Remove the air cleaner filter element (see Chapter 1B for more details).

Refitting

6 Refit the air cleaner by following the removal procedure in reverse. Engage the mounting lug with the recess in the inner wing **(see illustration)**.

| 3 | Accelerator cable - removal, refitting and adjustment |

Note: *This Section only applies to engine codes 1Y and AAZ; all other engines are fitted with an electronic accelerator position sensor (see Section 13).*

Removal

Note: *On RHD models the accelerator pedal pivot shaft extends into the left-hand passenger compartment, behind the heater assembly.*

1 Remove the engine top cover (Chapter 2B, Section 17), then remove the clip and detach the end of the accelerator inner cable from the fuel injection pump lever **(see illustration)**.
2 Slide out the adjustment ferrule and extract the rubber grommet from the mounting bracket **(see illustration)**. Leave the adjustment clip in position on the ferrule.
3 Using a screwdriver, carefully prise the cap/grommet from the bulkhead. The cap is retained by three tags, and if necessary have an assistant insert a screwdriver from inside the car to help release the tags. On RHD models, the pedal lever extension is located behind the heater assembly.
4 Have the assistant lift the accelerator pedal so that the top of the extension is visible through the hole in the bulkhead on the engine compartment side. Unclip the accelerator cable end from the pedal extension lever.

4C

3.1 Detach the accelerator inner cable from the fuel injection pump lever

3.2 Extract the accelerator outer cable from the mounting bracket

TOOL TiP

Use a pair of water pump pliers to grip and rotate the fuel tank sender unit plastic securing ring

5 Release the cable from the supports then withdraw it from inside the engine compartment.

Refitting

6 Refitting is a reversal of removal, but if necessary adjust the cable as follows.

Adjustment

7 At the fuel injection pump, fix the position of the outer cable in its mounting bracket by inserting the metal clip in one of the locating slots, such that when the accelerator pedal is depressed fully, the throttle lever is held wide open to its end stop.

4 Cold Start Accelerator (CSA) cable - removal, refitting and adjustment

Note: *This Section only applies to certain early models fitted with engine codes 1Y and AAZ.*

Removal

1 Remove the engine top cover (Chapter 2B, Section 17), then loosen the locking screw and disconnect the CSA cable inner from the injection pump lever.

2 Prise off the retaining clip and withdraw the cable outer from the mounting bracket on the side of the injection pump. Recover the washer.

3 Release the cable from the clips that secure it in position in the engine compartment.

4 Remove the parcel shelf from under the steering column (see Chapter 11).

5 Pull the cold start knob out to expose its rear surface, then prise off the clip and remove the knob from the cable inner.

6 Unscrew and remove the retaining nut to release the cable outer from the facia.

7 Pull the cable through into the passenger compartment, guiding it through the bulkhead grommet.

Refitting

8 Refit the CSA cable by reversing the removal procedure.

Adjustment

9 Push the cold start knob into the fully off position.

10 Thread the CSA cable inner through the drilled clevis on the injection pump lever. Hold the injection pump cold start lever in the closed position, then pull the cable inner taught to take up the slack and tighten the locking screw.

11 Operate the cold start knob from inside the car and check that the injection pump lever moves through its full range of travel.

12 Push the cold start knob in to its fully off position, then start the engine and check the idle speed, as described in Chapter 1B.

13 Pull the cold start knob fully out and check that the idle speed rises to approximately 1050 rpm. Adjust the cable if necessary.

5 Fuel tank sender unit - removal and refitting

⚠ **Warning: Avoid direct contact skin contact with diesel fuel - wear protective clothing and gloves when handling fuel system components. Ensure that the work area is well ventilated to prevent the build-up of diesel fuel vapour.**

1 The fuel tank sender unit is on the top of the fuel tank and is accessible via a hatch in the load space floor. The unit provides a variable voltage signal that drives the facia mounted fuel gauge and also serves as a connection point for the fuel supply and return hoses.

2 The unit protrudes into the fuel tank and its removal involves exposing the contents of the tank to the atmosphere.

Removal

3 Ensure that the vehicle is parked on a level surface, then disconnect the battery negative cable and position it away from the terminal.

4 Tilt the rear seat backrest forwards.

5 Slacken and withdraw the access hatch screws and lift the hatch away from the floorpan.

6 Unplug the wiring harness connector from the sender unit.

7 Pad the area around the supply and return fuel hoses with rags to absorb any spilt fuel, then slacken the hose clips and remove them from the ports at the sender unit. Observe the supply and return arrows markings on the ports - label the fuel hoses accordingly to ensure correct refitting later.

8 Unscrew the plastic securing ring and lift it out **(see Tool Tip)**. Turn the sender unit anticlockwise to release it from its bayonet fitting and lift it out, holding it above the level of the fuel in the tank until the excess fuel has drained out. Recover the rubber seal **(see illustrations)**.

9 Remove the sender unit from the vehicle and lay it on an absorbent card or rag. Inspect the float at the end of the swinging arm for punctures and fuel ingress - renew the sender unit if it appears damaged.

10 The fuel pick-up incorporated in the sender unit is spring loaded to ensure that it always draws fuel from the lowest part of the tank. Check that the pick-up is free to move under spring tension with respect to the sender unit body.

11 Recover the rubber seal from the fuel tank aperture and inspect for signs of fatigue - renew it if necessary.

12 Inspect the sender unit wiper and track; clean off any dirt and debris that may have accumulated and look for breaks in the track **(see illustration)**. An electrical specification for the sender unit is not quoted by Seat, but the integrity of the wiper and track may be verified by connecting a multimeter, set to the resistance function, across the sender unit connector terminals. The resistance should

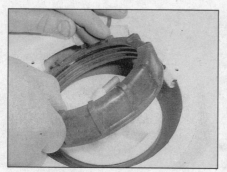

5.8a Lift out the sender unit . . .

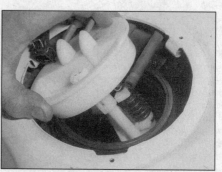

5.8b . . . and recover the rubber seal

vary as the float arm is moved up and down, and an open circuit reading indicates that the sender is faulty and should be renewed.

Refitting

13 Refitting is a reversal of removal, noting the following points:

a) The arrow markings on the sender unit body and the fuel tank must be aligned **(see illustration)**.

b) Smear the tank aperture rubber seal with clean fuel before fitting it in position.

c) Reconnect the fuel hoses to the correct ports - observe the direction of flow arrow markings.

6 Fuel tank -
removal and refitting

Refer to the information in Chapter 4A, Section 8.

7 Fuel injection pump -
removal and refitting

Note: *On engine code AEY, 1Z, AHU, and AFN, the injection pump commencement of injection setting must be checked and if necessary adjusted after refitting the injection pump. The commencement of injection is controlled by the fuel injection ECU and is influenced by several other engine parameters,*

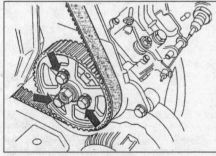

7.3 On engine codes 1Y and AAZ from October 1994 on, the sprocket is a two-piece assembly - loosen ONLY the bolts arrowed

7.5a Lift off the pump sprocket . . .

7.5b . . . and recover the Woodruff key

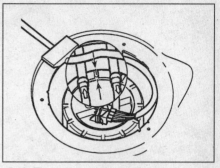

5.12 Look for breaks in the sender unit wiper track

including coolant temperature, and engine speed and position. Although the adjustment is a mechanical operation, checking can only be carried out by a Seat dealer, as dedicated electronic test equipment is needed to interface with the fuel injection ECU.

Removal

1 Disconnect the battery negative (earth) lead (see Chapter 5A), then remove the engine top cover (Chapter 2B, Section 17).

2 With reference to Chapter 2B, carry out the following:

a) Remove the air cleaner (and airflow meter on engine codes 1Z, AHU, AFN) and the associated ducting.

b) Remove the camshaft cover and timing belt outer cover(s).

c) Set the engine to TDC on cylinder No 1.

d) Remove the timing belt from the camshaft and fuel injection pump sprockets.

7.4 Attach a two-legged puller to the injection pump sprocket

7.6a Slacken the rigid fuel pipe unions at the rear of the injection pump

5.13 The arrow marks on the sender unit body and the fuel tank must be aligned

3 Loosen the nut or bolts (as applicable) that secure the timing belt sprocket to the injection pump shaft. The sprocket must be held stationary while doing this - a home made tool can easily be fabricated for this purpose; refer to Section 5 of Chapter 2B for further details.

Caution: On engine codes 1Y and AAZ from October 1994 on, the sprocket is a two-piece assembly, secured with three bolts - on no account should the shaft centre nut be slackened, as this will alter the basic injection timing (see illustration).

4 Attach a two-legged puller to the injection pump sprocket, then gradually tighten the puller until the sprocket is under firm tension **(see illustration)**.

Caution: To prevent damage to the injection pump shaft, insert a piece of scrap metal between the end of the shaft and the puller centre bolt.

5 Tap sharply on the puller centre bolt with a hammer - this will free the sprocket from the tapered shaft. Detach the puller, then fully slacken and remove the sprocket fixings, lift off the sprocket and recover the Woodruff key **(see illustrations)**.

6 Using a pair of spanners, slacken the rigid fuel pipe unions at the rear of the injection pump and at the injectors, then lift the fuel pipe assembly away from the engine **(see illustrations)**.

Caution: Be prepared for some fuel leakage during this operation by placing cloth rags beneath the unions. Take care to avoid stressing the rigid fuel pipes as they are removed.

4C

7.6b Lift the fuel pipe assembly away from the engine

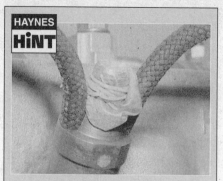

Hint 1: Cut the fingertips from an old pair of rubber gloves and secure them over the fuel ports with elastic bands

Hint 2: Fit a short length of hose over the banjo bolt (arrowed) so that the drillings are covered, then thread the bolt back into its injection pump port

7 Cover the open pipes and ports to prevent the ingress of dirt and excess fuel leakage **(see Haynes Hint 1)**.

8 Slacken the fuel supply and return banjo bolts at the injection pump ports, again taking precautions to minimise fuel spillage. Cover the open pipes and ports to prevent the ingress of dirt and excess fuel leakage **(see Haynes Hint 2)**.

9 Disconnect the injector bleed hose from the port on the fuel return union **(see illustration)**.

10 Refer to Section 12 and disconnect the wiring from the stop control valve.

11 On engine codes 1Y and AAZ, refer to Sections 3 and 4 and disconnect the accelerator cable and (where applicable) the cold start accelerator cable from the injection pump.

12 On all engine codes except 1Y and AAZ, unplug the electrical wiring from the fuel cut-off valve/commencement of injection valve and the quantity adjuster module at the connectors, labelling the cables to aid refitting later.

13 On engine codes 1Y and AAZ, if the existing injection pump is to be refitted later, use a scriber or a pen to mark the relationship between the injection pump body and the front mounting bracket. This will allow an approximate injection timing setting to be achieved when the pump is refitted.

14 As applicable, unplug the electrical wiring from the following components, labelling the connectors to aid refitting later:

a) *Commencement of injection valve.*
b) *Injection period sensor.*

c) *On engine code AAZ, the boost pressure enrichment cut-off valve.*
d) *On engine code 1Y, the full throttle stop valve.*
e) *On vehicles with air conditioning, the idle speed boost actuator.*

15 On later models, where the injection pump wiring is not provided with individual connectors, free the engine harness multiway connector from its bracket, and unbolt the earth connection. **Note:** *New injection pumps are not supplied with harness multiway connector housings, therefore if the pump is to be renewed, the relevant spade terminal pins must be pushed out of the existing connector housing, to allow those from the new pump to be inserted.*

16 On vehicles with air conditioning, disconnect the vacuum hose from the idle speed boost actuator.

17 On turbocharged engines, disconnect the wiring from the load switch.

All models

18 Unscrew and remove the bolt that secures the injection pump to the rear mounting bracket **(see illustration)**.

Caution: Do not slacken the pump distributor head bolts, as this could cause serious internal damage to the injection pump.

19 Slacken and withdraw the three nuts/bolts that secure the injection pump to the front

mounting bracket. Note that where fixing bolts are used, the two outer bolts are held captive with metal brackets. Support the pump body as the last fixing is removed. Check that nothing remains connected to the injection pump, then lift it away from the engine.

Refitting

20 Offer up the injection pump to the engine, then insert the mounting nuts/bolts and tighten to the specified torque. **Note:** *If the existing pump is being refitted, use the markings made during removal for alignment. If a new pump is being fitted, and the mounting holes are elongated, mount it such that the bolts are initially at the centre of the holes to allow the maximum range of pump timing adjustment.*

21 Prime the injection pump by fitting a small funnel to the fuel return pipe union and filling the cavity with clean diesel. Pad the area around the union with clean dry rags to absorb any spillage.

22 Reconnect the fuel injector delivery pipes to the injectors and injection pump head, then tighten the unions to the correct torque using a pair of spanners.

23 Reconnect the fuel supply and return pipes using new sealing washers, then tighten the banjo bolts to the specified torque. **Note:** *The inside diameter of the banjo bolt for the fuel return pipe is smaller than that of the fuel supply line and is marked OUT.*

24 Fit the timing belt sprocket to the injection pump shaft, ensuring that the Woodruff key is correctly seated. Fit the washer and retaining nut/bolts (as applicable), hand tightening them only at this stage.

25 Lock the injection pump sprocket in position by inserting a bar or bolt through its alignment hole and into the drilling in the pump front mounting bracket.

26 Refit and tension the timing belt as described in Chapter 2B. Tighten the fuel injection pump sprocket nut or bolts to the specified torque **(see illustration)**.

27 The rest of the refitting procedure is a direct reversal of removal, however, on engine codes 1Y and AAZ check and if necessary adjust the injection pump static timing as described in

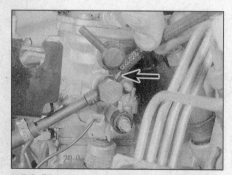

7.9 Disconnect the injector bleed hose from the fuel return union port (arrowed)

7.18 Withdraw the injection pump rear mounting bolt

Section 10, then check the idling speed (Chapter 1B), maximum no-load engine speed (Section 8 of this Chapter), and engine idle boost speed where applicable (Section 9 of this Chapter). On all other engine codes, the commencement of injection must now be dynamically checked and if necessary adjusted by a Seat dealer.

8 Maximum engine speed - checking and adjustment

Note: *This Section only applies to engine codes 1Y and AAZ.*

1 Connect a diesel tachometer to the engine.
2 Start the engine and with the handbrake applied and the transmission in neutral, have an assistant depress the accelerator fully.
Caution: Do not maintain maximum engine speed for more than two or three seconds.
3 Check that the maximum engine speed is as quoted in the Specifications.
4 If necessary, adjust the maximum engine speed by slackening the locknut and rotating the adjusting screw **(see illustration)**. On completion, tighten the locknut.
5 Disconnect the tachometer from the engine.

9 Fast idle speed - checking and adjustment

Note: *This Section only applies to certain early models fitted with engine codes 1Y and AAZ.*
1 Connect a diesel tachometer to the engine.

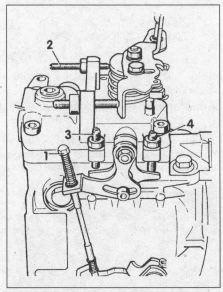

8.4 Fuel injection pump adjustment points (engine codes 1Y and AAZ)

1 Idling speed adjustment screw
2 Maximum engine speed adjustment screw
3 Minimum idling speed stop screw
4 Maximum idling speed stop screw

7.26 Tightening the fuel injection pump sprocket, using a home-made locking tool

2 With reference to Chapter 1B, check and if necessary adjust the engine idling speed.
3 Pull the facia cold start knob fully out and check that the idle speed rises to that given in the Specifications.
4 If necessary, adjust the setting by slackening the locknut and rotating the adjusting screw (refer to illustration 8.4). On completion, tighten the locknut.

10 Fuel injection pump timing - testing and adjustment

Note: *This Section only applies to engine codes 1Y and AAZ. On engine codes AEY, 1Z, AHU, and AFN, the fuel injection pump timing can only be tested and adjusted using dedicated test equipment. Refer to a Seat dealer for advice.*

Testing

1 With reference to Chapter 2B, set the engine to TDC on cylinder No 1. Where applicable, make sure that the cold start control cable is pushed fully in.
2 At the rear of the injection pump, unscrew the plug from the pump head and recover the seal **(see illustration)**.
3 Using a suitably threaded adapter, screw a DTI gauge into the pump head **(see illustration)**. Pre-load the gauge by a reading of approximately 2.5 mm.
4 Using a socket and wrench on the crankshaft bolt, slowly rotate the crankshaft anti-clockwise; the DTI gauge will indicate

10.2 Unscrew the plug (arrowed) from the pump head and recover the seal

movement - keep turning the crankshaft until the movement just ceases.
5 Zero the DTI gauge, with a pre-load of approximately 1.0 mm.
6 Now turn the crankshaft clockwise to bring the engine back up to TDC on cylinder No 1. Observe the reading indicated by the DTI gauge and compare it with the Specifications.
7 If the reading is within the test tolerance quoted in the Specifications, remove the DTI gauge and refit the pump head plug. Use a new seal and tighten the plug to the specified torque.
8 If the reading is out of tolerance, proceed as follows.

Adjustment

9 Slacken the pump securing bolts at the front and rear brackets (see Section 7).
10 Rotate the injection pump body until the setting reading (see specifications) is indicated on the DTI gauge.
11 On completion, tighten the pump securing bolts to the specified torque.
12 Remove the DTI gauge and refit the pump head plug. Use a new seal and tighten the plug to the specified torque.

11 Injectors - general information, removal and refitting

Warning: Exercise extreme caution when working on the fuel injectors. Never expose the hands or any part of the body to injector spray, as the high working pressure can cause the fuel to penetrate the skin, with possibly fatal results. You are strongly advised to have any work which involves testing the injectors under pressure carried out by a dealer or fuel injection specialist. Refer to the precautions given in Section 1 of this Chapter before proceeding.

General information

1 Injectors do deteriorate with prolonged use and it is reasonable to expect them to need reconditioning or renewal after 60 000 miles (100 000 km) or so. Accurate testing, overhaul and calibration of the injectors must be left to

10.3 Screw a DTI gauge into the pump head

4C

11.6a Removing an injector from the cylinder head (engine codes 1Y and AAZ)

11.6b Recover the heat shield washer (engine codes 1Y and AAZ)

a specialist. A defective injector which is causing knocking or smoking can be located without dismantling as follows.

2 Run the engine at a fast idle. Slacken each injector union in turn, placing rag around the union to catch spilt fuel and being careful not to expose the skin to any spray. When the union on the defective injector is slackened, the knocking or smoking will stop.

Removal

Note: *Take care not to allow dirt into the injectors or fuel pipes during this procedure. Do not drop the injectors or allow the needles at their tips to become damaged. The injectors are precision-made to fine limits and must not be handled roughly.*

3 Cover the alternator with a clean cloth or plastic bag to prevent the possibility of fuel being spilt onto it. Remove the engine top cover (Chapter 2B, Section 17).

4 Carefully clean around the injectors and pipe union nuts and disconnect the return pipe from the injector.

5 Wipe clean the pipe unions then slacken the union nut securing the relevant injector pipes to each injector and the relevant union nuts securing the pipes to the rear of the injection pump (the pipes are removed as one assembly); as each pump union nut is slackened, retain the adapter with a suitable open-ended spanner to prevent it being unscrewed from the pump. With the union nuts undone remove the injector pipes from the engine. Cover the injector and pipe unions to prevent the entry of dirt into the system.

HAYNES HINT *Cut the fingertips from an old rubber glove and secure them over the open unions with elastic bands to prevent dirt ingress (see Section 7).*

Engine codes 1Y and AAZ

6 Unscrew each injector using a 27 mm deep socket or box spanner, and remove them from the cylinder head. Recover the heat shield washers, and discard them - new washers must be used when refitting **(see illustrations)**.

Engine codes AEY, 1Z, AHU and AFN

7 Disconnect the wiring for the needle stroke transmitter from injector No 3.

8 Unscrew and remove the retaining nut or bolt, and recover the washer, retaining plate and mounting collar. Note the fitted position of all components, for use when refitting. Withdraw the injector from the cylinder head, and recover the heat shield washer - new washers must be obtained for refitting.

Refitting

Engine codes 1Y and AAZ

9 Fit new heat shield washers to the cylinder head, noting that they must be fitted the correct way round as shown in the accompanying illustration **(see illustration)**.

10 Screw the injector into position and tighten it to the specified torque **(see illustration)**.

Engine codes AEY, 1Z, AHU and AFN

11 Insert the injector into position, using a new heat shield washer. Make sure that the injector with the needle stroke transmitter is located in No 3 position.

12 Fit the mounting collar and retaining plate, and secure in position with the nut and washer, tightened to the specified torque.

13 Reconnect the wiring for the needle stroke transmitter on injector No 3.

All engines

14 Refit the injector pipes and tighten the union nuts to the specified torque setting. Position any clips attached to the pipes as noted before removal.

15 Reconnect the return pipe to the injector.

16 Reconnect the battery negative (earth) lead (see Chapter 5A), then start the engine and check that it runs correctly. Refit the engine top cover.

12 Fuel cut-off solenoid valve - removal and refitting

Removal

1 The fuel cut-off valve is located at the upper, rear of the injection pump.

2 Disconnect the wiring **(see illustration)**.

3 Unscrew and withdraw the valve body from the injection pump. Recover the sealing washer, O-ring seal and the plunger.

Refitting

4 Refitting is a reversal of removal. Use a new sealing washer and O-ring seal.

13 Diesel engine management system - component removal and refitting

Note: *This Section only applies to engine codes AEY, 1Z, AHU, AFN.*

Accelerator position sensor

Removal

1 Refer to Chapter 11 and remove the trim panels from under the steering column area of the facia, to gain access to the pedal cluster.

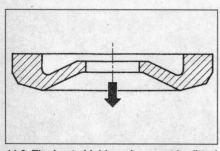

11.9 The heat shield washer must be fitted with its convex side facing downwards (arrow faces the cylinder head) (engine codes 1Y and AAZ)

11.10 Screw the injector into position and tighten it to the specified torque (engine codes 1Y and AAZ)

12.2 Disconnect the fuel cut-off valve wiring connector (arrowed)

2 The pivot shaft must now be removed from the accelerator pedal. To do this, insert a 6.0 mm Allen key in the left-hand end of the shaft, then carefully turn the shaft while depressing the arm through the small hole in the mounting bracket **(see illustration)**.

3 Disconnect the pedal from the pulley cable end fitting.

4 Disconnect the position sensor wiring at the connector.

5 Undo the screws securing the sensor to the mounting bracket, and lift out the sensor. If necessary, remove the nut and washer and detach the cable cam plate from the spindle.

Refitting

6 Refitting is a reversal of removal, noting the following points:

a) The cable cam plate must be fitted to the position sensor spindle according to the dimensions shown **(see illustration)**.

b) On completion, the adjustment of the position sensor must be verified electron-ically, using dedicated test equipment - refer to a Seat dealer for advice.

Coolant temperature sensor

Removal

7 Refer to Chapter 3 and drain approximately one quarter of the coolant from the engine. Remove the engine top cover (Chapter 2B, Section 17).

8 The sensor is at the top coolant outlet elbow, at the front of the cylinder head. Unplug the wiring from it at the connector.

9 Remove the securing clip then extract the sensor from its housing and recover the O-ring seal.

Refitting

10 Refit the coolant temperature sensor by reversing the removal procedure, using a new O-ring seal. Refer to Chapter 1B and top-up the cooling system.

Fuel temperature sensor

Removal

11 Slacken and withdraw the retaining screws and lift the top cover from the injection pump. Recover the gasket.

12 Remove the screws and lift out the fuel temperature sensor.

Refitting

13 Refitting is a reversal of removal. Tighten the pump top cover screws to the specified torque.

Inlet air temperature sensor

Removal

14 The sensor is mounted on the air cleaner cover (engine code AEY) or in the air duct between the intercooler and the inlet manifold (engine codes 1Z, AHU, AFN). Unplug the wiring harness from it at the connector **(see illustration)**.

15 Remove the securing clip and extract the

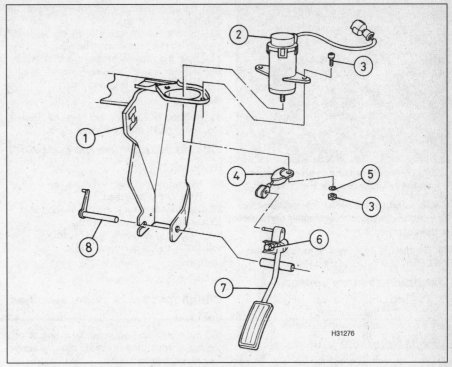

13.2 Accelerator pedal position sensor components

1	Mounting bracket	3	Securing screw	6	Adjustment bolt
2	Accelerator position sensor	4	Cable cam plate	7	Accelerator pedal
		5	Spring washer	8	Accelerator pedal spindle

sensor from its housing and recover the O-ring seal.

Refitting

16 Refit the inlet air temperature sensor by reversing the removal procedure, using a new O-ring seal.

Engine speed signal sensor

Removal

17 The engine speed sensor is mounted on the front cylinder block, adjacent to the mating surface of the block and transmission bellhousing.

18 Disconnect the wiring from the sensor.

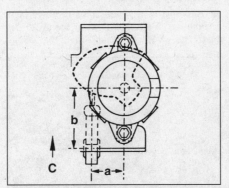

13.6 Mounting arrangement of accelerator position sensor cable cam plate

a 22 ± 0.5 mm   C To front of car
b 41± 0.5 mm

19 Remove the retaining screw and withdraw the sensor from the cylinder block.

Refitting

20 Refit the sensor by reversing the removal procedure.

Airflow meter (engine codes 1Z, AHU, AFN)

Removal

21 With reference to Section 2 , slacken the clips and disconnect the air ducting from the airflow meter, at the rear of the air cleaner housing.

22 Disconnect the wiring from the airflow meter.

23 Remove the retaining screws and extract the meter from the air cleaner housing. Recover the O-ring seal.

13.14 Inlet air temperature sensor

4C

13.27 The boost pressure valve is mounted on the left-hand rear of the bulkhead

Caution: Handle the airflow meter carefully - its internal components are easily damaged.

Refitting

24 Refitting is a reversal of removal. Renew the O-ring seal if it appears damaged.

Manifold pressure sensor

25 The manifold pressure sensor is an integral part of the Electronic Control Unit and hence cannot be renewed separately.

Absolute pressure (altitude) sensor

26 The absolute pressure sensor is an integral part of the Electronic Control Unit and hence cannot be renewed separately.

Boost pressure valve (engine codes 1Z, AHU, AFN)

Removal

27 The boost pressure valve is mounted on the left-hand rear of the bulkhead (see illustration).
28 Disconnect the wiring from the boost pressure valve.
29 Remove the vacuum hoses from the ports on the boost control valve, noting their order of connection carefully to aid correct refitting.
30 Remove the retaining screw and withdraw the valve.

Refitting

31 Refitting is a reversal of removal.

Throttle valve housing (engine code AEY)

Removal

32 With reference to Section 2, loosen the

14.4a Slacken the clips . . .

clip and disconnect the air trunking from the throttle valve housing.
33 Disconnect the hose from the vacuum capsule on the throttle valve housing.
34 Undo the retaining screws and withdraw the throttle valve housing from the inlet manifold. Recover the O-ring seal.

Refitting

35 Refitting is a reversal of removal. Renew the O-ring seal if it appears damaged.

Throttle actuator (engine code AEY)

Removal

36 The throttle actuator is located on the left-hand rear of the bulkhead.
37 Disconnect the wiring from the actuator.
38 Disconnect the vacuum hoses, then undo the retaining screws and withdraw the actuator from the bulkhead.

Refitting

39 Refitting is a reversal of removal.

Clutch and brake pedal switches

Removal

40 The clutch and brake pedal switches are clipped to mounting brackets directly above their respective pedals.
41 The brake pedal switch operates as a safety device, in the event of a problem with the accelerator position sensor. If the brake pedal switch is depressed while the accelerator pedal is held at a constant position, the engine speed will drop to idle. Thus, a faulty or incorrectly-adjusted brake pedal switch may result in a running problem.
42 The clutch pedal switch operation causes the injection pump to momentarily reduce its output while the clutch is disengaged, to permit smoother gear changing.
43 To remove either switch, refer to Chapter 11 and remove the trim panels from under the steering column area of the facia, to gain access to the pedal cluster.
44 The switches can be removed by unclipping them from their mountings and disconnecting the wiring plugs.

Refitting

45 Refitting is a reversal of removal. On completion, the adjustment of the switches must be verified electronically, using

14.4b . . . and remove the turbocharger-to-inlet manifold ducting

dedicated test equipment - refer to a Seat dealer for advice.

Needle stroke transmitter

46 The needle stroke transmitter is integral with No 3 injector. Refer to Section 11 for the removal and refitting procedure.

Electronic control unit (ECU)

47 The ECU is located beneath one of the windscreen cowl panels. On right-hand drive models it is located on the right-hand side, and on left-hand drive models it is located on the left-hand side. The unit is coded, and should not be removed without consulting a Seat dealer, otherwise it may not function correctly when the multi-plug is reconnected. If a new ECU is fitted, it must be adapted to the immobiliser by a Seat dealer using special equipment.

14 Turbocharger - general information, removal and refitting

General information

1 A turbocharger is fitted on engine codes AAZ, 1Z, AHU and AFN, and is mounted directly on the exhaust manifold. Lubrication is provided by an oil supply pipe that runs from the engine oil filter mounting. Oil is returned to the sump via a return pipe that connects to the side of the cylinder block. The turbocharger unit has an integral wastegate valve and vacuum actuator diaphragm, which is used to control the boost pressure applied to the inlet manifold.
2 The turbocharger's internal components rotate at very high speed, and as such are very sensitive to contamination; a great deal of damage can be caused by small particles of dirt, particularly if they strike the delicate turbine blades.
Caution: Thoroughly clean the area around all oil pipe unions before disconnecting them, to prevent the ingress of dirt. Store dismantled components in a sealed container to prevent contamination. Cover the turbocharger air inlet ducts to prevent debris entering, and clean using lint-free cloths only.

Removal

3 Disconnect the battery negative (earth) lead (see Chapter 5A). Apply the handbrake, then jack up the front of the vehicle and support it on axle stands (see *Jacking and vehicle support*).

Engine code AAZ

4 Slacken the clips and remove the turbocharger-to-inlet manifold (see illustrations) and air cleaner-to-turbocharger ducting. If necessary, remove the air cleaner assembly complete as described in Section 2.
5 Disconnect the vacuum hoses from the wastegate actuator diaphragm housing; note their order of connection and colour coding to aid correct refitting later.

6 Loosen the unions and disconnect the oil supply and return pipes from the turbocharger unit **(see illustrations)**. Recover the sealing washers and discard them - new items must be used on refitting. Free the supply pipe from the clip on the inlet manifold.

7 Remove the nuts and disconnect the exhaust downpipe from the turbocharger outlet. Recover and discard the gasket - a new item must be used on refitting **(see illustrations)**.

8 Slacken the mountings and remove the downpipe from the exhaust manifold support bracket.

9 Slacken and withdraw the turbocharger-to-exhaust manifold bolts. **Note:** *Access to the lowest bolt is restricted; a universal-joint extension bar will ease its removal.* Discard the bolts - new ones must be used on refitting.

10 Lift the turbocharger unit away from the exhaust manifold.

Engine codes 1Z and AHU

11 Remove the engine top cover where applicable.

12 Slacken the clips and remove the turbocharger-to-inlet manifold and air cleaner-to-turbocharger ducting. If necessary, remove the air cleaner assembly complete as described in Section 2.

13 Disconnect the hoses then unbolt the air inlet tube from the turbocharger.

14 Disconnect the boost control valve vacuum hoses from the wastegate actuator diaphragm housing; note their order of connection and colour coding to aid correct refitting later. Also disconnect the vacuum hoses from the inlet manifold and turbocharger.

15 Remove the nuts and disconnect the exhaust downpipe from the turbocharger outlet. Recover and discard the gasket - a new item must be used on refitting.

16 Loosen the unions and disconnect the oil supply and return pipes from the turbocharger

14.6a Slackening the oil return pipe union at the turbocharger

14.6b Disconnecting the oil supply pipe at the turbocharger

unit. Recover the sealing washers and discard them - new items must be used on refitting. Free the supply pipe from the clip on the inlet manifold.

17 Remove the retaining screws and detach the downpipe from the cylinder head support bracket.

18 Slacken and withdraw the two turbocharger-to-inlet manifold bolts from above, then working underneath the exhaust manifold, slacken and remove the retaining nut. Discard the bolts as new items must be used on refitting.

19 Lift the turbocharger unit away from the exhaust manifold.

Engine code AFN

20 Disconnect the battery negative lead and position it away from the terminal. Remove the engine top cover. Slacken the clips and remove the turbocharger-to-intercooler ducting.

21 Pull off the boost control valve vacuum hose from the wastegate actuator diaphragm housing.

22 Loosen the union and disconnect the oil feed pipe from the turbocharger. Recover the O-ring from the pipe and discard it - a new one must be used on refitting. Unscrew the retaining nut and bolt, and release the feed pipe from the bracket on the inlet manifold.

23 Remove the nuts and disconnect the exhaust downpipe from the turbocharger outlet. Recover and discard the gasket - a new one must be used on refitting.

24 Unbolt the turbocharger mounting bracket from the turbocharger and the cylinder head.

25 Unscrew and remove the two bolts from the oil return connection on the base of the turbocharger. When the turbocharger is removed, recover and discard the gasket - a new one will be needed for reassembly.

26 Slacken and remove the two turbocharger-to-manifold nuts from below, then slacken and remove the retaining nut from above. Discard the nuts, as new items must be used on refitting.

27 Lift the turbocharger away from the exhaust manifold.

Refitting

All engines

28 Refit the turbocharger by following the removal procedure in reverse, noting the following points:

a) *Offer up the turbocharger to the exhaust manifold, then fit and hand tighten the exhaust downpipe nuts.*

b) *On engine codes 1Z and AHU, fit the turbocharger-to-exhaust manifold nut and tighten it to the specified torque.*

4C

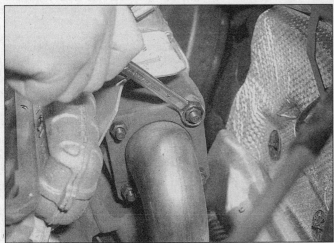

14.7a Remove the nuts and disconnect the downpipe from the turbocharger outlet

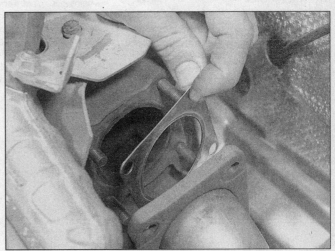

14.7b Recover and discard the gasket

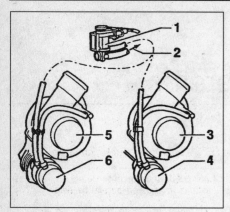

14.28a **Wastegate vacuum hose connections: engine code AAZ**

1 Two-way valve
2 To vacuum pump
3 Turbocharger (KKK)
4 Wastegate actuator
5 Turbocharger (Garrett)
6 Wastegate actuator

c) Apply high temperature grease to the threads and heads of the new turbocharger-to-exhaust manifold bolts, then fit and tighten them to the specified torque.
d) Tighten the exhaust downpipe nuts to the specified torque (see Chapter 4D).
e) Prime the oil supply pipe and turbocharger oil inlet port with clean engine oil before reconnecting the union and tightening it to the specified torque. Fit a new gasket.
f) Tighten the oil return union to the specified torque.
g) Reconnect the wastegate actuator vacuum hoses according to the notes made during removal **(see illustrations)**.
h) When the engine is started after refitting, allow it idle for approximately one minute to give the oil time to circulate around the turbine shaft bearings.

15 Intercooler -
removal and refitting

Note: *This Section only applies to engine codes 1Z, AHU and AFN.*

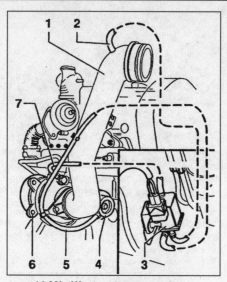

14.28b **Wastegate vacuum hose connections: engine code 1Z**

1 Inlet hose
2 Hose colour-coded black
3 Boost pressure control solenoid
4 Wastegate actuator
5 Hose colour-coded blue
6 Turbocharger
7 Hose colour-coded red

Removal

1 Apply the handbrake, then jack up the front of the vehicle and support it on axle stands (see *Jacking and vehicle support*). Where applicable, remove the engine compartment undertray.
2 Disconnect the battery negative (earth) lead (see Chapter 5A).
3 Loosen the clip and disconnect the intercooler air inlet duct from the inlet manifold.
4 Refer to Chapter 11 and remove the front bumper under-skirt.
5 Loosen the clip and disconnect the remaining air duct from the intercooler.
6 Unscrew the two lower and single upper mounting bolts, and lower the intercooler from under the car **(see illustration)**.
7 Loosen the clip and disconnect the air inlet duct from the intercooler.

15.6 **Intercooler viewed from under the engine compartment**

Refitting

8 Refitting is a reversal of removal.

16 Inlet manifold -
removal and refitting

Removal

1 On engine codes AAZ, 1Z, AHU and AFN remove the turbocharger (see Section 14).
2 On engine code AEY, remove the throttle valve housing as described in Section 13.
3 Where applicable, undo the nuts and remove the cover from the inlet manifold.
4 Remove the EGR valve and flexible pipe with reference to Chapter 4D. Note, however, that on engine code AFN the valve forms part of the inlet manifold and cannot be removed separately -
5 Progressively unscrew and remove the inlet manifold retaining nuts/bolts
6 Withdraw the inlet manifold from the cylinder head, and recover the gasket.

Refitting

7 Refitting is a reversal of removal, using a new manifold gasket.

Chapter 4 Part D:
Emission control and exhaust systems

Contents

Degrees of difficulty

Easy, suitable for novice with little experience	Fairly easy, suitable for beginner with some experience	Fairly difficult, suitable for competent DIY mechanic	Difficult, suitable for experienced DIY mechanic	Very difficult, suitable for expert DIY or professional

Specifications

Torque wrench settings	Nm	lbf ft
Downpipe to catalytic converter	40	30
Downpipe to manifold	40	30
Downpipe to turbocharger	25	18
EGR tube to EGR valve:		
Clamp	10	7
Bolt	25	18
EGR tube to exhaust manifold	25	18
EGR valve to inlet manifold	25	18
Exhaust manifold	25	18
Exhaust manifold hot air shroud	10	7
Exhaust system clamp bolts	40	30
Exhaust tailpipe mounting to underbody:		
Stage 1	20	30
Stage 2	Angle-tighten 90°	
Front exhaust bracket to underbody	20	15

4D

1 General information

Emission control systems

All petrol engine models have the ability to use unleaded petrol and are controlled by engine management systems that are tuned to give the best compromise between driveability, fuel consumption and exhaust emission production. In addition, a number of systems are fitted that help to minimise other harmful emissions. All models are fitted with a crankcase emission-control system that reduces the release of pollutants from the engines lubrication system, and a catalytic converter that reduces exhaust gas pollutant. Petrol engine model have an evaporative loss emission control system that reduces the release of gaseous hydrocarbons from the fuel tank.

All diesel-engined models have a crankcase emission control system, and in addition, except for engine code 1Y, are fitted with a catalytic converter. All diesel engines are fitted with an Exhaust Gas Recirculation (EGR) system to reduce exhaust emissions.

Crankcase emission control

To reduce the emission of unburned hydrocarbons from the crankcase into the atmosphere, the engine is sealed and the blow-by gases and oil vapour are drawn from inside the crankcase, through a wire mesh oil separator, into the inlet tract to be burned by the engine during normal combustion.

Under conditions of high manifold depression the gases will be sucked positively out of the crankcase. Under conditions of low manifold depression the gases are forced out of the crankcase by the (relatively) higher crankcase pressure. If the engine is worn, the raised crankcase pressure (due to increased blow-by) will cause some of the flow to return under all manifold conditions. All diesel engines have a pressure regulating valve on the camshaft cover, to control the flow of gases from the crankcase. Petrol engine codes 1F, 2E and AGG also have a pressure regulator on top of the camshaft cover, however all other petrol engines have an oil separator mounted on the side of the cylinder block.

Exhaust emission control - petrol models

To minimise the amount of pollutants which escape into the atmosphere, all petrol models are fitted with a three-way catalytic converter in the exhaust system. The fuelling system is of the closed-loop type, in which a Lambda sensor in the exhaust system provides the engine management system ECU with constant feedback, enabling the ECU to adjust the air/fuel mixture to optimise combustion.

The Lambda sensor has a heating element built-in that is controlled by the ECU through the Lambda sensor relay to quickly bring the sensor's tip to its optimum operating temperature. The sensor's tip is sensitive to oxygen and relays a voltage signal to the ECU that varies according on the amount of oxygen in the exhaust gas. If the inlet air/fuel mixture is too rich, the exhaust gases are low in oxygen so the sensor sends a low-voltage signal, the voltage rising as the mixture weakens and the amount of oxygen rises in the exhaust gases. Peak conversion efficiency of all major pollutants occurs if the inlet air/fuel mixture is maintained at the chemically-correct ratio for the complete combustion of petrol of 14.7 parts (by weight) of air to 1 part of fuel (the stoichiometric ratio). The sensor output voltage alters in a large step at this point, the ECU using the signal change as a reference point and correcting the inlet air/fuel mixture accordingly by altering the fuel injector pulse width. Details of the Lambda sensor removal and refitting are given in Chapter 4A or 4B as applicable.

Exhaust emission control - diesel models

An oxidation catalyst is fitted in the exhaust system of all diesel engined models. This has the effect of removing a large proportion of the gaseous hydrocarbons, carbon monoxide and particulates present in the exhaust gas.

An Exhaust Gas Recirculation (EGR) system is fitted to all diesel engined models. This reduces the level of nitrogen oxides produced during combustion by introducing a proportion of the exhaust gas back into the inlet manifold, under certain engine operating conditions, via a plunger valve. The system is controlled electronically by the glow plug control module on engine codes 1Y and AAZ, or by the diesel engine management ECU on engine codes AEY, 1Z, AHU and AFN.

Evaporative emission control - petrol models

To minimise the escape of unburned hydrocarbons into the atmosphere, an evaporative loss emission control system is fitted to all petrol models. The fuel tank filler cap is sealed and a charcoal canister is mounted underneath the right-hand wing to collect the petrol vapours released from the fuel contained in the fuel tank. It stores them until they can be drawn from the canister (under the control of the fuel-injection/ignition system ECU) via the purge valve(s) into the inlet tract, where they are then burned by the engine during normal combustion.

To ensure that the engine runs correctly when it is cold and/or idling and to protect the catalytic converter from the effects of an over-rich mixture, the purge control valve(s) are not opened by the ECU until the engine has warmed up, and the engine is under load; the valve solenoid is then modulated on and off to allow the stored vapour to pass into the inlet tract.

Exhaust systems

The exhaust system comprises the exhaust manifold, front pipe, catalytic converter, intermediate pipe and silencer, and tailpipe and silencer. Initially, the intermediate and rear sections are manufactured as one unit, however they are available separately as service items. The system is supported by rubber bushes and/or rubber mounting rings.

On diesel engine codes AAZ, 1Z, AHU and AFN, a turbocharger is fitted to the exhaust manifold.

2 Evaporative loss emission control system - information and component renewal

General information

1 The evaporative loss emission control system consists of the purge valve, the activated charcoal filter canister and a series of connecting vacuum hoses.

2 The purge valve is located in the front right-hand corner of the engine compartment, in the vacuum line between the charcoal canister and the throttle housing. The charcoal canister is mounted inside the right-hand front wheel housing. On models with a rectangular air cleaner mounted on the right-hand side of the engine compartment, the canister is located beneath the air cleaner body.

Component renewal

Purge valve

3 Ensure that the ignition is switched off, then unplug the wiring harness from the purge valve at the connector **(see illustration)**.
4 Slacken the clips and pull the vacuum hoses off the purge valve ports. Make a note of their position to aid refitting later.
5 Slide the purge valve out of its retaining ring and remove it.
6 Refitting is a reversal of removal.

Charcoal canister

7 Apply the handbrake, then jack up the front of the vehicle and support it on axle stands (see *Jacking and vehicle support*). Remove the right-hand front roadwheel.
8 Refer to Chapter 11, and partially remove the right-hand front wheel arch liner to give access to the charcoal canister.
9 Disconnect the vacuum hoses, noting which ports they connect to. Depress the

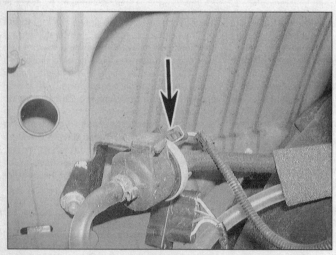

2.3 Unplug the wiring harness from the purge valve at the connector (arrowed)

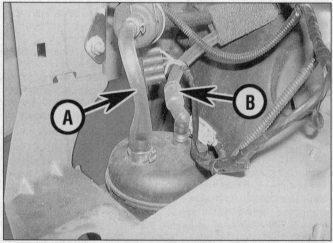

2.9a Charcoal canister pipe to purge valve (A) and pipe to fuel tank (B)

2.9c Charcoal canister viewed with the front lock carrier removed from the car

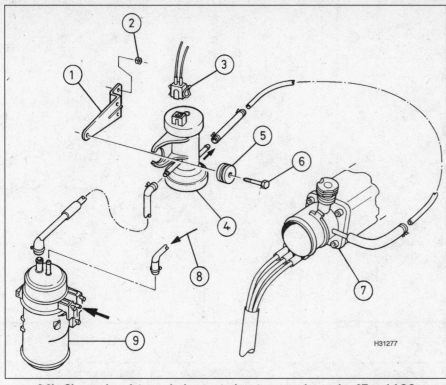

H31277

2.9b Charcoal canister emission control system - engine codes 2E and AGG

1 Mounting bracket in right-hand front wheel housing	3 Wiring connector	7 Throttle valve housing
	4 Solenoid valve	8 Vapour line from fuel
2 Nut	5 Rubber block	tank
	6 Bolt	9 Charcoal canister

Note: *Arrow indicates locking tab position and direction to depress*

locking tab and lift the canister out of the wheel housing **(see illustrations).**
10 Refitting is a reversal of removal.

3 Crankcase emission system - general information

1 The crankcase emission control system consists of hoses connecting the crankcase to the air cleaner or inlet manifold. A pressure regulating valve is fitted to all diesel engines, and petrol engines with the codes 1F, 2E, and AGG. Oil separator units are fitted to some petrol engines **(see illustration).**
2 The system requires no attention other than to check at regular intervals that the hoses, valve and oil separator are free of blockages and in good condition **(see illustrations).**

4 Exhaust Gas Recirculation (EGR) system - information and component removal

Note: *The EGR system is only fitted to diesel engines.*

General information

1 The EGR system consists of the EGR valve, the EGR control valve and a series of connecting vacuum hoses.
2 The EGR valve is mounted on a flange joint at the inlet manifold and is connected to a second flange joint at the exhaust manifold by a semi-flexible pipe on all engines except code AFN. On engine code AFN, the valve is integral with the inlet manifold, and cannot be removed separately.
3 The EGR control valve is mounted on the bulkhead at the rear of the engine compartment.

Component renewal

EGR valve (except engine code AFN)

4 Where applicable, unbolt the hot air shroud from the exhaust manifold.

4D

3.1 Oil separator unit on the rear of engine code APQ

3.2a Oil separator unit retaining bolts (seen with engine removed, for clarity)

3.2b Oil separator unit removed, showing O-ring seals (arrowed)

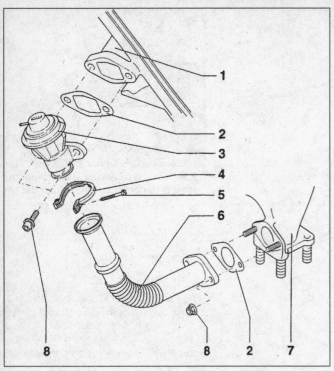

4.6a EGR valve details - engine code 1Y shown

1	Inlet manifold	4	Retaining clamp	7	Exhaust manifold
2	Gasket	5	Clamp screw	8	Retaining nut
3	EGR valve	6	Connecting pipe		

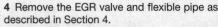

4.6b EGR valve details - engine code 1Z

1	Nut	3	Semi-flexible pipe	6	Inlet manifold
2	Oil supply pipe bracket	4	Screw	7	EGR valve
		5	Gaskets	8	Exhaust manifold

5 Disconnect the vacuum hose from the port at the top of the EGR valve.

6 Disconnect the semi-flexible connecting pipe from the EGR valve flange, and where necessary from the exhaust manifold. The pipe is attached to the exhaust manifold by two nuts, and to the EGR valve by bolts except on engine code 1Y where it is attached by a clamp **(see illustrations)**. Unscrew and remove the bolt(s) and disconnect the pipe - recover and discard the gasket(s) where necessary.

7 Remove the bolts securing the EGR valve to the inlet manifold flange and lift off the EGR valve. Recover and discard the gasket.

8 Refitting is a reversal of removal, but use new flange joint gaskets and self-locking nuts.

EGR control valve

9 Ensure that the ignition is switched off, then unplug the wiring harness from the valve at the connector.

10 Pull the vacuum hoses off the valve ports. Make a *careful* note of their orientation to aid refitting later.

11 Remove the retaining screws and lift off the valve.

12 Refitting is a reversal of removal.

Caution: Ensure that the vacuum hoses are refitted correctly; combustion and exhaust smoke production can be drastically affected by an incorrectly operating EGR system.

5 Exhaust manifold - removal and refitting

Removal

1 Apply the handbrake, then jack up the front of the vehicle and support it on axle stands (see *Jacking and vehicle support*).

2 Remove the air cleaner and trunking as described in Chapters 4A, 4B, or 4C (as applicable). Also remove the engine top cover where necessary.

3 Where applicable, unbolt the hot air shroud from the exhaust manifold and remove the stub **(see illustration)**.

4 Remove the EGR valve and flexible pipe as described in Section 4.

5 Unscrew the nuts and separate the downpipe from the exhaust manifold. Recover the gasket and support the downpipe on an axle stand.

6 Note the location of any support brackets, then progressively unscrew the nuts securing the exhaust manifold to the cylinder head **(see illustration)**. Withdraw the manifold and recover the gasket(s).

Refitting

7 Clean thoroughly the mating surfaces of the manifold and cylinder head.

8 Refitting is a reversal of removal, but fit new gaskets and tighten the nuts and bolts to the specified torque.

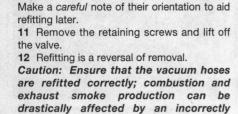

5.3 Removing the hot air shroud and stub

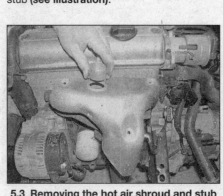

5.6 Exhaust manifold retaining nuts (engine code APQ)

6.2 Oxidation catalyst fitted to Diesel engine models - engine codes AEY, 1Z, AHU, AFN

6 Exhaust system - general information and component renewal

General information

1 On all petrol engines the exhaust system is made up of the downpipe, catalytic converter, intermediate section and silencer, and the rear section and silencer. A twin-branch downpipe is fitted to engine codes 2E, AGG, AEE, ALM and ABF.

2 On diesel engine codes AEY, 1Z, AHU, and AFN the exhaust system is made up of the downpipe and catalytic converter **(see illustration)**, intermediate section and silencer, and the rear section and silencer. On later models with these engine codes, the catalytic converter is integral with the downpipe. On engine code 1Y a plain downpipe is connected to the intermediate and rear sections. On engine code AAZ the system is similar to that fitted to AEY but the catalytic converter is separate. On engine code AFT, the system consists of a twin-branch downpipe, catalytic converter, intermediate section and silencer, and rear section silencer.

3 The intermediate and rear exhaust sections are manufactured as one unit on new cars from the factory, however the original pipe can be cut for fitment of individual sections **(see illustration)**.

4 On all models, the system is suspended throughout its entire length by rubber mountings **(see illustration)**.

Removal

⚠ **Warning: Allow ample time for the exhaust system to cool before starting work. In particular, the catalytic converter (where applicable) runs at very high temperatures, and severe burns will result if it is carelessly handled. If there is any chance that the system may still be hot, wear suitable gloves.**

5 Each exhaust section can be removed individually, however because the system is located above the rear axle and front subframe, the complete system cannot be removed complete **(see illustration)**.

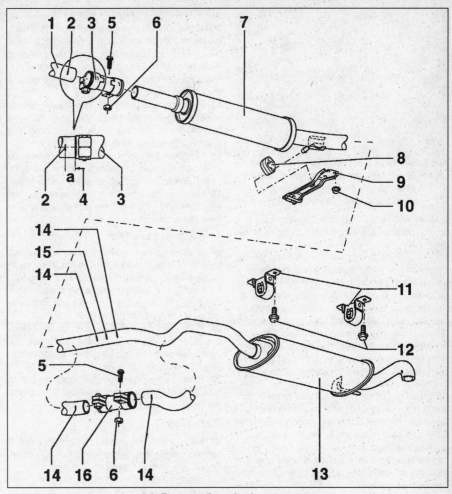

6.3 Rear section of exhaust system

1 Front pipe from catalyst	7 Front silencer with balance weight
2 Fitted position marking	8 Mounting rubber
3 Exhaust clamp	9 Cross-bracket
4 Dimension a = 5 mm approx	10 Nut
5 Clamp bolt	11 Rubber mounting bracket
6 Nut	

12 Bolt	
13 Rear silencer	
14 Fitted position marking	
15 Cutting point for original system	
16 Exhaust clamp	

6 To remove part of the system, first jack up the front or rear of the car and support it on axle stands (see *Jacking and vehicle support*). Alternatively position the car over an inspection pit or on car ramps.

Downpipe

7 Support the catalytic converter/front silencer on a trolley jack or wooden blocks.
8 Where applicable, refer to Chapter 4A or 4B and remove the Lambda sensor from the exhaust pipe.

6.4 Exhaust system rubber mounting

6.5 The exhaust rear section is located over the rear axle

4D

6.11 Short adapter and clamps between the intermediate section and downpipe/catalytic converter

9 Unscrew the nuts and separate the downpipe from the exhaust manifold. Recover the gasket.

10 On models where the downpipe is attached to the catalytic converter with a flange joint, unscrew and remove the bolts, separate the joint and recover the sealing ring.

11 On models where the catalytic converter is integral with the downpipe, unscrew and remove the clamp bolts and separate the downpipe from the intermediate section, then remove the short adapter and clamps **(see illustration)**. On these models it is necessary to partially lower the front subframe as follows. Attach a suitable hoist to the engine and support the weight of the engine/transmission. Beneath the car, unscrew and remove the subframe rear mounting bolts, then lower the subframe a little.

12 Where necessary, unbolt and remove the heatshield, then lift out the downpipe and catalytic converter.

Catalytic converter

Note: *Where the catalytic converter is integral with the downpipe, follow the previous paragraphs.*

13 Support the catalytic converter on a trolley jack or wooden blocks.

14 Unscrew and remove the bolts securing the downpipe to the catalytic converter. Separate the joint and recover the sealing ring.

15 Unscrew and remove the clamp bolts and separate the intermediate section from the catalytic converter, then remove the short adapter and clamps. Withdraw the catalytic converter from under the car.

Intermediate pipe and silencer

16 If the original exhaust system is fitted, locate the three marks on the length of pipe between the intermediate and rear silencers indicating the cutting and clamp positions. Cut through the centre mark at right-angles to the pipe, using a hacksaw.

17 If a service section has been fitted, unscrew the clamp bolts and separate the intermediate and rear sections. Remove the short adapter and clamps.

18 Unscrew the clamp bolts and separate the intermediate section from the catalytic converter. Remove the short adapter and clamps.

19 Release the pipe from the mounting, then withdraw the intermediate pipe and silencer from under the car.

Tailpipe and silencer

20 If the original exhaust system is fitted, locate the three marks on the length of pipe between the intermediate and rear silencers indicating the cutting and clamp positions. Cut through the centre mark at right-angles to the pipe, using a hacksaw.

21 If a service section has been fitted, unscrew the clamp bolts and separate the intermediate and rear sections. Remove the short adapter and clamps.

22 Release the pipe from the mounting, then withdraw the tailpipe and silencer from under the car.

Refitting

23 Each section is refitted by a reversal of the removal sequence, noting the following points.

a) *Ensure that all traces of corrosion have been removed from the flanges and renew all necessary gaskets.*

b) *Where the original intermediate and rear sections have been cut, locate the ends of the clamp on the marks already made on the pipe.*

c) *Inspect the rubber mountings for signs of damage or deterioration and renew as necessary.*

d) *If necessary, renew the sealing ring in the catalytic converter/front silencer-to-downpipe joint.*

e) *Prior to tightening the exhaust system fasteners, ensure that all rubber mountings are correctly located and that there is adequate clearance between the exhaust system and vehicle underbody.*

7 Catalytic converter - general information and precautions

1 The catalytic converter is a reliable and simple device which needs no maintenance in itself, but there are some facts which an owner should be aware of if the converter is to function properly for its full service life.

Petrol models

a) *DO NOT use leaded petrol in a car with a catalytic converter - the lead will coat the internal precious metals, reducing their converting efficiency and will eventually destroy the converter.*

b) *Always keep the ignition and fuel systems well-maintained in accordance with the manufacturer's schedule.*

c) *If the engine develops a misfire, do not drive the car at all (or at least as little as possible) until the fault is cured.*

d) *DO NOT push- or tow-start the car - this will soak the catalytic converter in unburned fuel, causing it to overheat when the engine does start.*

e) *DO NOT switch off the ignition at high engine speeds.*

f) *The catalytic converter, used on a well-maintained and well-driven car, should last between 50 000 and 100 000 miles - if the converter is no longer effective it must be renewed.*

Petrol and diesel models

g) *DO NOT use fuel or engine oil additives - these may contain substances harmful to the catalytic converter.*

h) *DO NOT continue to use the car if the engine burns oil to the extent of leaving a visible trail of blue smoke.*

i) *Remember that the catalytic converter operates at very high temperatures. DO NOT, therefore, park the car in dry undergrowth, over long grass or piles of dead leaves after a long run.*

j) *Remember that the catalytic converter is FRAGILE - do not strike it with tools during servicing work.*

Chapter 5 Part A:
Starting and charging systems

Contents

Degrees of difficulty

Easy, suitable for novice with little experience 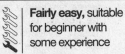	**Fairly easy,** suitable for beginner with some experience	**Fairly difficult,** suitable for competent DIY mechanic	**Difficult,** suitable for experienced DIY mechanic	**Very difficult,** suitable for expert DIY or professional

Specifications

General
System type .... 12-volt, negative earth

Starter motor
Rating:
1.05 and 1.3 litre engines	12V, 0.8 kW
1.4 and 1.6 litre engines	12V, 0.95 kW
1.8 and 2.0 litre engines	12V, 1.1 kW
All diesel engines	12V, 1.8 kW

Battery
Ratings .... 36 to 72 Ah (depending on model and market)

Alternator
Rating	55, 60, 70 or 90 amp
Minimum brush length	5.0 mm

Torque wrench settings

	Nm	lbf ft
Alternator mounting bolts:		
1.05 and 1.3 litre petrol engines	35	26
1.4, 1.6 and 2.0 litre petrol engines	23	17
All diesel engines	23	17
Alternator mounting bracket	45	33
Battery clamping plate bolt	20	15
Starter mounting bolts:		
1.05, 1.3, 1.4 and 1.6 litre petrol engines	20	15
2.0 litre petrol engines and all diesel engines:		
Long bolts	60	44
Short bolt	45	33

1 General information and precautions

General information

The engine electrical system consists mainly of the charging and starting systems. Because of their engine-related functions, these are covered separately from the body electrical devices such as the lights, instruments, etc (which are covered in Chapter 12). On petrol engine models refer to Part B of this Chapter for information on the ignition system, and on diesel models refer to Part C for the pre-heating system.

The electrical system is of the 12-volt negative earth type.

The battery may of the low maintenance or maintenance-free (sealed for life) type and is charged by the alternator, which is belt-driven from the crankshaft pulley.

The starter motor is of the pre-engaged type, with an integral solenoid. On starting, the solenoid moves the drive pinion into engagement with the flywheel ring gear before the starter motor is energised. Once the engine has started, a one-way clutch prevents the motor armature being driven by the engine until the pinion disengages from the flywheel.

Further details of the various systems are given in the relevant Sections of this Chapter. While some repair procedures are given, the usual course of action is to renew the component concerned. The owner whose interest extends beyond mere component renewal should obtain a copy of the *Automobile Electrical & Electronic Systems Manual*, available from the publishers of this manual.

Precautions

⚠ *Warning: It is necessary to take extra care when working on the electrical system to avoid damage to semi-conductor devices (diodes and transistors), and to avoid the risk of personal injury. In addition to the precautions given in Safety first!, observe the following when working on the system:*

Always remove rings, watches, etc before working on the electrical system. Even with the battery disconnected, capacitive discharge could occur if a component's live terminal is earthed through a metal object. This could cause a shock or nasty burn.

Do not reverse the battery connections. Components such as the alternator, electronic control units, or any other components having semi-conductor circuitry could be irreparably damaged.

Never disconnect the battery terminals, the alternator, any electrical wiring or any test instruments when the engine is running.

Do not allow the engine to turn the alternator when the alternator is not connected.

Never test for alternator output by flashing the output lead to earth.

Always ensure that the battery negative lead is disconnected when working on the electrical system.

If the engine is being started using jump leads and a slave battery, connect the batteries *positive-to-positive* and *negative-to-negative* (see *Jump starting* at the beginning of the manual). This also applies when connecting a battery charger.

Before using electric-arc welding equipment on the car, *disconnect the battery, alternator and components such as the electronic control units* (where applicable) to protect them from the risk of damage.

Caution: Certain radio/cassettes fitted as standard equipment by Seat have a built-in security code to deter thieves. If the power source to the unit is cut, the anti-theft system will activate. Even if the power source is immediately reconnected, the radio/cassette unit will not function until the correct security code has been entered. Therefore, if you do not know the correct security code for the radio/cassette unit do not disconnect the battery negative terminal or remove the radio/cassette unit from the vehicle. Refer to your Seat dealer for further information on whether the unit fitted to your car has a security code.

2 Battery - testing and charging

Standard and low-maintenance battery - testing

1 If the vehicle covers a small annual mileage, it is worthwhile checking the specific gravity of the electrolyte every three months to determine the state of charge of the battery. Use a hydrometer to make the check, and compare the results with the following table. Note that the specific gravity readings assume an electrolyte temperature of 15°C (60°F); for every 10°C (18°F) below 15°C (60°F) subtract 0.007. For every 10°C (18°F) above 15°C (60°F) add 0.007.

	Above 25°C	Below 25°C
Fully charged	1.210 to 1.230	1.270 to 1.290
70% charged	1.170 to 1.190	1.230 to 1.250
Discharged	1.050 to 1.070	1.110 to 1.130

2 If the battery condition is suspect, first check the specific gravity of electrolyte in each cell. A variation of 0.040 or more between any cells indicates loss of electrolyte or deterioration of the internal plates.

3 If the specific gravity variation is 0.040 or more, the battery should be renewed. If the cell variation is satisfactory but the battery is discharged, it should be charged as described later in this Section.

Maintenance-free battery - testing

4 In cases where a sealed for life maintenance-free battery is fitted, topping-up and testing of the electrolyte in each cell is not possible. The condition of the battery can therefore only be tested using a battery condition indicator or a voltmeter.

5 Certain models my be fitted with a maintenance-free battery, with a built-in charge condition indicator. The indicator is located in the top of the battery casing, and indicates the condition of the battery from its colour. If the indicator shows green, then the battery is in a good state of charge. If the indicator turns darker, eventually to black, then the battery requires charging, as described later in this Section. If the indicator shows clear/yellow, then the electrolyte level in the battery is too low to allow further use, and the battery should be renewed. **Do not** attempt to charge, load or jump start a battery when the indicator shows clear/yellow.

6 If testing the battery using a voltmeter, connect the voltmeter across the battery and note the voltage. The test is only accurate if the battery has not been subjected to any kind of charge for the previous six hours. If this is not the case, switch on the headlights for 30 seconds, then wait four to five minutes before testing the battery after switching off the headlights. All other electrical circuits must be switched off, so check that the doors and tailgate are fully shut when making the test.

7 If the voltage reading is less than 12.2 volts, then the battery is discharged, whilst a reading of 12.2 to 12.4 volts indicates a partially discharged condition.

8 If the battery is to be charged, remove it from the vehicle and charge it as described later in this Section.

Standard and low maintenance battery - charging

Note: *The following is intended as a guide only. Always refer to the manufacturer's recommendations (often printed on a label attached to the battery) before charging a battery.*

9 Charge the battery at a rate equivalent to 10% of the battery capacity (eg for a 45 Ah battery charge at 4.5 A) and continue to charge the battery at this rate until no further rise in specific gravity is noted over a four-hour period.

10 Alternatively, a trickle charger charging at the rate of 1.5 amps can safely be used overnight.

11 Specially rapid boost charges which are claimed to restore the power of the battery in 1 to 2 hours are not recommended, as they can cause serious damage to the battery plates through overheating.

12 While charging the battery, note that the temperature of the electrolyte should never exceed 37.8°C (100°F).

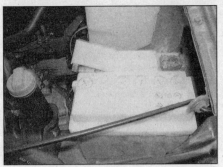

3.1 The battery is located in the left-hand front corner of the engine compartment

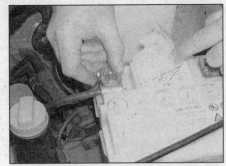

3.3 Disconnecting the battery positive lead

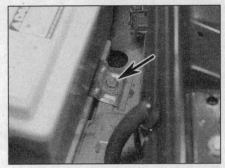

3.4 Battery clamping plate screw (arrowed)

Maintenance-free battery - charging

Note: *The following is intended as a guide only. Always refer to the manufacturer's recommendations (often printed on a label attached to the battery) before charging a battery.*

13 This battery type takes considerably longer to fully recharge than the standard type, the time taken being dependent on the extent of discharge, but it can take anything up to three days.

14 A constant voltage type charger is required, to be set, when connected, to 13.9 to 14.9 volts with a charger current below 25 amps. Using this method, the battery should be useable within three hours, giving a voltage reading of 12.5 volts, but this is for a partially-discharged battery and, as mentioned, full charging can take far longer.

15 If the battery is to be charged from a fully-discharged state (condition reading less than 12.2 volts), have it recharged by your local automotive electrician, as the charge rate is higher and constant supervision during charging is necessary.

3 Battery - removal and refitting

Note: *If the vehicle has a security-coded radio, check that you have a copy of the code number before disconnecting the battery cable; refer to the caution in Section 1.*

Removal

1 The battery is located in the front left-hand corner of the engine compartment **(see illustration)**.

2 Loosen the clamp nut and disconnect the battery negative (-) lead from the terminal.

3 Lift the plastic flap where fitted, then loosen the clamp nut and disconnect the battery positive (+) lead from the terminal **(see illustration)**.

4 At the base of the battery, unscrew the retaining clamp bolt and remove the clamp **(see illustration)**.

5 Carefully lift the battery from the engine compartment

Refitting

6 Refit the battery by following the removal procedure in reverse. Tighten the clamp bolt to the correct torque.

4 Alternator/charging system - testing in vehicle

Note: *Refer to Section 1 of this Chapter before starting work.*

1 If the charge warning light fails to illuminate when the ignition is switched on, first check the alternator wiring connections for security. If satisfactory, check that the warning light bulb has not blown, and that the bulbholder is secure in its location in the instrument panel. If the light still fails to illuminate, check the continuity of the warning light feed wire from the alternator to the bulbholder. If all is satisfactory, the alternator is at fault and should be renewed or taken to an auto-electrician for testing and repair.

2 Similarly, if the charge warning light comes on with the ignition, but is then slow to go out when the engine is started, this may indicate an impending alternator problem. Check all the items listed in the preceding paragraph, and refer to an auto-electrical specialist if no obvious faults are found.

3 If the charge warning light illuminates when the engine is running, stop the engine and check that the drivebelt is correctly tensioned (see Chapter 2A or 2B) and that the alternator connections are secure. If all is so far satisfactory, check the alternator brushes and slip rings as described in Section 6. If the fault persists, the alternator should be renewed, or taken to an auto-electrician for testing and repair.

4 If the alternator output is suspect even though the warning light functions correctly, the regulated voltage may be checked as follows.

5 Connect a voltmeter across the battery terminals, and start the engine.

6 Increase the engine speed until the voltmeter reading remains steady; the reading should be approximately 12 to 13 volts, and no more than 14 volts.

7 Switch on as many electrical accessories (eg, the headlights, heated rear window and heater blower) as possible, and check that the alternator maintains the regulated voltage at around 13 to 14 volts.

8 If the regulated voltage is not as stated, this may be due to worn brushes, weak brush springs, a faulty voltage regulator, a faulty diode, a severed phase winding or worn or damaged slip rings. The brushes and slip rings may be checked (see Section 6), but if the fault persists, the alternator should be renewed or taken to an auto-electrician.

5 Alternator - removal and refitting

Removal

1 Disconnect the battery negative lead and position it away from the terminal - refer to the precautions in Section 1.

2 Remove the auxiliary drivebelt from the alternator pulley (see Chapter 2A or 2B). Mark the drivebelt for direction to ensure it is refitted in the same position.

3 On 1.4 litre engine codes AEX, APQ and ABD fitted with air conditioning, refer to Chapter 3 and unbolt the air conditioning compressor from the engine without disconnecting the refrigerant lines. Support the compressor to one side.

4 Unscrew the nut and disconnect the warning lamp wiring from the alternator **(see illustration)**.

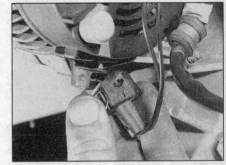

5.4 Disconnect the warning lamp wiring from the alternator at the connector

5A

5.5a Remove the protective cap . . .

5.5b . . . remove the nut and washers, then disconnect the power cable

5.5c Where applicable, unbolt and remove the cable guide

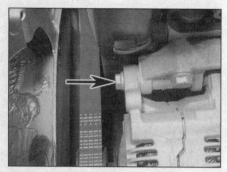

5.6a Alternator upper mounting bolt

5.6b Alternator lower mounting bolt on models with a drivebelt tensioning spring

5.6c Alternator lower mounting bolt (engine code APQ)

5 Remove the protective cap, unscrew and remove the nut and washers, then disconnect the battery positive cable from the alternator terminal. Where applicable, unscrew the nut and remove the cable guide **(see illustrations)**.

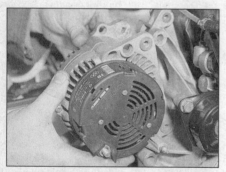

5.6d Lifting the alternator away from its mounting bracket (diesel engine shown)

6 Unscrew and remove the lower, then upper bolts, then lift the alternator away from its bracket. Where applicable, note the location of the drivebelt tensioning spring **(see illustrations)**.

Refitting

7 Refitting is a reversal of removal. Refer to Chapter 2A or 2B as applicable for details of refitting and tensioning the auxiliary drivebelt. Tighten the alternator mounting bolts to the specified torque.

6 Alternator -
brush holder/regulator
module renewal

1 Remove the alternator, as described in Section 5.

2 Place the alternator on a clean work surface, with the pulley facing down.

3 Where applicable, remove the plastic cover from the rear of the alternator. To do this, undo the retaining screws, then prise open the clips and lift off the plastic cover **(see illustrations)**.

4 Undo the screws then lift the brush holder/voltage regulator module away from the alternator **(see illustrations)**.

5 Measure the free length of the brush contacts - where applicable, take the measurement from the manufacturer's emblem (A) etched on the side of the brush contact, to the shallowest part of the curved end face of the brush (B) **(see illustration)**. Check the measure-ment with the Specifications; renew the module if the brushes are worn below the minimum limit.

6.3a Where applicable, remove the retaining screws (arrowed) . . .

6.3b . . . then prise open the clips . . .

6.3c . . . and lift the plastic cover from the rear of the alternator

6.4a Remove the brush holder/voltage regulator module screws . . .

6.4b . . . then lift the module away from the alternator

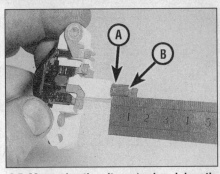

6.5 Measuring the alternator brush length - for A and B, see text

6 Clean and inspect the surfaces of the slip rings, at the end of the alternator shaft **(see illustration)**. If they are excessively worn, or damaged, the alternator must be renewed.

7 Reassemble the alternator by following the dismantling procedure in reverse. On completion, refer to Section 5 and refit the alternator.

7 Starting system - testing

Note: *Refer to Section 1 of this Chapter before starting work.*

1 If the starter motor fails to operate when the ignition key is turned to the appropriate position, the following possible causes may be to blame:

 a) *The battery is faulty.*
 b) *The electrical connections between the switch, solenoid, battery and starter motor are somewhere failing to pass the necessary current from the battery through the starter to earth.*
 c) *The solenoid is faulty.*
 d) *The starter motor is mechanically or electrically defective.*

2 To check the battery, switch on the headlights. If they dim after a few seconds, this indicates that the battery is discharged - recharge (see Section 2) or renew the battery. If the headlights glow brightly, operate the ignition switch and observe the lights. If they dim, then this indicates that current is reaching the starter motor, therefore the fault must lie in the starter motor. If the lights continue to glow brightly (and no clicking sound can be heard from the starter motor solenoid), this indicates that there is a fault in the circuit or solenoid - see following paragraphs. If the starter motor turns slowly when operated, but the battery is in good condition, then this indicates that either the starter motor is faulty, or there is considerable resistance somewhere in the circuit.

3 If a fault in the circuit is suspected, disconnect the battery leads (including the earth connection to the body), the starter/solenoid wiring and the engine/transmission earth strap. Thoroughly clean the connections, and reconnect the leads and wiring, then use a

voltmeter or test light to check that full battery voltage is available at the battery positive lead connection to the solenoid, and that the earth is sound. Smear petroleum jelly around the battery terminals to prevent corrosion - corroded connections are amongst the most frequent causes of electrical system faults.

4 If the battery and all connections are in good condition, check the circuit by disconnecting the wire from the solenoid blade terminal. Connect a voltmeter or test light between the wire end and a good earth (such as the battery negative terminal), and check that the wire is live when the ignition switch is turned to the start position. If it is, then the circuit is sound - if not the circuit wiring can be checked as described in Chapter 12.

5 The solenoid contacts can be checked by connecting a voltmeter or test light between the battery positive feed connection on the starter side of the solenoid, and earth. When the ignition switch is turned to the start position, there should be a reading or lighted bulb, as applicable. If there is no reading or lighted bulb, the solenoid is faulty and should be renewed.

6 If the circuit and solenoid are proved sound, the fault must lie in the starter motor. Begin checking the starter motor by removing it (see Section 8), and checking the brushes. If the fault does not lie in the brushes, the motor windings must be faulty. In this event, it may be possible to have the starter motor overhauled by a specialist, but check on the availability and cost of spares before proceeding, as it may prove more economical to obtain a new or exchange motor.

8 Starter motor - removal and refitting

On engine codes AER, AEX, APQ, AEE, ALM, AAU, AAV, ABD, ABU, the starter motor is located on the rear of the engine and is bolted to the transmission bellhousing. On engine codes AFT, 1F, 2E, AGG, ABF, 1Y, AAZ, 1Z, AHU, AEY, AFN, the starter is situated on the bellhousing at the front of the engine and shares its mounting bolts with the front engine mounting bracket. **Note:**

6.6 Inspect the surfaces of the slip rings (arrowed), at the end of the alternator shaft

Removal of the front engine mounting bracket involves supporting the engine with either a lifting beam or an engine hoist whilst the bracket is removed - refer to Chapter 2A or 2B as applicable for greater detail.

Removal

Engine codes AFT, 1F, 2E, AGG, ABF, 1Y, AAZ, 1Z, AHU, AEY, AFN

1 Disconnect the battery negative (earth) lead (see Chapter 5A).

2 Where applicable, remove the air cleaner assembly as described in Chapter 4A, 4B or 4C.

3 Refer to Chapter 2A or 2B as applicable and remove the front engine mounting bracket from the starter motor **(see illustration)**. Support the weight of the engine and transmission using a suitable hoist or alternatively a trolley jack and block of wood beneath the sump.

5A

8.3 Front engine mounting bracket (engine codes AFT, 1F, 2E, AGG, ABF, 1Y, AAZ, 1Z, AHU, AEY, AFN)

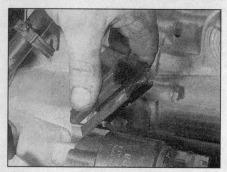

8.4a Remove the cable guide from above the solenoid housing . . .

8.4b . . . then unplug the solenoid supply cabling at the connector

8.6 Remove the nut and washer, and take off the power cable

4 Unhook the wiring connector from the cable guide above the solenoid housing, then remove the cable guide. Unplug the solenoid supply cabling at the connector **(see illustrations).**

5 Where applicable, unbolt the PAS hose guide from the starter motor mountings.

6 At the rear of the solenoid housing, remove the nut and washer from the power cable terminal post and take off the power cables **(see illustration).**

7 Remove the starter upper mounting bolt, then unscrew the nut from the mounting stud underneath the starter motor.

8 Guide the starter and solenoid assembly out of the bellhousing aperture **(see illustration).**

Engine codes AER, AEX, APQ, AEE, ALM, AAU, AAV, ABD, ABU

9 Disconnect the battery negative (earth) lead (see Chapter 5A).

10 Where applicable, remove the air cleaner assembly as described in Chapter 4A, 4B or 4C.

11 Apply the handbrake, then jack up the front of the vehicle and support it on axle stands (see *Jacking and vehicle support*).

12 Unplug the solenoid supply wiring at the connector **(see illustration).**

8.8 Guide the starter motor and solenoid assembly out of the bellhousing aperture

13 On the solenoid, remove the nut and washer from the power cable terminal post and take off the power cable. Where applicable, release the wiring from the cable tie.

14 Remove the starter mounting bolts, then remove the starter motor.

Refitting

15 Refit the starter motor by following the removal procedure in reverse. Tighten the mounting bolts to the specified torque. Where applicable, refer to Chapter 2A or 2B and refit the front engine mounting bracket.

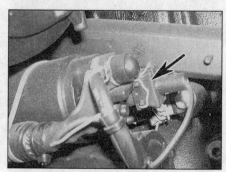

8.12 Starter motor solenoid supply wiring connector

9 Starter motor - testing and overhaul

If the starter motor is thought to be defective, it should be removed from the vehicle and taken to an auto-electrician for assessment. In the majority of cases, new starter motor brushes can be fitted at a reasonable cost. However, check the cost of repairs first as it may prove more economical to purchase a new or exchange motor.

Chapter 5 Part B:
Ignition system - petrol engines

Contents

Degrees of difficulty

Easy, suitable for novice with little experience	Fairly easy, suitable for beginner with some experience	Fairly difficult, suitable for competent DIY mechanic	Difficult, suitable for experienced DIY mechanic	Very difficult, suitable for expert DIY or professional

Specifications

General

Type:

Engine code AER, AEX, APQ	Bosch Motronic 9.0
Engine codes AAU, AAV, ABD, ABU, 1F	Bosch Mono-Motronic
Engine code AEE, ALM	Magneti-Marelli 1AV
Engine code AFT, AGG	Simos
Engine code 2E, ABF	Digifant

Ignition coil

Primary winding resistance:

Engine codes AER, AAU, AAV, ABD, ABU, AEX, APQ, AEE, ALM, 1F, 2E	0.5 to 0.7 ohms
Engine code AFT, AGG	0.5 to 1.5 ohms

Secondary resistance:

Engine code AER, AFT, AGG	2500 to 4000 ohms
Engine codes AAU, AAV, ABD, ABU, AEX, APQ, AEE, ALM, 1F, 2E . .	3000 to 4000 ohms

Distributor

Type	Breakerless
Ignition timing	Controlled by engine management system
Rotor resistance	600 to 1400 ohms

Spark plugs

See Chapter 1A Specifications

Torque wrench settings

	Nm	lbf ft
Distributor clamp bolts (engine codes AER, AAU, AAV, ABD, ABU, 1F, AEX, APQ, AEE, ALM)	10	7
Distributor clamp plate bolt (engine codes AFT, 2E, AGG)	25	18
Knock sensor mounting bolt (engine codes AER, AEX, APQ, AEE, ALM, AFT, 2E, ABF)	20	15

5B

1 General information

The Bosch Motronic, Bosch Mono-Motronic, Magneti-Marelli 1AV, Simos and Digifant systems are self-contained engine management systems, which control both the fuel injection and ignition. This Chapter deals with the ignition system components only - refer to Chapter 4A or 4B for details of the fuel system components.

The ignition system comprises the spark plugs, HT leads, distributor, electronic ignition coil, and Electronic Control Unit (ECU) together with its associated sensors, actuators and wiring. The component layout varies from system to system but the basic operation is the same for all models.

The basic operation is as follows: the ECU supplies a voltage to the input stage of the ignition coil which causes the primary windings in the coil to be energised. The supply voltage is periodically interrupted by the ECU and this results in the collapse of primary magnetic field, which then induces a much larger voltage in the secondary coil, called the HT voltage. This voltage is directed, by the distributor via the HT leads, to the spark plug in the cylinder currently on its ignition stroke. The spark plug electrodes form a gap small enough for the HT voltage to arc across, and the resulting spark ignites the fuel/air mixture in the cylinder. The timing of this sequence of events is critical and is regulated solely by the ECU.

The ECU calculates and controls the ignition timing primarily according to engine speed, crankshaft position and inlet manifold depression (or inlet air volume flow rate, depending on system type) information, received from sensors mounted on and around the engine. Other parameters that affect ignition timing are throttle position and rate of opening, inlet air temperature, coolant temperature and on certain systems, engine knock. Again, these are monitored via sensors mounted on the engine. On all engines, the coil dwell angle is controlled by a Hall transmitter in the distributor.

On systems where knock control is employed, a knock sensor is mounted on the cylinder block in order to detect engine pre-ignition (or pinking) before it actually becomes audible. If pre-ignition occurs, the ECU retards the ignition timing of the cylinder that is pre-igniting in steps until the pre-ignition ceases. The ECU then advances the ignition timing of that cylinder in steps until it is restored to normal, or until pre-ignition occurs again.

Except on engines fitted with the Simos or Digifant engine management systems, idle speed control is achieved partly by an electronic throttle valve positioning module, mounted on the side of the throttle body and partly by the ignition system, which gives fine control of the idle speed by altering the ignition timing. On Simos systems, the ECU controls the idle speed through ignition timing and injector period. On Digifant systems, idle speed is controlled by a stabilization valve located in a throttle body by-pass hose. Manual adjustment of the engine idle speed is not necessary or possible.

On certain systems, the ECU has the ability to perform multiple ignition cycles during cold starting. During cranking, each spark plug fires several times per ignition stroke, until the engine starts. This greatly improves the engine's cold starting performance.

It should be noted that comprehensive fault diagnosis of all the engine management systems described in this Chapter is only possible with dedicated electronic test equipment. Problems with the systems operation that cannot be pinpointed by following the basic guidelines in Section 2 should therefore be referred to a Seat dealer for assessment. Once the fault has been identified, the removal/refitting sequences detailed in the following Sections will then allow the appropriate component(s) to be renewed as required.

Note: *Throughout this Chapter, vehicles are frequently referred to by their engine code, rather than by engine capacity - refer to Chapter 2A for engine code listings.*

2 Ignition system - testing

⚠️ **Warning: Extreme care must be taken when working on the system with the ignition switched on; it is possible to get a substantial electric shock from a vehicle's ignition system. Persons with cardiac pacemaker devices should keep well clear of the ignition circuits, components and test equipment. Always switch off the ignition before disconnecting or connecting any component and when using a multi-meter to check resistances.**

General

1 Most ignition system faults are likely to be due to loose or dirty connections or to tracking (unintentional earthing) of HT voltage due to dirt, dampness or damaged insulation, rather than by the failure of any of the system's components. Always check all wiring thoroughly before condemning an electrical component and work methodically to eliminate all other possibilities before deciding that a particular component is faulty.

2 The old practice of checking for a spark by holding the live end of an HT lead a short distance away from the engine is not recommended; not only is there a high risk of an electric shock, but the HT coil could be damaged. Similarly, **never** try to diagnose misfires by pulling off one HT lead at a time.

Engine will not start

3 If the engine either will not turn over at all, or only turns very slowly, check the battery and starter motor. Connect a voltmeter across the battery terminals (meter positive probe to battery positive terminal), disconnect the ignition coil HT lead from the distributor cap and earth it, then note the voltage reading obtained while turning over the engine on the starter for (no more than) ten seconds. If the reading obtained is less than approximately 9.5 volts, first check the battery, starter motor and charging systems (see Chapter 5A).

4 If the engine turns over at normal speed but will not start, check the HT circuit by connecting a timing light (following the manufacturer's instructions) and turning the engine over on the starter motor; if the light flashes, voltage is reaching the spark plugs, so these should be checked first. If the light does not flash, check the HT leads themselves followed by the distributor cap, carbon brush and rotor arm using the information given in Chapter 1.

5 If there is a spark, check the fuel system for faults referring to the relevant part of Chapter 4 for further information.

6 If there is still no spark, then the problem must lie within the engine management system. In these cases, the vehicle should be referred to a Seat dealer for assessment.

Engine misfires

7 An irregular misfire suggests either a loose connection or intermittent fault on the primary circuit, or an HT fault on the coil side of the rotor arm.

8 With the ignition switched off, check carefully through the system ensuring that all connections are clean and securely fastened. If the equipment is available, check the LT circuit as described above.

9 Check that the HT coil, the distributor cap and the HT leads are clean and dry. Check the leads themselves and the spark plugs (by substitution, if necessary), then check the distributor cap, carbon brush and rotor arm.

10 Regular misfiring is almost certainly due to a fault in the distributor cap, HT leads or spark plugs. Use a timing light (paragraph 4 above) to check whether HT voltage is present at all leads.

11 If HT voltage is not present on one particular lead, the fault will be in that lead or in the distributor cap. If HT is present on all leads, the fault will be in the spark plugs; check and renew them if there is any doubt about their condition.

12 If no HT voltage is present, check the HT coil; its secondary windings may be breaking down under load.

Other problems

13 Problems with the system's operation that cannot be pinpointed by following the guidelines in the preceding paragraphs should be referred to a Seat dealer for assessment.

3.1 The ignition coil is mounted on the engine compartment bulkhead

3.3 Unplug the HT lead from the ignition coil at the connector

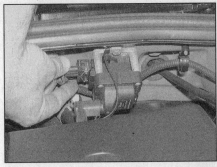

3.4 Disconnect the LT wiring plug from the ignition coil

3 HT coil - removal and refitting

Removal

1 On all models, the ignition coil is mounted on the engine compartment bulkhead **(see illustration)**.

2 Make sure the ignition is switched off.

3 Unplug the HT lead from the ignition coil at the connector. Note which way round the collar on the lead end fitting is located **(see illustration)**.

4 Disconnect the LT wiring from the ignition coil at the multiway connector **(see illustration)**.

5 Lift up the weatherstrip from the top of the engine compartment bulkhead, and lift up the plastic cowl panel for access to the coil mounting nuts.

3.6a One of the ignition coil mounting bolts is used to secure the coil earth strap

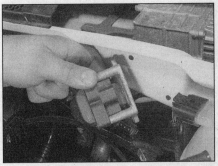

3.6b Removing the ignition coil

6 Unscrew the mounting nuts or bolts, and remove the ignition coil. Note that one of the mounting bolts is used to retain the coil earth strap **(see illustrations)**.

7 On some models, the coil output stage can be unbolted from the main body and renewed separately if required.

Refitting

8 Refitting is a reversal of removal.

4 Distributor - removal, inspection and refitting

Removal

1 Make sure the ignition is switched off. Also remove the engine top cover where necessary.

2 Set the engine to TDC on cylinder No 1, referring to Section 2 of Chapter 2A for guidance.

3 If required, unplug all five HT leads from the distributor cap, labelling them to aid refitting later. It is preferable, however, to remove the distributor cap with all leads attached as described later - the leads can then be transferred one at a time to a new cap, if one is being fitted **(see illustration)**.

4 Where applicable, unplug the earth braid from the metal screening cap **(see illustration)**.

5 Unplug the Hall sensor cable from the distributor body at the connector **(see illustration)**.

6 Prise off the retaining clips/remove the screws (as applicable), then lift off the distributor cap. Check at this point that the centre of the rotor arm electrode is aligned with the cylinder No 1 marking on the distributor body **(see illustrations)**.

5B

4.3 Disconnecting the HT leads from the distributor cap

4.4 Disconnecting the distributor cap earth braid

4.5 Unplug the Hall sensor cable from the distributor body at the connector

4.6a Using a suitable screwdriver, release the spring clips . . .

4.6b . . . and lift away the distributor cap

7 Mark the relationship between the distributor body and the cylinder head/block by scribing arrows on each, or painting an alignment mark between them (see illustration).

8 On engine codes AER, AAU, AAV, ABD, ABU, AEX, APQ, AEE, ALM, ABF unscrew and remove the clamp bolts, then withdraw the distributor body from the cylinder head and recover the seals (see illustrations). Note: On engine code ABF, the rotor arm is bonded to the distributor shaft - see Section 7.

9 On engine codes AFT, 1F, 2E, AGG, unscrew and remove the bolt, then lift off the clamp plate and withdraw the distributor body from the cylinder block (see illustration). Recover the O-ring seal.

Inspection

10 Recover the O-ring seal(s) from the bottom of the distributor and inspect them. Renew them if they appear at all worn or damaged.

Refitting

11 Check that the engine is still set to TDC on cylinder No 1.

Engine codes AER, AAU, AAV, ABD, ABU, AEX, APQ, AEE, ALM, ABF

12 Install the distributor and loosely fit the clamp bolts; it may be necessary to rotate the shaft slightly to allow it to engage with the camshaft. Rotate the distributor body such that the alignment marks made during removal line up. The centre of the rotor arm electrode should point directly at the No 1 cylinder mark on the distributor body (see illustration).

Engine codes AFT, 1F, 2E, AGG

13 On engine codes 1F, 2E, AGG, check at this point that the oil pump shaft drive tongue is aligned with the threaded hole, adjacent to the distributor aperture (see illustration).

14 On engine code AFT, check at this point that the oil pump shaft drive tongue is aligned with the axis of the crankshaft (see illustration).

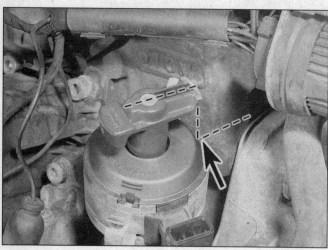

4.6c Centre of the rotor arm electrode aligned with cylinder No 1 mark on engine codes AFT, 1F, 2E and AGG (arrowed)

4.7 Alignment marks (arrowed) painted between distributor body and cylinder head

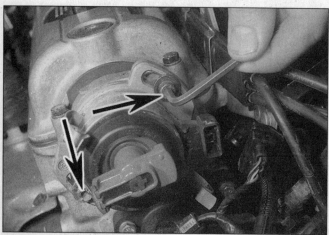

4.8a On engine codes AER, AAU, AAV, ABD, ABU, AEX, APQ, AEE, ALM and ABF, loosen the clamp bolts (arrowed) using an Allen key . . .

4.8b . . . and remove the distributor - note the large O-ring seal (arrowed)

4.9 Unscrew and remove the bolt, then lift off the clamp plate (engine code 2E shown)

4.12 Rotor arm contact aligned with raised notch in distributor body on engine codes AER, AAU, AAV, ABD, ABU, AEX, APQ, AEE, ALM and ABF (arrowed)

15 Install the distributor, then loosely fit the clamp plate and securing bolt; it may be necessary to rotate the shaft slightly to allow it to engage with the intermediate shaft drive gear. Rotate the distributor body such that the alignment marks made during removal line up.

16 The shaft is engaged at the correct angle when the centre of the rotor arm electrode is pointing directly at the No 1 cylinder mark on the distributor body - it may take a few attempts to get this right, as the helical drive gears make the alignment difficult to judge. Tighten the distributor clamp bolt to its specified torque. **Note:** *If alignment proves impossible, check that the intermediate shaft sprocket is correctly aligned with the crankshaft pulley - refer to Chapter 2A for further guidance.*

All engine codes

17 Refit the distributor cap, pressing the retaining clips firmly into place or tightening the retaining screws (as applicable).

18 Reconnect the Hall sensor wiring to the distributor.

19 Reconnect the earth braid to the metal screening cap.

20 Working from the No 1 terminal, connect the HT leads between the spark plugs and the distributor cap. The firing order is 1-3-4-2.

21 Fit the HT king lead between the coil and the centre terminal on the distributor cap.

22 It will now be necessary to have the ignition timing checked and if necessary adjusted - refer to the notes in Section 5.

5 Ignition timing - checking and adjusting

The ignition timing is under the control of the engine management system ECU and is not manually adjustable without access to dedicated electronic test equipment. A basic setting cannot be quoted because the ignition timing is constantly being altered to control engine idle speed (see Section 1 for details).

The vehicle must be taken to a Seat dealer if the timing requires checking or adjustment.

6 Ignition system sensors - removal and refitting

1 Many of the engine management system sensors provide signals for both the fuel injection and ignition systems. Those specific to the ignition system are detailed in this Section.

2 Those sensors that are common to both systems are detailed in Chapter 4A or 4B as applicable. These include the coolant temperature sensor, the inlet air temperature sensor, the air flow/mass meter, the engine speed/TDC sensor, the throttle potentiometer, the idle switch and the inlet manifold depression sensor.

5B

4.13 Oil pump shaft drive tongue is aligned with the threaded hole (arrowed), adjacent to the distributor aperture (engine codes 1F, 2E, AGG)

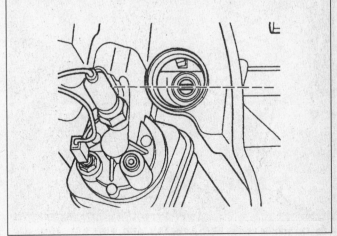

4.14 Oil pump shaft drive tongue is aligned with the axis of the crankshaft (engine code AFT)

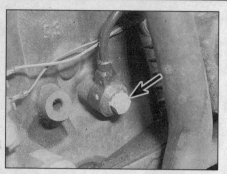

6.5 Slacken and withdraw the mounting bolt (arrowed) and lift off the knock sensor

Knock sensor (engine codes AER, AEX, APQ, AEE, ALM, AFT, 2E, ABF)

Removal

3 The knock sensor is located on the front, right-hand end of the cylinder block. On engine code ABF there are two sensors located next to each other.
4 Unplug the harness wiring from the sensor at the connector.
5 Unscrew and remove the mounting bolt and lift off the sensor **(see illustration)**.

7.2 Pull the rotor arm from the end of the distributor shaft (engine code 2E shown)

Refitting

6 Refitting is a reversal of removal, but note that the sensor's operation will be affected if its mounting bolt is not tightened to exactly the right torque.

Hall-effect sensor

7 This sensor is an integral part of the distributor assembly. It can be removed and renewed separately, however special tooling may be required to dismantle the distributor. It is therefore recommended that this operation is entrusted to a automotive electrical specialist.

7 Rotor arm - renewal

1 With reference to Section 4, remove the distributor cap and its screening shield (where applicable).
2 Pull the rotor arm from the end of the distributor shaft **(see illustration)**. **Note:** *On engine code ABF, the rotor arm is bonded to the distributor shaft, and it can only be removed by destroying it. It strongly recommended that this operation is carried out by a Seat dealer who will have the equipment necessary to complete the task without risking further damage to the distributor shaft bearings.*
3 Inspect the distributor cap contacts and clean them if necessary.
4 Fit the new rotor arm using a reversal of the removal procedure - ensure that the rotor arm alignment lug engages with the recess in the distributor shaft, before refitting the distributor cap.

Chapter 5 Part C:
Pre-heating systems - diesel models

Contents

Degrees of difficulty

Easy, suitable for novice with little experience	**Fairly easy,** suitable for beginner with some experience	**Fairly difficult,** suitable for competent DIY mechanic	**Difficult,** suitable for experienced DIY mechanic	**Very difficult,** suitable for expert DIY or professional 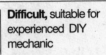

Specifications

Glow plugs

Electrical resistance:
Engine codes 1Y, AAZ:
   Beru glow plugs .... 0.45 ± 0.05 ohms
   Bosch glow plugs .... 0.46 ± 0.05 ohms
Engine codes AEY, 1Z, AHU, AFN .... N/A
Pre-heating relay operating times:
Engine codes 1Y, AAZ:
   Pre-heating .... 4.0 ± 0.5 seconds to 20°C
   Starting readiness .... 10.0 ± 1.0 seconds
   Post-heating .... 180.0 ± 2.0 seconds
Engine codes AEY, 1Z, AHU, AFN .... N/A
Current consumption:
Engine codes 1Y, AAZ .... 8 amps (per glow plug)
Engine codes AEY, 1Z, AHU, AFN .... N/A

Torque wrench settings

	Nm	lbf ft
Glow plug to cylinder head:		
Engine codes 1Y, AAZ	25	18
Engine codes AEY, 1Z, AHU, AFN	15	11

5C

1 General information

To assist cold starting, diesel engined models are fitted with a pre-heating system, which comprises four glow plugs, a glow plug control unit (incorporated in the ECU on engine codes AEY, 1Z, AHU, AFN), a facia mounted warning lamp and the associated electrical wiring.

The glow plugs are miniature electric heating elements, encapsulated in a metal case with a probe at one end and electrical connection at the other. Each swirl chamber (engine codes 1Y, AAZ) or inlet tract (engine codes AEY, 1Z, AHU, AFN) has a glow plug threaded into it, which is positioned directly in line with the incoming spray of fuel. When the glow plug is energised, the fuel passing over it is heated, allowing its optimum combustion temperature to be achieved more readily in the combustion chamber.

The duration of the pre-heating period is governed by the glow plug control unit, which monitors the temperature of the engine via the coolant temperature sensor and alters the pre-heating time to suit the conditions.

A facia mounted warning lamp informs the driver that pre-heating is taking place. The lamp extinguishes when sufficient pre-heating has taken place to allow the engine to be started, but power will still be supplied to the glow plugs for a further period until the engine is started. If no attempt is made to start the engine, the power supply to the glow plugs is switched off to prevent battery drain and glow plug burn-out. Note that on certain models, the warning lamp will also illuminate during normal driving if a pre-heating system malfunction occurs.

Generally, pre-heating is triggered by the ignition key being turned to the second position. However, certain models are equipped with a pre-heating system that activates when the drivers door is opened then shut. Refer to the vehicle's handbook for further information.

After the engine has been started, the glow plugs continue to operate for a further period of time. This helps to improve fuel combustion whilst the engine is warming up, resulting in quieter, smoother running and reduced exhaust emissions.

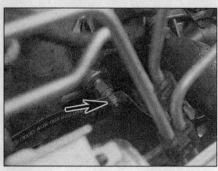

3.4 Glow plug and supply cable retaining nut (arrowed)

3.6 Supply cable (arrowed) removed from No 4 cylinder glow plug

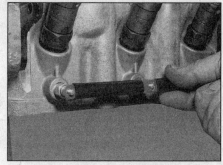

3.10 Remove the nuts and washers from the glow plug terminal. Lift off the bus bar/supply cable (engine code 1Y/AAZ shown)

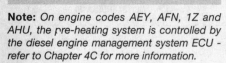

2 Glow plug control unit (engine codes 1Y and AAZ) - removal and refitting

Note: *On engine codes AEY, AFN, 1Z and AHU, the pre-heating system is controlled by the diesel engine management system ECU - refer to Chapter 4C for more information.*

Removal

1 The glow plug control unit is located on or just above the main fusebox/relay board behind the facia (see Chapter 12). The power supply relay for the control unit is located at the No 12 position on the relay board, and a 50 amp fuse for the system is located in the auxiliary fusebox in the engine compartment.
2 Disconnect the battery negative (earth) lead (see Chapter 5A).
3 Where the control unit is mounted above the fusebox, disconnect the wiring and detach the unit.
4 Where the control unit is plugged into the relay board, carefully pull it from the socket.

Refitting

5 Refitting is a reversal of removal.

3 Glow plugs - testing, removal and refitting

Testing

1 If the system malfunctions, testing is ultimately by substitution of known good units, but some preliminary checks may be made as described in the following paragraphs.
2 Connect a voltmeter or 12 volt test lamp between the glow plug supply cable and a good earth point on the engine.

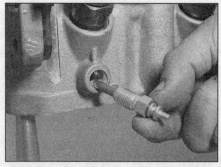

3.11 Unscrew and remove the glow plug (engine code 1Y/AAZ shown)

Caution: Make sure that the live connection is kept well clear of the engine and bodywork.
3 Have an assistant activate the pre-heating system (either using the ignition key, or opening and closing the drivers door as applicable) and check that the battery voltage is applied to the glow plug electrical connection. (Note that the voltage will drop to zero when the pre-heating period ends).
4 If no supply voltage can be detected at the glow plug, then either the glow plug relay (where applicable) or the supply cabling must be faulty **(see illustration)**.
5 To locate a faulty glow plug, first disconnect the battery negative cable and position it away from the terminal.
6 Refer to the next sub-Section and remove the supply cabling from the glow plug terminal **(see illustration)**. Measure the electrical resistance between the glow plug terminal and the engine earth. Where given, compare the reading with the information in Specifications. Where information is not available, a resistance of more than a few Ohms indicates that the plug is defective.
7 If a suitable ammeter is available, connect it between the glow plug and its supply cable

3.13 Tighten the glow plug to the specified torque (engine code 1Y/AAZ shown)

and measure the steady state current consumption (ignore the initial current surge which will be about 50% higher). Compare the result with the Specifications - high current consumption (or no current draw at all) indicates a faulty glow plug.
8 As a final check, remove the glow plugs and inspect them visually, as described in the next sub-Section.

Removal

9 Disconnect the battery negative (earth) lead (see Chapter 5A).
10 Remove the nuts and washers from the glow plug terminals. Lift off the bus bar **(see illustration)**.
11 Unscrew and remove the glow plug(s) **(see illustration)**.
12 Inspect the glow plug stems for signs of damage. A badly burned or charred stem may be an indication of a faulty fuel injector; refer to Chapter 4C for greater detail.

Refitting

13 Refitting is a reversal of removal, but tighten the glow plug to the specified torque **(see illustration)**.

Chapter 6
Clutch

Contents

Degrees of difficulty

Easy, suitable for novice with little experience	Fairly easy, suitable for beginner with some experience	Fairly difficult, suitable for competent DIY mechanic	Difficult, suitable for experienced DIY mechanic	Very difficult, suitable for expert DIY or professional

Specifications

General
Clutch type	Single dry plate, diaphragm spring pressure plate with spring-loaded hub
Operation	Cable or hydraulic operation according to market

Clutch disc
Diameter:
085 transmission	190 mm
020 transmission	210 mm
02A transmission	228 mm
Run-out (measured 2.5 mm from outer edge)	0.8 mm

Clutch pressure plate
Maximum distortion	0.2 mm

Clutch pedal
Pedal free-play (manually-adjusted cable)	25.0 ± 5.0 mm

Torque wrench settings
	Nm	lbf ft
Clutch hydraulic unions	20	15
Flywheel to pressure plate (020 transmission)	20	15
Master cylinder to bulkhead	25	18
Pedal bracket	25	18
Pressure plate to crankshaft (020 transmission):		
Stage 1	60	44
Stage 2	Angle-tighten 60°	
Pressure plate to flywheel:		
02A transmission	20	15
085 transmission	25	18
Release bearing guide to transmission (085 and 02A transmissions)	18	13
Slave cylinder to transmission	25	18

6

1 General description

The clutch is of single dry plate type, incorporating a diaphragm spring pressure plate, and is cable or hydraulic operated. When the clutch pedal is depressed, effort is transmitted to the clutch release mechanism either mechanically by means of a cable, or hydraulically by means of master and slave cylinders. The release mechanism transfers effort to the pressure plate diaphragm spring, which withdraws from the flywheel and releases the friction disc. The mounting arrangement of the flywheel and clutch components depends on the type of transmission fitted.

On vehicles fitted with the 020 transmission (see Chapter 7), the clutch system comprises the clutch pedal, clutch release components, the pressure plate and the friction disc. The clutch pressure plate is bolted directly to the crankshaft flange - the dished flywheel is then mounted on the pressure plate. With this arrangement, the removal and refitting of the flywheel and pressure plate is described in this Chapter.

On vehicles fitted with the 085 and 02A transmissions (see Chapter 7), the layout is conventional. The flywheel is mounted on the crankshaft, with the pressure plate bolted to it. In this case, removal of the flywheel is described in Chapter 2A.

Where a cable operated clutch is fitted, adjustment may be either manual or automatic. Where a hydraulic system is used, adjustment is automatic; the hydraulic fluid employed is the same as that used in the braking system, hence fluid is supplied to the master cylinder from a tapping on the brake fluid reservoir. The clutch hydraulic system must be sealed before work is carried out on any of its components to prevent entry of dust and dirt, and then, on completion, topped up and bled to remove any trapped air.

As the linings wear on the friction disc, the pressure plate rest position moves closer to the flywheel resulting in the rest position of the diaphragm spring fingers being raised.

3.5 Compressing the adjustment mechanism using the locking strap

Some models fitted with a cable-operated clutch incorporate an adjustment nut and locknut, however other models have an automatic adjuster fitted into the cable at the pedal end. The hydraulically-operated clutch requires no adjustment; the quantity of hydraulic fluid in the circuit automatically compensates for wear every time the clutch pedal is operated.

2 Clutch pedal - removal, inspection and refitting

Removal

1 Disconnect the battery negative (earth) lead (see Chapter 5A).
2 Working inside the car, remove the parcel tray from the driver's side of the facia panel for access to the clutch pedal.
3 Release the relay carrier plate from the bracket, then unhook the pedal cover from the bracket.
4 On models with a cable operated clutch, working in the engine compartment pull the cable from the bracket on the transmission and release the outer cable. Inside the car unhook the end of the cable from the top of the pedal.
5 On models with a hydraulic operated clutch, working inside the car release the retaining clip and extract the pedal to pushrod clevis pin.
6 Extract the retaining clips from each end of the pedal shaft.
7 Note that where an over-centre spring is fitted to the clutch pedal, a special tool is required to compress it for refitting. If the tool is not available, it may be possible to hold the spring in compression at this stage using a suitable piece of bent metal. This will make the refitting procedure easier.
8 Push the pedal shaft to the right until the clutch pedal is free to be removed. Where applicable, disengage the pedal from the over-centre spring.

Inspection

9 If the pedal bush is badly worn, it can be renewed by drifting it out, and pressing in a new bush between vice jaws. Where applicable, the over-centre spring can be removed by releasing its retaining clip and washer.

Refitting

10 Refitting is a reversal of the removal procedure. When refitting the over-centre spring, it will need to be compressed and fitted to Seat tool U-40005 before locating it in position. Alternatively, a holding tool may be made out of strip of metal, bent at each end to locate on each end of the spring.
11 Where applicable on cable-operated models, adjust the cable as described in Section 3.

3 Clutch cable - removal, refitting and adjustment

020 transmission

Removal

1 A self-adjusting clutch cable is fitted to models with the 020 transmission. First, depress the clutch pedal several times, to settle the automatic adjustment mechanism.
2 Working inside the car, remove the parcel tray from the driver's side of the facia panel for access to the clutch pedal.
3 Release the relay carrier plate from the bracket, then unhook the pedal cover from the bracket.
4 Working in the engine compartment, slide the locking strap down the cable to the top of the adjustment mechanism protective boot.
5 Grasp the top and bottom of the adjustment mechanism and compress it - at the same time, hook the ends of the locking strap over the lugs protruding from the side of the adjustment mechanism **(see illustration)**.
Note: *If the locking strap is no longer attached to the clutch cable, a home made strap can be fabricated using nylon cable-ties or a length of electrical cable.*
6 Lift the clutch release lever up and disconnect the inner cable together with the locking plates and rubber damper. Also disconnect the outer cable from the bracket.
7 Inside the car, unhook the end of the inner cable from the top of the clutch pedal.
8 Unscrew the nuts and remove the clutch/brake pedal bracket from the floor.
9 Refer to Chapter 10 and lower the steering column from the bulkhead without disconnecting it from the steering gear.
10 From inside the engine compartment, push the cable through the bulkhead until the metal bush is released, then remove the cover and withdraw the cable from inside the car.

Refitting

11 Feed the clutch cable through the bulkhead grommet, into the passenger area. Apply a smear of multi-purpose grease to the inner clutch cable nipple, then fit the nipple to the top of the clutch pedal. Refit the cover.
12 At this point check that the automatic adjuster is held compressed with the locking strap. If necessary, grasp the inner and outer cables and pull them in opposite directions to compress the adjuster, then fit the strap.
13 Refit the steering column to the bulkhead and tighten the bolts with reference to Chapter 10.
14 Refit the clutch/brake pedal bracket to the floor and tighten the nuts.
15 Working in the engine compartment, attach the inner cable to the release lever together with the locking plates and rubber damper. Also locate the outer cable on the bracket **(see illustration)**.

3.15 Fit the base of the adjustment mechanism into the retaining bracket on the transmission casing (020 transmission)

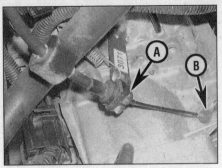

3.23 Clutch cable mounting arrangement (085 transmission)

A Release lever   *B Anchor bracket*

3.39 Clutch cable end fitting on the top of the pedal

16 Unhook the locking strap from the lugs at the side of the adjustment mechanism, then depress the clutch pedal at least five times, until the cable tension is set. Now move the release lever on the transmission about 10 mm in the opposite direction to its normal direction of travel, and check that it moves freely. This indicates that the automatic adjuster is functioning correctly.

17 Refit the pedal cover and relay carrier plate, then refit the parcel tray.

18 On completion, assess the feel of the clutch pedal. If it exhibits any stiffness or shows signs of binding, check the routing of the cable and ensure that there are no sharp bends or kinks along its length.

19 Finally, road test the vehicle and check the operation of the clutch.

085 and 02A transmissions with self-adjusting cable

Removal

20 Depress the clutch pedal approximately five times, to settle the automatic adjustment mechanism.

21 Working inside the car, remove the parcel tray from the driver's side of the facia panel for access to the clutch pedal.

22 Release the relay carrier plate from the bracket, then unhook the pedal cover from the bracket.

23 Working in the engine compartment, move the release lever to disconnect the inner cable from the bracket on the transmission, then disconnect the outer cable from the release lever **(see illustrations)**.

24 Inside the car, unhook the end of the inner cable from the top of the clutch pedal.

25 Unscrew the nuts and remove the clutch/brake pedal bracket from the floor.

26 Refer to Chapter 10 and lower the steering column from the bulkhead without disconnecting it from the steering gear.

27 From inside the engine compartment, push the cable through the bulkhead until the metal bush is released, then remove the cover and withdraw the cable from inside the car.

Refitting

28 Feed the clutch cable through the bulkhead grommet, into the passenger area.

Apply a smear of multi-purpose grease to the inner clutch cable nipple, then fit the nipple into the recess at the top of the clutch pedal. Refit the cover.

29 Refit the steering column to the bulkhead and tighten the bolts with reference to Chapter 10.

30 Refit the clutch/brake pedal bracket to the floor and tighten the nuts.

31 Working in the engine compartment, connect the inner cable inner to the bracket on the transmission casing.

32 Engage the outer cable with the fork at the end of the clutch release lever.

33 Refit the pedal cover and relay carrier plate, then refit the parcel tray.

34 On completion, assess the feel of the clutch pedal. If it exhibits any stiffness or shows signs of binding, check the routing of the cable and ensure that there are no sharp bends or kinks along its length.

35 Finally, road test the vehicle and check the operation of the clutch.

085 and 02A transmissions with manually-adjusted cable

Removal

36 Working in the engine compartment, move the release lever against the tension of the return spring and disconnect the outer cable from the fork on the end of the lever, then disconnect the inner cable from the bracket on the transmission.

37 Working inside the car, remove the parcel

tray from the driver's side of the facia panel for access to the clutch pedal.

38 Release the relay carrier plate from the bracket, then unhook the pedal cover from the bracket.

39 Unhook the end of the inner cable from the top of the clutch pedal and release the rubber boot from the pedal bracket **(see illustration)**.

40 In the engine compartment, pull the cable from the bulkhead then release it from the supports and withdraw it from the car.

Refitting

41 Feed the clutch cable through the bulkhead grommet, into the passenger area. Apply a smear of multi-purpose grease to the inner clutch cable nipple, then fit the nipple to the top of the clutch pedal. Refit the rubber boot.

42 In the engine compartment, locate the outer cable in the supports, then fit the inner cable to the bracket on the transmission. Locate the outer cable in the fork on the end of the release lever.

43 Inside the car, refit the pedal cover and relay carrier plate, then refit the parcel tray.

44 The cable must now be adjusted to provide freeplay of 25.0 ± 5.0 mm at the pedal. Use a steel rule to check the pedal freeplay, and make the adjustment by loosening the locknut and turning the adjustment nut on the inner cable end fitting. Tighten the locknut on completion **(see illustrations)**.

6

3.44a Checking the clutch pedal freeplay with a steel rule

3.44b Adjusting the clutch cable (085 and 02A transmissions with manually-adjusted cable)

45 On completion, assess the feel of the clutch pedal. If it exhibits any stiffness or shows signs of binding, check the routing of the cable and ensure that there are no sharp bends or kinks along its length.
46 Finally, road test the vehicle and check the operation of the clutch.

4 Clutch hydraulic system - bleeding

⚠️ *Warning: Hydraulic fluid is poisonous - wash off immediately and thoroughly in the case of skin contact, and seek immediate medical advice if any fluid is swallowed or gets into the eyes. Certain types of hydraulic fluid are flammable, and may ignite when allowed into contact with hot components. When servicing any hydraulic system, it is safest to assume that the fluid is flammable, and to take precautions against the risk of fire. Hydraulic fluid is also an effective paint stripper, and will attack plastics - if any is spilt, it should be washed off immediately, using copious quantities of fresh water. Finally, it is hygroscopic (it absorbs moisture from the air) - old fluid may be contaminated and unfit for further use. When topping-up or renewing the fluid, always use the recommended type, and ensure that it comes from a freshly opened sealed container.*
Note: *Refer to Chapter 9 for details of alternative one-man bleeding kits which may be used to bleed the clutch hydraulic system.*
1 The correct operation of any hydraulic system is only possible after removing all air from the components and circuit. This is achieved by bleeding the system. Observe the following points:
a) *During the bleeding procedure, add only clean, unused hydraulic fluid of the recommended type. Never re-use fluid that has already been bled from the system. Ensure that sufficient fluid is available before starting work.*
b) *If there is any possibility of incorrect fluid being already in the system, the hydraulic circuit must be flushed completely with uncontaminated, correct fluid.*

4.3 Bleeding the clutch slave cylinder

c) *If hydraulic fluid has been lost from the system, or air has entered because of a leak, ensure that the fault is cured before continuing further.*
2 For improved access to the bleed screw on the slave cylinder, raise the front of the car and support it on axle stands (see *Jacking and vehicle support*).
3 Remove the rubber cap from the slave cylinder bleed screw. Fit the bleed tube onto the bleed screw, and place the other end of the tube in a jar with some brake fluid in it **(see illustration).**
4 Check that the fluid level in the brake/clutch reservoir is topped up to the maximum level, and have ready some fresh brake fluid for topping-up purposes.
5 Unscrew the bleed screw half a turn, and have an assistant fully depress the clutch pedal. As the pedal reaches the end of the downstroke close the bleed nipple. With the bleed nipple closed, release the clutch pedal. Repeat this procedure until the fluid entering the jar is free of air bubbles. Make sure that the fluid level in the reservoir does not drop to the level of the cylinder outlet, otherwise air will be drawn into the system.
6 Tighten the bleed screw with the clutch pedal depressed, release the pedal, then top up the fluid level as necessary.
7 Disconnect the bleed tube, and refit the rubber cap.
8 On completion, detach the bleed tube, refit the rubber cap and then lower the vehicle.
9 Discard any hydraulic fluid that has been bled from the system, since it will not be fit for re-use.

5 Clutch slave cylinder - removal, overhaul and refitting

Removal

1 If a suitable hose clamp is available, clamp the slave cylinder's hydraulic hose at a point near its union. This will minimise fluid loss when the hose is detached and simplify the bleeding procedure when refitting.
2 Loosen the hydraulic pipe union on the slave cylinder. Do not fully unscrew the hydraulic hose, since it will be easier to unscrew the slave cylinder from the hose later.
3 Unscrew the retaining bolts and withdraw the slave cylinder from the transmission, then unscrew the cylinder from the hose **(see illustrations).** If the hose is not clamped, plug the hose to prevent fluid loss and the possible ingress of dirt. Where applicable, it may be necessary to loosen off the gear selector unit from the transmission and withdraw it sufficiently to allow removal of the slave cylinder; leave the cables attached to the unit.
4 Do not operate the clutch pedal whilst the slave cylinder is removed.

Overhaul

5 At the time of writing, repair kits are not available from Seat, but they may be available from other sources.
6 To overhaul the slave cylinder, first clean the exterior surfaces.
7 Prise off the rubber boot and remove the pushrod.
8 Extract the special spring clip from the mouth of the cylinder, and withdraw the piston and spring.
9 Clean the components, and examine them for wear and deterioration. If the piston and bore are worn excessively, or if corrosion is evident, renew the complete cylinder. If they are in good condition, remove the seal from the piston and renew it.
10 Dip the new seal in the hydraulic fluid, and fit it on the piston, using the fingers only to manipulate it into position. Make sure that the seal lip faces the spring end of the piston.
11 Insert the spring in the cylinder, then dip the piston in hydraulic fluid and carefully insert it.
12 Hold the piston depressed with a screwdriver, then press a new spring clip into the mouth of the cylinder, making sure that the legs of the clip grip the cylinder.
13 Fit the pushrod, then the rubber boot.

Refitting

14 Refitting is a reversal of removal, but bleed the system as described in Section 4. The end of the pushrod which contacts the release lever should be lightly lubricated with a molybdenum disulphide grease. Where a plastic support ring is fitted, the outer surface should also be lubricated with the same grease.

5.3a Unscrew the retaining bolts ...

5.3b ... and remove the clutch slave cylinder

6 Clutch master cylinder -
removal, overhaul and refitting

Removal

1 The clutch master cylinder is mounted at the rear of the engine compartment, next to the brake servo unit.

2 Working inside the car, remove the glovebox and facia panel from under the steering column (refer to Chapter 11).

3 Prise off the clip, and extract the clevis pin securing the master cylinder pushrod to the clutch pedal.

4 If a suitable hose clamp is available, clamp the hydraulic hose from the combined brake/clutch cylinder reservoir at the clutch master cylinder end to prevent excess fluid loss **(see illustration)**, then detach the hose from the clutch master cylinder. Plug the fluid lines to prevent the ingress of dirt (and fluid loss from the fluid reservoir if the hose has not been clamped).

5 Undo the union nut and detach the fluid line to the clutch slave cylinder at the master cylinder. Plug the fluid line connections to prevent the ingress of dirt.

6 Working inside the car, prise free the gaiter from the bulkhead.

7 Unscrew the mounting nuts and withdraw the clutch master cylinder.

Overhaul

8 At the time of writing, repair kits are not available from Seat, but they may be available from other sources.

9 To overhaul the master cylinder, first clean the exterior surfaces.

10 Prise off the rubber boot and remove the pushrod. If necessary loosen the locknut, unscrew the clevis and locknut, and remove the pushrod from the rubber boot.

11 Extract the circlip from the mouth of the cylinder, and withdraw the washer, piston, and spring, noting that the smaller end of the spring contacts the piston.

12 Clean the components with methylated spirit, and examine them for wear and deterioration. If the piston and bore are worn excessively, renew the complete cylinder, but if they are in good condition, remove the seals from the piston and obtain new ones.

13 Dip the new seals in hydraulic fluid, and fit them on the piston, using the fingers only to manipulate them into position. Make sure that the seal lips face the spring end of the piston.

14 Insert the spring into the cylinder, large end first. Dip the piston in hydraulic fluid, locate it on the spring, and carefully insert it.

15 Fit the washer, then locate the circlip in the groove.

16 Apply a little grease to the end of the pushrod, then locate it on the piston and fit the rubber boot. Screw on the locknut and clevis and tighten the locknut.

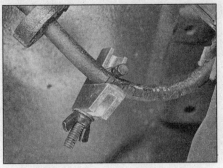

6.4 Hydraulic hose clamp in use

Refitting

17 Refitting is a reversal of removal, but finally bleed the hydraulic system as described in Section 4.

7 Clutch assembly -
removal, inspection and refitting

⚠️ *Warning: Dust created by clutch wear and deposited on the clutch components may contain asbestos, which is a health hazard. DO NOT blow it out with compressed air, or inhale any of it. DO NOT use petrol or petroleum-based solvents to clean off the dust. Brake system cleaner or methylated spirit should be used to flush the dust into a suitable receptacle. After the clutch components are wiped clean with rags, dispose of the contaminated rags and cleaner in a sealed, marked container.*
Note: *Although some friction materials may no longer contain asbestos, it is safest to assume that they do, and to take precautions accordingly.*

General information

1 The mounting arrangement of the flywheel and clutch components depends on the type of transmission fitted.

2 On vehicles fitted with the 020 transmission, the clutch pressure plate is bolted directly to the end of the crankshaft. The dished flywheel is then bolted to the

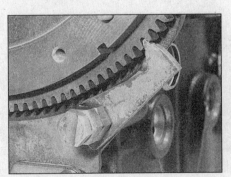

7.5 Home-made flywheel locking tool in use

pressure plate. Removal of these components is described in the following paragraphs.

3 On vehicles fitted with the 085 and 02A transmissions, the layout is conventional; the flywheel is mounted on the crankshaft, with the pressure plate bolted to it. Removal of the flywheel is as described in Chapter 2A or 2B as appropriate and removal of the clutch components is described in the following paragraphs.

Removal

020 transmission

4 Remove the transmission as described in Chapter 7.

5 Before the flywheel bolts can be removed, the flywheel must be locked in position - a home made flywheel locking tool can be fabricated from scrap metal **(see illustration)**.

6 Loosen the flywheel bolts progressively, then lift the flywheel away from the clutch pressure plate and recover the friction plate.

7 Prise off the spring clip and lift the clutch release plate away.

8 Lock the pressure plate in position by bolting a piece of scrap metal between it and one of the bellhousing mounting bolt holes **(see illustration)**.

9 Progressively loosen the pressure plate bolts until they can be removed by hand. Recover the intermediate plate.

10 Lift the pressure plate away from the crankshaft flange.

085 and 02A transmissions

11 Refer to Chapter 7 and remove the transmission from the engine.

12 Lock the flywheel in position using a home-made tool (see illustration 7.5).

13 Progressively slacken the pressure plate bolts until they can be removed. Lift off the pressure plate and recover the friction plate.

Inspection

Note: *Due to the amount of work necessary to remove and refit clutch components, it is usually considered good practice to renew the clutch friction disc, pressure plate assembly and release bearing as a matched set, even if only one of these is actually worn enough to require renewal. It is also worth considering the renewal of the clutch components on a*

7.8 Lock the pressure plate in position with a piece of scrap metal (020 transmission)

6

7.21a Lift the pressure plate up to the crankshaft flange . . .

7.21b . . . together with the intermediate plate . . .

7.21c . . . then insert a new set of retaining bolts (020 transmission)

preventive basis if the engine and/or transmission have been removed for some other reason.

14 When cleaning clutch components, read first the warning at the beginning of this Section. Remove dust using a clean, dry cloth, and working in a well-ventilated atmosphere.

15 Check the friction disc linings for signs of wear, damage or oil contamination. If the friction material is cracked, burnt, scored or damaged, or if it is contaminated with oil or grease (shown by shiny black patches), the friction disc must be renewed. Check the depth of the rivets below the friction material surface. If any are at or near the surface of the friction material, then the friction disc must be renewed.

16 If the friction material is still serviceable, check that the centre boss splines are

unworn, that the torsion springs are in good condition and securely fastened, and that all the rivets are tight. If any wear or damage is found, the friction disc must be renewed.

17 If the friction material is contaminated with oil, this must be due to an oil leak from the crankshaft oil seal, from the sump-to-cylinder block joint, or from the transmission input shaft. Renew the seal or repair the joint, as appropriate, as described in Chapter 2 or 7, before installing the new friction disc.

18 Check the pressure plate assembly for obvious signs of wear or damage; shake it to check for loose rivets or a worn or damaged fulcrum ring, and check that the drive straps securing the pressure plate to the cover do not show signs of overheating (such as a deep yellow or blue discoloration). If the diaphragm spring is worn or damaged, or if its pressure is in any way suspect, the pressure plate assembly should be renewed.

19 Examine the machined bearing surfaces of the pressure plate and of the flywheel. They should be clean, completely flat, and free from scratches or scoring. If either is discoloured from excessive heat, or shows signs of cracks, it should be renewed - although minor damage of this nature can sometimes be polished away using emery paper.

20 Check that the release bearing contact surface rotates smoothly and easily, with no sign of noise or roughness. Also check that the surface itself is smooth and unworn, with no signs of cracks, pitting or scoring. If there is any doubt about its condition, the bearing must be renewed.

Refitting

020 transmission

21 If a new pressure plate is to be fitted, first wipe the protective grease from the friction surface only. Lift the pressure plate up to the crankshaft flange together with the intermediate plate then insert a new set of retaining bolts. Coat the bolt threads with a suitable locking compound, if they are not supplied already coated **(see illustrations)**.

22 Hold the pressure plate still using the method described during removal and tighten the retaining bolts progressively to the specified torque and angle **(see illustration)**.

23 Fit the release plate and secure it in position with the spring clip **(see illustrations)**. Apply a smear of high temperature grease to the centre of the release plate.

24 Smear a little high temperature grease on the splines at the centre of the friction plate - take care to avoid contaminating the friction surfaces.

25 Hold the friction plate up to the pressure plate, with the spring loaded boss facing outwards, then offer up the flywheel, ensuring that the locating dowels engage with the recess on the edge of the pressure plate **(see illustrations)**. Insert a new set of flywheel retaining bolts - hand tighten them only at this stage.

26 Centre the friction plate using vernier calipers; ensure that there is uniform gap between outer edge of the friction plate and

7.22 Tighten the pressure plate retaining bolts progressively to the specified torque (020 transmission)

7.23a Fit the release plate . . .

7.23b . . . and secure it in position with the spring clip (020 transmission)

7.25a Fit the friction plate, with the spring-loaded boss facing outwards (020 transmission)

7.25b Ensure that the locating dowels (arrowed) engage with . . .

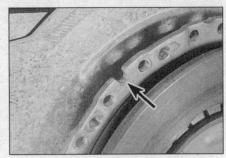

7.25c . . . the recesses on the edge of the pressure plate (arrowed) (020 transmission)

7.26 Centre the friction plate using vernier calipers (020 transmission)

the inner edge of the flywheel, around the whole circumference **(see illustration)**.

27 Tighten the flywheel retaining bolts diagonally and progressively to the specified torque. Re-check the friction plate centralisation.

28 Refer to Chapter 7 and refit the transmission.

085 and 02A transmissions

29 Smear a little high temperature grease on the splines at the centre of the friction plate - take care to avoid contaminating the friction surfaces.

30 If a new pressure plate is to be fitted, first wipe the protective grease from the friction surface only. Hold the friction plate up to the pressure plate, with the spring loaded boss facing outwards, then offer up the pressure plate, ensuring that the locating dowels engage with the flywheel **(see illustration)**.

Insert a new set of pressure plate retaining bolts - hand tighten them only at this stage.

31 The friction disc must now be centralised, to ensure correct alignment of the transmission input shaft with the clutch components. To do this, a proprietary tool may be used, or alternatively, use a wooden mandrel can be made to suit. Insert the tool through the friction disc into the crankshaft spigot bearing, and make sure that it is central. Failure to centralise the friction disc will mean that the transmission input shaft will not be able to pass through the friction disc hub, making reconnecting the engine and transmission impossible. Time spent getting the centralisation correct will be well justified.

32 Tighten the clutch pressure plate bolts progressively and in diagonal sequence to the specified torque, then remove the centralising tool.

33 Refer to Chapter 7 and refit the transmission.

8 Clutch release lever - removal, inspection and refitting

085 transmission

Removal

1 The release bearing and lever are only accessible with the transmission removed from the engine (see Chapter 7) **(see illustration)**.

2 Extract the circlips securing the release lever to the release shaft, then withdraw the shaft from its bushes and the release lever **(see illustration)**. Note that there is a master spline on the shaft and lever allowing refitting in only one position.

7.30 Fitting the clutch friction disc and pressure plate (085 transmission)

8.1 Clutch release lever (085 transmission)

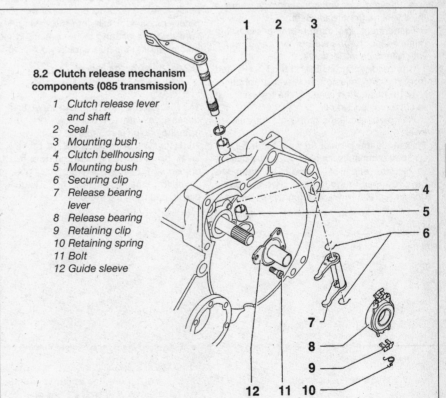

8.2 Clutch release mechanism components (085 transmission)

1 Clutch release lever and shaft
2 Seal
3 Mounting bush
4 Clutch bellhousing
5 Mounting bush
6 Securing clip
7 Release bearing lever
8 Release bearing
9 Retaining clip
10 Retaining spring
11 Bolt
12 Guide sleeve

6

8.17 Clutch release lever and bearing removal (02A transmission)

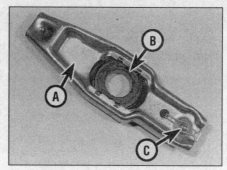

8.18 Clutch release lever (A), bearing (B) and ball stud socket (C)

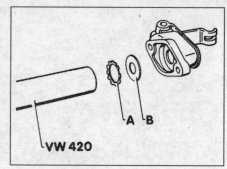

8.21 Release lever on cable-operated clutch models showing star washer (A), flat washer (B) and the fitting tool

Inspection

3 Check the bushes and bearing surfaces of the shaft for wear, and also check the release bearing guide sleeve for scoring. The bushes may be removed using a drift, and new bushes fitted in a similar fashion. Fit the bushes so that the oil seal will be flush with the housing when in position.

Refitting

4 Refitting is a reversal of removal, but lubricate all bearing surfaces with a high-melting-point grease.

020 transmission

Removal

5 Apply the handbrake, then jack up the front of the vehicle and support it on axle stands (see Jacking and vehicle support). Remove the left-hand front roadwheel.

6 Disconnect the clutch cable from the release lever on the side of the transmission with reference to Section 3.

7 It is recommended that the oil is drained from the transmission, however a container may be positioned beneath the transmission to catch any spilled oil.

8 Remove the plastic stop from the release lever.

9 Remove the circular lid from the left-hand end of the transmission. The lid is very difficult to remove, and it will usually be damaged beyond repair in the removal process. Use a drift to tap the lid off, or alternatively pierce it

with a screwdriver and lever it off. Do not damage the surface of the transmission casing.

10 Prise the safety clip from the top of the clutch operating finger.

11 Note how the return spring is fitted, then slide the release arm and shaft from the front of the transmission, and remove the finger and spring. Note that the finger and shaft incorporate master splines to ensure correct refitting.

12 Using a magnet, withdraw the release bearing and rod from the end of the transmission.

13 Using a screwdriver, carefully prise out the shaft oil seal from the transmission casing.

Refitting

14 Refitting is a reversal of removal, but apply a little grease to the lips of the oil seal before pressing it fully into the casing. Make sure that the seating in the casing is clean before refitting the new circular lid.

02A transmission

Removal

15 The release bearing and lever are only accessible with the transmission removed from the engine (see Chapter 7).

16 Using a screwdriver, prise the release lever from the ball stud on the gearbox housing. If this proves difficult, push the spring from the release lever first. Remove the plastic pad from the stud.

17 Slide the release bearing, together with the lever, from the guide sleeve, and withdraw it over the transmission input shaft (see illustration).

18 Separate the release bearing from the lever (see illustration).

19 Spin the release bearing by hand, and check it for smooth running. Any tendency to seize or run rough will necessitate renewal of the bearing. If it is to be re-used, wipe it clean with a dry cloth; on no account should the bearing be washed in a liquid solvent, otherwise the internal grease will be removed.

20 Clean the release lever, ball stud, and guide sleeve.

21 If a replacement release lever is to be fitted on cable-operated clutch models, insert the washers as shown (see illustration). The star washer must fit with its convex face towards the housing. Use a tube of suitable diameter to drive it into position but when fitted, ensure that the flat washer (B) is free to move.

Refitting

22 Refitting is a reversal of removal, but lubricate the ball stud with molybdenum disulphide grease. Smear a little grease on the release bearing surface which contacts the diaphragm spring fingers in the clutch cover. Fit the spring onto the release lever. Press the release lever onto the ball stud until the spring holds it in position.

23 Refit the transmission with reference to Chapter 7.

Chapter 7
Manual transmission

Contents

Degrees of difficulty

Easy, suitable for novice with little experience		Fairly easy, suitable for beginner with some experience		Fairly difficult, suitable for competent DIY mechanic		Difficult, suitable for experienced DIY mechanic		Very difficult, suitable for expert DIY or professional	

Specifications

General

Type	Transverse mounted, front wheel drive layout with integral transaxle differential/final drive. 5 forward speeds, 1 reverse
Lubricant capacities	See Chapter 1A or 1B

Torque wrench settings

	Nm	lbf ft
Bellhousing lower cover:		
085 transmission	16	12
020 and 02A transmissions	10	7
Gearchange rod to selector rod (085 transmission)	20	15
Gear lever knob (020 and 02A transmissions)	10	7
Gear lever housing	20	15
Release bearing guide to transmission (085 transmission)	18	13
Transmission to engine	80	59

1 General information

The manual transmission is bolted directly to the left-hand end of the engine. This layout has the advantage of providing the shortest possible drive path to the front wheels, as well as locating the transmission in the airflow through engine bay, optimising cooling. The unit is cased in aluminium alloy.

Drive from the crankshaft is transmitted via the clutch to the gearbox input shaft, which is splined to accept the clutch friction plate.

All forward gears are fitted with synchromesh. The floor-mounted gear lever is connected to the gearbox either by a selector rod, or selector and shift cables, depending on the transmission type. This in turn actuates selector forks inside the gearbox which are slotted onto the synchromesh sleeves. The sleeves, which are locked to the gearbox shafts but can slide axially by means of splined hubs, press baulk rings into contact with the respective gear/pinion. The coned surfaces between the baulk rings and the pinion/gear act as a friction clutch, that progressively matches the speed of the synchromesh sleeve (and hence the gearbox shaft) with that of the gear/pinion. This allows gear changes to be carried out smoothly.

Drive is transmitted to the differential crown-wheel, which rotates the differential case and planetary gears, thus driving the sun gears and driveshafts. The rotation of the differential planetary gears on their shaft allows the inner roadwheel to rotate at a slower speed than the outer roadwheel during cornering.

The transmission identification numbers are marked on the gearbox casing, in the following locations:

a) *085 transmission - the gearbox type number is engraved around the opening for the left-hand driveshaft, between the oil filler/level and drain plugs: its individual identifying three-letter code and the date of manufacture are engraved on the top of the clutch bellhousing, next to the clutch release lever*

b) *020 transmission - the gearbox type number is cast on the webs around the opening for the left-hand driveshaft, just above the oil drain plug: its individual identifying three-letter code and the date of manufacture are engraved on a flat on the bottom of the clutch bellhousing*

c) *02A transmission - the gearbox type number is cast on the webs above the opening for the left-hand driveshaft: its individual identifying three-letter code and the date of manufacture are engraved on the top of the gearbox housing, beneath the clutch release cylinder/mechanism*

7

2.2 Releasing the gear change lever gaiter from the floor bracket

2 Gearchange linkage - adjustment

085 and 020 transmissions

1 If the gearchange quality proves unsatisfactory following transmission refitting, proceed as described in the following paragraphs.

2 Remove the gearchange lever gaiter from the floor bracket, to expose the adjustment collar **(see illustration)**. Pull the gaiter up the lever.

3 Select first gear, then take up the play in the gear change mechanism by gently pressing the gear change lever to the left. Do not press it hard.

4 Using feeler blades, measure the clearance between the gear change lever stop and the side of the lever housing **(see illustrations)**.

5 If the clearance is not 1.0 ± 0.5 mm, unscrew the adjustment collar clamping bolt using an Allen key, then rotate the collar until the correct clearance is achieved **(see illustration)**. Tighten the clamping bolt.

6 On completion, refit the gear change lever gaiter to the floor bracket.

02A transmission

7 To accurately adjust the operation of the gear selector and shift cables, precisely machined jigs are required to set the gear change lever in a reference position. It is recommended, therefore that this operation be entrusted to a Seat dealer.

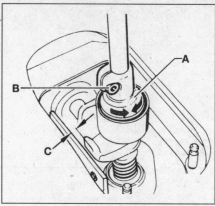

2.4a Gearchange lever adjustment collar (085 and 020 transmissions)

A Adjustment collar
B Clamp bolt
C Clearance 1.0 ± 0.5 mm

3 Manual transmission - removal and refitting

Removal

1 Select a solid, level surface to park the vehicle upon. Give yourself enough space to move around it easily. Apply the handbrake and chock the rear wheels.

2 Raise the front of the vehicle and support it securely on axle stands (see *Jacking and vehicle support*). Position a suitable container beneath the transmission, then unscrew the drain plug and drain the transmission oil **(see illustration)**.

3 Refer to Chapter 11 and remove the bonnet from its hinges.

4 Disconnect the battery negative (earth) lead (see Chapter 5A). Also remove the engine top cover where necessary.

5 The lock carrier is a panel assembly comprising the front bumper moulding, radiator and grille, cooling fan(s), headlight units, front valance and bonnet lock mechanism. Although its removal is not essential, its does give greatly improved access to the engine. Its removal is relatively simple and is described at the beginning of the engine

removal procedure - refer to Chapter 2C for details.

6 Extra working space may be gained on engine codes AER, AAU, AAV, ABD, ABU, AEX, APQ, AEE, ALM by removing the exhaust downpipe; refer to Chapter 4D for details.

085 and 02A transmissions

7 On the 085 transmission, disconnect the clutch cable from the transmission release lever with reference to Chapter 6 and position it to one side.

8 On the 02A transmission, remove the slave cylinder from the transmission with reference to Chapter 6, then insert a 35 mm M8 bolt through the drilling above the slave cylinder aperture, to hold the clutch release lever in position. Tie the slave cylinder to one side without disconnecting the hydraulic hose.

9 Disconnect the wiring from the speedometer sender.

10 Unbolt the support bracket for the starter and speedometer wiring.

11 Unscrew the nut and remove the exhaust pipe bracket, then unscrew and remove the starter motor mounting bolts.

12 Note the location of the earth cable on the transmission to engine mounting bolt, then unscrew and remove the bolt.

13 Unscrew and remove the upper transmission to engine mounting bolts.

14 Using a suitable hoist, support the weight of the engine. Where necessary, remove the engine wiring support bracket.

15 Unbolt the left-hand engine mounting from the transmission.

16 At the front of the engine, unscrew and remove the centre bolt from the front engine mounting.

17 Disconnect the wiring from the reversing light switch on the front of the transmission, and also remove the wiring support bracket.

18 Disconnect the remaining earth wiring from the transmission.

19 Unbolt the front engine mounting bracket from the transmission.

20 On the 085 transmission, mark the position of the gearchange rod on the transmission selector rod, then unscrew the clamp bolt, separate the rod and support it to

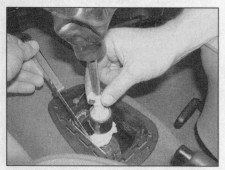

2.4b Using feeler blades, check the clearance between the gear change lever stop and the side of the lever housing

2.5 Use an Allen key to loosen the clamping bolt when adjusting the gear lever clearance

3.2 Transmission drain plug (085 transmission)

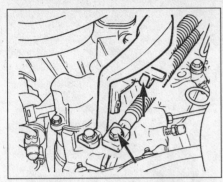

3.20 Disconnect the shift and selector cables (02A transmission)

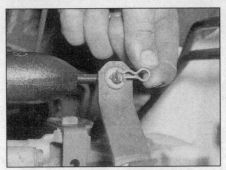

3.31a Pull out the clip to disconnect the control rod from the front selector lever ...

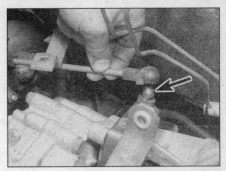

3.31b ... then disconnect the rods from the rear selector lever (020 transmission)

one side. Note that there are two possible positions for the rod on the selector rod, and it is important that it is fitted to the correct position. On the 02A transmission, disconnect the two cable ends from the transmission lever **(see illustration)**. Where necessary, unbolt the cable support bracket from the top of the transmission.

21 Unbolt and remove the bellhousing lower cover.

22 Using a multi-spline key, unscrew and remove the bolts securing the driveshafts to the transmission output flanges. Tie the right-hand driveshaft to one side. Turn the steering fully to the left, then support the left-hand driveshaft on an axle stand. Alternatively, completely remove the left-hand driveshaft as described in Chapter 8.

23 At the rear of the transmission, unscrew the bolts and disconnect the rear engine mounting.

24 Using a trolley jack, support the transmission. Position the jack so that it can be withdrawn from the left-hand side of the car.

25 At the rear of the engine, unscrew the transmission mounting bolt. Move the exhaust pipe bracket to the rear, or alternatively unbolt the bracket and lower the pipe to the ground.

26 Unscrew and remove the remaining bolts securing the transmission to the engine. Where necessary, bend the coolant support to one side.

27 Carefully pull the transmission directly away from the engine, taking care not to allow its weight to rest on the clutch friction plate hub.

⚠️ **Warning: Support the transmission to ensure that it remains steady on the jack head. Keep the transmission level until the input shaft is fully withdrawn from the clutch friction plate.**

28 When the transmission is clear of the locating dowels and clutch components, lower the transmission to the ground and withdraw from under the car.

020 transmission

29 Disconnect the clutch cable from the transmission release lever with reference to Chapter 6 and position it to one side.

30 Disconnect the wiring from the reversing light switch and speedometer sender located on top of the transmission.

31 Note how the gearchange control rods are fitted. Extract the clip and disconnect the rod from the front selector lever, then disconnect the two remaining rods from the rear selector lever by prising open the plastic clips **(see illustrations)**.

32 Unscrew the two bolts and remove the relay lever support bracket from the rear of the transmission casing **(see illustration)**.

33 Disconnect the wiring from the starter motor and remove the wiring support bracket.

34 Unscrew the starter motor upper mounting bolt.

35 At the front of the engine, unbolt the oil cooler from the front engine mounting, then unscrew and remove the mounting centre bolt.

36 Unscrew and nut securing the earth cable to the upper transmission mounting bolt, then unscrew and remove the two upper mounting bolts **(see illustration)**.

37 Using a suitable hoist, support the weight of the engine.

38 Using a trolley jack, support the transmission. Position the jack so that it can be withdrawn from the left-hand side of the car.

39 Unbolt the left-hand engine mounting bracket from the transmission and subframe.

40 On models with air conditioning, release the high pressure line from the support, then unbolt the support from the transmission.

41 On models with power steering, unscrew the bolt/nut and detach the power steering

hydraulic lines from the transmission. Tie the lines to one side.

42 Unscrew the lower starter motor mounting bolt and withdraw the starter motor from the engine.

43 Unbolt the front engine mounting bracket from the transmission.

44 Unbolt and remove bellhousing lower cover.

45 Using a multi-spline key, unscrew and remove the bolts securing the driveshafts to the transmission output flanges. Tie the right-hand driveshaft to one side. Turn the steering fully to the left, then support the left-hand driveshaft on an axle stand. Alternatively, completely remove the left-hand driveshaft as described in Chapter 8.

46 At the rear of the transmission, unbolt and remove the rear engine mounting bracket.

47 Unbolt and remove the protection plate located behind the right-hand driveshaft flange.

48 At the rear of the engine, unscrew the lower bolt securing the transmission to the engine.

49 Carefully pull the transmission directly away from the engine, taking care not to allow its weight to rest on the clutch friction plate hub **(see illustration)**.

⚠️ **Warning: Support the transmission to ensure that it remains steady on the jack head. Keep the transmission level until the input shaft is fully withdrawn from the clutch friction plate.**

50 When the transmission is clear of the

3.32 Unbolt and remove the relay lever support bracket (020 transmission)

3.36 Removing the upper transmission mounting bolt which secures the earth cable

3.49 Removing the transmission from the engine (transmission 020 shown)

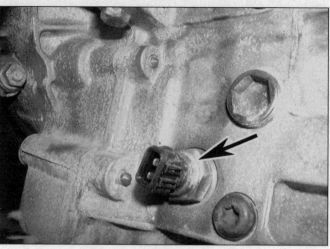

5.7 Reversing light switch location (085 transmission shown)

locating dowels and clutch components, lower the transmission to the ground and withdraw from under the car.

Refitting

51 Refitting the transmission is essentially a reversal of the removal procedure, but note the following points:

a) Apply a smear of high-melting-point grease to the clutch friction plate hub splines; take care to avoid contaminating the friction surfaces.

b) Tighten the transmission-to-engine bolts to the specified torque

c) Refer to Chapter 2A, 2B or 2C (as applicable) and tighten the engine mounting bolts to the correct torque.

d) Refer to Chapter 8 and tighten the driveshaft bolts to the specified torque.

e) On models fitted with transmission 02A, refer to Chapter 6 and refit the slave cylinder.

f) On models fitted with transmissions 085 and 020, refer to Chapter 6 and refit the clutch cable.

g) On completion, refer to Section 2 and check the gearchange linkage adjustment (where possible).

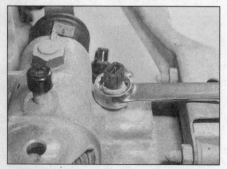

5.8 Slacken the switch body using a ring spanner and withdraw it from the transmission casing (020 transmission)

4 Manual transmission overhaul - general information

The overhaul of a manual transmission is a complex (and often expensive) task for the DIY home mechanic to undertake, which requires access to specialist equipment. It involves dismantling and reassembly of many small components, measuring clearances precisely and if necessary, adjusting them by selecting shims and spacers. Internal transmission components are also often difficult to obtain and in many instances, extremely expensive. Because of this, if the transmission develops a fault or becomes noisy, the best course of action is to have the unit overhauled by a specialist repairer or to obtain an exchange reconditioned unit.

Nevertheless, it is not impossible for the more experienced mechanic to overhaul the trans-mission if the special tools are available and the job is carried out in a deliberate step-by-step manner, to ensure nothing is overlooked.

The tools necessary for an overhaul include internal and external circlip pliers, bearing pullers, a slide hammer, a set of pin punches, a dial test indicator and possibly a hydraulic press. In addition, a large, sturdy workbench and a vice will be required.

During dismantling of the transmission, make careful notes of how each component is fitted to make reassembly easier and accurate.

Before dismantling the transmission, it will help if you have some idea of where the problem lies. Certain problems can be closely related to specific areas in the transmission which can make component examination and renewal easier. Refer to the Fault finding Section in this manual for more information.

5 Reversing light switch - testing, removal and refitting

Testing

1 Ensure that the ignition switch is turned to the OFF position.

2 Unplug the wiring harness from the reversing light switch at the connector. The switch is located on the top of the transmission casing on the 020 and 02A transmissions, and on the underside of the transmission casing on the 085 transmission. For access to the latter, apply the handbrake then jack up the front of the vehicle and support it on axle stands (see *Jacking and vehicle support*).

3 Connect the probes of a continuity tester, or multimeter set to the resistance measurement function, across the terminals of the reverse light switch.

4 The switch contacts are normally open, so with any gear other than reverse selected, the tester/meter should indicate an open circuit or infinity resistance. When reverse gear is selected, the switch contacts should close, causing the tester/meter to indicate continuity or zero resistance.

5 If the switch does not operate correctly, it should be renewed.

Removal

6 Ensure that the ignition switch is turned to the OFF position.

7 Unplug the wiring harness from the reversing light switch at the connector **(see illustration)**

8 Unscrew the switch from the transmission casing, and recover the sealing ring **(see illustration).**

Refitting

9 Refitting is a reversal of removal.

6.4 Roadspeed sensor/speedometer drive location (085 transmission)

6.5a Remove the transducer retaining screw using an Allen key . . .

6.5b . . . and withdraw the unit from the transmission casing (020 transmission)

6 Roadspeed sensor/ speedometer drive - removal and refitting

General information

1 All transmissions are fitted with an electronic speedometer transducer. This device measures the rotational speed of the transmission final drive and converts the information into an electronic signal, which is then sent to the speedometer module in the instrument panel. On certain models, the signal is also used as an input by the engine management system ECU.

Removal

Note: *A new gasket/sealing ring should be used on refitting.*

2 Ensure that the ignition switch is turned to the OFF position.

3 Locate the speed transducer, at the top of the transmission casing. Unplug the wiring harness from the transducer, at the connector.

4 On the 085 transmission, the transducer and pinion housing is screwed directly into the casing **(see illustration)**. If required, hold the housing with a spanner, then unscrew the transducer from the top of the pinion housing and recover the washer. If necessary, unscrew the pinion housing and withdraw it together with the pinion.

5 On the 020 and 02A transmissions, the transducer and pinion unit is retained by a single screw. Undo the retaining screw using an Allen key and withdraw the unit from the transmission casing **(see illustrations)**. Recover the gasket where applicable.

Refitting

6 Refitting is a reversal of removal.

Chapter 8
Driveshafts

Contents

Degrees of difficulty

Easy, suitable for novice with little experience	**Fairly easy,** suitable for beginner with some experience	**Fairly difficult,** suitable for competent DIY mechanic	**Difficult,** suitable for experienced DIY mechanic	**Very difficult,** suitable for expert DIY or professional

Specifications

Type . . . . Steel shafts with ball-and-cage type constant velocity joint at each end

Driveshaft grease
Type . . . . Seat/VW G 000 633
Quantity (per joint):
  Inner joints:
    1.0, 1.05, 1.3 and 1.4 litre engine models . . . . 90 grams
    Diesel engine models and 1.6 & 2.0 litre petrol engine models . . . 120 grams
  Outer joints:
    1.0, 1.05, 1.3 and 1.4 litre engine models . . . . 90 grams
    Diesel engine models and 1.6 & 2.0 litre petrol engine models . . . 110 grams

Torque wrench settings

	Nm	lbf ft
Driveshaft retaining nut	265	196
Inner constant velocity joint-to-transmission flange bolts	45	33
Lower arm balljoint retaining bolts	35	26
Roadwheel bolts	110	81

1 General information

Drive is transmitted from the differential to the front wheels by means of two solid-steel driveshafts of unequal length. The right-hand driveshaft is longer than the left-hand driveshaft, due to the position of the transmission.

Both driveshafts are splined at their outer ends to accept the wheel hubs, and are threaded so that each hub can be fastened by a large nut. The inner end of each driveshaft is bolted to the transmission drive flanges.

Constant velocity (CV) joints are fitted to each end of the driveshafts, to ensure the smooth and efficient transmission of drive at all the angles possible as the roadwheels move up and down with the suspension, and as they turn from side to side under steering. Both inner and outer constant velocity joints are of the ball-and-cage type.

Some models have a vibration damper fitted to the right-hand driveshaft.

2 Driveshaft - removal and refitting

Note: *A new driveshaft retaining nut and a new inner constant velocity joint-to-transmission gasket will be required on refitting. All self-locking nuts should be renewed.*

Removal

1 Remove the wheel trim/hub cap (as applicable) and slacken the driveshaft retaining nut with the vehicle resting on its wheels – note that the nut is very tight, and a swing-bar will probably be required to slacken it **(see illustration).** Also slacken the wheel bolts.

2 Chock the rear wheels of the car, firmly apply the handbrake, then jack up the front of the car and support it on axle stands. Remove the front roadwheel.

3 Slacken and remove the bolts securing the inner driveshaft joint to the transmission flange and, where applicable, recover the retaining plates from underneath the bolts.

2.1 Remove the trim/hub cap and slacken the driveshaft retaining nut

8

2.3a Slacken the inner driveshaft joint retaining bolts . . .

2.3b . . . and remove them along with their retaining plates (arrowed)

Where applicable, unbolt the driveshaft shield from the engine to improve access to the bolts. Support the driveshaft by suspending it with wire or string - do not allow it to hang under its own weight, or the joint may be damaged **(see illustrations)**.

4 Using a suitable marker pen, draw around the end of the suspension lower arm, marking the correct fitted position of balljoint. Unscrew the balljoint retaining bolts and remove the retaining plate from the top of the lower arm. **Note:** *On some models the balljoint inner retaining bolt hole is slotted; on these models the inner retaining bolt can be slackened, leaving the retaining plate and bolt in position in the arm, and the balljoint can be disengaged from the bolt.*

5 Unscrew the driveshaft retaining nut and (where applicable) remove its washer.

6 Carefully pull the hub carrier assembly outwards, and withdraw the driveshaft outer constant velocity joint from the hub assembly. The outer joint will be very tight, tap the joint out of the hub using a soft-faced mallet. If this fails to free the outer joint, the joint will have to be pressed out using a suitable tool bolted to the hub.

7 Manoeuvre the driveshaft out from underneath the vehicle and (where fitted) recover the gasket from the end of the inner

constant velocity joint. Discard the gasket - a new one should be used on refitting.

8 *Do not allow the vehicle to rest on its wheels with one or both driveshaft(s) removed, as damage to the wheel bearing(s) may result.* If moving the vehicle is unavoidable, temporarily insert the outer end of the driveshaft(s) in the hub(s), and tighten the driveshaft retaining nut(s); in this case, the inner end(s) of the driveshaft(s) must be supported, for example by suspending with string from the vehicle underbody. *Do not allow the driveshaft to hang down under its own weight, or the joint may be damaged.*

Refitting

9 Ensure that the transmission flange and inner joint mating surfaces are clean and dry. Where necessary, fit a new gasket to the joint by peeling off its backing foil and sticking it in position.

10 Ensure that the outer joint and hub splines are clean and dry.

11 Manoeuvre the driveshaft into position, and engage the outer joint with the hub. Ensure that the threads are clean, and apply a smear of oil to the contact face of the new driveshaft retaining nut. Fit the washer (where applicable) and nut and tighten it to draw the

joint fully into position. Do not attempt to fully tighten the nut at this stage.

12 Refit the suspension lower arm balljoint retaining bolts, and tighten them to the specified torque setting, using the marks made on removal to ensure that the balljoint is correctly positioned on the lower arm.

13 Align the driveshaft inner joint with the transmission flange, and refit the retaining bolts and (where necessary) plates. Tighten the retaining bolts to the specified torque.

14 Ensure that the outer joint is drawn fully into position in the hub, then refit the road-wheel and lower the vehicle to the ground.

15 Tighten the driveshaft nut to the specified torque.

16 Once the driveshaft nut is correctly tightened, tighten the wheel bolts to the specified torque and refit the wheel trim/hub cap.

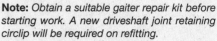

3 Driveshaft inner joint gaiter – renewal

Note: *Obtain a suitable gaiter repair kit before starting work. A new driveshaft joint retaining circlip will be required on refitting.*

1 With the driveshaft removed as described in Section 2, proceed as follows.

2 Remove the inner CV joint retaining circlip from the inner end of the driveshaft, using circlip pliers **(see illustration)**.

3 Using a screwdriver, work around the joint, and carefully prise the metal gaiter retaining plate away from the edge of the joint **(see illustration)**.

4 Note which way round the joint is fitted on the driveshaft (mark the joint if necessary). Support the joint outer member then, using a metal bar or tube of suitable diameter bearing on the end of the driveshaft, press or drive the end of the driveshaft from the joint. This job will be eased greatly if access can be obtained to a hydraulic press.

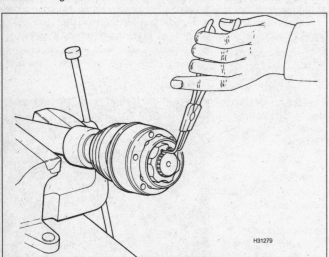

3.2 Remove the inner CV joint retaining circlip

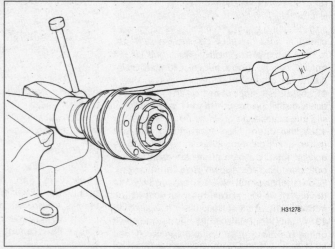

3.3 Carefully prise the metal gaiter retaining plate away from the edge of the joint

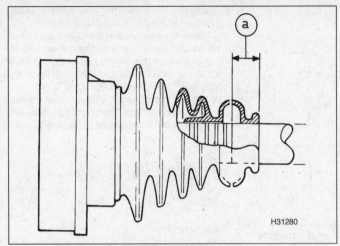

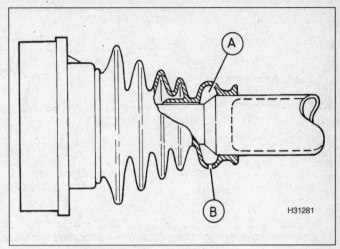

3.12 Mark the correct fitted position of the gaiter using paint or adhesive tape – left-hand inner driveshaft gaiter

a = 17.0 mm

3.13 Correct fitted position of right-hand inner driveshaft gaiter

A Venting chamber
B Venting hole (not applicable to all models)

5 Wipe out the grease from the joint and the gaiter.

6 Recover the dished washer from the driveshaft, then release the clip securing the outboard end of the gaiter to the driveshaft, and slide the gaiter from the end of the driveshaft.

7 Thoroughly clean the driveshaft joint using paraffin or a suitable solvent, then inspect the components as follows.

8 Move the inner splined driving member from side to side to expose each ball in turn at the top of its track. Examine the balls for cracks, flat spots or signs of surface pitting.

9 Inspect the ball tracks on the inner and outer members. If the tracks have widened, the balls will no longer be a tight fit. At the same time, check the ball cage windows for wear or cracking between the windows.

10 If on inspection any of the constant velocity joint components are found to be worn or damaged, it will be necessary to renew the complete joint assembly. If the joint is in satisfactory condition, obtain a new gaiter and retaining clips, a constant velocity joint circlip, and the correct type of grease. Grease is often supplied with the joint repair kit – if not, use a good-quality molybdenum disulphide grease.

11 Tape over the splines on the end of the driveshaft, to protect the new gaiter as it is slid into place.

12 When fitting the left-hand driveshaft gaiter, using paint or adhesive tape, mark the correct fitted position of the driveshaft gaiter outboard end, as shown **(see illustration)**. Slide the new gaiter onto the end of the driveshaft, then remove the protective tape from the driveshaft splines.

13 When fitting the right-hand driveshaft gaiter, make sure that the gaiter is positioned as shown, with the gaiter venting chamber (B) resting on the larger diameter of the driveshaft **(see illustration)**.

14 Slide on the dished washer, making sure that its convex side is facing the gaiter.

15 Engage the splines of the joint inner member with the end of the driveshaft, ensuring that the joint is fitted the correct way round as noted before removal, then carefully tap or press the joint onto the end of the driveshaft, using a metal tube bearing on only the joint inner member. Press the joint onto the driveshaft until it contacts the shoulder, then fit a new circlip to retain the joint.

16 Pack half the specified quantity of fresh grease into the joint, then spread the remaining half evenly inside the joint gaiter.

17 Push the metal gaiter retaining plate onto the joint outer member, then align the outboard end of the gaiter with the mark made in paragraph 12, and secure with a new retaining clip. Pull the clip as tight as possible, and locate the hooks on the clip in their slots. Remove any slack in the gaiter retaining clip by carefully compressing the raised section of the clip. In the absence of the special tool, a pair of side cutters may be used, taking care not to cut the clip.

18 Refit the driveshaft as described in Section 2.

---

4   Driveshaft outer joint gaiter – renewal

Note: *Obtain a suitable gaiter repair kit before starting work. A new driveshaft joint retaining circlip will be required on refitting.*

1 With the driveshaft removed as described in Section 2, proceed as follows.

2 Secure the driveshaft in a vice equipped with soft jaws, and release the two outer joint gaiter retaining clips. If necessary, the retaining clips can be cut to release them.

3 Slide the rubber gaiter down the shaft to expose the constant velocity joint, and scoop out excess grease.

4 Using a soft-faced mallet, tap the joint off the end of the driveshaft **(see illustration)**.

5 Remove the circlip from the driveshaft groove, and slide off the thrustwasher and dished washer, noting which way around it is fitted.

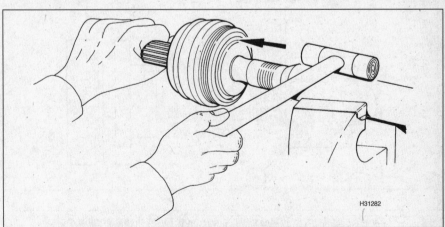

4.4 Using a soft-faced mallet, tap the outer joint from the driveshaft

8

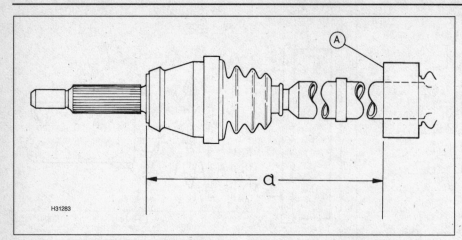

5.5a Driveshaft damper fitting dimension – petrol and turbo diesel engine models

A Driveshaft damper   a = 175.0 mm

6 Slide the rubber gaiter off the driveshaft and discard it.

7 Thoroughly clean the constant velocity joint using paraffin, or a suitable solvent, and dry thoroughly. Carry out a visual inspection as follows.

8 Move the inner splined driving member from side to side to expose each ball in turn at the top of its track. Examine the balls for cracks, flat spots or signs of surface pitting.

9 Inspect the ball tracks on the inner and outer members. If the tracks have widened, the balls will no longer be a tight fit. At the same time, check the ball cage windows for wear or cracking between the windows.

10 If on inspection any of the constant velocity joint components are found to be worn or damaged, it will be necessary to renew the complete joint assembly. If the joint is in satisfactory condition, obtain a new gaiter and retaining clips, a constant velocity joint circlip and the correct type of grease. Grease is often supplied with the joint repair kit - if not, use a good-quality molybdenum disulphide grease.

11 Tape over the splines on the end of the driveshaft, to protect the new gaiter as it is slid into place.

12 Slide the new gaiter onto the end of the driveshaft, then remove the protective tape from the driveshaft splines.

13 Slide on the dished washer, making sure its convex side is innermost, followed by the thrustwasher.

14 Fit a new circlip to the driveshaft, then tap the joint onto the driveshaft until the circlip engages in its groove. Make sure that the joint is securely retained by the circlip.

15 Pack the joint with the specified type of grease. Work the grease well into the bearing tracks whilst twisting the joint, and fill the rubber gaiter with any excess.

16 Ease the gaiter over the joint, and ensure that the gaiter lips are correctly located on both the driveshaft and constant velocity joint. Lift the outer sealing lip of the gaiter to equalise air pressure within the gaiter.

17 Fit the large metal retaining clip to the gaiter. Pull the clip as tight as possible, and locate the hooks on the clip in their slots. Remove any slack in the gaiter retaining clip by carefully compressing the raised section of the clip. In the absence of the special tool, a pair of side cutters may be used, taking care not to cut the clip. Secure the small retaining clip using the same procedure.

18 Check the constant velocity joint moves freely in all directions, then refit the driveshaft to the vehicle, as described in Section 2.

5 Driveshaft damper – removal and refitting

Removal

1 Remove the inner joint as described in Section 3.

2 Clearly mark the position of the damper on the driveshaft.

3 Use a long-reach puller or a press to remove the damper from the inner end of the driveshaft.

Refitting

4 Ensure that the mating surfaces of the driveshaft and the damper are clean and free from oil or grease.

5 Press or drive the vibration damper along the driveshaft, until it is aligned as shown (if the original components are being reassembled, the mark made on removal can be used as a guide (**see illustrations**).

6 Refit the inner joint as described in Section 3.

6 Driveshaft overhaul - general information

1 If any of the checks described in Chapter 1 reveal wear in any driveshaft joint, first remove the roadwheel trim or centre cap (as appropriate) and check that the driveshaft retaining nut is tight.

2 If the nut is tight, refit the centre cap or trim. Repeat this check on the remaining driveshaft nut.

3 Road test the vehicle, and listen for a metallic clicking from the front as the vehicle is driven slowly in a circle on full lock. If a clicking noise is heard, this indicates wear in the outer constant velocity joint. This means that the joint must be renewed; reconditioning is not possible.

4 If vibration, consistent with road speed, is felt through the car when accelerating, there is a possibility of wear in the inner constant velocity joints.

5 To check the joints for wear, the driveshaft must be dismantled. The constant velocity joints can be removed and checked as described in Sections 3 and 4; if any wear or free play is found, the affected joint must be renewed.

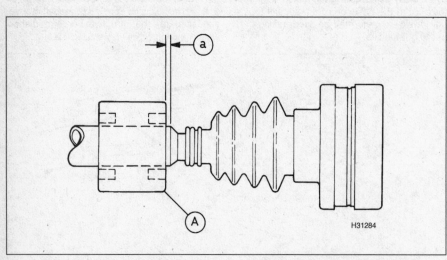

5.5b Driveshaft damper fitting dimension – non-turbo diesel engine models

A Driveshaft damper   a = 4.0 mm

Chapter 9
Braking system

Contents

Degrees of difficulty

Easy, suitable for novice with little experience	**Fairly easy,** suitable for beginner with some experience	**Fairly difficult,** suitable for competent DIY mechanic	**Difficult,** suitable for experienced DIY mechanic	**Very difficult,** suitable for expert DIY or professional

Specifications

Front brakes

Disc diameter:
All except 2.0 litre models .... 239 mm
2.0 litre models .... 256 mm

Disc thickness:	**New**	**Minimum permissible thickness**
1.0, 1.3 and 1.4 litre models	10.0 mm	8.0 mm
1.6 litre models and 1.9 litre (diesel) models	12.0 mm	10.0 mm
2.0 litre models	20.0 mm	18.0 mm
Maximum disc run-out	0.1 mm	

Brake pad thickness:	**New**	**Minimum thickness**
1.0, 1.3 and 1.4 litre models	12.0 mm	7.0 mm
1.6 litre and 1.9 litre (diesel) models	14.0 mm	7.0 mm
2.0 litre engines	11.0 mm	7.0 mm

Rear drum brakes

Drum diameter:	**New**	**Maximum diameter**
Petrol models	180 mm	181 mm
Diesel models	200 mm	201 mm
Maximum drum out-of-round	0.1 mm	

Brake shoe friction material thickness:
New .... 5.0 mm
Minimum thickness .... 2.5 mm

Rear disc brakes

Disc diameter .... 226 mm
Disc thickness:
New .... 10.0 mm
Minimum thickness .... 8.0 mm
Maximum disc run-out .... 0.1 mm
Brake pad thickness:
New .... 10.0 mm
Minimum .... 7.0 mm

9

Torque wrench settings

	Nm	lbf ft
ABS wheel sensor retaining bolts	10	7
Front brake caliper:		
Girling caliper:		
Guide pin bolts	35	26
Mounting bracket bolts	125	92
VW caliper mounting bolts	25	18
Master cylinder mounting nuts	20	15
Rear brake caliper:		
Guide pin bolts	25	18
Mounting bracket bolts	65	48
Rear brake wheel cylinder bolts	10	7
Roadwheel bolts	110	81
Servo unit mounting nuts	25	18

1 General information and precautions

General information

The braking system is of the servo-assisted, dual-circuit hydraulic type. The arrangement of the hydraulic system is such that each circuit operates one front and one rear brake from a tandem master cylinder. Under normal circumstances, both circuits operate in unison. However, if there is hydraulic failure in one circuit, full braking force will still be available at two wheels.

Most large-capacity engine models have disc brakes all round as standard; all other models are fitted with front disc brakes and rear drum brakes. ABS is fitted as standard to some models, and was offered as an option on most other models (refer to Section 24 for further information on ABS operation).

The front disc brakes are actuated by single-piston sliding type calipers, which ensure that equal pressure is applied to each disc pad.

On models with rear drum brakes, the rear brakes incorporate leading and trailing shoes, which are actuated by twin-piston wheel cylinders. A self-adjust mechanism is incorporated, to compensate for brake shoe wear.

On models with rear disc brakes, the brakes are actuated by single-piston sliding calipers which incorporate mechanical handbrake mechanisms.

A pressure-regulating mechanism is incorporated in the braking system, this helps to prevent rear wheel lock-up during emergency braking. The system is controlled either by a single load-dependent valve which is linked to the rear torsion beam assembly, or by a pair of pressure-dependent valves which are screwed into the master cylinder outlet ports, one valve fitted in each rear brake line.

The handbrake provides an independent mechanical means of rear brake application.

Precautions

When servicing any part of the system, work carefully and methodically; also observe scrupulous cleanliness when overhauling any part of the hydraulic system. Always renew components (in axle sets, where applicable) if in doubt about their condition, and use only genuine Seat replacement parts, or at least those of known good quality. Note the warnings given in Safety first and at relevant points in this Chapter concerning the dangers of asbestos dust and hydraulic fluid.

2 Hydraulic system – bleeding

⚠️ *Warning: Hydraulic fluid is poisonous; wash off immediately and thoroughly in the case of skin contact, and seek immediate medical advice if any fluid is swallowed or gets into the eyes. Certain types of hydraulic fluid are flammable, and may ignite when allowed into contact with hot components; when servicing any hydraulic system, it is safest to assume that the fluid is flammable, and to take precautions against the risk of fire as though it is petrol that is being handled. Hydraulic fluid is also an effective paint stripper, and will attack plastics; if any is spilt, it should be washed off immediately, using copious quantities of fresh water. Finally, it is hygroscopic (it absorbs moisture from the air) - old fluid may be contaminated and unfit for further use. When topping-up or renewing the fluid, always use the recommended type, and ensure that it comes from a freshly-opened sealed container.*

General

1 The correct operation of any hydraulic system is only possible after removing all air from the components and circuit; this is achieved by bleeding the system.

2 During the bleeding procedure, add only clean, unused hydraulic fluid of the recommended type; never re-use fluid that has already been bled from the system. Ensure that sufficient fluid is available before starting work.

3 If there is any possibility of incorrect fluid being already in the system, the brake components and circuit must be flushed completely with uncontaminated, correct fluid, and new seals should be fitted to the various components.

4 If hydraulic fluid has been lost from the system, or air has entered because of a leak, ensure that the fault is cured before continuing further.

5 Park the vehicle on level ground, switch off the engine and select first or reverse gear, then chock the wheels and release the handbrake.

6 Check that all pipes and hoses are secure, unions tight and bleed screws closed. Clean any dirt from around the bleed screws.

7 Unscrew the master cylinder reservoir cap, and top the reservoir up to the MAX level line; refit the cap loosely, and remember to maintain the fluid level at least above the MIN level line throughout the procedure, or there is a risk of further air entering the system.

8 There are a number of one-man, do-it-yourself brake bleeding kits currently available from motor accessory shops. It is recommended that one of these kits is used whenever possible, as they greatly simplify the bleeding operation, and reduce the risk of expelled air and fluid being drawn back into the system. If such a kit is not available, the basic (two-man) method must be used, which is described in detail below.

9 If a kit is to be used, prepare the vehicle as described previously, and follow the kit manufacturer's instructions, as the procedure may vary slightly according to the type being used; generally, they are as outlined below in the relevant sub-section.

10 Whichever method is used, the same sequence must be followed (paragraphs 11 and 12) to ensure the removal of all air from the system.

Bleeding sequence

11 If the system has been only partially disconnected, and suitable precautions were taken to minimise fluid loss, it should be necessary only to bleed that part of the system (ie the primary or secondary circuit).

12 If the complete system is to be bled, then it should be done working in the following sequence:

  a) *Right-hand rear brake.*
  b) *Left-hand rear brake.*
  c) *Right-hand front brake.*
  d) *Left-hand front brake.*

Note: *On models fitted with a load-dependent rear brake pressure-regulating valve, when bleeding the rear brakes, push the pressure-regulating valve operating lever firmly upwards towards the rear torsion bar assembly.*

⚠️ **Warning: On models with ABS, under no circumstances should the hydraulic unit bleed screws be opened.**

Bleeding - basic (two-man) method

13 Collect together a clean glass jar of reasonable size, a suitable length of plastic or rubber tubing which is a tight fit over the bleed screw, and a ring spanner to fit the screw. The help of an assistant will also be required.

14 Remove the dust cap from the first screw in the sequence **(see illustration)**. Fit the spanner and tube to the screw, place the other end of the tube in the jar, and pour in sufficient fluid to cover the end of the tube.

15 Ensure that the master cylinder reservoir fluid level is maintained at least above the MIN level line throughout the procedure.

16 Have the assistant fully depress the brake pedal several times to build up pressure, then maintain it on the final downstroke.

17 While pedal pressure is maintained, unscrew the bleed screw (approximately one turn) and allow the compressed fluid and air to flow into the jar. The assistant should maintain pedal pressure, following it down to the floor if necessary, and should not release it until instructed to do so. When the flow stops, tighten the bleed screw again, have the assistant release the pedal slowly, and recheck the reservoir fluid level.

18 Repeat the steps given in paragraphs 16 and 17 until the fluid emerging from the bleed screw is free from air bubbles. If the master cylinder has been drained and refilled, and air is being bled from the first screw in the sequence, allow approximately five seconds between cycles for the master cylinder passages to refill.

19 When no more air bubbles appear, tighten the bleed screw securely, remove the tube and spanner, and refit the dust cap. Do not overtighten the bleed screw.

20 Repeat the procedure on the remaining screws in the sequence, until all air is removed from the system and the brake pedal feels firm again.

Bleeding - using a one-way valve kit

21 As their name implies, these kits consist of a length of tubing with a one-way valve fitted, to prevent expelled air and fluid being drawn back into the system; some kits include a translucent container, which can be positioned so that the air bubbles can be more easily seen flowing from the end of the tube.

22 The kit is connected to the bleed screw, which is then opened. The user returns to the driver's seat, depresses the brake pedal with

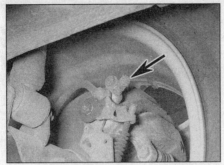

2.14 Remove the dust cap (arrowed) from the first screw in the sequence

a smooth, steady stroke, and slowly releases it; this is repeated until the expelled fluid is clear of air bubbles **(see illustration)**.

23 Note that these kits simplify work so much that it is easy to forget the master cylinder reservoir fluid level; ensure that this is maintained at least above the MIN level line at all times.

Bleeding - using a pressure-bleeding kit

24 These kits are usually operated by the reservoir of pressurised air contained in the spare tyre. However, note that it will probably be necessary to reduce the pressure to a lower level than normal; refer to the instructions supplied with the kit.

25 By connecting a pressurised, fluid-filled container to the master cylinder reservoir, bleeding can be carried out simply by opening each screw in turn (in the specified sequence), and allowing the fluid to flow out until no more air bubbles can be seen in the expelled fluid.

26 This method has the advantage that the large reservoir of fluid provides an additional safeguard against air being drawn into the system during bleeding.

27 Pressure-bleeding is particularly effective when bleeding difficult systems, or when bleeding the complete system at the time of routine fluid renewal.

All methods

28 When bleeding is complete, and firm pedal feel is restored, wash off any spilt fluid, tighten the bleed screws securely, and refit their dust caps.

2.22 Bleeding a brake using a one-way valve kit

29 Check the hydraulic fluid level in the master cylinder reservoir, and top-up if necessary (see *Weekly Checks*).

30 Discard any hydraulic fluid that has been bled from the system; it will not be fit for re-use.

31 Check the feel of the brake pedal. If it feels at all spongy, air must still be present in the system, and further bleeding is required. Failure to bleed satisfactorily after a reasonable repetition of the bleeding procedure may be due to worn master cylinder seals.

3 Hydraulic pipes and hoses - inspection, removal and refitting

Note: *Refer to the note in Section 2 concerning the dangers of hydraulic fluid.*

1 If any pipe or hose is to be renewed, minimise fluid loss by first removing the master cylinder reservoir cap, then tightening it down onto a piece of polythene to obtain an airtight seal. Alternatively, flexible hoses can be sealed, if required, using a proprietary brake hose clamp; metal brake pipe unions can be plugged (if care is taken not to allow dirt into the system) or capped immediately they are disconnected. Place a wad of rag under any union that is to be disconnected, to catch any spilt fluid.

2 If a flexible hose is to be disconnected, unscrew the brake pipe union nut before removing the spring clip which secures the hose to its mounting bracket.

3 To unscrew the union nuts, it is preferable to obtain a brake pipe spanner of the correct size; these are available from most large motor accessory shops. Failing this, a close-fitting open-ended spanner will be required, though if the nuts are tight or corroded, their flats may be rounded-off if the spanner slips. In such a case, a self-locking wrench is often the only way to unscrew a stubborn union, but it follows that the pipe and the damaged nuts must be renewed on reassembly. Always clean a union and surrounding area before disconnecting it. If disconnecting a component with more than one union, make a careful note of the connections before disturbing any of them.

4 If a brake pipe is to be renewed, it can be obtained, cut to length and with the union nuts and end flares in place, from Seat dealers. All that is then necessary is to bend it to shape, following the line of the original, before fitting it to the car. Alternatively, most motor accessory shops can make up brake pipes from kits, but this requires very careful measurement of the original, to ensure that the replacement is of the correct length. The safest answer is usually to take the original to the shop as a pattern.

5 On refitting, do not overtighten the union nuts. It is not necessary to exercise brute force to obtain a sound joint.

9

4.4 On VW calipers, remove the caliper mounting bolts

4.10a Fit the anti-rattle springs to the hub carrier, making sure they are correctly positioned . . .

4.10b . . . then fit the pads with the friction material facing the disc

6 Ensure that the pipes and hoses are correctly routed, with no kinks, and that they are secured in the clips or brackets provided. After fitting, remove the polythene from the reservoir, and bleed the hydraulic system as described in Section 2. Wash off any spilt fluid, and check carefully for fluid leaks.

4 Front brake pads –
removal, inspection and refitting

⚠️ *Warning: Renew both sets of brake pads/shoes at the same time - never renew the pads/shoes on only one wheel, as uneven braking may result. Note that the dust created by wear of the pads may contain asbestos, which is a health hazard. Never blow it out with compressed air, and do not inhale any of it. An approved filtering mask should be worn when working on the brakes. DO NOT use petrol or petroleum-based solvents to clean brake parts; use brake cleaner or methylated spirit only.*

VW calipers

Removal

Note: *New brake pad anti-rattle springs should be used on refitting.*

1 Apply the handbrake, then jack up the front of the vehicle and support it on axle stands. Remove the front roadwheels.
2 Trace the brake pad wear sensor wiring (where fitted) back from the pads, and disconnect it from the wiring connector. Note

4.11 Position the caliper over the pads

the routing of the wiring, and free it from any relevant retaining clips. Continue as described under the relevant sub-heading.
3 Where applicable, to improve access, undo the retaining bolts and remove the air deflector shield from the caliper.
4 Slacken and remove the two caliper mounting bolts, then lift the caliper away from the brake pads and hub, and tie it to the suspension strut using a suitable piece of wire (see illustration). Do not allow the caliper to hang unsupported on the flexible brake hose.
5 Withdraw the two brake pads from the hub carrier and recover the anti-rattle springs, noting their correct fitted locations. Note that the springs are different and are not interchangeable. If the original pads are to be refitted, mark them so that they can be refitted in their original positions.

Inspection

6 First measure the thickness of each brake pad (including the backing plate). If either pad is worn at any point to the specified minimum thickness or less, all four pads must be renewed. Also, the pads should be renewed if any are fouled with oil or grease; there is no satisfactory way of degreasing friction material, once contaminated. If any of the brake pads are worn unevenly, or are fouled with oil or grease, trace and rectify the cause before reassembly. New brake pad kits are available from Seat dealers.
7 If the brake pads are still serviceable, carefully clean them using a clean, fine wire brush or similar, paying particular attention to the sides and back of the metal backing. Clean out the grooves in the friction material (where applicable), and pick out any large embedded particles of dirt or debris. Carefully clean the pad locations in the caliper body/mounting bracket.
8 Prior to fitting the pads, check that the spacers are free to slide easily in the caliper body bushes, and are a reasonably tight fit. Brush the dust and dirt from the caliper and piston, but *do not* inhale it, as it is injurious to health. Inspect the dust seal around the piston for damage, and the piston for evidence of fluid leaks, corrosion or damage. If attention to any of these components is necessary, refer to Section 5.

Refitting

9 If new brake pads are to be fitted, the caliper piston must be pushed back into the cylinder to make room for them. Either use a G-clamp or similar tool, or use suitable pieces of wood as levers. Provided that the master cylinder reservoir has not been overfilled with hydraulic fluid, there should be no spillage, but keep a careful watch on the fluid level while retracting the piston. If the fluid level rises above the MAX level line at any time, the surplus should be syphoned off or ejected through a plastic tube connected to the bleed screw (see Section 2). **Note:** *Do not syphon the fluid by mouth, as it is poisonous; use a syringe or an old poultry baster.*
10 Fit the new anti-rattle springs to the hub carrier, making sure they are correctly positioned, then fit the pads, ensuring that the friction material of each pad is against the brake disc. If the original pads are being refitted, ensure that they are refitted to their original locations as noted before removal. Note that, where applicable, the pad with the wear sensor wire should be installed as the inner pad (see illustrations).
11 Position the caliper over the pads, and pass the pad warning sensor wiring (where fitted) through the caliper aperture (see illustration).
12 Press the caliper into position sufficiently until it is possible to install caliper mounting bolts. Tighten the mounting bolts to the specified torque. **Note:** *Do not exert excess pressure on the caliper, as this will deform the pad springs, resulting in noisy operation of the brakes.*
13 Where applicable, reconnect the brake pad wear sensor wiring connectors, ensuring that the wiring is correctly routed. Where applicable, refit the air deflector shield to the caliper.
14 Depress the brake pedal repeatedly, until the pads are pressed into firm contact with the brake disc, and normal (non-assisted) pedal pressure is restored.
15 Repeat the above procedure on the remaining front brake caliper.
16 Refit the roadwheels, then lower the vehicle to the ground and tighten the roadwheel bolts to the specified torque.

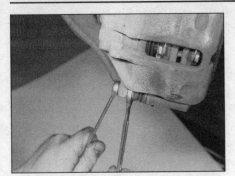

4.19 On Girling calipers, remove the lower guide pin bolt, holding the pin as shown

4.20a Pivot the caliper upwards . . .

4.20b . . . then remove the shim from the caliper piston . . .

17 New pads will not give full braking efficiency until they have bedded-in. Be prepared for this, and avoid hard braking as far as possible for the first hundred miles or so after pad renewal.

Girling caliper

Removal

Note: *A new lower caliper guide pin bolt will be required on refitting.*

18 Proceed as described in paragraphs 1 and 2.

19 Slacken and remove the lower caliper guide pin bolt, using a slim open-ended spanner to prevent the guide pin itself from rotating **(see illustration)**. Discard the guide pin bolt - a new bolt must be used on refitting.

20 With the lower guide pin bolt removed, pivot the caliper upwards until it is clear of the brake pads and mounting bracket. Remove the shim from the caliper piston **(see illustrations)**.

21 Withdraw the two brake pads from the caliper mounting bracket **(see illustration)**. If the original pads are to be refitted, identify them so that they can be refitted in their original locations. Where applicable, disconnect the pad wear sensor wiring connector.

Inspection

22 Examine the pads and caliper as described previously in paragraphs 6 to 9, substituting 'guide pins' for references to spacers and bushes.

Refitting

23 Install the pads in the caliper mounting bracket, ensuring that the friction material of each pad is against the brake disc. If the original pads are being refitted, ensure that they are refitted to their original locations as noted before removal. Where applicable, note that the pad with the wear sensor wiring should be installed as the inner pad.

24 Refit the shim to the caliper piston. Pivot the caliper down into position and, where applicable, pass the pad warning sensor wiring through the caliper aperture. If the threads of the new guide pin bolt are not already pre-coated with locking compound, apply suitable thread-locking compound to them. Press the caliper into position whilst

ensuring that the pad anti-rattle springs locate correctly in the caliper. Install the guide pin bolt, tightening it to the specified torque while retaining the guide pin with an open-ended spanner **(see illustration)**.

25 Where applicable, reconnect the brake pad wear sensor wiring connectors, ensuring that the wiring is correctly routed.

26 Depress the brake pedal repeatedly, until the pads are pressed into firm contact with the brake disc, and normal (non-assisted) pedal pressure is restored.

27 Repeat the above procedure on the remaining front brake caliper.

28 Refit the roadwheels, then lower the vehicle to the ground and tighten the roadwheel bolts to the specified torque.

29 Check the hydraulic fluid level as described in *Weekly Checks*.

5 Front brake caliper -
removal, overhaul and refitting

Note: *Before starting work, refer to the note at the beginning of Section 2 concerning the dangers of hydraulic fluid, and to the warning at the beginning of Section 4 concerning the dangers of asbestos dust. On models with Girling calipers, new guide pin bolts will be required on refitting.*

Removal

1 Apply the handbrake, then jack up the front of the vehicle and support it on axle stands. Remove the appropriate roadwheel.

4.21 . . . and withdraw the pads from the caliper mounting bracket

2 Minimise fluid loss by first removing the master cylinder reservoir cap, and then tightening it down onto a piece of polythene, to obtain an airtight seal. Alternatively, use a brake hose clamp, a G-clamp or a similar tool to clamp the flexible hose.

3 Clean the area around the union, then loosen the brake hose union nut.

4 Remove the brake pads as described in Section 4.

5 On models with VW brake calipers, unscrew the caliper from the end of the brake hose and remove it from the vehicle.

6 On Girling calipers, slacken and remove the caliper upper guide pin bolt, using a slim open-ended spanner to prevent the guide pin itself from rotating, then unscrew the caliper from the brake hose and remove it from the vehicle. Discard the guide pin bolt - a new bolt must be used on refitting.

Overhaul

7 With the caliper on the bench, wipe away all traces of dust and dirt, but *avoid inhaling the dust, as it is injurious to health.*

8 Withdraw the partially-ejected piston from the caliper body, and remove the dust seal.

> **HAYNES HINT** *If the piston cannot be withdrawn by hand, it can be pushed out by applying compressed air to the brake hose union hole. Only low pressure should be required, such as is generated by a foot pump. As the piston is expelled, take great care not to trap your fingers between the piston and caliper.*

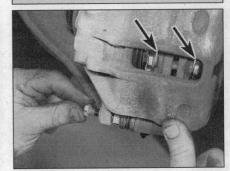

4.24 Ensure that the pad anti-rattle springs (arrowed) locate correctly in the caliper

9

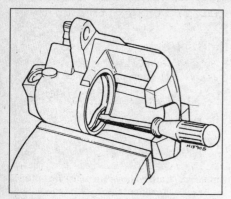

5.9 Use a small screwdriver to extract the caliper piston hydraulic seal

9 Using a small screwdriver, extract the piston hydraulic seal, taking great care not to damage the caliper bore **(see illustration)**.
10 Thoroughly clean all components, using only methylated spirit, isopropyl alcohol or clean hydraulic fluid as a cleaning medium. Never use mineral-based solvents such as petrol or paraffin, as they will attack the hydraulic system rubber components. Dry the components immediately, using compressed air or a clean, lint-free cloth. Use compressed air to blow clear the fluid passages.
11 On VW calipers, withdraw the spacers from the caliper body bushes.
12 On Girling calipers, withdraw the guide pins from the caliper mounting bracket, and remove the rubber gaiters.
13 Check all components, and renew any that are worn or damaged. Check particularly the cylinder bore and piston; these should be renewed (note that this means the renewal of the complete caliper body assembly) if they are scratched, worn or corroded in any way. Similarly check the condition of the spacers/guide pins and their bushes/bores (as applicable); both spacers/pins should be undamaged and (when cleaned) a reasonably tight sliding fit in their bores. If there is any doubt about the condition of any component, renew it.
14 If the assembly is fit for further use, obtain the appropriate repair kit; the components are available from Seat dealers in various combinations.
15 Renew all rubber seals, dust covers and caps disturbed on dismantling as a matter of course; these should never be re-used.
16 On reassembly, ensure that all components are clean and dry.
17 Soak the piston and the new piston (fluid) seal in clean hydraulic fluid. Smear clean fluid on the cylinder bore surface.
18 Fit the new piston (fluid) seal, using only your fingers (no tools) to manipulate it into the cylinder bore groove. Fit the new dust seal to the piston, and refit the piston to the cylinder bore using a twisting motion; ensure that the piston enters squarely into the bore. Press the piston fully into the bore, then press the dust seal into the caliper body.

19 On VW calipers, apply the grease supplied in the repair kit, or a copper-based high-temperature brake grease or anti-seize compound to the spacers and insert them into their bushes.
20 On Girling calipers, apply the grease supplied in the repair kit, or a copper-based high-temperature brake grease or anti-seize compound to the guide pins, and fit the new gaiters. Fit the guide pins to the caliper mounting bracket, ensuring that the gaiters are correctly located in the grooves on both the sleeve and mounting bracket.

Refitting

21 Screw the caliper fully onto the flexible hose union.
22 On Girling calipers, fit a new caliper upper guide pin bolt, and tighten to the specified torque, using a slim open-ended spanner to prevent the guide pin itself from rotating.
23 Refit the brake pads as described in Section 4.
24 Securely tighten the brake pipe union nut.
25 Remove the brake hose clamp or polythene, as applicable, and bleed the hydraulic system as described in Section 2. Note that, providing the precautions described were taken to minimise brake fluid loss, it should only be necessary to bleed the relevant front brake.
26 Refit the roadwheel, then lower the vehicle to the ground and tighten the roadwheel bolts to the specified torque.

6	Brake disc - inspection, removal and refitting

Note: *Before starting work, refer to the note at the beginning of Section 4 concerning the dangers of asbestos dust.*

Front brake disc

Inspection

Note: *If either disc requires renewal, BOTH should be renewed at the same time, to ensure even and consistent braking. New brake pads should also be fitted.*
1 Apply the handbrake, then jack up the front of the car and support it on axle stands.

6.8 Removing a front brake disc securing screw

6.3 Measuring front brake disc thickness using a micrometer

Remove the appropriate front roadwheel.
2 Slowly rotate the brake disc so that the full area of both sides can be checked; remove the brake pads if better access is required to the inboard surface. Light scoring is normal in the area swept by the brake pads, but if heavy scoring or cracks are found, the disc must be renewed.
3 It is normal to find a lip of rust and brake dust around the perimeter of the disc; this can be scraped off if required. If, however, a lip has formed due to excessive wear of the brake pad swept area, then the disc thickness must be measured using a micrometer **(see illustration)**. Take measurements at several places around the disc, at the inside and outside of the pad swept area; if the disc has worn at any point to the specified minimum thickness or less, the disc must be renewed.
4 If the disc is thought to be warped, it can be checked for run-out. Either use a dial gauge mounted on any convenient fixed point, while the disc is slowly rotated, or use feeler blades to measure (at several points all around the disc) the clearance between the disc and a fixed point, such as the caliper mounting bracket. If the measurements obtained are at the specified maximum or beyond, the disc is excessively warped, and must be renewed; however, it is worth checking first that the hub bearing is in good condition (Chapters 1 and/or 10). If the run-out is excessive, the disc must be renewed.
5 Check the disc for cracks, especially around the wheel bolt holes, and any other wear or damage, and renew if necessary.

Removal

6 On models with VW front brake calipers, remove the brake pads as described in Section 4.
7 On models with Girling front brake calipers, unscrew the two bolts securing the brake caliper mounting bracket to the hub carrier, then slide the caliper assembly off the disc. Using a piece of wire or string, tie the caliper to the front suspension coil spring, to avoid placing any strain on the brake hose.
8 Use chalk or paint to mark the relationship of the disc to the hub, then remove the screw securing the brake disc to the hub, and remove the disc **(see illustration)**. If it is tight, tap its rear face with a hide or plastic mallet.

Refitting

9 Refitting is the reverse of the removal procedure, noting the following points:

a) *Ensure that the mating surfaces of the disc and hub are clean and flat.*

b) *Align (if applicable) the marks made on removal, and securely tighten the disc retaining screw.*

c) *If a new disc has been fitted, use a suitable solvent to wipe any preservative coating from the disc, before refitting the caliper.*

d) *On models with Girling brake calipers, slide the caliper into position over the disc, making sure the pads pass either side of the disc. Tighten the caliper bracket mounting bolts to the specified torque.*

e) *On models with VW brake calipers, refit the pads as described in Section 4.*

f) *Refit the roadwheel, then lower the vehicle to the ground and tighten the roadwheel bolts to the specified torque. On completion, repeatedly depress the brake pedal until normal (non-assisted) pedal pressure returns.*

Rear brake disc

Inspection

Note: *If either disc requires renewal, BOTH should be renewed at the same time, to ensure even and consistent braking. New brake pads should be fitted also.*

10 Firmly chock the front wheels, then jack up the rear of the car and support it on axle stands. Remove the appropriate rear roadwheel.

11 Inspect the disc as described in paragraphs 2 to 5.

Removal

Note: *A new rear hub nut split pin will be required on refitting.*

12 Unscrew the two bolts securing the brake caliper mounting bracket in position, then slide the caliper assembly off the disc. Using a piece of wire or string, tie the caliper to the rear suspension coil spring, to avoid placing any strain on the hydraulic brake hose.

13 Using a hammer and a large flat-bladed screwdriver, carefully tap and prise the cap out of the centre of the brake disc. Renew the cap if it is damaged during removal.

14 Extract the split pin from the hub nut, and remove the locking cap. Discard the split pin; a new one must be used on refitting.

15 Slacken and remove the rear hub nut, then slide off the toothed washer and remove the outer bearing from the centre of the disc.

16 The disc can now be slide off the stub axle.

Refitting

17 If a new disc is being fitted, use a suitable solvent to wipe any preservative coating from the disc. If necessary, install the bearing races, inner bearing and oil seal as described in Chapter 10, and thoroughly grease the outer bearing.

18 Apply a smear of grease to the disc oil seal, and slide the assembly onto the stub axle.

19 Fit the outer bearing and toothed thrustwasher, ensuring that its tooth is correctly engaged in the stub axle slot.

20 Refit the hub nut, tightening it to the point where it just contacts the washer, whilst rotating the brake disc to settle the hub bearings in position. Gradually slacken the hub nut until the position is found where it is just possible to move the toothed washer from side-to-side using a screwdriver. **Note:** *Only a small amount of force should be needed to move the washer.* When the hub nut is correctly positioned, secure it in position with a new split pin.

21 Fit the cap to the centre of the brake disc, driving it fully into position.

22 Slide the caliper into position over the disc, making sure the pads pass either side of the disc. Tighten the caliper mounting bolts to the specified torque.

23 Refit the roadwheel, then lower the vehicle to the ground and tighten the wheel bolts to the specified torque.

7 Front brake disc shield - removal and refitting

Removal

1 Remove the brake disc as described in Section 6.

2 Unscrew the securing bolts, and remove the brake disc shield.

Refitting

3 Refitting is a reversal of removal. Refit the brake disc with reference to Section 6.

8 Rear brake shoes – inspection, removal and refitting

Note: *Before starting work, refer to the note at the beginning of Section 4 concerning the dangers of asbestos dust.*

Inspection

1 Remove the brake drum as described in Section 9.

2 Working carefully, and taking the necessary precautions, remove all traces of brake dust from the brake drum, backplate and shoes.

3 Measure the thickness of the friction material of each brake shoe at several points; if either shoe is worn at any point to the specified minimum thickness or less, **all four** shoes must be renewed as a set. The shoes should also be renewed if any are fouled with oil or grease; there is no way of degreasing friction material, once contaminated.

4 If any of the brake shoes are worn unevenly, or fouled with oil or grease, trace and rectify the cause before reassembly.

Removal

5 To renew the brake shoes, continue as follows. If all is well, refit the brake drum as described in Section 9.

6 Note the position of the brake shoes and springs, and make identifying marks on the webs of the shoes, if necessary, to aid refitting.

7 Using a pair of pliers, remove the shoe retainer spring cups by depressing and turning them through 90°. With the cups removed, lift off the springs and withdraw the retainer pins **(see illustrations)**.

8 Ease the shoes out one at a time from the lower pivot point, to release the tension of the return spring, then disconnect the lower return spring from both shoes **(see illustration)**.

8.7a Remove the shoe retainer spring cups . . .

8.7b . . . then lift off the springs . . .

8.7c . . . and withdraw the retainer pins

8.8 Ease the shoes out, then disconnect the lower return spring

8.9a Ease the upper ends of the shoes from the wheel cylinder. Note elastic band (arrowed) used to retain pistons

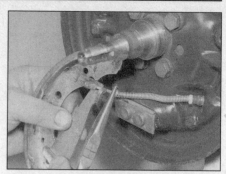

8.9b Disconnecting the handbrake cable from the trailing shoe

9 Ease the upper ends of both shoes out from their wheel cylinder locations, taking care not to damage the wheel cylinder seals, and disconnect the handbrake cable from the trailing shoe. The brake shoe assembly can then be manoeuvred out of position and away from the backplate. Do not depress the brake pedal until the brakes are reassembled; wrap a strong elastic band around the wheel cylinder pistons to retain them **(see illustrations)**.

10 Make a note of the correct fitted positions of all components **(see illustrations)**, then unhook the upper return spring, and disengage the wedge key spring.

11 Unhook the tensioning spring, and remove the pushrod from the trailing shoe, together with the wedge key.

12 Examine all components for signs of wear or damage, and renew as necessary. All return springs should be renewed, regardless of their apparent condition. Although linings are available separately (without shoes) from Seat dealers, renewal of the shoes complete with linings is to be preferred, unless the necessary skills and equipment are available to fit new linings to the old shoes.

13 Peel back the rubber protective caps, and check the wheel cylinder for fluid leaks or other damage; check that both cylinder pistons are free to move easily. Refer to Section 12, if necessary, for information on wheel cylinder overhaul.

Refitting

14 Apply a little brake grease to the contact areas of the pushrod and handbrake lever.

15 Hook the tensioning spring into the trailing shoe. Engage the pushrod with the opposite

end of the spring, and pivot the pushrod into position on the trailing shoe **(see illustrations)**.

16 Fit the wedge key between the trailing shoe and pushrod, making sure it is fitted the correct way around **(see illustration)**.

17 Locate the handbrake lever on the leading shoe in the pushrod, and fit the upper return spring using a pair of pliers **(see illustrations)**.

18 Fit the spring to the wedge key, and hook it onto the trailing shoe **(see illustration)**.

19 Prior to installation, clean the backplate, and apply a thin smear of high-temperature brake grease or anti-seize compound to all those surfaces of the backplate which bear on the shoes, particularly the wheel cylinder pistons and lower pivot point. Do not allow the lubricant to foul the friction material.

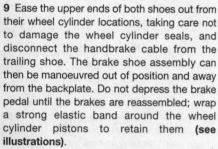

8.10a Make a note of the correct fitted positions of all components

8.10b Alternative adjuster strut component layout

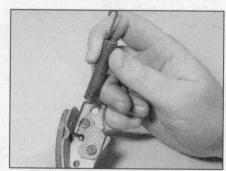

8.15a Hook the tensioning spring into the trailing shoe . . .

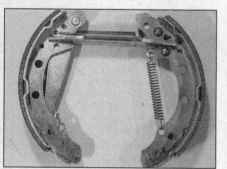

8.15b . . . then engage the pushrod with the opposite end of the spring . . .

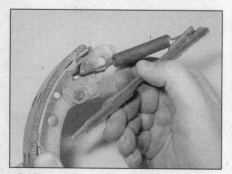

8.15c . . . and pivot the pushrod into position on the trailing shoe

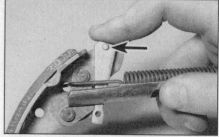

8.16 Fit the wedge key between the trailing shoe and the pushrod. Ensure that the raised dot (arrowed) is facing away from the shoe

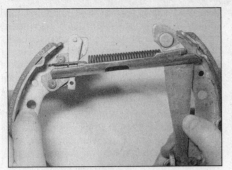

8.17a Locate the handbrake lever in the pushrod . . .

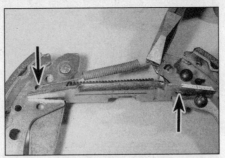

8.17b . . . and hook the upper return spring into the leading shoe and pushrod (arrowed)

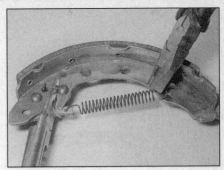

8.18 Fit the spring to the wedge key, and hook it into the trailing shoe

20 Remove the elastic band fitted to the wheel cylinder, and offer up the shoe assembly.

21 Connect the handbrake cable to the handbrake lever, and locate the top of the shoes in the wheel cylinder piston slots.

22 Fit the lower return spring to the shoes, then lever the bottom of the shoes onto the bottom anchor.

23 Tap the shoes to centralise them with the backplate, then refit the shoe retainer pins and springs, and secure them in position with the spring cups.

24 Refit the brake drum as described in Section 9.

25 Repeat the above procedure on the remaining rear brake assembly.

26 Once both sets of rear shoes have been renewed, adjust the lining-to-drum clearance by repeatedly depressing the brake pedal until

normally (non-assisted) pedal pressure returns.

27 Check and, if necessary, adjust the handbrake as described in Section 18.

28 On completion, check the hydraulic fluid level as described in *Weekly Checks*.

29 New shoes will not give full braking efficiency until they have bedded-in. Be prepared for this, and avoid hard braking as far as possible for the first hundred miles or so after shoe renewal.

9 Rear brake drum - removal, inspection and refitting

Note: *Before starting work, refer to the note at the beginning of Section 4 concerning the dangers of asbestos dust. A new rear hub nut split-pin will be required on refitting.*

Removal

1 Chock the front wheels, then jack up the rear of the vehicle and support it on axle stands. Remove the appropriate rear wheel.

2 Using a hammer and a large flat-bladed screwdriver, carefully tap and prise the cap out of the centre of the brake drum **(see illustration)**. Discard the cap if it is damaged during removal.

3 Extract the split pin from the hub nut and remove the locking cap **(see illustration)**. Discard the split pin; a new one must be used on refitting.

4 Slacken and remove the rear hub nut, then slide off the toothed washer and remove the outer bearing from the centre of the drum **(see illustrations)**.

5 It should now be possible to withdraw the brake drum assembly from the stub axle by hand **(see illustration)**. It may be difficult to remove the drum, due to the tightness of the hub bearing on the stub axle, or due to the brake shoes binding on the inner circumference of the drum. If the bearing is tight, tap the periphery of the drum using a hide or plastic mallet, or use a universal puller, secured to the drum with the wheel bolts, to pull it off. If the brake shoes are binding, first check that the handbrake is fully released, then continue as follows.

6 Referring to Section 18, fully slacken the handbrake adjustment, to obtain maximum free play in the cable.

7 Insert a screwdriver through one of the wheel bolt holes in the brake drum, and lever

9.2 Prise the cap out of the centre of the brake drum

9.3 Extract the split pin and remove the locking cap from the hub nut

9.4a Remove the hub nut and the toothed washer . . .

9.4b . . . and remove the outer bearing

9.5 Withdrawing the brake drum from the stub axle

9

9.7a Insert a screwdriver through one of the wheel bolt holes to retract the brake shoes . . .

9.7b . . . by levering the wedge key (arrowed) upwards

up the wedge key in order to allow the brake shoes to retract fully **(see illustrations)**. The brake drum can now be withdrawn.

Inspection

Note: *If either drum requires renewal, BOTH should be renewed at the same time, to ensure even and consistent braking. New brake shoes should also be fitted.*

8 Working carefully, remove all traces of brake dust from the drum, but avoid inhaling the dust, as it is injurious to health.

9 Clean the outside of the drum, and check it for obvious signs of wear or damage, such as cracks around the roadwheel bolt holes; renew the drum if necessary.

10 Examine carefully the inside of the drum. Light scoring of the friction surface is normal, but if heavy scoring is found, the drum must be renewed. It is usual to find a lip on the drum's inboard edge which consists of a mixture of rust and brake dust; this should be scraped away, to leave a smooth surface which can be polished with fine (120- to 150-grade) emery paper. If, however, the lip is due to the friction surface being recessed by wear, then the drum must be renewed.

11 If the drum is thought to be excessively worn, or oval, its internal diameter must be measured at several points using an internal micrometer. Take measurements in pairs, the second at right-angles to the first, and compare the two, to check for signs of ovality. Provided that it does not enlarge the drum to beyond the specified maximum diameter, it may be possible to have the drum refinished by skimming or grinding; if this is not possible, the drums on both sides must be renewed. Note that if the drum is to be skimmed, BOTH drums must be refinished, to maintain a consistent internal diameter on both sides.

Refitting

12 If a new brake drum is to be installed, use a suitable solvent to remove any preservative coating that may have been applied to its interior. If necessary, install the bearing races, inner bearing and oil seal as described in Chapter 10, and thoroughly grease the outer bearing.

13 Prior to refitting, fully retract the brakes shoes by lifting up the wedge key.

14 Apply a smear of grease to the drum oil seal, and carefully slide the assembly onto the stub axle.

15 Fit the outer bearing and toothed thrustwasher, ensuring its tooth is correctly engaged in the stub axle slot.

16 Refit the hub nut, tightening it to the point where it just contacts the washer whilst rotating the brake drum to settle the hub bearings in position. Gradually slacken the hub nut until the position is found where it is just possible to move the toothed washer from side-to-side using a screwdriver. **Note:** *Only a small amount of force should be needed to move the washer.* When the hub nut is correctly positioned, refit the locking cap and secure the nut in position with a new split pin.

17 Fit the cap to the centre of the brake drum, driving it fully into position.

18 Depress the footbrake several times to operate the self-adjusting mechanism.

19 Repeat the above procedure on the remaining rear brake assembly (where necessary), then check and, if necessary, adjust the handbrake cable as described in Section 17.

20 On completion, refit the roadwheel(s), then lower the vehicle to the ground and tighten the wheel bolts to the specified torque.

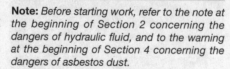

10 Rear wheel cylinder -
removal, overhaul and refitting

Note: *Before starting work, refer to the note at the beginning of Section 2 concerning the dangers of hydraulic fluid, and to the warning at the beginning of Section 4 concerning the dangers of asbestos dust.*

Removal

1 Remove the brake drum as described in Section 9.

2 Using pliers, carefully unhook the upper brake shoe return spring, and remove it from both brake shoes. Pull the upper ends of the shoes away from the wheel cylinder to disengage them from the pistons.

3 Minimise fluid loss by first removing the master cylinder reservoir cap, and then tightening it down onto a piece of polythene, to obtain an airtight seal. Alternatively, use a brake hose clamp, a G-clamp or a similar tool to clamp the flexible hose at the nearest convenient point to the wheel cylinder.

4 Wipe away all traces of dirt around the brake pipe union at the rear of the wheel cylinder, and unscrew the union nut. Carefully ease the pipe out of the wheel cylinder, and plug or tape over its end to prevent dirt entry. Wipe off any spilt fluid immediately.

5 Unscrew the two wheel cylinder retaining bolts from the rear of the backplate, and remove the cylinder, taking great care not to allow leaking hydraulic fluid to contaminate the brake shoe linings.

Overhaul

6 Brush the dirt and dust from the wheel cylinder, but take care not to inhale it.

7 Pull the rubber dust seals from the ends of the cylinder body.

8 The pistons will normally be ejected by the pressure of the coil spring, but if they are not, tap the end of the cylinder body on a piece of wood, or apply low air pressure - eg, from a foot pump - to the hydraulic fluid union hole to eject the pistons from their bores.

9 Inspect the surfaces of the pistons and their bores in the cylinder body for scoring, or evidence of metal-to-metal contact. If evident, renew the complete wheel cylinder assembly.

10 If the pistons and bores are in good condition, discard the seals and obtain a repair kit, which will contain all the necessary renewable items.

11 Remove the seals from the pistons noting their orientation. Lubricate the new piston seals with clean brake fluid, and fit them onto the pistons with their larger diameters innermost.

12 Dip the pistons in clean brake fluid, then fit the spring to the cylinder.

13 Insert the pistons into the cylinder bores using a twisting motion.

14 Fit the dust seals, and check that the pistons can move freely in their bores.

Refitting

15 Ensure that the backplate and wheel cylinder mating surfaces are clean, then spread the brake shoes and manoeuvre the wheel cylinder into position.

16 Engage the brake pipe, and screw in the union nut two or three turns to ensure that the thread has started.

17 Insert the two wheel cylinder retaining bolts, and tighten them to the specified torque. Now fully tighten the brake pipe union nut.

18 Remove the clamp from the flexible brake hose, or the polythene from the master cylinder reservoir (as applicable).

19 Ensure that the brake shoes are correctly located in the wheel cylinder pistons, then refit the brake shoe upper return spring, using a screwdriver to stretch the spring into position.

11.2 Disconnect the handbrake cable from the caliper

11.3 Slacken the caliper guide pin bolts, using a slim open-ended spanner to prevent the guide pins from rotating

11.4 Lift the caliper away from the pads . . .

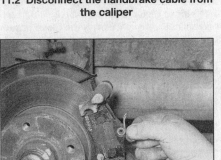

11.5a . . . then withdraw the outer . . .

11.5b . . . and inner pads from the caliper bracket . . .

11.5c . . . and recover the anti-rattle springs

20 Refit the brake drum as described in Section 9.

21 Bleed the brake hydraulic system as described in Section 2. Providing suitable precautions were taken to minimise loss of fluid, it should only be necessary to bleed the relevant rear brake.

11 Rear brake pads (rear disc brakes) – removal, inspection and refitting

Note: *Before starting work, refer to the note at the beginning of Section 4 concerning the dangers of asbestos dust. New caliper guide pin bolts will be required on refitting.*

Removal

1 Chock the front wheels, then jack up the rear of the vehicle and support it on axle stands. Remove the rear wheels.

2 Slacken the handbrake cable and detach it from the caliper as described in Section 20 **(see illustration)**.

3 Slacken and remove the caliper guide pin bolts, using a slim open-ended spanner to prevent the guide pins from rotating **(see illustration)**. Discard the guide pin bolts - new bolts must be used on refitting.

4 Lift the caliper away from the brake pads, and tie it to the suspension strut using a suitable piece of wire **(see illustration)**. Do not allow the caliper to hang unsupported on the flexible brake hose.

5 Withdraw the two brake pads from the caliper mounting bracket and recover the anti-rattle springs from the mounting bracket, noting their correct fitted locations **(see illustrations)**.

Inspection

6 First measure the thickness of each brake pad (including the backing plate). If either pad is worn at any point to the specified minimum thickness or less, **all four** pads must be renewed. Also, the pads should be renewed if any are fouled with oil or grease; there is no satisfactory way of degreasing friction material, once contaminated. If any of the brake pads are worn unevenly, or fouled with oil or grease, trace and rectify the cause before reassembly. New brake pads are available from Seat dealers.

7 If the brake pads are still serviceable, carefully clean them using a clean, fine wire brush or similar, paying particular attention to the sides and back of the metal backing. Clean out the grooves in the friction material (where applicable), and pick out any large embedded particles of dirt or debris. Carefully clean the pad locations in the caliper body/mounting bracket.

8 Prior to fitting the pads, check that the guide pins are free to slide easily in the caliper bracket, and check that the rubber guide pin gaiters are undamaged. Brush the dust and dirt from the caliper and piston, but **do not** inhale it, as it is injurious to health. Inspect the dust seal around the piston for damage, and the piston for evidence of fluid leaks, corrosion or damage. If attention to any of these components is necessary, refer to Section 11.

Refitting

9 If new brake pads are to be fitted, it will be necessary to retract the piston fully into the caliper bore, by rotating it in a clockwise direction **(see Tool Tip)**. Provided that the master cylinder reservoir has not been overfilled with hydraulic fluid, there should be no spillage, but keep a careful watch on the fluid level while retracting the piston. If the fluid level rises above the MAX level line at any time, the surplus should be syphoned off, or ejected through a plastic tube connected to the bleed screw (see Section 2). **Note:** *Do not syphon the fluid by mouth, as it is poisonous; use a syringe or an old poultry baster.*

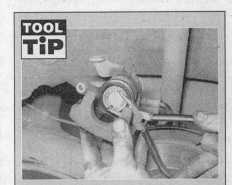

TOOL TIP

In the absence of the special tool, the piston can be screwed back into the caliper using a pair of circlip pliers

10 Fit the anti-rattle springs to the caliper mounting bracket, ensuring that they are correctly located. Install the pads in the mounting bracket, ensuring that each pad's friction material is against the brake disc.

11 Slide the caliper back into position over the pads.

12 If the threads of the new guide pin bolts are not already pre-coated with locking compound, apply a suitable thread-locking compound to them. Press the caliper into position, then install the bolts, tightening them to the specified torque setting while retaining the guide pin with an open-ended spanner.

13 Depress the brake pedal repeatedly, until the pads are pressed into firm contact with the brake disc, and normal (non-assisted) pedal pressure is restored.

14 Repeat the above procedure on the remaining rear brake caliper.

15 Reconnect the handbrake cables to the calipers, and adjust the handbrake as described in Section 17.

16 Refit the roadwheels, then lower the vehicle to the ground and tighten the road-wheel bolts to the specified torque setting.

17 Check the hydraulic fluid level as described in *Weekly Checks*.

18 New pads will not give full braking efficiency until they have bedded-in. Be prepared for this, and avoid hard braking as far as possible for the first hundred miles or so after pad renewal.

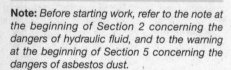

12 Rear brake caliper (rear disc brakes) - removal, overhaul and refitting

Note: *Before starting work, refer to the note at the beginning of Section 2 concerning the dangers of hydraulic fluid, and to the warning at the beginning of Section 5 concerning the dangers of asbestos dust.*

Removal

1 Chock the front wheels, then jack up the rear of the vehicle and support on axle stands. Remove the relevant rear wheel.

2 Minimise fluid loss by first removing the master cylinder reservoir cap, and then tightening it down onto a piece of polythene, to obtain an airtight seal. Alternatively, use a brake hose clamp, a G-clamp or a similar tool to clamp the flexible hose.

3 Clean the area around the union on the caliper, then loosen the brake hose union nut.

4 Remove the brake pads as described in Section 11.

5 Unscrew the caliper from the end of the flexible hose and remove it from the vehicle.

Overhaul

Note: *It is not possible to overhaul the brake caliper handbrake mechanism. If the mechanism is faulty, or fluid is leaking from the handbrake lever seal the caliper assembly must be renewed.*

6 With the caliper on the bench, wipe away all traces of dust and dirt, but avoid inhaling the dust, as it is injurious to health.

7 Using a small screwdriver, carefully prise out the dust seal from the caliper bore, taking care not to damage the piston.

8 Remove the piston from the caliper bore by rotating it in an anti-clockwise direction. This can be achieved using a suitable pair of circlip pliers engaged in the caliper piston slots. Once the piston turns freely but does not come out any further, the piston can be withdrawn by hand.

> **HAYNES HINT** *If the piston cannot be withdrawn by hand, it can be pushed out by applying compressed air to the brake hose union hole. Only low pressure should be required, such as is generated by a foot pump. As the piston is expelled, take care not to trap your fingers between the piston and caliper.*

9 Using a small screwdriver, extract the piston hydraulic seal(s), taking care not to damage the caliper bore.

10 Withdraw the guide pins from the caliper mounting bracket, and remove the guide sleeve gaiters.

11 Thoroughly clean all components, using only methylated spirit, isopropyl alcohol or clean hydraulic fluid as a cleaning medium. Never use mineral-based solvents such as petrol or paraffin, as they will attack the hydraulic system rubber components. Dry the components immediately, using compressed air or a clean, lint-free cloth. Use compressed air to blow clear the fluid passages.

12 Check all components, and renew any that are worn or damaged. Check particularly the cylinder bore and piston; these should be renewed (note that this means the renewal of the complete caliper body assembly) if they are scratched, worn or corroded in any way. Similarly check the condition of the spacers/guide pins and their bushes/bores (as applicable); both spacers/pins should be undamaged and (when cleaned) a reasonably tight sliding fit in their bores. If there is any doubt about the condition of any component, renew it.

13 If the assembly is fit for further use, obtain the appropriate repair kit; the components are available from Seat dealers in various combinations.

14 Renew all rubber seals, dust covers and caps disturbed on dismantling as a matter of course; these should never be re-used.

15 On reassembly, ensure that all components are clean and dry.

16 Soak the piston and the new piston (fluid) seal in clean hydraulic fluid. Smear clean fluid on the cylinder bore surface. Fit the new piston (fluid) seal(s), using only the fingers (no tools) to manipulate into the cylinder bore groove(s).

17 Fit the new dust seal to the piston groove, then refit the piston assembly. Turn the piston in a clockwise direction, using the method employed on dismantling, until it is fully retracted into the caliper bore.

18 Press the dust seal into position in the caliper housing.

19 Apply the grease supplied in the repair kit, or a copper-based brake grease or anti-seize compound, to the guide pins. Fit the new gaiters to the guide pins and fit the pins to the caliper mounting bracket, ensuring that the gaiters are correctly located in the grooves on both the pins and caliper bracket.

20 Prior to refitting, fill the caliper with fresh hydraulic fluid by slackening the bleed screw and pumping the fluid through the caliper until bubble-free fluid is expelled from the union hole.

Refitting

21 Screw the caliper fully onto the flexible hose union.

22 Refit the brake pads as described in paragraphs 10 to 12 of Section 11.

23 Securely tighten the brake pipe union nut.

24 Remove the brake hose clamp or remove the polythene from the fluid reservoir, as applicable, and bleed the hydraulic system as described in Section 2. Note that, providing the precautions described were taken to minimise brake fluid loss, it should only be necessary to bleed the relevant rear brake.

25 Connect the handbrake cable to the caliper, and adjust the handbrake as described in Section 18.

26 Refit the roadwheel, then lower the vehicle to the ground and tighten the roadwheel bolts to the specified torque. On completion, check the hydraulic fluid level as described in *Weekly Checks*.

13 Rear brake backplate - removal and refitting

Rear brake backplate removal is described as part of the rear stub axle removal and refitting procedure in Chapter 10, Section 12. Where applicable, the brake shoe and wheel cylinder components can be removed from the backplate as described in the relevant Sections of this Chapter.

14 Brake pedal - removal and refitting

Removal

1 Disconnect the battery negative lead.

2 Working in the driver's footwell, remove the glovebox (see Chapter 11, Section 31), and the lower facia panel.

3 Remove the brake light switch as described in Section 23.

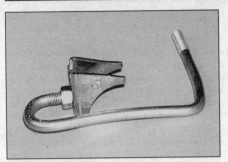

14.4a Improvised special tool constructed from a modified exhaust clamp, used to release the brake pedal from the vacuum servo pushrod

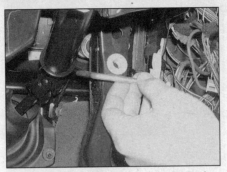

14.4b Using the tool to release the brake pedal from the servo pushrod

14.4c Rear view of brake pedal (pedal removed) showing plastic lugs (arrowed) securing pedal to servo pushrod

4 It is now necessary to release the brake pedal from the ball on the vacuum servo pushrod. To do this, a Seat special tool is available, but a suitable alternative can be improvised as shown. Note that the plastic lugs in the pedal are very stiff, and it will not be possible to release them by hand. Using the tool, release the securing lugs, and pull the pedal from the servo pushrod (see illustrations).

5 Carefully prise the retaining clip from the right-hand end of the pedal pivot shaft, noting its location and orientation to aid refitting (see illustration).

6 Slide the pedal pivot shaft to the left, until the brake pedal is free, then remove the pedal, unhooking the return spring from the pedal bracket as the pedal is withdrawn (see illustrations).

7 Carefully clean all components, and renew any that are worn or damaged.

Refitting

8 Prior to refitting, apply a smear of multi-purpose grease to the pivot shaft and pedal bearing surfaces.

9 Manoeuvre the pedal into position, and engage the end of the return spring with the pedal bracket.

10 Slide the pivot shaft into position. Make sure the flats on the end of the pivot shaft are positioned vertically, and slide on the right-hand shaft retaining clip, making sure it is securely clipped in position as noted before removal.

11 Hold the servo unit pushrod, and push the pedal back onto the pushrod ball. Make sure the pedal is securely fastened to the pushrod.

12 Refit the brake light switch as described in Section 22, then refit the lower facia panel and the glovebox. Reconnect the battery.

---

15 Servo unit -
testing, removal and refitting

Testing

1 To test the operation of the servo unit, depress the footbrake several times to exhaust the vacuum, then start the engine whilst keeping the pedal firmly depressed. As the engine starts, there should be a noticeable give in the brake pedal as the vacuum builds up. Allow the engine to run for at least two minutes, then switch it off. If the brake pedal is now depressed, it should feel normal, but further applications should result in the pedal feeling firmer, with the pedal stroke decreasing with each application.

2 If the servo does not operate as described, first inspect the servo unit non-return valve as described in Section 16. On diesel models, also check the operation of the vacuum pump as described in Section 27.

3 If the servo unit still fails to operate satisfactorily, the fault lies within the unit itself. Repairs to the unit are not possible - if faulty, the servo unit must be renewed.

Removal

Note: *On left-hand drive models equipped with ABS, it is not possible to remove the vacuum servo unit without first removing the hydraulic unit (see Section 25). Therefore, servo unit removal and refitting should be entrusted to a Seat dealer. A new servo unit gasket will be required on refitting.*

4 Remove the master cylinder as described in Section 17.

5 On models fitted with a hydraulic clutch, remove the clutch master cylinder as described in Chapter 6.

6 On models equipped with ABS, remove the brake pedal position sensor as described in Section 25.

7 Where applicable remove the heatshield from the servo, then carefully ease the vacuum hose out from the sealing grommet in the front of the servo.

8 Working in the driver's footwell, remove the glovebox (see Chapter 11, Section 31), and the facia lower trim panel, then remove the brake light switch as described in Section 22.

9 It is now necessary to release the brake pedal from the ball on the vacuum servo pushrod. To do this, a Seat special tool is available, but a suitable alternative can be improvised as shown. Note that the plastic lugs in the pedal are very stiff, and it will not be possible to release them by hand. Using the tool, release the securing lugs, and pull the pedal from the servo pushrod (see illustrations 14.4a to 14.4c).

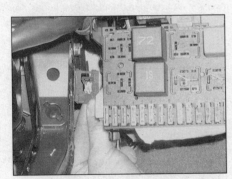

14.5 Prise the retaining clip from the right-hand end of the pedal pivot shaft

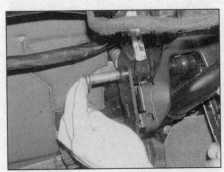

14.6a Slide out the pedal pivot shaft . . .

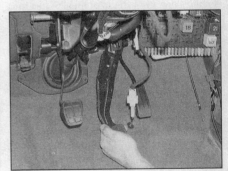

14.6b . . . then remove the pedal

9

10 Again working in the footwell, undo the three nuts securing the servo unit to the bulkhead, then return to the engine compartment and manoeuvre the servo unit out of position, noting the gasket which is fitted to the rear of the unit **(see illustration)**. Note that on some models, it may be necessary to remove the inlet manifold (see Chapter 4) to give sufficient clearance to withdraw the servo.

Refitting

11 Check the servo unit vacuum hose sealing grommet for signs of damage or deterioration, and renew if necessary.
12 Fit a new gasket to the rear of the servo unit, and reposition the unit in the engine compartment.
13 From inside the vehicle, ensure that the servo unit pushrod is correctly engaged with the brake pedal, and push the pedal onto the pushrod ball. Check the pushrod ball is securely engaged, then refit the servo unit mounting nuts and tighten them to the specified torque.
14 Carefully ease the vacuum hose back into position in the servo, taking great care not to displace the sealing grommet. Where applicable, refit the heatshield to the servo.
15 On models equipped with ABS, refit the brake pedal position sensor with reference to Section 25.
16 Refit the master cylinder as described in Section 17 of this Chapter. Where applicable, also refit the clutch master cylinder as described in Chapter 6.
17 Refit the brake light switch as described in Section 22.
18 Refit the lower facia panel, and refit the glovebox.
19 Where applicable, refit the inlet manifold as described in Chapter 4.
20 On completion, start the engine and check for air leaks at the vacuum hose-to-servo unit connection; check the operation of the braking system.

16 Servo non-return valve - testing, removal and refitting

1 The non-return valve is located in the vacuum hose from the inlet manifold to the brake servo. If the valve is to be renewed, the complete hose/valve assembly should be replaced.

Removal

2 Ease the vacuum hose out of the servo unit, taking care not to displace the grommet.
3 Note the routing of the hose, then slacken the retaining clip and disconnect the opposite end of the hose assembly from the manifold/pump hose, and remove it from the car.

Testing

4 Examine the check valve and vacuum hose for signs of damage, and renew if necessary.

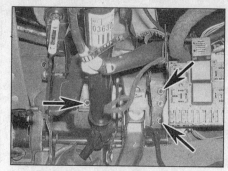

15.10 Vacuum servo securing nuts (arrowed)

5 The valve may be tested by blowing through it in both directions, air should flow through the valve in one direction only; when blown through from the servo unit end of the valve. Renew the valve if this is not the case.
6 Examine the servo unit rubber sealing grommet for signs of damage or deterioration, and renew as necessary.

Refitting

7 Ensure that the sealing grommet is correctly fitted to the servo unit.
8 Ease the hose union into position in the servo, taking great care not to displace or damage the grommet.
9 Ensure that the hose is correctly routed, and connect it to the inlet manifold/pump hose, tightening its retaining clip securely.
10 On completion, start the engine and check the valve-to-servo unit connection for signs of air leaks.

17 Master cylinder - removal, overhaul and refitting

Note: *Before starting work, refer to the warning at the beginning of Section 2 concerning the dangers of hydraulic fluid. A new master cylinder O-ring will be required on refitting.*

Removal

1 On models with ABS, the ABS hydraulic unit must be removed before the master cylinder can be removed.

17.5 Master cylinder-to-vacuum servo securing nut (arrowed)

Warning: Removal and refitting of the hydraulic unit should be entrusted to a Seat dealer. Great care has to be taken not to allow any fluid to escape from the unit as the pipes are disconnected. If the fluid is allowed to escape, air can enter the unit, causing air locks which cause the hydraulic unit to malfunction.

2 Disconnect the battery negative lead. Where necessary, to improve access to the master cylinder, remove the air inlet trunking. Similarly, on left-hand-drive models, if necessary, unbolt the coolant expansion tank from the body, and move it to one side leaving the hoses connected.
3 Remove the master cylinder reservoir cap (disconnect the wiring plug from the brake fluid level sender unit), and syphon the hydraulic fluid from the reservoir. **Note:** *Do not syphon the fluid by mouth, as it is poisonous; use a syringe or an old poultry baster.* Alternatively, open any convenient bleed screw in the system, and gently pump the brake pedal to expel the fluid through a plastic tube connected to the screw (see Section 2).
4 Wipe clean the area around the brake pipe unions on the side of the master cylinder, and place absorbent rags beneath the pipe unions to catch any leaking fluid. Make a note of the correct fitted positions of the unions, then unscrew the union nuts and carefully withdraw the pipes. Plug or tape over the pipe ends and master cylinder orifices, to minimise the loss of brake fluid, and to prevent the entry of dirt into the system. Wash off any spilt fluid immediately with cold water.
5 Slacken and remove the two nuts and washers securing the master cylinder to the vacuum servo unit, then withdraw the unit from the engine compartment **(see illustration)**. Remove the O-ring from the rear of the master cylinder, and discard it.

Overhaul

6 If the master cylinder is faulty, it must be renewed. Repair kits are not available from Seat dealer, so the cylinder must be treated as a sealed unit.
7 The only items which can be renewed are the mounting seals for the fluid reservoir; if these show signs of deterioration, pull off the reservoir and remove the old seals. Lubricate the new seals with clean brake fluid, and press them into the master cylinder ports. Ease the fluid reservoir into position, and push it fully home.

Refitting

8 Remove all traces of dirt from the master cylinder and servo unit mating surfaces, and fit a new O-ring to the groove on the master cylinder body.
9 Fit the master cylinder to the servo unit, ensuring that the servo unit pushrod enters the master cylinder bore centrally. Refit the master cylinder mounting nuts and washers, and tighten them to the specified torque.

10 Wipe clean the brake pipe unions, then refit them to the master cylinder ports and tighten them securely.

11 Refill the master cylinder reservoir with new fluid, and bleed the complete hydraulic system as described in Section 2.

18 Handbrake - adjustment

1 To check the handbrake adjustment, first apply the footbrake firmly several times to establish correct shoe-to-drum/pad-to-disc clearance, then apply and release the handbrake several times.

2 Applying normal moderate pressure, pull the handbrake lever to the fully-applied position, counting the number of clicks from the handbrake ratchet mechanism. If adjustment is correct, there should be approximately 4 to 7 clicks before the handbrake is fully applied. If this is not the case, adjust as follows.

3 Remove the handbrake cover or the centre console (see Chapter 11), as applicable, to gain access to the handbrake lever.

4 Chock the front wheels, then jack up the rear of the vehicle and support it on axle stands. Continue as described under the relevant sub-heading.

Rear drum brake models

5 With the handbrake set on the 4th notch of the ratchet mechanism, slacken the locknuts and rotate the adjusting nuts equally until it is difficult to turn both rear wheels/drums **(see illustration)**. Once this is so, release the handbrake lever, and check that the wheels/hubs rotate freely. Check the adjustment by applying the handbrake fully, and counting the clicks from the handbrake ratchet (see paragraph 2). If necessary re-adjust.

6 Once adjustment is correct, hold the adjusting nuts and securely tighten the locknuts. Refit the handbrake cover or the centre console, as applicable.

Rear disc brake models

7 With the handbrake fully released, equally slacken the handbrake adjuster locknuts and

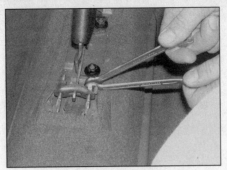

18.5 Slackening a handbrake adjuster locknut

adjusting nuts until both the rear caliper handbrake levers are back against their stops.

8 From this point, equally tighten both adjusting nuts until both handbrake levers just move off the caliper stops. Ensure that the gap between each caliper handbrake lever and its stop is less than 1.5 mm, and ensure both the right- and left-hand gaps are equal **(see illustration)**. Check that both wheels/discs rotate freely, then check the adjustment by applying the handbrake fully and counting the clicks from the handbrake ratchet (see paragraph 2). If necessary, re-adjust.

9 Once adjustment is correct, hold the adjusting nuts and securely tighten the locknuts. Refit the handbrake cover or the centre console, as applicable.

19 Handbrake lever - removal, overhaul and refitting

Removal

1 On models fitted with a centre console, remove the centre console as described in Chapter 11.

2 On models without a centre console, remove the handbrake lever cover as follows.

a) Lever up the flap at the rear of the handbrake cover to reveal the two cover securing screws.

b) Remove the screws and lift off the handbrake cover.

18.8 Adjust the handbrake to that the clearance between the handbrake lever and caliper (arrowed) is a stated

3 If desired, remove the handbrake lever cover sleeve by depressing the locating tag with a screwdriver, then sliding the sleeve from the lever.

4 Disconnect the wiring plug from the handbrake 'on' warning light switch **(see illustration)**.

5 Slacken the handbrake cable locknuts and adjuster nuts, then unscrew the two handbrake lever securing nuts **(see illustration)**.

6 Twist the lever to release the lever rod from the cable equaliser, then withdraw the lever **(see illustration)**.

Refitting

7 Refitting is a reversal of removal, bearing in mind the following points.

a) Prior to refitting the handbrake cover or centre console, as applicable, adjust the handbrake as described in Section 18.

b) On models without a centre console, when refitting the handbrake cover, make sure that the tang on the floor engages with the corresponding hole in the cover.

20 Handbrake cables - removal and refitting

Removal

1 Remove the handbrake lever cover, or the centre console, as applicable, to gain access to the handbrake lever. The handbrake cable

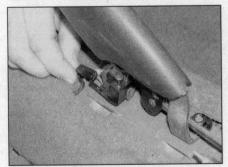

19.4 Disconnect the wiring plug from the handbrake 'on' warning light switch

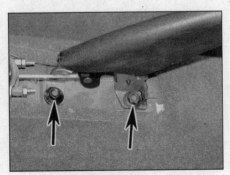

19.5 Handbrake lever securing nuts (arrowed)

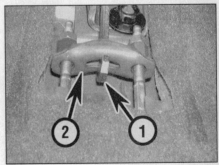

19.6 Twist the lever to release the lever rod (1) from the cable equaliser (2)

9

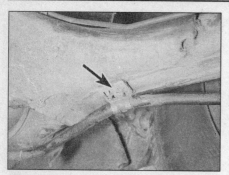

20.4 Release the retaining clip (arrowed) and detach the handbrake cable from the trailing arm

20.5 On models with drum brakes, release the cable from the brake backplate

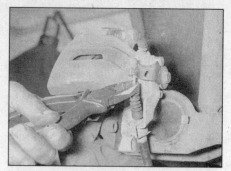

20.6a On models with rear disc brakes, disengage the inner cable from the caliper lever . . .

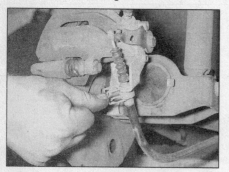

20.6b . . . then remove the outer cable retaining clip . . .

20.6c . . . and free the cable from the caliper bracket

consists of two sections, a right- and a left-hand section, which are linked to the lever by an equaliser plate. Each section can be removed individually.

2 Remove the relevant handbrake cable locknut and adjusting nut, and detach the cable from the compensator plate.

3 Chock the front wheels, then jack up the rear of the car and support it on axle stands.

4 Working back along the length of the cable, noting its correct routing, and free it from all the relevant guides and retaining clips **(see illustration)**.

5 On models with rear drum brakes, remove the rear brake shoes from the relevant side as described in Section 8. Using a hammer and pin punch, carefully tap the outer cable out from the brake backplate, then withdraw the cable from underneath the vehicle **(see illustration)**.

6 On models with rear disc brakes, disengage the inner cable from the caliper handbrake lever, then remove the outer cable retaining clip and detach the cable from the caliper **(see illustrations)**. Withdraw the cable from underneath the vehicle.

Refitting

7 Refitting is a reversal of removal, bearing in mind the following points.

a) When locating the handbrake cable sheath in the guide on the rear trailing arm, align the paint mark on the cable sheath with the guide.

b) On models with rear drum brakes, refit the brake shoes as described in Section 8.

c) Before refitting the handbrake cover to the centre console, adjust the handbrake as described in Section 18.

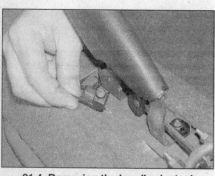

21.4 Removing the handbrake 'on' warning light switch

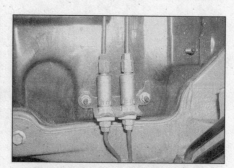

22.1 Pressure-sensitive rear brake pressure regulating valves mounted on engine compartment bulkhead

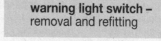

21 Handbrake 'on' warning light switch – removal and refitting

Removal

1 Disconnect the battery negative lead.

2 Remove the handbrake cover or the centre console, as applicable, with reference to Chapter 11 if necessary.

3 Disconnect the wiring plug from the switch.

4 Squeeze the securing lugs, and withdraw the switch from the handbrake lever assembly **(see illustration)**.

Refitting

5 Refitting is a reversal of removal.

22 Rear brake pressure-regulating valve - removal, refitting and adjustment

Pressure-sensitive valve

Removal

1 On models with pressure-sensitive valves, a separate valve is used for each rear brake circuit, and the valves are screwed into the master cylinder outlet ports, or fitted to a bracket on the engine compartment bulkhead, depending on model **(see illustration)**. To remove a valve, proceed as follows.

2 Minimise fluid loss by first removing the master cylinder reservoir cap, and then tightening it down onto a piece of polythene to obtain an airtight seal.

3 Wipe the area around the relevant regulating valve brake pipe union(s), and place rags beneath the pipe union(s) to catch any leaking fluid.

4 Unscrew the union nut(s) which connect(s) the brake pipe(s) to the end of the regulating valve, and carefully withdraw the pipe(s). Plug or tape over the pipe end(s) to prevent fluid leakage and the entry of dirt into the system.

5 On models with valves fitted to the master cylinder, unscrew the valve from the master cylinder, and plug or tape over the master

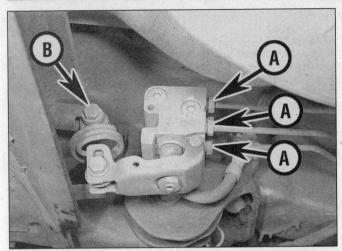

22.9 Load-dependent rear brake pressure regulating valve brake pipe unions (A) and spring pivot bolt (B)

22.11 Remove the nut and bolt (arrowed) securing the valve spring to the torsion beam

cylinder orifice to minimise the loss of brake fluid, and to prevent the entry of dirt into the system. Wash off any spilt fluid with cold water.

6 On models with valves mounted on the bulkhead, remove the clip securing the valve to the bracket, and remove the valve. Wash off any spilt fluid with cold water.

Refitting

7 Refitting is the reverse of the removal procedure, ensuring that the valve and pipe union nut(s) are securely tightened. On completion, bleed the complete braking system as described in Section 2.

Adjustment

8 No adjustment of the valves is necessary or possible.

Load-dependant valve

Removal

9 On models with a load-dependant valve, the valve is mounted on the left-hand rear torsion beam pivot bracket, and is connected to the torsion beam by a spring **(see illustration)**. As the load being carried by the vehicle is altered, the suspension moves in relation to the vehicle body, altering the tension in the spring. The spring moves the pressure-regulating valve lever so that the correct pressure is applied to the rear brakes to suit the load being carried. To remove the valve, proceed as follows.

10 Minimise fluid loss by first removing the master cylinder reservoir cap, and then tightening it down onto a piece of polythene to obtain an airtight seal.

11 Slacken and remove the nut and bolt securing the valve spring to the torsion beam **(see illustration)**.

12 Wipe clean the area around the brake pipe unions on the valve, and place rags beneath the pipe unions to catch any leaking fluid. Make identification marks on the brake

pipes; these marks can then be used on refitting to ensure each pipe is correctly reconnected.

13 Slacken the union nuts and disconnect the brake pipes from the valve. Plug or tape over the pipe ends and valve orifices, to minimise the loss of brake fluid and to prevent the entry of dirt into the system. Wash off any spilt fluid immediately with cold water.

14 Unscrew the two valve securing bolts and remove the pressure-regulating valve and spring from below the car **(see illustration)**.

Refitting

15 Refitting is the reverse of the removal procedure, noting the following points:

a) If a new valve is being fitted, set the spring adjustment bolt to the same position as the one on the old valve, and tighten it securely.

b) Ensure that the brake pipes are correctly connected to the valve, and that their union nuts are securely tightened.

c) Coat the ends of the spring with grease prior to installation.

d) Bleed the braking system (see Section 2).

e) On completion, adjust the valve as follows.

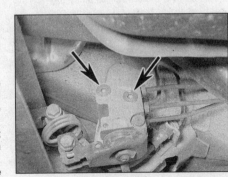

22.14 Load-dependent rear brake pressure regulating valve securing bolts (arrowed)

Adjustment

16 Before starting the adjustment procedure, the vehicle must be resting on its wheels, in an unladen condition (luggage compartment empty, fuel tank full, and driver's seat occupied).

17 Slacken the bolt securing the spring to the valve lever.

18 Adjust the position of the lever until the dimension shown between the centre of the lower valve securing bolt and the hole in the valve lever is as specified.

19 Adjust the position of the spring so that there is no free play (note that the spring securing bolt slot in the valve lever is slotted to allow adjustment), and re-check the dimension described in paragraph 18.

20 When the dimension described in paragraph 18 is correct, with no free play in the spring, tighten the bolt securing the spring to the valve lever.

21 If desired, a Seat dealer will be able to carry out a pressure check to ensure that the valve is operating correctly.

23 Brake light switch - removal and refitting

Removal

1 The brake light switch is located on the pedal bracket beneath the facia. Disconnect the battery negative lead.

2 Working in the driver's footwell, remove the lower facia panel. If desired to further improve access, the driver's side glovebox can be removed as described in Chapter 11, Section 31.

3 Reach up behind the facia and disconnect the wiring connector from the switch.

4 Twist the switch through 90° and release it from the mounting bracket **(see illustration)**.

9

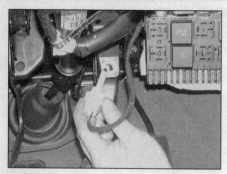

23.4 Removing the brake light switch

Refitting

5 Prior to installation, fully extend the brake light switch plunger.

6 Fully depress and hold the brake pedal, then manoeuvre the switch into position. Secure the switch in position it by pushing it into the bracket and twisting it through 90°, then release the brake pedal.

7 Reconnect the wiring connector, and check the operation of the brake lights. The brake lights should illuminate after the brake pedal has travelled approximately 5 mm. If the switch is not functioning correctly, it is faulty and must be renewed; no adjustment is possible.

8 On completion, refit the lower facia panel and, where applicable, the glovebox.

24 Anti-lock braking system (ABS) – general information and precautions

Note: *On models equipped with traction control, the ABS unit is a dual function unit, controlling both the anti-lock braking system (ABS) and the electronic differential locking (EDL) system functions.*

ABS is available as an option on most models covered in this manual. The system comprises a hydraulic unit (which contains the hydraulic solenoid valves and accumulators), the electrically-driven fluid return pump, four roadwheel sensors (one fitted to each wheel), the electronic control unit (ECU) and the brake pedal position sensor. The purpose of the system is to prevent wheel(s) locking during heavy braking. This is achieved by automatic release of the brake on the relevant wheel, followed by re-application of the brake.

The solenoids are controlled by the ECU, which itself receives signals from the four wheel sensors (one fitted on each hub), which monitor the speed of rotation of each wheel. By comparing these speed signals, the ECU can determine the speed at which the car is travelling. It can then use this speed to determine when a wheel is decelerating at an abnormal rate, compared to the speed of the car, and therefore predicts when a wheel is about to lock. During normal operation, the system functions in the same way as a non-

ABS braking system. In addition, the brake pedal position sensor (which is fitted to the vacuum servo unit) also informs the ECU of how hard the brake pedal is being depressed.

If the ECU senses that a wheel is about to lock, it operates the relevant solenoid valve in the hydraulic unit, which then isolates the brake caliper on the wheel which is about to lock from the master cylinder, effectively sealing-in the hydraulic pressure.

If the speed of rotation of the wheel continues to decrease at an abnormal rate, the ECU switches on the electrically-driven return pump, which pumps the hydraulic fluid back into the master cylinder, releasing pressure on the brake caliper so that the brake is released. Once the speed of rotation of the wheel returns to an acceptable rate, the pump stops; the solenoid valve opens, allowing the hydraulic master cylinder pressure to return to the caliper, which then re-applies the brake. This cycle can be carried out at up to 10 times a second.

The action of the solenoid valves and return pump creates pulses in the hydraulic circuit. When the ABS system is functioning, these pulses can be felt through the brake pedal.

The operation of the ABS system is entirely dependent on electrical signals. To prevent the system responding to any inaccurate signals, a built-in safety circuit monitors all signals received by the ECU. If an inaccurate signal or low battery voltage is detected, the ABS system is automatically shut down, and the warning light on the instrument panel is illuminated, to inform the driver that the ABS system is not operational. Normal braking should still be available, however.

If a fault does develop in the ABS system, the car must be taken to a Seat dealer for fault diagnosis and repair.

25 Anti-lock braking system (ABS) components – removal and refitting

Hydraulic unit

1 Removal and refitting of the hydraulic unit should be entrusted to a Seat dealer. Great care has to be taken not to allow any fluid to escape from the unit as the pipes are disconnected. If the fluid is allowed to escape, air can enter the unit, causing air locks which cause the hydraulic unit to malfunction.

Electronic control unit (ECU)

Removal

2 The ECU is located in the scuttle at the rear of the engine compartment, on the right-hand side on left-hand-drive models, or on the left-hand side on right-hand-drive models.

3 Disconnect the battery negative lead.

4 Remove the windscreen cowl panels as described in Chapter 11.

5 Release the securing clip, and disconnect the ECU wiring connector.

6 Release the wiring from the clips attached to the ECU mounting bracket.

7 Unscrew the nut and the bolt securing the ECU mounting bracket to the scuttle, then manipulate the ECU/mounting bracket assembly out from the scuttle.

8 If desired, the ECU can now be unbolted from the mounting bracket.

Refitting

9 Refitting is a reversal of removal.

Front wheel sensor

Removal

10 Chock the rear wheels, then firmly apply the handbrake, jack up the front of the car and support on axle stands. Remove the appropriate front roadwheel.

11 Trace the wiring back from the sensor to the connector, freeing it from all the relevant retaining clips, and disconnect the connector from the main loom (the sensor connectors are normally located on the sides of the suspension turrets in the engine compartment).

12 Slacken and remove the bolt securing the sensor to the hub carrier, and remove the sensor and lead assembly from the car.

Refitting

13 Prior to refitting, apply a thin coat of multi-purpose grease to the sensor tip (Seat recommend the use of lubricating paste G 000 650 - available from your dealer).

14 Ensure that the sensor and hub carrier sealing faces are clean, then fit the sensor to the hub carrier. Refit the retaining bolt and tighten it to the specified torque.

15 Ensure that the sensor wiring is correctly routed and retained by all the necessary clips, and reconnect the wiring connector.

16 Refit the roadwheel, then lower the car to the ground and tighten the roadwheel bolts to the specified torque.

Rear wheel sensor

Removal

17 Chock the front wheels, then jack up the rear of the car and support it on axle stands. Remove the appropriate roadwheel.

18 Remove the sensor as described in paragraphs 11 and 12, noting the following points.

a) *The sensors are fitted to the rear stub axle carriers.*

b) *The sensor wiring connectors are normally located inside the vehicle, under the rear seat cushion.*

Refitting

19 Refit the sensor as described above in paragraphs 13 to 16.

Front reluctor rings

20 The front reluctor rings are secured to the rear of the wheel hubs by three screws. Examine the rings for damage such as chipped or missing teeth. If renewal is necessary, the complete hub assembly must

be removed from the hub carrier and the bearings renewed as described in Chapter 10. With the hub removed, the reluctor ring can be removed after removing the securing screws.

Rear reluctor rings

21 The rear reluctor rings are pressed onto the inside of the rear brake drum/disc. Examine the rings for signs of damage such as chipped or missing teeth, and renew as necessary. If renewal is necessary, remove the drum/disc as described in Section 9 or 6 (as applicable) and take it to a Seat dealer, who will have access to the necessary tools required to extract the old ring and press on the new one.

Brake pedal position sensor

Removal

22 Release the vacuum from inside the servo unit by depressing the brake pedal several times. If desired, for improved access, unbolt the coolant expansion tank from the body, and move it to one side leaving the hoses connected.
23 Disconnect the battery negative lead, then disconnect the sensor wiring connector.
24 Using a small screwdriver, carefully lever off the sensor retaining clip, then withdraw the sensor from the front of the vacuum servo unit. Recover the sealing ring and clip.

Refitting

25 If a new sensor is being fitted, it will be supplied in a kit consisting of a sensor, sealing ring, circlip, and four spacers of different colours. Note the colour of the spacer fitted to the original sensor, and fit the relevant colour spacer to the new sensor. This is vital to ensure the correct operation of the ABS.
26 Fit the new circlip to the groove on the front of the vacuum servo unit, positioning its end gap over the servo unit sensor lower locating slot.
27 Fit the new sealing ring to the sensor, and lubricate it with a smear of oil to aid installation.

26.2 Servo unit vacuum pump retaining bolt (arrowed) – diesel model

28 Fit the sensor to the vacuum servo, aligning its locating notch with the servo unit upper groove. Push the sensor until it clicks into position, and check that it is securely retained by the circlip.
29 Reconnect the sensor wiring connector, and reconnect the battery negative lead.

26 Servo unit vacuum pump (diesel models) – removal and refitting

Removal

Note: *A new pump O-ring will be required on refitting.*
1 Release the retaining clip, and disconnect the vacuum hose from the top of pump.
2 Slacken and remove the retaining bolt, and remove the pump retaining clamp from the cylinder block **(see illustration)**.
3 Withdraw the vacuum pump from the cylinder block, and recover the O-ring seal. Discard the O-ring - a new one should be used on refitting.

Refitting

4 Fit the new O-ring to the vacuum pump, and apply a smear of oil to the O-ring to aid installation.
5 Manoeuvre the vacuum pump into position, making sure that the slot in the pump drive

26.5 Make sure that the slot in the pump drive gear aligns with the dog on the pump driveshaft

gear aligns with the dog on the pump driveshaft **(see illustration)**.
6 Refit the pump retaining clamp and securely tighten its retaining bolt.
7 Reconnect the vacuum hose to the pump, and secure it in position with the retaining clip.

27 Servo unit vacuum pump (diesel models) - testing and overhaul

1 The operation of the braking system vacuum pump can be checked using a vacuum gauge.
2 Disconnect the vacuum pipe from the pump, and connect the gauge to the pump union using a suitable length of hose.
3 Start the engine and allow it to idle, then measure the vacuum created by the pump. As a guide, after one minute, a minimum of approximately 500 mm Hg should be recorded. If the vacuum registered is significantly less than this, it is likely that the pump is faulty. However, seek the advice of a Seat dealer before condemning the pump.
4 Overhaul of the vacuum pump is not possible, since no major components are available separately for it; the only spare part readily available is the pump cover sealing ring. If faulty, the complete pump assembly must be renewed.

Chapter 10
Suspension and steering

Contents

Degrees of difficulty

Easy, suitable for novice with little experience	**Fairly easy,** suitable for beginner with some experience	**Fairly difficult,** suitable for competent DIY mechanic	**Difficult,** suitable for experienced DIY mechanic	**Very difficult,** suitable for expert DIY or professional

Specifications

Front suspension

Type .... Independent, with MacPherson struts incorporating coil springs and telescopic shock absorbers. Anti-roll bar fitted to most models

Rear suspension

Type .... Transverse torsion beam with trailing arms. Coil spring struts incorporating telescopic shock absorbers. Anti-roll bar on some models

Steering

Type .... Rack-and-pinion. Power assistance standard on certain models, optional on others

Number of turns from lock-to-lock:
  Manual steering 3.827
  Power steering 3.2

Wheel alignment and steering angles*

Front wheel alignment:
  Camber angle:
    All models except Sport .... -30' ± 20'
    Sport models .... -35' ± 20'
    Maximum difference in camber angle between sides .... 30'
  Castor angle (not adjustable):
    All models except Vario and Sport .... 1° 26' ± 30'
    Vario models .... 1° 12' ± 30'
    Sport models .... 1° 32' ± 30'
    Maximum difference in castor angle between sides .... 30'
  Toe setting (all models) .... 0° ± 10'
Rear wheel alignment:
  Camber angle (not adjustable) .... -1° 30' ± 30'
  Maximum difference in camber angle between sides .... 30'
  Toe setting .... 20' ± 10' toe-in

Refer to a Seat dealer for the latest recommendations – all values are for an unladen vehicle.

10

Roadwheels

Type .... Pressed-steel or aluminium alloy (depending on model)
Size:
  Roadwheels .... 5J x 13, 5.5J x 13, 6J x 14, 6J x 15 or 6J x 16
  'Space saver' spare wheel .... 3.5J x 14 or 3.5J x 15

Tyres

Pressures - Refer to the sticker attached to the rear of the fuel filler cap or *Weekly checks* on Page 0•17
Sizes:*
  Roadwheels:
    5J x 13 wheels .... 155 R 13, 155/80 R 13 or 175/70 R 13
    5.5J x 13 wheels .... 175/70 R 13
    6J x 14 wheels .... 185/60 R 14
    6J x 15 wheels .... 185/55 R 15
    6J x 16 wheels .... 195/45 R 16
  Spare wheel:
    3.5J x 14 wheel .... 105/70 R 14
    3.5J x 15 wheel .... 115/70 R 15
Consult your handbook, a Seat dealer or a suitable tyre dealer for the correct size for your vehicle

Torque wrench settings

	Nm	lbf ft
Front suspension		
Anti-roll bar connecting link retaining nut	25	18
Lower arm balljoint:		
Clamp bolt nut	50	37
Retaining bolts	35	26
Lower arm front pivot bolt:		
Stage 1	50	37
Stage 2	Angle-tighten a further 90°	
Lower arm rear mounting bolt:		
Stage 1	70	52
Stage 2	Angle-tighten a further 90°	
Subframe mounting bolts:		
Front mounting bolts:		
Stage 1	70	52
Stage 2	Angle-tighten a further 90°	
Rear mounting bolts	65	48
Subframe vibration damper mounting nuts	25	18
Suspension strut spring seat retaining nut	40	30
Suspension strut-to-hub carrier bolt nut	95	70
Suspension strut upper mounting nuts	60	44
Rear suspension		
Rear suspension torsion beam/trailing arms assembly pivot bolts	60	44
Stub axle/backplate retaining bolts	60	44
Suspension strut:		
Lower mounting bolt	70	52
Spring retaining plate nut	15	11
Upper mounting bottom nut	15	11
Upper mounting top nut	25	18
Steering		
Intermediate shaft clamp bolts	30	22
Intermediate shaft connecting piece nuts	25	18
Power steering pump:		
Feed pipe union bolt	30	22
Mounting bolts	20	15
Pulley retaining bolts	20	15
Swivel bracket and mounting bracket bolts	25	18
Steering gear:		
Power steering pipe union nuts	30	22
Retaining nuts	30	22
Steering wheel nut	40	30
Track rod balljoint:		
Locknut	50	37
Retaining nut	35	26
Roadwheels		
Roadwheel bolts	110	81

2.6 Separating the track rod balljoint from the hub carrier. Leave the nut (arrowed) in place to protect the balljoint threads

2.7 Remove the retaining plate from the top of the lower arm

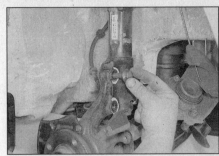

2.8 Mark their positions on the strut, then remove the suspension strut-to-hub carrier bolts

1 General information

The independent front suspension is of the MacPherson strut type, incorporating coil springs and integral telescopic shock absorbers. The struts are located by transverse lower suspension arms, which are mounted on a subframe, via rubber inner mounting bushes, and incorporate a balljoint at the outer ends. The front hub carriers, which carry the wheel bearings, brake calipers and the hub/disc assemblies, are bolted to the MacPherson struts, and connected to the lower arms through the balljoints. A front anti-roll bar is fitted to most models. The anti-roll bar is rubber-mounted, and is connected to both lower suspension arms.

The rear suspension consists of a torsion beam/trailing arm assembly, with the rear ends of the trailing arms located by suspension struts. On certain models, an anti-roll bar is incorporated into the torsion beam/trailing arm assembly; this links both trailing arms, and is situated just to the rear of the torsion beam.

The steering column incorporates a universal joint, and is connected to the steering gear by a second universal joint.

The steering gear is mounted onto the front subframe, and is connected by two track rods, with balljoints at their outer ends, to the steering arms projecting rearwards from the hub carriers. The track rod ends are threaded, to facilitate adjustment.

Power-assisted steering is fitted as standard on some models, and is available as an option on all others. The hydraulic steering system is powered by a belt-driven pump, which is driven from the crankshaft pulley.

2 Front hub carrier – removal and refitting

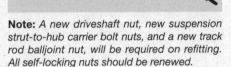

Note: *A new driveshaft nut, new suspension strut-to-hub carrier bolt nuts, and a new track rod balljoint nut, will be required on refitting. All self-locking nuts should be renewed.*

Removal

1 Remove the wheel trim/hub cap (as applicable) and slacken the driveshaft retaining nut with the vehicle resting on its wheels. Also slacken the wheel bolts.
2 Chock the rear wheels, firmly apply the handbrake, then jack up the front of the car and support it on axle stands. Remove the front roadwheel.
3 Remove the driveshaft retaining nut and (where fitted) its washer.
4 On models with ABS, remove the wheel sensor as described in Chapter 9.
5 If the hub bearings are to be disturbed, remove the brake disc as described in Chapter 9. If no work is to be carried out on the hub bearings, remove the brake pads as described in Chapter 9, but additionally, on models with Girling calipers, unscrew the upper caliper guide pin bolt (discard the bolt – a new bolt must be used on refitting). Using a piece of wire or string, tie the caliper to the front suspension coil spring, to avoid placing any strain on the hydraulic brake hose.
6 Slacken the nut securing the steering gear track rod balljoint to the hub carrier – leave the nut in place on the end of the balljoint threads to protect the threads. Release the balljoint tapered shank using a universal balljoint separator, then remove the nut completely once the taper has been released **(see illustration)**.
7 Using a suitable marker pen, draw around the end of the suspension lower arm, marking the correct fitted position of the balljoint. Unscrew the balljoint retaining bolts, and remove the retaining plate from the top of the lower arm **(see illustration)**. **Note:** *On certain models, the inner retaining bolt hole in the balljoint is slotted;*

on these models, the inner retaining bolt can be slackened, leaving the retaining plate and bolt in position in the arm, and the balljoint can then be disengaged from the bolt.
8 Using a suitable marker pen, draw around the outline of each suspension strut-to-hub carrier bolt, marking their positions on the strut. Slacken and remove both nuts and bolts **(see illustration)**.
9 Free the hub carrier from the strut, then carefully pull the hub assembly outwards and withdraw the driveshaft outer constant velocity joint from the hub assembly **(see illustration)**. The driveshaft outer joint will be a tight fit in the hub - tap the joint out of the hub using a soft-faced mallet. If this fails, the joint will have to be pressed out of the hub using a suitable tool bolted to the hub.

Refitting

10 Note that all self-locking nuts disturbed on removal must be renewed as a matter of course. These nuts have threads which are pre-coated with locking compound (this is only effective once), and include the driveshaft nut, the track rod balljoint nut, and the suspension strut-to-hub carrier bolt nuts.
11 Ensure that the outer joint and hub splines are clean and dry.
12 Manoeuvre the hub carrier assembly into position, and engage the hub with the driveshaft outer joint. Ensure that the threads on the end of the driveshaft are clean, and apply a smear of oil to the contact face of the new driveshaft nut. Fit the washer (where applicable) and nut, and use the nut to draw the joint fully into position in the hub **(see illustration)**.

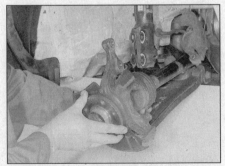

2.9 Free the hub carrier from the strut, and withdraw the assembly from the vehicle

2.12 Fit the washer and driveshaft nut, and use the nut to draw the driveshaft into position

10

13 Engage the hub carrier with the suspension strut, whilst aligning the balljoint with the lower arm.

14 Insert the strut-to-hub carrier bolts, and fit the new retaining nuts. Align the bolts with the marks made prior to removal, and tighten the nuts to the specified torque.

15 Refit the lower arm balljoint retaining bolts. Align the balljoint with the marks made prior to removal, then tighten the retaining bolts to the specified torque.

16 Engage the track rod balljoint with the hub carrier, then fit a new retaining nut and tighten it to the specified torque.

17 Where necessary, refit the brake disc to the hub, with reference to Chapter 9.

18 Refit the brake pads and the caliper as described in Chapter 9.

19 Where necessary, refit the ABS wheel sensor as described in Chapter 9.

20 Ensure that the driveshaft outer joint is drawn fully into position in the hub, then refit

the roadwheel and lower the vehicle to the ground.

21 Tighten the driveshaft retaining nut to the specified torque (see Chapter 8), then tighten the roadwheel bolts to the specified torque.

Note: *On completion, it is advisable to have the front wheel camber angle checked and, if necessary, adjusted (see Section 25).*

3 Front hub bearings – renewal

Note: *The bearing is a sealed, pre-adjusted and pre-lubricated, double-row roller type, and is intended to last the car's entire service life without maintenance or attention. Never overtighten the driveshaft nut beyond the specified torque wrench setting in an attempt to adjust the bearing.*

Note: *A press will be required to dismantle and rebuild the assembly; if such a tool is not*

available, a large bench vice and spacers (such as large sockets) will serve as an adequate substitute. The bearing inner races are an interference fit on the hub; if the inner race remains on the hub when the hub is pressed out of the hub carrier, a knife-edged bearing puller will be required to remove it. New bearing retaining circlips will be required on refitting.

1 Remove the hub carrier assembly as described in Section 2 **(see illustration)**.

2 If not already done, remove the brake disc, with reference to Chapter 9 if necessary.

3 Support the hub carrier securely on blocks or in a vice. Using a tubular spacer which bears only on the inner end of the hub flange, press the hub flange out of the bearing. If the bearing outboard inner race remains on the hub, remove it using a bearing puller (see note above). If necessary, unscrew the retaining screws and remove the ABS rotor from the rear of the hub. If desired, the brake disc shield can now be unbolted from the hub carrier.

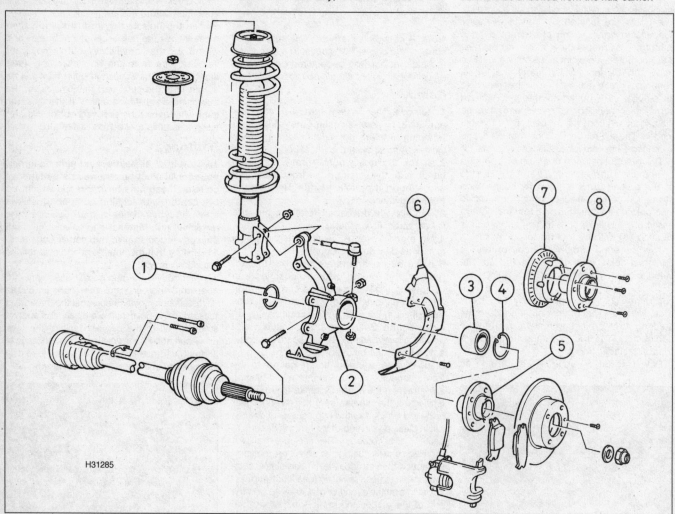

H31285

3.1 Exploded view of front hub components

1 *Bearing inboard retaining circlip*	4 *Bearing outboard retaining circlip*	6 *Brake disc shield*
2 *Hub carrier*		7 *ABS rotor*
3 *Bearing*	5 *Hub flange*	8 *Hub flange*

3.4 Removing the front hub bearing inboard retaining circlip

4.3 Remove the strut-to-hub carrier bolts, and unclip the brake hose (arrowed) from the strut

4.4a Remove the plastic cover . . .

4 Extract the bearing inboard and outboard bearing retaining circlips from the hub carrier assembly, using a large pair of circlip pliers **(see illustration)**.

5 Securely support the outer face of the hub carrier. Using a tubular spacer, press the complete bearing assembly out of the hub carrier.

6 Thoroughly clean the hub and hub carrier, removing all traces of dirt and grease, and polish away any burrs or raised edges which might hinder reassembly. Check the hub carrier and the hub for cracks or any other signs of wear or damage, and renew them if necessary. Renew the circlips, regardless of their apparent condition.

7 On reassembly, apply a light coating of molybdenum disulphide grease to the bearing outer race and the bearing surface in the hub carrier.

8 Fit the new outboard bearing retaining circlip, ensuring that it locates correctly in the groove in the hub carrier.

9 Securely support the outboard face of the hub carrier, and locate the bearing in the hub carrier. Press the bearing fully into position, ensuring that it enters the hub carrier squarely, using a tubular spacer which bears only on the bearing outer race. Press the bearing into position until it contacts the shoulder in the hub carrier, or the outboard bearing retaining circlip, as applicable.

10 Once the bearing is correctly seated, secure the bearing in position with the new inboard circlip, ensuring that it is correctly located in the groove in the hub carrier.

11 Where applicable, refit the ABS rotor to the

rear of the hub, and securely tighten the retaining screws. Make sure that the mating faces of the hub and rotor are clean and dry before fitting.

12 Support the outer face of the hub flange, and locate the hub bearing inner race over the end of the hub. Press the bearing onto the hub, using a tubular spacer which bears only on the inner race of the bearing, until it seats against the shoulder on the hub. Check that the hub rotates freely, and wipe off any excess oil or grease.

13 Refit the brake disc, with reference to Chapter 9 if necessary, then refit the hub carrier assembly as described in Section 2.

---

4 Front suspension strut – removal, overhaul and refitting

Note: *New suspension strut upper and lower retaining nuts will be required on refitting.*

Removal

1 Chock the rear wheels, apply the handbrake, then jack up the front of the vehicle and support securely on axle stands. Remove the appropriate roadwheel.

2 Unbolt the brake fluid hose/ABS sensor wiring bracket from the lower end of the strut, and move the hose/wiring to one side.

3 Using a suitable marker pen, draw around the outline of each suspension strut-to-hub carrier bolt, marking their positions on the strut. Slacken and remove both nuts and bolts, and unclip the brake hose from the strut **(see illustration)**.

4 Working in the engine compartment, unclip the plastic cover (where fitted) from the strut upper mounting, then slacken and remove the strut upper mounting nut and recover the mounting plate. Note that it may be necessary to counterhold the strut piston with a suitable Allen key, to prevent it from rotating as the nut is slackened **(see illustrations)**.

5 Free the strut from the hub carrier and manoeuvre it out from underneath the wheel arch. Where necessary, recover the mounting bush from the top of the strut.

Overhaul

> ⚠️ **Warning: Before attempting to dismantle the suspension strut, a suitable tool to hold the coil spring in compression must be obtained. Adjustable coil spring compressors are readily available, and are recommended for this operation. Any attempt to dismantle the strut without such a tool is likely to result in damage or personal injury.**

Note: *A special slotted socket is required to remove and refit the upper spring seat retaining nut; alternatives from the manufacturer's tool are available from specialist automotive tool manufacturers* **(see Tool Tip)**.

4.4b . . . then unscrew the strut upper mounting nut . . .

4.4c . . . and lift off the mounting plate

TOOL TiP

In the absence of the special Seat/VW tool, an alternative can be fabricated from a long-reach 13 mm socket. Cut the lower end of the socket to leave two teeth (A) which will engage with the slots in the strut nut, and file the upper end of the socket (B) so that it can be held with an open-ended spanner

10

4.14a Slide the rubber damper and protective sleeve onto the strut . . .

4.14b . . . and refit the washer to the piston

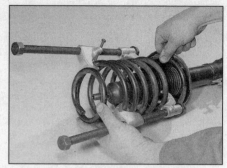

4.14c Fit the coil spring to the strut . . .

4.14d . . . and fit the upper spring seat to the top of the spring

4.14e Fit the strut mounting assembly . . .

4.14f . . . and screw the slotted nut onto the strut piston

6 With the strut removed from the car, clean away all external dirt, then mount it upright in a vice.

7 Fit the spring compressor, and compress the coil spring until all tension is relieved from the upper spring seat.

8 Using the special slotted socket, slacken and remove the upper spring seat retaining nut and lift off the strut mounting, upper spring seat and washer.

9 Lift off the coil spring, and remove the rubber damper and sleeve from the strut.

10 With the strut assembly now completely dismantled, examine all the components for wear, damage or deformation, and check the bearing for smoothness of operation. Renew any of the components as necessary.

11 Examine the strut for signs of fluid leakage. Check the strut piston for signs of pitting along its entire length, and check the strut body for

signs of damage. While holding it in an upright position, test the operation of the strut by moving the piston through a full stroke, and then through short strokes of 50 to 100 mm. In both cases, the resistance felt should be smooth and continuous. If the resistance is jerky, or uneven, or if there is any visible sign of wear or damage to the strut, renewal is necessary.

12 If any doubt exists about the condition of the coil spring, carefully remove the spring compressors, and check the spring for distortion and signs of cracking. Renew the spring if it is damaged or distorted, or if there is any doubt as to its condition.

13 Inspect all other components for signs of damage or deterioration, and renew any that are suspect.

14 To reassemble the strut, follow the accompanying photos, beginning with illustration 4.14a. Be sure to stay in order, and

carefully read the caption underneath each **(see illustrations)**.

Refitting

15 Ensure that the mounting bush (where fitted) is in position on the top of the strut, then manoeuvre the strut into position and engage it with the hub carrier.

16 Make sure the top of the strut is correctly located, then insert the strut-to-hub carrier bolts and fit the new retaining nuts.

17 Fit the mounting plate to the top of the strut, and fit the new upper mounting nut. Tighten the nut to the specified torque setting and (where applicable) refit the cover.

18 Align the strut-to-hub carrier bolts with the marks made on removal, and tighten the retaining new nuts to the specified torque **(see illustration)**. Refit the brake fluid hose/ABS sensor wiring bracket to the lower

4.14g Tighten the slotted nut to the specified torque setting . . .

4.14h . . . then release the compressors, ensuring that the spring ends are located against the stops on the upper and lower seats

4.18 Align the marks made prior to removal, and tighten the strut-to-hub carrier bolts to the specified torque

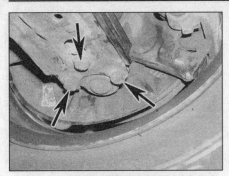

5.3 Lower arm balljoint retaining bolts (arrowed)

5.4a Remove the lower arm pivot bolt . . .

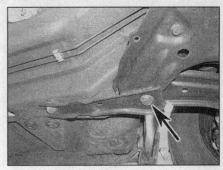

5.4b . . . and rear mounting bolt (arrowed)

end of the strut, and securely tighten the retaining bolt.

19 Refit the roadwheel, and tighten the wheel bolts to the specified torque. **Note:** *On completion, it is advisable to have the front wheel camber angle checked and, if necessary, adjusted (see Section 25).*

5 Front suspension lower arm – removal and refitting

Note: *A new lower arm pivot bolt and rear mounting bolt will be required on refitting.*

Removal

1 Chock the rear wheels, firmly apply the handbrake, then jack up the front of the vehicle and support securely on axle stands. Remove the appropriate front roadwheel.

2 Where applicable, remove the anti-roll bar connecting link as described in Section 8.

3 Using a suitable marker pen, draw around the end of the suspension lower arm, marking the correct fitted position of balljoint, then slacken and remove the balljoint retaining bolts and lift off the retaining plate from the top of the lower arm **(see illustration)**.

4 Slacken and remove the lower arm pivot bolt and rear mounting bolt **(see illustrations)**.

5 Lower the arm out of position, and remove it from underneath the vehicle.

Overhaul

6 Thoroughly clean the lower arm and the area around the arm mountings, removing all traces of dirt and underseal if necessary, then check carefully for cracks, distortion or any other signs of wear or damage, paying particular attention to the pivot and rear mounting bushes. If either bush requires renewal, the lower arm should be taken to a Seat dealer or suitably-equipped garage. A hydraulic press and suitable spacers are required to press the bushes out of the arm and install the new ones. To remove the rear mounting bush, it is necessary to saw through the rubber and metal bush – the new rear bush must be fitted as shown **(see illustration)**.

Refitting

7 Manoeuvre the lower arm into position, engaging it with the balljoint.

8 Fit the new pivot bolt and rear mounting bolt.

9 Position the balljoint retaining plate on the top of the arm, then refit the lower arm balljoint retaining bolts. Align the balljoint with the marks made prior to removal, then tighten the retaining bolts to the specified torque.

10 Tighten the lower arm rear mounting bolt to the specified stage 1 torque setting, then angle-tighten it through the specified stage 2 angle **(see illustration)**. Tighten the pivot bolt lightly only at this stage.

11 Where applicable, refit the connecting link as described in Section 8.

12 Refit the roadwheel, then lower the vehicle and tighten the roadwheel bolts to the specified torque. Rock the vehicle to settle the disturbed components into position, then tighten the lower arm front pivot bolt first to the specified stage 1 torque setting, then through the specified stage 2 angle **(see illustration)**. **Note:** *On completion, it is advisable to have the camber angle checked and, if necessary, adjusted (see Section 25).*

6 Front suspension lower arm balljoint – removal and refitting

Note: *A new balljoint retaining nut/clamp bolt nut (as applicable) will be required on refitting*

Removal

1 Chock the rear wheels, firmly apply the handbrake, then jack up the front of the vehicle and support securely on axle stands. Remove the appropriate front roadwheel.

2 Slacken and remove the bolts securing the inner driveshaft joint to the transmission flange. Recover the spacer plates if they are loose. Support the driveshaft by suspending it with wire or string - do not allow it to hang under its own weight.

3 Using a suitable marker pen, draw around the end of the suspension lower arm, marking the correct fitted position of the balljoint. Unscrew the balljoint retaining bolts and

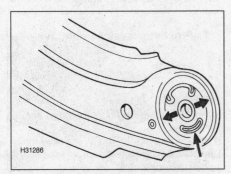

5.6 The lower arm rear mounting bush must be fitted as shown

5.10 Tightening the lower arm rear mounting bolt to the specified Stage 1 torque

5.12 Tightening the lower arm front pivot bolt to the specified Stage 1 torque

10

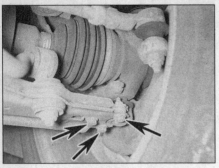

6.3 Lower arm balljoint retaining bolts (arrowed)

6.9 Tightening the lower arm balljoint retaining bolts to the specified torque

remove the retaining plate from the top of the lower arm **(see illustration)**. Note: *On certain models, the balljoint inner retaining bolt hole is slotted; on these models the inner retaining bolt can be slackened, leaving the retaining plate and bolt in position in the arm, and the balljoint can be disengaged from the bolt.*

4 Pull the hub carrier assembly outwards, and disengage the balljoint from the lower arm.

5 Slacken and remove the nut and withdraw the balljoint clamp bolt from the hub carrier. Free the balljoint shank from the hub carrier, and remove the balljoint from the vehicle.

6 Check that there is no excessive play in the balljoint. Check also that the balljoint gaiter shows no sign of deterioration, and is free from cracks and splits. Renew worn or damaged components as necessary.

Refitting

7 Slide the balljoint into the hub carrier and refit the clamp bolt. Fit a new nut to the clamp bolt, and tighten it to the specified torque.

8 Align the balljoint with the lower suspension arm, and slot it into position.

9 Refit the lower arm balljoint retaining bolts. Align the balljoint with the marks made prior to removal, then tighten the retaining bolts to the specified torque **(see illustration)**.

10 Align the driveshaft inner joint with the transmission flange, then refit the spacer plates (where applicable). Refit the driveshaft-to-transmission flange bolts, and tighten them to the specified torque (see Chapter 8).

11 Refit the roadwheel, then lower the vehicle to the ground and tighten the wheel bolts to the specified torque.

7 Front suspension anti-roll bar – removal and refitting

Removal

1 Chock the rear wheels, firmly apply the handbrake, then jack up the front of the vehicle and support securely on axle stands. Remove both front roadwheels.

2 Remove both anti-roll bar connecting links, as described in Section 8.

3 Make alignment marks between the mounting bushes and anti-roll bar, then remove the two anti-roll bar mounting clamp bolts from the subframe **(see illustration)**.

4 Remove the subframe rear securing bolts **(see illustration 9.9b)** and manoeuvre the anti-roll bar out from underneath the vehicle, levering the subframe down if necessary. Remove the mounting bushes from the bar.

5 Carefully examine the anti-roll bar components for signs of wear, damage or deterioration, paying particular attention to the mounting bushes. Renew worn components as necessary.

Refitting

6 Fit the rubber mounting bushes to the anti-roll bar, aligning them with the marks made prior to removal. Rotate each bush so that its split is positioned towards the rear of the vehicle.

7 Offer up the anti-roll bar, and manoeuvre it into position. Refit the subframe rear securing bolts. Refit the mounting clamps, ensuring that their ends are correctly located in the

hooks on the subframe, and refit the retaining bolts. Ensure that the bush markings are still aligned with the marks on the bars, then securely tighten the mounting clamp retaining bolts.

8 Refit the connecting links as described in Section 8.

9 Refit the roadwheels, then lower the vehicle to the ground and tighten the wheel bolts to the specified torque.

8 Front suspension anti-roll bar connecting links – removal and refitting

Removal

Note: *Any self-locking nuts should be renewed on refitting.*

1 Apply the handbrake, then jack up the front of the car and support securely on axle stands.

2 Slacken and remove the nut and washer securing the connecting link to the lower arm **(see illustration)**. Recover the lower mounting rubber, noting which way round it is fitted.

3 Disengage the connecting link from the end of the anti-roll bar, and remove it from the lower arm, complete with the upper mounting rubber.

4 Inspect the mounting rubbers for signs of damage or deterioration, and renew as necessary. The connecting link bush can be pressed out of the link. Coat the new bush with washing-up liquid to ease installation, and press it into position.

Refitting

5 Apply a smear of washing-up liquid to the connecting link rubber, to aid installation.

6 Fit the upper mounting rubber to the connecting link, making sure that the conical side is facing towards the lower arm.

7 Manoeuvre the link into position, and locate it on the end of the anti-roll bar.

8 Fit the lower mounting rubber with its conical surface facing the lower arm, then refit the washer with its collar facing away from the mounting rubber.

9 Refit the connecting link retaining nut, tighten it to the specified torque setting, then lower the vehicle to the ground.

9 Front suspension subframe – removal and refitting

Removal

Note: *All self-locking nuts must be renewed on refitting.*

1 The subframe is most easily removed complete with the lower arms and the anti-roll bar (where applicable).

2 Apply the handbrake, then jack up the front of the vehicle and support securely on axle stands. Remove the front roadwheels.

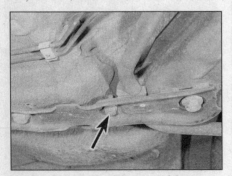

7.3 Front anti-roll bar-to-subframe mounting bolt (arrowed)

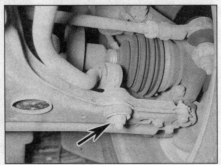

8.2 Anti-roll bar connecting link-to-lower arm nut (arrowed)

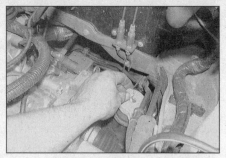

9.3 Unscrew the bolt securing the transmission support bracket to the rubber mounting on the subframe

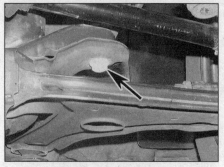

9.9a Subframe front . . .

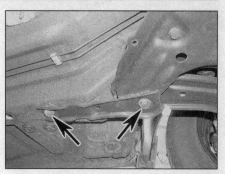

9.9b . . . and rear securing bolts (arrowed)

3 Working on the left-hand side of the engine compartment, unscrew and remove the bolt securing the transmission support bracket to the rubber mounting on the subframe **(see illustration)**. If necessary to improve access, move the coolant expansion tank to one side, without disconnecting the coolant hoses. Release any hoses and/or wiring harnesses from the mounting.

4 Attach a hoist and suitable lifting tackle to the engine lifting brackets on the engine. Raise the hoist to just take the weight of the engine/transmission assembly.

5 Working on each side of the vehicle in turn, slacken and remove the nut and withdraw the lower arm balljoint clamp bolt from the hub carrier. Free the balljoint shank from the hub carrier.

6 Working under the right-hand wheel arch, slacken and remove the two bolts securing the engine mounting to the bracket on the subframe.

7 Slacken and remove the bolts securing the steering gear to the subframe, and remove the steering gear mounting clamps.

8 Place a trolley jack and a block of wood under the centre of the subframe, and raise the jack to take the weight of the subframe.

9 Progressively unscrew and remove the bolts securing the subframe to the vehicle body, then carefully lower the jack and withdraw the assembly from under the vehicle **(see illustrations)**.

10 If desired, the lower arms and the anti-roll bar can be removed from the subframe with reference to the relevant Sections of this Chapter.

Refitting

11 Refitting is a reversal of removal, bearing in mind the following points.
   a) *Renew all self-locking nuts.*
   b) *Before fully tightening the engine and transmission mounting bolts, grasp the engine/transmission assembly and move it firmly from side-to-side to settle the mountings.*
   c) *Tighten all fixings to the specified torque.*
   d) *On completion, check the front wheel alignment with reference to Section 25.*

10 Rear hub assembly – removal and refitting

The rear hub is an integral part of the brake drum/disc. Refer to Chapter 9 for removal and refitting details.

11 Rear hub bearings – renewal

Note: *A suitable wheel bearing repair kit, complete with new oil seal will be required.*

1 Remove the rear brake drum/disc (as applicable) as described in Chapter 9.

2 On disc brake models, where applicable, lever off the cover ring from the rear of the hub.

3 On all models, using a flat-bladed screwdriver, lever the oil seal out of the rear of

the hub, noting which way round it is fitted.

4 Remove the inner bearing from the drum/disc.

5 Support the outer end of the hub, and tap the outer bearing outer race out of position **(see illustration)**.

6 Turn the drum/disc over, and tap the inner bearing outer race out of position.

7 Thoroughly clean the hub, removing all traces of dirt and grease, and polish away any burrs or raised edges which might hinder reassembly. Check the hub surface for cracks or any other signs of wear or damage, and renew if necessary. The bearings and oil seal must be renewed whenever they are disturbed, as removal will almost certainly damage the outer races. Obtain new bearings, an oil seal and a small quantity of the special grease, from your Seat dealer.

8 On reassembly, apply a light film of clean engine oil to each bearing outer race, to aid installation.

9 Securely support the hub, and locate the outer bearing outer race in the hub. Tap the outer race fully into position, ensuring that it enters the hub squarely, using a suitable tubular spacer which bears only on the race outer edge **(see illustration)**.

10 Turn the drum/disc over, and install the inner bearing outer race in the same way.

11 Ensure that both outer races are correctly seated in the hub, and wipe them clean.

12 Work grease well into both the taper roller bearings, and apply a smear of grease to the outer races **(see illustration)**.

13 Fit the taper roller bearing to the inner bearing outer race.

11.5 Drive the bearing outer races out of position using a hammer and punch

11.9 Tap the outer races securely into position using a socket on the race outer edge

11.12 Work grease well into the bearings before fitting them to the hub

10

11.14 Grease the lips of the oil seal, and press it into the rear of the hub

14 Press the oil seal into the rear of the hub, ensuring that its sealing lip is facing inwards **(see illustration)**. Position the seal so that it is flush with the hub face, or until its lip abuts the rear of the hub. If necessary, the seal can be tapped into position using a suitable tubular drift with bears only on the hard outer edge of the seal.

15 On disc brake models, where applicable, press a new cover ring fully onto the rear of the hub.

16 Turn the drum/disc over, fit the taper roller bearing to the outer race, and install the toothed washer.

17 Pack the hub bearings with grease, and install the brake drum/disc as described in Chapter 9.

12 Rear stub axle – removal and refitting

Removal

Note: *On rear disc brake models, a new oil seal guard plate may be required on refitting – see text.*

1 Chock the front wheels, then jack up the rear of the car and support it on axle stands. Remove the relevant rear roadwheel.

Rear drum brake models

2 Remove the brake drum as described in Chapter 9.

3 Minimise fluid loss by first removing the master cylinder reservoir cap, and then

tightening it down onto a piece of polythene, to obtain an airtight seal. Alternatively, use a brake hose clamp, a G-clamp or a similar tool to clamp the flexible hose at the nearest possible point to the relevant wheel cylinder.

4 Wipe away all traces of dirt around the brake pipe union at the rear of the wheel cylinder, and unscrew the union nut. Carefully ease the pipe out of the wheel cylinder, and plug or tape over its end to prevent dirt entry. Wipe off any spilt fluid immediately.

5 Slacken and remove the bolts (and washers) securing the brake backplate assembly in position, and remove it along with the stub axle.

6 Inspect the stub axle surface for damage such as scoring, and renew if necessary. Do not attempt to straighten the stub axle if it is suspected of being bent.

Rear disc brake models

7 Remove the brake disc as described in Chapter 9.

8 Where applicable, prise the oil seal guard plate from the stub axle to allow access to the disc backplate/stub axle securing bolts – the guard plate will be destroyed on removal.

9 Slacken and remove the bolts (and washers) securing the disc backplate in position and remove it along with the stub axle.

10 Inspect the stub axle for signs of damage such as scoring and renew if necessary. Do not attempt to straighten the stub axle if it is suspected of being bent.

Refitting

Rear drum brake models

11 Ensure the mating surfaces of the trailing arm, stub axle and backplate are clean and dry. Check the backplate for signs of damage, and remove any burrs with a fine file or emery cloth.

12 Offer up the stub axle and backplate assembly, and fit the washers and retaining bolts. Note that the washers are dished, and should be fitted with their concave surface facing towards the backplate. Tighten the retaining bolts to the specified torque.

13 Unplug the brake pipe, wipe it clean, and connect it to the rear of the wheel cylinder.

Securely tighten the brake pipe union nut.

14 Remove the hose clamp or polythene (as applicable), then refit the brake drum as described in Chapter 9.

15 Bleed the hydraulic system as described in Chapter 9. Providing precautions were taken to minimise brake fluid loss, it should only be necessary to bleed the relevant rear brake.

Rear disc brake models

16 Refit the stub axle and backplate as described in paragraphs 11 and 12.

17 Where applicable, press or drive a new oil seal guard plate into position on the stub axle, using a tube of suitable diameter. Press the guard plate into position until is contacts the shoulder on the stub axle.

18 Refit the brake disc as described in Chapter 9.

13 Rear suspension strut – removal, overhaul and refitting

Removal

Note: *Any self-locking nuts must be renewed on refitting.*

1 Chock the front wheels, then jack up the rear of the car and support it on axle stands. Remove the relevant rear roadwheel.

2 Working in the luggage compartment, where applicable remove any relevant trim panels for access to the strut top mounting, then remove the trim cap from the top of the strut mounting **(see illustration)**.

3 Slacken and remove the upper mounting top nut and remove the dished washer, noting which way round it is fitted **(see illustration)**.

4 Unscrew the upper mounting bottom nut and lift off the cover plate, upper mounting rubber and shaped washer, noting each component's correct fitted location **(see illustrations)**.

5 From underneath the car, slacken and remove the strut lower mounting nut and bolt, then manoeuvre the strut assembly out of position. Recover the lower mounting rubber from the top of the strut **(see illustrations)**.

13.2 Remove the trim cap from the top of the strut mounting

13.3 Unscrew the upper mounting top nut and remove the dished washer . . .

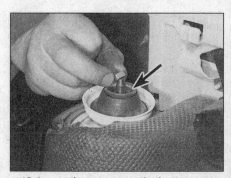

13.4a . . . then unscrew the bottom nut and lift off the cover plate (arrowed) . . .

13.4b . . . followed by the upper mounting rubber . . .

13.4c . . . and shaped washer

13.5a Free the lower end of the strut from the trailing arm . . .

13.5b . . . then manoeuvre the strut out from under the wheelarch . . .

13.5c . . . and recover the lower mounting rubber from the top of the strut

13.8 Hold the strut piston with a spanner whilst slackening the spring plate nut

Overhaul

⚠️ **Warning: Before attempting to dismantle the suspension strut, a suitable tool to hold the coil spring in compression must be obtained.**

Adjustable coil spring compressors are readily available, and are recommended for this operation. Any attempt to dismantle the strut without such a tool is likely to result in damage or personal injury.

6 With the strut removed from the car, clean away all external dirt, then mount it upright in a vice.

7 Fit the spring compressor, and compress the coil spring until all tension is relieved from the upper spring seat.

8 Slacken and remove the spring retaining plate nut whilst retaining the strut piston with an open-ended spanner, then remove the spacer, spring retaining plate, rubber spring seat and washer from the strut **(see illustration)**.

9 Remove the coil spring, and recover rubber damper stop and protective sleeve.

10 Inspect the strut components as described in paragraphs 10 to 13 of Section 4.

11 To reassemble the strut, follow the accompanying photos, beginning with illustration 12.11a. Be sure to stay in order, and carefully read the caption underneath each **(see illustrations)**.

13.11a Ensure that the cap is securely clipped onto the strut . . .

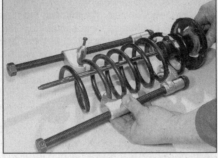

13.11b . . . and fit the coil spring, making sure that it is fitted the correct way round

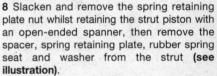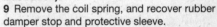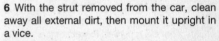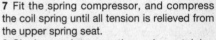

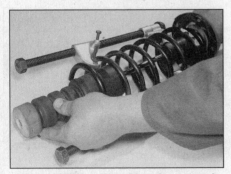

13.11c Slide on the rubber damper and protective sleeve . . .

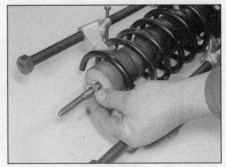

13.11d . . . and fit the washer to the strut piston

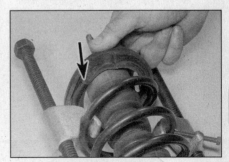

13.11e Fit the rubber spring seat, ensuring that it is located against the spring end (arrowed)

10

13.11f Refit the spring retaining plate

13.11g Slide on the spacer, and refit the retaining nut. Tighten the nut to the specified torque setting

13.11h Carefully release the spring compressors, ensuring that the coil spring ends are correctly located

Refitting

12 Fit the lower mounting rubber to the top of the strut, and manoeuvre the strut into position. Make sure the strut upper end is correctly located, and refit the lower mounting bolt, tightening its nut by hand only at this stage.
13 From inside the car, refit the washer, upper mounting rubber and cover plate. The rubber should be fitted with its tapered serrated face downwards, and the cover with its convex surface towards the rubber.
14 Fit the upper mounting bottom nut, and tighten it to the specified torque.
15 Fit the dished washer with its convex surface downwards, then fit the top mounting nut and tighten it to the specified torque. Fit any trim panels removed to gain access to the strut mounting.
16 Refit the roadwheel, then lower the car to the ground and tighten the wheel bolts to the specified torque.
17 With the car standing on its wheels, rock the car to settle the strut in position, then tighten the lower mounting bolt to the specified torque.

14 Rear anti-roll bar – removal and refitting

The rear anti-roll bar (where fitted) runs along the length of the axle beam. It is an integral part of the axle assembly, and cannot be removed. If the anti roll bar is damaged,

which is unlikely, the complete axle assembly must be renewed.

15 Rear suspension torsion beam/trailing arms assembly - removal and refitting

Removal

Note: *Any self-locking nuts must be renewed on refitting.*
1 Firmly chock the front wheels, then jack up the rear of the car and support it on axle stands. Remove both rear roadwheels.
2 Referring to Chapter 9, fully slacken the handbrake cable adjuster nut.
3 On models with rear drum brakes, disconnect both handbrake cables from the handbrake lever. Working underneath the car, free the handbrake cables from any retaining clips on the car underbody.
4 On models with rear disc brakes, free the ends of the handbrake inner cables from the caliper handbrake levers, then remove the retaining clips and detach the cables from the calipers. Work back along the cables, freeing them from their retaining clips on the torsion beam/trailing arms assembly.
5 On models equipped with ABS, disconnect the ABS wheel sensor wiring harnesses at the wiring connectors, and free the wiring from any retaining clips so the sensors are free to be removed with the torsion beam/trailing arms assembly.
6 Referring to Chapter 9, on models with

pressure-dependent rear brake regulating valves, trace the brake pipes back from the caliper/brake backplate to the connectors located just in front of the torsion beam/trailing arms assembly **(see illustration)**. On models with a load-dependent rear brake regulating valve, trace the brake pipes back from the caliper/brake backplate to the valve, then remove all traces of dirt from the valve, and mark the pipes for identification purposes. On all models, slacken the union nuts and disconnect the pipes from the connectors or valve, as applicable. Plug the pipe ends, to minimise fluid loss and prevent the entry of dirt into the hydraulic system. Release the pipes from any brackets or clips on the car underbody.
7 On models with a load-dependent rear brake regulating valve, unscrew the bolt securing the valve spring to the torsion beam/trailing arms assembly.
8 Make a final check to ensure that all necessary components have been disconnected and positioned so that they will not hinder the removal procedure, then position a trolley jack beneath the centre of the rear torsion beam/trailing arms assembly. Raise the jack until it is supporting the weight of the assembly.
9 Slacken, but do not remove both the left- and right-hand suspension strut lower mounting nuts and bolts **(see illustration)**.
10 Unscrew and remove the pivot bolts and nuts securing the torsion beam/trailing arms assembly to the brackets on the underbody **(see illustration)**. Lower the jack, and lower

15.6 Brake pipe-to-hose connector (arrowed) in front of rear suspension torsion beam/trailing arms assembly

15.9 Slacken the suspension strut lower mounting bolts (arrowed)

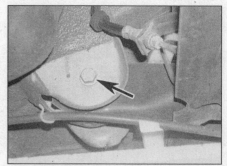

15.10 Torsion beam/trailing arms assembly pivot bolt (arrowed)

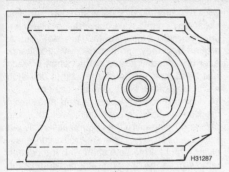

15.12 The torsion beam/trailing arms assembly mounting bushes must be positioned as shown

15.15a With the vehicle resting on its wheels, tighten the rear axle pivot bolts . . .

15.15b . . . and the strut lower mounting bolts to their specified torque settings

the torsion beam assembly from the mounting brackets. The rear of the assembly will be supported by the suspension struts.

11 Remove the suspension strut lower mounting nuts and bolts, then withdraw the assembly from under the car.

12 Inspect the torsion beam/trailing arms assembly mountings for signs or damage or deterioration. If renewal of the mounting bushes is necessary, the task should be entrusted to a Seat dealer, who will have the necessary tools required to press out the old bushes and install the new ones. Note that the bushes must be positioned as shown **(see illustration)**.

Refitting

13 Raise the torsion beam/trailing arms assembly into position, and insert the suspension strut lower mounting bolts and nuts. Do not fully tighten the bolts and nuts until the car is resting on its wheels.

14 Lift the trailing arms into their mounting brackets on the underbody, then fit the pivot bolts and nuts, noting that the nuts fit on the outboard sides of the trailing arms. Do not fully tighten the pivot bolts and nuts until the car is resting on its wheels.

15 The remainder of refitting is a reversal of the removal procedure, bearing in mind the following points:

a) *Ensure that the brake pipes, handbrake cables and wiring (as applicable) are correctly routed, and retained by all the necessary retaining clips.*

b) *Renew any self-locking nuts.*

c) *Securely tighten the brake pipe union nuts.*

d) *Adjust the handbrake cable as described in Chapter 9.*

e) *Bleed the complete braking system hydraulic circuit as described in Chapter 9.*

f) *On completion, lower the car to the ground. With the car resting on its wheels, rock the car to settle all disturbed components in position, then tighten the strut lower mounting bolt nuts and the axle pivot bolt nuts to their specified torque settings* **(see illustrations)**.

16 Steering wheel – removal and refitting

Removal

Note: *It is advisable to use a new steering wheel securing nut on refitting.*

1 Set the front wheels in the straight-ahead position, and release the steering lock by inserting the ignition key.

Models without an airbag

2 Prise the horn pad out from the centre of the wheel, and disconnect the horn wiring connectors **(see illustration)**.

3 Slacken and remove the steering wheel retaining nut **(see illustration)**.

4 Mark the steering wheel and steering

column shaft in relation to each other, then lift the steering wheel off the column splines **(see illustration)**. If it is tight, tap it up near the centre, using the palm of your hand, or twist it from side to side, whilst pulling upwards to release it from the shaft splines.

Models with an airbag

5 Remove the airbag unit from the centre of the steering wheel, as described in Chapter 12.

6 Slacken and remove the retaining screws, and remove the steering column lower shroud.

7 Trace the wiring back from the airbag contact unit in the steering wheel, and disconnect it at the wiring connector.

8 Remove the steering wheel as described above in paragraphs 3 and 4.

9 With the steering wheel removed, rotate the contact unit ring slightly so its wiring connector is at the bottom (steering wheel in the straight-ahead position); this will lock the contact unit in the central position, and prevent it from being turned.

Refitting

Models without an airbag

10 Refitting is a reversal of removal, aligning the marks made on removal. Note that it is advisable to use a new steering wheel securing nut, particularly if the steering wheel has been removed and refitted a number of times using the original nut **(see illustration)**. Tighten the steering wheel retaining nut to the specified torque setting.

10

16.2 Prise out the horn pad and disconnect the horn wiring connectors

16.3 Slacken and remove the steering wheel retaining nut . . .

16.4 . . . then lift the steering wheel off the column splines

Models with an airbag

11 Manoeuvre the wheel into position, making sure the wiring contact unit is correctly positioned, and engage it with the column splines.

12 Refit the steering wheel retaining nut, and tighten it to the specified torque setting.

13 Reconnect the contact unit wiring connector, making sure the wiring is correctly routed.

14 Refit the steering column shroud, and securely tighten the retaining screws.

15 Refit the airbag unit as described in Chapter 12.

17 Steering column –
removal and refitting

Note: *New steering column shear-bolts, and a new steering column shaft-to-intermediate shaft retaining plate nuts will be required on refitting.*

Removal

1 Disconnect the battery negative lead.

2 Remove the steering wheel as described in Section 16.

3 Slacken and remove the retaining screws, and remove the steering column lower shroud.

4 Working under the steering column, disconnect the steering column stalk switch and ignition switch wiring connectors, and free the wiring from any clips on the steering column. Similarly, where applicable, disconnect

17.7 Prise out the clip and remove the cover sleeve from the base of the steering column

17.8b ... then withdraw the retaining plate ...

16.10 It is advisable to use a new steering wheel securing nut on refitting

the immobiliser module wiring connector (the immobiliser module is fitted to the ignition switch housing), and free the wiring from any clips on the steering column. If desired for improved access, remove the stalk switches with reference to Chapter 12.

5 Remove the driver's side glove compartment as described in Chapter 11, Section 31.

6 Working in the driver's footwell, remove the footwell trim panel for access to the steering column universal joint.

7 Prise out the retaining clip(s) or remove the screw(s) and remove the cover sleeve from the base of the steering column **(see illustration)**.

8 Slacken and remove the nuts from the intermediate shaft connecting piece, and slide out the retaining plate. Slide the connecting piece upwards, then separate the intermediate shaft halves and recover the connecting piece **(see illustrations)**.

9 The steering column is secured in position

17.8a Unscrew the two retaining nuts ...

17.8c ... and slide off the connecting piece securing the shaft halves together

with two shear-bolts **(see illustration)**. The shear-bolts can be extracted using a hammer and suitable chisel to tap the bolt heads around until they can be unscrewed by hand. Alternatively, drill a hole in the centre of each bolt head, and extract them using a bolt/stud extractor (sometimes called an 'easy-out').

10 Pull the column upwards and away from the bulkhead, to release the lower retaining clip, and manoeuvre the column assembly out from the car. Do not operate the steering gear or turn the intermediate shaft with the column removed, as the steering gear centre position will be lost.

Inspection

11 The steering column incorporates a telescopic safety feature. In the event of a front-end crash, the shaft collapses and prevents the steering wheel from injuring the driver. Before refitting the steering column, examine the column and mountings for signs of damage and deformation, and renew as necessary.

12 Check the steering shaft for signs of free play in the column bushes. If any damage or wear is found on the steering column bushes, the column should be renewed as an assembly. Inspect the intermediate shaft universal joint as described in Section 19.

Refitting

13 Offer the steering column into position (ensure that the upper column shroud is in position), ensuring that the lower retaining clip engages.

14 Manoeuvre the column bracket into position, then fit two new shear-bolts, and tighten them evenly until the heads break off.

15 Working in the driver's footwell, slide the intermediate shaft connecting piece onto the upper half of the shaft, then align the shaft halves and joint them with the connecting piece. Insert the retaining plate and fit the new nuts, tightening them to the specified torque.

16 Refit the cover sleeve to the base of the steering column and secure with the clip.

17 Refit the footwell trim panel.

18 Refit the driver's side glove compartment.

19 Where applicable, refit the stalk switches, then reconnect the stalk switch and ignition switch wiring connectors, ensuring that the

17.9 Steering column shear-bolt (arrowed)

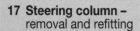

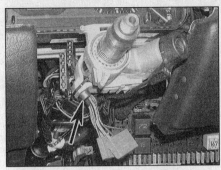

18.5 Unscrew the bolt (arrowed) securing the steering column lock housing to the steering column bracket

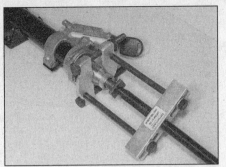

18.6 Draw the splined collar off the steering column using a suitable puller (column removed for clarity)

18.8a Slacken the retaining screw . . .

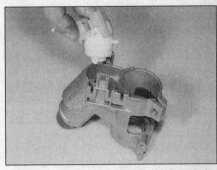

18.8b . . . and remove the ignition switch from the steering column lock assembly

wiring is correctly routed. Similarly, where applicable, reconnect the immobiliser module wiring connector.

20 Refit the steering column lower shroud and tighten the retaining screws.

21 Refit the steering wheel as described in Section 16, then reconnect the battery negative lead.

18 Ignition switch/ steering column lock - removal and refitting

Note: *A new lock assembly shear-bolt will be required on refitting. A suitable puller will be required to remove the splined collar from the steering column.*

Removal

1 Remove the steering wheel as described in Section 16.

2 On models with a height-adjustable steering column, lower the column to enable the steering column upper shroud to be unclipped from the top of the column. On models with a fixed steering column, remove the instrument panel surround as described in Chapter 12, Section 10, then unclip the steering column upper shroud from the top of the column.

3 Remove the steering column stalk switches as described in Chapter 12, Section 4.

4 On models fitted with an immobiliser,

depress the two securing clips, and slide the immobiliser module from the steering column lock housing (if necessary, trace the wiring back from the module and disconnect the connector, or release the wiring from the clips on the steering column to allow the module to be removed).

5 Unscrew and remove the bolt securing the steering column lock housing to the steering column bracket **(see illustration)**.

6 Using a puller, carefully draw the splined collar off from the top of the steering column and recover the spring **(see illustration)**.

7 Note the alignment of the lock assembly and the steering column to aid refitting. Insert the ignition key, and ensure that the steering column lock is released, then slide the lock assembly from the end of the steering column.

8 With the lock assembly removed, slacken the retaining screw and remove the ignition switch from the base of the lock assembly **(see illustrations)**.

9 To renew the lock cylinder, carefully drill a 3 mm diameter hole in the side of the lock casting at the point shown **(see illustration)**. Insert a rod or twist drill into the hole, depress the lock detent plunger, and withdraw the cylinder from the casting. Slide the new lock cylinder into position, and check that it is securely retained by the detent plunger. **Note:** *Renewal of the lock cylinder is a tricky operation, and it is recommended that it is entrusted to a Seat dealer. If the hole is not accurately drilled, the lock assembly casting*

will be ruined, and the complete lock assembly will have to be renewed.

Refitting

10 Fit the ignition switch (where removed) to the lock assembly, making sure that it is correctly engaged with the lock cylinder, and securely tighten the switch retaining screw.

11 Slide the lock assembly onto the column, aligning it with the column lug, then refit and tighten the bolt securing the lock housing to the steering column.

12 Fit the spring to the top of the column, and fit the splined collar to the shaft. Fit a washer over the end of the collar, then refit the steering wheel retaining nut, and use the nut to press the collar fully onto the steering column shaft **(see illustrations)**. Once the collar is securely seated, unscrew the nut and remove the washer.

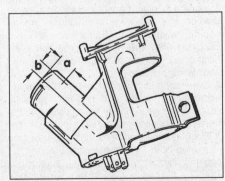

18.9 Drill a 3 mm hole at the point shown to reveal the lock cylinder detent plunger

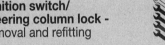

a 12 mm   b 10 mm

18.12a Refit the spring and splined collar to the top of the steering column . . .

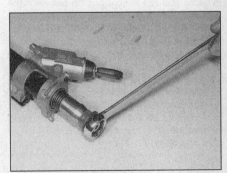

18.12b . . . then press them into place by fitting and tightening the steering wheel nut

10

13 Where applicable, refit the immobiliser module, ensuring that the securing clips are correctly engaged, and that the wiring is clipped into position on the steering column.

14 Refit the steering column stalk switches, ensuring that they are correctly located as noted before removal, then refit and tighten the switch securing screws.

15 Reconnect the column stalk switch and ignition switch wiring connectors, and where applicable clip the wiring back into position.

16 Refit the steering column upper shroud and where applicable, the instrument panel surround, then refit the steering wheel as described in Section 16.

19 Steering column intermediate shaft - removal and refitting

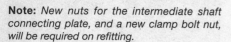

Note: *New nuts for the intermediate shaft connecting plate, and a new clamp bolt nut, will be required on refitting.*

Removal

1 Chock the rear wheels, firmly apply the handbrake, then jack up the front of the car and support on axle stands. Set the front wheels in the straight-ahead position.

2 Working under the car, release the rubber gaiter from the bulkhead, then cut the cable-tie and free the gaiter from the steering gear. Slide the gaiter downwards to gain access to the intermediate shaft.

3 Slacken and remove the nuts from the intermediate shaft connecting plate, and slide out the connecting plate. Slide the connecting sleeve upwards, then separate the intermediate shaft halves and recover the connecting sleeve.

4 Remove the rubber gaiter from the steering gear.

5 Using a hammer and punch, white paint or similar, mark the exact relationship between the intermediate shaft universal joint and the steering gear pinion. Slacken and remove the clamp bolt securing the joint to the pinion, then free the joint from the pinion, and remove it from the car.

6 Mark the exact relationship between the intermediate shaft upper universal joint and steering column shaft. Slacken and remove the clamp nut and bolt, then disengage the universal joint from the column shaft splines and remove it from the car.

7 Inspect the intermediate shaft universal joints for ease of movement, and signs of excess play. If either joint is damaged or worn, it should be renewed. Renew the bulkhead rubber gaiter if it shows signs of damage or deterioration.

Refitting

8 Check that the front wheels are still in the straight-ahead position and that the steering wheel is correctly positioned.

9 Aligning the marks made on removal, engage the upper universal joint with the steering column shaft splines. Install the clamp bolt and fit the new retaining nut, tightening it to the specified torque setting.

10 Slide the bulkhead rubber gaiter into position.

11 Manoeuvre the lower universal joint into position and, aligning the marks made prior to removal, engage it with the steering gear pinion splines. Refit the clamp bolt, and tighten it to the specified torque setting.

12 Slide the intermediate shaft connecting sleeve onto the upper half of the shaft, then align the shaft halves and join them with the connecting sleeve. Insert the connecting plate and fit the new nuts, tightening them to the specified torque.

13 Seat the rubber gaiter correctly in the bulkhead, then locate it on the steering gear and secure it in position with a new cable-tie. Lower the car to the ground.

20 Steering gear rubber gaiters – renewal

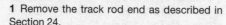

1 Remove the track rod end as described in Section 24.

2 Mark the correct fitted position of the outboard end of the gaiter on the track rod, then release the retaining clip(s) and slide the gaiter off the steering gear housing, and off the end of the track rod.

3 Thoroughly clean the track rod and the steering gear housing, using fine abrasive paper to polish off any corrosion, burrs or sharp edges, which might damage the new gaiter's sealing lips on installation. Scrape off all the grease from the old gaiter, and apply it to the track rod inner balljoint. (This assumes that grease has not been lost or contaminated as a result of damage to the old gaiter. Use fresh grease if in doubt).

4 Carefully slide the new gaiter onto the track rod, and locate it on the steering gear housing. Align the outboard edge of the gaiter with the mark made on the track rod prior to removal. Make sure that the gaiter is not twisted, then lift the outer sealing lip of the gaiter to equalise air pressure within the gaiter.

5 Secure the gaiter in position with new retaining clip(s). Where crimped-type clips are used, pull the clip as tight as possible, and locate the hooks on the clip in their slots. Remove any slack in the gaiter retaining clip by carefully compressing the raised section of the clip. In the absence of the special tool, a pair of side cutters may be used, taking care not to actually cut the clip.

6 Refit the track rod end as described in Section 24.

21 Steering gear – removal and refitting

Note: *New subframe mounting bolts, track rod balljoint nuts, steering gear retaining nuts, and intermediate shaft connecting piece retaining plate nuts, will be required on refitting.*

Note: *The manufacturers suggest that on some models, the manual steering gear can be removed through one of the wheel arches, without lowering the subframe. In this case, the subframe vibration damper must be removed, and the cover must be unbolted from the steering gear pinion housing, to provide additional clearance when removing the steering gear. DO NOT alter the position of the central bolt in the cover, as this bolt is used to adjust the steering gear. Take care not to allow dirt to enter the steering gear mechanism.*

Removal

1 Chock the rear wheels, firmly apply the handbrake, then jack up the front of the car and support on axle stands. Remove both front roadwheels.

2 Working on each side of the car in turn, slacken the nut securing the steering gear track rod balljoint to the hub carrier – leave the nut in place on the end of the balljoint threads to protect the threads. Release the balljoint tapered shank using a universal balljoint separator, then remove the nut completely once the taper has been released.

3 Working under the car, release the rubber gaiter from the bulkhead, then cut the cable-tie and free the gaiter from the steering gear. Slide the gaiter downwards to gain access to the intermediate shaft.

4 Slacken and remove the nuts from the intermediate shaft connecting plate, and slide out the connecting plate. Slide the connecting sleeve upwards, then separate the intermediate shaft halves and recover the connecting sleeve.

5 Remove the rubber gaiter from the steering gear.

6 Place a jack with a block of wood beneath the engine, to take the weight of the engine/transmission. Alternatively, attach a couple of lifting eyes to the engine, and use a hoist or support bar to take the weight of the engine/transmission.

7 On manual transmission models, where necessary, slacken and remove the bolts securing the gearchange linkage pivot to the top of the steering gear (see Chapter 7).

8 Slacken and remove all the front subframe mounting bolts, whilst making sure that the engine/transmission is adequately supported.

Manual steering gear

9 Slacken and remove the steering gear retaining nuts, and remove the mounting clamps **(see illustration)**.

10 Lower the subframe slightly, and manoeuvre the steering gear out towards the rear of the subframe. Remove the mounting rubbers from the steering gear, and inspect them for signs of damage or deterioration, renewing them if necessary. **Note:** *If the steering rack is to be removed for some time, lift the subframe back into position and refit the mounting bolts to support the engine/transmission.*

Power-assisted steering gear

11 Using suitable clamps, clamp both the fluid supply and return hoses near the power steering fluid reservoir. This will minimise fluid loss during subsequent operations.

12 Identify the fluid supply and return pipes on the steering gear to ensure that they are correctly positioned on reassembly, then unscrew the feed and return pipe union nuts from the steering gear assembly; be prepared for fluid spillage, and position a suitable container beneath the pipes to catch escaping fluid **(see illustration)**. Disconnect both pipes, and recover their sealing rings. Plug the pipe ends and steering gear orifices, to prevent fluid leakage and to keep dirt out of the hydraulic system. Release the pipes from any brackets or clips to allow removal of the steering gear.

13 Remove the steering gear as described in paragraphs 9 and 10.

Overhaul

14 Examine the steering gear assembly for signs of wear or damage, and check that the rack moves freely throughout the full length of its travel, with no signs of roughness or excessive free play between the steering gear pinion and rack. It is not possible to overhaul the steering gear assembly housing components; if it is faulty, the assembly must be renewed. The only components which can be renewed individually are the steering gear gaiters, the track rod ends and the track rods. Track rod end and steering gear gaiter renewal procedures are covered later in this Chapter. Track rod renewal should be entrusted to a Seat dealer as it is a fiddly task, requiring special tools if it is to be carried out correctly and safely.

Refitting

Manual steering gear

15 Fit the mounting rubbers to the steering gear, and manoeuvre the assembly into position on the subframe.

16 Refit the mounting clamps and fit the new retaining nuts. Tighten the retaining nuts to the specified torque setting **(see illustration)**.

17 Carefully raise the subframe into position, and fit the new mounting bolts. Tighten the subframe mounting bolts first to the specified Stage 1 torque setting, then go around and tighten all the bolts through the specified Stage 2 angle.

18 Slide the intermediate shaft connecting sleeve onto the upper half of the shaft, then align the shaft halves and join them with the

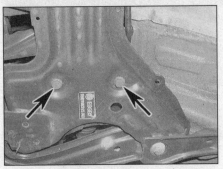

21.9 Two of the steering gear retaining nuts (arrowed)

connecting sleeve. Insert the connecting plate and fit the new nuts, tightening them to the specified torque.

19 Seat the rubber gaiter correctly in the bulkhead, then locate it correctly on the steering gear and secure it in position with a new cable-tie.

20 Reconnect the track rod balljoints to the hub carriers and fit the new retaining nuts, tightening them to the specified torque.

21 On manual transmission models, where applicable refit and tighten the bolts securing the gearchange linkage pivot to the top of the steering gear.

22 Refit the front wheels, and lower the car to the ground. On completion check and, if necessary, adjust the front wheel alignment as described in Section 25.

Power-assisted steering gear

23 Refit the steering gear as described in paragraphs 15 and 16.

24 Wipe clean the feed and return pipe unions, then refit them to their respective positions on the steering gear, and tighten the union nuts securely. Ensure that the pipes are correctly routed, and are securely held by all the necessary retaining clips.

25 Carry out the operations described in paragraphs 17 to 22.

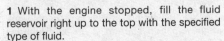

22 Power steering hydraulic system – bleeding

1 With the engine stopped, fill the fluid reservoir right up to the top with the specified type of fluid.

2 Slowly move the steering from lock-to-lock several times to purge out the trapped air, then top-up the level in the fluid reservoir. Repeat this procedure until the fluid level in the reservoir does not drop any further.

3 Have an assistant start the engine, whilst you keep watch on the fluid level. Be prepared to add more fluid as the engine starts, as the fluid level is likely to drop quickly. The fluid level must be kept above the MIN mark at all times.

4 With the engine running at idle speed, turn the steering wheel slowly two or three times approximately 45° to the left and right of

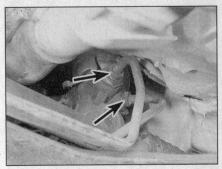

21.12 Power-assisted steering gear union nuts (arrowed)

centre, then turn the wheel twice from lock to lock. Do not hold the wheel on either lock, as this imposes excessive strain upon the hydraulic system. Repeat this procedure until bubbles cease to appear in fluid reservoir.

5 If, when turning the steering, an odd noise is heard from the fluid lines, it indicates there is still air in the system. Check this by turning the wheels to the straight-ahead position and switching off the engine. If the fluid level in the reservoir rises, then air is present in the system, and further bleeding is necessary.

6 Once all traces of air have been removed from the power steering hydraulic system, stop the engine and allow the system to cool. Once cool, check that fluid level is up to the maximum mark on the power steering fluid reservoir, topping-up if necessary.

23 Power steering pump - removal and refitting

Note: *New feed pipe union bolt sealing washers will be required on refitting*

Removal

1 Slacken the steering pump pulley retaining bolts. Working as described in Chapter 1, release the drivebelt tension and unhook the drivebelt from the pump pulley.

2 Using brake hose clamps, clamp both the supply and return hoses near the power steering fluid reservoir. This will minimise fluid loss during subsequent operations. Continue as described under the relevant sub-heading.

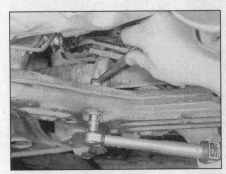

21.16 Tighten the steering gear mounting clamp nuts to the specified torque

1.0, 1.3, 1.4 and 1.6 litre models (except 1.6 litre models with engine code AFT)

3 Unscrew the retaining bolts and remove the pulley from the power steering pump, noting which way around it is fitted.

4 Slacken the retaining clip, and disconnect the fluid supply hose from the pump. Where a crimp-type clip is still fitted, cut the clip and discard it; replace it with a standard worm-drive hose clip on refitting. Slacken the union bolt, and disconnect the feed pipe from the pump, along with its sealing washers; discard the washers - new ones should be used on refitting. Be prepared for some fluid spillage as the pipe and hose are disconnected, and plug the hose/pipe end and pump unions, to minimise fluid loss and prevent the entry of dirt into the system.

5 Slacken and remove the two or three bolts securing the power steering pump to its mounting bracket, and remove the pump from the engine compartment **(see illustration)**.

1.6 litre models with engine code AFT, 1.9 and 2.0 litre models

6 Carry out the operations described in paragraphs 3 and 4.

7 Slacken and remove the power steering pump pivot bolt and the adjuster bolt, and remove the pump and swivel bracket assembly from the main mounting bracket. If necessary, slacken and remove the pump mounting bolts, and separate the pump and swivel bracket; the mounting bracket can also be unbolted from the engine.

Refitting

1.0, 1.3, 1.4 and 1.6 litre models (except 1.6 litre models with engine code AFT)

8 Prior to fitting, ensure that the pump is primed by injecting hydraulic fluid in through the supply hose union and rotating the pump shaft.

9 Manoeuvre the pump into position and refit the mounting bolts, tightening them to the specified torque setting.

10 Position a new sealing washer on each side of the feed pipe union, then fit the union bolt and tighten it to the specified torque setting. Refit the supply pipe to the pump, and

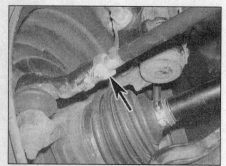

24.3 Unscrew the track rod end locknut (arrowed) by a quarter of a turn

23.5 Removing a power steering pump mounting bolt – 1.4 litre engine

securely tighten its retaining clip. Remove the brake hose clamps used to minimise fluid loss.

11 Refit the drive pulley, making sure it is the correct way around, and fit its retaining bolts.

12 Refit the drivebelt to the pump pulley, and tension it as described in Chapter 1. Once the belt is tensioned, tighten the pulley retaining bolts to the specified torque setting.

13 On completion, bleed the hydraulic system as described in Section 22.

1.6 litre models with engine code AFT, 1.9 and 2.0 litre models

14 Where necessary, refit the mounting bracket to the engine, and tighten its mounting bolts to the specified torque.

15 Join the pump and swivel bracket, and tighten the mounting bolts to the specified torque setting.

16 Prime the pump as described in paragraph 8.

17 Move the pump assembly into position and insert the pivot bolt and adjuster bolt, tighten them loosely only at this stage.

18 Carry out the operations described in paragraphs 10 to 13.

24 Track-rod end – removal and refitting

Note: *A new balljoint retaining nut will be required on refitting.*

Removal

1 Apply the handbrake, then jack up the front of the car and support it on axle stands. Remove the appropriate front roadwheel.

2 If the track rod end is to be re-used, use a straight-edge and a scriber, or similar, to mark its relationship to the track rod.

3 Hold the track rod, and unscrew the track rod end locknut by a quarter of a turn **(see illustration)**. Do not move the locknut from this position, as it will serve as a handy reference mark on refitting.

4 Slacken the nut securing the track rod end balljoint to the hub carrier – leave the nut in place on the end of the balljoint threads to protect the threads. Release the balljoint tapered shank using a universal balljoint

separator, then remove the nut completely once the taper has been released

5 Counting the **exact** number of turns necessary to do so, unscrew the track rod end from the track rod.

6 Carefully clean the track rod end and the threads. Renew the track rod end if its movement is sloppy or too stiff, if excessively worn, or if damaged in any way; carefully check the stud taper and threads. If the balljoint gaiter is damaged, the complete track rod end assembly must be renewed; it is not possible to obtain the gaiter separately.

Refitting

7 Screw the track rod end onto the track rod by the number of turns noted on removal. This should bring the end of the track rod end to within a quarter of a turn from the locknut, with the alignment marks that were made on removal (if applicable) lined up.

8 Refit the balljoint shank to the hub carrier, then fit a new retaining nut and tighten it to the specified torque **(see illustration)**.

9 Refit the roadwheel, then lower the car to the ground and tighten the roadwheel bolts to the specified torque.

10 Check and, if necessary, adjust the front wheel toe setting as described in Section 25, then tighten the track rod end locknut to the specified torque.

25 Wheel alignment and steering angles – general information

Definitions

1 A car's steering and suspension geometry is defined in three basic settings - all angles are expressed in degrees (toe settings are also expressed as a measurement); the steering axis is defined as an imaginary line drawn through the axis of the suspension strut, extended where necessary to contact the ground.

2 **Camber** is the angle between each roadwheel and a vertical line drawn through its centre and tyre contact patch, when viewed from the front or rear of the car. Positive camber is when the roadwheels are

24.8 Tightening the track rod balljoint retaining nut to the specified torque

tilted outwards from the vertical at the top; negative camber is when they are tilted inwards.

3 Camber angle is adjustable, and can be checked using a camber checking gauge.

4 Castor is the angle between the steering axis and a vertical line drawn through each roadwheel's centre and tyre contact patch, when viewed from the side of the car. Positive castor is when the steering axis is tilted so that it contacts the ground ahead of the vertical; negative castor is when it contacts the ground behind the vertical.

5 Castor is not adjustable, and is given for reference only; while it can be checked using a castor checking gauge, if the figure obtained is significantly different from that specified, the car must be taken for careful checking by a professional, as the fault can only be caused by wear or damage to the body or suspension components.

6 Toe is the amount by which the roadwheels point outwards or inwards, viewed from above. Toe-in is when the roadwheels point inwards, towards each other at the front, while toe-out is when they splay outwards from each other at the front. The value for toe can be expressed as an angle (taking the centre-line of the car as zero), or as a measurement of length (taking measurements between the inside rims of the wheels at hub height).

7 The front wheel toe setting is adjusted by screwing the right-hand track rod in or out of its track rod end, to alter the effective length of the steering gear/track rod assembly.

8 Rear wheel toe setting is not adjustable, and is given for reference only. While it can be checked, if the figure obtained is significantly different from that specified, the car must be taken for careful checking by a professional, as the fault can only be caused by wear or damage to the body or suspension components.

Checking and adjustment

Front wheel toe setting

9 Due to the special measuring equipment necessary to check the wheel alignment, and the skill required to use it properly, the checking and adjustment of these settings is best left to a Seat dealer or similar expert. Note that most tyre-fitting centres now possess sophisticated checking equipment.

10 To check the toe setting, a tracking gauge must first be obtained. Two types of gauge are available, and can be obtained from motor accessory shops. The first type measures the distance between the front and rear inside edges of the roadwheels, as previously described, with the car stationary. The second type, known as a scuff plate, measures the actual position of the contact surface of the tyre, in relation to the road surface, with the car in motion. This is achieved by pushing or driving the front tyre over a plate, which then moves slightly according to the scuff of the tyre, and shows this movement on a scale. Both types have their advantages and disadvantages, but either can give satisfactory results if used correctly and carefully.

11 Make sure that the steering is in the straight-ahead position when making measurements.

12 If adjustment is necessary, apply the handbrake, then jack up the front of the car and support it securely on axle stands. Adjustment is made on the right-hand track rod (right- and left-hand are as seen from the driver's seat).

13 First clean the track rod threads; if they are corroded, apply penetrating fluid before starting adjustment. Release the steering gear rubber gaiter outboard clips, peel back the gaiter and apply a smear of grease. This will ensure that the gaiter is free and will not be twisted or strained as the track rod is rotated.

14 Retain the track rod with a suitable spanner, and slacken the track rod end locknut fully. Alter the length of the track rod, by screwing it into or out of the track rod end. Rotate the track rod using an open-ended spanner fitted to the flats provided; shortening the track rod (screwing it into the track rod end) will reduce toe-in/increase toe-out.

15 When the setting is correct, hold the track rod and tighten the track rod end locknut securely. If after adjustment, the steering wheel spokes are no longer horizontal when the wheels are in the straight-ahead position, remove the steering wheel and reposition it (see Section 16).

16 Check that the toe setting has been correctly adjusted by lowering the car to the ground and re-checking the toe setting; re-adjust if necessary. Ensure that the rubber gaiter is seated correctly and is not twisted or strained, and secure in position with the retaining clip; where necessary, fit a new retaining clip (refer to Section 20).

Rear wheel toe setting

17 The procedure for checking the rear toe setting is the same as described for the front setting in paragraph 10. The setting is not adjustable - see paragraph 8.

Front wheel camber angle

18 Checking and adjusting the front wheel camber angle should be entrusted to a Seat dealer or other suitably-equipped specialist. Note that most tyre-fitting centres now possess sophisticated checking equipment. For reference, adjustments are made by slackening the suspension strut-to-hub carrier mounting bolts, and repositioning the hub carrier assembly.

10

Chapter 11
Bodywork and fittings

Contents

Degrees of difficulty

Easy, suitable for novice with little experience	Fairly easy, suitable for beginner with some experience	Fairly difficult, suitable for competent DIY mechanic	Difficult, suitable for experienced DIY mechanic	Very difficult, suitable for expert DIY or professional

Specifications

Torque wrench settings	Nm	lbf ft
Bonnet lock retaining bolts	12	9
Door hinge retaining bolts	36	27
Door hinge pin grub bolt	23	17
Door check link pivot bolt nut	7	5
Door handle retaining bolt	8	6
Door lock retaining bolts	8	6
Door window glass clamp nuts	10	7
Door window glass regulator retaining bolts	10	7
Front seat mounting bolt nut	8	6
Seat belt anchor bolts	40	30

1 General information

The bodyshell is made of pressed-steel sections, and is available in both three- and five-door Hatchback (Ibiza), four-door Saloon and 2-door Coupe (Cordoba), and Estate (Cordoba Vario) versions. Most components are welded together, but some use is made of structural adhesives; the front wings are bolted on.

The bonnet, door, and some other vulnerable panels are made of zinc-coated metal, and are further protected by being coated with an anti-chip primer before being sprayed.

Extensive use is made of plastic materials, mainly in the interior, but also in exterior components. The front and rear bumpers and front grille are injection-moulded from a synthetic material which is very strong and yet light. Plastic components such as wheelarch liners are fitted to the underside of the vehicle, to improve the body's resistance to corrosion.

2 Maintenance – bodywork and underframe

The general condition of a vehicle's bodywork is the one thing that significantly affects its value. Maintenance is easy, but needs to be regular. Neglect, particularly after minor damage, can lead quickly to further deterioration and costly repair bills. It is important also to keep watch on those parts of the vehicle not immediately visible, for instance the underside, inside all the wheelarches, and the lower part of the engine compartment.

The basic maintenance routine for the bodywork is washing - preferably with a lot of water, from a hose. This will remove all the loose solids which may have stuck to the vehicle. It is important to flush these off in such a way as to prevent grit from scratching the finish. The wheelarches and underframe need washing in the same way, to remove any accumulated mud which will retain moisture and tend to encourage rust. Paradoxically enough, the best time to clean the underframe and wheelarches is in wet weather, when the mud is thoroughly wet and soft. In very wet weather, the underframe is usually cleaned of large accumulations automatically, and this is a good time for inspection.

Periodically, except on vehicles with a wax-based underbody protective coating, it is a good idea to have the whole of the underframe of the vehicle steam-cleaned, engine compartment included, so that a thorough inspection can be carried out to see what minor repairs and renovations are necessary. Steam cleaning is available at many garages, and is necessary for the removal of the accumulation of oily grime, which sometimes is allowed to become thick in certain areas. If steam-cleaning facilities are not available, there are some excellent grease solvents available which can be brush-applied; the dirt can then be simply hosed off. Note that these methods should not be used on vehicles with wax-based underbody protective coating, or the coating will be removed. Such vehicles should be inspected annually, preferably just before Winter, when the underbody should be washed down, and any damage to the wax coating repaired. Ideally, a completely fresh coat should be applied. It would also be worth considering the use of wax-based protection for injection into door panels, sills, box sections, etc, as an additional safeguard against rust damage, where such protection is not provided by the vehicle manufacturer.

After washing paintwork, wipe off with a chamois leather to give an unspotted clear finish. A coat of clear protective wax polish will give added protection against chemical pollutants in the air. If the paintwork sheen has dulled or oxidised, use a cleaner/polisher combination to restore the brilliance of the shine. This requires a little effort, but such dulling is usually caused because regular washing has been neglected. Care needs to be taken with metallic paintwork, as special non-abrasive cleaner/polisher is required to avoid damage to the finish. Always check that the door and ventilator opening drain holes and pipes are completely clear, so that water can be drained out. Brightwork should be treated in the same way as paintwork. Windscreens and windows can be kept clear of the smeary film which often appears, by proprietary glass cleaner. Never use any form of wax or other body or chromium polish on glass.

3 Maintenance - upholstery and carpets

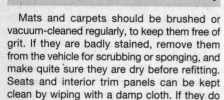

Mats and carpets should be brushed or vacuum-cleaned regularly, to keep them free of grit. If they are badly stained, remove them from the vehicle for scrubbing or sponging, and make quite sure they are dry before refitting. Seats and interior trim panels can be kept clean by wiping with a damp cloth. If they do become stained (which can be more apparent on light-coloured upholstery), use a little liquid detergent and a soft nail brush to scour the grime out of the grain of the material. Do not forget to keep the headlining clean in the same way as the upholstery. When using liquid cleaners inside the vehicle, do not over-wet the surfaces being cleaned. Excessive damp could get into the seams and padded interior, causing stains, offensive odours or even rot. If the inside of the vehicle gets wet accidentally, it is worthwhile taking some trouble to dry it out properly, particularly where carpets are involved. *Do not leave oil or electric heaters inside the vehicle for this purpose.*

4 Minor body damage – repair

Repairs of minor scratches in bodywork

If the scratch is very superficial, and does not penetrate to the metal of the bodywork, repair is very simple. Lightly rub the area of the scratch with a paintwork renovator or a very fine cutting paste to remove loose paint from the scratch, and to clear the surrounding bodywork of wax polish. Rinse the area with clean water.

Apply touch-up paint to the scratch using a fine paint brush; continue to apply fine layers of paint until the surface of the paint in the scratch is level with the surrounding paintwork. Allow the new paint at least two weeks to harden, then blend it into the surrounding paintwork by rubbing the scratch area with a paintwork renovator or a very fine cutting paste. Finally, apply wax polish.

Where the scratch has penetrated right through to the metal of the bodywork, causing the metal to rust, a different repair technique is required. Remove any loose rust from the bottom of the scratch with a penknife, then apply rust-inhibiting paint to prevent the formation of rust in the future. Using a rubber or nylon applicator, fill the scratch with bodystopper paste. If required, this paste can be mixed with cellulose thinners to provide a very thin paste which is ideal for filling narrow scratches. Before the stopper-paste in the scratch hardens, wrap a piece of smooth cotton rag around the top of a finger. Dip the finger in cellulose thinners, and quickly sweep it across the surface of the stopper-paste in the scratch; this will ensure that the surface of the stopper-paste is slightly hollowed. The scratch can now be painted over as described earlier in this Section.

Repairs of dents in bodywork

When deep denting of the vehicle's bodywork has taken place, the first task is to pull the dent out, until the affected bodywork almost attains its original shape. There is little point in trying to restore the original shape completely, as the metal in the damaged area will have stretched on impact, and cannot be reshaped fully to its original contour. It is better to bring the level of the dent up to a point which is about 3 mm below the level of the surrounding bodywork. In cases where the dent is very shallow anyway, it is not worth trying to pull it out at all. If the underside of the dent is accessible, it can be hammered out gently from behind, using a mallet with a wooden or plastic head. Whilst doing this, hold a suitable block of wood firmly against the outside of the panel, to absorb the impact from the hammer blows and thus prevent a large area of the bodywork from being 'belled-out'.

Should the dent be in a section of the bodywork which has a double skin, or some other factor making it inaccessible from behind, a different technique is called for. Drill several small holes through the metal inside the area - particularly in the deeper section. Then screw long self-tapping screws into the holes, just sufficiently for them to gain a good purchase in the metal. Now the dent can be pulled out by pulling on the protruding heads of the screws with a pair of pliers.

The next stage of the repair is the removal of the paint from the damaged area, and from an inch or so of the surrounding 'sound' bodywork. This is accomplished most easily by using a wire brush or abrasive pad on a power drill, although it can be done just as effectively by hand, using sheets of abrasive paper. To complete the preparation for filling, score the surface of the bare metal with a screwdriver or the tang of a file, or alternatively, drill small holes in the affected area. This will provide a good 'key' for the filler paste.

To complete the repair, see the Section on filling and respraying.

Repairs of rust holes or gashes in bodywork

Remove all paint from the affected area, and from an inch or so of the surrounding 'sound' bodywork, using an abrasive pad or a wire brush on a power drill. If these are not available, a few sheets of abrasive paper will do the job most effectively. With the paint removed, you will be able to judge the severity of the corrosion, and therefore decide whether to renew the whole panel (if this is possible) or to repair the affected area. New body panels are not as expensive as most people think, and it is often quicker and more satisfactory to fit a new panel than to attempt to repair large areas of corrosion.

Remove all fittings from the affected area, except those which will act as a guide to the original shape of the damaged bodywork (eg headlamp shells etc). Then, using tin snips or a hacksaw blade, remove all loose metal and any other metal badly affected by corrosion. Hammer the edges of the hole inwards, to create a slight depression for the filler paste.

Wire-brush the affected area to remove the powdery rust from the surface of the remaining metal. Paint the affected area with rust-inhibiting paint; if the back of the rusted area is accessible, treat this also.

Before filling can take place, it will be necessary to block the hole in some way. This can be achieved with aluminium or plastic mesh, or aluminium tape.

Aluminium or plastic mesh, or glass-fibre matting, is probably the best material to use for a large hole. Cut a piece to the approximate size and shape of the hole to be filled, then position it in the hole so that its edges are below the level of the surrounding bodywork. It can be retained in position by several blobs of filler paste around its periphery.

Aluminium tape should be used for small or very narrow holes. Pull a piece off the roll, trim it to the approximate size and shape required, then pull off the backing paper (if used) and stick the tape over the hole; it can be overlapped if the thickness of one piece is insufficient. Burnish down the edges of the tape with the handle of a screwdriver or similar, to ensure that the tape is securely attached to the metal underneath.

Bodywork repairs - filling and respraying

Before using this Section, see the Sections on dent, deep scratch, rust holes and gash repairs.

Many types of bodyfiller are available, but generally speaking, those proprietary kits which contain a tin of filler paste and a tube of resin hardener are best for this type of repair which can be used directly from the tube. A wide, flexible plastic or nylon applicator will be found invaluable for imparting a smooth and well-contoured finish to the surface of the filler.

Mix up a little filler on a clean piece of card or board - measure the hardener carefully (follow the maker's instructions on the pack), otherwise the filler will set too rapidly or too slowly. Using the applicator, apply the filler paste to the prepared area; draw the applicator across the surface of the filler to achieve the correct contour and to level the surface. When a contour that approximates to the correct one is achieved, stop working the paste - if you carry on too long, the paste will become sticky and begin to 'pick-up' on the applicator. Continue to add thin layers of filler paste at 20-minute intervals, until the level of the filler is just proud of the surrounding bodywork.

Once the filler has hardened, the excess can be removed using a metal plane or file. From then on, progressively-finer grades of abrasive paper should be used, starting with a 40-grade production paper, and finishing with a 400-grade wet-and-dry paper. Always wrap the abrasive paper around a flat rubber, cork, or wooden block - otherwise the surface of the filler will not be completely flat. During the smoothing of the filler surface, the wet-and-dry paper should be periodically rinsed in water. This will ensure that a very smooth finish is imparted to the filler at the final stage.

At this stage, the 'dent' should be surrounded by a ring of bare metal, which in turn should be encircled by the finely 'feathered' edge of the good paintwork. Rinse the repair area with clean water, until all the dust produced by the rubbing-down operation has gone.

Spray the whole area with a light coat of primer - this will show up any imperfections in the surface of the filler. Repair these imperfections with fresh filler paste or bodystopper, and again smooth the surface with abrasive paper. If bodystopper is used, it can be mixed with cellulose thinners, to form a thin paste which is ideal for filling small holes. Repeat this spray-and-repair procedure until you are satisfied that the surface of the filler, and the feathered edge of the paintwork, are perfect. Clean the repair area with clean water, and allow to dry fully.

The repair area is now ready for final spraying. Paint spraying must be carried out in a warm, dry, windless and dust-free atmosphere. This condition can be created artificially if you have access to a large indoor working area, but if you are forced to work in the open, you will have to pick your day very carefully. If you are working indoors, dousing the floor in the work area with water will help to settle the dust which would otherwise be in the atmosphere. If the repair area is confined to one body panel, mask off the surrounding panels; this will help to minimise the effects of a slight mis-match in paint colours. Bodywork fittings (eg chrome strips, door handles etc) will also need to be masked off. Use genuine masking tape, and several thickness of newspaper, for the masking operations.

Before starting to spray, agitate the aerosol can thoroughly, then spray a test area (an old tin, or similar) until the technique is mastered. Cover the repair area with a thick coat of primer; the thickness should be built up using several thin layers of paint, rather than one thick one. Using 400 grade wet-and-dry paper, rub down the surface of the primer until it is smooth. While doing this, the work area should be thoroughly doused with water, and the wet-and-dry paper periodically rinsed in water. Allow to dry before spraying on more paint.

Spray on the top coat, again building up the thickness by using several thin layers of paint. Start spraying in the centre of the repair area, and then, using a circular motion, work outwards until the whole repair area and about 2 inches of the surrounding original paintwork is covered. Remove all masking material 10 to 15 minutes after spraying on the final coat of paint.

Allow the new paint at least two weeks to harden, then, using a paintwork renovator or a very fine cutting paste, blend the edges of the paint into the existing paintwork. Finally, apply wax polish.

Plastic components

With the use of more and more plastic body components by the vehicle manufacturers (eg bumpers, spoilers, and in some cases major body panels), rectification of more serious damage to such items has become a matter of either entrusting repair work to a specialist in this field, or renewing complete components. Repair of such damage by the DIY owner is not feasible, owing to the cost of the equipment and materials required for effecting such repairs. The basic technique involves making a groove along the line of the crack in the plastic, using a rotary burr in a power drill. The damaged part is then welded back together, using a hot air gun to heat up and fuse a plastic filler rod into the groove. Any excess plastic is then removed, and the area rubbed down to a smooth finish. It is important that a filler rod of the correct plastic is used, as body components can be made of a variety of different types (eg polycarbonate, ABS, polypropylene).

Damage of a less serious nature (abrasions, minor cracks etc) can be repaired by the DIY owner using a two-part epoxy filler repair material which can be used directly from the tube. Once mixed in equal proportions, this is used in similar fashion to the bodywork filler used on metal panels. The filler is usually cured in twenty to thirty minutes, ready for sanding and painting.

If the owner is renewing a complete component himself, or if he has repaired it with epoxy filler, he will be left with the problem of finding a suitable paint for finishing which is compatible with the type of plastic used. At one time, the use of a universal paint was not possible, owing to the complex range of plastics met with in body component applications. Standard paints, generally speaking, will not bond to plastic or rubber satisfactorily, but professional matched paints, to match any plastic or rubber finish, can be obtained from some dealers. However, it is now possible to obtain a plastic body parts finishing kit which consists of a pre-primer treatment, a primer and coloured top coat. Full instructions are normally supplied with a kit, but basically the method of use is to first apply the pre-primer to the component concerned, and allow it to dry for up to 30 minutes. Then the primer is applied, and left to dry for about an hour before finally applying the special-coloured top coat. The result is a correctly coloured component, where the paint will flex with the plastic or rubber, a property that standard paint does not normally possess.

5 Major body damage – repair

Where serious damage has occurred, or large areas need renewal due to neglect, it means that complete new panels will need welding-in, and this is best left to professionals. If the damage is due to impact, it will also be necessary to check completely the alignment of the bodyshell, and this can only be carried out accurately by a Seat dealer using special jigs. If the body is left misaligned, it is primarily dangerous, as the car will not handle properly, and secondly, uneven stresses will be imposed on the steering, suspension and possibly transmission, causing abnormal wear, or complete failure, particularly to such items as the tyres.

11

6.2 Release the wheel arch liner from the bumper

6.3a Unscrew the upper . . .

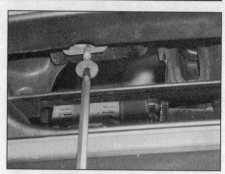

6.3b . . . and lower bumper securing bolts

6 Bumpers - removal and refitting

Front bumper

Removal

1 Remove the radiator grille panel, with reference to Section 8.

2 Remove any clips or screws securing the wheel arch liner(s) to the bumper **(see illustration)**.

3 Unscrew the two upper bumper securing bolts, accessible through the radiator grille panel aperture, and the two lower bumper securing bolts, accessible through the top of the bumper lower grille panel aperture **(see illustrations)**. If desired, to improve access to the lower bumper securing bolts, the bumper

lower grille panel can be removed after unscrewing the three screws securing it to the bumper.

4 Working on each side of the bumper in turn, release the bumper side fixing clips, then pull the bumper forwards to release it from the fitting on the front wing panel **(see illustrations)**.

5 On models fitted with a headlamp wash/wipe system, disconnect the headlight washer nozzle hoses. Similarly, on models fitted with front foglights, disconnect the foglight wiring connector(s).

6 Withdraw the bumper from the front of the vehicle.

7 If desired, the two halves of the front spoiler can be removed from the bumper after unscrewing the securing screws.

Refitting

8 Refitting is a reversal of removal, but make

sure that the locating tangs on each side of the bumper engage with the corresponding slots in the body.

Rear bumper – Ibiza models

Removal

9 Where applicable, working inside the luggage compartment, carefully pull the trim from the lower rear corners of the luggage compartment to expose the two bumper lower securing bolts. Unscrew the two lower securing bolts. Note that not all models have these lower bolts.

10 Remove any clips or screws securing the wheel arch liner(s) to the bumper **(see illustration)**.

11 Where applicable, remove the four screws securing the lower edge of the bumper to the body **(see illustration)**.

12 Unscrew the three bolts securing the top of the bumper to the lower edge of the tailgate aperture **(see illustration)**.

13 Carefully pull the sides of the bumper rearwards to release them from the bumper side fittings, then withdraw the bumper from the vehicle **(see illustration)**.

Refitting

14 Refitting is a reversal of removal, but make sure that the locating tangs on each side of the bumper engage with the corresponding slots in the body.

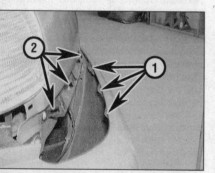

6.4a Release the bumper side fixing clips (1) from the locating grooves (2) . . .

6.4b . . . then pull the bumper from the vehicle

6.10 Unscrewing a wheel arch liner-to-rear bumper nut

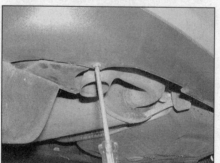

6.11 Remove the screws securing the lower edge of the bumper to the body

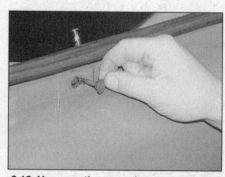

6.12 Unscrew the upper bumper securing bolts

6.13 Withdrawing the rear bumper from the vehicle

6.16 Remove the screws securing the lower edge of the bumper to the body – Cordoba Saloon model

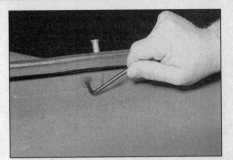

6.17 Unscrew the bolts securing the bumper to the lower edge of the boot lid aperture – Cordoba Saloon model

Rear bumper – Cordoba Saloon and Coupe models

Removal

15 Proceed as described in paragraphs 9 and 10.

16 Where applicable, remove the eight screws securing the lower edge of the bumper to the body **(see illustration)**.

17 Unscrew the three bolts securing the top of the bumper to the lower edge of the boot lid aperture **(see illustration)**.

18 Carefully pull the sides of the bumper rearwards to release them from the bumper side fittings, then withdraw the bumper from the vehicle.

Refitting

19 Refitting is a reversal of removal, but make sure that the locating tangs on each side of the bumper engage with the corresponding slots in the body.

Rear bumper – Cordoba Vario models

Removal

20 Remove any clips or screws securing the wheel arch liner(s) to the bumper.

21 Where applicable, remove the eight screws securing the lower edge of the bumper to the body **(see illustration)**

22 Open the tailgate, and unscrew the five bolts securing the top of the bumper to the lower edge of the tailgate aperture **(see illustration)**.

23 Carefully pull the sides of the bumper

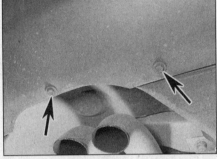

6.21 Two of the screws (arrowed) securing the lower edge of the bumper to the body – Cordoba Vario model

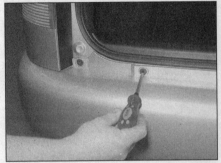

6.22 Unscrew the bolts securing the top of the bumper to the edge of the tailgate aperture – Cordoba Vario model

rearwards to release them from the bumper side fittings, then withdraw the bumper from the vehicle.

Refitting

24 Refitting is a reversal of removal.

7 Body front panel – removal and refitting

Removal

1 Disconnect the battery negative lead.

2 Remove the front bumper as described in Section 6.

3 Remove the radiator as described in Chapter 3.

4 Where applicable, unscrew the three securing bolts on each side, and remove the

lower front trim/spoiler panel from the front of the vehicle.

5 Remove the front direction indicator light units as described in Chapter 12.

6 Working at the right-hand side of the engine compartment, locate the bonnet release cable connector. Open the connector cover, then pull the cable from the connector **(see illustration)**. Release the front section of the cable from the clips. The front section of the cable can now be removed complete with the front body panel. On models without a cable connector, the cable will have to be disconnected from the bonnet lock with reference to Section 12.

7 Disconnect the headlight wiring plugs, and where applicable, disconnect the wiring plugs from the headlight beam adjustment motors. Release the wiring harness from the right-hand side of the body front panel **(see illustrations)**.

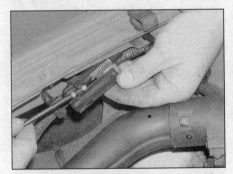

7.6 Disconnect the bonnet release cable from the connector

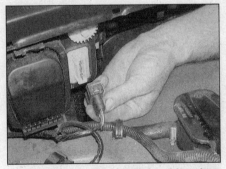

7.7a Disconnect the headlight wiring plugs

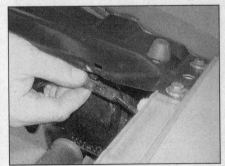

7.7b Release the wiring from the body front panel

11

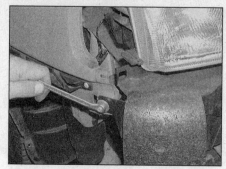

7.8a Unscrew the front . . .

7.8b . . . and side lower securing bolts on each side

from the vehicle **(see illustration)**. Store the front panel carefully to avoid damage.

Refitting

11 Refitting is a reversal of removal, but on completion, check the operation of the bonnet lock and adjust if necessary with reference to Section 11.

8 Radiator grille -
removal and refitting

Early models

Removal

1 Open the bonnet and unscrew the three upper grille panel securing bolts.
2 Carefully lever the lower edge of the grill panel to release the four lower retaining clips – take care not to damage the grill panel or the bumper. Lift the grille panel from the front of the vehicle.

Refitting

3 Refitting is a reversal of removal, but make sure that the lower retaining clips are securely engaged.

Later models

Removal

4 Open the bonnet and unscrew the three upper grille panel securing bolts **(see illustration)**.
5 Using a long flat-bladed screwdriver, reach down behind the grille panel and release the two grille panel lower securing clips **(see illustrations)**.
6 Remove the front direction indicator lights as described in Chapter 12.
7 Working through the direction indicator light apertures, unscrew the plastic nut on each side, securing the edges of the front grille panel to the front wing panels, then withdraw the grille panel **(see illustration)**.

Refitting

8 Refitting is a reversal of removal, but make sure that the lower retaining clips are securely engaged.

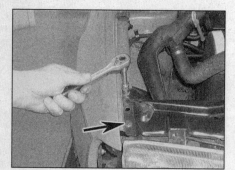

7.9 Unscrew the two bolts securing the body front panel to the front wing

7.10 Carefully lift the front body panel from the vehicle

8 Working on each side of the vehicle in turn, unscrew the three lower body front panel securing bolts on each side **(see illustrations)**.
9 Again working on each side of the vehicle in

turn, unscrew the two bolts on each side securing the body front panel to the front wing **(see illustration)**.
10 With the aid of an assistant, carefully lift the body front panel forwards, and remove it

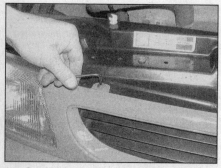

8.4 Unscrew the upper grille panel securing bolts

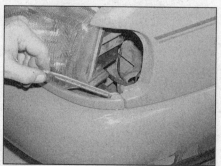

8.5a Using a long flat-bladed screwdriver . . .

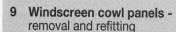

9 Windscreen cowl panels -
removal and refitting

Removal

1 Disconnect the battery negative lead.
2 Remove the windscreen wiper arms as described in Chapter 12.
3 Unscrew the four plastic securing screws, then pull out the four clip centres, and lift off the two halves of the upper windscreen cowl panel **(see illustrations)**.
4 Carefully pull the weather seal from the front edge of the scuttle **(see illustration)**.

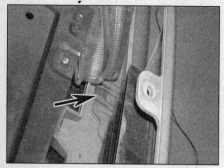

8.5b . . . release the grille panel lower securing clips (arrowed)

8.7 Unscrew the nuts securing the edges of the grille panel to the front wing panels

9.3a Unscrew the four plastic securing screws . . .

9.3b . . . then pull out the clip centres . . .

9.3c . . . and lift off the upper windscreen cowl panel

9.4 Pull the weather seal from the front of the scuttle

9.5 Unscrew the nuts from the windscreen wiper arm spindles

9.6 Manipulate the cowl panel from the scuttle

5 Unscrew the plastic nuts from the windscreen wiper arm spindles **(see illustration)**.
6 Unclip the front edge of the lower windscreen cowl panel from the body panel, then carefully manipulate the cowl panel out from the scuttle **(see illustration)**.

Refitting

7 Refitting is a reversal of removal, but ensure that the weather seal is correctly refitted, and refit the windscreen wiper arms as described in Chapter 12.

---

10 Bonnet and hinges –
removal, refitting and adjustment

Bonnet

Removal

1 Open the bonnet and have an assistant support it. Using a pencil or felt tip pen, mark the outline of each bonnet hinge relative to the bonnet, to use as a guide on refitting.
2 Where applicable, undo the retaining nut and free the earth strap from the left-hand bonnet retaining bolt.
3 Disconnect the washer fluid hose from the connector under the bonnet and, where necessary, disconnect the wiring from the washer jet heating elements **(see illustration)**.
4 Unscrew the bolts securing the bonnet to the hinges and, with the help of an assistant, carefully lift the bonnet clear **(see illustration)**. Store the bonnet out of the way in a safe place.

Refitting and adjustment

5 With the aid of an assistant, offer up the bonnet and loosely fit the retaining bolts. Align the hinges with the marks made on removal, then tighten the retaining bolts securely. Where applicable, reconnect the earth strap and securely tighten its retaining nut.
6 Close the bonnet, and check for alignment with the adjacent panels. If necessary, slacken the hinge bolts and re-align the bonnet to suit. Once the bonnet is correctly aligned, securely tighten the hinge bolts, then check that the bonnet fastens and releases satisfactorily. If necessary, adjust the operation of the bonnet lock as described in Section 11.
7 On completion, reconnect the washer hose and, where applicable, reconnect the wiring to the washer jet heating elements and reconnect the earth strap.

Bonnet hinges

Removal

8 Remove the bonnet as described previously in this Section.
9 Inspect the bonnet hinges for signs of wear and free play at the pivots, and if necessary renew. Each hinge is secured to the body by two bolts; note that on models with a bonnet earth strap, one of the left-hand hinge retaining bolts will have the earth strap attached to it.
10 Mark the position of the hinge on the body then unscrew the retaining bolts and remove the hinge from the vehicle.

Refitting

11 Refitting is a reversal of removal, but align the hinge with the marks made before removal and securely tighten the retaining bolts. Refit the bonnet as described previously in this Section.

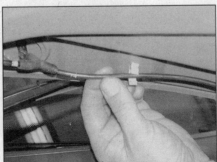

10.3 Disconnect the washer fluid hose from the connector

10.4 Unscrew the bolts securing the bonnet to the hinges

11

11 Bonnet lock –
removal, refitting and adjustment

Removal

1 Open the bonnet.
2 Using a suitable marker pen, mark the outline of the bonnet lock on the crossmember, then slacken and remove the two lock retaining bolts (see illustration).
3 Free the release inner cable from the lock lever then detach the outer cable from the lock bracket and remove the lock from the vehicle (see illustration).

Refitting and adjustment

4 Locate the bonnet release outer cable in the lock bracket and reconnect the inner cable to the lever. Seat the lock on the crossmember.
5 Align the lock with the marks made prior to removal, then refit the bolts and tighten them to the specified torque.
6 Check that the lock operates smoothly, without any sign of undue resistance. Check that the bonnet fastens and releases satisfactorily. If adjustment is necessary, slacken the bonnet lock retaining bolts, and adjust the position of the lock to suit. Once the lock is operating correctly, tighten its retaining bolts to the specified torque.

12 Bonnet release cable -
removal and refitting

Removal

1 Open the bonnet. Where applicable, working at the right-hand side of the engine compartment, locate the bonnet release cable connector. Open the connector cover, then pull the cable from the connector (see illustration). Release the front section of the cable from the clips. The front section of the cable can now be removed complete with the bonnet lock as described in paragraphs 3 and 4.
2 On models without a cable connector, the cable will have to be disconnected from the bonnet lock as described in the following

11.2 Remove the bonnet lock retaining bolts

paragraph, then the whole cable will have to be withdrawn from inside the vehicle.
3 Mark the position of the bonnet lock on the crossmember with a suitable marker pen, then slacken and remove the two bonnet lock retaining bolts. Free the lock from the crossmember then release the inner cable from the lock lever and detach the outer cable from the lock body.
4 Work back along the length of the cable, noting its correct routing, and free it from any retaining clips and ties.
5 On models with a cable connector (see paragraph 1) the front section of the cable can now be withdrawn. Tie a length of string to the end of the cable in the engine compartment.
6 From inside the vehicle, slacken and remove the screws securing the bonnet release handle to the vehicle, then disconnect the cable from the release handle (see illustrations).
7 Release the cable grommet from the bulkhead and withdraw the lever and cable assembly from inside the vehicle. On models with a cable connector, the rear section of the cable can now be withdrawn. On models with a one-piece cable, withdraw the complete cable into the passenger compartment. Once the cable is free, untie the string and leave it in position in the vehicle; the string can then be used to draw the new cable into position.

Refitting

8 Tie the inner end of the string to the end of the cable, then use the string to draw the cable through into the engine compartment.

11.3 Free the inner cable from the lock lever and detach the outer cable from the lock bracket

Once the cable is in position, untie the string.
9 Manoeuvre the bonnet release lever back into position, and securely tighten its retaining screws. Seat the rubber grommet in the bulkhead.
10 Ensure that the cable is correctly routed, and secured by all the relevant retaining clips.
11 Refit the bonnet lock with reference to Section 11.
12 Where applicable, reconnect the two sections of the cable to the cable connector, then close the connector cover and clip the connector back into position at the side of the engine compartment.

13 Door inner trim panels –
removal and refitting

Models up to April 1996
Removal

1 Disconnect the battery negative lead.
2 Prise off the screw covers, then remove the two securing screws, and withdraw the door interior handle trim panel/grab handle.
3 On models with manually-operated windows, push the spacer behind the window regulator handle directly away from the handle knob to release the retaining clip. Pull the handle from the regulator spindle, and remove the spacer (see illustrations).
4 Unscrew the door lock operating button from the operating rod (see illustration).

12.1 Pull the bonnet release cable from the connector

12.6a Remove the screws securing the bonnet release handle . . .

12.6b . . . and disconnect the cable from the handle

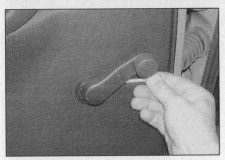

13.3a Push the spacer behind the window regulator handle directly away from the handle knob to release the retaining clip . . .

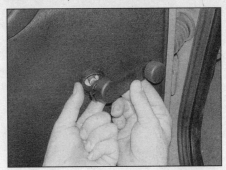

13.3b . . . then remove the handle and trim plate

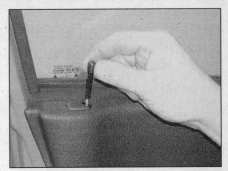

13.4 Unscrew the door lock operating button

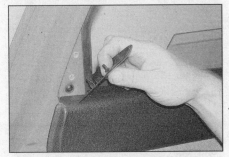

13.5 On the rear door, prise the trim panel from the rear edge of the door window aperture

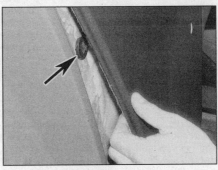

13.6a Release the securing clips (arrowed) . . .

13.6b . . . then remove the trim panel from the door

5 When working on the rear door, where applicable, carefully prise the trim panel from the rear edge of the door window aperture **(see illustration)**.

6 Release the door trim panel securing studs, carefully levering between the panel and door with a flat-bladed screwdriver. Work around the outside edges of the panel, and when all the studs are released, ease the panel away from the door, pulling the top of the panel from the window weatherstrip **(see illustrations)**. Where applicable, disconnect the wiring from the loudspeaker as it becomes accessible.

7 If work is to be carried out on components inside the door, carefully prise the trim panel securing clips from the door, and where applicable remove the door interior handle (see Section 15), then peel away the plastic sealing sheet for access to the door components **(see illustrations)**. If the sheet is torn during removal, a new sheet should be fitted before refitting the door trim panel.

Refitting

8 Refitting is a reversal of removal, bearing in mind the following points.
a) Ensure that the sealing sheet is securely refitted, and if the sheet was damaged during removal, fit a new sealing sheet.
b) Check whether any of the trim panel retaining studs or clips were broken on removal, and renew them as necessary.

Models from May 1996

Removal

9 Disconnect the battery negative lead.
10 Prise the centre cover from the interior handle surround to reveal the two upper door trim panel securing screws. Remove the securing screws **(see illustrations)**.

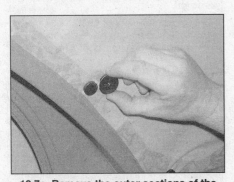

13.7a Remove the outer sections of the trim panel securing clips . . .

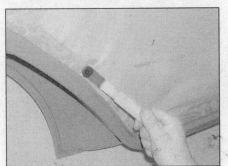

13.7b . . . then prise out the inner sections of the clips . . .

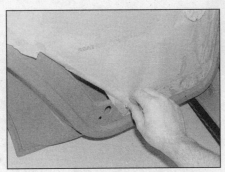

13.7c . . . then peel away the plastic sealing sheet

13.10a Prise the centre cover from the interior handle surround . . .

11

13.10b ... then remove the two upper door trim panel securing screws

11 Unscrew the small screw securing the interior handle to the door trim panel **(see illustration)**.

12 Proceed as described in paragraphs 3 to 7.

Refitting

13 Refer to paragraph 8. When offering the panel into position, make sure that the lugs on the panel engage with the slots in the interior handle.

14 Doors - removal, refitting and adjustment

Removal

1 On models with a door wiring plug, carefully pull the rubber gaiter from the door wiring plug at the body front pillar, then turn the wiring plug locking ring anti-clockwise and pull the plug from connector on the door pillar **(see illustration)**.

2 On models without a door wiring plug, but with electrical components inside the door, remove the door inner trim panel and the plastic sealing sheet as described in Section 13.

3 On models without a door wiring plug, where applicable, reach inside the door, and disconnect the wiring plugs from all relevant electrical components inside the door. Release the wiring harness from any clips and brackets in the door to enable it to pass through the aperture in the front of the door as the door is removed. On models fitted with

13.11 Unscrew the screw securing the interior handle to the door trim panel

central locking, also disconnect the vacuum pipe from the door lock unit.

4 Unscrew and remove the nut and pivot bolt securing the door check link to the body pillar **(see illustration)**.

5 Remove the trim caps, then slacken the two hinge pin grub screws and, with the aid of an assistant, lift the door upwards and off the hinge pins **(see illustration)**. Where applicable, as the door is withdrawn, release the wiring gaiter, and feed the wiring harness and the central locking vacuum pipe through the aperture in the front of the door.

6 Examine the hinges for signs of wear or damage. If renewal is necessary, mark the position of the hinge(s) then undo the retaining bolts and remove them from the vehicle. Fit the new hinge(s) and align with the marks made before removal and lightly tighten the retaining bolts.

Refitting

7 Apply a smear of multi-purpose grease to the hinge pins then, with the aid of an assistant, refit the door to the vehicle. Where applicable, feed the wiring harness and the central locking vacuum pipe through the aperture in the front of the door, and push the wiring gaiter into position as the door is refitted. Once the door is correctly positioned, tighten the grub screws securely, then refit the trim caps.

8 Align the check link with its bracket and refit the pivot bolt and nut, tightening securely.

9 Check the door alignment and adjust if necessary as described in the following

paragraphs, then reconnect the battery negative lead. If the paintwork around the hinges has been damaged, paint the area with a suitable touch-in brush to prevent corrosion.

10 On models without a door wiring plug, where applicable, reconnect the wiring plugs to the electrical components inside the door, reconnect the vacuum pipe to the door lock actuator, and refit the plastic sealing sheet and the door inner trim panel as described in Section 13.

11 On models with a door wiring plug, reconnect the door wiring plug to the connector on the front body pillar (ensure that the gaiter is correctly refitted).

Adjustment

12 Close the door and check the door alignment with surrounding body panels. If necessary, slight adjustment of the door position can be made by slackening the hinge retaining bolts and repositioning the hinge/door as necessary. Once the door is correctly positioned, tighten the hinge bolts securely. If the paintwork around the hinges has been damaged, paint the affected area with a suitable touch-in brush to prevent corrosion.

15 Door handle and lock components - removal and refitting

Interior door handle

Removal

1 On models up to April 1996, prise off the screw covers, then remove the two securing screws, and withdraw the door interior handle trim panel/grab handle.

2 On models from May 1996, remove the door inner trim panel as described in Section 13.

3 The interior handle is held in place by a locating tab, and is released from the door by pushing the handle towards the front of the door and simultaneously depressing the locating tab **(see illustration)**.

4 Once the handle has been released from the door, disconnect the lock operating rod and remove the handle **(see illustration)**.

14.1 Disconnect the door wiring plug from the connector on the door pillar

14.4 Unscrew the nut and pivot bolt securing the door check link to the body pillar

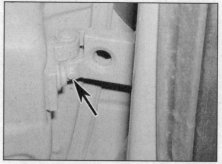

14.5 Door hinge pin grub screw (arrowed)

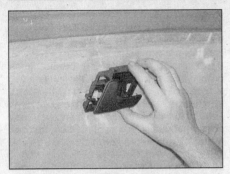

15.3 Push the handle towards the front of the door to release it . . .

15.4 . . . then disconnect the lock operating rod

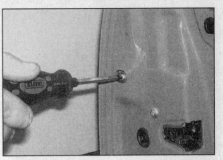

15.7a Remove the exterior handle retaining bolt from the rear edge of the door . . .

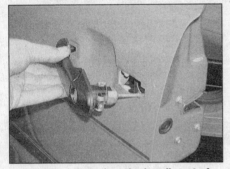

15.7b . . . then pivot the handle out of position

15.11a Prise off the lock cylinder retaining clip and lift off the lock rod . . .

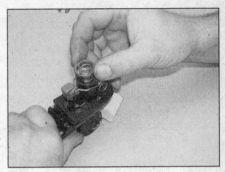

15.11b . . . spacer . . .

Refitting

5 Engage the handle with the lock operating rod and clip it back into position. Make sure the handle operates correctly, then refit the trim panel as described in Section 13.

Exterior door handle

Note: *On most models, this task can be performed with the door inner trim panel in position. Note however that when working on the front door of certain models, it may be necessary to remove the door inner trim panel to allow the handle lever to be disengaged from the lock lever by pushing from inside the door.*

Removal

6 If work is being carried out on the front door, insert the key into the lock.
7 Prise out the grommet, then slacken and remove the handle retaining bolt from the rear edge of the door, move the handle assembly forwards and pivot it out of position **(see illustrations)**.

Refitting

8 Hook the lock front pivot into place, then clip the rear of the handle into position.
9 Check the operation of the handle, then refit the retaining bolt and tighten it securely. Refit the retaining bolt grommet on completion.

Front door lock cylinder

Removal

10 Remove the exterior door handle as described previously in this Section.
11 With the key in the lock, carefully prise off the lock cylinder retaining clip, then lift off the lock rod, spacer, spring and seat, noting the orientation of all components to ensure correct refitting **(see illustrations)**.
12 Pull out the lock cylinder using the key **(see illustration)**.
13 Recover the sealing ring from the handle and renew it if it is damaged.

Refitting

16 Refit the lock cylinder using the key.
17 Refit the spring seat, the spring, the lock rod and the spacer, ensuring that all components are correctly orientated as noted before removal, and that the spring is correctly located. Hold the components in position, and refit the lock cylinder retaining clip.
18 Refit the exterior door handle as described previously in this Section.

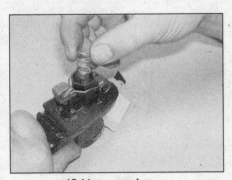

15.11c . . . spring . . .

15.11d . . . and seat

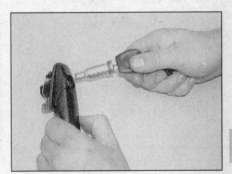

15.12 Pull out the lock cylinder using the key

11

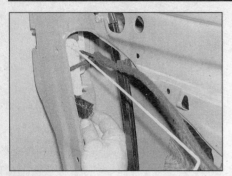

15.21 Disconnect the wiring plug from the central locking unit

Front door lock

Removal

19 Ensure that the window glass is in the fully closed position, then remove the interior door handle as described previously in this Section.

20 If not already done, remove the door inner trim panel as described in Section 13, then remove the exterior door handle as described previously in this Section.

21 On models with central locking, disconnect the vacuum pipe from the lock assembly and disconnect the wiring from the central locking unit (see illustration).

22 Working at the rear edge of the door, slacken and remove the lock retaining bolts, then disengage the lock from the lock operating rod and remove it from the door. Note that on some models it may be

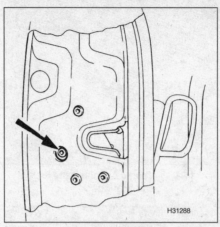

15.28 Front door lock adjustment screw location (arrowed)

necessary to loosen the window regulator retaining bolts and release the guide rail from the door (see Section 16) to gain the clearance required to remove the lock assembly.

Refitting

23 Before refitting, slacken the lock adjusting (Torx) screw; on the left-hand door the screw has a right-handed thread and on the right-hand door it has a left-handed thread.

24 Manoeuvre the lock assembly into position and engage it with the lock operating rod.

25 Refit the lock bolts and tighten them securely. Where applicable, reconnect the

vacuum pipe and/or wiring connector(s) to the lock assembly.

26 Refit the exterior handle as described previously in this Section.

27 Open and close the door several times using the exterior handle; this will automatically adjust the lock.

28 Remove the rubber plug from the rear edge of the door to gain access to the lock adjustment screw. Tighten the screw to 3 Nm (2 lbf ft), then refit the rubber plug (see illustration).

29 Where applicable, refit the window regulator guide rail retaining bolts and adjust as described in Section 16.

30 Check the operation of the lock and handle, then press the polythene insulating panel back onto the door. Press the trim panel retaining clips back into position.

31 Refit the door inner trim panel as described in Section 13, and the interior door handle as described previously in this Section.

Rear door lock

Removal

32 Ensure that the window glass is in the fully closed position, then remove the interior door handle as described previously in this Section.

33 If not already done, remove the door inner trim panel as described in Section 13, then remove the exterior door handle as described previously in this Section.

34 Slacken the two window rear guide rail securing bolts, then slide the guide rail forwards. Unclip the weatherstrip from the guide rail, then withdraw the guide rail through the aperture in the door (see illustrations).

35 Where applicable, disconnect the vacuum pipe from the lock assembly (see illustration).

36 Press out the retaining pin from the centre of the interior lock button operating rod bellcrank, and free the bellcrank from the door. Recover the retaining pin and detach the bellcrank from the lock operating rod (see illustrations).

37 Unclip the lock operating rod guide clips from the door (see illustration).

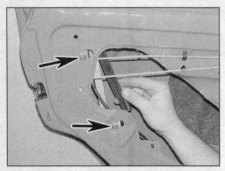

15.34a Slacken the window rear guide rail securing bolts (arrowed), and unclip the weatherstrip from the guide rail . . .

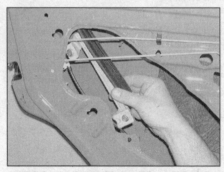

15.34b . . . then withdraw the guide rail

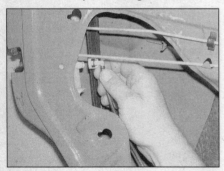

15.35 Disconnect the vacuum pipe from the lock assembly

15.36a Press out the retaining pin . . .

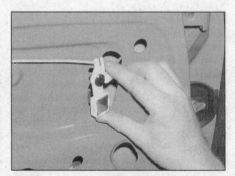

15.36b . . . and free the bellcrank from the door

15.37 Unclip the lock operating rod guide clips from the door

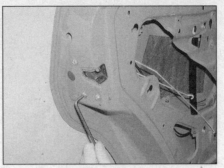

15.38a Slacken and remove the lock retaining bolts . . .

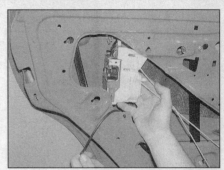

15.38b . . . and manoeuvre the lock out from the door

38 Working at the rear edge of the door, slacken and remove the lock retaining bolts and manoeuvre the lock and operating rod assembly out from the door **(see illustrations)**. If necessary, detach the operating rods from the lock, noting their correct fitted locations; the operating rods are different and must not be interchanged.

Refitting

39 Refit the operating rods to the lock, making sure that they are correctly fitted.
40 Before refitting, slacken the lock adjusting (Torx) screw; on the left-hand door the screw has a right-handed thread and on the right-hand door it has a left-handed thread.
41 Manoeuvre the lock assembly into position and tighten the retaining bolts securely. Where applicable, reconnect the vacuum pipe and/or wiring connector(s) to the lock assembly.

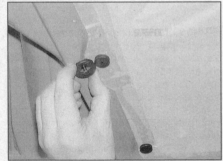

16.3a Prise the trim panel securing clips from the door . . .

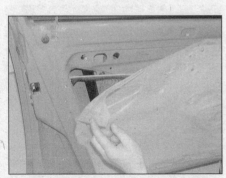

16.3b . . . and peel away the plastic sealing sheet

42 Attach the operating rod to the bellcrank and clip the bellcrank into the door. Secure the bellcrank in position with the retaining pin.
43 Proceed as described previously for the front door lock in paragraphs 26 to 28.
44 Clip the weatherstrip into the window rear guide rail, then refit the guide rail, and refit and tighten the two securing bolts.
45 Check the operation of the lock and handle, then press the polythene insulating panel back onto the door. Press the trim panel retaining clips back into position.
46 Refit the interior door handle as described previously in this Section, and the door inner trim panel as described in Section 13.

16 Door window glass and regulators - removal and refitting

Front door window glass

Removal

1 Fully lower the door window glass.
2 Remove the interior door handle as described in Section 15.
3 If not already done, remove the door inner trim panel as described in Section 13, then carefully prise the trim panel securing clips from the door, and peel away the plastic sealing sheet for access to the door components **(see illustrations)**.
4 Slacken the window glass clamp bolts and release the clamps from the glass, then

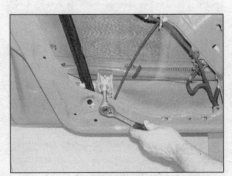

16.4a Slacken the window glass clamp bolts . . .

carefully manoeuvre the window glass out through the outside of the window aperture **(see illustrations)**.

Refitting

5 Manoeuvre the window glass into position and engage it with the regulator clamps. Make sure that the glass is correctly seated, then lightly tighten the regulator clamp bolts.
6 Check that the window glass moves smoothly and easily and closes fully. If necessary, slacken the regulator clamp bolts, then reposition the glass as necessary. Once the window operation is correct, tighten the clamp bolts securely.
7 Once the window is operating correctly, press the polythene insulating panel back into position, making sure it is correctly seated, and refit the trim panel clips. Refit the inner trim panel as described in Section 13.

Rear door window glass

Removal

8 Remove the interior door handle as described in Section 15.
9 If not already done, remove the door inner trim panel as described in Section 13, then carefully prise the trim panel securing clips from the door, and peel away the plastic sealing sheet for access to the door components.
10 Carefully ease the window inner sealing strip from the edge of the window aperture **(see illustration)**.
11 With the window glass raised, unscrew the two bolts securing the window rear guide

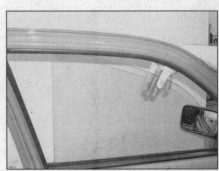

16.4b . . . and withdraw the window glass

11

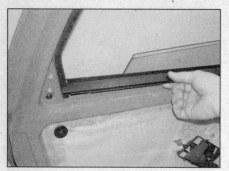

16.10 Ease the window inner sealing strip from the window aperture

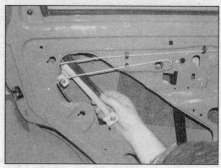

16.11 Lifting out the window rear guide rail

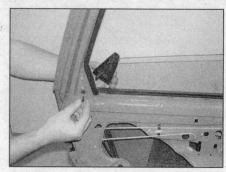

16.13 Remove the securing screw and remove the trim plate from the rear edge of the door

16.14a Carefully pull the weatherstrips from the front . . .

16.14b . . . and rear edges of the window aperture

rail to the door, then lift out the rear guide rail **(see illustration)**.

12 Position the window glass so that the glass clamps on the regulator mechanism are accessible through the door panel cutaways. On models with electric windows, temporarily reconnect the battery negative lead to enable the window glass to be moved.

13 Remove the securing screw, and remove the trim plate from the outside rear edge of the door **(see illustration)**.

14 Carefully pull the weatherstrips from the front and rear edges of the door window aperture **(see illustrations)**.

15 Slacken the window glass clamp bolts and release the clamps from the glass, then carefully manoeuvre the window glass out through the top of the door **(see illustrations)**.

Refitting

16 Manoeuvre the window glass into position and engage it with the regulator clamps. Make sure that the glass is correctly seated, then lightly tighten the regulator clamp bolts.

17 Raise the window glass to enable the rear guide rail to be fitted, then refit the guide rail, ensuring that it engages correctly with the glass, and tighten the securing bolts.

18 Refit the inner sealing strip to the top of the door.

19 Refit the weatherstrips to the front and rear edges of the window aperture, then refit the trim plate to the outside rear edge of the door, and secure with the screw.

20 Check that the window glass moves smoothly and easily and closes fully. If necessary, slacken the regulator clamp bolts,

then reposition the glass as necessary. Once the window operation is correct, tighten the clamp bolts securely.

21 Once the window is operating correctly, press the polythene insulating panel back into position, making sure it is correctly seated, and refit the trim panel clips. Refit the inner trim panel as described in Section 13.

Door window regulator

Removal

22 Remove the window glass as described previously in this Section. Alternatively, the glass can be unbolted from the regulator mechanism, then fully raised, and held in position in the window aperture using strong adhesive tape.

23 Where applicable, release the retaining clip and free the regulator cables from the door. On models with electric windows disconnect the wiring connector from the regulator motor **(see illustration)**.

24 When working on the front door, slacken the three bolts securing the motor/regulator assembly to the door, and the two bolts securing the guide rail (there is no need to remove the bolts), then manipulate the regulator mechanism out through the door **(see illustrations)**.

25 When working on the rear door, slacken the four regulator assembly securing bolts (there is no need to remove the bolts), then

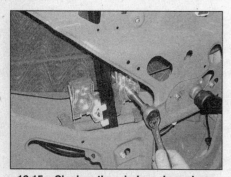

16.15a Slacken the window glass clamp bolts . . .

16.15b and manoeuvre the glass out through the top of the door

16.23 Disconnecting the wiring plug from a front door electric window regulator motor

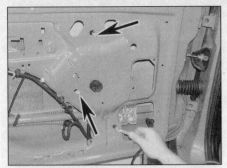

16.24a Slacken the three bolts securing the front door motor/regulator assembly . . .

16.24b . . . and the bolts securing the guide rail . . .

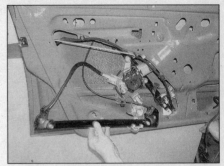

16.24c . . . then manipulate the regulator mechanism out through the aperture in the door

manipulate the regulator mechanism out through the aperture in the door **(see illustrations)**.

Refitting

26 Manipulate the regulator mechanism into position, then tighten the four securing bolts.
27 Where applicable, clip the regulator cables into position in the door, and reconnect the regulator motor wiring connector.
28 Refit the window glass as described previously in this Section.

17 Boot lid and support struts - removal and refitting

Boot lid

Removal

1 Disconnect the battery negative lead.
2 Open the boot lid, then carefully prise out the securing clips and withdraw the boot lid trim panel.
3 Disconnect the wiring from the rear lights and any other electrical components in the boot lid, and release the wiring harness(es) from any clips inside the boot lid. Tie a length of string to the wiring harness(es). Noting the correct routing of the wiring harness(es), release the harness rubber grommet(s) from the boot lid and withdraw the wiring **(see illustration)**. When the end of the wiring appears, untie the string and leave it in position in the boot lid; it can then be used on

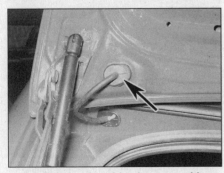

17.3 Release the wiring harness rubber grommet (arrowed) from the boot lid

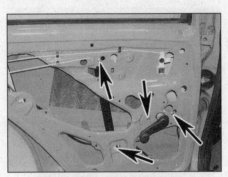

16.25a Slacken the four rear door regulator assembly securing bolts . . .

refitting to draw the wiring into position. Similarly, on models with central locking, disconnect the vacuum pipe from the central locking actuator in the boot lid, and withdraw the pipe from the boot lid.
4 Support the boot lid with the aid of an assistant. Using a pencil or felt tip pen, mark the outline of each boot lid hinge relative to the boot lid, to use as a guide on refitting.
5 Unscrew the four bolts securing the boot lid to the hinges, then carefully lift the boot lid from the vehicle.
6 Inspect the hinges for signs of wear or damage, and renew if necessary; the hinges are secured to the vehicle by bolts.

Refitting

7 Refitting is a reversal of removal, bearing in mind the following points.
  a) *Align the hinges with the marks made on the boot lid before removal.*
  b) *Use the string to draw the wiring harness(es) into position.*
  c) *On completion, close the boot lid and check its alignment with the surrounding panels. If necessary, slight adjustment can be made by slackening the retaining bolts and repositioning the boot lid on its hinges.*

Support struts

Removal

8 Support the boot lid in the open position. Using a small flat-bladed screwdriver, release the spring clip, and pull the support strut off

16.25b . . . then manipulate the regulator mechanism out through the aperture in the door

its upper mounting. Repeat the procedure on the lower strut mounting and remove the strut from the vehicle.

Refitting

9 Refitting is a reversal of removal, ensuring that the retaining clips are securely engaged.

18 Boot lid handle and lock components - removal and refitting

Lock

Removal

1 Open the boot lid, then carefully release the securing clips and withdraw the boot lid trim panel **(see illustration)**.

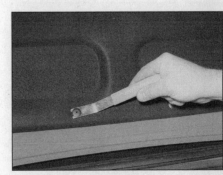

18.1 Prising out a boot lid trim panel securing clip

18.2a Unscrew the securing screws . . .

18.2b . . . then withdraw the boot lid lock and disconnect the wiring plug

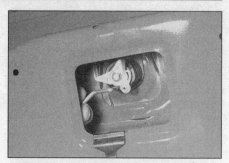

18.5 Disconnecting the central locking actuator rod from the boot lid handle/pushbutton assembly

2 Working at the rear edge of the boot lid, unscrew the two lock securing screws, and withdraw the lock. Where applicable, disconnect the luggage compartment light switch wiring plug from the switch, which is integral with the lock **(see illustrations)**.

3 Check the operation of the lock, and if necessary adjust the position of the lock striker to achieve satisfactory lock operation.

Refitting

4 Refitting is a reversal of removal, but ensure that the lock operating lever is correctly engaged with the lock.

Handle/pushbutton assembly

Removal

5 Remove the lock as described previously in this Section and, where applicable, disconnect the central locking actuator rod from the lever on the rear of the assembly **(see illustration)**.

6 Working at the rear of the boot lid, unscrew the handle/pushbutton assembly securing screw **(see illustration)**.

7 Release the locating tang at the top of the handle/pushbutton assembly, then release the assembly from the boot lid.

8 Note that it may be necessary to insert the key into the lock and depress the lock button in order to allow the lever on the rear of the assembly to clear the boot lid **(see illustration)**.

Refitting

9 Refitting is a reversal of removal.

18.6 Unscrewing the boot lid handle/pushbutton assembly securing screw

Lock striker

Removal

10 Open the boot lid, then unscrew the two securing bolts, and remove the lock striker.

Refitting

11 Refitting is a reversal of removal, but note that if necessary, the lock striker can be adjusted within its elongated securing bolt holes to achieve satisfactory lock operation.

---

19 Tailgate, hinges and support struts - removal and refitting

---

Ibiza Hatchback models

Tailgate

1 Disconnect the battery negative lead.

2 Open the tailgate, then carefully release the securing clips and withdraw the tailgate trim panel.

3 Disconnect the wiring connectors from the electrical components inside the tailgate, and free the washer fluid hose from the tailgate wiper motor (be prepared for fluid spillage). Disconnect the wiring connectors from the heated rear window terminals, and free the wiring grommets from the tailgate **(see illustration)**.

4 Tie a length of string to the wiring harness(es) and the washer fluid hose. Noting the correct routing of the wiring harness(es) and hose, release the harness rubber

18.8 Insert the key and depress the lock button to allow the lock lever to clear the boot lid

grommet(s) from the tailgate and withdraw the wiring and hose. When the end of the wiring appears, untie the string and leave it in position in the tailgate; it can then be used on refitting to draw the wiring and hose into position. Similarly, on models with central locking, disconnect the vacuum pipe from the central locking actuator in the tailgate, and withdraw the pipe from the tailgate.

5 Using a marker pen, draw around the outline of each hinge, marking its correct position on the tailgate.

6 Have an assistant support the tailgate, then using a small flat-bladed screwdriver, release the spring clips and pull the support struts off their balljoints on the tailgate.

7 Slacken and remove the bolts securing the tailgate to the hinges, and lift the tailgate from the vehicle **(see illustration)**. Where applicable,

19.3 Disconnect the wiring connectors from the heater rear window terminals – Hatchback model

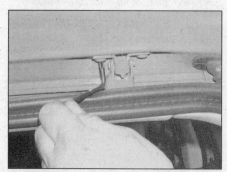

19.7 Slacken and remove the bolts securing the tailgate to the hinges – Ibiza Hatchback model

recover the shims which are fitted between the hinges and the tailgate.

8 Inspect the hinges for signs of wear or damage, and renew if necessary. The hinges are secured to the vehicle by nuts or bolts (depending on model), which can be accessed once the headlining has been freed from trim strip and peeled back. Note the locations of the hinge shims where applicable.

9 Refitting is a reversal of removal, bearing in mind the following points.

a) Align the hinges with the marks made on the tailgate before removal.

b) Use the string to draw the wiring harness(es) and fluid hose into position.

c) On completion, close the tailgate and check its alignment with the surrounding panels. If necessary, slight adjustment can be made by slackening the retaining bolts and repositioning the tailgate on its hinges.

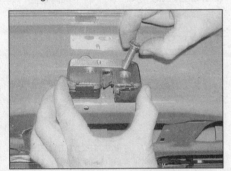

20.1a Removing the tailgate lock – Ibiza Hatchback model

20.1b Disconnecting the central locking actuator rod – Ibiza Hatchback model

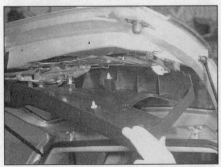

20.2b . . . and withdraw the trim panel – Cordoba Vario model

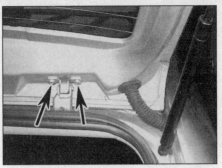

19.13 Tailgate-to-hinge securing bolts (arrowed) – Cordoba Vario model

Support struts

10 Proceed as described for the boot lid support struts in Section 17.

Cordoba Vario models

Tailgate

11 Disconnect the battery negative lead.

12 Unscrew the two tailgate trim panel securing screws, then pull the trim panel away from the tailgate to release the securing clips, and withdraw the trim panel.

13 Proceed as described for Hatchback models in paragraphs 3 to 9 **(see illustration)**.

Support struts

14 Proceed as described for the boot lid support struts in Section 17.

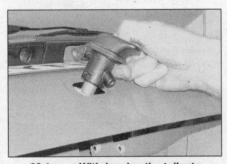

20.1c . . . Withdrawing the tailgate handle/pushbutton assembly – Ibiza Hatchback model

20.3 Tailgate lock securing screws (arrowed) – Cordoba Vario model

20 Tailgate handle and lock components – removal and refitting

Ibiza Hatchback models

1 The procedures for lock, handle/push-button assembly and lock striker removal and refitting are as described for Saloon models in Section 18 **(see illustrations)**.

Cordoba Vario models

Lock

2 Unscrew the two tailgate trim panel securing screws, then pull the trim panel away from the tailgate to release the securing clips, and withdraw the trim panel **(see illustration)**.

3 Working at the lower edge of the tailgate, unscrew the two lock securing screws, and withdraw the lock, disconnecting the lock operating rod(s) and, where applicable, the luggage compartment light switch wiring plug, as the lock is withdrawn **(see illustration)**.

4 Refitting is a reversal of removal, but ensure that the lock operating rods are correctly reconnected.

Exterior handle

5 Remove the rear light panel from the tailgate as follows **(see illustrations)**.

a) Unscrew the two tailgate trim panel securing screws, then pull the trim panel away from the tailgate to release the securing clips, and withdraw the trim panel.

20.2a Unscrew the tailgate trim panel securing screws . . .

20.5a Unscrew the nuts securing the rear light panel to the tailgate . . .

11

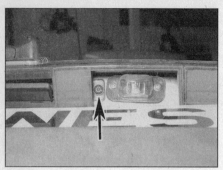

20.5b . . . then remove the securing screw
(arrowed) . . .

20.5c . . . and withdraw the rear light panel
from the tailgate – Cordoba Vario model

20.11 Disconnect the lock operating rods
from the lock cylinder . . .

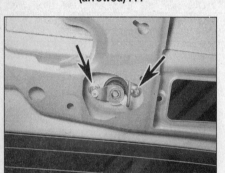

20.12a . . . then unscrew the two securing
nuts (arrowed) . . .

20.12b . . . and withdraw the lock cylinder
from the tailgate – Cordoba Vario model

Lock cylinder

10 Proceed as described in paragraph 5.
11 Reach inside the door, and disconnect the lock operating rod(s) from the lock cylinder **(see illustration)**.
12 Unscrew the two securing nuts, and withdraw the lock cylinder from the tailgate **(see illustrations)**.
13 Refitting is a reversal of removal.

**21 Central locking
 system components -**
removal and refitting

Central locking vacuum pump –
all models except Cordoba Vario

Removal

1 The central locking vacuum pump is located on the right-hand side of the luggage compartment.
2 Disconnect the battery negative lead.
3 Where necessary, unbolt the rear right-hand seat belt inertia reel from the side of the luggage compartment, then carefully prise out the securing clip(s) and pull the trim away from the side of the luggage compartment **(see illustrations)**.
4 Where applicable, press the lugs to release the pump retaining bracket from the body panel, then lift out the retaining strap and pump through the body aperture **(see illustrations)**.
5 Where applicable, release the insulation from around the pump, then disconnect the

b) *Working inside the tailgate, twist the bulbholders anti-clockwise, and remove the foglight bulbholders from the light units.*

c) *Unscrew the nuts securing the rear light panel to the tailgate.*
d) *Working on the outside of the tailgate, remove the rear light panel securing screw, located next to the right-hand number plate light.*
e) *Withdraw the rear light panel from the tailgate.*

6 Remove the tailgate wiper motor as described in Chapter 12.
7 Once the wiper motor has been removed, access can be obtained to the two exterior handle securing nuts.
8 Disconnect the lock operating rod(s) from the exterior handle, noting the location of the rod(s) to aid refitting.
9 Unscrew the two securing nuts, and withdraw the exterior handle.
10 Refitting is a reversal of removal, but ensure that the lock operating rod(s) is/are correctly reconnected as noted before removal.

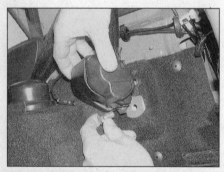

21.3a Unbolt the inertial reel . . .

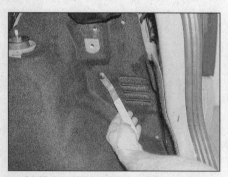

21.3b . . . then prise out the securing
clips . . .

21.3c . . . and pull the trim from the side of
the luggage compartment –
Ibiza Hatchback model

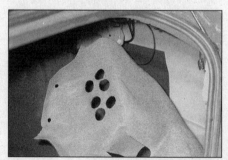

21.3d Pulling the trim from the side of the
luggage compartment –
Cordoba Saloon model

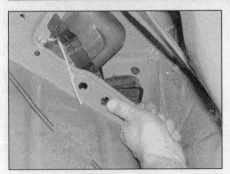

21.4a Press the lugs . . .

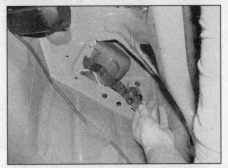

21.4b . . . to release the pump retaining bracket – Ibiza Hatchback model

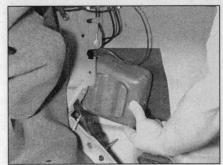

21.4c Lifting out the central locking vacuum pump – Cordoba Saloon model

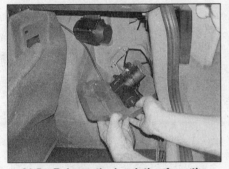

21.5a Release the insulation from the pump . . .

21.5b . . . then disconnect the vacuum pipe . . .

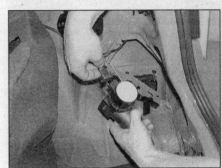

21.5c . . . and the wiring plug, and withdraw the pump – Ibiza Hatchback model

vacuum pipe and the wiring plug from the pump (squeeze the connector to disconnect the vacuum pipe) (see illustrations).

6 Withdraw the pump from the luggage compartment.

Refitting

7 Refitting is a reversal of removal, but ensure that the vacuum pipe is securely reconnected, and check the operation of the central locking system on refitting.

Central locking vacuum pump – Cordoba Vario models

Removal

8 The central locking vacuum pump is located under the spare wheel cover at the right-hand rear corner of the luggage compartment.

9 Working in the luggage compartment, lift the spare wheel cover and support it with the support hook.

10 Where applicable, release the rubber securing strap from the pump cover, then lift the pump and foam surround its housing (see illustration).

11 Lift the surround from the pump, then lift out the pump and disconnect the wiring plug and the vacuum pipe (see illustration).

12 Withdraw the pump from the luggage compartment.

Refitting

13 Refitting is a reversal of removal, but ensure that the vacuum pipe is securely

reconnected, and check the operation of the central locking system on refitting.

Central locking door microswitch

Removal

14 Remove the door lock as described in Section 15.

15 Carefully release the two securing clips, and prise the switch from the door lock actuator.

Refitting

16 Refitting is a reversal of removal.

Door lock actuator

Removal

17 Remove the door lock as described in Section 15.

18 Turn the lock latch to the locked position,

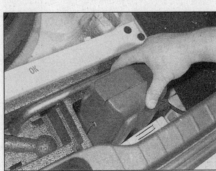

21.10 Lift the pump and foam surround from housing . . .

then unscrew the lock actuator retaining screw. Release the retaining clips, and remove the actuator from the lock, noting how the actuator plunger engages with the lock lever.

Refitting

19 Refitting is a reversal of removal, but refit the lock as described in Section 15, and on completion, check the operation of the central locking system.

Tailgate lock actuator

Removal

20 Open the tailgate, then carefully release the securing clips and withdraw the tailgate trim panel.

21 Disconnect the lock operating rod from the lock or linkage, as applicable.

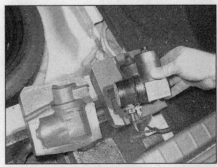

21.11 . . . then lift the foam surround from the pump – Cordoba Vario model

11

21.22a Slacken the securing screws . . .

21.22b . . . then withdraw the tailgate lock actuator and disconnect the vacuum pipe – Hatchback model

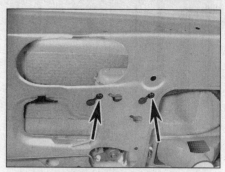

21.22c Tailgate lock actuator securing screws – Cordoba Vario models

22 Slacken the securing screws (there is no need to remove them completely), and withdraw the actuator from the tailgate, complete with the lock operating rod **(see illustrations)**. Disconnect the vacuum pipe from the actuator by squeezing the connector.

Refitting

23 Refitting is a reversal of removal, but make sure that the vacuum pipe is securely reconnected, and on completion check the operation of the central locking system.

Boot lid lock actuator

Removal

24 Open the boot lid, then carefully prise out the securing clips and withdraw the boot lid trim panel.
25 Unscrew the securing screws and remove

the lock actuator and operating rod from the boot lid (disconnect the operating rod from the lock as the actuator is removed) **(see illustration)**..
26 Disconnect the vacuum pipe, and remove the actuator **(see illustration)**.

Refitting

27 Refitting is a reversal of removal, but make sure that the vacuum pipe is securely reconnected, and on completion check the operation of the central locking system.

Fuel filler flap actuator – all models except Cordoba Vario

Removal

28 Remove the central locking vacuum pump as described previously in this Section.
29 Slacken the two fuel filler flap actuator securing screws, then carefully pull out the

actuator and disconnect the vacuum pipe by squeezing the connector **(see illustrations)**.

Refitting

30 Refitting is a reversal of removal, but make sure that the vacuum pipe is securely reconnected, and make sure that the actuator plunger is correctly positioned in the plunger hole. On completion check the operation of the central locking system.

Fuel filler flap actuator – Cordoba Vario models

Removal

31 Working in the luggage compartment, remove the luggage load cover side support panel as follows.
  a) Unscrew the two securing screws from the front edge of the panel (behind the rear seat back catch striker).
  b) Working in the luggage compartment, unscrew the two lower panel securing screws, then pull the panel away from the body to release the securing clips, and remove the panel.
32 Carefully prise out the retaining clips and remove the netting pocket from the side of the luggage compartment.
33 Prise out the remaining securing clips, and carefully pull the side trim panel from the luggage compartment.
34 Slacken the two fuel filler flap actuator securing screws, then carefully pull out the actuator and disconnect the vacuum pipe by squeezing the connector **(see illustration)**.

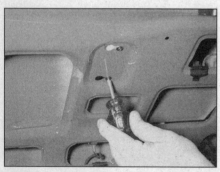

21.25 Unscrew the securing screws . . .

21.26 . . . then withdraw the boot lid lock actuator and disconnect the vacuum pipe

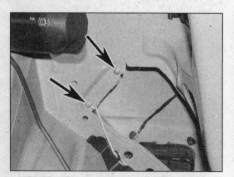

21.29a Slacken the securing screws (arrowed) . . .

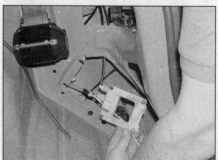

21.29b . . . and remove the fuel filler flap actuator – Ibiza Hatchback model

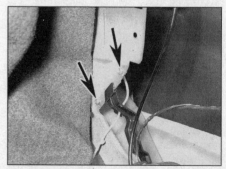

21.29c Fuel filler flap actuator securing screws (arrowed) – Cordoba Saloon model

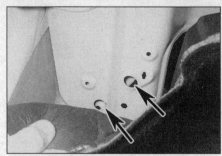

21.34 Fuel filler flap actuator securing screw locations (arrowed) – Cordoba Vario model

Refitting

35 Refitting is a reversal of removal, but make sure that the vacuum pipe is securely reconnected, and make sure that the actuator plunger is correctly positioned in the plunger hole. On completion check the operation of the central locking system.

Remote-control central locking receiver unit

36 The receiver unit is incorporated in the interior rear view mirror. Refer to Section 23 for details of mirror removal and refitting.

Remote-control central locking transmitter unit batteries - renewal

37 Insert a screwdriver into the slot next to the manufacturer's logo on the key, and carefully lever the key body from the blade.
38 Carefully lever the clips to separate the two halves of the key body.
39 Lever apart the two clips to release the batteries from the key body, then lift out the batteries, noting the position of the metal spacer between the batteries.
40 Fit the new batteries using a reversal of the removal procedure, noting that the correct orientation of the batteries is marked inside the key body. Make sure that the spacer is refitted between the two batteries.

22 Electric window components - removal and refitting

Window switches
1 Refer to Chapter 12.

Window regulator motors

Removal

2 Remove the regulator assembly as described in Section 16.
3 Remove the screw shown (A), and refit it to location (B) – this is vital to prevent the regulator cable drum from coming out of its housing **(see illustration)**.
4 Release the motor wiring connector from the bracket on the regulator assembly, and remove the tape securing the wiring to the bracket.

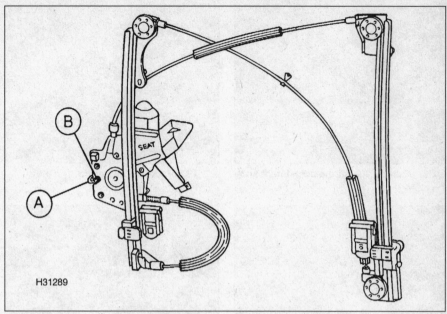

22.3 Remove screw (A) and refit it to location (B)

5 Unscrew the ten securing screws, noting their locations, then carefully withdraw the motor from the regulator assembly. Recover the gasket and the seal.

Refitting

6 Refitting is a reversal of removal, but ensure that the motor wiring is taped back into position on the regulator bracket, and on completion, remove the cable drum retaining screw from location (B), and screw it back into position in location (A) – see paragraph 3.

23 Mirror components – removal and refitting

Interior rear view mirror

Note: *On models equipped with remote-control central locking, the receiver unit is incorporated in the interior rear view mirror.*

Removal

1 On models with remote-control central locking, insert a small flat-bladed screwdriver

23.2 Removing the interior rear view mirror

into the joint between the two mirror stalk covers, and prise off the covers for access to the remote-control receiver wiring connector.
2 Grasp the mirror stalk, and carefully twist the assembly in the vertical plane (approximately 15 to 20°) until the assembly is released from the mounting plate on the windscreen **(see illustration)**. Do not pull the mirror stalk down, as this may damage the roof lining.

Refitting

3 Refitting is a reversal of removal. Where applicable, ensure that the remote-control central locking receiver wiring connector is securely reconnected.

Exterior rear view mirror

Removal

4 On models fitted with electric mirrors, disconnect the battery negative lead.
5 On models fitted with manually-operated mirrors, pull the rubber cover from the adjustment knob, then pull off the adjustment knob **(see illustrations)**.

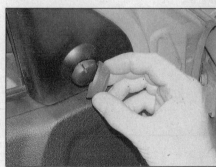

23.5a Pull the rubber cover from the adjustment knob . . .

11

23.5b . . . then pull off the adjustment knob

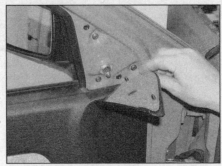

23.6 Prise off the mirror trim plate

23.7a Unscrew the nut securing the adjuster to the door . . .

23.7b . . . then unscrew the three mirror securing screws . . .

23.7c . . . and withdraw the mirror from outside the door

6 Working at the inner front edge of the door, carefully prise off the mirror trim plate **(see illustration)**.

7 Unscrew the three now-exposed mirror securing screws, and on models with manually-adjustable mirrors, unscrew the nut securing the adjuster to the door, then carefully withdraw the mirror from outside the door, taking care not to damage the paint **(see illustrations)**. On models with electric mirrors, disconnect the mirror wiring plug.

Refitting

8 Refitting is a reversal of removal.

Exterior rear view mirror glass
Removal

9 Using two large flat-bladed instruments, such as spatulas, carefully prise behind the centre of the glass at the top and bottom, to release it from the balljoints **(see illustrations)**.

23.8a Prise behind the centre of the glass at the top and bottom . . .

23.8b . . . to release it from the balljoints

Refitting

10 To refit, align the mirror glass with the guide pins, then push the centre of the glass to engage it with the balljoint. Take care, as the glass is easily broken.

24 Windscreen, rear window and fixed rear quarterlight glass - general

These areas of glass are secured by the tight fit of the weatherstrip in the body aperture, and are bonded in position with a special adhesive. Renewal of such fixed glass is a difficult, messy and time-consuming task, which is beyond the scope of the home mechanic. It is difficult, unless one has plenty of practice, to obtain a secure, waterproof fit. Furthermore, the task carries a high risk of breakage; this applies especially to the laminated glass windscreen.

In view of this, owners are strongly advised to have this sort of work carried out by one of the many specialist windscreen fitters.

25 Rear quarter windows (opening) - removal and refitting

Removal

1 Have an assistant support the glass from outside the vehicle then, working inside the car, unscrew the screws securing the glass to the hinges and the stud securing the catch to the glass, and withdraw the glass.

Refitting

2 Refitting is a reversal of removal.

26 Sunroof components – general information

Due to the complexity of the sunroof mechanism, considerable expertise is needed to repair, replace or adjust the sunroof components successfully. Removal of the roof first requires the headlining to be removed, which is a complex and tedious operation, and not a task to be undertaken lightly. Therefore, any problems with the sunroof should be referred to a Seat dealer.

27 Body exterior fittings – removal and refitting

Wheel arch liners and body under-panels

1 The various plastic covers fitted to the underside of the vehicle are secured in position by a mixture of screws, nuts and retaining clips, and removal will be fairly obvious on inspection **(see illustration)**. Work methodically around the panel removing its retaining screws, nuts and/or releasing its retaining clips until the panel is free and can be removed from the underside of the vehicle.

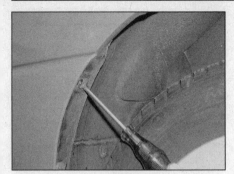

27.1 Removing a wheel arch liner securing screw

Most clips used on the vehicle are simply prised out of position. Some two-part plastic clips are released by pressing out their centre pins and then removing the outer section of the clip; new clips will be required on refitting if the centre pins are not recovered.
2 On refitting, renew any retaining clips that may have been broken on removal, and ensure that the panel is securely retained by all the relevant clips, screws and nuts, as applicable.

Body trim strips and badges

3 The various body trim strips and badges are held in position with a special adhesive tape. Removal requires the trim/badge to be heated, to soften the adhesive, and then cut away from the surface. Due to the high risk of damage to the vehicle's paintwork during this operation, it is recommended that this task should be entrusted to a Seat dealer.

28.1a Unclip the plastic trim covers from the inner . . .

28.2 . . . then unscrew the seat travel stop nut and bolt

Fuel filler flap

Removal

4 Open the filler flap and unscrew the two securing bolts.

Refitting

5 Refitting is a reversal of removal, but if necessary adjust the position of the flap within the elongated bolt holes, to achieve an even gap all round between the edge of the flap and the surrounding body panel.

28 Seats – removal and refitting

Front seat

Removal

1 Slide the seat fully forwards, and unclip the plastic trim covers from the rear of the inner and outer seat rails **(see illustrations)**.
2 Slide the seat backwards, then unscrew and remove the seat travel stop nut and bolt from the centre of the seat **(see illustration)**.
3 Carefully slide the seat out from the rear of the rails, and lift it out from the vehicle. Note that the rails are normally lubricated with grease, which can easily contaminate the vehicle trim or clothes.

Refitting

4 Refitting is a reversal of removal, but make sure that the seat stop nut and bolt are tightened securely.

28.1b . . . and outer seat rails . . .

28.7a Carefully push the seat back retaining levers over

Rear seat assembly

Removal

5 Lift up the rear seat cushion(s) then slacken and remove the hinge retaining bolts and remove the seat cushion(s) from the vehicle.
6 Fold down the rear seat backs.
7 Using a screwdriver, carefully push the retaining levers over, then lift out the seat back assembly. On models with split rear seats, prise off the spring clip securing the relevant seat back to the centre hinge before lifting it out **(see illustrations)**.

Refitting

8 Refitting is the reverse of removal making sure the seat backs are clipped securely in position.

29 Seat belt tensioner system – general information and precautions

General information

Most models covered in this manual are fitted with a front seat belt tensioner system. The system is designed to instantaneously take up any slack in the seat belt in the case of a sudden frontal impact, therefore reducing the possibility of injury to the front seat occupants. Each front seat is fitted with its system, the tensioner being situated behind the sill trim panel.

The seat belt tensioner is triggered by a frontal impact above a pre-determined force. Lesser impacts, including impacts from behind, will not trigger the system.

When the system is triggered, the explosive gas in the tensioner mechanism retracts and locks the seat belt through a cable which acts on the inertia reel. This prevents the seat belt moving and keeps the occupant firmly in position in the seat. Once the tensioner has been triggered, the seat belt will be permanently locked and the assembly must be renewed.

There is a risk of injury if the system is triggered inadvertently when working on the vehicle, and it is therefore strongly recommended that any work involving the seat belt tensioner system is entrusted to a Seat dealer.

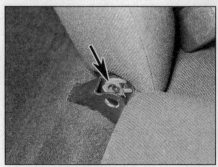

28.7b Prise off the spring clip (arrowed) securing the seat back to the centre hinge

11

30.1 Pull the front door sill trim panel from the sill – five-door Ibiza model

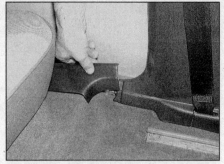

30.2 Pull up the front edge of the rear door sill trim panel – five-door Ibiza model

30.3 Remove the centre pillar trim panel – five-door Ibiza model

Note the following warnings before contemplating any work on the front seat belts.

Precautions

⚠️ **Warning: Do not expose the tensioner mechanism to temperatures in excess of 100° C (212° F).**

If the tensioner mechanism is dropped, it must be renewed, even it has suffered no apparent damage.

Do not allow any solvents to come into contact with the tensioner mechanism.

Do not attempt to open the tensioner mechanism as it contains explosive gas.

Tensioners must be discharged before they are disposed of, but this task should be entrusted to a Seat dealer.

30 Seat belt components - removal and refitting

⚠️ **Warning: On models equipped with seat belt tensioners refer to Section 29 before proceeding; under no circumstances should you attempt to separate the tensioner assembly from the inertia reel.**

Front seat belt – five-door Ibiza Hatchback, Cordoba Saloon and Cordoba Vario models

Removal

1 Carefully pull the front door sill trim panel from the sill **(see illustration)**.

2 Carefully pull up the front edge of the rear door sill trim panel to release it from the centre pillar trim panel **(see illustration)**.
3 Remove the centre pillar trim panel by pulling it upwards **(see illustration)**.
4 Unbolt the trim bracket from the centre pillar **(see illustration)**.
5 Prise the trim plate from the seat belt upper anchor bolt **(see illustration)**.
6 Unbolt the seat belt lower anchor, then unbolt the upper anchor from the centre pillar **(see illustrations)**.
7 Unscrew the inertia reel securing bolt and, where applicable, unscrew the bolt securing the seat belt tensioner to the sill **(see illustrations)**.
8 Lift out the seat belt/tensioner assembly **(see illustration)**.

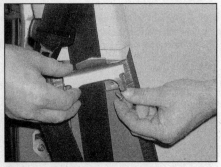

30.4 Unbolt the trim bracket from the centre pillar – five-door Ibiza model

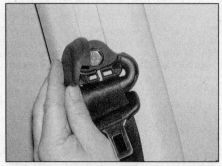

30.5 Prise the trim plate from the seat belt upper anchor bolt – five-door Ibiza model

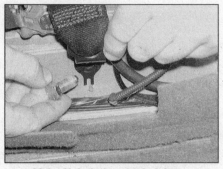

30.6a Unbolt the seat belt lower anchor . . .

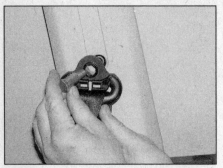

30.6b . . . then unbolt the upper anchor – five-door Ibiza model

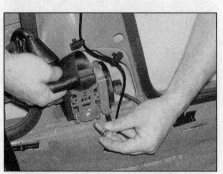

30.7a Unscrew the inertia reel securing bolt . . .

30.7b . . . and the bolt securing the tensioner to the sill . . .

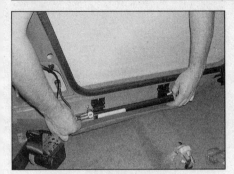

30.8 . . . then lift out the seat belt/tensioner assembly – five-door Ibiza model

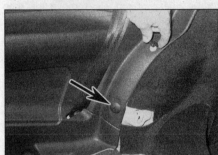

30.11 Remove the screw securing the rear edge of the sill trim panel – three-door Ibiza model

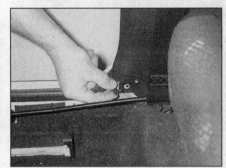

30.13 Unscrew the passenger compartment side trim panel securing screw – three-door Ibiza model

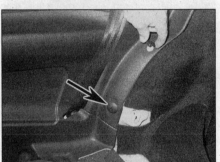

30.14a Unscrew the plastic securing nuts . . .

30.14b . . . then prise the securing clip from the lower edge of the panel – three-door Ibiza model

Refitting

9 Refitting is a reversal of the removal procedure, ensuring that all the seat belt mounting bolts are tightened to the specified torque, and all disturbed trim panels are securely retained by all the relevant retaining clips.

Front seat belt - three-door Ibiza Hatchback models and Cordoba Coupe models

Removal

10 Remove the rear seats as described in Section 28.

11 Remove the screw securing the rear edge of the sill trim panel, then carefully pull the sill trim panel from the sill (see illustration).

12 On Ibiza Hatchback models, working in the luggage compartment, remove the rear parcel shelf, then remove the relevant parcel shelf side support panel as follows.

a) Disconnect the wiring plug from the loudspeaker, and where applicable, disconnect the wiring plug from the luggage compartment light.

b) Unscrew the four side support panel securing nuts accessible in the luggage compartment beneath the panel, and the single nut at the front of the panel (accessible from the passenger compartment).

c) Carefully withdraw the panel, feeding the rear seat belt webbing through the panel as it is withdrawn.

13 Unscrew the passenger compartment side trim panel securing screw, located next to the rear seat back catch striker (see illustration).

14 Unscrew the three side trim panel plastic securing nuts, then carefully prise the plastic securing clip from the lower edge of the panel (see illustrations).

15 Pull the side trim panel upwards to release the upper securing clips from the holes in the body, then withdraw the panel, feeding the rear seat belt webbing through the slot in the panel as it is withdrawn.

16 Unbolt the trim bracket located behind the rear edge of the door aperture (the seat belt webbing passes through the bracket).

17 Prise the trim plate from the seat belt upper anchor bolt, then unscrew the upper anchor bolt.

18 Unscrew the bolt securing the seat belt lower anchor rail to the sill, then slide the seat belt webbing from the anchor rail (see illustration).

19 Unscrew the inertia reel securing bolt and, where applicable, unscrew the screw securing the seat belt tensioner to the body panel (see illustration).

20 Lift out the seat belt/tensioner assembly (see illustration).

Refitting

21 Refitting is a reversal of the removal procedure, ensuring that all the seat belt mounting bolts are tightened to the specified torque, and all disturbed trim panels are securely retained by all the relevant retaining clips.

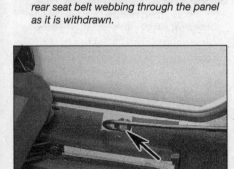

30.18 Unscrew the bolt (arrowed) securing the seat belt lower anchor rail to the sill – three-door Ibiza model

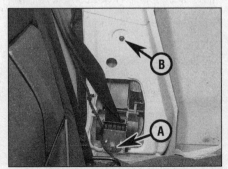

30.19 Unscrew the inertia reel securing bolt (A) and the screw (B) securing the seat belt tensioner to the body panel – three-door Ibiza model

30.20 Lift out the seat belt/tensioner assembly – three-door Ibiza model

11

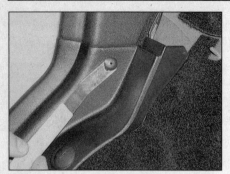

30.26a Prise the retaining clip from the top of the rear sill/rear wheel arch trim panel . . .

30.26b . . . then unscrew the plastic nuts . . .

30.26c . . . and pull the panel away from the body, noting that it is clipped into the rear pillar trim panel – Ibiza Hatchback model

Front seat belt stalk

Removal

22 Remove the seat as described in Section 28.
23 Slacken and remove the bolt securing the stalk to the seat, and remove the stalk.

Refitting

24 Refitting is a reversal of removal, ensuring that the stalk securing bolt is securely tightened. Refit the seat with reference to Section 28.

Rear side seat belt – Ibiza Hatchback models

Removal

25 On three-door models remove the passenger compartment side trim panel as described in paragraphs 10 to 15.

26 On five-door models, remove the rear sill/rear wheel arch trim panel as follows **(see illustrations)**.
 a) *Remove the rear seats as described in Section 28.*
 b) *Using a suitable forked tool, or a large flat-bladed screwdriver, prise the retaining clip from the top of the trim panel.*
 c) *Unscrew the three large plastic nuts – two on the wheel arch, and one on the sill.*
 d) *Carefully pull the rear sill/rear wheel arch trim panel away from the body, noting that the panel is clipped into the rear pillar trim panel – take care not to break the clip as the panel is removed.*
27 On five-door models, slacken and remove the retaining nuts securing the relevant parcel shelf side trim panel in position. Where applicable, disconnect the wiring from the loudspeaker, then unclip the panel from the

rear pillar trim panel and remove it from the vehicle, feeding the seat belt webbing through the panel as it is removed; where necessary free the luggage compartment light from the panel as it is removed **(see illustrations)**.
28 Slacken and remove the seat belt lower anchor bolt **(see illustration)**.
29 Prise off the trim plate, then slacken and remove the seat belt upper anchor bolt and free the belt from the rear pillar **(see illustration)**. Where necessary, recover the spacer from behind the belt anchorage.
30 Working in the luggage compartment, unscrew the inertia reel mounting bolt, then free the reel from the pillar and remove the seat belt from the vehicle **(see illustration)**. If necessary, unscrew the retaining bolt and remove the height adjuster mechanism from the pillar (where fitted).

30.27a Remove the front securing nut (arrowed) . . .

30.27b . . . the two rear securing nuts and the two side securing nuts (arrowed) . . .

30.27c . . . then remove the parcel shelf side trim panel – five-door Ibiza model

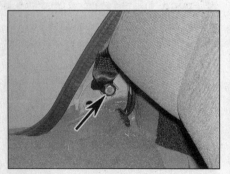

30.28 Remove the seat belt lower anchor bolt (arrowed) – Ibiza Hatchback model

30.29 Prise off the trim plate, then remove the seat belt upper anchor bolt - Ibiza Hatchback model

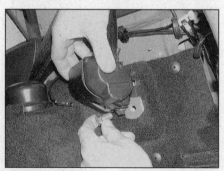

30.30 Unscrew the mounting bolt and lift out the inertia reel – Ibiza Hatchback model

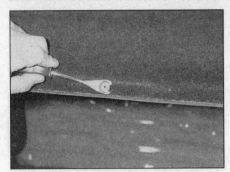

30.34a Prise out the retaining clips . . .

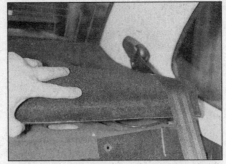

30.34b . . . and lift the parcel shelf away from the body – Cordoba Saloon model

30.35a Prising out the rear wheel arch/rear pillar trim panel upper securing clip – Cordoba Saloon model

Upper securing screw arrowed

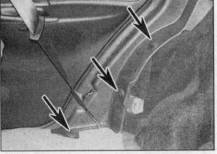

30.35b Rear wheel arch/rear pillar trim panel plastic fasteners (arrowed) – Cordoba Saloon model

30.35c Removing the rear wheel arch liner/rear pillar trim panel – Cordoba Saloon model

disturbed trim panels are securely retained by all the relevant retaining clips.

> **HAYNES HiNT** *When refitting the rear parcel shelf, remove the rear shelf retaining clips from the shelf, and slide them into position on the lugs on the body. Refit the shelf and push down on the rear edge to engage the clips.*

Refitting

31 Refitting is a reversal of the removal procedure, ensuring that all the seat belt mounting bolts are tightened to the specified torque, and that all disturbed trim panels are securely retained by all the relevant retaining clips.

Rear side seat belt – Cordoba Saloon models

Removal

32 Remove the rear seats as described in Section 28.
33 Where applicable, remove the rear parcel shelf-mounted loudspeakers as described in Chapter 12.
34 Working at the lower edge of the rear parcel shelf, carefully prise out the retaining clips, and lift the parcel shelf away from the

body (see illustrations). As the parcel shelf is removed, feed the seat belt webbing through the slots in the side of the panel.
35 Remove the rear wheel arch/rear pillar trim panel as follows (see illustrations).
  a) *Unscrew the upper panel securing screw.*
  b) *Prise out the upper panel securing clip.*
  c) *Unscrew the three plastic fasteners from the panel.*
  d) *Pull the lower edge of the panel from the sill.*
  e) *Pull the panel forwards to release it from the body, then remove the panel.*
36 Proceed as described in paragraphs 28 to 30 (see illustration).

Refitting

37 Refitting is a reversal of the removal procedure, ensuring that all the seat belt anchor bolts are securely tightened, and all

disturbed trim panels are securely retained by all the relevant retaining clips.

Rear side seat belt – Cordoba Coupe models

Removal

38 Proceed as described for the front seat belt in paragraphs 10 to 15.
39 Partially unclip the rear parcel tray.
40 Proceed as described in paragraphs 28 to 30, feeding the belt webbing and anchor plates through the hole in the rear parcel shelf as the belt is removed.

Refitting

41 Refitting is a reversal of the removal procedure, ensuring that all the seat belt anchor bolts are securely tightened, and all disturbed trim panels are securely retained by all the relevant retaining clips.

Rear side seat belt – Cordoba Vario models

Removal

42 Remove the rear seats as described in Section 28.
43 Working in the luggage compartment, remove the luggage load cover side support panel as follows (see illustrations).
  a) *Unscrew the two securing screws from the front edge of the panel (behind the rear seat back catch striker).*
  b) *Working in the luggage compartment, unscrew the two lower panel securing screws, then pull the panel away from the body to release the securing clips, and remove the panel.*
44 Working in the passenger compartment, remove the rear wheel arch trim panel as follows.

30.36 Rear side seat belt lower anchor bolt (arrowed) – Cordoba Saloon model

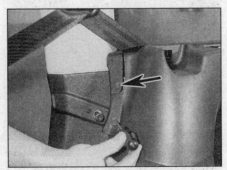

30.43a Unscrew the two securing screws from the front edge of the panel . . .

11

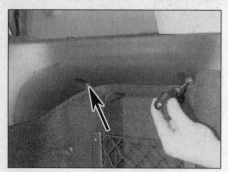

30.43b . . . and the two lower panel securing screws . . .

30.43c . . . then pull the load cover support panel from the body – Cordoba Vario model

30.45 Remove the seat belt guide bracket (arrowed) – Cordoba Vario model

a) *Unscrew upper retaining screw.*
b) *Unscrew the three plastic retaining clips, then carefully pull the trim panel from the body.*

45 Unscrew the two securing bolts, and remove the seat belt guide bracket from the body panel above the rear suspension strut top mounting **(see illustration)**.

46 Proceed as described in paragraphs 28 to 30.

Refitting

47 Refitting is a reversal of the removal procedure, ensuring that all the seat belt anchor bolts are securely tightened, and all disturbed trim panels are securely retained by all the relevant retaining clips.

Rear centre belt and buckles

Removal

48 Fold the rear seat cushion forwards then slacken and remove the bolt and washers

securing the centre belt and/or buckle assembly to the floor, and remove it from the vehicle **(see illustration)**.

Refitting

49 Refitting is a reversal of the removal procedure, ensuring that all the seat belt mounting bolts are securely tightened.

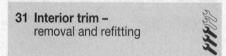

31 Interior trim –
removal and refitting

Note: *Specific details for most interior panels are contained within Section 30.*

General information

1 The interior trim panels are secured using either screws or various types of trim fasteners, usually studs or clips.

2 Check that there are no other panels overlapping the one to be removed; usually

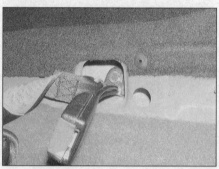

30.48 Centre seat belt/buckle mounting viewed with rear seats removed

there is a sequence that has to be followed, and this will only become obvious on close inspection.

3 Remove all obvious fasteners, such as screws. If the panel will not come free, it is held by hidden clips or fasteners. These are usually situated around the edge of the panel and can be prised up to release them; note, however that they can break quite easily so replacements should be available. The best way of releasing such clips without the correct type of tool, is to use a large flat-bladed screwdriver. Note in many cases that the adjacent sealing strip must be prised back to release a panel.

4 When removing a panel, **never** use excessive force or the panel may be damaged; always check carefully that all fasteners or other relevant components have been removed or released before attempting to withdraw a panel.

5 Refitting is the reverse of the removal procedure; secure the fasteners by pressing them firmly into place and ensure that all disturbed components are correctly secured to prevent rattles.

Passenger's side glovebox

Removal

6 Open up the glovebox lid then slacken and remove the two upper and two lower retaining screws. Remove the screw securing the glovebox catch, and remove the catch assembly. Lift the glovebox upwards, complete with the oddments tray, and remove the glovebox/oddments tray assembly from the facia **(see illustrations)**.

31.6a Remove the two upper . . .

31.6b . . . and two lower retaining screws . . .

31.6c . . . then remove the glovebox catch . . .

31.6d . . . and remove the passenger's glovebox/oddments tray assembly from the facia

Refitting

7 Refitting is the reverse of removal.

Driver's side glovebox

Removal

8 Open the glovebox, then push the glovebox lid side supports inwards so that the glovebox can be lowered and released from its hinge pins **(see illustration)**.

Refitting

9 Refitting is a reversal of removal.

Carpets

10 The passenger compartment floor carpet is in one piece and is secured at its edges by screws or clips, usually the same fasteners used to secure the various adjoining trim panels.
11 Carpet removal and refitting is reasonably

31.8 Push the driver's side glovebox lid side supports inwards, then release the glovebox from its hinge pins

straightforward but very time-consuming because all adjoining trim panels must be removed first, as must components such as the seats, the centre console and seat belt lower anchorages.

Headlining

12 The headlining is clipped to the roof and can be withdrawn only once all fittings such as the grab handles, sun visors, sunroof (if fitted), windscreen and rear quarter windows and related trim panels have been removed and the door, tailgate and sunroof aperture sealing strips have been prised clear.
13 Note that headlining removal requires considerable skill and experience if it is to be carried out without damage and is therefore best entrusted to an expert.

32 Centre console - removal and refitting

Removal

1 Unclip the ashtray from its housing.
2 Where applicable, remove the cassette storage trays by pulling them carefully from their locations in the centre console.
3 Where applicable, carefully prise the auxiliary gauge trim plate from the centre console.
4 Working at the rear of the console, prise out the screw covers, then unscrew the two screws securing the console to the floor **(see illustrations)**.
5 Unclip the handbrake lever gaiter from the centre console, and slide the gaiter up the handbrake lever **(see illustration)**.
6 Similarly, unclip the gear lever gaiter from the centre console, and slide it up the gear lever **(see illustration)**.
7 Unscrew the two centre console securing nuts, revealed by unclipping the gear lever gaiter **(see illustration)**.
8 Pull the rear section of the console upwards to release it from the front section of the console, then withdraw the rear section of the console over the gear lever and the handbrake lever **(see illustrations)**.
9 Unscrew the screw securing the front section of the console to the facia bracket, then withdraw the front section of the console **(see illustrations overleaf)**. Where applicable, disconnect the battery negative lead, then

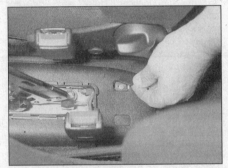

32.4a Prise out the screw covers . . .

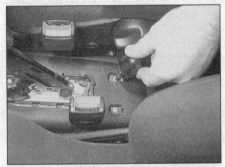

32.4b . . . and unscrew the two screws securing the console to the floor

32.5 Unclip the handbrake lever gaiter from the centre console

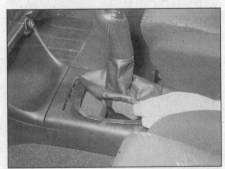

32.6 Unclip the gear lever gaiter from the centre console

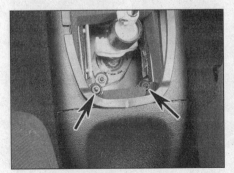

32.7 Unscrew the two centre console securing nuts (arrowed)

32.8a Pull the console upwards . . .

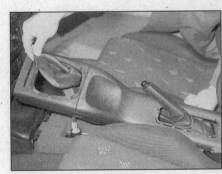

32.8b . . . then withdraw it over the gear lever and handbrake lever

11

32.9a Unscrew the securing screw (arrowed) . . .

disconnect the auxiliary gauge wiring connectors as the front section of the console is withdrawn.

Refitting

10 Refitting is the reverse of removal making sure all fasteners are securely tightened.

---

33 Facia assembly -
removal and refitting

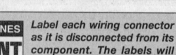

 Label each wiring connector as it is disconnected from its component. The labels will prove useful on refitting, when routing the wiring and feeding the wiring through the facia apertures.

32.9b . . . and withdraw the front section of the console

Removal

1 Disconnect the battery negative lead.
2 On models equipped with a passenger side airbag, remove the airbag unit as described in Chapter 12.
3 Remove the steering wheel as described in Chapter 10.
4 Remove the instrument panel as described in Chapter 12.
5 Where applicable, remove the centre console as described in Section 32.
6 Slacken and remove the retaining screws, and remove the steering column lower shroud, then unclip the upper shroud (see illustrations).
7 Unscrew the three column stalk switch securing screws, then remove the indicator stalk switch assembly by pulling it from the lighting stalk switch (see illustration).
8 Working under the steering column, dis-

connect the wiring plugs from the wash/wipe stalk switch, then slide the wash/wipe stalk switch from the steering column (see illustration).
9 Remove the lighting switch from the driver's side of the facia, as described in Chapter 12.
10 Using a suitable screwdriver, carefully prise the ventilation nozzle from the driver's side of the facia. Similarly, carefully prise the ventilation nozzle from the passenger's side of the facia (see Chapter 3).
11 Again using a small screwdriver, carefully prise the centre ventilation nozzles from the facia. Prise gently at both sides of each nozzle, and take care not to damage the surrounding trim (see Chapter 3).
12 Prise the switch(es) from the facia centre panel, next to the centre ventilation nozzle housing, and disconnect the wiring plug(s) (see illustration).
13 Remove the radio/cassette player as described in Chapter 12, and on models not fitted with electric windows or mirrors, remove the radio/cassette player housing.
14 Carefully prise off the heater control panel trim plate (see illustration).
15 Remove the two screws securing the switch mounting plate in position below the heater controls. Disconnect the wiring plugs from the switches, and remove the mounting plate/switch assembly (see illustrations).
16 Where applicable, reach behind the facia panel and disconnect the wiring from the rear of the cigarette lighter housing.
17 Working at the top of the centre facia ventilation nozzle housings, unscrew the two

33.6a Remove the securing screws . . .

33.6b . . . and remove the steering column lower shroud . . .

33.6c . . . then unclip the upper shroud

33.7 Remove the indicator stalk switch . . .

33.8 . . . and the wash/wipe stalk switch

33.12 Prising a switch from the facia centre panel

33.14 Prise off the heater control trim plate

33.15a Remove the screws securing the switch mounting plate . . .

33.15b . . . the disconnect the wiring plugs and remove the mounting plate/switch assembly

upper screws securing the facia centre panel to the facia **(see illustration).**

18 Remove the four screws securing the heater control panel to the facia centre panel, then unscrew the three screws from the bottom of the facia centre panel, then withdraw the facia centre panel **(see illustrations).** Where applicable, cut the cable-tie securing the wiring harness to the panel to allow the panel to be withdrawn.

19 Where applicable, remove the passenger's side glovebox with reference to Section 31.

20 Where applicable, remove the securing screws and withdraw the passenger's side lower facia panel from under the facia.

21 Working at the passenger's side end of the facia, prise out the cover, and unscrew the facia side securing bolt **(see illustrations).**

22 Remove the driver's side glovebox with reference to Section 31.

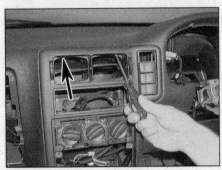

33.17 Unscrew the two facia centre panel upper screws

23 Remove the securing screws and withdraw the driver's side lower facia panel from under the facia **(see illustration).**

24 Working at the driver's side end of the facia, prise out the cover, and unscrew the

33.18a Remove the heater control panel securing screws (arrowed) . . .

remaining facia side securing bolt **(see illustration).**

25 Unclip the cover from the lower centre facia bracket, on top of the floor centre tunnel, then unscrew the two screws securing the facia to

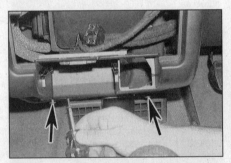

33.18b . . . then unscrew the three screws (arrowed) from the bottom of the facia centre panel . . .

33.18c . . . and withdraw the facia centre panel

33.21a Prise out the cover . . .

33.21b . . . and unscrew the facia side securing bolt

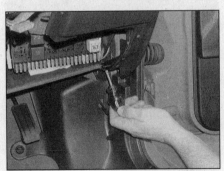

33.23a Remove the securing screws . . .

33.23b . . . and withdraw the driver's side lower facia panel

11

33.24 Unscrew the remaining facia side securing bolt

33.25a Unclip the cover from the lower centre facia bracket . . .

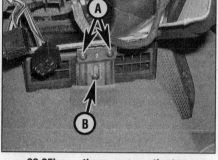

33.25b . . . then unscrew the two screws (A) securing the facia to the lower bracket, and the screw (B) securing the bracket to the heater ducting

33.25c Unscrew the nut securing the bracket to the floor . . .

33.25d . . . and remove the bracket

27 Working through the instrument panel aperture, unclip the heater ducting for access to the two upper facia securing nuts, then unscrew and remove the nuts **(see illustration)**.

28 Working under the steering column, unscrew the two screws securing the facia to the bracket above the steering column **(see illustration)**.

29 Working through the passenger's side glovebox aperture, unscrew the remaining two upper facia securing nuts **(see illustration)**.

30 The facia assembly should now be free from the bulkhead, but before it can be removed, various wiring connectors must be disconnected and wiring harnesses must be released from the facia to facilitate removal. These details will vary according to model and equipment, but the following will act as a guide.

31 Working on the passenger's side of the facia, unscrew the two screws securing the footwell trim panel, then carefully unclip the panel from the surrounding panels, and withdraw it. Pull back the carpet and insulation panels for access to the facia wiring connectors – the connectors may be loose, or they may be wrapped in foam. Where applicable, release the connectors from the foam insulation, and disconnect all relevant facia wiring connectors (including the radio aerial lead, where applicable) **(see illustrations)**.

32 Similarly, unscrew the two screws securing the driver's side footwell trim panel, then

the lower bracket, and the screw securing the bracket to the lower heater ducting. Unscrew the plastic nut securing the bracket to the floor, and remove the bracket **(see illustrations)**.

26 Working at the side of the floor centre tunnel, unscrew the lower centre securing bolt from the passenger's side of the tunnel **(see illustration)**.

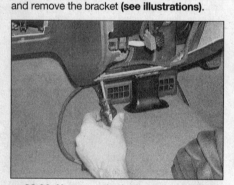

33.26 Unscrew the lower centre facia securing bolt

33.27 Working through the instrument panel aperture, unscrew the two upper facia securing nuts (arrowed)

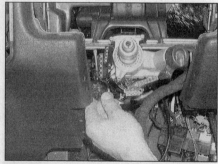

33.28 Unscrew the two screws (arrowed) securing the facia to the bracket above the steering column

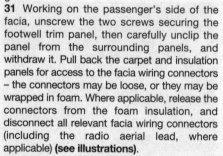

33.29 Working through the glovebox aperture, unscrew the remaining two facia securing screws (arrowed)

33.31a Withdraw the passenger's side footwell trim panel . . .

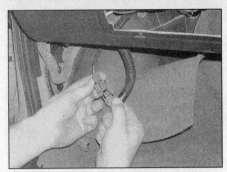

33.31b ... then disconnect the facia wiring connectors ...

33.31c ... including the radio aerial lead

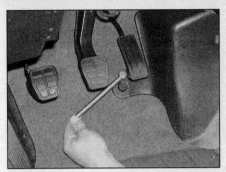

33.32a Unscrew the throttle pedal stop ...

33.32b ... and remove the bonnet release lever ...

33.32c ... then unclip the footwell trim panel

33.33 Unclip the wiring cover plate from the facia

unscrew the throttle pedal stop. Remove the two screws securing the bonnet release lever, then disconnect the bonnet release cable from the lever. Carefully unclip the footwell trim panel from the surrounding panels for access

33.34 Release the catches and lower the fusebox ...

to the facia wiring connectors. Disconnect all relevant connectors, noting their locations (see illustrations).

33 Working at the top of the instrument panel aperture, unclip the wiring cover plate from the facia to allow the wiring harness(es) to be released from the facia (see illustration).

34 Working on the driver's side of the facia, release the catches on either side of the fusebox, and carefully lower the fusebox from the facia for access to the connectors at the rear of the fusebox assembly (see illustration).

35 Trace the facia wiring harnesses to the relevant connectors in the fusebox, then disconnect the relevant connectors, noting their locations to aid refitting. Note that there is a locking clip accessible at the outboard end of the fusebox, which must be pulled out to release some of the connectors (see illustrations).

36 Carefully pull the facia forwards from the

bulkhead, and disconnect any remaining wiring connectors, including the immobiliser/alarm control unit wiring connectors (the control unit is secured to the rear of the facia) and the OBD (On-Board Diagnostics) wiring connector, where applicable.

37 Reach behind the facia, and release all relevant wires and wiring harnesses from the clips and brackets on the rear of the facia. Note that some of the wiring harnesses are removed with the facia, whilst others remain in the vehicle. Note the routing of all wiring to aid refitting. Note that it may be necessary to cut some cable-ties to release the wiring.

38 Make a final check to ensure that all wiring has been disconnected and released as necessary then, with the aid of an assistant, lift the facia from the bulkhead, and withdraw it through one of the front door apertures (see illustration).

33.35a ... then pull out the locking clip ...

33.35b ... and disconnect the wiring connectors

33.38 Withdrawing the facia

11

Refitting

39 Refitting is a reversal of the removal procedure, noting the following points:

a) Manoeuvre the facia into position, ensuring that the wiring is correctly routed and securely retained by all relevant clips.

b) Ensure that the heater air ducts are correctly clipped into position.

b) Refit the steering wheel with reference to Chapter 10.

c) Where applicable, refit the passenger's side airbag as described in Chapter 12.

d) On completion, reconnect the battery and check that all the electrical components and switches function correctly.

Chapter 12
Body electrical system

Contents

Degrees of difficulty

Easy, suitable for novice with little experience	**Fairly easy,** suitable for beginner with some experience	**Fairly difficult,** suitable for competent DIY mechanic

Difficult, suitable for experienced DIY mechanic	**Very difficult,** suitable for expert DIY or professional

Specifications

System type . . . . 12-volt negative earth

Fuses . . . . See Wiring diagrams starting on page 12•20

Bulbs   Rating and type
Headlights . . . . 60/55 W, H4
Front foglights . . . . 55 W, H3
Front sidelights . . . . 5 W, capless
Front and rear direction indicator lights . . . . . . 21 W, bayonet
Direction indicator side repeaters . . . . 5 W, capless
Stop/tail lights . . . . 21/5 W, bayonet
Rear sidelights . . . . 5 W, bayonet
Rear foglights . . . . 21 W, bayonet
Reversing lights . . . . 21 W, bayonet
Number plate lighting . . . . 5 W, capless
High-level brake light:
  Except Vario . . . . 5 W, capless
  Vario . . . . Not available
Courtesy lights . . . . 10 W, festoon
Front reading light/courtesy light . . . . 5 W, capless
Luggage compartment light . . . . 3 W, festoon
Glovebox illumination . . . . 3 W, festoon
Instrument panel illumination/warning lights . . . . 1.1 W, integral in bulbholder

1 General information and precautions

Warning: Before carrying out any work on the electrical system, read through the precautions given in Safety first! at the beginning of this manual, and in Chapter 5.

The electrical system is of 12-volt negative earth type. Power for the lights and all electrical accessories is supplied by a lead/acid type battery which is charged by the alternator.

This Chapter covers repair and service procedures for the various electrical components not associated with the engine. Information on the battery, alternator and starter motor can be found in Chapter 5.

It should be noted that prior to working on any component in the electrical system, the battery negative terminal should first be disconnected to prevent the possibility of electrical short circuits and/or fires.

Caution: Before disconnecting the battery, refer to the information given in Chapter 5A, Sections 1 and 3.

12

2 Electrical fault-finding - general information

Note: *Refer to the precautions given in Safety first! and in Chapter 5 before starting work. The following tests relate to testing of the main electrical circuits, and should not be used to test delicate electronic circuits (such as anti-lock braking systems), particularly where an electronic control module is used.*

General

1 A typical electrical circuit consists of an electrical component, any switches, relays, motors, fuses, fusible links or circuit breakers related to that component, and the wiring and connectors which link the component to both the battery and the chassis. To help to pinpoint a problem in an electrical circuit, wiring diagrams are included at the end of this Chapter.

2 Before attempting to diagnose an electrical fault, first study the appropriate wiring diagram to obtain a complete understanding of the components included in the particular circuit concerned. The possible sources of a fault can be narrowed down by noting if other components related to the circuit are operating properly. If several components or circuits fail at one time, the problem is likely to be related to a shared fuse or earth connection.

3 Electrical problems usually stem from simple causes, such as loose or corroded connections, a faulty earth connection, a blown fuse, a melted fusible link, or a faulty relay (refer to Section 3 for details of testing relays). Visually inspect the condition of all fuses, wires and connections in a problem circuit before testing the components. Use the wiring diagrams to determine which terminal connections will need to be checked in order to pinpoint the trouble spot.

4 The basic tools required for electrical fault-finding include a circuit tester or voltmeter (a 12-volt bulb with a set of test leads can also be used for certain tests); a self-powered test light (sometimes known as a continuity tester); an ohmmeter (to measure resistance); a battery and set of test leads; and a jumper wire, preferably with a circuit breaker or fuse incorporated, which can be used to bypass suspect wires or electrical components. Before attempting to locate a problem with test instruments, use the wiring diagram to determine where to make the connections.

5 To find the source of an intermittent wiring fault (usually due to a poor or dirty connection, or damaged wiring insulation), a wiggle test can be performed on the wiring. This involves wiggling the wiring by hand to see if the fault occurs as the wiring is moved. It should be possible to narrow down the source of the fault to a particular section of wiring. This method of testing can be used in conjunction with any of the tests described in the following sub-Sections.

6 Apart from problems due to poor connections, two basic types of fault can occur in an electrical circuit - open-circuit, or short-circuit.

7 Open-circuit faults are caused by a break somewhere in the circuit, which prevents current from flowing. An open-circuit fault will prevent a component from working, but will not cause the relevant circuit fuse to blow.

8 Short-circuit faults are caused by a short somewhere in the circuit, which allows the current flowing in the circuit to escape along an alternative route, usually to earth. Short-circuit faults are normally caused by a breakdown in wiring insulation, which allows a feed wire to touch either another wire, or an earthed component such as the bodyshell. A short circuit fault will normally cause the relevant circuit fuse to blow.

Finding an open-circuit

9 To check for an open-circuit, connect one lead of a circuit tester or voltmeter to either the negative battery terminal or a known good earth.

10 Connect the other lead to a connector in the circuit being tested, preferably nearest to the battery or fuse.

11 Switch on the circuit, bearing in mind that some circuits are live only when the ignition switch is moved to a particular position.

12 If voltage is present (indicated either by the tester bulb lighting or a voltmeter reading, as applicable), this means that the section of the circuit between the relevant connector and the battery is problem-free.

13 Continue to check the remainder of the circuit in the same fashion.

14 When a point is reached at which no voltage is present, the problem must lie between that point and the previous test point with voltage. Most problems can be traced to a broken, corroded or loose connection.

Finding a short-circuit

15 To check for a short-circuit, first disconnect the load(s) from the circuit (loads are the components which draw current from a circuit, such as bulbs, motors, heating elements, etc).

16 Remove the relevant fuse from the circuit, and connect a circuit tester or voltmeter to the fuse connections.

17 Switch on the circuit, bearing in mind that some circuits are live only when the ignition switch is moved to a particular position.

18 If voltage is present (indicated either by the tester bulb lighting or a voltmeter reading, as applicable), this means that there is a short circuit.

19 If no voltage is present, but the fuse still blows with the load(s) connected, this indicates an internal fault in the load(s).

Finding an earth fault

20 The battery negative terminal is connected to earth - the metal of the engine/transmission and the car body - and most systems are wired so that they only receive a positive feed, the current returning through the metal of the car body. This means that the component mounting and the body form part of that circuit. Loose or corroded mountings can therefore cause a range of electrical faults, ranging from total failure of a circuit, to a puzzling partial fault. In particular, lights may shine dimly (especially when another circuit sharing the same earth point is in operation), motors (eg. wiper motors or the radiator cooling fan motor) may run slowly, and the operation of one circuit may have an apparently unrelated effect on another. Note that on many vehicles, earth straps are used between certain components, such as the engine/transmission and the body, usually where there is no metal-to-metal contact between components due to flexible rubber mountings, etc.

21 To check whether a component is properly earthed, disconnect the battery and connect one lead of an ohmmeter to a known good earth point. Connect the other lead to the wire or earth connection being tested. The resistance reading should be zero; if not, check the connection as follows.

22 If an earth connection is thought to be faulty, dismantle the connection and clean back to bare metal both the bodyshell and the wire terminal or the component earth connection mating surface. Be careful to remove all traces of dirt and corrosion, then use a knife to trim away any paint, so that a clean metal-to-metal joint is made. On reassembly, tighten the joint fasteners securely; if a wire terminal is being refitted, use serrated washers between the terminal and the bodyshell to ensure a clean and secure connection. When the connection is remade, prevent the onset of corrosion in the future by applying a coat of petroleum jelly or silicone-based grease or by spraying on (at regular intervals) a proprietary ignition sealer or a water dispersant lubricant.

3 Fuses and relays - general information

Fuses

1 Fuses are designed to break a circuit when a predetermined current is reached, in order to protect the components and wiring which could be damaged by excessive current flow. Any excessive current flow will be due to a fault in the circuit, usually a short-circuit (see Section 2).

2 The main fuses are located in the fusebox, below the driver's side of the facia. The fuse locations and identifications are stamped into the rear of the driver's side glovebox or fusebox cover, as applicable.

3 For access to the fuses on models fitted with a driver's side glovebox, open the glovebox, then push the glovebox lid side supports inwards so that the glovebox can be lowered further for access to the fuses **(see illustration)**.

3.3 Push the side supports inwards and lower the glovebox lid

3.6 Pull the fuse from its location

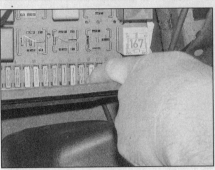

3.9 Push the new fuse into position

4 For access to the fuses on models not equipped with a driver's side glovebox, turn the fusebox cover retaining catch anti-clockwise to release the cover. Carefully pull the cover out from the facia to release the locating tangs.

5 A blown fuse can be recognised from its melted or broken wire.

6 To remove a fuse, first ensure that the relevant circuit is switched off, then pull the fuse from its location **(see illustration)**.

7 Before renewing a blown fuse, trace and rectify the cause, and always use a fuse of the correct rating. Never substitute a fuse of a higher rating, or make temporary repairs using wire or metal foil; more serious damage, or even fire, could result.

8 Note that the fuses are colour-coded as follows.

Colour	Rating
Orange	5A
Red	10A
Blue	15A
Yellow	20A
Clear or white	25A
Green	30A

9 Fit the new fuse by simply pushing it into position **(see illustration)**.

Relays

10 A relay is an electrically-operated switch, which is used for the following reasons:

a) A relay can switch a heavy current remotely from the circuit in which the current is flowing, allowing the use of lighter-gauge wiring and switch contacts.

b) A relay can receive more than one control input, unlike a mechanical switch.

c) A relay can have a timer function - for example, the intermittent wiper relay.

11 Most of the relays are located in the main fusebox, above the fuses.

12 Access to the relays can be obtained after removing the driver's side glovebox or the fusebox cover, as applicable.

13 If a circuit or system controlled by a relay develops a fault, and the relay is suspect, operate the system. If the relay is functioning, it should be possible to hear it click as it is energised. If this is the case, the fault lies with the components or wiring of the system. If the relay is not being energised, then either the relay is not receiving a main supply or a switching voltage, or the relay itself is faulty. Testing is by the substitution of a known good unit, but be careful - while some relays are identical in appearance and in operation, others look similar but perform different functions.

14 To remove a relay, first ensure that the relevant circuit is switched off. The relay can then simply be pulled out from the socket, and pushed back into position.

15 The direction indicator/hazard flasher relay is located at the top right-hand side of the group of relays in the fusebox **(see illustration)**.

---

4 Switches -
removal and refitting

Note: *Disconnect the battery negative lead before removing any switch, and reconnect the lead after refitting the switch.*

3.15 Direction indicator/hazard flasher relay location (arrowed)

Ignition switch/ steering column lock

1 Refer to Chapter 10.

Steering column stalk switches

Removal

2 Remove the steering wheel as described in Chapter 10.

3 Slacken and remove the retaining screws, and remove the steering column lower shroud, then unclip the upper shroud. Note that on models fitted with a fixed steering column, the upper shroud cannot be removed until the instrument panel surround has been removed (there is no need to remove the upper shroud completely to remove the stalk switches) **(see illustrations)**.

4 Unscrew the three securing screws, and pull the direction indicator stalk switch from the steering column **(see illustrations)**.

4.3a Remove the retaining screws . . .

4.3b . . . and remove the steering column lower shroud

4.4a Unscrew the securing screws . . .

12

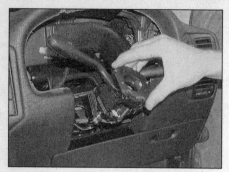

4.4b . . . and remove the direction indicator stalk switch

4.5 Removing the wash/wipe stalk switch

4.8 Push to release the switch knob securing lug

5 Once the indicator stalk switch has been removed, disconnect the wiring connectors from the wash/wipe switch, then slide the wash/wipe switch from the steering column **(see illustration)**.

Refitting

6 Refitting is a reversal of removal, but refit the steering wheel as described in Chapter 10.

Lighting switch (incorporating instrument panel dimmer and headlight levelling switch)

Removal

7 Turn the lighting switch to the 'headlights on' position, and pull the switch out to the 'foglights on' position.
8 Insert a 2 mm diameter twist drill or punch into the hole in the lower end of the switch, and push to release the switch knob securing lug **(see illustration)**.

9 Insert a small screwdriver into the hole in the right-hand side of the switch, and push upwards to release the lower switch assembly securing lug, whilst carefully prising out the bottom of the switch assembly. Prise out the top of the switch assembly and pull the assembly out from the facia **(see illustrations)**.
10 Disconnect the wiring plugs, and withdraw the assembly **(see illustration)**.

Refitting

11 Refitting is a reversal of removal, but ensure that the switch assembly and switch knob securing lugs are fully engaged.

Heated rear window switch and heated front seat switches

Removal

12 Carefully prise the switch from its location in the facia panel, using a small flat-bladed

screwdriver. Take care not to damage the surrounding trim **(see illustration)**.
13 Disconnect the wiring plug(s) and withdraw the switch **(see illustration)**.

Refitting

14 Reconnect the switch wiring plug, and push the switch firmly into position.

Facia-mounted electric window switches

Removal

15 Carefully prise off the heater control panel trim plate **(see illustration)**.
16 Remove the two screws securing the switch mounting plate in position below the heater controls **(see illustration)**.
17 Pull the panel forwards to release the lower retaining clips, then disconnect the wiring plugs from the switches and withdraw the panel **(see illustration)**.

4.9a Push upwards through the hole in the right-hand side of the switch, whilst prising out the bottom of the switch assembly

4.9b Prise out the top of the switch assembly . . .

4.10 . . . then disconnect the wiring plugs and withdraw the assembly

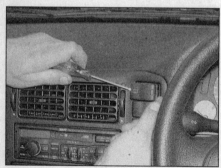

4.12 Prise the heated rear window switch from its location . . .

4.13 . . . then disconnect the wiring plug

4.15 Prise off the heater control panel trim plate

18 To remove a switch, squeeze the retaining clips at the top and bottom of the switch, and push the switch out through the front of the mounting plate **(see illustration)**.

Refitting

19 Refitting is a reversal of removal.

Door-mounted electric window switches

Removal

20 The switch can be removed by carefully prising it from the top of the door pocket. Disconnect the wiring plug and withdraw the switch.

Refitting

21 Refitting is a reversal of removal.

Electric mirror switch

Removal

22 Proceed as described for the facia-mounted electric window switches in paragraphs 15 to 18.
23 Squeeze the switch retaining tabs, two at the bottom of the switch, and one at the top, and withdraw the switch from the mounting plate.

Refitting

24 Refitting is a reversal of removal.

Hazard warning light switch

25 The hazard warning light switch is integral with the direction indicator stalk switch, and cannot be removed separately. Refer to paragraphs 2 to 6 for details of direction indicator stalk switch removal and refitting.

Air conditioning system switches

26 The switches are integral with the heater control panel, and cannot be removed separately. Refer to Chapter 3 for details of heater control panel removal and refitting.

Heater blower motor switch

27 The switch is integral with the heater control panel, and cannot be removed separately. Refer to Chapter 3 for details of heater control panel removal and refitting.

Handbrake 'on' warning light switch

28 Refer to Chapter 9.

Brake light switch

29 Refer to Chapter 9.

Reversing light switch

30 Refer to Chapter 7.

Courtesy light switches

Removal

31 The switches are located in the rear door pillars. Open the relevant door, and carefully prise the switch rubber grommet from the door pillar.
32 Carefully prise the switch from the door pillar and disconnect the wiring plug **(see illustration)**.

4.16 Remove the two screws securing the switch mounting plate

4.18 Removing an electric windows switch from the mounting plate

Refitting

33 Refitting is a reversal of removal.

Luggage compartment light switch

Removal

34 Remove the lock as described in Chapter 11.
35 Squeeze the retaining tabs at the side of the switch, and withdraw the switch from the lock.

Refitting

36 Refitting is a reversal of removal, but refit the lock with reference to Chapter 11.

Glovebox light switch

Removal

37 The switch is integral with the light assembly. Carefully prise the light assembly from the glovebox and disconnect the wiring plug.

Refitting

38 Refitting is a reversal of removal.

---

5 Bulbs (exterior lights) – renewal

General

1 Whenever a bulb is renewed, note the following points:
a) Disconnect the battery negative lead before starting work.

4.17 Pull the panel forwards, then disconnect the wiring plugs

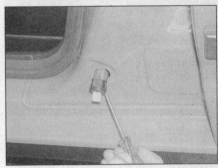
4.32 Prising out a courtesy light switch

b) Remember that if the light has just been in use the bulb may be extremely hot.
c) Always check the bulb contacts and holder, ensuring that there is clean metal-to-metal contact between the bulb and its live(s) and earth. Clean off any corrosion or dirt before fitting a new bulb.
d) Wherever bayonet-type bulbs are fitted ensure that the live contact(s) bear firmly against the bulb contact.
e) Always ensure that the new bulb is of the correct rating and that it is completely clean before fitting it; this applies particularly to headlight/foglight bulbs (see below).

Headlight

2 Working in the engine compartment, release the securing clip, and remove the plastic cover from the rear of the headlight **(see illustration)**.

5.2 Remove the plastic cover from the rear of the headlight

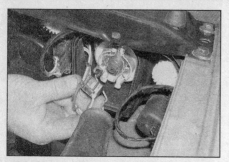

5.3 Disconnect the wiring plug from the bulb . . .

5.4a . . . then release the retaining clip . . .

5.4b . . . and withdraw the bulb

5.9a Pull the sidelight bulbholder from the headlight unit . . .

5.9b . . . then pull the bulb from the bulbholder

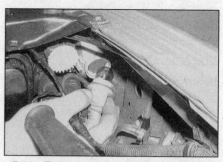

5.11a Twist the front direction indicator bulbholder anti-clockwise to release it . . .

3 Disconnect the wiring plug from the rear of the bulb (see illustration).
4 Unhook and release the ends of the bulb retaining clip and release it from the light unit, then withdraw the bulb (see illustrations).
5 When handling the new bulb, use a tissue or clean cloth to avoid touching the glass with the fingers; moisture and grease from the skin can cause blackening and rapid failure of this type of bulb. If the glass is accidentally touched, wipe it clean using methylated spirit.
6 Install the new bulb, ensuring that its locating tabs are correctly located in the light cut-outs, and secure it in position with the retaining clip.
7 Reconnect the wiring plug and refit the headlight cover, making sure that it is secure.

Front sidelight

8 Working in the engine compartment, release the securing clip, and remove the plastic cover from the rear of the headlight.
9 Carefully pull the sidelight bulbholder from the headlight unit. The bulb is a push-fit in the holder and can be removed by grasping the end of the bulb and pulling it out (see illustrations).
10 Refitting is a reversal of removal, making sure that the headlight cover is securely refitted.

Front direction indicator light

11 Working in the engine compartment, twist the bulbholder anti-clockwise to release it from the rear of the indicator light unit. The bulb is a bayonet-fit in the bulbholder (see illustrations).
12 Fit the new bulb using a reversal of the removal procedure.

Front direction indicator side repeater

13 Carefully prise the light unit from the front wing panel, using a small flat-bladed screwdriver – prise the left-hand light unit forwards, and prise the right-hand light unit rearwards (see illustration). Take care not to damage the vehicle paint.
14 Twist the bulbholder clockwise to remove it from the light unit. The bulb is a push-fit in the bulbholder (see illustrations).
15 Fit the new bulb using a reversal of the removal procedure.

Front foglight
Models up to August 1996

16 Unscrew the three securing screws, and remove the lower grille panel from the front spoiler.
17 Unscrew the two bolts securing the light unit to the front spoiler, then withdraw the

5.11b . . . then remove the bayonet-fit bulb

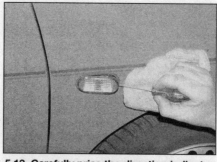

5.13 Carefully prise the direction indicator side repeater from the wing panel

5.14a Twist the bulbholder clockwise . . .

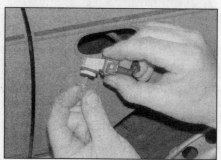

5.14b . . . then remove the push-fit bulb

5.23 Prise foglight trim panel from the front spoiler

5.24a Unscrew the two foglight securing bolts (arrowed) . . .

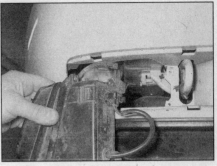

5.24b . . . then withdraw the foglight and disconnect the wiring plug

light unit from the spoiler. If there is insufficient slack in the wiring to enable the light unit to be withdrawn, the foglight unit wiring connector can be disconnected after removing the front direction indicator light unit (see Section 7) for access.

18 Unscrew the three screws securing the rear cover to the foglight unit, then withdraw the cover and disconnect the bulb wiring connector(s).

19 Unhook and release the ends of the bulb retaining clip and release it from the light unit, then withdraw the bulb.

20 When handling the new bulb, use a tissue or clean cloth to avoid touching the glass with the fingers; moisture and grease from the skin can cause blackening and rapid failure of this type of bulb. If the glass is accidentally touched, wipe it clean using methylated spirit.

21 Install the new bulb, ensuring that its locating tabs are correctly located in the light

cut-outs, and secure it in position with the retaining clip.

22 Refit the light unit using a reversal of the removal procedure. Note that the horizontal adjustment of the foglight can be adjusted using the screw fitted to the inboard edge of the light unit.

Models from September 1996

23 Carefully prise the foglight trim panel from the front spoiler (see illustration).

24 Unscrew the two foglight securing bolts from the inboard end of the foglight, then manipulate the foglight to release the lug securing the outboard end of the light unit to the spoiler. Withdraw the light unit from the spoiler. If there is insufficient slack in the wiring to enable the light unit to be withdrawn, the foglight unit wiring connector can be disconnected after removing the front direction indicator light unit (see Section 7) for access (see illustration).

25 Proceed as described in paragraphs 18 to 21 (see illustrations).

26 Refit the light unit using a reversal of the removal procedure. Note that the horizontal adjustment of the foglight can be adjusted (with the foglight trim panel removed) using the screw fitted to the inboard edge of the light unit.

Rear light cluster

Ibiza models

27 Working in the luggage compartment, depress the two retaining tabs and remove the bulbholder from the light unit. The bulbs are a bayonet-fit in the bulbholder (see illustrations).

28 Fit the new bulb using a reversal of removal procedure.

Cordoba Saloon and Coupe models – rear wing-mounted lights

29 Lift the access panel in the luggage

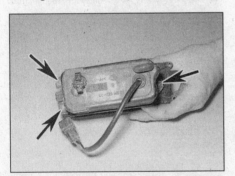

5.25a Unscrew the three screws (arrowed) securing the rear cover to the foglight

5.25b Disconnect the bulb wiring connector . . .

5.25c . . . then release the bulb retaining clip . . .

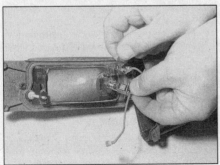

5.25d . . . and withdraw the bulb

5.27a Depress the two retaining tabs . . .

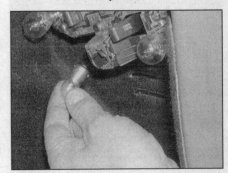

5.27b . . . and remove the bulbholder – the bulbs are a bayonet-fit (Ibiza models)

12

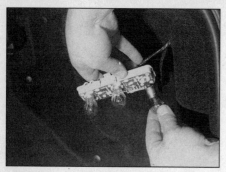

5.30 Removing a rear direction indicator light bulb – Cordoba Saloon model

5.32 Unclip the access panel from the boot lid trim panel . . .

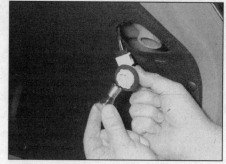

5.33 . . . then withdraw the bulbholder and remove the foglight bulb – Cordoba Saloon model

compartment trim, then reach in through the opening, and disconnect the wiring connector from the bulbholder.

30 Depress the retaining clips, and remove the bulbholder from the light unit. The bulbs are a bayonet-fit in the bulbholder **(see illustration)**.

31 Fit the new bulb using a reversal of the removal procedure.

Cordoba Saloon and Coupe models – boot lid-mounted lights (foglights)

32 Open the boot lid, then unclip the access panel from the boot lid trim panel **(see illustration)**.

33 Twist the bulbholder anti-clockwise, and withdraw it from the light unit. The bulb is a bayonet-fit in the bulbholder **(see illustration)**.

34 Fit the new bulb using a reversal of the removal procedure.

Cordoba Vario models – rear wing-mounted lights

35 Working in the luggage compartment, release the securing clips and open the rear light access panel. Where applicable, unclip the netting pocket securing clips to enable the panel to be opened **(see illustrations)**.

36 Depress the two retaining clips and remove the bulbholder from the light unit. The bulbs are a bayonet-fit in the bulbholder **(see illustration)**.

37 Fit the new bulb using a reversal of removal procedure.

Cordoba Vario models – tailgate-mounted lights (foglights)

38 Open the tailgate.

39 Carefully prise the bulbholder cover panel from the tailgate trim panel **(see illustration)**.

40 Twist the bulbholder anti-clockwise to release it from the reflector/light panel. The bulb is a bayonet-fit in the bulbholder **(see illustration)**.

41 Fit the new bulb using a reversal of the removal procedure.

High level brake light

All models except Cordoba Vario

42 Working inside the rear window, squeeze the retaining clips at the sides of the light unit, and carefully withdraw the rear section of the light – take care as the retaining clips are easily broken **(see illustration)**.

43 The bulbs are a push-fit in the rear section of the light **(see illustration)**.

44 Fit the new bulb, then refit the rear section of the light unit, taking care not to break the retaining clips.

5.35a Unclip the netting pocket . . .

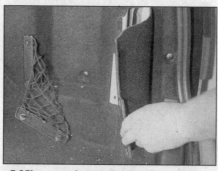

5.35b . . . and open the rear light access panel – Cordoba Vario model

5.36 The bulbs are a bayonet-fit in the bulbholder – Cordoba Vario model

5.39 Prise the bulbholder cover panel from the tailgate trim panel – Cordoba Vario model

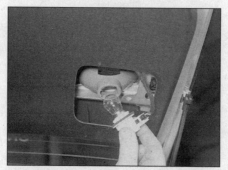

5.40 Twist the bulbholder anti-clockwise to release it from the reflector/light panel – Cordoba Vario model

5.42 Squeeze the retaining clips at the sides of the light unit, and withdraw the rear section of the light – Ibiza Hatchback model

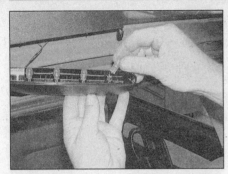

5.43 The bulbs are a push-fit in the rear section of the light – Ibiza Hatchback model

5.46 Carefully prise open the high level brake light rear cover – Cordoba Vario model

5.47a Disconnect the wiring connector . . .

5.47b . . . then unscrew the two light unit securing screws – Cordoba Vario model

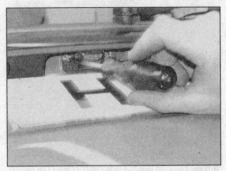

5.49 Unscrew the two number plate light securing screws

5.50a Unclip the lens from the light unit . . .

Cordoba Vario models

45 The bulbs cannot be renewed individually. If one or two bulbs have failed, the light unit can continue to be used. If more than two bulbs have failed, the complete unit must be renewed as follows.

46 Working inside the rear window, carefully prise open the light unit rear cover **(see illustration)**.

47 Disconnect the wiring connector, unscrew the two securing screws, and withdraw the light unit **(see illustrations)**.

48 Refitting is a reversal of removal.

Rear number plate light

49 Unscrew the two securing screws, and withdraw the light unit from the tailgate **(see illustration)**.

50 Unclip the lens from the light unit. The bulb is a push-fit in the bulbholder **(see illustrations)**.

51 Fit the new bulb using a reversal of the removal procedure.

6 Bulbs (interior lights) – renewal

General

1 Refer to Section 5, paragraph 1.

Courtesy light – models without front reading light

2 Carefully prise the lens from the light unit, using a small flat-bladed screwdriver **(see illustration)**.

3 Pull the bulb from the spring contacts **(see illustration)**.

4 Fit the new bulb using a reversal of the removal procedure.

Courtesy light – models with front reading light

5 Carefully prise the lens from the light. The bulb is a push-fit in the spring contacts.

6 Fit the new bulb using a reversal of the removal procedure.

Front reading light

7 The procedure is as described in paragraphs 5 and 6 for the courtesy light.

Luggage compartment light

8 Carefully prise the light unit from its location in the luggage compartment or boot lid, as applicable. The bulb is a push-fit in the spring contacts.

9 Fit the new bulb using a reversal of the removal procedure.

5.50b . . . then pull out the bulb

6.2 Prise the lens from the courtesy light unit . . .

6.3 . . . then pull the bulb from the spring contacts

6.10a Prise the light unit from its location in the glovebox . . .

6.10b . . . then pull the bulb from the spring contacts

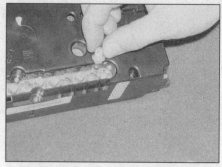

6.12 Removing an instrument panel bulb

Glovebox illumination light bulb

10 Proceed as described previously for the luggage compartment light (see illustrations).

Instrument panel illumination/warning lights

11 Remove the instrument panel as described in Section 10.

12 Twist the relevant bulbholder clockwise and withdraw it from the rear of the panel (see illustration).

13 All bulbs are integral with their holders. Be very careful to ensure that the new bulbs are of the correct rating, the same as those removed; this is especially important in the case of the ignition/battery charging warning light.

14 Refit the bulbholder to the rear of the instrument panel then refit the instrument panel as described in Section 10.

Auxiliary gauge illumination bulbs

15 Remove the auxiliary gauge as described in Section 12.

16 Carefully pull the bulbholder from the gauge. The bulb is integral with the bulbholder.

17 Fit the new bulb, then refit the gauge as described in Section 12.

Cigarette lighter/ashtray illumination bulb

18 Remove the cigarette lighter as described in Section 15.

19 Pull the bulbholder from the rear of the

6.22a Unclip the bulb housing from the rear of the heater/ventilation control panel . . .

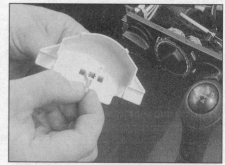

6.22b . . . then pull the bulb from the housing

assembly and disconnect the wiring plug. The bulb is integral with the bulbholder.

20 Fit the new bulb using a reversal of the removal procedure.

Heater/ventilation control panel illumination bulb

21 Remove the heater/ventilation control panel as described in Chapter 3, noting that there is no need to disconnect the control cables.

22 Unclip the plastic bulb housing from the rear of the control panel. The bulb is a push-fit in the bulb housing (see illustrations).

23 Fit the new bulb using a reversal of the removal procedure.

Switch illumination bulbs

24 The switch illumination bulbs are integral with the switches. If a bulb fails, the complete switch must be renewed.

7 Exterior light units - removal and refitting

Note: Disconnect the battery negative lead before removing any light unit, and reconnect the lead after refitting the light unit.

Headlight

Removal

1 Remove the front grille panel as described in Chapter 11.

2 Remove the front direction indicator light unit as described later in this Section.

3 Unscrew the single upper and two lower headlight securing bolts (see illustrations).

4 Disconnect the headlight wiring connector and, where applicable, the headlight adjust-

7.3a Unscrew the upper headlight securing bolt . . .

7.3b . . . and the outboard lower . . .

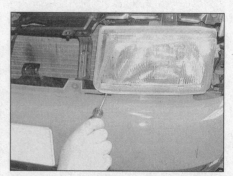

7.3c . . . and inboard lower securing bolts . . .

7.4 . . . then withdraw the headlight

7.6a Press the direction indicator light unit retaining lug . . .

7.6b . . . then withdraw the light unit

ment motor wiring connector, then withdraw the headlight **(see illustration)**.

Refitting

5 Refitting is a reversal of removal, but on completion, have the headlight alignment checked at the earliest opportunity.

Front direction indicator light

Removal

6 Working in the engine compartment, press the direction indicator light unit retaining lug on the inboard end of the light unit away from the headlight, then slide the direction indicator unit out from the front wing panel **(see illustrations)**.

7 Disconnect the wiring plug, and withdraw the light unit.

Refitting

8 Refitting is a reversal of removal, but ensure

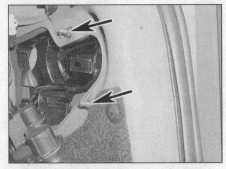

7.12a Unscrew the two securing nuts (arrowed) . . .

that the light unit retaining lug is securely engaged.

Front direction indicator side repeater

9 The procedure is described as part of the bulb renewal procedure in Section 5.

Front foglight

10 The procedure is described as part of the bulb renewal procedure in Section 5.

Rear wing-mounted light cluster

Removal

11 Remove the rear light bulbholder, as described in Section 5.

12 Working inside the wing panel, unscrew the securing nuts (two nuts on Ibiza models, three nuts on Cordoba Saloon and Coupe models, and four nuts on Cordoba Vario models), and withdraw the light unit from the wing panel **(see illustrations)**.

Refitting

13 Refitting is a reversal of removal.

Boot lid/tailgate-mounted lights (foglights)

14 The light units are integral with the boot lid/tailgate light/reflector trim panel, and cannot be removed separately.

High level brake light

All models except Cordoba Vario

15 On Hatchback models, open the tailgate.

16 Carefully release the two securing tangs at the rear of the light unit, and slide the unit towards the centre of the window glass to remove it **(see illustration)**.

17 Refitting is a reversal of removal.

Cordoba Vario models

18 The procedure is described as part of the bulb renewal procedure in Section 5.

Rear number plate light

19 The procedure is described as part of the rear number plate light bulb renewal procedure in Section 5.

8 Headlight beam adjustment components – removal and refitting

Headlight adjustment switch

1 The switch is integral with the lighting switch. Removal and refitting of the switch assembly is covered in Section 4.

Headlight adjustment motor

Removal

2 Disconnect the battery negative lead.

3 Working in the engine compartment, disconnect the wiring plug from the headlight adjustment motor at the outboard edge of the headlight.

4 Twist the headlight adjustment motor anti-clockwise to release the motor body from the headlight housing, then slide the unit out to

7.12b . . . and withdraw the rear light unit – Ibiza model

7.12c Withdrawing the rear light unit – Cordoba Saloon model

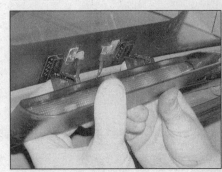

7.16 Removing the high level brake light – Ibiza model

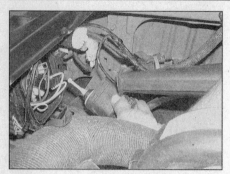

8.4 Removing a headlight adjustment motor

release the balljoint from the headlight reflector. Withdraw the motor assembly **(see illustration)**.

Refitting

5 Refitting is a reversal of removal, but remove the plastic cover from the rear of the headlight, and hold the headlight reflector whilst pushing the motor balljoint into position. On completion, check the operation of the headlight beam adjustment mechanism.

9 Headlight beam alignment - general information

1 Accurate adjustment of the headlight beam is only possible using optical beam setting equipment and this work should therefore be carried out by a Seat dealer or suitably equipped workshop.

2 For reference, the headlights can be adjusted using the adjuster assemblies fitted to the top of each light unit. The outer adjuster alters the vertical position of the beam whilst the inner adjuster alters the horizontal aim of the beam **(see illustration)**.

3 Some models are equipped with an electrically operated headlight beam adjustment system which is controlled through the switch in the facia. On these models ensure that the switch is set to the off position before adjusting the headlight aim.

10 Instrument panel - removal and refitting

Removal

Note: *On models fitted with an airbag, it may be necessary to remove the airbag unit (Section 28) and steering wheel (Chapter 10) to allow sufficient clearance to remove the instrument panel.*

1 Disconnect the battery negative lead.
2 Working at the top of the instrument panel unscrew the two instrument panel surround securing screws, then pull the surround upwards to release the two lower securing clips, and carefully withdraw the surround **(see illustrations)**.
3 Working at each side of the instrument panel in turn, unscrew the two instrument panel side securing screws **(see illustration)**.
4 Tilt the instrument panel forwards, and disconnect the wiring plugs from the rear of the panel **(see illustration)**.

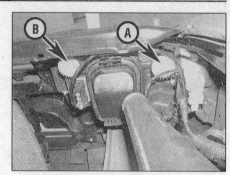

9.2 Headlight adjuster assemblies

1 *Vertical adjuster*
2 *Horizontal adjuster*

5 Withdraw the instrument panel by passing it through the gap between the steering wheel spokes **(see illustration)**.

Refitting

6 Refitting is a reversal of removal, making sure that the wiring plugs are securely reconnected.

11 Instrument panel components - removal and refitting

With the exception of the panel illumination/warning light bulbs, it is not possible to dismantle the instrument panel. If any of the gauges are faulty, the complete instrument panel must be renewed. Refer to Section 6 for details of instrument panel illumination/warning light bulb renewal.

10.2a Unscrew the two instrument panel surround securing screws . . .

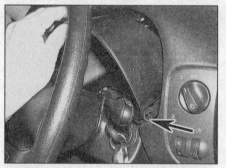

10.2b . . . then pull the surround up to release the lower clips (one arrowed) . . .

10.2c . . . and withdraw the surround

10.3 Unscrew the instrument panel securing screws

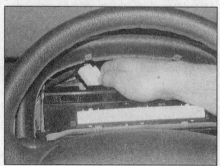

10.4 Disconnect the wiring plugs from the rear of the panel . . .

10.5 . . . then withdraw the panel through the steering wheel spokes

12 Auxiliary gauges – removal and refitting

Removal

1 On certain models, a voltmeter and engine oil pressure gauge are fitted to the centre console.
2 Remove the centre console as described in Chapter 11.
3 Unscrew the upper and lower bolts securing the auxiliary gauge panel to the front section of the centre console.
4 To remove a gauge from the panel, unscrew the two nuts securing the gauge to the locating bracket, then withdraw the gauge through the front of the panel.

Refitting

5 Refitting is a reversal of removal.

13 Trip computer – general information

A trip computer is fitted to certain models, and the trip computer display is incorporated into the tachometer in the instrument panel.

The trip computer receives data from a vehicle speed sensor, an outside air temperature sensor, and oil temperature sensor, and the engine management electronic control unit, and analyses this data to give the following information:

- a) Driving time.
- b) Distance driven.
- c) Average speed.
- d) Average fuel consumption.
- e) Engine oil temperature.
- f) Outside air temperature.

At the time of writing, no information was available for the removal and refitting of the trip computer components. Any problems should be referred to a Seat dealer. Note that the trip computer display is integral with the tachometer, and cannot be removed separately.

14 Service interval indicator – general information and resetting

1 All Ibiza and Cordoba models are equipped with a service interval indicator. After all necessary maintenance work has been completed (see Chapter 1), the relevant service interval display code must be reset. If more than one service schedule is carried out, note that the relevant display intervals must be reset individually.
2 The display is reset using the reset button on the left-hand side of the instrument panel (below the speedometer) and the clock setting button on the right-hand side of the panel (below the clock/tachometer); on models with a digital clock the lower (minute) button is used. Resetting is carried out as follows.

17.3 Horn location (arrowed) viewed from underneath vehicle

3 Turn the ignition switch and check that the speedometer mileage indicator is set to the mileage setting and not the trip meter setting. When this is so, press and hold in the button on the left of the instrument panel. Keeping the button depressed, switch off the ignition and release the button. The word OEL should be shown on the display, by depressing the left-hand button again the display will change to IN 01 followed by IN 02. Set the display to the relevant service which has just been performed, then depress the clock adjustment button briefly until ----- is displayed; this indicates that the service interval display has been reset. Repeat the reset procedure for all the relevant service display intervals.
4 Once the resetting procedure is complete, switch on the ignition and check that IN 00 is shown in the display.

15 Clock – removal and refitting

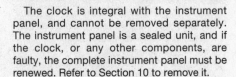

The clock is integral with the instrument panel, and cannot be removed separately. The instrument panel is a sealed unit, and if the clock, or any other components, are faulty, the complete instrument panel must be renewed. Refer to Section 10 to remove it.

16 Cigarette lighter – removal and refitting

Removal

1 Disconnect the battery negative lead.
2 Pull the ashtray from its housing.
3 Carefully prise off the heater control panel trim plate.
4 Remove the two screws securing the electric windows/electric mirror switch mounting plate/blanking plate in position below the heater controls.
5 Withdraw the switch mounting plate, taking care not to strain the switch wiring.
6 Carefully prise the cigarette lighter assembly from the facia, and disconnect the wiring plug.

Refitting

7 Refitting is a reversal of removal.

17 Horn – removal and refitting

Removal

1 Disconnect the battery negative lead.
2 To improve access to the horn(s), apply the handbrake then jack up the front of the vehicle and support securely on axle stands.
3 Working under the left-hand front wing, disconnect the horn wiring plug, then unscrew the securing nut, and withdraw the horn from its mounting bracket (see illustration).

Refitting

4 Refitting is a reversal of removal.

18 Speedometer sensor – removal and refitting

General information

1 All models are fitted with an electronic speedometer sensor (see illustration). This device measures the rotational speed of the transmission final drive and converts the information into an electronic signal, which is then sent to the speedometer module in the instrument panel. On certain models, the signal is also used as an input by the engine management system ECU, and the trip computer.

Removal and refitting

2 Refer to Chapter 7, Section 6.

19 Wiper arm – removal and refitting

Removal

1 Operate the wiper motor, then switch off so that the wiper arm(s) return(s) to the at-rest position.
2 Stick a piece of masking tape to the glass along the edge of the wiper blade to use as an alignment aid on refitting.

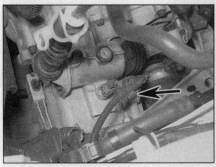

18.1 Speedometer sensor securing bolt (arrowed) – 1.4 litre model

19.3a Remove the wiper arm spindle nut . . .

19.3b . . . then pull the wiper arm from the spindle

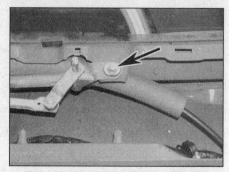

20.2a Unscrew the bolts securing the wiper linkage . . .

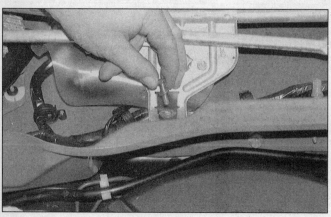

20.2b . . . and the motor mounting plate . . .

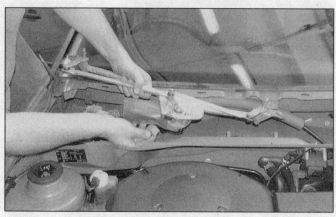

20.2c . . . then withdraw the wiper motor/linkage assembly and disconnect the wiring plug

3 Prise off the wiper arm spindle nut cover, then slacken and remove the spindle nut. Lift the blade off the glass and pull the wiper arm off its spindle **(see illustrations)**. If necessary the arm can be levered off the spindle using a suitable flat-bladed screwdriver. **Note:** *If both windscreen wiper arms are to be removed at the same time mark them for identification; the arms are not interchangeable.*

Refitting

4 Ensure that the wiper arm and spindle splines are clean and dry, then refit the arm to the spindle, aligning the wiper blade with the tape fitted on removal. Refit the spindle nut, tightening it securely, and clip the nut cover back in position.

20 Windscreen wiper motor and linkage - removal and refitting

Removal

1 Remove the windscreen cowl panels as described in Chapter 11.
2 Unscrew the three securing bolts, then carefully manipulate the windscreen wiper motor and linkage out from the scuttle and disconnect the wiring plug **(see illustrations)**.
3 Recover the washers and spacers from the motor mounting rubbers, noting their

locations, then inspect the rubbers for signs of damage or deterioration, and renew if necessary.
4 To separate the motor from the linkage, proceed as follows.
  a) *Make alignment marks between the motor spindle and the linkage to ensure correct alignment on refitting, and note the orientation of the linkage.*
  b) *Unscrew the nut securing the linkage to the motor spindle.*
  c) *Unscrew the three bolts securing the motor to the mounting plate, then withdraw the motor.*

Refitting

5 Refitting is a reversal of removal, bearing in mind the following points.

21.3a Unscrew the nut securing the tailgate wiper motor shaft to the tailgate . . .

  a) *If the motor has been separated from the linkage, ensure that the marks made on the motor spindle and linkage before removal are aligned, and ensure that the linkage is orientated as noted before removal.*
  b) *Ensure that the washers and spacers are fitted to the motor mounting rubbers as noted before removal.*
  c) *Refit the wiper arms with reference to Section 19.*

21 Tailgate wiper motor - removal and refitting

Removal

1 Disconnect the battery negative lead.
2 Remove the wiper arm as described in Section 19.
3 Unscrew the nut securing the tailgate wiper motor shaft to the tailgate. Recover the plastic washer and the rubber sealing ring **(see illustrations)**.
4 Open the tailgate, then carefully release the securing clips and withdraw the tailgate trim panel **(see illustration)**. On Cordoba Vario models, in addition to the securing clips, the tailgate trim panel has two securing screws located in the recesses at the bottom of the panel.

21.3b . . . then recover the plastic washer and rubber sealing ring

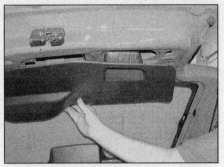

21.4 Remove the tailgate trim panel

21.5 Disconnecting the tailgate wiper motor wiring plug

5 Unplug the wiring connector from the motor, or unclip the motor wiring connector from its bracket, then separate the two halves of the connector, as applicable **(see illustration)**.
6 Disconnect the washer fluid hose from the washer nozzle connector on the motor assembly **(see illustration)**.
7 Unscrew the two bolts securing the motor/bracket assembly to the tailgate, then withdraw the assembly **(see illustration)**.

Refitting

8 Refitting is a reversal of removal, but ensure that the motor shaft rubber sealing ring is correctly refitted to prevent water leaks, and refit the wiper arm with reference to Section 19.

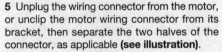

22 Windscreen/tailgate/headlight washer system components - removal and refitting

Washer fluid reservoir

Removal

1 Disconnect the battery negative lead.
2 Slacken and remove the securing nut from the front of the reservoir, then lift the reservoir from its location in the engine compartment **(see illustrations)**.
3 Disconnect the wiring plug(s) from the fluid pump(s) in the reservoir.
4 Have a container ready to catch escaping washer fluid, then disconnect the fluid hose(s) from the pump(s), noting their locations, and withdraw the reservoir.

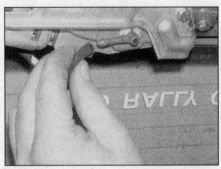

21.6 Disconnecting the washer fluid hose from the connector on the motor assembly

Refitting

5 Refitting is a reversal of removal. On models with tailgate and/or headlight washers, ensure that the fluid hoses are correctly reconnected as noted before removal.

Washer fluid pumps

Removal

6 Disconnect the battery negative lead.
7 If desired, to improve access, remove the washer fluid reservoir as described previously in this Section.
8 Carefully pull the pump from its grommet in the reservoir. If not already done, disconnect the washer fluid hose(s) and the wiring plug from the pump.

Refitting

9 Refitting is a reversal of removal, but take care not to push the pump grommet into the

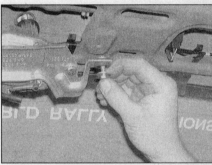

21.7 Unscrew the securing bolts and withdraw the motor/bracket assembly

reservoir. Use a little soapy water to ease the pump into the grommet.

Windscreen washer jets

Removal

10 Open the bonnet, and on models with heater washer jets, disconnect the battery negative lead.
11 Where applicable, unclip the washer jet heating element wiring connector from the bonnet and separate the two halves of the connector.
12 Disconnect the fluid hose from the washer jet, being prepared for fluid spillage, then working from the top of the bonnet, push the jet towards the windscreen, then lift the jet up and tilt it to allow the washer fluid tube to pass through the hole in the bonnet **(see illustration)**.

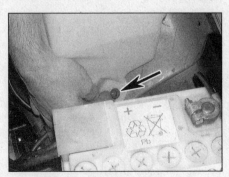

22.2a Remove the securing nut (arrowed) . . .

22.2b . . . then lift out the washer fluid reservoir

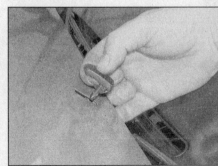

22.12 Removing a windscreen washer jet

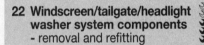

Refitting

13 Refitting is a reversal of removal. Note that the air of the washer jet can be adjusted by inserting a thin piece of wire or a pin into the jet and using it to lever the jet to the required position.

Tailgate washer jet

Removal

14 Unclip the cover from the wiper arm spindle for access to the washer jet, and pull the jet from the centre of the spindle.

Refitting

15 On refitting, ensure that the jet is securely pushed into position. Check the operation of the jet. If necessary, adjust the nozzle using a pin, aiming the spray at a point slightly above the area of glass swept by the wiper blade.

Headlight washer jets

Removal

16 Remove the front bumper as described in Chapter 11.
17 Disconnect the fluid hose from the washer nozzle.
18 Unscrew the securing nut and recover the spacer ring, and withdraw the washer nozzle from the bumper.

Refitting

19 Refitting is a reversal of removal, but refit the bumper with reference to Chapter 11.

24.2 Prise the loudspeaker cover panel from the facia

24.5a Disconnect the loudspeaker wiring plug . . .

23.3a Using DIN standard tools, pull out the radio/cassette player . . .

23 Radio/cassette player -
removal and refitting

Removal

1 The radio/cassette players have DIN standard fixings. Two special tools, obtainable from most car accessory shops, are required for removal. Alternatively suitable tools can be fabricated from 3 mm diameter wire, such as welding rod.
2 Disconnect the battery negative lead.
3 Insert the tools into the slots on each side of the unit and push them until they snap into place. The radio/cassette player can then be pulled out of the facia using the tools, and the wiring connectors and aerial disconnected **(see illustrations)**.

Refitting

4 Reconnect the wiring connector and aerial lead then push the unit into the facia until the retaining lugs snap into place.

24 Loudspeakers -
removal and refitting

Facia-mounted loudspeaker

Removal

1 Disconnect the battery negative lead.
2 Carefully prise the loudspeaker cover panel

24.5b . . . then squeeze the securing clips and push the loudspeaker from the facia

23.3b . . . then disconnect the wiring connectors and the aerial

from the top of the facia – take care not to damage the facia **(see illustration)**.
3 If the passenger's side loudspeaker is to be removed, remove the passenger's side glovebox as described in Chapter 11.
4 If the driver's side loudspeaker is to be removed, remove the lighting switch as described in Section 4, then carefully prise the driver's side ventilation nozzle from the facia.
5 Reach in through the aperture in the facia, and disconnect the loudspeaker wiring plug, then squeeze the loudspeaker securing clips, and carefully push the loudspeaker out through the top of the facia **(see illustrations)**.

Refitting

6 On refitting, note that the loudspeaker will only fit in one position – ensure that the lug on the loudspeaker engages with the cut-out in the facia.
7 Reconnect the wiring plug, then push the loudspeaker into position, and refit the cover panel.
8 Refit the passenger's side glovebox, or refit the ventilation nozzle and the lighting switch (refer to Section 4), as applicable.

Door-mounted loudspeaker

Removal

9 Disconnect the battery negative lead.
10 Open the door, and working at the front edge, unscrew the loudspeaker cover securing screw **(see illustration)**.
11 Carefully prise the loudspeaker cover from the door to release the securing clips **(see illustration)**.

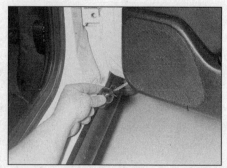

24.10 Unscrew the loudspeaker cover securing screw . . .

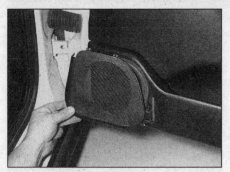

24.11 . . . then prise the loudspeaker cover from the door

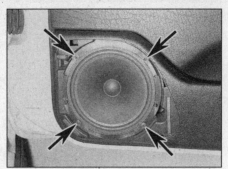

24.12 Loudspeaker securing screws (arrowed)

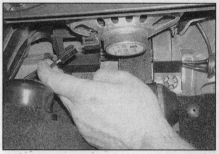

24.15 Disconnecting a rear parcel shelf-mounted loudspeaker wiring plug – Hatchback model

12 Unscrew the four securing screws and lift the loudspeaker from the door, then disconnect the loudspeaker wiring plug (**see illustration**).

Refitting

13 Refitting is a reversal of removal.

Rear parcel shelf-mounted loudspeaker – Hatchback models

Removal

14 Disconnect the battery negative lead.
15 Working in the luggage compartment, disconnect the wiring plug from the rear of the loudspeaker (**see illustration**).
16 On models where the loudspeaker is secured by nuts, unscrew the four nuts securing the loudspeaker to the parcel shelf support panel, then recover the rubber spacers (where applicable) and remove the loudspeaker.
17 On models where the loudspeaker is secured by metal clips, prise off the four metal clips, then withdraw the loudspeaker from the parcel shelf support panel.

Refitting

18 Refitting is a reversal of removal.

Rear parcel shelf-mounted loudspeakers – Cordoba Saloon and Coupe models

Removal

19 Disconnect the battery negative lead.
20 Carefully prise out the loudspeaker/cover panel from the rear parcel shelf, and disconnect the wiring plug (**see illustrations**).

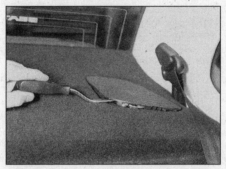

24.20a Prise out the loudspeaker/cover panel . . .

21 If desired, the loudspeaker can be separated from the cover panel after unscrewing the four securing nuts.

Refitting

22 Refitting is a reversal of removal.

Rear parcel shelf-mounted loudspeakers – Cordoba Vario models

Removal

23 Disconnect the battery negative lead.
24 Carefully prise out the loudspeaker cover panel from the parcel shelf side support panel (**see illustration**).
25 Unscrew the two securing screws, and manipulate the loudspeaker out from the parcel shelf side support panel. Disconnect the wiring plug and remove the loudspeaker (**see illustrations**).

24.20b . . . and disconnect the wiring plug – Cordoba Saloon model

Refitting

26 Refitting is a reversal of removal.

---

25 Radio aerial - removal and refitting

Front wing-mounted aerial

Removal

1 Remove the front wheel arch liner, with reference to Chapter 11.
2 Open the bonnet and, where applicable, unscrew the bolt securing the bonnet hinge and the aerial earth strap to the front wing.
3 Working under the front wing panel, unscrew the nut securing the aerial mounting bracket to the wing.

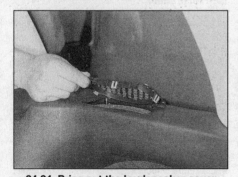

24.24 Prise out the loudspeaker cover panel . . .

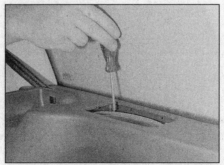

24.25a . . . then unscrew the two securing screws . . .

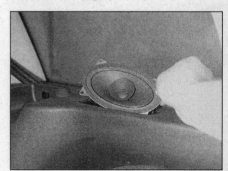

24.25b . . . and lift out the loudspeaker – Cordoba Vario model

12

4 Lower the aerial from the wing, pulling the aerial mast down through the grommet, and disconnect the aerial lead from the base of the aerial.

Refitting

5 Refitting is a reversal of removal.

Roof-mounted aerial

Removal

6 The aerial mast can be unscrewed from the base by twisting anti-clockwise, although note that it cannot be removed completely.
7 If the aerial base is to be removed, the rear of the headlining must be lowered for access (refer to Chapter 11, Section 30).
8 Once the headlining has been lowered, disconnect the aerial lead at the connector, then unscrew the securing nut, and withdraw the aerial base from the roof. Hold the aerial base as the nut is being unscrewed to prevent the base from rotating and scratching the roof panel. Recover the rubber spacer.

Refitting

9 Refitting is a reversal of removal.

26 Anti-theft alarm system and engine immobiliser - general information

Note: *This information is applicable only to the anti-theft alarm system fitted by Seat as standard equipment.*

Some models in the range are fitted with an anti-theft alarm system as standard equipment. The alarm has switches on all the doors (including the tailgate/boot lid), the bonnet and the ignition switch. If the tailgate/boot lid, bonnet or either of the doors are opened or the ignition switch is switched on whilst the alarm is set, the alarm horn will sound and the hazard warning lights will flash.

The alarm is set using the key in the driver's or passenger's front door lock, or via the central locking remote control transmitter. When the system is armed, the warning light near the driver's door lock button starts to flash. The alarm system will then start to monitor its various switches approximately 30 seconds later.

With the alarm set, if the tailgate/boot lid is unlocked, the lock switch sensing will automatically be switched off but the door and bonnet switches will still be active. Once the tailgate/boot lid is shut and locked again, the switch sensing will be switched back on.

Certain later models are fitted with an immobiliser system, which is activated via the ignition switch. A module incorporated in the ignition switch reads a code contained within the ignition key. The module sends a signal to the engine management electronic control unit (ECU) which allows the engine to start if the code is correct. If an incorrect ignition key is used, the engine will not start.

28.2 Remove the airbag retaining screws . . .

If a fault is suspected with the alarm or immobiliser systems, the vehicle should be taken to a Seat dealer for examination. They will have access to a special diagnostic tester which will quickly trace any fault present in the system.

27 Air bag system - general information and precautions

⚠️ *Warning: Before carrying out any operations on the airbag system, disconnect the battery negative terminal. When operations are complete, make sure no one is inside the vehicle when the battery is reconnected.*

Note that the airbag(s) must not be subjected to temperatures in excess of 90°C (194°F). When the airbag is removed, ensure that it is stored the correct way up to prevent possible inflation.

Do not allow any solvents or cleaning agents to contact the airbag assemblies. They must be cleaned using only a damp cloth.

The airbags and control unit are both sensitive to impact. If either is dropped or damaged they should be renewed.

Remove the airbag units prior to using arc-welding equipment on the vehicle.

Both a driver's and passenger's airbag were fitted as standard to some models in the Ibiza/Cordoba range; on other models they are available as an optional extra. Models fitted with a driver's side airbag have the word

28.3 . . . then lift out the airbag and disconnect the wiring connector

AIRBAG stamped on the airbag unit, which is fitted to the centre of the steering wheel. Models also equipped with a passenger's side airbag also have the word AIRBAG stamped on the passenger's end of the facia. The airbag system comprises of the airbag unit (complete with gas generator) which is fitted to the steering wheel (driver's side) or facia (passenger's side), an impact sensor, the control unit and a warning light in the instrument panel.

The airbag system is triggered in the event of a heavy frontal impact above a predetermined force; depending on the point of impact. The airbag is inflated within milliseconds and forms a safety cushion between the driver and the steering wheel and (where fitted) the passenger and the facia. This prevents contact between the upper body and the wheel/facia and therefore greatly reduces the risk of injury. The airbag then deflates almost immediately.

Every time the ignition is switched on, the airbag control unit performs a self-test. The self-test takes approximately 3 seconds and during this time the airbag warning light on the facia is illuminated. After the self-test has been completed the warning light should go out. If the warning light fails to come on, remains illuminated after the initial 3 second period or comes on at any time when the vehicle is being driven, there is a fault in the airbag system. The vehicle should then be taken to a Seat dealer for examination at the earliest possible opportunity.

28 Air bag system components – removal and refitting

Note: *Refer to the warnings in Section 27 before carrying out the following operations.*
1 Disconnect the battery negative terminal, then continue as described under the relevant heading.

Driver's side airbag

Note: *New airbag retaining screws will be required on refitting.*

Removal

2 Slacken and remove the two airbag retaining screws from the rear of the steering wheel, rotating the wheel as necessary to gain access to the screws **(see illustration)**.
3 Return the steering wheel to the straight-ahead position, then carefully lift the airbag assembly away from the steering wheel and disconnect the wiring connector from the rear of the unit **(see illustration)**. Note that the airbag must not be knocked or dropped and should be stored the correct way up with its padded surface uppermost.

Refitting

4 On refitting reconnect the wiring connector and seat the airbag unit in the steering wheel, making sure that the wire does not become

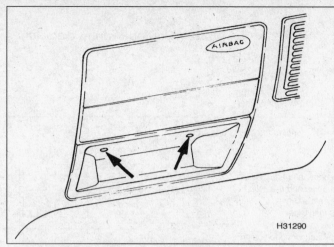

28.5 Remove the passenger's side oddments tray retaining screws (arrowed)

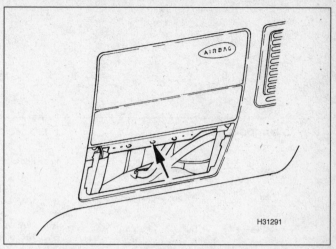

28.6 Passenger's side airbag securing bolt (arrowed)

trapped. Fit the new retaining screws and tighten them securely. Reconnect the battery negative lead, ensuring that no-one is inside the vehicle as the lead is connected.

Passenger's side airbag

Removal

5 Slacken and remove the two passenger's side oddments tray retaining screws, then remove the oddments tray from the facia **(see illustration)**.
6 Unscrew the bolt securing the lower edge of the airbag module to the facia **(see illustration)**.
7 Carefully withdraw the airbag unit from the facia, and separate the two halves of the wiring connector.

Refitting

8 On refitting, manoeuvre the airbag into position and reconnect the wiring connector.
9 Refit the airbag securing bolt, and tighten it securely.
10 Refit the oddments tray, then reconnect the battery negative lead, ensuring that no-one is inside the vehicle as the lead is connected.

Airbag control unit

Removal

11 The control unit is located under the facia, in front of the centre console **(see illustration)**.
12 Disconnect the battery negative lead.

13 Remove the centre console as described in Chapter 11.
14 Working on the passenger's side of the facia centre section, reach up behind the facia, depress the retaining clip, and disconnect the control unit wiring plug.
15 Working on the driver's side of the facia centre section, reach up behind the facia and unscrew the three nuts securing the control unit to the floor, then manipulate the control unit out from behind the facia.

Refitting

16 Refitting is the reverse of removal making sure the wiring connector is securely reconnected. Reconnect the battery negative lead, ensuring that no-one is inside the vehicle as the lead is connected.

Airbag wiring contact unit

Removal

17 Remove the steering wheel as described in Chapter 10.
18 Taking care not to rotate the contact unit, undo the three retaining screws and remove it from the steering wheel.

Refitting

19 On refitting, fit the unit to the steering wheel and securely tighten its retaining screws. If a new contact unit is being fitted, cut the cable-tie which is fitted to prevent the unit accidentally rotating.
20 Refit the steering wheel as described in

28.11 Airbag control unit location (arrowed)

Chapter 10, then reconnect the battery negative lead, ensuring that no-one is inside the vehicle as the lead is connected

Airbag warning light

Removal

21 Carefully prise the light unit from its location in the facia, taking care not to damage the surrounding trim.
22 Disconnect the wiring plug and remove the light unit.

Refitting

23 Reconnect the wiring plug and push the light unit into position in the facia. Reconnect the battery negative lead, ensuring that no-one is inside the vehicle as the lead is connected.

H31600

Key to symbols

20	Item number
	Pin and socket contact
	Bulb
	Switch
	Multiple contact switch (ganged)
	Fuse/ fusible link
	Solenoid actuator
	Resistor
	Variable resistor
	Connecting wires
	Wire splice
Gn/Ge	Wire colour (green wire with yellow tracer)
	Interconnecting line (thin line)
	Denotes alternative wiring variation
Diagram 5, Arrow B **RH indicator signal** B	Connections to other circuits
	Earth point with location code
G102	
M	Pump/motor
	Dashed outline denotes part of a larger item, containing in this case an electronic or solid state device
	Gauge/meter

Fuse / relay box *(behind the glove compartment)*

Fuse allocation

1	10A	LH dip beam and adjuster
2	10A	RH dip beam and adjuster
3	10A	Number plate light
4	15A	Rear screen wiper
5	15A	Windscreen wash/wipe
6	20A	Fresh air fan, air conditioning
7	10A	RH sidelight and rear light, engine compartment lighting
8	10A	LH sidelight and rear light
9	20A	Heated mirrors, rear window
10	15A	Front, rear fog lamps
11	10A	LH main beam, warning lights
12	10A	RH main beam
13	10A	Horn
14	10A	Reversing lights, heated seats
15	10A	Engine equipment
16	15A	Instrument panel, clock, interior light, lights on buzzer
17	10A	Indicators
18	20A	Fuel pump, lambda probe, injectors
19	30A	Coolant fan unit
20	10A	Brake lights
21	15A	Central locking, boot light, radio
22	10A	Cigarette lighter

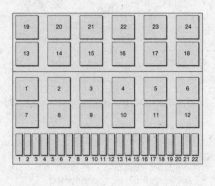

Earth locations

E1	Earth strap, battery to bodywork
E2	Next to relay plate
E3	In coolant fan wire bundle
E4	In engine compartment wire bundle
E5	In engine compartment wire bundle
E6	In engine compartment wire bundle
E7	In engine compartment wire bundle
E8	At gearbox
E9	In monomotronic wire bundle
E10	Instrument panel wire bundle
E11	In rear wire bundle
E12	In rear RH door wire bundle
E13	In front lighting wire bundle
E14	LH boot wiring
E15	RH boot wiring
E16	Headlamp wire bundle
E17	In tailgate, on left
E18	Interior light wire bundle
E19	Under RH rear seat
E20	Near roof
E21	In dash board
E22	In motronic wire bundle
E23	In engine compartment wire bundle
E24	Cylinder head wire bundle
E25	In engine compartment wire bundle
E26	In rear wiring bundle

Relay allocation

1	-
2	Rear window wash/wipe relay
3	Power supply relay
4	'X' contact relay
5	-
6	Hazard warning lights relay
7	Headlight wiper relay
8	Windscreen wash/wipe timer relay
9	Lights on warning buzzer relay
10	Fog lamps relay, or plug bridge
11	Twin tone horn relay, or plug bridge
12	Fuel pump or glow plug relay

Note.. these relay positions may vary.

13	-
14	Central locking, with remote control (160) or relay for 2nd speed of electric fan (80)
15	Inlet manifold relay (1)
16	Electric fan 2nd speed
15 and 16	Electronic terminal box relay for diesel engine control (144), turbodiesel (166)
17	Diesel glow plug fuse or ABS relay (178)
18	ABS relay (178) or relay for double light models (145)/(200)
19	Central locking, with remote control (160)
20	Electric windows fuse (53)
21	Engine relay (31)/electric fan 2nd speed (53)
22	Automatic transmission relay (150)
23	Diesel glow plug relay or ABS fuse
24	EDS relay (79) or Automatic transmission relay (150)

Wire colours

Ws White
Ro Red
Ge Yellow
Br Brown
Bl Blue
Gr Grey
Gn Green
Sw Black
Li Lilac

H31601

Key to items

1 Battery
2 Fuse/relay box
   R12 = glow plug relay
3 Ignition switch
4 Starter motor
5 Alternator
6 Glow plugs fuse (50A)
7 Glow plugs

Diagram 1

Starting and charging - Diesel models

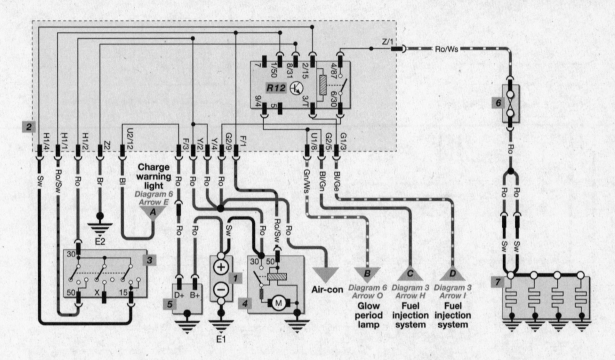

Starting and charging - Petrol models

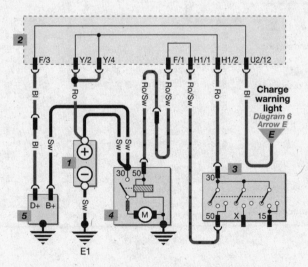

12

Wire colours

Ws	White
Ro	Red
Ge	Yellow
Br	Brown
Bl	Blue
Gr	Grey
Gn	Green
Sw	Black
Li	Lilac

H31602

Key to items

1 Battery
2 Fuse/relay box
  R4 = 'X' contact relay
3 Ignition switch
4 Starter motor
5 Alternator
6 Fresh air fan switch
7 Engine coolant fan switch
8 Fresh air fan
9 Fan speed control
  (with 8A fuse)
10 Engine coolant fan
11 Luggage compartment light
12 Front interior light (delayed)
13 Side lights warning buzzer
14 Glove compartment light
15 Door switch - driver's side
16 Door switch - passenger side
17 Door switch - rear left
18 Door switch - rear right
19 Boot light switch

Diagram 2

Heater blower, engine cooling fan

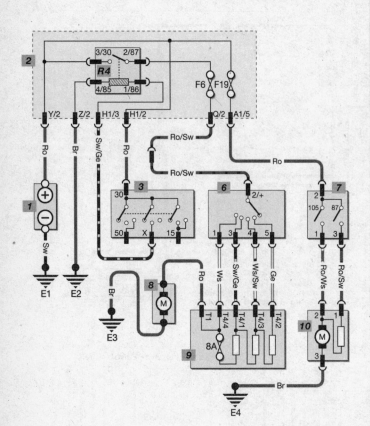

Interior lighting, lights on buzzer

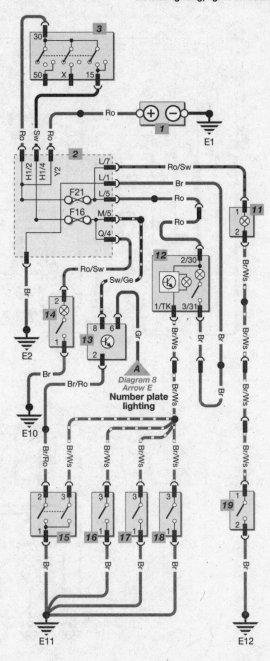

Diagram 8
Arrow E
**Number plate
lighting**

Wire colours

Ws White
Ro Red
Ge Yellow
Br Brown
Bl Blue
Gr Grey
Gn Green
Sw Black
Li Lilac

H31603

Key to items

1 Battery
2 Fuse/relay box
   R3 = power supply relay
3 Ignition switch
4 Starter motor
20 Injection start valve
21 EGR valve
22 Throttle valve
23 Speedometer transmitter
24 Injection control unit
25 Engine temp. transmitter
26 Fuel control unit
27 Throttle position transmitter
28 Clutch pedal switch
29 Brake pedal switch
30 Inlet air temp. transmitter
31 Engine rpm transmitter
32 Needle stroke transmitter
33 Fuel cut off valve

Diagram 3

Typical diesel injection system

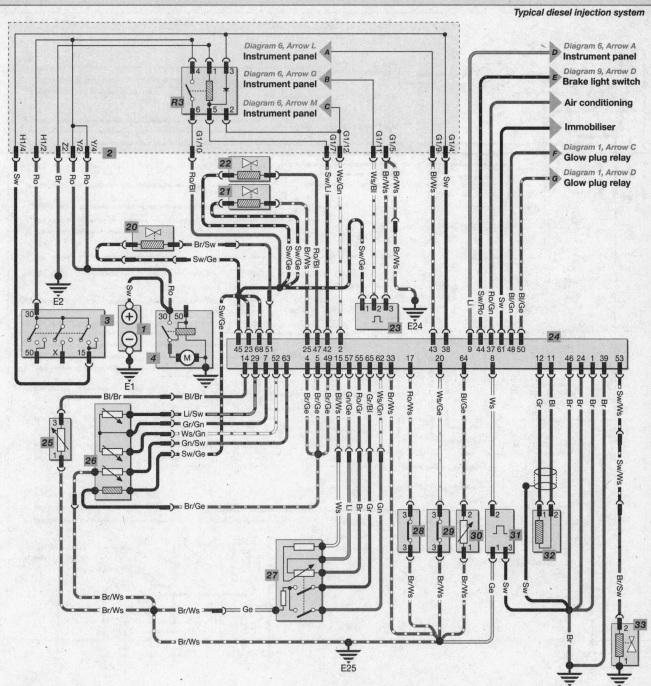

12

Wire colours

Ws White
Ro Red
Ge Yellow
Br Brown
Bl Blue
Gr Grey
Gn Green
Sw Black
Li Lilac

H31604

Key to items

1 Battery
2 Fuse / relay box
  R12 = Fuel pump relay
3 Ignition switch
22 Inlet manifold preheating relay
23 Inlet manifold preheater
24 Monomotronic control unit
25 Lambda probe
26 Coolant temp. sender
27 Injector / inlet air temp sender

28 Fuel pump and level sender
29 Throttle valve potentiometer
30 Throttle valve controller
31 Diagnostic connector
32 Speed sensor
33 Ignition transformer
34 Hall transmitter
35 Distributor
36 Spark plugs

Diagram 4

Typical monomotronic fuel injection system

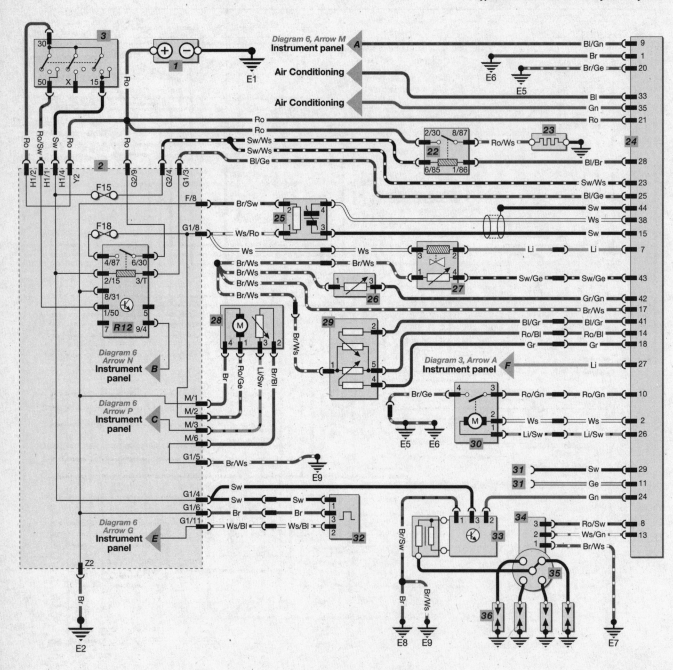

Wire colours

Ws	White
Ro	Red
Ge	Yellow
Br	Brown
Bl	Blue
Gr	Grey
Gn	Green
Sw	Black
Li	Lilac

H31605

Key to items

1	Battery
2	Fuse / relay box
	R12 = Fuel pump relay
3	Ignition switch
20	Injector
21	Cannister purge valve
24	Motronic control unit
25	Lambda probe
26	Coolant temp. sender
27	Inlet air temp and pressure senders
28	Fuel pump and level sender
29	Throttle valve controller and potentiometer
32	Speed sensor
33	Ignition transformer
34	Hall transmitter
35	Distributor
36	Spark plugs
37	Knock sensor

Diagram 5

Typical motronic-9 fuel injection system

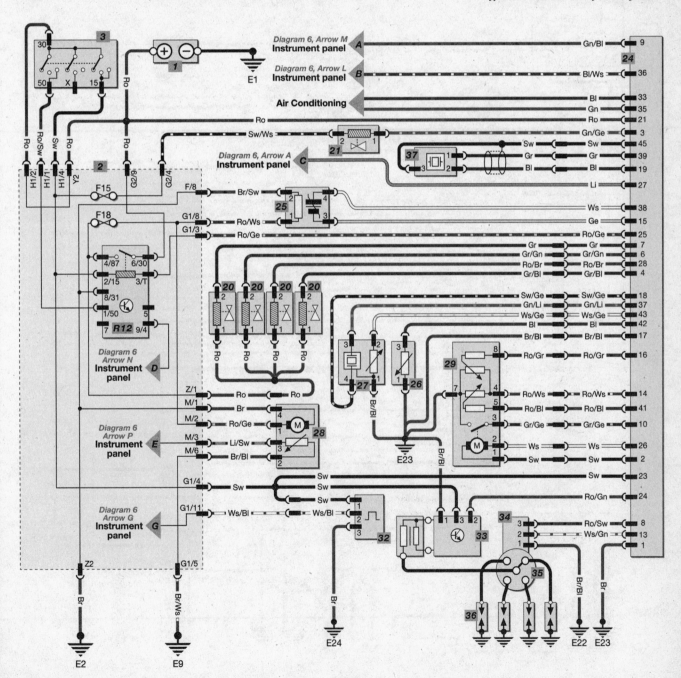

12

Wire colours

Ws White
Ro Red
Ge Yellow
Br Brown
Bl Blue
Gr Grey
Gn Green
Sw Black
Li Lilac

H31606

Key to items

1 Battery
2 Fuse / relay box
3 Ignition switch
40 Instrument panel
  a = Rear fog light warning light
  b = RH indicator warning light
  c = LH indicator warning light
  d = Alternator charge warning light
  e = ABS warning light
  f = Main beam warning light

g = Instrument panel illumination
h = Brake fluid and handbrake
warning light
i = Temperature warning light
j = Oil pressure warning light
k = Clock
l = Speedometer
m = Tachometer
n = Coolant temperature gauge
o = Fuel level gauge

p = Glow plug period light
41 Coolant level sender
42 Handbrake switch
43 Brake fluid level switch
44 Fuel level sender
46 Oil pressure switch

Diagram 6

Instrument panel

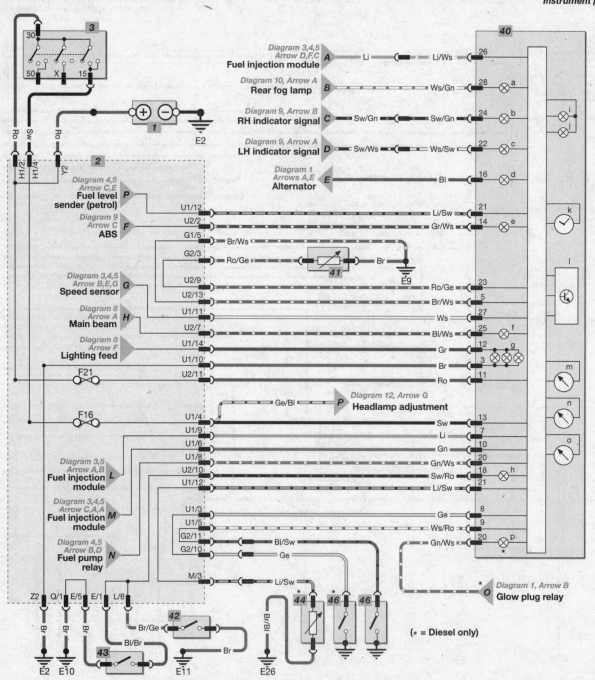

(* = Diesel only)

Wire colours

Ws	White
Ro	Red
Ge	Yellow
Br	Brown
Bl	Blue
Gr	Grey
Gn	Green
Sw	Black
Li	Lilac

H31607

Key to items

1 Battery
2 Fuse/relay box
  R4 = 'X' contact relay
  R11 or 58= Twin tone horn relay
  or link
3 Ignition switch
45 Cigar lighter
46 Radio
47 Electric aerial
48 Rear left speaker

49 Rear right speaker
50 Front left door speaker
51 Front left speaker
52 Front right door speaker
53 Front right speaker
54 Heated rear window switch
55 Heated rear window
56 Multifunction switch
   horn,wash/wipe
57 Horn

58 Link

Diagram 7

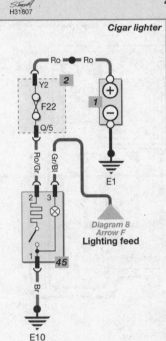

Cigar lighter

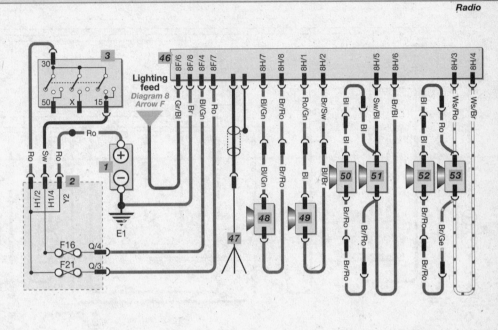

Radio

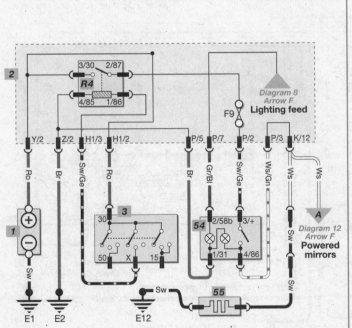

Heated rear window

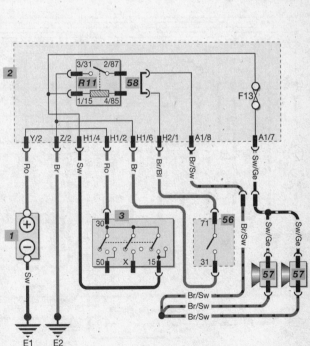

Twin tone horn

12

Wire colours

Ws White
Ro Red
Ge Yellow
Br Brown
Bl Blue
Gr Grey
Gn Green
Sw Black
Li Lilac

H31608

Key to items

1 Battery
2 Fuse/relay box
   R2 = rear window wash/wipe relay
   R4 = 'X' contact relay
   R8 = wash/wipe delay relay
3 Ignition switch
56 Multi-function switch
   horn, wash/wipe
60 Windscreen washer pump
61 Windscreen wiper motor

62 Rear window wiper motor
63 RH headlight unit
64 LH headlight unit
65 Headlight dip / flash switch
66 LH rear light
67 RH rear light
68 Light switch
69 Number plate lights

Diagram 8

Windscreen wash/wipe

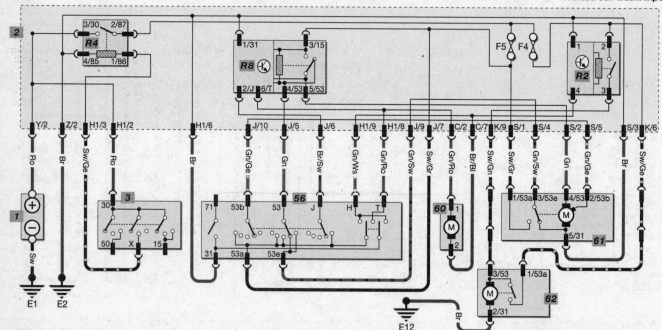

Exterior lighting - side and headlamps

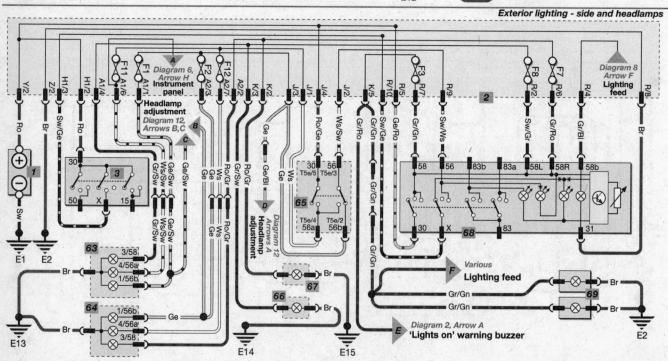

Wire colours

Ws White
Ro Red
Ge Yellow
Br Brown
Bl Blue
Gr Grey
Gn Green
Sw Black
Li Lilac

H31609

Key to items

1 Battery
2 Fuse/relay box
  R6 = hazard warning flasher relay
3 Ignition switch
65 Multi function switch
70 LH side indicator
71 LH front indicator
72 RH front indicator
73 RH side indicator
74 LH rear indicator

75 RH rear indicator
76 LH brake light
77 Centre brake light
78 RH brake light
79 Brake switch
80 LH reversing light
81 RH reversing light
82 Reversing light switch
   (manual transmission)
83 Automatic transmission relay

Diagram 9

Exterior lighting - indicators and hazard warning lights

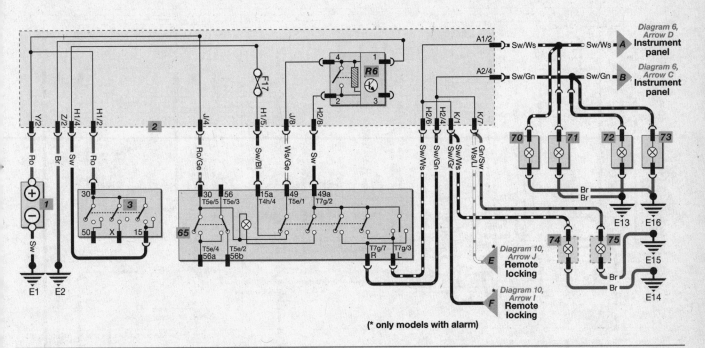

(* only models with alarm)

Exterior lighting - brake lights

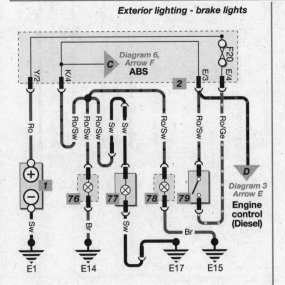

Exterior lighting - reversing lights

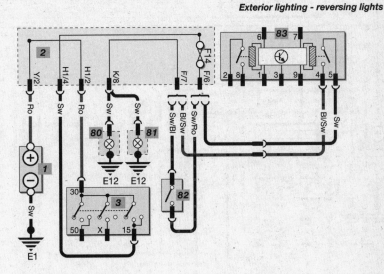

12

Wire colours

Ws White
Ro Red
Ge Yellow
Br Brown
Bl Blue
Gr Grey
Gn Green
Sw Black
Li Lilac

H31610

Key to items

1   Battery
2   Fuse/relay box
    R6 = hazard warning flasher relay
3   Ignition switch
68 Light switch
85 Rear fog light
86 Front LH fog light
87 Front RH fog light
88 Power closing switch
    (driver side)
89 Power closing switch
    (passenger side)
90 Central locking unit with pump
91 Control unit for radio frequency
    remote control

Diagram 10

Exterior lighting - front and rear fog lights

Central locking (radiofrequency remote control)

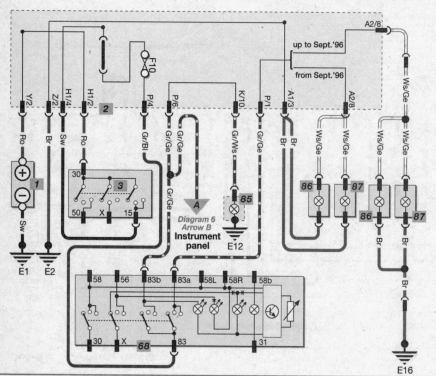

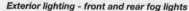

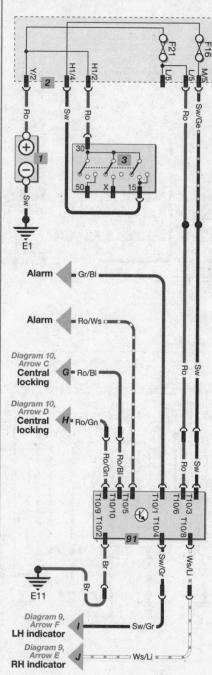

Central locking

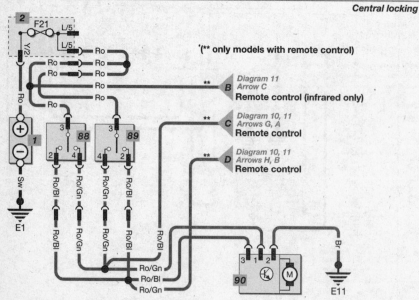

'(** only models with remote control)

Wire colours

Ws	White
Ro	Red
Ge	Yellow
Br	Brown
Bl	Blue
Gr	Grey
Gn	Green
Sw	Black
Li	Lilac

H31611

Key to items

1 Battery
2 Fuse/relay box
  R6 = hazard warning flasher relay
3 Ignition switch
92 Lock relay
93 Control unit for infrared remote control
94 Open relay
95 Front LH locking regulator
96 Window fuse (20A)

97 Automatic window closing relay
98 Front LH window motor
99 Front LH window switch
100 Front RH window motor
101 Front RH window switch
102 Rear window locking switch
103 Rear LH window switch (on dashboard)
104 Rear RH window switch (on dashboard)

105 Rear LH window switch (on door)
106 Rear RH window switch (on door)
107 Rear LH window motor
108 Rear RH window motor

Diagram 11

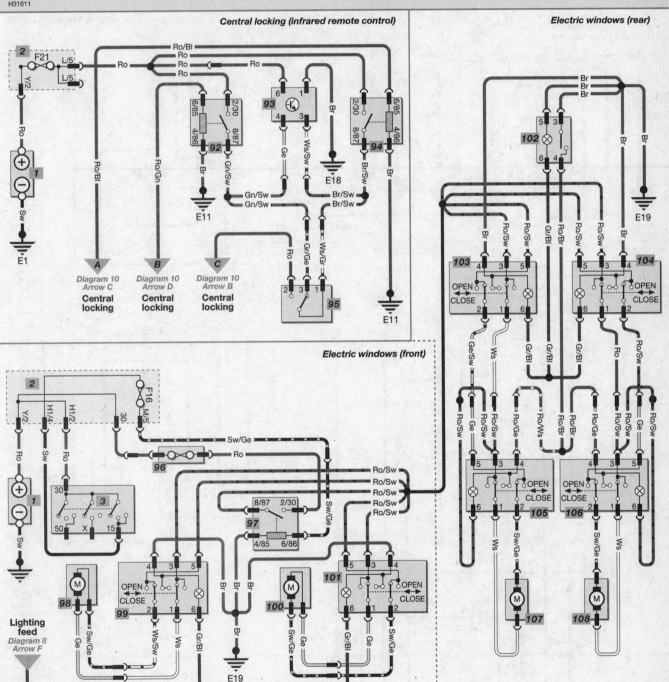

Central locking (infrared remote control)

Electric windows (rear)

Electric windows (front)

A Diagram 10 Arrow C Central locking

B Diagram 10 Arrow D Central locking

C Diagram 10 Arrow B Central locking

Lighting feed Diagram 8 Arrow F

Wire colours

Ws White
Ro Red
Ge Yellow
Br Brown
Bl Blue
Gr Grey
Gn Green
Sw Black
Li Lilac

H31612

Key to items

1 Battery
2 Fuse/relay box
3 Ignition switch
110 Light range controller
111 LH light range controller
112 RH light range controller
113 Door mirror switch
114 Door mirror motors and heating (Driver side)
115 Door mirror motors and heating (Passenger side)
116 Fuse 2 for ABS (30A)
117 Fuse 1 for ABS (30A)
118 ABS with EDS control unit
119 Rear left wheel sensor
120 Front left wheel sensor
121 Condensor (used up to Oct '97)
122 Front right wheel sensor
123 Rear right wheel sensor

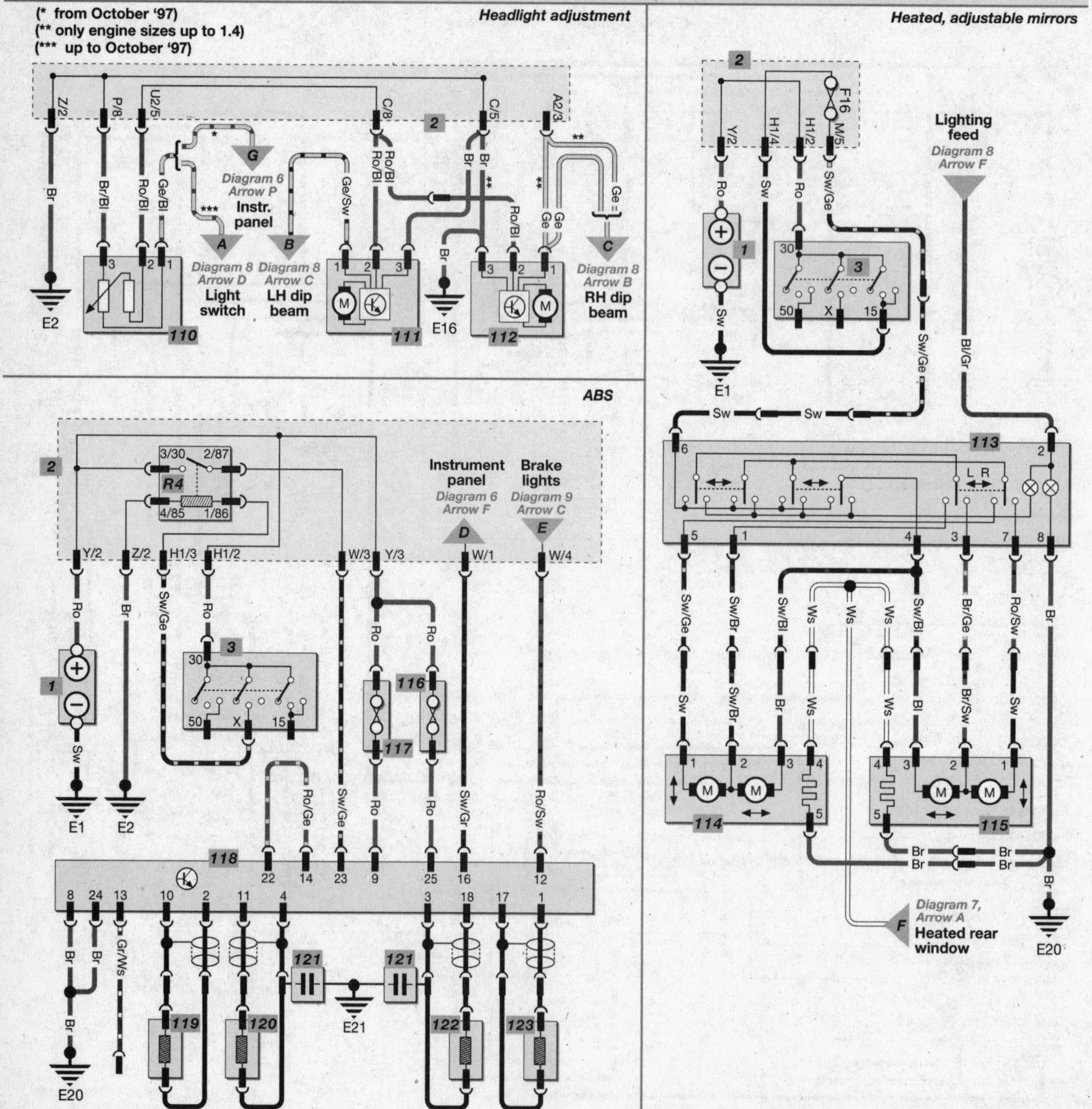

Diagram 12

(* from October '97)
(** only engine sizes up to 1.4)
(*** up to October '97)

Headlight adjustment

Heated, adjustable mirrors

Lighting feed
Diagram 8
Arrow F

Diagram 6
Arrow P
Instr. panel

Diagram 8
Arrow D
Light switch

Diagram 8
Arrow C
LH dip beam

Diagram 8
Arrow B
RH dip beam

110   111   112

E2   E16

ABS

Instrument panel
Diagram 6
Arrow F

Brake lights
Diagram 9
Arrow C

R4

116   117

118

119   120   121   122   123

E1   E2   E20   E21

113

114   115

Diagram 7,
Arrow A
Heated rear window

E1   E20

Dimensions and weights

Note: *All figures and dimensions are approximate and may vary according to model. Refer to manufacturer's data for exact figures.*

Overall length
Ibiza Hatchback models	3853 mm
Cordoba Saloon models	4144 mm
Cordoba Coupe models	4142 mm
Cordoba Vario models	4144 mm

Overall width
All models	1640 mm

Overall height (unladen)
Ibiza Hatchback 'standard' models	1422 mm
Ibiza Hatchback 'Sports' models	1409 mm
Cordoba Saloon models	1424 mm
Cordoba Coupe models	1409 mm
Cordoba Vario models	1496 mm

Wheelbase
All models	2443 mm

Turning circle
Standard models	10.4 m
Sports models	10.9 m

Weights

	Kerb weight *	Maximum gross vehicle weight **
Ibiza Hatchback models	900 to 1100 kg	1380 to 1560 kg
Cordoba Saloon models	1000 to 1100 kg	1485 to 1555 kg
Cordoba Coupe models	1100 to 1150 kg	1500 to 1600 kg
Cordoba Vario models	1000 to 1200 kg	1500 to 1600 kg

* *Exact kerb weights depend upon model and specification.*
** *Exact maximum gross vehicle weights depend upon model and specification – refer to VIN plate for details.*

Maximum roof rack load
All models	50 kg

Maximum towing hitch downward load (noseweight)
All models	50 kg

Maximum towing weights

	Unbraked trailer	Braked trailer
Petrol engines:		
1.0 and 1.3 litre models	400 kg	600 kg
1.4 litre models	400 kg	750 kg
1.6 litre single-point fuel injection models	450 kg	900 kg
1.6 litre multi-point fuel injection models	480 kg	1000 kg
2.0 litre SOHC engines	500 kg	1000 kg
2.0 litre DOHC engines	500 kg	1100 kg
Diesel engines:		
Models with mechanical fuel injection	480 kg	1000 kg
Models with electronic fuel injection	500 kg	1000 kg

Length (distance)

Inches (in)	x 25.4	= Millimetres (mm)	x 0.0394	= Inches (in)
Feet (ft)	x 0.305	= Metres (m)	x 3.281	= Feet (ft)
Miles	x 1.609	= Kilometres (km)	x 0.621	= Miles

Volume (capacity)

Cubic inches (cu in; in^3)	x 16.387	= Cubic centimetres (cc; cm^3)	x 0.061	= Cubic inches (cu in; in^3)
Imperial pints (Imp pt)	x 0.568	= Litres (l)	x 1.76	= Imperial pints (Imp pt)
Imperial quarts (Imp qt)	x 1.137	= Litres (l)	x 0.88	= Imperial quarts (Imp qt)
Imperial quarts (Imp qt)	x 1.201	= US quarts (US qt)	x 0.833	= Imperial quarts (Imp qt)
US quarts (US qt)	x 0.946	= Litres (l)	x 1.057	= US quarts (US qt)
Imperial gallons (Imp gal)	x 4.546	= Litres (l)	x 0.22	= Imperial gallons (Imp gal)
Imperial gallons (Imp gal)	x 1.201	= US gallons (US gal)	x 0.833	= Imperial gallons (Imp gal)
US gallons (US gal)	x 3.785	= Litres (l)	x 0.264	= US gallons (US gal)

Mass (weight)

Ounces (oz)	x 28.35	= Grams (g)	x 0.035	= Ounces (oz)
Pounds (lb)	x 0.454	= Kilograms (kg)	x 2.205	= Pounds (lb)

Force

Ounces-force (ozf; oz)	x 0.278	= Newtons (N)	x 3.6	= Ounces-force (ozf; oz)
Pounds-force (lbf; lb)	x 4.448	= Newtons (N)	x 0.225	= Pounds-force (lbf; lb)
Newtons (N)	x 0.1	= Kilograms-force (kgf; kg)	x 9.81	= Newtons (N)

Pressure

Pounds-force per square inch (psi; lbf/in^2; lb/in^2)	x 0.070	= Kilograms-force per square centimetre (kgf/cm^2; kg/cm^2)	x 14.223	= Pounds-force per square inch (psi; lbf/in^2; lb/in^2)
Pounds-force per square inch (psi; lbf/in^2; lb/in^2)	x 0.068	= Atmospheres (atm)	x 14.696	= Pounds-force per square inch (psi; lbf/in^2; lb/in^2)
Pounds-force per square inch (psi; lbf/in^2; lb/in^2)	x 0.069	= Bars	x 14.5	= Pounds-force per square inch (psi; lbf/in^2; lb/in^2)
Pounds-force per square inch (psi; lbf/in^2; lb/in^2)	x 6.895	= Kilopascals (kPa)	x 0.145	= Pounds-force per square inch (psi; lbf/in^2; lb/in^2)
Kilopascals (kPa)	x 0.01	= Kilograms-force per square centimetre (kgf/cm^2; kg/cm^2)	x 98.1	= Kilopascals (kPa)
Millibar (mbar)	x 100	= Pascals (Pa)	x 0.01	= Millibar (mbar)
Millibar (mbar)	x 0.0145	= Pounds-force per square inch (psi; lbf/in^2; lb/in^2)	x 68.947	= Millibar (mbar)
Millibar (mbar)	x 0.75	= Millimetres of mercury (mmHg)	x 1.333	= Millibar (mbar)
Millibar (mbar)	x 0.401	= Inches of water (inH$_2$O)	x 2.491	= Millibar (mbar)
Millimetres of mercury (mmHg)	x 0.535	= Inches of water (inH$_2$O)	x 1.868	= Millimetres of mercury (mmHg)
Inches of water (inH$_2$O)	x 0.036	= Pounds-force per square inch (psi; lbf/in^2; lb/in^2)	x 27.68	= Inches of water (inH$_2$O)

Torque (moment of force)

Pounds-force inches (lbf in; lb in)	x 1.152	= Kilograms-force centimetre (kgf cm; kg cm)	x 0.868	= Pounds-force inches (lbf in; lb in)
Pounds-force inches (lbf in; lb in)	x 0.113	= Newton metres (Nm)	x 8.85	= Pounds-force inches (lbf in; lb in)
Pounds-force inches (lbf in; lb in)	x 0.083	= Pounds-force feet (lbf ft; lb ft)	x 12	= Pounds-force inches (lbf in; lb in)
Pounds-force feet (lbf ft; lb ft)	x 0.138	= Kilograms-force metres (kgf m; kg m)	x 7.233	= Pounds-force feet (lbf ft; lb ft)
Pounds-force feet (lbf ft; lb ft)	x 1.356	= Newton metres (Nm)	x 0.738	= Pounds-force feet (lbf ft; lb ft)
Newton metres (Nm)	x 0.102	= Kilograms-force metres (kgf m; kg m)	x 9.804	= Newton metres (Nm)

Power

Horsepower (hp)	x 745.7	= Watts (W)	x 0.0013	= Horsepower (hp)

Velocity (speed)

Miles per hour (miles/hr; mph)	x 1.609	= Kilometres per hour (km/hr; kph)	x 0.621	= Miles per hour (miles/hr; mph)

Fuel consumption*

Miles per gallon, Imperial (mpg)	x 0.354	= Kilometres per litre (km/l)	x 2.825	= Miles per gallon, Imperial (mpg)
Miles per gallon, US (mpg)	x 0.425	= Kilometres per litre (km/l)	x 2.352	= Miles per gallon, US (mpg)

Temperature

Degrees Fahrenheit = (°C x 1.8) + 32   Degrees Celsius (Degrees Centigrade; °C) = (°F - 32) x 0.56

It is common practice to convert from miles per gallon (mpg) to litres/100 kilometres (l/100km), where mpg x l/100 km = 282

Spare parts are available from many sources, including maker's appointed garages, accessory shops, and motor factors. To be sure of obtaining the correct parts, it will sometimes be necessary to quote the vehicle identification number. If possible, it can also be useful to take the old parts along for positive identification. Items such as starter motors and alternators may be available under a service exchange scheme - any parts returned should be clean.

Our advice regarding spare parts is as follows.

Officially appointed garages

This is the best source of parts which are peculiar to your car, and which are not otherwise generally available (eg, badges, interior trim, certain body panels, etc). It is also the only place at which you should buy parts if the vehicle is still under warranty.

Accessory shops

These are very good places to buy materials and components needed for the maintenance of your car (oil, air and fuel filters, light bulbs, drivebelts, greases, brake pads, touch-up paint, etc). Components of this nature sold by a reputable shop are usually of the same standard as those used by the car manufacturer.

Besides components, these shops also sell tools and general accessories, usually have convenient opening hours, charge lower prices, and can often be found close to home. Some accessory shops have parts counters where components needed for almost any repair job can be purchased or ordered.

Motor factors

Good factors will stock all the more important components which wear out comparatively quickly, and can sometimes supply individual components needed for the overhaul of a larger assembly (eg, brake seals and hydraulic parts, bearing shells, pistons, valves). They may also handle work such as cylinder block reboring, crankshaft regrinding, etc.

Tyre and exhaust specialists

These outlets may be independent, or members of a local or national chain. They frequently offer competitive prices when compared with a main dealer or local garage, but it will pay to obtain several quotes before making a decision. When researching prices, also ask what extras may be added - for instance fitting a new valve and balancing the wheel are both commonly charged on top of the price of a new tyre.

Other sources

Beware of parts or materials obtained from market stalls, car boot sales or similar outlets. Such items are not invariably sub-standard, but there is little chance of compensation if they do prove unsatisfactory. in the case of safety-critical components such as brake pads, there is the risk not only of financial loss, but also of an accident causing injury or death.

Second-hand components or assemblies obtained from a car breaker can be a good buy in some circumstances, but this sort of purchase is best made by the experienced DIY mechanic.

Vehicle identification

Modifications are a continuing and unpublicised process in vehicle manufacture, quite apart from major model changes. Spare parts manuals and lists are compiled upon a numerical basis, the individual vehicle identification numbers being essential to correct identification of the component concerned.

When ordering spare parts, always give as much information as possible. Quote the car model, year of manufacture and registration, chassis and engine numbers as appropriate.

The *Vehicle Identification Number plate* is attached to the right-hand side of the bulkhead panel, behind the right-hand front suspension strut **(see illustration)**. In some territories it is attached to the right-hand inner wing panel, in front of the windscreen.

The *Chassis Identification Number* is stamped on the bulkhead panel in front of the windscreen, and is visible through a cut-out in the windscreen cowl panel **(see illustration)**.

The *engine number* is stamped into the front or the left-hand end of the cylinder block on petrol engines. On diesel engines it is stamped into the front of the cylinder block, near the injection pump. A barcode identification sticker is located on the top of the timing cover **(see illustrations)**.

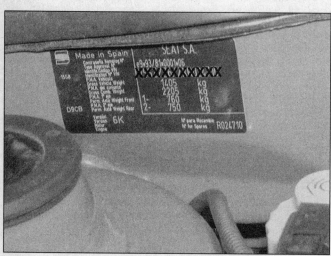

VIN plate on the engine compartment bulkhead

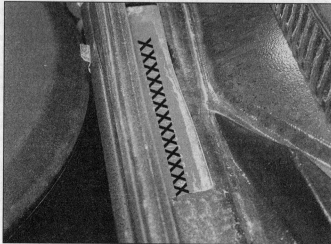

Chassis Identification Number on the bulkhead panel in front of the windscreen

Engine number location on the left-hand end of the cylinder block - petrol engines

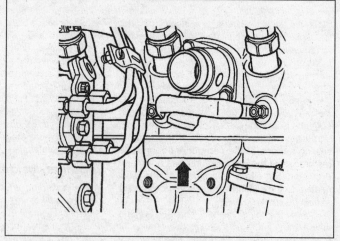

Engine number location on the front of the cylinder block - diesel engines

Whenever servicing, repair or overhaul work is carried out on the car or its components, observe the following procedures and instructions. This will assist in carrying out the operation efficiently and to a professional standard of workmanship.

Joint mating faces and gaskets

When separating components at their mating faces, never insert screwdrivers or similar implements into the joint between the faces in order to prise them apart. This can cause severe damage which results in oil leaks, coolant leaks, etc upon reassembly. Separation is usually achieved by tapping along the joint with a soft-faced hammer in order to break the seal. However, note that this method may not be suitable where dowels are used for component location.

Where a gasket is used between the mating faces of two components, a new one must be fitted on reassembly; fit it dry unless otherwise stated in the repair procedure. Make sure that the mating faces are clean and dry, with all traces of old gasket removed. When cleaning a joint face, use a tool which is unlikely to score or damage the face, and remove any burrs or nicks with an oilstone or fine file.

Make sure that tapped holes are cleaned with a pipe cleaner, and keep them free of jointing compound, if this is being used, unless specifically instructed otherwise.

Ensure that all orifices, channels or pipes are clear, and blow through them, preferably using compressed air.

Oil seals

Oil seals can be removed by levering them out with a wide flat-bladed screwdriver or similar implement. Alternatively, a number of self-tapping screws may be screwed into the seal, and these used as a purchase for pliers or some similar device in order to pull the seal free.

Whenever an oil seal is removed from its working location, either individually or as part of an assembly, it should be renewed.

The very fine sealing lip of the seal is easily damaged, and will not seal if the surface it contacts is not completely clean and free from scratches, nicks or grooves. If the original sealing surface of the component cannot be restored, and the manufacturer has not made provision for slight relocation of the seal relative to the sealing surface, the component should be renewed.

Protect the lips of the seal from any surface which may damage them in the course of fitting. Use tape or a conical sleeve where possible. Lubricate the seal lips with oil before fitting and, on dual-lipped seals, fill the space between the lips with grease.

Unless otherwise stated, oil seals must be fitted with their sealing lips toward the lubricant to be sealed.

Use a tubular drift or block of wood of the appropriate size to install the seal and, if the seal housing is shouldered, drive the seal down to the shoulder. If the seal housing is unshouldered, the seal should be fitted with its face flush with the housing top face (unless otherwise instructed).

Screw threads and fastenings

Seized nuts, bolts and screws are quite a common occurrence where corrosion has set in, and the use of penetrating oil or releasing fluid will often overcome this problem if the offending item is soaked for a while before attempting to release it. The use of an impact driver may also provide a means of releasing such stubborn fastening devices, when used in conjunction with the appropriate screwdriver bit or socket. If none of these methods works, it may be necessary to resort to the careful application of heat, or the use of a hacksaw or nut splitter device.

Studs are usually removed by locking two nuts together on the threaded part, and then using a spanner on the lower nut to unscrew the stud. Studs or bolts which have broken off below the surface of the component in which they are mounted can sometimes be removed using a stud extractor. Always ensure that a blind tapped hole is completely free from oil, grease, water or other fluid before installing the bolt or stud. Failure to do this could cause the housing to crack due to the hydraulic action of the bolt or stud as it is screwed in.

When tightening a castellated nut to accept a split pin, tighten the nut to the specified torque, where applicable, and then tighten further to the next split pin hole. Never slacken the nut to align the split pin hole, unless stated in the repair procedure.

When checking or retightening a nut or bolt to a specified torque setting, slacken the nut or bolt by a quarter of a turn, and then retighten to the specified setting. However, this should not be attempted where angular tightening has been used.

For some screw fastenings, notably cylinder head bolts or nuts, torque wrench settings are no longer specified for the latter stages of tightening, "angle-tightening" being called up instead. Typically, a fairly low torque wrench setting will be applied to the bolts/nuts in the correct sequence, followed by one or more stages of tightening through specified angles.

Locknuts, locktabs and washers

Any fastening which will rotate against a component or housing during tightening should always have a washer between it and the relevant component or housing.

Spring or split washers should always be renewed when they are used to lock a critical component such as a big-end bearing retaining bolt or nut. Locktabs which are folded over to retain a nut or bolt should always be renewed.

Self-locking nuts can be re-used in non-critical areas, providing resistance can be felt when the locking portion passes over the bolt or stud thread. However, it should be noted that self-locking stiffnuts tend to lose their effectiveness after long periods of use, and should then be renewed as a matter of course.

Split pins must always be replaced with new ones of the correct size for the hole.

When thread-locking compound is found on the threads of a fastener which is to be re-used, it should be cleaned off with a wire brush and solvent, and fresh compound applied on reassembly.

Special tools

Some repair procedures in this manual entail the use of special tools such as a press, two or three-legged pullers, spring compressors, etc. Wherever possible, suitable readily-available alternatives to the manufacturer's special tools are described, and are shown in use. In some instances, where no alternative is possible, it has been necessary to resort to the use of a manufacturer's tool, and this has been done for reasons of safety as well as the efficient completion of the repair operation. Unless you are highly-skilled and have a thorough understanding of the procedures described, never attempt to bypass the use of any special tool when the procedure described specifies its use. Not only is there a very great risk of personal injury, but expensive damage could be caused to the components involved.

Environmental considerations

When disposing of used engine oil, brake fluid, antifreeze, etc, give due consideration to any detrimental environmental effects. Do not, for instance, pour any of the above liquids down drains into the general sewage system, or onto the ground to soak away. Many local council refuse tips provide a facility for waste oil disposal, as do some garages. If none of these facilities are available, consult your local Environmental Health Department, or the National Rivers Authority, for further advice.

With the universal tightening-up of legislation regarding the emission of environmentally-harmful substances from motor vehicles, most vehicles have tamperproof devices fitted to the main adjustment points of the fuel system. These devices are primarily designed to prevent unqualified persons from adjusting the fuel/air mixture, with the chance of a consequent increase in toxic emissions. If such devices are found during servicing or overhaul, they should, wherever possible, be renewed or refitted in accordance with the manufacturer's requirements or current legislation.

OIL CARE
FOLLOW THE CODE

OIL BANK LINE
0800 66 33 66
www.oilbankline.org.uk

Note: It is antisocial and illegal to dump oil down the drain. To find the location of your local oil recycling bank, call this number free.

The jack supplied with the vehicle tool kit should only be used for changing roadwheels. When carrying out any other kind of work, raise the vehicle using a hydraulic jack, and always supplement the jack with axle stands positioned under the vehicle jacking points.

When jacking up the vehicle with a trolley jack, position the jack head under one of the relevant jacking points. Note that the jacking points for use with a hydraulic jack are located just inside the sill seam. **Do not** jack the vehicle under the sump or any of the steering or suspension components. Supplement the jack using axle stands. The jacking points and axle stand positions are shown in the accompanying illustrations (**see illustrations**).

⚠ *Warning: Never work under, around, or near a raised car, unless it is adequately supported in at least two places.*

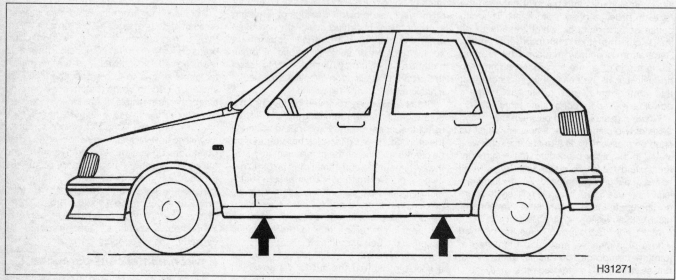

Front and rear jacking points (arrowed)

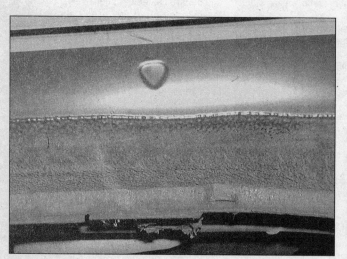

The jacking points are indicated by an arrow on the sill

The hydraulic jack jacking points are located just inside the sill seam

The radio/cassette unit fitted as standard equipment by Seat is equipped with a built-in security code, to deter thieves. If the power source to the unit is cut, the anti-theft system will activate. Even if the power source is immediately reconnected, the radio/ cassette unit will not function until the correct security code has been entered. Therefore, if you do not know the correct security code for the radio/cassette unit, **do not** disconnect the battery negative terminal of the battery, or remove the radio/cassette unit from the vehicle.

Refer to the Audio handbook supplied in the owners handbook pack, for further details of how to use the code.

If you should loose or forget the code, seek the advice of your Seat dealer. On presentation of proof of ownership, a Seat dealer will be able to unlock the unit and provide you with a new security code.

Devices known as memory-savers (or code-savers) can be used to avoid some of the above problems. Precise details vary according to the device used. Typically, it is plugged into the cigarette lighter, and is connected by its own wires to a spare battery; the vehicle's own battery is then disconnected from the electrical system, leaving the memory-saver to pass sufficient current to maintain audio unit security codes and any other memory values, and also to run permanently-live circuits such as the clock.

⚠️ *Warning: Some of these devices allow a considerable amount of current to pass, which can mean that many of the vehicle's systems are still operational when the main battery is disconnected. If a memory-saver is used, ensure that the circuit concerned is actually dead before carrying out any work on it!*

Introduction

A selection of good tools is a fundamental requirement for anyone contemplating the maintenance and repair of a motor vehicle. For the owner who does not possess any, their purchase will prove a considerable expense, offsetting some of the savings made by doing-it-yourself. However, provided that the tools purchased meet the relevant national safety standards and are of good quality, they will last for many years and prove an extremely worthwhile investment.

To help the average owner to decide which tools are needed to carry out the various tasks detailed in this manual, we have compiled three lists of tools under the following headings: *Maintenance and minor repair*, *Repair and overhaul*, and *Special*. Newcomers to practical mechanics should start off with the *Maintenance and minor repair* tool kit, and confine themselves to the simpler jobs around the vehicle. Then, as confidence and experience grow, more difficult tasks can be undertaken, with extra tools being purchased as, and when, they are needed. In this way, a *Maintenance and minor repair* tool kit can be built up into a *Repair and overhaul* tool kit over a considerable period of time, without any major cash outlays. The experienced do-it-yourselfer will have a tool kit good enough for most repair and overhaul procedures, and will add tools from the *Special* category when it is felt that the expense is justified by the amount of use to which these tools will be put.

Maintenance and minor repair tool kit

The tools given in this list should be considered as a minimum requirement if routine maintenance, servicing and minor repair operations are to be undertaken. We recommend the purchase of combination spanners (ring one end, open-ended the other); although more expensive than open-ended ones, they do give the advantages of both types of spanner.

☐ *Combination spanners:*
Metric - 8 to 19 mm inclusive
☐ *Adjustable spanner - 35 mm jaw (approx.)*
☐ *Spark plug spanner (with rubber insert) - petrol models*
☐ *Spark plug gap adjustment tool - petrol models*
☐ *Set of feeler gauges*
☐ *Brake bleed nipple spanner*
☐ *Screwdrivers:*
Flat blade - 100 mm long x 6 mm dia
Cross blade - 100 mm long x 6 mm dia
Torx - various sizes (not all vehicles)
☐ *Combination pliers*
☐ *Hacksaw (junior)*
☐ *Tyre pump*
☐ *Tyre pressure gauge*
☐ *Oil can*
☐ *Oil filter removal tool*
☐ *Fine emery cloth*
☐ *Wire brush (small)*
☐ *Funnel (medium size)*
☐ *Sump drain plug key (not all vehicles)*

Repair and overhaul tool kit

These tools are virtually essential for anyone undertaking any major repairs to a motor vehicle, and are additional to those given in the *Maintenance and minor repair* list. Included in this list is a comprehensive set of sockets. Although these are expensive, they will be found invaluable as they are so versatile - particularly if various drives are included in the set. We recommend the half-inch square-drive type, as this can be used with most proprietary torque wrenches.

The tools in this list will sometimes need to be supplemented by tools from the *Special* list:

☐ *Sockets (or box spanners) to cover range in previous list (including Torx sockets)*
☐ *Reversible ratchet drive (for use with sockets)*
☐ *Extension piece, 250 mm (for use with sockets)*
☐ *Universal joint (for use with sockets)*
☐ *Flexible handle or sliding T "breaker bar" (for use with sockets)*
☐ *Torque wrench (for use with sockets)*
☐ *Self-locking grips*
☐ *Ball pein hammer*
☐ *Soft-faced mallet (plastic or rubber)*
☐ *Screwdrivers:*
Flat blade - long & sturdy, short (chubby), and narrow (electrician's) types
Cross blade - long & sturdy, and short (chubby) types
☐ *Pliers:*
Long-nosed
Side cutters (electrician's)
Circlip (internal and external)
☐ *Cold chisel - 25 mm*
☐ *Scriber*
☐ *Scraper*
☐ *Centre-punch*
☐ *Pin punch*
☐ *Hacksaw*
☐ *Brake hose clamp*
☐ *Brake/clutch bleeding kit*
☐ *Selection of twist drills*
☐ *Steel rule/straight-edge*
☐ *Allen keys (inc. splined/Torx type)*
☐ *Selection of files*
☐ *Wire brush*
☐ *Axle stands*
☐ *Jack (strong trolley or hydraulic type)*
☐ *Light with extension lead*
☐ *Universal electrical multi-meter*

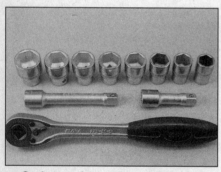

Sockets and reversible ratchet drive

Brake bleeding kit

Torx key, socket and bit

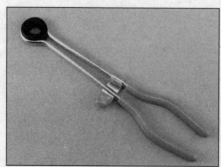

Hose clamp

Angular-tightening gauge

Special tools

The tools in this list are those which are not used regularly, are expensive to buy, or which need to be used in accordance with their manufacturers' instructions. Unless relatively difficult mechanical jobs are undertaken frequently, it will not be economic to buy many of these tools. Where this is the case, you could consider clubbing together with friends (or joining a motorists' club) to make a joint purchase, or borrowing the tools against a deposit from a local garage or tool hire specialist. It is worth noting that many of the larger DIY superstores now carry a large range of special tools for hire at modest rates.

The following list contains only those tools and instruments freely available to the public, and not those special tools produced by the vehicle manufacturer specifically for its dealer network. You will find occasional references to these manufacturers' special tools in the text of this manual. Generally, an alternative method of doing the job without the vehicle manufacturers' special tool is given. However, sometimes there is no alternative to using them. Where this is the case and the relevant tool cannot be bought or borrowed, you will have to entrust the work to a dealer.

- [ ] Angular-tightening gauge
- [ ] Valve spring compressor
- [ ] Valve grinding tool
- [ ] Piston ring compressor
- [ ] Piston ring removal/installation tool
- [ ] Cylinder bore hone
- [ ] Balljoint separator
- [ ] Coil spring compressors (where applicable)
- [ ] Two/three-legged hub and bearing puller
- [ ] Impact screwdriver
- [ ] Micrometer and/or vernier calipers
- [ ] Dial gauge
- [ ] Stroboscopic timing light
- [ ] Dwell angle meter/tachometer
- [ ] Fault code reader
- [ ] Cylinder compression gauge
- [ ] Hand-operated vacuum pump and gauge
- [ ] Clutch plate alignment set
- [ ] Brake shoe steady spring cup removal tool
- [ ] Bush and bearing removal/installation set
- [ ] Stud extractors
- [ ] Tap and die set
- [ ] Lifting tackle
- [ ] Trolley jack

Buying tools

Reputable motor accessory shops and superstores often offer excellent quality tools at discount prices, so it pays to shop around.

Remember, you don't have to buy the most expensive items on the shelf, but it is always advisable to steer clear of the very cheap tools. Beware of 'bargains' offered on market stalls or at car boot sales. There are plenty of good tools around at reasonable prices, but always aim to purchase items which meet the relevant national safety standards. If in doubt, ask the proprietor or manager of the shop for advice before making a purchase.

Care and maintenance of tools

Having purchased a reasonable tool kit, it is necessary to keep the tools in a clean and serviceable condition. After use, always wipe off any dirt, grease and metal particles using a clean, dry cloth, before putting the tools away. Never leave them lying around after they have been used. A simple tool rack on the garage or workshop wall for items such as screwdrivers and pliers is a good idea. Store all normal spanners and sockets in a metal box. Any measuring instruments, gauges, meters, etc, must be carefully stored where they cannot be damaged or become rusty.

Take a little care when tools are used. Hammer heads inevitably become marked, and screwdrivers lose the keen edge on their blades from time to time. A little timely attention with emery cloth or a file will soon restore items like this to a good finish.

Working facilities

Not to be forgotten when discussing tools is the workshop itself. If anything more than routine maintenance is to be carried out, a suitable working area becomes essential.

It is appreciated that many an owner-mechanic is forced by circumstances to remove an engine or similar item without the benefit of a garage or workshop. Having done this, any repairs should always be done under the cover of a roof.

Wherever possible, any dismantling should be done on a clean, flat workbench or table at a suitable working height.

Any workbench needs a vice; one with a jaw opening of 100 mm is suitable for most jobs. As mentioned previously, some clean dry storage space is also required for tools, as well as for any lubricants, cleaning fluids, touch-up paints etc, which become necessary.

Another item which may be required, and which has a much more general usage, is an electric drill with a chuck capacity of at least 8 mm. This, together with a good range of twist drills, is virtually essential for fitting accessories.

Last, but not least, always keep a supply of old newspapers and clean, lint-free rags available, and try to keep any working area as clean as possible.

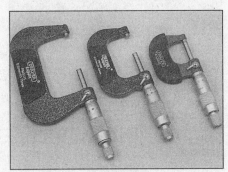
Micrometers

Dial test indicator ("dial gauge")

Strap wrench

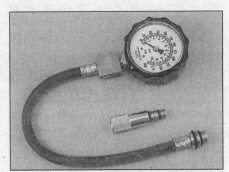
Compression tester

Fault code reader

This is a guide to getting your vehicle through the MOT test. Obviously it will not be possible to examine the vehicle to the same standard as the professional MOT tester. However, working through the following checks will enable you to identify any problem areas before submitting the vehicle for the test.

Where a testable component is in borderline condition, the tester has discretion in deciding whether to pass or fail it. The basis of such discretion is whether the tester would be happy for a close relative or friend to use the vehicle with the component in that condition. If the vehicle presented is clean and evidently well cared for, the tester may be more inclined to pass a borderline component than if the vehicle is scruffy and apparently neglected.

It has only been possible to summarise the test requirements here, based on the regulations in force at the time of printing. Test standards are becoming increasingly stringent, although there are some exemptions for older vehicles.

An assistant will be needed to help carry out some of these checks.

The checks have been sub-divided into four categories, as follows:

1 Checks carried out **FROM THE DRIVER'S SEAT**

2 Checks carried out **WITH THE VEHICLE ON THE GROUND**

3 Checks carried out **WITH THE VEHICLE RAISED AND THE WHEELS FREE TO TURN**

4 Checks carried out on **YOUR VEHICLE'S EXHAUST EMISSION SYSTEM**

---

1 Checks carried out **FROM THE DRIVER'S SEAT**

Handbrake

☐ Test the operation of the handbrake. Excessive travel (too many clicks) indicates incorrect brake or cable adjustment.
☐ Check that the handbrake cannot be released by tapping the lever sideways. Check the security of the lever mountings.

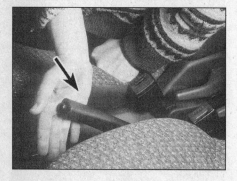

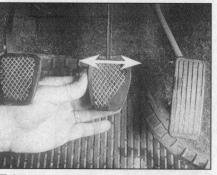

☐ Check that the brake pedal is secure and in good condition. Check also for signs of fluid leaks on the pedal, floor or carpets, which would indicate failed seals in the brake master cylinder.
☐ Check the servo unit (when applicable) by operating the brake pedal several times, then keeping the pedal depressed and starting the engine. As the engine starts, the pedal will move down slightly. If not, the vacuum hose or the servo itself may be faulty.

Footbrake

☐ Depress the brake pedal and check that it does not creep down to the floor, indicating a master cylinder fault. Release the pedal, wait a few seconds, then depress it again. If the pedal travels nearly to the floor before firm resistance is felt, brake adjustment or repair is necessary. If the pedal feels spongy, there is air in the hydraulic system which must be removed by bleeding.

Steering wheel and column

☐ Examine the steering wheel for fractures or looseness of the hub, spokes or rim.
☐ Move the steering wheel from side to side and then up and down. Check that the steering wheel is not loose on the column, indicating wear or a loose retaining nut. Continue moving the steering wheel as before, but also turn it slightly from left to right.
☐ Check that the steering wheel is not loose on the column, and that there is no abnormal

movement of the steering wheel, indicating wear in the column support bearings or couplings.

Windscreen, mirrors and sunvisor

☐ The windscreen must be free of cracks or other significant damage within the driver's field of view. (Small stone chips are acceptable.) Rear view mirrors must be secure, intact, and capable of being adjusted.

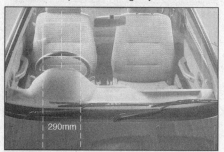

☐ The driver's sunvisor must be capable of being stored in the "up" position.

Seat belts and seats

Note: *The following checks are applicable to all seat belts, front and rear.*

☐ Examine the webbing of all the belts (including rear belts if fitted) for cuts, serious fraying or deterioration. Fasten and unfasten each belt to check the buckles. If applicable, check the retracting mechanism. Check the security of all seat belt mountings accessible from inside the vehicle.

☐ Seat belts with pre-tensioners, once activated, have a "flag" or similar showing on the seat belt stalk. This, in itself, is not a reason for test failure.

☐ The front seats themselves must be securely attached and the backrests must lock in the upright position.

Doors

☐ Both front doors must be able to be opened and closed from outside and inside, and must latch securely when closed.

2 Checks carried out WITH THE VEHICLE ON THE GROUND

Vehicle identification

☐ Number plates must be in good condition, secure and legible, with letters and numbers correctly spaced – spacing at (A) should be at least twice that at (B).

☐ The VIN plate and/or homologation plate must be legible.

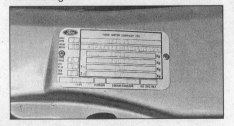

Electrical equipment

☐ Switch on the ignition and check the operation of the horn.

☐ Check the windscreen washers and wipers, examining the wiper blades; renew damaged or perished blades. Also check the operation of the stop-lights.

☐ Check the operation of the sidelights and number plate lights. The lenses and reflectors must be secure, clean and undamaged.

☐ Check the operation and alignment of the headlights. The headlight reflectors must not be tarnished and the lenses must be undamaged.

☐ Switch on the ignition and check the operation of the direction indicators (including the instrument panel tell-tale) and the hazard warning lights. Operation of the sidelights and stop-lights must not affect the indicators - if it does, the cause is usually a bad earth at the rear light cluster.

☐ Check the operation of the rear foglight(s), including the warning light on the instrument panel or in the switch.

☐ The ABS warning light must illuminate in accordance with the manufacturers' design. For most vehicles, the ABS warning light should illuminate when the ignition is switched on, and (if the system is operating properly) extinguish after a few seconds. Refer to the owner's handbook.

Footbrake

☐ Examine the master cylinder, brake pipes and servo unit for leaks, loose mountings, corrosion or other damage.

☐ The fluid reservoir must be secure and the fluid level must be between the upper (**A**) and lower (**B**) markings.

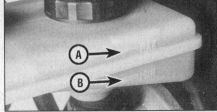

☐ Inspect both front brake flexible hoses for cracks or deterioration of the rubber. Turn the steering from lock to lock, and ensure that the hoses do not contact the wheel, tyre, or any part of the steering or suspension mechanism. With the brake pedal firmly depressed, check the hoses for bulges or leaks under pressure.

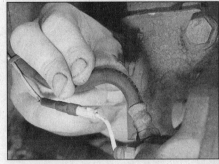

Steering and suspension

☐ Have your assistant turn the steering wheel from side to side slightly, up to the point where the steering gear just begins to transmit this movement to the roadwheels. Check for excessive free play between the steering wheel and the steering gear, indicating wear or insecurity of the steering column joints, the column-to-steering gear coupling, or the steering gear itself.

☐ Have your assistant turn the steering wheel more vigorously in each direction, so that the roadwheels just begin to turn. As this is done, examine all the steering joints, linkages, fittings and attachments. Renew any component that shows signs of wear or damage. On vehicles with power steering, check the security and condition of the steering pump, drivebelt and hoses.

☐ Check that the vehicle is standing level, and at approximately the correct ride height.

Shock absorbers

☐ Depress each corner of the vehicle in turn, then release it. The vehicle should rise and then settle in its normal position. If the vehicle continues to rise and fall, the shock absorber is defective. A shock absorber which has seized will also cause the vehicle to fail.

Exhaust system

☐ Start the engine. With your assistant holding a rag over the tailpipe, check the entire system for leaks. Repair or renew leaking sections.

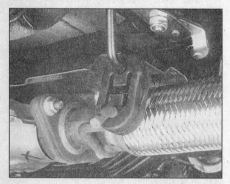

3 Checks carried out
WITH THE VEHICLE RAISED AND THE WHEELS FREE TO TURN

Jack up the front and rear of the vehicle, and securely support it on axle stands. Position the stands clear of the suspension assemblies. Ensure that the wheels are clear of the ground and that the steering can be turned from lock to lock.

Steering mechanism

☐ Have your assistant turn the steering from lock to lock. Check that the steering turns smoothly, and that no part of the steering mechanism, including a wheel or tyre, fouls any brake hose or pipe or any part of the body structure.

☐ Examine the steering rack rubber gaiters for damage or insecurity of the retaining clips. If power steering is fitted, check for signs of damage or leakage of the fluid hoses, pipes or connections. Also check for excessive stiffness or binding of the steering, a missing split pin or locking device, or severe corrosion of the body structure within 30 cm of any steering component attachment point.

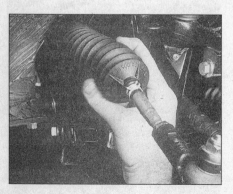

Front and rear suspension and wheel bearings

☐ Starting at the front right-hand side, grasp the roadwheel at the 3 o'clock and 9 o'clock positions and rock gently but firmly. Check for free play or insecurity at the wheel bearings, suspension balljoints, or suspension mountings, pivots and attachments.

☐ Now grasp the wheel at the 12 o'clock and 6 o'clock positions and repeat the previous inspection. Spin the wheel, and check for roughness or tightness of the front wheel bearing.

☐ If excess free play is suspected at a component pivot point, this can be confirmed by using a large screwdriver or similar tool and levering between the mounting and the component attachment. This will confirm whether the wear is in the pivot bush, its retaining bolt, or in the mounting itself (the bolt holes can often become elongated).

☐ Carry out all the above checks at the other front wheel, and then at both rear wheels.

Springs and shock absorbers

☐ Examine the suspension struts (when applicable) for serious fluid leakage, corrosion, or damage to the casing. Also check the security of the mounting points.

☐ If coil springs are fitted, check that the spring ends locate in their seats, and that the spring is not corroded, cracked or broken.

☐ If leaf springs are fitted, check that all leaves are intact, that the axle is securely attached to each spring, and that there is no deterioration of the spring eye mountings, bushes, and shackles.

☐ The same general checks apply to vehicles fitted with other suspension types, such as torsion bars, hydraulic displacer units, etc. Ensure that all mountings and attachments are secure, that there are no signs of excessive wear, corrosion or damage, and (on hydraulic types) that there are no fluid leaks or damaged pipes.

☐ Inspect the shock absorbers for signs of serious fluid leakage. Check for wear of the mounting bushes or attachments, or damage to the body of the unit.

Driveshafts (fwd vehicles only)

☐ Rotate each front wheel in turn and inspect the constant velocity joint gaiters for splits or damage. Also check that each driveshaft is straight and undamaged.

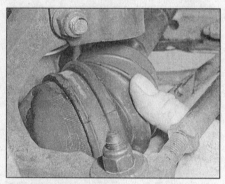

Braking system

☐ If possible without dismantling, check brake pad wear and disc condition. Ensure that the friction lining material has not worn excessively, (A) and that the discs are not fractured, pitted, scored or badly worn (B).

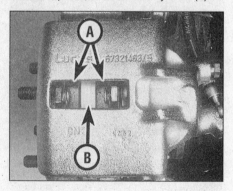

☐ Examine all the rigid brake pipes underneath the vehicle, and the flexible hose(s) at the rear. Look for corrosion, chafing or insecurity of the pipes, and for signs of bulging under pressure, chafing, splits or deterioration of the flexible hoses.

☐ Look for signs of fluid leaks at the brake calipers or on the brake backplates. Repair or renew leaking components.

☐ Slowly spin each wheel, while your assistant depresses and releases the footbrake. Ensure that each brake is operating and does not bind when the pedal is released.

□ Examine the handbrake mechanism, checking for frayed or broken cables, excessive corrosion, or wear or insecurity of the linkage. Check that the mechanism works on each relevant wheel, and releases fully, without binding.

□ It is not possible to test brake efficiency without special equipment, but a road test can be carried out later to check that the vehicle pulls up in a straight line.

Fuel and exhaust systems

□ Inspect the fuel tank (including the filler cap), fuel pipes, hoses and unions. All components must be secure and free from leaks.

□ Examine the exhaust system over its entire length, checking for any damaged, broken or missing mountings, security of the retaining clamps and rust or corrosion.

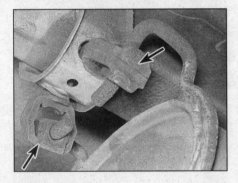

Wheels and tyres

□ Examine the sidewalls and tread area of each tyre in turn. Check for cuts, tears, lumps, bulges, separation of the tread, and exposure of the ply or cord due to wear or damage. Check that the tyre bead is correctly seated on the wheel rim, that the valve is sound and properly seated, and that the wheel is not distorted or damaged.

□ Check that the tyres are of the correct size for the vehicle, that they are of the same size and type on each axle, and that the pressures are correct.

□ Check the tyre tread depth. The legal minimum at the time of writing is 1.6 mm over at least three-quarters of the tread width. Abnormal tread wear may indicate incorrect front wheel alignment.

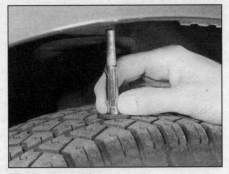

Body corrosion

□ Check the condition of the entire vehicle structure for signs of corrosion in load-bearing areas. (These include chassis box sections, side sills, cross-members, pillars, and all suspension, steering, braking system and seat belt mountings and anchorages.) Any corrosion which has seriously reduced the thickness of a load-bearing area is likely to cause the vehicle to fail. In this case professional repairs are likely to be needed.

□ Damage or corrosion which causes sharp or otherwise dangerous edges to be exposed will also cause the vehicle to fail.

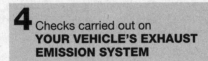

4 Checks carried out on **YOUR VEHICLE'S EXHAUST EMISSION SYSTEM**

Petrol models

□ Have the engine at normal operating temperature, and make sure that it is in good tune (ignition system in good order, air filter element clean, etc).

□ Before any measurements are carried out, raise the engine speed to around 2500 rpm, and hold it at this speed for 20 seconds. Allow the engine speed to return to idle, and watch for smoke emissions from the exhaust tailpipe. If the idle speed is obviously much too high, or if dense blue or clearly-visible black smoke comes from the tailpipe for more than 5 seconds, the vehicle will fail. As a rule of thumb, blue smoke signifies oil being burnt (engine wear) while black smoke signifies unburnt fuel (dirty air cleaner element, or other carburettor or fuel system fault).

□ An exhaust gas analyser capable of measuring carbon monoxide (CO) and hydrocarbons (HC) is now needed. If such an instrument cannot be hired or borrowed, a local garage may agree to perform the check for a small fee.

CO emissions (mixture)

□ At the time of writing, for vehicles first used between 1st August 1975 and 31st July 1986 (P to C registration), the CO level must not exceed 4.5% by volume. For vehicles first used between 1st August 1986 and 31st July 1992 (D to J registration), the CO level must not exceed 3.5% by volume. Vehicles first

used after 1st August 1992 (K registration) must conform to the manufacturer's specification. The MOT tester has access to a DOT database or emissions handbook, which lists the CO and HC limits for each make and model of vehicle. The CO level is measured with the engine at idle speed, and at "fast idle". The following limits are given as a general guide:

   At idle speed -
      CO level no more than 0.5%
   At "fast idle" (2500 to 3000 rpm) -
      CO level no more than 0.3%
      (Minimum oil temperature 60ºC)

□ If the CO level cannot be reduced far enough to pass the test (and the fuel and ignition systems are otherwise in good condition) then the carburettor is badly worn, or there is some problem in the fuel injection system or catalytic converter (as applicable).

HC emissions

□ With the CO within limits, HC emissions for vehicles first used between 1st August 1975 and 31st July 1992 (P to J registration) must not exceed 1200 ppm. Vehicles first used after 1st August 1992 (K registration) must conform to the manufacturer's specification. The MOT tester has access to a DOT database or emissions handbook, which lists the CO and HC limits for each make and model of vehicle. The HC level is measured with the engine at "fast idle". The following is given as a general guide:

   At "fast idle" (2500 to 3000 rpm) -
      HC level no more than 200 ppm
      (Minimum oil temperature 60ºC)

□ Excessive HC emissions are caused by incomplete combustion, the causes of which can include oil being burnt, mechanical wear and ignition/fuel system malfunction.

Diesel models

□ The only emission test applicable to Diesel engines is the measuring of exhaust smoke density. The test involves accelerating the engine several times to its maximum unloaded speed.

Note: *It is of the utmost importance that the engine timing belt is in good condition before the test is carried out.*

□ The limits for Diesel engine exhaust smoke, introduced in September 1995 are:
Vehicles first used before 1st August 1979:
   Exempt from metered smoke testing, but must not emit "dense blue or clearly visible black smoke for a period of more than 5 seconds at idle" or "dense blue or clearly visible black smoke during acceleration which would obscure the view of other road users".
Non-turbocharged vehicles first used after
   1st August 1979: 2.5m-1
Turbocharged vehicles first used after
   1st August 1979: 3.0m-1

□ Excessive smoke can be caused by a dirty air cleaner element. Otherwise, professional advice may be needed to find the cause.

Engine

- [ ] Engine fails to rotate when attempting to start
- [ ] Engine rotates, but will not start
- [ ] Engine difficult to start when cold
- [ ] Engine difficult to start when hot
- [ ] Starter motor noisy or excessively-rough in engagement
- [ ] Engine starts, but stops immediately
- [ ] Engine idles erratically
- [ ] Engine misfires at idle speed
- [ ] Engine misfires throughout the driving speed range
- [ ] Engine hesitates on acceleration
- [ ] Engine stalls
- [ ] Engine lacks power
- [ ] Engine backfires
- [ ] Oil pressure warning light illuminated with engine running
- [ ] Engine runs-on after switching off
- [ ] Engine noises

Cooling system

- [ ] Overheating
- [ ] Overcooling
- [ ] External coolant leakage
- [ ] Internal coolant leakage
- [ ] Corrosion

Fuel and exhaust systems

- [ ] Excessive fuel consumption
- [ ] Fuel leakage and/or fuel odour
- [ ] Excessive noise or fumes from exhaust system

Clutch

- [ ] Pedal travels to floor - no pressure or very little resistance
- [ ] Clutch fails to disengage (unable to select gears).
- [ ] Clutch slips (engine speed increases, with no increase in vehicle speed).
- [ ] Judder as clutch is engaged
- [ ] Noise when depressing or releasing clutch pedal

Manual transmission

- [ ] Noisy in neutral with engine running
- [ ] Noisy in one particular gear
- [ ] Difficulty engaging gears
- [ ] Jumps out of gear
- [ ] Vibration
- [ ] Lubricant leaks

Driveshafts

- [ ] Vibration when accelerating or decelerating
- [ ] Clicking or knocking noise on turns (at slow speed on full-lock)

Braking system

- [ ] Vehicle pulls to one side under braking
- [ ] Noise (grinding or high-pitched squeal) when brakes applied
- [ ] Brakes binding
- [ ] Excessive brake pedal travel
- [ ] Brake pedal feels spongy when depressed
- [ ] Excessive brake pedal effort required to stop vehicle
- [ ] Judder felt through brake pedal or steering wheel when braking
- [ ] Rear wheels locking under normal braking

Suspension and steering

- [ ] Vehicle pulls to one side
- [ ] Excessive pitching and/or rolling around corners, or during braking
- [ ] Lack of power assistance
- [ ] Wandering or general instability
- [ ] Excessively-stiff steering
- [ ] Excessive play in steering
- [ ] Wheel wobble and vibration
- [ ] Tyre wear excessive

Electrical system

- [ ] Battery will not hold a charge for more than a few days
- [ ] Ignition/no-charge warning light remains illuminated with engine running
- [ ] Ignition/no-charge warning light fails to come on
- [ ] Lights inoperative
- [ ] Instrument readings inaccurate or erratic
- [ ] Horn inoperative, or unsatisfactory in operation
- [ ] Windscreen wipers inoperative, or unsatisfactory in operation
- [ ] Windscreen washers inoperative, or unsatisfactory in operation
- [ ] Electric windows inoperative, or unsatisfactory in operation
- [ ] Central locking system inoperative, or unsatisfactory in operation

Introduction

The vehicle owner who does his or her own maintenance according to the recommended service schedules should not have to use this section of the manual very often. Modern com-ponent reliability is such that, provided those items subject to wear or deterioration are inspected or renewed at the specified intervals, sudden failure is comparatively rare. Faults do not usually just happen as a result of sudden failure, but develop over a period of time. Major mechanical failures in particular are usually preceded by characteristic symptoms over hundreds or even thousands of miles. Those components that do occasionally fail without warning are often small and easily carried in the vehicle.

With any fault-finding, the first step is to decide where to begin investigations.

Sometimes this is obvious, but on other occasions, a little detective work will be necessary. The owner who makes half a dozen haphazard adjustments or replacements may be successful in curing a fault (or its symptoms). However, will be none the wiser if the fault recurs, and ultimately may have spent more time and money than was necessary. A calm and logical approach will be found to be more satisfactory in the long run. Always take into account any warning signs or abnormalities that may have been noticed in the period preceding the fault - power loss, high or low gauge readings, unusual smells, etc. - and remember that failure of compo-nents such as fuses or spark plugs may only be pointers to some underlying fault.

The pages that follow provide an easy-

reference guide to the more common problems that may occur during the operation of the vehicle. These problems and their possible causes are grouped under headings denoting various components or systems, such as Engine, Cooling system, etc. The Chapter and/or Section that deals with the problem is also shown in brackets. Whatever the fault, certain basic principles apply. These are as follows:

Verify the fault. This is simply a matter of being sure that you know what the symptoms are before starting work. This is particularly important if you are investigating a fault for someone else, who may not have described it very accurately.

Do not overlook the obvious. For example, if the vehicle will not start, is there petrol in the tank? (Do not take anyone else's word on this particular point, and do not trust the fuel gauge either!) If an electrical fault is indicated, look for loose or broken wires before digging out the test gear.

Cure the disease, not the symptom. Substituting a flat battery with a fully charged one will get you off the hard shoulder, but if the underlying cause is not attended to, the new battery will go the same way. Similarly, changing oil-fouled spark plugs for a new set will get you moving again, but remember that the reason for the fouling (if it was not simply an incorrect grade of plug) will have to be established and corrected.

Do not take anything for granted. Particularly, do not forget that a new component may itself be defective (especially if it's been rattling around in the boot for months). Also do not leave components out of a fault diagnosis sequence just because they are new or recently fitted. When you do finally diagnose a difficult fault, you will probably realise that all the evidence was there from the start.

Engine

Engine fails to rotate when attempting to start

- ☐ Battery terminal connections loose or corroded (*Weekly checks*).
- ☐ Battery discharged or faulty (Chapter 5A).
- ☐ Broken, loose or disconnected wiring in the starting circuit (Chapter 5A).
- ☐ Defective starter solenoid or switch (Chapter 5A).
- ☐ Defective starter motor (Chapter 5A).
- ☐ Starter pinion or flywheel ring gear teeth loose or broken (Chapters 2A, 2B and 5A).
- ☐ Engine earth strap broken or disconnected (Chapter 5A).

Engine rotates, but will not start

- ☐ Fuel tank empty.
- ☐ Battery discharged (engine rotates slowly) (Chapter 5A).
- ☐ Battery terminal connections loose or corroded (*Weekly checks*).
- ☐ Ignition components damp or damaged – petrol models (Chapters 1A and 5B).
- ☐ Broken, loose or disconnected wiring in the ignition circuit - petrol models (Chapters 1A and 5B).
- ☐ Worn, faulty or incorrectly gapped spark plugs – petrol models (Chapter 1A).
- ☐ Fuel injection system fault – petrol models (Chapter 4A and 4B).
- ☐ Stop solenoid faulty – diesel models (Chapter 4C).
- ☐ Air in fuel system – diesel models (Chapter 4C).
- ☐ Major mechanical failure (e.g. camshaft drive) (Chapter 2A or 2B).

Engine difficult to start when cold

- ☐ Battery discharged (Chapter 5A).
- ☐ Battery terminal connections loose or corroded (*Weekly checks*).
- ☐ Worn, faulty or incorrectly gapped spark plugs – petrol models (Chapter 1A).
- ☐ Fuel injection system fault - petrol models (Chapter 4A and 4B).
- ☐ Other ignition system fault – petrol models (Chapters 1A and 5B).
- ☐ Preheating system fault – diesel models (Chapter 5C).
- ☐ Low cylinder compressions (Chapter 2A or 2B).

Engine difficult to start when hot

- ☐ Air filter element dirty or clogged (Chapter 1A or 1B).
- ☐ Fuel injection system fault - petrol models (Chapter 4A and 4B).
- ☐ Low cylinder compressions (Chapter 2A or 2B).

Starter motor noisy or excessively rough in engagement

- ☐ Starter pinion or flywheel ring gear teeth loose or broken (Chapters 2A, 2B and 5A).
- ☐ Starter motor mounting bolts loose or missing (Chapter 5A).
- ☐ Starter motor internal components worn or damaged (Chapter 5A).

Engine starts, but stops immediately

- ☐ Loose or faulty electrical connections in the ignition circuit – petrol models (Chapters 1A and 5B).
- ☐ Vacuum leak at the throttle body or inlet manifold – petrol models (Chapter 4A or 4B).
- ☐ Blocked injector/fuel injection system fault - petrol models (Chapter 4A or 4B).
- ☐ Faulty injector(s) – diesel models (Chapter 4C).
- ☐ Air in fuel system – diesel models (Chapter 4C).

Engine idles erratically

- ☐ Air filter element clogged (Chapter 1A or 1B).
- ☐ Vacuum leak at the throttle body, inlet manifold or associated hoses – petrol models (Chapter 4A or 4B).
- ☐ Worn, faulty or incorrectly gapped spark plugs – petrol models (Chapter 1A).
- ☐ Uneven or low cylinder compressions (Chapter 2A or 2B).
- ☐ Camshaft lobes worn (Chapter 2A or 2B).
- ☐ Timing belt incorrectly tensioned (Chapter 2A or 2B).
- ☐ Blocked injector/fuel injection system fault - petrol models (Chapter 4B).
- ☐ Faulty injector(s) – diesel models (Chapter 4C).

Engine misfires at idle speed

- ☐ Worn, faulty or incorrectly gapped spark plugs – petrol models (Chapter 1A).
- ☐ Faulty spark plug HT leads – petrol models (Chapter 5B).
- ☐ Vacuum leak at the throttle body, inlet manifold or associated hoses (Chapter 4A or 4B).
- ☐ Blocked injector/fuel injection system fault - petrol models (Chapter 4A and 4B).
- ☐ Faulty injector(s) – diesel models (Chapter 4C).
- ☐ Distributor cap cracked or tracking internally – petrol models (where applicable) (Chapter 5B).
- ☐ Uneven or low cylinder compressions (Chapter 2A or 2B).
- ☐ Disconnected, leaking, or perished crankcase ventilation hoses (Chapter 4D).

Engine misfires throughout the driving speed range

- ☐ Fuel filter choked (Chapter 1A or 1B).
- ☐ Fuel pump faulty, or delivery pressure low (Chapter 4A or 4B).
- ☐ Fuel tank vent blocked, or fuel pipes restricted (Chapter 4A, 4B or 4C).
- ☐ Vacuum leak at the throttle body, inlet manifold or associated hoses – petrol models (Chapter 4A or 4B).
- ☐ Worn, faulty or incorrectly gapped spark plugs – petrol models (Chapter 1A).
- ☐ Faulty spark plug HT leads (Chapter 5B).
- ☐ Faulty injector(s) – diesel models (Chapter 4C).
- ☐ Distributor cap cracked or tracking internally – petrol models (where applicable) (Chapter 5B).
- ☐ Faulty ignition coil – petrol models (Chapter 5B).
- ☐ Uneven or low cylinder compressions (Chapter 2A or 2B).
- ☐ Blocked injector/fuel injection system fault - petrol models (Chapter 4A or 4B).

Engine hesitates on acceleration

- ☐ Worn, faulty or incorrectly gapped spark plugs – petrol models (Chapter 1A).
- ☐ Vacuum leak at the throttle body, inlet manifold or associated hoses – petrol models (Chapter 4A or 4B).
- ☐ Blocked injector/fuel injection system fault - petrol models (Chapter 4B).
- ☐ Faulty injector(s) – diesel models (Chapter 4C).
- ☐ Incorrect injection pump timing – diesel models (Chapter 4C).

Engine (continued)

Engine stalls

- [ ] Vacuum leak at the throttle body, inlet manifold or associated hoses – petrol models (Chapter 4A or 4B).
- [ ] Fuel filter choked (Chapter 1A or 1B).
- [ ] Fuel pump faulty, or delivery pressure low – petrol models (Chapter 4A or 4B).
- [ ] Fuel tank vent blocked, or fuel pipes restricted (Chapter 4A, 4B or 4C).
- [ ] Blocked injector/fuel injection system fault - petrol models (Chapter 4B).
- [ ] Faulty injector(s) – diesel models (Chapter 4C).
- [ ] Air in fuel system – diesel models (Chapter 4C).

Engine lacks power

- [ ] Timing belt incorrectly fitted or tensioned (Chapter 2A or 2B).
- [ ] Fuel filter choked (Chapter 1A or 1B).
- [ ] Fuel pump faulty, or delivery pressure low – petrol models (Chapter 4A or 4B).
- [ ] Uneven or low cylinder compressions (Chapter 2A or 2B).
- [ ] Worn, faulty or incorrectly gapped spark plugs – petrol models (Chapter 1A).
- [ ] Vacuum leak at the throttle body, inlet manifold or associated hoses – petrol models (Chapter 4A or 4B).
- [ ] Blocked injector/fuel injection system fault - petrol models (Chapter 4A or 4B).
- [ ] Injection pump timing incorrect – diesel models (Chapter 4C).
- [ ] Brakes binding (Chapters 1A or 1B and 9).
- [ ] Clutch slipping (Chapter 6).

Engine backfires

- [ ] Timing belt incorrectly fitted or tensioned (Chapter 2A or 2B).
- [ ] Vacuum leak at the throttle body, inlet manifold or associated hoses – petrol models (Chapter 4A or 4B).
- [ ] Blocked injector/fuel injection system fault - petrol models (Chapter 4A or 4B).

Oil pressure warning light illuminated with engine running

- [ ] Low oil level, or incorrect oil grade (*Weekly checks*).
- [ ] Faulty oil pressure warning light switch (Chapter 2A or 2B).
- [ ] Worn engine bearings and/or oil pump (Chapter 2A, 2B or 2C).
- [ ] High engine operating temperature (Chapter 3).
- [ ] Oil pressure relief valve defective (Chapter 2A or 2B).
- [ ] Oil pick-up strainer clogged (Chapter 2A or 2B).

Engine runs-on after switching off

- [ ] Excessive carbon build-up in engine (Chapter 2A, 2B or 2C).
- [ ] High engine operating temperature (Chapter 3).
- [ ] Fuel injection system fault - petrol models (Chapter 4B).
- [ ] Faulty stop solenoid – diesel models (Chapter 4C).

Engine noises

Pre-ignition (pinking) or knocking during acceleration or under load

- [ ] Ignition timing incorrect/ignition system fault – petrol models (Chapters 1A and 5B).
- [ ] Incorrect grade of spark plug – petrol models (Chapter 1A).
- [ ] Incorrect grade of fuel (Chapter 1A).
- [ ] Vacuum leak at the throttle body, inlet manifold or associated hoses – petrol models (Chapter 4A or 4B).
- [ ] Excessive carbon build-up in engine (Chapter 2A, 2B or 2C).
- [ ] Blocked injector/fuel injection system fault - petrol models (Chapter 4B).

Whistling or wheezing noises

- [ ] Leaking inlet manifold or throttle body gasket – petrol models (Chapter 4A or 4B).
- [ ] Leaking exhaust manifold gasket or pipe-to-manifold joint (Chapter 4D).
- [ ] Leaking vacuum hose (Chapters 4A, 4B, 4C, 4D, 5B, 9 and 12).
- [ ] Blowing cylinder head gasket (Chapter 2A or 2B).

Tapping or rattling noises

- [ ] Worn valve gear or camshaft (Chapter 2A or 2B).
- [ ] Ancillary component fault (coolant pump, alternator, etc.) (Chapters 3, 5A, etc.).

Knocking or thumping noises

- [ ] Worn big-end bearings (regular heavy knocking, perhaps less under load) (Chapter 2C).
- [ ] Worn main bearings (rumbling and knocking, perhaps worsening under load) (Chapter 2C).
- [ ] Piston slap (most noticeable when cold) (Chapter 2C).
- [ ] Ancillary component fault (coolant pump, alternator, etc.) (Chapters 3, 5A, etc.).

Cooling system

Overheating

- ☐ Insufficient coolant in system (*Weekly checks*).
- ☐ Thermostat faulty (Chapter 3).
- ☐ Radiator core blocked, or grille restricted (Chapter 3).
- ☐ Electric cooling fan or thermoswitch faulty (Chapter 3).
- ☐ Pressure cap faulty (Chapter 3).
- ☐ Ignition timing incorrect/ignition system fault – petrol engines (Chapters 1A and 5B).
- ☐ Inaccurate temperature gauge sender unit (Chapter 3).
- ☐ Airlock in cooling system.

Overcooling

- ☐ Thermostat faulty (Chapter 3).
- ☐ Inaccurate temperature gauge sender unit (Chapter 3).

Internal coolant leakage

- ☐ Leaking cylinder head gasket (Chapter 2A or 2B).
- ☐ Cracked cylinder head or cylinder bore (Chapter 2C).

External coolant leakage

- ☐ Deteriorated or damaged hoses or hose clips (Chapter 1A or 1B).
- ☐ Radiator core or heater matrix leaking (Chapter 3).
- ☐ Pressure cap faulty (Chapter 3).
- ☐ Water pump seal leaking (Chapter 3).
- ☐ Boiling due to overheating (Chapter 3).
- ☐ Core plug leaking (Chapter 2C).

Corrosion

- ☐ Infrequent draining and flushing (Chapter 1A or 1B).
- ☐ Incorrect coolant mixture or inappropriate coolant type (Chapter 1A or 1B).

Fuel and exhaust systems

Excessive fuel consumption

- ☐ Air filter element dirty or clogged (Chapter 1A or 1B).
- ☐ Fuel injection system fault - petrol models (Chapter 4A or 4B).
- ☐ Ignition timing incorrect/ignition system fault – petrol models (Chapters 1A and 5B).
- ☐ Faulty injector(s) – diesel models (Chapter 4C).
- ☐ Tyres under-inflated (*Weekly checks*).

Fuel leakage and/or fuel odour

- ☐ Damaged or corroded fuel tank, pipes or connections (Chapter 4A or 4B).

Excessive noise or fumes from exhaust system

- ☐ Leaking exhaust system or manifold joints (Chapters 1A or 1B and 4D).
- ☐ Leaking, corroded or damaged silencers or pipe (Chapters 1A or 1B and 4D).
- ☐ Broken mountings causing body or suspension contact (Chapter 1A or 1B).

Clutch

Pedal travels to floor - no pressure or very little resistance

- ☐ Broken clutch cable – where applicable (Chapter 6).
- ☐ Incorrect clutch cable adjustment – where applicable (Chapter 6).
- ☐ Hydraulic fluid level low/air in hydraulic system – where applicable (Chapter 6).
- ☐ Broken clutch release bearing or fork (Chapter 6).
- ☐ Broken diaphragm spring in clutch pressure plate (Chapter 6).

Noise when depressing or releasing clutch pedal

- ☐ Worn clutch release bearing (Chapter 6).
- ☐ Worn or dry clutch pedal bushes (Chapter 6).
- ☐ Faulty pressure plate assembly (Chapter 6).
- ☐ Pressure plate diaphragm spring broken (Chapter 6).
- ☐ Broken clutch disc cushioning springs (Chapter 6).

Clutch slips (engine speed increases, with no increase in vehicle speed)

- ☐ Incorrect clutch cable adjustment – where applicable (Chapter 6).
- ☐ Hydraulic fluid level too high – where applicable (Chapter 6).
- ☐ Clutch disc linings excessively worn (Chapter 6).
- ☐ Clutch disc linings contaminated with oil or grease (Chapter 6).
- ☐ Faulty pressure plate or weak diaphragm spring (Chapter 6).

Clutch fails to disengage (unable to select gears)

- ☐ Incorrect clutch cable adjustment – where applicable (Chapter 6).
- ☐ Hydraulic fluid level too high (Chapter 6).
- ☐ Clutch disc sticking on transmission input shaft splines (Chapter 6).
- ☐ Clutch disc sticking to flywheel or pressure plate (Chapter 6).
- ☐ Faulty pressure plate assembly (Chapter 6).
- ☐ Clutch release mechanism worn or incorrectly assembled (Chapter 6).

Judder as clutch is engaged

- ☐ Clutch disc linings contaminated with oil or grease (Chapter 6).
- ☐ Clutch disc linings excessively worn (Chapter 6).
- ☐ Clutch cable sticking or frayed – where applicable (Chapter 6).
- ☐ Faulty or distorted pressure plate or diaphragm spring (Chapter 6).
- ☐ Worn or loose engine or transmission mountings (Chapter 2A or 2B).
- ☐ Clutch disc hub or transmission input shaft splines worn (Chapter 6).

Manual transmission

Noisy in neutral with engine running

- ☐ Input shaft bearings worn (noise apparent with clutch pedal released, but not when depressed) (Chapter 7).*
- ☐ Clutch release bearing worn (noise apparent with clutch pedal depressed, possibly less when released) (Chapter 6).

Noisy in one particular gear

- ☐ Worn, damaged or chipped gear teeth (Chapter 7).*

Difficulty engaging gears

- ☐ Clutch fault (Chapter 6).
- ☐ Worn or damaged gear linkage (Chapter 7).
- ☐ Incorrectly adjusted gear linkage (Chapter 7).
- ☐ Worn synchroniser units (Chapter 7).*

Vibration

- ☐ Lack of oil (Chapter 1A or 1B).
- ☐ Worn bearings (Chapter 7).*

Jumps out of gear

- ☐ Worn or damaged gear linkage (Chapter 7).
- ☐ Incorrectly adjusted gear linkage (Chapter 7).
- ☐ Worn synchroniser units (Chapter 7).*
- ☐ Worn selector forks (Chapter 7).*

Lubricant leaks

- ☐ Leaking differential output oil seal (Chapter 7).
- ☐ Leaking housing joint (Chapter 7).*
- ☐ Leaking input shaft oil seal (Chapter 7).*

* Although the corrective action necessary to remedy the symptoms described is beyond the scope of the home mechanic, the above information should be helpful in isolating the cause of the condition. This should enable the owner can communicate clearly with a professional mechanic.

Driveshafts

Clicking or knocking noise on turns (at slow speed on full-lock)

- [ ] Lack of constant velocity joint lubricant, possibly due to damaged gaiter (Chapter 8).
- [ ] Worn outer constant velocity joint (Chapter 8).

Vibration when accelerating or decelerating

- [ ] Worn inner constant velocity joint (Chapter 8).
- [ ] Bent or distorted driveshaft (Chapter 8).

Braking system

Note: *Before assuming that a brake problem exists, make sure that the tyres are in good condition and correctly inflated, that the front wheel alignment is correct, and that the vehicle is not loaded with weight in an unequal manner. Apart from checking the condition of all pipe and hose connections, any faults occurring on the anti-lock braking system should be referred to a Seat dealer for diagnosis.*

Vehicle pulls to one side under braking

- [ ] Worn, defective, damaged or contaminated brake pads/shoes on one side (Chapters 1A or 1B and 9).
- [ ] Seized or partially seized brake caliper/wheel cylinder piston (Chapters 1A or 1B and 9).
- [ ] A mixture of brake pad/shoe lining materials fitted between sides (Chapters 1A or 1B and 9).
- [ ] Brake caliper or backplate mounting bolts loose (Chapter 9).
- [ ] Worn or damaged steering or suspension components (Chapters 1A or 1B and 10).

Noise (grinding or high-pitched squeal) when brakes applied

- [ ] Brake pad or shoe friction lining material worn down to metal backing (Chapters 1A or 1B and 9).
- [ ] Excessive corrosion of brake disc or drum. This may be apparent after the vehicle has been standing for some time (Chapters 1A or 1B and 9).
- [ ] Foreign object (stone chipping, etc.) trapped between brake disc and shield (Chapters 1A or 1B and 9).

Brakes binding

- [ ] Seized brake caliper or wheel cylinder piston(s) (Chapter 9).
- [ ] Incorrectly adjusted handbrake mechanism (Chapter 9).
- [ ] Faulty master cylinder (Chapter 9).

Excessive brake pedal travel

- [ ] Inoperative rear brake self-adjust mechanism - drum brakes (Chapters 1A or 1B and 9).
- [ ] Faulty master cylinder (Chapter 9).
- [ ] Air in hydraulic system (Chapters 1A or 1B and 9).
- [ ] Faulty vacuum servo unit (Chapter 9).

Brake pedal feels spongy when depressed

- [ ] Air in hydraulic system (Chapters 1A or 1B and 9).
- [ ] Deteriorated flexible rubber brake hoses (Chapters 1A or 1B and 9).
- [ ] Master cylinder mounting nuts loose (Chapter 9).
- [ ] Faulty master cylinder (Chapter 9).

Excessive brake pedal effort required to stop vehicle

- [ ] Faulty vacuum servo unit (Chapter 9).
- [ ] Faulty brake vacuum pump – diesel models (Chapter 9).
- [ ] Disconnected, damaged or insecure brake servo vacuum hose (Chapter 9).
- [ ] Primary or secondary hydraulic circuit failure (Chapter 9).
- [ ] Seized brake caliper or wheel cylinder piston(s) (Chapter 9).
- [ ] Brake pads or brake shoes incorrectly fitted (Chapters 1A or 1B and 9).
- [ ] Incorrect grade of brake pads or brake shoes fitted (Chapters 1A or 1B and 9).
- [ ] Brake pads or brake shoe linings contaminated (Chapters 1A or 1B and 9).

Judder felt through brake pedal or steering wheel when braking

Note: *Judder felt through the brake pedal is a normal feature of models fitted with ABS.*

- [ ] Excessive run-out or distortion of discs/drums (Chapters 1A or 1B and 9).
- [ ] Brake pad or brake shoe linings worn (Chapters 1A or 1B and 9).
- [ ] Brake caliper or brake backplate mounting bolts loose (Chapter 9).
- [ ] Wear in suspension or steering components or mountings (Chapters 1A or 1B and 10).

Rear wheels locking under normal braking

- [ ] Rear brake shoe linings contaminated (Chapters 1A or 1B and 9).
- [ ] Faulty brake pressure regulator (Chapter 9).

Suspension and steering

Note: *Before diagnosing suspension or steering faults, be sure that the trouble is not due to incorrect tyre pressures, mixtures of tyre types, or binding brakes.*

Vehicle pulls to one side

- ☐ Defective tyre (*Weekly checks*).
- ☐ Excessive wear in suspension or steering components (Chapters 1A or 1B and 10).
- ☐ Incorrect front wheel alignment (Chapter 10).
- ☐ Accident damage to steering or suspension components (Chapter 1A, 1B or 10).

Excessive pitching and/or rolling around corners, or during braking

- ☐ Defective shock absorbers (Chapters 1A or 1B and 10).
- ☐ Broken or weak spring and/or suspension component (Chapters 1A or 1B and 10).
- ☐ Worn or damaged anti-roll bar or mountings – where applicable (Chapter 10).

Lack of power assistance

- ☐ Broken or incorrectly adjusted auxiliary drivebelt (Chapter 1A or 1B).
- ☐ Incorrect power steering fluid level (*Weekly checks*).
- ☐ Restriction in power steering fluid hoses (Chapter 1A or 1B).
- ☐ Faulty power steering pump (Chapter 10).
- ☐ Faulty rack-and-pinion steering gear (Chapter 10).

Wandering or general instability

- ☐ Incorrect front wheel alignment (Chapter 10).
- ☐ Worn steering or suspension joints, bushes or components (Chapters 1A or 1B and 10).
- ☐ Roadwheels out of balance (Chapters 1A or 1B and 10).
- ☐ Faulty or damaged tyre (*Weekly checks*).
- ☐ Wheel bolts loose (Chapters 1A or 1B and 10).
- ☐ Defective shock absorbers (Chapters 1A or 1B and 10).

Excessively stiff steering

- ☐ Lack of steering gear lubricant (Chapter 10).
- ☐ Seized track rod end balljoint or suspension balljoint (Chapters 1A or 1B and 10).
- ☐ Broken or incorrectly adjusted auxiliary drivebelt - power steering (Chapter 1A or 1B).
- ☐ Incorrect front wheel alignment (Chapter 10).
- ☐ Steering rack or column bent or damaged (Chapter 10).

Excessive play in steering

- ☐ Worn steering column intermediate shaft universal joint (Chapter 10).
- ☐ Worn steering track rod end balljoints (Chapters 1A or 1B and 10).
- ☐ Worn rack-and-pinion steering gear (Chapter 10).
- ☐ Worn steering or suspension joints, bushes or components (Chapters 1A or 1B and 10).

Wheel wobble and vibration

- ☐ Front roadwheels out of balance (vibration felt mainly through the steering wheel) (Chapters 1A or 1B and 10).
- ☐ Rear roadwheels out of balance (vibration felt throughout the vehicle) (Chapters 1A or 1B and 10).
- ☐ Roadwheels damaged or distorted (Chapters 1A or 1B and 10).
- ☐ Faulty or damaged tyre (*Weekly checks*).
- ☐ Worn steering or suspension joints, bushes or components (Chapters 1A or 1B and 10).
- ☐ Wheel bolts loose (Chapters 1A or 1B and 10).

Tyre wear excessive

Tyres worn on inside or outside edges

- ☐ Tyres under-inflated (wear on both edges) (*Weekly checks*).
- ☐ Incorrect camber or castor angles (wear on one edge only) (Chapter 10).
- ☐ Worn steering or suspension joints, bushes or components (Chapters 1A or 1B and 10).
- ☐ Excessively hard cornering.
- ☐ Accident damage.

Tyre treads exhibit feathered edges

- ☐ Incorrect toe setting (Chapter 10).

Tyres worn in centre of tread

- ☐ Tyres over-inflated (*Weekly checks*).

Tyres worn on inside and outside edges

- ☐ Tyres under-inflated (*Weekly checks*).

Tyres worn unevenly

- ☐ Tyres/wheels out of balance (Chapter 1A, 1B or 10).
- ☐ Excessive wheel or tyre run-out (Chapter 1A, 1B or 10).
- ☐ Worn shock absorbers (Chapters 1A or 1B and 10).
- ☐ Faulty tyre (*Weekly checks*).

Electrical system

Note: *For problems associated with the starting system, refer to the faults listed under Engine earlier in this Section.*

Battery will not hold a charge for more than a few days

- [ ] Battery defective internally (Chapter 5A).
- [ ] Battery terminal connections loose or corroded (*Weekly checks*).
- [ ] Auxiliary drivebelt worn or incorrectly adjusted (Chapter 1A or 1B).
- [ ] Alternator not charging at correct output (Chapter 5A).
- [ ] Alternator or voltage regulator faulty (Chapter 5A).
- [ ] Short-circuit causing continual battery drain (Chapters 5A and 12).

Ignition/no-charge warning light remains illuminated with engine running

- [ ] Auxiliary drivebelt broken, worn, or incorrectly adjusted (Chapter 1A or 1B).
- [ ] Alternator brushes worn, sticking, or dirty (Chapter 5A).
- [ ] Alternator brush springs weak or broken (Chapter 5A).
- [ ] Internal fault in alternator or voltage regulator (Chapter 5A).
- [ ] Broken, disconnected, or loose wiring in charging circuit (Chapter 5A).

Ignition/no-charge warning light fails to come on

- [ ] Warning light bulb blown (Chapter 12).
- [ ] Broken, disconnected, or loose wiring in warning light circuit (Chapter 12).
- [ ] Alternator faulty (Chapter 5A).

Lights inoperative

- [ ] Bulb blown (Chapter 12).
- [ ] Corrosion of bulb or bulbholder contacts (Chapter 12).
- [ ] Blown fuse (Chapter 12).
- [ ] Faulty relay (Chapter 12).
- [ ] Broken, loose, or disconnected wiring (Chapter 12).
- [ ] Faulty switch (Chapter 12).

Instrument readings inaccurate or erratic

Instrument readings increase with engine speed

- [ ] Faulty voltage regulator (Chapter 12).

Fuel or temperature gauges give no reading

- [ ] Faulty gauge sender unit (Chapters 3, 4A or 4B).
- [ ] Wiring open-circuit (Chapter 12).
- [ ] Faulty gauge (Chapter 12).

Fuel or temperature gauges give continuous maximum reading

- [ ] Faulty gauge sender unit (Chapters 3, 4A or 4B).
- [ ] Wiring short-circuit (Chapter 12).
- [ ] Faulty gauge (Chapter 12).

Horn inoperative, or unsatisfactory in operation

Horn operates all the time

- [ ] Horn push either earthed or stuck down (Chapter 12).
- [ ] Horn cable-to-horn push earthed (Chapter 12).

Horn fails to operate

- [ ] Blown fuse (Chapter 12).
- [ ] Cable or cable connections loose, broken or disconnected (Chapter 12).
- [ ] Faulty horn (Chapter 12).

Horn emits intermittent or unsatisfactory sound

- [ ] Cable connections loose (Chapter 12).
- [ ] Horn mountings loose (Chapter 12).
- [ ] Faulty horn (Chapter 12).

Windscreen/tailgate wipers inoperative, or unsatisfactory in operation

Wipers fail to operate, or operate very slowly

- [ ] Wiper blades stuck to screen, or linkage seized or binding (Chapters 1A or 1B and 12).
- [ ] Blown fuse (Chapter 12).
- [ ] Cable or cable connections loose, broken or disconnected (Chapter 12).
- [ ] Faulty relay (Chapter 12).
- [ ] Faulty wiper motor (Chapter 12).

Wiper blades sweep over too large or too small an area of the glass

- [ ] Wiper arms incorrectly positioned on spindles (Chapter 12).
- [ ] Excessive wear of wiper linkage (Chapter 12).
- [ ] Wiper motor or linkage mountings loose or insecure (Chapter 12).

Wiper blades fail to clean the glass effectively

- [ ] Wiper blade rubbers worn or perished (*Weekly checks*).
- [ ] Wiper arm tension springs broken, or arm pivots seized (Chapter 12).
- [ ] Insufficient windscreen washer additive to adequately remove road film (Chapter 1A or 1B).

Windscreen/tailgate washers inoperative, or unsatisfactory in operation

One or more washer jets inoperative

- [ ] Blocked washer jet (Chapter 1A or 1B).
- [ ] Disconnected, kinked or restricted fluid hose (Chapter 12).
- [ ] Insufficient fluid in washer reservoir (Chapter 1A or 1B).

Washer pump fails to operate

- [ ] Broken or disconnected wiring or connections (Chapter 12).
- [ ] Blown fuse (Chapter 12).
- [ ] Faulty washer switch (Chapter 12).
- [ ] Faulty washer pump (Chapter 12).

Washer pump runs for some time before fluid is emitted from jets

- [ ] Faulty one-way valve in fluid supply hose (Chapter 12).

Electric windows inoperative, or unsatisfactory in operation

Window glass will only move in one direction

- [ ] Faulty switch (Chapter 12).

Window glass slow to move

- [ ] Regulator seized or damaged, or in need of lubrication (Chapter 11).
- [ ] Door internal components or trim fouling regulator (Chapter 11).
- [ ] Faulty motor (Chapter 11).

Window glass fails to move

- [ ] Blown fuse (Chapter 12).
- [ ] Faulty relay (Chapter 12).
- [ ] Broken or disconnected wiring or connections (Chapter 12).
- [ ] Faulty motor (Chapter 11).

Electrical system (continued)

Central locking system inoperative, or unsatisfactory in operation

Complete system failure

☐ Blown fuse (Chapter 12).
☐ Faulty relay (Chapter 12).
☐ Broken or disconnected wiring or connections (Chapter 12).
☐ Faulty control module (Chapter 11).
☐ Faulty vacuum pump (Chapter 11).
☐ Broken or leaking vacuum hose (Chapter 11).

Latch locks but will not unlock, or unlocks but will not lock

☐ Faulty master switch (Chapter 11).
☐ Broken or disconnected latch operating rods or levers (Chapter 11).
☐ Faulty relay (Chapter 12).
☐ Faulty control module (Chapter 11).

One actuator fails to operate

☐ Broken or disconnected wiring or connections (Chapter 12).
☐ Faulty actuator (Chapter 11).
☐ Leak in vacuum line (Chapter 11).
☐ Broken, binding or disconnected latch operating rods or levers (Chapter 11).
☐ Fault in door lock (Chapter 11).

A

ABS (Anti-lock brake system) A system, usually electronically controlled, that senses incipient wheel lockup during braking and relieves hydraulic pressure at wheels that are about to skid.

Air bag An inflatable bag hidden in the steering wheel (driver's side) or the dash or glovebox (passenger side). In a head-on collision, the bags inflate, preventing the driver and front passenger from being thrown forward into the steering wheel or windscreen.

Air cleaner A metal or plastic housing, containing a filter element, which removes dust and dirt from the air being drawn into the engine.

Air filter element The actual filter in an air cleaner system, usually manufactured from pleated paper and requiring renewal at regular intervals.

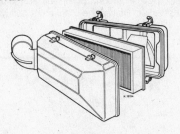

Air filter

Allen key A hexagonal wrench which fits into a recessed hexagonal hole.

Alligator clip A long-nosed spring-loaded metal clip with meshing teeth. Used to make temporary electrical connections.

Alternator A component in the electrical system which converts mechanical energy from a drivebelt into electrical energy to charge the battery and to operate the starting system, ignition system and electrical accessories.

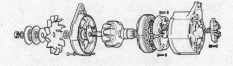

Alternator (exploded view)

Ampere (amp) A unit of measurement for the flow of electric current. One amp is the amount of current produced by one volt acting through a resistance of one ohm.

Anaerobic sealer A substance used to prevent bolts and screws from loosening. Anaerobic means that it does not require oxygen for activation. The Loctite brand is widely used.

Antifreeze A substance (usually ethylene glycol) mixed with water, and added to a vehicle's cooling system, to prevent freezing of the coolant in winter. Antifreeze also contains chemicals to inhibit corrosion and the formation of rust and other deposits that

would tend to clog the radiator and coolant passages and reduce cooling efficiency.

Anti-seize compound A coating that reduces the risk of seizing on fasteners that are subjected to high temperatures, such as exhaust manifold bolts and nuts.

Anti-seize compound

Asbestos A natural fibrous mineral with great heat resistance, commonly used in the composition of brake friction materials. Asbestos is a health hazard and the dust created by brake systems should never be inhaled or ingested.

Axle A shaft on which a wheel revolves, or which revolves with a wheel. Also, a solid beam that connects the two wheels at one end of the vehicle. An axle which also transmits power to the wheels is known as a live axle.

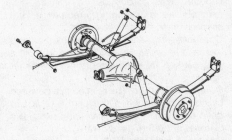

Axle assembly

Axleshaft A single rotating shaft, on either side of the differential, which delivers power from the final drive assembly to the drive wheels. Also called a driveshaft or a halfshaft.

B

Ball bearing An anti-friction bearing consisting of a hardened inner and outer race with hardened steel balls between two races.

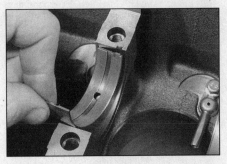

Bearing

Bearing The curved surface on a shaft or in a bore, or the part assembled into either, that permits relative motion between them with minimum wear and friction.

Big-end bearing The bearing in the end of the connecting rod that's attached to the crankshaft.

Bleed nipple A valve on a brake wheel cylinder, caliper or other hydraulic component that is opened to purge the hydraulic system of air. Also called a bleed screw.

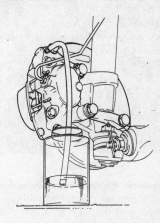

Brake bleeding

Brake bleeding Procedure for removing air from lines of a hydraulic brake system.

Brake disc The component of a disc brake that rotates with the wheels.

Brake drum The component of a drum brake that rotates with the wheels.

Brake linings The friction material which contacts the brake disc or drum to retard the vehicle's speed. The linings are bonded or riveted to the brake pads or shoes.

Brake pads The replaceable friction pads that pinch the brake disc when the brakes are applied. Brake pads consist of a friction material bonded or riveted to a rigid backing plate.

Brake shoe The crescent-shaped carrier to which the brake linings are mounted and which forces the lining against the rotating drum during braking.

Braking systems For more information on braking systems, consult the *Haynes Automotive Brake Manual*.

Breaker bar A long socket wrench handle providing greater leverage.

Bulkhead The insulated partition between the engine and the passenger compartment.

C

Caliper The non-rotating part of a disc-brake assembly that straddles the disc and carries the brake pads. The caliper also contains the hydraulic components that cause the pads to pinch the disc when the brakes are applied. A caliper is also a measuring tool that can be set to measure inside or outside dimensions of an object.

Camshaft A rotating shaft on which a series of cam lobes operate the valve mechanisms. The camshaft may be driven by gears, by sprockets and chain or by sprockets and a belt.

Canister A container in an evaporative emission control system; contains activated charcoal granules to trap vapours from the fuel system.

Canister

Carburettor A device which mixes fuel with air in the proper proportions to provide a desired power output from a spark ignition internal combustion engine.

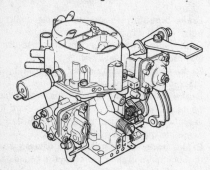

Carburettor

Castellated Resembling the parapets along the top of a castle wall. For example, a castellated balljoint stud nut.

Castellated nut

Castor In wheel alignment, the backward or forward tilt of the steering axis. Castor is positive when the steering axis is inclined rearward at the top.

Catalytic converter A silencer-like device in the exhaust system which converts certain pollutants in the exhaust gases into less harmful substances.

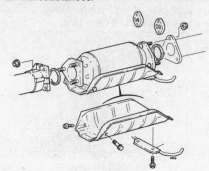

Catalytic converter

Circlip A ring-shaped clip used to prevent endwise movement of cylindrical parts and shafts. An internal circlip is installed in a groove in a housing; an external circlip fits into a groove on the outside of a cylindrical piece such as a shaft.

Clearance The amount of space between two parts. For example, between a piston and a cylinder, between a bearing and a journal, etc.

Coil spring A spiral of elastic steel found in various sizes throughout a vehicle, for example as a springing medium in the suspension and in the valve train.

Compression Reduction in volume, and increase in pressure and temperature, of a gas, caused by squeezing it into a smaller space.

Compression ratio The relationship between cylinder volume when the piston is at top dead centre and cylinder volume when the piston is at bottom dead centre.

Constant velocity (CV) joint A type of universal joint that cancels out vibrations caused by driving power being transmitted through an angle.

Core plug A disc or cup-shaped metal device inserted in a hole in a casting through which core was removed when the casting was formed. Also known as a freeze plug or expansion plug.

Crankcase The lower part of the engine block in which the crankshaft rotates.

Crankshaft The main rotating member, or shaft, running the length of the crankcase, with offset "throws" to which the connecting rods are attached.

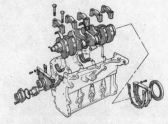

Crankshaft assembly

Crocodile clip See Alligator clip

D

Diagnostic code Code numbers obtained by accessing the diagnostic mode of an engine management computer. This code can be used to determine the area in the system where a malfunction may be located.

Disc brake A brake design incorporating a rotating disc onto which brake pads are squeezed. The resulting friction converts the energy of a moving vehicle into heat.

Double-overhead cam (DOHC) An engine that uses two overhead camshafts, usually one for the intake valves and one for the exhaust valves.

Drivebelt(s) The belt(s) used to drive accessories such as the alternator, water pump, power steering pump, air conditioning compressor, etc. off the crankshaft pulley.

Accessory drivebelts

Driveshaft Any shaft used to transmit motion. Commonly used when referring to the axleshafts on a front wheel drive vehicle.

Driveshaft

Drum brake A type of brake using a drum-shaped metal cylinder attached to the inner surface of the wheel. When the brake pedal is pressed, curved brake shoes with friction linings press against the inside of the drum to slow or stop the vehicle.

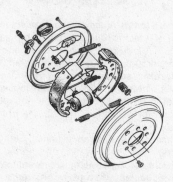

Drum brake assembly

E

EGR valve A valve used to introduce exhaust gases into the intake air stream.

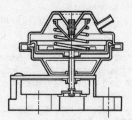

EGR valve

Electronic control unit (ECU) A computer which controls (for instance) ignition and fuel injection systems, or an anti-lock braking system. For more information refer to the *Haynes Automotive Electrical and Electronic Systems Manual*.

Electronic Fuel Injection (EFI) A computer controlled fuel system that distributes fuel through an injector located in each intake port of the engine.

Emergency brake A braking system, independent of the main hydraulic system, that can be used to slow or stop the vehicle if the primary brakes fail, or to hold the vehicle stationary even though the brake pedal isn't depressed. It usually consists of a hand lever that actuates either front or rear brakes mechanically through a series of cables and linkages. Also known as a handbrake or parking brake.

Endfloat The amount of lengthwise movement between two parts. As applied to a crankshaft, the distance that the crankshaft can move forward and back in the cylinder block.

Engine management system (EMS) A computer controlled system which manages the fuel injection and the ignition systems in an integrated fashion.

Exhaust manifold A part with several passages through which exhaust gases leave the engine combustion chambers and enter the exhaust pipe.

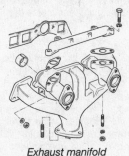

Exhaust manifold

F

Fan clutch A viscous (fluid) drive coupling device which permits variable engine fan speeds in relation to engine speeds.

Feeler blade A thin strip or blade of hardened steel, ground to an exact thickness, used to check or measure clearances between parts.

Feeler blade

Firing order The order in which the engine cylinders fire, or deliver their power strokes, beginning with the number one cylinder.

Flywheel A heavy spinning wheel in which energy is absorbed and stored by means of momentum. On cars, the flywheel is attached to the crankshaft to smooth out firing impulses.

Free play The amount of travel before any action takes place. The "looseness" in a linkage, or an assembly of parts, between the initial application of force and actual movement. For example, the distance the brake pedal moves before the pistons in the master cylinder are actuated.

Fuse An electrical device which protects a circuit against accidental overload. The typical fuse contains a soft piece of metal which is calibrated to melt at a predetermined current flow (expressed as amps) and break the circuit.

Fusible link A circuit protection device consisting of a conductor surrounded by heat-resistant insulation. The conductor is smaller than the wire it protects, so it acts as the weakest link in the circuit. Unlike a blown fuse, a failed fusible link must frequently be cut from the wire for replacement.

G

Gap The distance the spark must travel in jumping from the centre electrode to the side

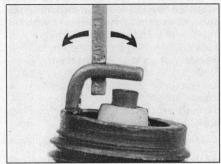

Adjusting spark plug gap

electrode in a spark plug. Also refers to the spacing between the points in a contact breaker assembly in a conventional points-type ignition, or to the distance between the reluctor or rotor and the pickup coil in an electronic ignition.

Gasket Any thin, soft material - usually cork, cardboard, asbestos or soft metal - installed between two metal surfaces to ensure a good seal. For instance, the cylinder head gasket seals the joint between the block and the cylinder head.

Gasket

Gauge An instrument panel display used to monitor engine conditions. A gauge with a movable pointer on a dial or a fixed scale is an analogue gauge. A gauge with a numerical readout is called a digital gauge.

H

Halfshaft A rotating shaft that transmits power from the final drive unit to a drive wheel, usually when referring to a live rear axle.

Harmonic balancer A device designed to reduce torsion or twisting vibration in the crankshaft. May be incorporated in the crankshaft pulley. Also known as a vibration damper.

Hone An abrasive tool for correcting small irregularities or differences in diameter in an engine cylinder, brake cylinder, etc.

Hydraulic tappet A tappet that utilises hydraulic pressure from the engine's lubrication system to maintain zero clearance (constant contact with both camshaft and valve stem). Automatically adjusts to variation in valve stem length. Hydraulic tappets also reduce valve noise.

I

Ignition timing The moment at which the spark plug fires, usually expressed in the number of crankshaft degrees before the piston reaches the top of its stroke.

Inlet manifold A tube or housing with passages through which flows the air-fuel mixture (carburettor vehicles and vehicles with throttle body injection) or air only (port fuel-injected vehicles) to the port openings in the cylinder head.

J

Jump start Starting the engine of a vehicle with a discharged or weak battery by attaching jump leads from the weak battery to a charged or helper battery.

L

Load Sensing Proportioning Valve (LSPV) A brake hydraulic system control valve that works like a proportioning valve, but also takes into consideration the amount of weight carried by the rear axle.

Locknut A nut used to lock an adjustment nut, or other threaded component, in place. For example, a locknut is employed to keep the adjusting nut on the rocker arm in position.

Lockwasher A form of washer designed to prevent an attaching nut from working loose.

M

MacPherson strut A type of front suspension system devised by Earle MacPherson at Ford of England. In its original form, a simple lateral link with the anti-roll bar creates the lower control arm. A long strut - an integral coil spring and shock absorber - is mounted between the body and the steering knuckle. Many modern so-called MacPherson strut systems use a conventional lower A-arm and don't rely on the anti-roll bar for location.

Multimeter An electrical test instrument with the capability to measure voltage, current and resistance.

N

NOx Oxides of Nitrogen. A common toxic pollutant emitted by petrol and diesel engines at higher temperatures.

O

Ohm The unit of electrical resistance. One volt applied to a resistance of one ohm will produce a current of one amp.

Ohmmeter An instrument for measuring electrical resistance.

O-ring A type of sealing ring made of a special rubber-like material; in use, the O-ring is compressed into a groove to provide the sealing action.

O-ring

Overhead cam (ohc) engine An engine with the camshaft(s) located on top of the cylinder head(s).

Overhead valve (ohv) engine An engine with the valves located in the cylinder head, but with the camshaft located in the engine block.

Oxygen sensor A device installed in the engine exhaust manifold, which senses the oxygen content in the exhaust and converts this information into an electric current. Also called a Lambda sensor.

P

Phillips screw A type of screw head having a cross instead of a slot for a corresponding type of screwdriver.

Plastigage A thin strip of plastic thread, available in different sizes, used for measuring clearances. For example, a strip of Plastigage is laid across a bearing journal. The parts are assembled and dismantled; the width of the crushed strip indicates the clearance between journal and bearing.

Plastigage

Propeller shaft The long hollow tube with universal joints at both ends that carries power from the transmission to the differential on front-engined rear wheel drive vehicles.

Proportioning valve A hydraulic control valve which limits the amount of pressure to the rear brakes during panic stops to prevent wheel lock-up.

R

Rack-and-pinion steering A steering system with a pinion gear on the end of the steering shaft that mates with a rack (think of a geared wheel opened up and laid flat). When the steering wheel is turned, the pinion turns, moving the rack to the left or right. This movement is transmitted through the track rods to the steering arms at the wheels.

Radiator A liquid-to-air heat transfer device designed to reduce the temperature of the coolant in an internal combustion engine cooling system.

Refrigerant Any substance used as a heat transfer agent in an air-conditioning system. R-12 has been the principle refrigerant for many years; recently, however, manufacturers have begun using R-134a, a non-CFC substance that is considered less harmful to the ozone in the upper atmosphere.

Rocker arm A lever arm that rocks on a shaft or pivots on a stud. In an overhead valve engine, the rocker arm converts the upward movement of the pushrod into a downward movement to open a valve.

Rotor In a distributor, the rotating device inside the cap that connects the centre electrode and the outer terminals as it turns, distributing the high voltage from the coil secondary winding to the proper spark plug. Also, that part of an alternator which rotates inside the stator. Also, the rotating assembly of a turbocharger, including the compressor wheel, shaft and turbine wheel.

Runout The amount of wobble (in-and-out movement) of a gear or wheel as it's rotated. The amount a shaft rotates "out-of-true." The out-of-round condition of a rotating part.

S

Sealant A liquid or paste used to prevent leakage at a joint. Sometimes used in conjunction with a gasket.

Sealed beam lamp An older headlight design which integrates the reflector, lens and filaments into a hermetically-sealed one-piece unit. When a filament burns out or the lens cracks, the entire unit is simply replaced.

Serpentine drivebelt A single, long, wide accessory drivebelt that's used on some newer vehicles to drive all the accessories, instead of a series of smaller, shorter belts. Serpentine drivebelts are usually tensioned by an automatic tensioner.

Serpentine drivebelt

Shim Thin spacer, commonly used to adjust the clearance or relative positions between two parts. For example, shims inserted into or under bucket tappets control valve clearances. Clearance is adjusted by changing the thickness of the shim.

Slide hammer A special puller that screws into or hooks onto a component such as a shaft or bearing; a heavy sliding handle on the shaft bottoms against the end of the shaft to knock the component free.

Sprocket A tooth or projection on the periphery of a wheel, shaped to engage with a chain or drivebelt. Commonly used to refer to the sprocket wheel itself.

Starter inhibitor switch On vehicles with an automatic transmission, a switch that prevents starting if the vehicle is not in Neutral or Park.

Strut See MacPherson strut.

T

Tappet A cylindrical component which transmits motion from the cam to the valve stem, either directly or via a pushrod and rocker arm. Also called a cam follower.

Thermostat A heat-controlled valve that regulates the flow of coolant between the cylinder block and the radiator, so maintaining optimum engine operating temperature. A thermostat is also used in some air cleaners in which the temperature is regulated.

Thrust bearing The bearing in the clutch assembly that is moved in to the release levers by clutch pedal action to disengage the clutch. Also referred to as a release bearing.

Timing belt A toothed belt which drives the camshaft. Serious engine damage may result if it breaks in service.

Timing chain A chain which drives the camshaft.

Toe-in The amount the front wheels are closer together at the front than at the rear. On rear wheel drive vehicles, a slight amount of toe-in is usually specified to keep the front wheels running parallel on the road by offsetting other forces that tend to spread the wheels apart.

Toe-out The amount the front wheels are closer together at the rear than at the front. On front wheel drive vehicles, a slight amount of toe-out is usually specified.

Tools For full information on choosing and using tools, refer to the *Haynes Automotive Tools Manual*.

Tracer A stripe of a second colour applied to a wire insulator to distinguish that wire from another one with the same colour insulator.

Tune-up A process of accurate and careful adjustments and parts replacement to obtain the best possible engine performance.

Turbocharger A centrifugal device, driven by exhaust gases, that pressurises the intake air. Normally used to increase the power output from a given engine displacement, but can also be used primarily to reduce exhaust emissions (as on VW's "Umwelt" Diesel engine).

U

Universal joint or U-joint A double-pivoted connection for transmitting power from a driving to a driven shaft through an angle. A U-joint consists of two Y-shaped yokes and a cross-shaped member called the spider.

V

Valve A device through which the flow of liquid, gas, vacuum, or loose material in bulk may be started, stopped, or regulated by a movable part that opens, shuts, or partially obstructs one or more ports or passageways. A valve is also the movable part of such a device.

Valve clearance The clearance between the valve tip (the end of the valve stem) and the rocker arm or tappet. The valve clearance is measured when the valve is closed.

Vernier caliper A precision measuring instrument that measures inside and outside dimensions. Not quite as accurate as a micrometer, but more convenient.

Viscosity The thickness of a liquid or its resistance to flow.

Volt A unit for expressing electrical "pressure" in a circuit. One volt that will produce a current of one ampere through a resistance of one ohm.

W

Welding Various processes used to join metal items by heating the areas to be joined to a molten state and fusing them together. For more information refer to the *Haynes Automotive Welding Manual*.

Wiring diagram A drawing portraying the components and wires in a vehicle's electrical system, using standardised symbols. For more information refer to the *Haynes Automotive Electrical and Electronic Systems Manual*.

Note: *References throughout this index are in the form* **"Chapter number"** • **"Page number"**

Haynes Manuals – The Complete List

Title	Book No.
ALFA ROMEO	
Alfa Romeo Alfasud/Sprint (74 - 88) up to F	0292
Alfa Romeo Alfetta (73 - 87) up to E	0531
AUDI	
Audi 80 (72 - Feb 79) up to T	0207
Audi 80, 90 (79 - Oct 86) up to D & Coupe (81 - Nov 88) up to F	0605
Audi 80, 90 (Oct 86 - 90) D to H & Coupe (Nov 88 - 90) F to H	1491
Audi 100 (Oct 82 - 90) up to H & 200 (Feb 84 - Oct 89) A to G	0907
Audi 100 & A6 Petrol & Diesel (May 91 - May 97) H to P	3504
Audi A4 (95 - Feb 00) M to V	3575
AUSTIN	
Austin A35 & A40 (56 - 67) *	0118
Austin Allegro 1100, 1300, 1.0, 1.1 & 1.3 (73 - 82)*	0164
Austin Healey 100/6 & 3000 (56 - 68) *	0049
Austin/MG/Rover Maestro 1.3 & 1.6 (83 - May 95) up to M	0922
Austin/MG Metro (80 - May 90) up to G	0718
Austin/Rover Montego 1.3 & 1.6 (84 - 94) A to L	1066
Austin/MG/Rover Montego 2.0 (84 - 95) A to M	1067
Mini (59 - 69) up to H	0527
Mini (69 - Oct 96) up to P	0646
Austin/Rover 2.0 litre Diesel Engine (86 - 93) C to L	1857
BEDFORD	
Bedford CF (69 - 87) up to E	0163
Bedford/Vauxhall Rascal & Suzuki Supercarry (86 - Oct 94) C to M	3015
BMW	
BMW 1500, 1502, 1600, 1602, 2000 & 2002 (59 - 77)*	0240
BMW 316, 320 & 320i (4-cyl) (75 - Feb 83) up to Y	0276
BMW 320, 320i, 323i & 325i (6-cyl) (Oct 77 - Sept 87) up to E	0815
BMW 3-Series (Apr 91 - 96) H to N	3210
BMW 3- & 5-Series (sohc) (81 - 91) up to J	1948
BMW 520i & 525e (Oct 81 - June 88) up to E	1560
BMW 525, 528 & 528i (73 - Sept 81) up to X	0632
CITROËN	
Citroën 2CV, Ami & Dyane (67 - 90) up to H	0196
Citroën AX Petrol & Diesel (87 - 97) D to P	3014
Citroën BX (83 - 94) A to L	0908
Citroën C15 Van Petrol & Diesel (89 - Oct 98) F to S	3509
Citroën CX (75 - 88) up to F	0528
Citroën Saxo Petrol & Diesel (96 - 01) N to X	3506
Citroën Visa (79 - 88) up to F	0620
Citroën Xantia Petrol & Diesel (93 - 98) K to S	3082
Citroën XM Petrol & Diesel (89 - 00) G to X	3451
Citroën Xsara Petrol & Diesel (97 - Sept 00) R to W	3751
Citroën ZX Diesel (91 - 98) J to S	1922
Citroën ZX Petrol (91 - 98) H to S	1881
Citroën 1.7 & 1.9 litre Diesel Engine (84 - 96) A to N	1379
FIAT	
Fiat 126 (73 - 87) *	0305
Fiat 500 (57 - 73) up to M	0090
Fiat Bravo & Brava (95 - 00) N to W	3572
Fiat Cinquecento (93 - 98) K to R	3501
Fiat Panda (81 - 95) up to M	0793
Fiat Punto Petrol & Diesel (94 - Oct 99) L to V	3251
Fiat Regata (84 - 88) A to F	1167
Fiat Tipo (88 - 91) E to J	1625
Fiat Uno (83 - 95) up to M	0923
Fiat X1/9 (74 - 89) up to G	0273
FORD	
Ford Anglia (59 - 68) *	0001
Ford Capri II (& III) 1.6 & 2.0 (74 - 87) up to E	0283
Ford Capri II (& III) 2.8 & 3.0 (74 - 87) up to E	1309
Ford Cortina Mk III 1300 & 1600 (70 - 76) *	0070
Ford Cortina Mk IV (& V) 1.6 & 2.0 (76 - 83) *	0343
Ford Cortina Mk IV (& V) 2.3 V6 (77 - 83) *	0426
Ford Escort Mk I 1100 & 1300 (68 - 74) *	0171
Ford Escort Mk I Mexico, RS 1600 & RS 2000 (70 - 74)*	0139
Ford Escort Mk II Mexico, RS 1800 & RS 2000 (75 - 80)*	0735
Ford Escort (75 - Aug 80) *	0280
Ford Escort (Sept 80 - Sept 90) up to H	0686
Ford Escort & Orion (Sept 90 - 00) H to X	1737
Ford Fiesta (76 - Aug 83) up to Y	0334
Ford Fiesta (Aug 83 - Feb 89) A to F	1030
Ford Fiesta (Feb 89 - Oct 95) F to N	1595
Ford Fiesta (Oct 95 - 01) N-reg. onwards	3397
Ford Focus (98 - 01) S to Y	3759
Ford Granada (Sept 77 - Feb 85) up to B	0481
Ford Granada & Scorpio (Mar 85 - 94) B to M	1245
Ford Ka (96 - 02) P-reg. onwards	3570
Ford Mondeo Petrol (93 - 99) K to T	1923
Ford Mondeo Diesel (93 - 96) L to N	3465
Ford Orion (83 - Sept 90) up to H	1009
Ford Sierra 4 cyl. (82 - 93) up to K	0903
Ford Sierra V6 (82 - 91) up to J	0904
Ford Transit Petrol (Mk 2) (78 - Jan 86) up to C	0719
Ford Transit Petrol (Mk 3) (Feb 86 - 89) C to G	1468
Ford Transit Diesel (Feb 86 - 99) C to T	3019
Ford 1.6 & 1.8 litre Diesel Engine (84 - 96) A to N	1172
Ford 2.1, 2.3 & 2.5 litre Diesel Engine (77 - 90) up to H	1606
FREIGHT ROVER	
Freight Rover Sherpa (74 - 87) up to E	0463
HILLMAN	
Hillman Avenger (70 - 82) up to Y	0037
Hillman Imp (63 - 76) *	0022
HONDA	
Honda Accord (76 - Feb 84) up to A	0351
Honda Civic (Feb 84 - Oct 87) A to E	1226
Honda Civic (Nov 91 - 96) J to N	3199
HYUNDAI	
Hyundai Pony (85 - 94) C to M	3398
JAGUAR	
Jaguar E Type (61 - 72) up to L	0140
Jaguar MkI & II, 240 & 340 (55 - 69) *	0098
Jaguar XJ6, XJ & Sovereign; Daimler Sovereign (68 - Oct 86) up to D	0242
Jaguar XJ6 & Sovereign (Oct 86 - Sept 94) D to M	3261
Jaguar XJ12, XJS & Sovereign; Daimler Double Six (72 - 88) up to F	0478
JEEP	
Jeep Cherokee Petrol (93 - 96) K to N	1943
LADA	
Lada 1200, 1300, 1500 & 1600 (74 - 91) up to J	0413
Lada Samara (87 - 91) D to J	1610
LAND ROVER	
Land Rover 90, 110 & Defender Diesel (83 - 95) up to N	3017
Land Rover Discovery Petrol & Diesel (89 - 98) G to S	3016
Land Rover Series IIA & III Diesel (58 - 85) up to C	0529
Land Rover Series II, IIA & III Petrol (58 - 85) up to C	0314
MAZDA	
Mazda 323 (Mar 81 - Oct 89) up to G	1608
Mazda 323 (Oct 89 - 98) G to R	3455
Mazda 626 (May 83 - Sept 87) up to E	0929
Mazda B-1600, B-1800 & B-2000 Pick-up (72 - 88) up to F	0267
Mazda RX-7 (79 - 85) *	0460
MERCEDES-BENZ	
Mercedes-Benz 190, 190E & 190D Petrol & Diesel (83 - 93) A to L	3450
Mercedes-Benz 200, 240, 300 Diesel (Oct 76 - 85) up to C	1114
Mercedes-Benz 250 & 280 (68 - 72) up to L	0346
Mercedes-Benz 250 & 280 (123 Series) (Oct 76 - 84) up to B	0677
Mercedes-Benz 124 Series (85 - Aug 93) C to K	3253
Mercedes-Benz C-Class Petrol & Diesel (93 - Aug 00) L to W	3511
MG	
MGA (55 - 62) *	0475
MGB (62 - 80) up to W	0111
MG Midget & AH Sprite (58 - 80) up to W	0265
MITSUBISHI	
Mitsubishi Shogun & L200 Pick-Ups (83 - 94) up to M	1944
MORRIS	
Morris Ital 1.3 (80 - 84) up to B	0705
Morris Minor 1000 (56 - 71) up to K	0024
NISSAN	
Nissan Bluebird (May 84 - Mar 86) A to C	1223
Nissan Bluebird (Mar 86 - 90) C to H	1473
Nissan Cherry (Sept 82 - 86) up to D	1031
Nissan Micra (83 - Jan 93) up to K	0931
Nissan Micra (93 - 99) K to T	3254
Nissan Primera (90 - Aug 99) H to T	1851
Nissan Stanza (82 - 86) up to D	0824
Nissan Sunny (May 82 - Oct 86) up to D	0895
Nissan Sunny (Oct 86 - Mar 91) D to H	1378
Nissan Sunny (Apr 91 - 95) H to N	3219
OPEL	
Opel Ascona & Manta (B Series) (Sept 75 - 88) up to F	0316
Opel Ascona (81 - 88) (Not available in UK see Vauxhall Cavalier 0812)	3215
Opel Astra (Oct 91 - Feb 98) (Not available in UK see Vauxhall Astra 1832)	3156
Opel Astra & Zafira Diesel (Feb 98 - Sept 00) (See Astra & Zafira Diesel Book No. 3797)	
Opel Astra & Zafira Petrol (Feb 98 - Sept 00) (See Vauxhall/Opel Astra & Zafira Petrol Book No. 3758)	
Opel Calibra (90 - 98) (See Vauxhall/Opel Calibra Book No. 3502)	
Opel Corsa (83 - Mar 93) (Not available in UK see Vauxhall Nova 0909)	3160
Opel Corsa (Mar 93 - 97) (Not available in UK see Vauxhall Corsa 1985)	3159
Opel Frontera Petrol & Diesel (91 - 98) (See Vauxhall/Opel Frontera Book No. 3454)	
Opel Kadett (Nov 79 - Oct 84) up to B	0634
Opel Kadett (Oct 84 - Oct 91) (Not available in UK see Vauxhall Astra & Belmont 1136)	3196
Opel Omega & Senator (86 - 94) (Not available in UK see Vauxhall Carlton & Senator 1469)	3157
Opel Omega (94 - 99) (See Vauxhall/Opel Omega Book No. 3510)	
Opel Rekord (Feb 78 - Oct 86) up to D	0543
Opel Vectra (Oct 88 - Oct 95) (Not available in UK see Vauxhall Cavalier 1570)	3158
Opel Vectra Petrol & Diesel (95 - 98) (Not available in UK see Vauxhall Vectra 3396)	3523
PEUGEOT	
Peugeot 106 Petrol & Diesel (91 - 01) J to X	1882
Peugeot 205 Petrol (83 - 97) A to P	0932
Peugeot 206 Petrol and Diesel (98 - 01) S to X	3757
Peugeot 305 (78 - 89) up to G	0538

* Classic reprint

Title	Book No.
Peugeot 306 Petrol & Diesel (93 - 99) K to T	3073
Peugeot 309 (86 - 93) C to K	1266
Peugeot 405 Petrol (88 - 97) E to P	1559
Peugeot 405 Diesel (88 - 97) E to P	3198
Peugeot 406 Petrol & Diesel (96 - 97) N to R	3394
Peugeot 505 (79 - 89) up to G	0762
Peugeot 1.7/1.8 & 1.9 litre Diesel Engine (82 - 96) up to N	0950
Peugeot 2.0, 2.1, 2.3 & 2.5 litre Diesel Engines (74 - 90) up to H	1607

PORSCHE
Title	Book No.
Porsche 911 (65 - 85) up to C	0264
Porsche 924 & 924 Turbo (76 - 85) up to C	0397

PROTON
Title	Book No.
Proton (89 - 97) F to P	3255

RANGE ROVER
Title	Book No.
Range Rover V8 (70 - Oct 92) up to K	0606

RELIANT
Title	Book No.
Reliant Robin & Kitten (73 - 83) up to A	0436

RENAULT
Title	Book No.
Renault 4 (61 - 86) *	0072
Renault 5 (Feb 85 - 96) B to N	1219
Renault 9 & 11 (82 - 89) up to F	0822
Renault 18 (79 - 86) up to D	0598
Renault 19 Petrol (89 - 94) F to M	1646
Renault 19 Diesel (89 - 96) F to N	1946
Renault 21 (86 - 94) C to M	1397
Renault 25 (84 - 92) B to K	1228
Renault Clio Petrol (91 - May 98) H to R	1853
Renault Clio Diesel (91 - June 96) H to N	3031
Renault Clio Petrol & Diesel (May 98 - May 01) R to Y	3906
Renault Espace Petrol & Diesel (85 - 96) C to N	3197
Renault Fuego (80 - 86) *	0764
Renault Laguna Petrol & Diesel (94 - 00) L to W	3252
Renault Mégane & Scénic Petrol & Diesel (96 - 98) N to R	3395
Renault Mégane & Scénic (Apr 99 - 02) T-reg onwards	3916

ROVER
Title	Book No.
Rover 213 & 216 (84 - 89) A to G	1116
Rover 214 & 414 (89 - 96) G to N	1689
Rover 216 & 416 (89 - 96) G to N	1830
Rover 211, 214, 216, 218 & 220 Petrol & Diesel (Dec 95 - 98) N to R	3399
Rover 414, 416 & 420 Petrol & Diesel (May 95 - 98) M to R	3453
Rover 618, 620 & 623 (93 - 97) K to P	3257
Rover 820, 825 & 827 (86 - 95) D to N	1380
Rover 3500 (76 - 87) up to E	0365
Rover Metro, 111 & 114 (May 90 - 98) G to S	1711

SAAB
Title	Book No.
Saab 90, 99 & 900 (79 - Oct 93) up to L	0765
Saab 95 & 96 (66 - 76) *	0198
Saab 99 (69 - 79) *	0247
Saab 900 (Oct 93 - 98) L to R	3512
Saab 9000 (4-cyl) (85 - 98) C to S	1686

SEAT
Title	Book No.
Seat Ibiza & Cordoba Petrol & Diesel (Oct 93 - Oct 99) L to V	3571
Seat Ibiza & Malaga (85 - 92) B to K	1609

SKODA
Title	Book No.
Skoda Estelle (77 - 89) up to G	0604
Skoda Favorit (89 - 96) F to N	1801
Skoda Felicia Petrol & Diesel (95 - 01) M to X	3505

SUBARU
Title	Book No.
Subaru 1600 & 1800 (Nov 79 - 90) up to H	0995

SUNBEAM
Title	Book No.
Sunbeam Alpine, Rapier & H120 (67 - 76) *	0051

SUZUKI
Title	Book No.
Suzuki SJ Series, Samurai & Vitara (4-cyl) (82 - 97) up to P	1942
Suzuki Supercarry & Bedford/Vauxhall Rascal (86 - Oct 94) C to M	3015

TALBOT
Title	Book No.
Talbot Alpine, Solara, Minx & Rapier (75 - 86) up to D	0337
Talbot Horizon (78 - 86) up to D	0473
Talbot Samba (82 - 86) up to D	0823

TOYOTA
Title	Book No.
Toyota Carina E (May 92 - 97) J to P	3256
Toyota Corolla (Sept 83 - Sept 87) A to E	1024
Toyota Corolla (80 - 85) up to C	0683
Toyota Corolla (Sept 87 - Aug 92) E to K	1683
Toyota Corolla (Aug 92 - 97) K to P	3259
Toyota Hi-Ace & Hi-Lux (69 - Oct 83) up to A	0304

TRIUMPH
Title	Book No.
Triumph Acclaim (81 - 84) *	0792
Triumph GT6 & Vitesse (62 - 74) *	0112
Triumph Herald (59 - 71) *	0010
Triumph Spitfire (62 - 81) up to X	0113
Triumph Stag (70 - 78) up to T	0441
Triumph TR2, TR3, TR3A, TR4 & TR4A (52 - 67)*	0028
Triumph TR5 & 6 (67 - 75) *	0031
Triumph TR7 (75 - 82) *	0322

VAUXHALL
Title	Book No.
Vauxhall Astra (80 - Oct 84) up to B	0635
Vauxhall Astra & Belmont (Oct 84 - Oct 91) B to J	1136
Vauxhall Astra (Oct 91 - Feb 98) J to R	1832
Vauxhall/Opel Astra & Zafira Diesel (Feb 98 - Sept 00) R to W	3797
Vauxhall/Opel Astra & Zafira Petrol (Feb 98 - Sept 00) R to W	3758
Vauxhall/Opel Calibra (90 - 98) G to S	3502
Vauxhall Carlton (Oct 78 - Oct 86) up to D	0480
Vauxhall Carlton & Senator (Nov 86 - 94) D to L	1469
Vauxhall Cavalier 1300 (77 - July 81) *	0461
Vauxhall Cavalier 1600, 1900 & 2000 (75 - July 81) up to W	0315
Vauxhall Cavalier (81 - Oct 88) up to F	0812
Vauxhall Cavalier (Oct 88 - 95) F to N	1570
Vauxhall Chevette (75 - 84) up to B	0285
Vauxhall Corsa (Mar 93 - 97) K to R	1985
Vauxhall/Opel Corsa (Apr 97 - Oct 00) P to X	3921
Vauxhall/Opel Frontera Petrol & Diesel (91 - Sept 98) J to S	3454
Vauxhall Nova (83 - 93) up to K	0909
Vauxhall/Opel Omega (94 - 99) L to T	3510
Vauxhall Vectra Petrol & Diesel (95 - 98) N to R	3396
Vauxhall/Opel 1.5, 1.6 & 1.7 litre Diesel Engine (82 - 96) up to N	1222

VOLKSWAGEN
Title	Book No.
Volkswagen 411 & 412 (68 - 75) *	0091
Volkswagen Beetle 1200 (54 - 77) up to S	0036
Volkswagen Beetle 1300 & 1500 (65 - 75) up to P	0039
Volkswagen Beetle 1302 & 1302S (70 - 72) up to L	0110
Volkswagen Beetle 1303, 1303S & GT (72 - 75) up to P	0159
Volkswagen Beetle Petrol & Diesel (Apr 99 - 01) T reg onwards	3798
Volkswagen Golf & Bora Petrol & Diesel (April 98 - 00) R to X	3727
Volkswagen Golf & Jetta Mk 1 1.1 & 1.3 (74 - 84) up to A	0716
Volkswagen Golf, Jetta & Scirocco Mk 1 1.5, 1.6 & 1.8 (74 - 84) up to A	0726
Volkswagen Golf & Jetta Mk 1 Diesel (78 - 84) up to A	0451
Volkswagen Golf & Jetta Mk 2 (Mar 84 - Feb 92) A to J	1081
Volkswagen Golf & Vento Petrol & Diesel (Feb 92 - 96) J to N	3097
Volkswagen LT vans & light trucks (76 - 87) up to E	0637
Volkswagen Passat & Santana (Sept 81 - May 88) up to E	0814
Volkswagen Passat Petrol & Diesel (May 88 - 96) E to P	3498
Volkswagen Passat 4-cyl Petrol & Diesel (Dec 96 - Nov 00) P to X	3917
Volkswagen Polo & Derby (76 - Jan 82) up to X	0335
Volkswagen Polo (82 - Oct 90) up to H	0813
Volkswagen Polo (Nov 90 - Aug 94) H to L	3245
Volkswagen Polo Hatchback Petrol & Diesel (94 - 99) M to S	3500
Volkswagen Scirocco (82 - 90) up to H	1224
Volkswagen Transporter 1600 (68 - 79) up to V	0082
Volkswagen Transporter 1700, 1800 & 2000 (72 - 79) up to V	0226
Volkswagen Transporter (air-cooled) (79 - 82) up to Y	0638
Volkswagen Transporter (water-cooled) (82 - 90) up to H	3452
Volkswagen Type 3 (63 - 73) *	0084

VOLVO
Title	Book No.
Volvo 120 & 130 Series (& P1800) (61 - 73) *	0203
Volvo 142, 144 & 145 (66 - 74) up to N	0129
Volvo 240 Series (74 - 93) up to K	0270
Volvo 262, 264 & 260/265 (75 - 85) *	0400
Volvo 340, 343, 345 & 360 (76 - 91) up to J	0715
Volvo 440, 460 & 480 (87 - 97) D to P	1691
Volvo 740 & 760 (82 - 91) up to J	1258
Volvo 850 (92 - 96) J to P	3260
Volvo 940 (90 - 96) H to N	3249
Volvo S40 & V40 (96 - 99) N to V	3569
Volvo S70, V70 & C70 (96 - 99) P to V	3573

AUTOMOTIVE TECHBOOKS
Title	Book No.
Automotive Air Conditioning Systems	3740
Automotive Brake Manual	3050
Automotive Carburettor Manual	3288
Automotive Diagnostic Fault Codes Manual	3472
Automotive Diesel Engine Service Guide	3286
Automotive Electrical and Electronic Systems Manual	3049
Automotive Engine Management and Fuel Injection Systems Manual	3344
Automotive Gearbox Overhaul Manual	3473
Automotive Service Summaries Manual	3475
Automotive Timing Belts Manual – Austin/Rover	3549
Automotive Timing Belts Manual – Ford	3474
Automotive Timing Belts Manual – Peugeot/Citroën	3568
Automotive Timing Belts Manual – Vauxhall/Opel	3577
Automotive Welding Manual	3053
In-Car Entertainment Manual (3rd Edition)	3363

* Classic reprint

CL13.4/02

Preserving Our Motoring Heritage

< The Model J Duesenberg Derham Tourster. Only eight of these magnificent cars were ever built – this is the only example to be found outside the United States of America

Almost every car you've ever loved, loathed or desired is gathered under one roof at the Haynes Motor Museum. Over 300 immaculately presented cars and motorbikes represent every aspect of our motoring heritage, from elegant reminders of bygone days, such as the superb Model J Duesenberg to curiosities like the bug-eyed BMW Isetta. There are also many old friends and flames. Perhaps you remember the 1959 Ford Popular that you did your courting in? The magnificent 'Red Collection' is a spectacle of classic sports cars including AC, Alfa Romeo, Austin Healey, Ferrari, Lamborghini, Maserati, MG, Riley, Porsche and Triumph.

A Perfect Day Out

Each and every vehicle at the Haynes Motor Museum has played its part in the history and culture of Motoring. Today, they make a wonderful spectacle and a great day out for all the family. Bring the kids, bring Mum and Dad, but above all bring your camera to capture those golden memories for ever. You will also find an impressive array of motoring memorabilia, a comfortable 70 seat video cinema and one of the most extensive transport book shops in Britain. The Pit Stop Cafe serves everything from a cup of tea to wholesome, home-made meals or, if you prefer, you can enjoy the large picnic area nestled in the beautiful rural surroundings of Somerset.

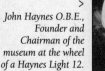

> John Haynes O.B.E., Founder and Chairman of the museum at the wheel of a Haynes Light 12.

< Graham Hill's Lola Cosworth Formula 1 car next to a 1934 Riley Sports.

The Museum is situated on the A359 Yeovil to Frome road at Sparkford, just off the A303 in Somerset. It is about 40 miles south of Bristol, and 25 minutes drive from the M5 intersection at Taunton.

Open 9.30am - 5.30pm (10.00am - 4.00pm Winter) 7 days a week, *except Christmas Day, Boxing Day and New Years Day*

Special rates available for schools, coach parties and outings Charitable Trust No. 292048